FIRST AND SECOND CORINTHIANS

Cover Photo Description

This historical site of the *bema* is in Corinth. The Greek word for *judgment seat* is *bema*. The Corinthians were familiar with the *bema,* for there the Romans punished crime in public. The judge sat in the open at the top of stairs to a government building. There, the public watched and listened. Some citizens served as a jury as the judge heard cases before him. Some Jews accused Paul in Corinth and brought him to the *bema* court to be judged (See Figure 11.14). When Gallio refused to judge Paul's case, the Jews beat Sosthenes, the synagogue ruler, in front of the *bema* (Acts 18:12-17).

The Bible teaches that believers will one day give an account, at the *bema*—the judgment seat of Christ. (In the *Full Life Study Bible* or *Life in the Spirit Study Bible,* see the article "The Judgment of Believers" (2 Cor. 5:10). Truth about the *bema* judgment is very important. Lesson 35 presents facts about the *bema* judgment of believers.

Contact Information

Order your copy from:

Faith & Action
3728 W. Chestnut Expressway
Springfield, Missouri 65802 U.S.A.

Telephone: 417-881-4698

Fax: 417-881-1037

E-mail: Orders@FaithAndActionSeries.org

Web: www.FaithAndActionSeries.org

FIRST AND SECOND CORINTHIANS

Student Manual

by
Dr. George O. Wood, Dr. James Hernando,
Rev. Floyd Woodworth, Rev. Edgardo Muñoz, and
Dr. Quentin McGhee

Instructional Design by
Dr. Quentin McGhee,
Senior Editor

Faith & Action Series

Faith & Action
3728 W. Chestnut Expressway
Springfield, Missouri 65802 U.S.A.

Photo Credits

	Figure #
Assemblies of God World Missions	2.1, 8.9
Ken Berg	2.1, 5-three crosses, 9.10a
Robert Cooley	1.6, 4.6, 6.3a, 8.28, 11.13
Corel Photo Stock	7.6, 7.8, 7.9, 7.10a, 7.10c, 7.11, 9.1, 9.10a, 9.12, 10.6
DesignPics.com	2.5a, 2.5b, 5.1, 5-introspection
Doré	8.2
Ralph Harris	3.1, 4.1, 4.2, 4.5, 4.10, 11.2
http://breadsite.org	4.17, Clip art 3 LEV 1
http://www.journalofamericanhistory.org	11.1
iStock	11.3
LaVista Church	4.16
Johnston Studio	5.2b
Edith LaFon	2.6, 2.7, 2.8a, 5.5, 9.14
James Macharia	3.3, 3.12
Brian Morely	11.14
Photos.com	1.8, 2.1, 2.2, 3.9, 3.10b, 5.2a, 5-spiritual body, 9.2, 9.13, 11.6, 11.7, 11.8a, 11.11, 11.15, 11.22, 12.3, 12.4, 12.5, 13.1, 13.2, 13.3, 13.4
Rockafellow Studio	8.1, 11.8b
Pat M. Smith	5-2nd coming, 11.17
sxc.hu	4.9, 4.18, 6.1, 7.10b
Adam Weatherly	2.1
Wikipedia	2.3, 4.8, 7.1, 8.4, 8.5, 11.20
Lucinda Zilverberg	5.4, 6.3b, 9.10b, 12.1, 12.2a, 12.2b

Copyright Information

Cover layout and logo design: Grace Artworks; www.GraceArtworks.com, 406 W. Commercial St, Spgfd, MO 65803

Front cover photos:
 "Bema Seat - Corinth", Brian Morley, Ph.D; www.BrianMorely.com Made in the Image Photography
 Doric Columns in Corinth, Dr. Robert Cooley, Ph.D.

Any art not listed above was found in free domain.

All rights reserved on all photos in this book.

The Holy Bible: New International Version, International Bible Societies, Grand Rapids, Michigan: Zondervan Publishing House, ©1984. All Scripture quotes from Corinthians are from the NIV.

The Holy Bible: King James Version, Cleveland and New York: The World Publishing Company.

The Holy Bible: New American Standard Bible, Philadelphia and New York: A. J. Holman Company, ©1973. All Scripture quotes other than Corinthians are from NASB.

The Message © 1993, 1994, 1995, 1996, 2000, 2001, 2002. Used by permission of NavPress Publishing Group.

New English Bible @ 1970 England: Oxford University Press and Cambridge University Press.

First Edition 2011

Faith & Action Series—First and Second Corinthians, First Edition
©2011 Faith & Action Team

Course # BIB2033

ISBN 978-1-60382-036-3

Item # 4411-23E0

Table of Contents

	Page
List of Charts	6
Faith & Action Series Overview	8
Faith & Action Series Three-Year Bible School Plan	10
About This Book	12
Dedication	13

Chapters

Unit 1: Christian Freedom—Preferences, Choices, and Rights (1 Cor. 1–10)

1	Introduction to First Corinthians	16
2	Christian Preferences	26
3	Christian Choices	46
4	Christian Rights	70

Unit 2: Guidelines for Worship (1 Cor. 11–16)

5	Christian Worship	94
6	Spiritual Gifts in Worship	108
7	Ministry and Love in Worship	130
8	Christian Edification and Spiritual Gifts	152
9	Doctrine and Worship	174

Unit 3: Paul's Apostolic Ministry (2 Cor. 1–13)

10	Paul Reviews His Recent Past	194
11	Paul Defends His Apostolic Ministry	212
12	Paul Teaches Principles of Giving	266
13	Paul Confronts His Critics	**278**

Definitions	308
Scripture List	310
Bibliography	314
Endnotes	320
Plan of Salvation	326

List of Charts

Figure 1.1	House of New Testament Books	16
Figure 1.2	Groups, sub-groups, dates, and authors of New Testament books	17
Figure 1.3	Dates and events related to 1 and 2 Corinthians	18
Figure 1.5	Outline of 1 Corinthians	19
Figure 1.9	Three aspects of holiness	22
Figure 2.4	There are three types of people in the world, and each lives on a different level.	31
Figure 2.6	Spiritual believers grow in grace by facing the Lord and taking small steps day by day.	37
Figure 3.4	There are three aspects or sides of holiness in Christ.	54
Figure 3.5	Holiness (sanctification) includes three aspects: our position, our orientation, and our condition.	54
Figure 3.6	The process of sanctification (holiness) begins at regeneration (the new birth) and reaches its highest level at glorification.	57
Figure 3.8	First Corinthians 6:12-14 is a mixture of Corinthian proverbs and Paul's responses.	59
Figure 3.10	Some people spread as many as 18 sexual diseases.	61
Figure 3.11	At least eight of the diseases spread through sexual sins can kill you.	61
Figure 4.3	Some believers boast about knowledge, but others have knowledge with love.	73
Figure 4.4	A list of things that may cause people to stumble	75
Figure 4.7	Four reasons why Paul had the right to receive financial support from the Corinthians	76
Figure 4.11	The themes of 1 Corinthians 8–10 in relation to rights and freedom	82
Figure 4.12	Five warnings from Israel's past sins	83
Figure 4.17	Four types of tables in 1 Corinthians 10:14–11:1	90
Figure 5.3	Headship is a part of God's design for heaven and earth.	96
Figure 6.2	God gives some spiritual gifts to help each person and some gifts to edify the whole body.	110
Figure 6.4	The gifts of the Spirit may overlap.	118
Figure 6.5	Biblical faith ranges from faith in Christ to faith that can move mountains.	120
Figure 7.2	There are many chiasms in Scripture, such as in 1 Corinthians 12:12.	131
Figure 7.4	Some churches have as many as 200 different ministries that church members are doing.	133
Figure 7.7	Ten characteristics of love in 1 Corinthians 13:4-7	140
Figure 7.12	Paul mentions at least ten characteristics of love.	144
Figure 7.13	First Corinthians 13 and 15 contrast *now* and *then*.	149
Figure 8.3	Human speech may vary in its level of inspiration from 0% to 100%.	159
Figure 8.6	Tongues and prophecy may be a sign for unbelievers or believers, depending on the context.	168
Figure 8.7	Paul encouraged women to minister in church, but he emphasized order.	170
Figure 9.4	Four parts of the gospel that we believe in order to be saved (1 Cor. 15:1-2)	178
Figure 9.3	Biblical verses emphasizing that truth and certainty are based on two or more witnesses	178
Figure 9.5	If/then statements about the Resurrection (1 Cor. 15:14-32)	178
Figure 9.6	Jesus died on the Day of Passover, and arose on the Day of Firstfruits.	180
Figure 9.7	The New Testament explains the prophetic fulfillment of four spring feasts of the Old Testament.	181
Figure 9.8	Contrasts on how the resurrection body is sown and how it is raised (1 Cor. 15:42-44)	184
Figure 9.9	Contrasts of the first Adam and the Last Adam	184
Figure 9.13	Shall we make regular payments for earthly things, but not spiritual things?	189
Figure 9.15	Brothers and sisters Paul mentions in the family of God (1 Cor. 16)	191
Figure 10.2	Dates and events related to 1 and 2 Corinthians	197
Figure 10.3	Outline of 2 Corinthians	198
Figure 10.4	The Scriptures are a major source of comfort for believers in tight places.	200
Figure 11.4	Paul compared the Roman march of triumph to our journey as Christians.	216
Figure 11.5	Seven contrasts between the ministries of the old and new covenants	217
Figure 11.9	Summary of the Spirit's ministry	222

Figure 11.10 Some contrasts in 2 Corinthians 3–5 223
Figure 11.11 Belief speaks words of faith, and words of faith strengthen belief. 226
Figure 11.12 Second Corinthians 4:17 contrasts present troubles with future glory. 226
Figure 11.18 Second Corinthians 6:2 has parallel lines that are synonymous. 242
Figure 11.19 Grace, integrity, and cheerful endurance were foundation stones of Paul's ministry. 243
Figure 11.23 God divides all people into two groups: holy and unholy. 253
Figure 11.26 Characteristics of repentance, based on 2 Corinthians 7:8-11 261

Figure 12.2 Map showing regions related to the Corinthian letters 267

Faith & Action Series Overview

Bible	Theology	Church Ministries
Survey of the Old Testament	God & the Bible (Theology 1)	Evangelism & Discipleship
Survey of the New Testament	Angels, Man, & Sin (Theology 2)	Marriage & Family
Pentateuch	Christ & Salvation (Theology 3)	Pastoral Ministry
Historical Books	The Holy Spirit & the Church (Theology 4)	Ministerial Ethics
Poetic Books	General Principles for Interpreting Scripture (Hermeneutics 1)	Preach the Word (Homiletics 1)
Major Prophets	Hermeneutics 2	Homiletics 2
Minor Prophets		Principles of Teaching
Life & Teachings of Christ (Synoptic Gospels)		Biblical Counseling
John		Children's Ministry
Acts of the Holy Spirit		Youth Ministry
Romans & Galatians		Missions 1
First and Second Corinthians		Cross Cultural Communications (Missions 2)
Prison Epistles		Teaching Literacy
Pastoral Epistles		Leadership
Hebrews		Church Government & Administration
General Epistles		Church History 1
Revelation & Daniel		Church History 2

Faith & Action Series
Three-Year Bible School Plan (103 credits)

First Year

First Semester

Course #	Title	Credits
BIB1013	Survey of the New Testament	3
BIB1023	Pentateuch	3
BIB1033	Synoptic Gospels	3
THE1012	God & the Bible (Theology 1)	2
THE1022	Hermeneutics 1	2
MIN3023	Children's Ministry	3
		16

Second Semester

Course #	Title	Credits
BIB1043	Survey of the Old Testament	3
BIB1052	John	2
BIB1063	Acts	3
THE1032	Angels, Man, & Sin (Theology 2)	2
MIN1013	Homiletics 1	3
MIN1033	Evangelism & Discipleship	3
		16

Second Year

First Semester

Course #	Title	Credits
BIB2013	Romans & Galatians	3
BIB2023	Historical Books	3
BIB2072	Hebrews	2
MIN2012	Church History 1	2
MIN2023	Missions 1	3
THE2013	Christ & Salvation (Theology 3)	3
THE2032	Hermeneutics 2	2
		18

Second Semester

Course #	Title	Credits
BIB2043	First and Second Corinthians	3
BIB2052	Prison Epistles	2
BIB2063	Poetic Books	3
MIN2032	Church History 2	2
THE2042	The Holy Spirit & the Church (Theology 4)	2
THE2052	Leadership	2
MIN3073	Marriage & Family	3
		17

Third Year

First Semester

Course #	Title	Credits
BIB3012	Pastoral Epistles	2
BIB3022	General Epistles	2
BIB3033	Major Prophets	3
MIN3013	Pastoral Ministry	3
MIN3022	Church Government & Admin.	2
MIN3033	Cross Cultural Communications	3
MIN3043	Homiletics 2	3
		18

Second Semester

Course #	Title	Credits
BIB3043	Revelation & Daniel	3
MIN1032	Teaching Literacy	2
MIN3053	Biblical Counseling	3
BIB3053	Minor Prophets	3
MIN3063	Principles of Teaching	3
MIN3072	Ministerial Ethics	2
MIN3082	Youth Ministry	2
		18

About This Book

1. **The Lesson Headings** divide each chapter into several parts. Each of these lessons focuses on principles related to one theme. We number the lessons consecutively throughout the book.

2. **The Lesson Goals** are listed at the beginning of each chapter. Also, when a lesson begins, the goal for that lesson is printed there. You will find that there is at least one goal for each lesson.

3. **Key Words** are defined in a section called "Definitions" at the end of the book. The symbol * comes before all words that are defined. To help some students, we have also defined a few words that are not key words.

4. **Teaching Method:** These courses are designed for the *guided discovery* method of learning. This method focuses on the student, rather than the teacher. When this course is used in a classroom, lectures are not intended. Rather, most of the class time should be used for students to discuss the questions in the margins and related questions from the teacher and other students. At least 25% of the student's grade should be on how faithfully the student has tried to answer questions *before* class.

   It is VERY important for each student to own his or her book. We encourage Bible schools to require students to buy their texts at the time they pay tuition. It is a shame for students to leave school without their books, because they need them for a lifetime of ministry. Owning the book enables a student to write notes in it and underline important ideas. Also, when students own their books, they do not waste class time by copying things that are already written in the text. Rather, they spend their time discussing questions related to the Bible and ministry.

   In a classroom the teacher and students should discuss key questions together. The best teachers never answer their own questions. Some students will complain at first when the teacher requires them to think, read, and search for answers. But a good teacher knows that children who are always carried never learn to walk. And students who are always told the answer learn to memorize, but not to think and solve problems. In many ways, a good teacher is like a coach—guiding others to succeed.

   The questions in this course are like a path that leads straight to the goal. If the questions are too hard for a student, the teacher can ask easier questions that are like stairs toward harder questions. Also, the teacher should ask questions that guide students to apply the text to local issues. Often, a good teacher will add a story or illustration that emphasizes a truth for students.

5. **Schedule:** This *Faith & Action Series* course is for three credits. For a Bible school course, it is good to plan 40 contact hours between the teacher and students. This allows one lesson for a class hour.

6. **The Questions:** Most questions in the margins are identified by the hammer ⚒ and nail ⚓ symbols. Questions are steps toward a goal. As a student answers the questions, he or she is sure to reach the goals. The hammer introduces *content questions* and the nail precedes *application questions*. Our logo for this book includes the hammer hitting the nail. A student must grasp content before being able to apply it. The answers to all content questions are in the text, near the question. We encourage students to answer nail or application questions from their local settings.

   In some books there is the symbol of a shovel before certain questions. Questions beside the shovel symbol are inductive questions. The word *induce* means "to lead." These questions lead students to discover truth for themselves.

7. *Sabio* is a Spanish word that means "wise man." This symbol in the margin signifies a proverb or wise saying.

8. **The Illustrations**, such as stories and examples, are preceded by the candle symbol.

9. **Figures** include pictures, photos, charts, and maps. We number the figures in order throughout the chapter. For example, the first three figures in chapter one are numbered 1.1, 1.2, and 1.3. There is a list of maps and charts near the front of the book.

10. **The Test Yourself** questions come at the end of each chapter and are indicated by the balance symbol ⚖. There are always ten of these questions. As a rule, there are two test questions for each goal in the chapter. If students miss any of these questions, they need to understand why they missed them. Knowing why an answer is right is as important as knowing the right answer.

11. **Essay Test Topics** are at the end of each chapter, indicated by the pencil symbol ✎. Note that these essay topics are the lesson goals of the chapter. A student should be able to summarize these goals, writing 50-100 words on each one. These essay topics test students at a much higher level than the multiple choice, Test Yourself questions.

12. **Sample Answers** to the hammer questions, some comments on the nail questions, and answers for the Test Yourself questions and Essay Topics are in the Teacher's Guide. Students should answer questions so they will grow and become strong in their mental skills.

13. **Bible quotations** are usually from the New International Version (NIV). In this Corinthians book, all Scripture quotes from Corinthans are from the NIV. All other quotes are from the New American Standard Bible (NASB). We also use the New Century Version (NCV), the New English Bible (NEB), The Message, and the King James Version (KJV). We encourage students to compare biblical passages in several versions of the Bible.

14. **The Scripture List** includes key Scripture references in this course. It is located near the back of the book.

15. **The Bibliography** is near the endnotes page. It is a complete list of books the author refers to in this course. Some students will want to do further research in these books.

16. **Endnotes** identify the sources of thoughts and quotes. They are listed by chapter at the end of the book.

17. **The Unit Exams and Final Exam** are in the Teacher's Guide. In the Teacher's Guide there are also other useful items for the teacher and potential projects for the students.

18. **Course Description (BIB2033):** A thorough study of 1 and 2 Corinthians, beginning with an analysis of the authorship, date, readers, purpose, outline, and introduction of the book. Throughout the course, lesson by lesson, care is taken to examine the meaning of each passage to the first readers and identify timeless principles. Case studies and illustrations guide students to apply these principles to the problems believers face today.

19. **Course Goals for each chapter of this book:**
    1. Analyze the authorship, date, readers, purpose, outline, and introduction of 1 Corinthians.
    2. Explain the causes of division in the Corinthian church and Paul's principles to restore unity (1 Cor. 1–4).
    3. Identify and apply principles related to Christian choices about discipline, legal disputes, immorality, and marriage (1 Cor. 5–7).
    4. Contrast the attitudes of mature and immature believers on the topic of personal rights (1 Cor. 8–11).
    5. Discover principles from Paul's teachings on relationships in 1 Corinthians 11.
    6–8. Explain each of the nine spiritual gifts in 1 Corinthians 12–14, and state principles that govern the use of these gifts today.
    9. Answer questions the Corinthians had on the Resurrection, and relate these answers to questions of modern believers (1 Cor. 15).
       State principles for financial stewardship, based on 1 Corinthians 16.
    10. Review the background of 2 Corinthians, and trace the flow of the letter from Ephesus to Corinth.
        Explain and apply six principles for relationships (2 Cor. 1:12–2:11).
    11. Identify problems and solutions in 2 Corinthians 2–7.
    12. Explain, illustrate, and apply principles of giving (2 Cor. 8–9).
    13. Derive principles for daily living from Paul's defense of his apostolic ministry (2 Cor. 10–13).

20. Author

Dr. George O. Wood provided tapes and manuscripts of his preaching and teaching through Corinthians. His insights and illustrations were vital to this course. He is co-author of the *Faith & Action* book, *Acts of the Holy Spirit*. He is the son of missionary parents to China and Tibet. He completed his undergraduate degree from Evangel College (now Evangel University). Later, he earned a doctorate in theology from Fuller Theological Seminary, and a juris doctorate from Western State University College of Law. He was assistant district superintendent of Southern California for 4 years and pastored Newport-Mesa Christian Center in Costa Mesa for 17 years. Dr. Wood has authored a number of books including a college textbook on Acts. Dr. Wood served as General Secretary of the Assemblies of God from 1993, until he was elected as General Superintendent in 2007.

Dr. James Hernando has earned the following degrees: B.S. in Education (State University of New York), B.A. in Bible (Northeast Bible College), M.S. in Education (State University of New York), M.Div. (Assemblies of God Theological Seminary), M. Phil. and Ph. D. (Drew University, 1990).

Jim's ministry experience includes teaching elementary school (4 years), teaching at Trinity Bible College and serving as Chairman of the Dept. of Biblical Studies (1980-1986); and serving as Associate Professor of New Testament at AGTS from 1990 to the present (2011), where he serves as the full-time Chair of the Biblical Theology Department. Internationally, Jim has taught Hermeneutics and New Testament Theology in Ukraine; and preached a number of times in Ukraine, as well as San Jose, Costa Rica.

His most recent publications are:
- 2 Corinthians in *Full Life Bible Commentary to the New Testament*. Edited by F. L. Arrington and Roger Stronstad. Grand Rapids, Michigan: Zondervan Publishing House, 1999.
- *Dictionary of Hermeneutics: A Concise Guide to Terms, Names, Methods and Expressions,* Springfield, Missouri: Gospel Publishing House, 2005.
- *Studies in the Letters of Paul,* B.A. level, Springfield Missouri: Global University, 2006.
- *1 & 2 Corinthians* in the *Faith & Action Series* (Co-author), 2011.

Jim has been awarded many honors, such as: Who's Who in American High Schools; Who's Who in American Colleges and University; FTE Hispanic Doctoral Scholarship; Outstanding Alumnus of Valley Forge Christian College; Member of the Advisory Board for the Foundation of Pentecostal Scholarship; Assemblies of God Distinguished Educator's Award for 25 years of service.

Jim and his wife, Moira, attend King's Chapel in Springfield, Missouri, and have three sons: Matthew, Eric, and Daniel.

Floyd Woodworth is the son of Assemblies of God pioneers in the United States. He completed studies at Central Bible Institute in Springfield, Missouri, and later graduated with a B.A. from Bethany Peniel College in Oklahoma.

Floyd started his missionary work with a "hitch-hiked" trip to Mexico City, where he enrolled for classes at the university to learn the language of Cervantes. Soon, at the request of the Assemblies of God, Floyd went to Cuba to help teach pastors. He remained there for 10 years as professor and Director of the Bible School.

In 1964, Floyd and his wife, Mildred, and their three children moved to Colombia to train teachers and pastors. Floyd strengthened his writing skills by earning an M.A. in Latin American Literature from the University of Southern California. He then began training Latin-American evangelical writers.

Floyd started CONOZCA, a magazine that reached evangelical ministers across Latin America and in some European countries. He authored several books, including *La escalera de la predicación, Hacia el arte de escribir, Hacia la meta, y Verdades fundamentales*. With his colleagues at Servicio de Educación Cristiana (Christian Education Services), he led workshops on editing, helped edit several textbooks for Latin American Seminaries, and taught classes in Bible, Theology, and Ministry for Instituto de Superación Ministerial (ISUM), as well as M.A. studies for Facultad de Teología.

In his 58 years of missionary ministry, Floyd has taught in every Latin American country, as well as in Haiti, Jamaica, Canada, Belgium, Spain, and the Canary Islands. In more recent years, he has served as an editor for books on the history of the Assemblies of God in Latin America. His contribution to God's kingdom has impacted thousands of Latin-American pastors, evangelists, writers, and missionaries.

Edgardo Rolando Muñoz has an M.A. in Theology. Since 1981 he has served as pastor of Avance Cristiano Church in Temperley, Buenos Aires, Argentina. He has taught at Río de la Plata Bible Institute in Lomas de Zamora, Buenos Aires since 1981, and served there as Dean from 1985 to 1997. Since then, he has served as Assistant Director of that institution. From 1988 to 2003 he was a member of the Board of Directors of Christian Education Services. In 1996 he was named Secretary of Instituto de Superación Ministerial (ISUM), and continues in that position. Along with his duties as pastor, teacher, Assistant Director, and secretary, he presently serves as National President of the Christian Education Department of the Assemblies of God in Argentina (since 1998); National Director of the Bible Institutes in Argentina (since 1990); and Chief Editor of CONOZCA Magazine (since 1997).

Dr. Quentin McGhee added and integrated pastoral/missionary insights, along with other teaching material on Corinthians. He is the founder and senior editor of the *Faith & Action Series*. He earned a B.A. from Southwestern College in Oklahoma City, and a B.S. from Oral Roberts University (ORU). Later he completed an M.Div. at the Assemblies of God Theological Seminary, where he taught beginning Greek. He earned a D.Min. from ORU in 1987. Dr. McGhee and his wife, Elizabeth, pioneered a church in Oklahoma. They went on to serve as missionaries in Kenya for 15 years. There they helped start many churches, developed an extension Bible school for full-time ministers, and assisted in curriculum development. Currently, Dr. McGhee serves as Director for the *Faith & Action Series*.

20. Contributors and Consultants

Dr. Warren Bullock is the author of *"When the Spirit Speaks: Making Sense of Tongues, Interpretation & Prophecy"* (Amazon.com). His past ministry includes: Senior pastor for 25 years in four churches, Dean of the College of Ministry at Northwest University, Superintendent of the Northwest Ministry Network (District). He presently serves as: General Council Executive Presbyter for the Northwest Region; adjunct faculty member for Northwest University and for Assemblies of God Theological Seminary; board member of Northwest University and of AGTS; writer, preacher, and teacher in the US and various nations. Warren and his wife Judi have two children and five grandchildren.

Dr. Stanley M. Horton approved this course for biblical and theological accuracy. His degrees include a B.S. from the University of California, an M.Div. from Gordon-Conwell Theological Seminary, an S.T.M. from Harvard University, and a Th.D. from Central Baptist Theological Seminary. He is Distinguished Professor of Bible and Theology Emeritus at the Assemblies of God Theological Seminary in Springfield, Missouri. Dr. Horton has written 400 articles and book reviews, and authored 46 books on topics such as Genesis, Amos, Matthew, John, Acts, First and Second Corinthians, Revelation, and the Holy Spirit.

Reverend Jimmy Beggs added pastoral insights, illustrations, and cross-cultural applications. He graduated from Southwestern Assemblies of God University with a B.A. in Biblical Studies, and from the Assemblies of God Theological Seminary with an M.A. in Communications. His 44 years of ministry include 14 years in pastoral ministry, and 30 years in missions, teaching in Bible Schools and planting churches. He has served as the Missionary Field Chairman in Tanzania, Kenya, and Uganda. His wife, Mary, has served beside him, as the National Women's Ministry leader for 20 years—8 in Tanzania and 12 in Kenya. Jimmy and Mary have two children, both in ministry. Their son, Greg, is the Assemblies of God Area Director of Missions in East Africa. Their daughter, Suzan Triplett, has served as a pastor's wife in Texas.

Dedication

This book, *First and Second Corinthians,* was made possible by a generous donation from Dr. Daniel T. and Bonnie Sheaffer.

Daniel Thomas Sheaffer was born November 29, 1929 to Reverend Gerald and Jeanette Sheaffer. Dan was named after his uncle, Daniel Thomas Muse, a bishop of the Pentecostal Holiness Church.

Dan first began preaching at the age of 17. Like many Pentecostal pioneers, when he did not have a church to speak in, he preached on street corners or used schools to hold revivals.

In 1950, at the age of 21, Dan married Bonnie Rose Benson, who became his faithful companion for the next 60 years. They conducted evangelistic meetings for several years, and Dan was ordained by the Assemblies of God Oklahoma District in 1958.

Dan and Bonnie pastored First Assembly in Miami, Oklahoma from 1961–1969. Then they accepted the pastorate of a small AG church in Oklahoma City. This proved to be a step of destiny into a ministry that would impact multitudes of people in many nations of the world. In the first 3 years, from 1969 to 1971, the small church grew from 42 to 1250 members, with a new building. Then in 1979 the Sheaffers led the congregation to build Crossroads Cathedral, located on two major highways. This was one of the first and largest mega-churches in the Assemblies of God. It seated about 6,000 people each Sunday morning, contained more than 200,000 square feet, and was built debt free—partly because the Sheaffers founded a successful business to build homes and do general contracting in order to expand their ministry.

Thousands of people came to Christ in this strategic mega-city church at the crossroads. But as AG General Superintendent George O. Wood noted, Dan and Bonnie had a heart for Oklahoma City and the world. Their generosity is a legend. Here are a few of the projects made possible by their ministry and the millions of dollars they gave:

- The *Faith & Action* book *First and Second Corinthians*, which more than 3 million students will study worldwide;
- Churches they founded and built in Liberia, Kenya, Nigeria, South Africa, Paraguay, Colombia, Jamaica, Chile and Burundi;
- 1,000 churches they funded in Malawi, and sponsorships that helped the Malawi AG Church grow from 200 to 4,000 churches with 800,000 members;
- Malawi Assemblies of God School of Theology that trains students from across Africa;
- The Sheaffer Full Life Center at Southwestern AG University in Waxahachie, Texas—this building has 111,000 square feet, and contains a cafeteria, classrooms, offices, an athletic center, two gymnasiums, and a chapel;
- Participation in the construction of Bridges and Teeter Halls on the Southwestern AG University campus;
- The financial undergirding of the Doctor of Ministry program at Assemblies of God Theological Seminary (AGTS) in Springfield, Missouri;
- The Assemblies of God Center for Holy Land Studies, funded during their final pastorate at Harvest AG;
- Initial funding for the Daniel T. Sheaffer Chair of Practical Ministry at AGTS.

Dan held degrees from Oklahoma City Southwestern College, Oklahoma City University, East Central State University, Tulsa University, Luther Rice Seminary, and Southwestern Assemblies of God University. Pastor Sheaffer and Bonnie hosted the popular Trinity Broadcasting Network program, "The Answer" for 17 years and were frequent hosts and guests of TBN's "Praise the Lord" program. Dan authored two books of Bible questions and answers and a church growth book entitled *Together We Grow.*

To Dan and Bonnie Sheaffer, we gratefully dedicate this book. Their legacy endures forever. And we express our thankfulness to their daughter, Terri and her husband, Gary King; and their son, Mike and his wife, Starla, who continue to pastor Harvest AG and fulfill the Great Commission as Dan and Bonnie cheer from heaven.

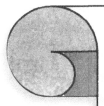

Unit 1: Christian Freedom—Preferences, Choices, and Rights (1 Cor. 1–10)

Some say, "Jesus, YES! Church, NO!". Likewise, *Ghandi once said his problem was not with Christ, but with Christians. Comments like these remind us of the church at Corinth. Many in that sinful city had received Jesus Christ as Savior. Yet the church there was young. These childish believers needed a lot of love and teaching to grow in Christ. The Corinthian church was divided into four groups. Each group had a favorite leader. Meanwhile some committed sexual sins. Other "believers" swindled, which led to lawsuits in public courts. And at pagan feasts, believers ate meat sacrificed to idols and had sex with temple prostitutes. So Paul wrote to help them find the way to heaven.

Chapter 1 introduces the letters to the Corinthians. We will guide you to:
- *Identify the author and date of 1 Corinthians.*
- *Summarize the purposes of 1 Corinthians, as you look at its outline.*
- *Comment on the size, location, and reputation of Corinth.*
- *Trace the Corinthian church from its beginning to the first letter Paul wrote to its members.*
- *Explain why Paul emphasized that he was an apostle.*
- *Describe three types of holiness in 1 Corinthians 1:2.*
- *Summarize what 1 Corinthians 1:7 teaches about spiritual gifts.*

Chapter 2 explores the motivation of Christian preferences (1 Cor. 1–4). By the end of this chapter you will be able to:
- *Explain the problem Paul writes about in 1 Corinthians 1:10-17.*
- *Summarize three illustrations contrasting human and divine wisdom (1 Cor. 1:18–2:5).*
- *Identify three types of people and state characteristics of each (1 Cor. 2:6–3:4).*
- *Explain three illustrations that show the Church belongs to God (1 Cor. 3:5–17).*
- *Explain the sense in which all things belong to the saints (1 Cor. 3:18-23).*
- *Explain a principle about each of these: faithfulness, conscience, God's Word, spiritual children, and God's kingdom.*

Chapter 3 examines principles for choice as members of Christ's body (1 Cor. 5–7). As you study this chapter you will learn to:
- *Summarize four principles on discipline in the local church.*
- *Summarize three reasons believers should settle disputes outside of court.*
- *Explain three ways in which God is holy.*
- *Explain what it means to be holy in our position in Christ. Cite Bible references.*
- *Draw the triangle of holiness, and explain its sides and corners.*
- *Compare and contrast three aspects of holiness. Match Scriptures with each aspect.*
- *Explain how sexual sins are against self and God.*
- *List and explain four ways to honor God with your body and avoid sexual sins.*
- *Explain four biblical principles related to marriage.*

Chapter 4 guides us to give up some of our rights for several reasons (1 Cor. 8:1–11:1). In this chapter we will enable you to:
- *State and illustrate two principles about conscience.*
- *Explain the proper relationship between knowledge and love.*
- *Analyze the balance between personal freedom and concern for others.*
- *Summarize four reasons why Paul had the right to be paid at Corinth.*
- *Explain and illustrate three principles about giving up some of our rights.*
- *Identify five warnings from Israel's history. Apply these to us.*
- *Summarize three keys to overcoming temptations and trials.*
- *Explain why it was wrong for the Corinthians to eat meat at pagan feasts. Apply this.*

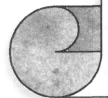

Chapter 1:
Introduction to First Corinthians

Introduction

Q 1 *Fill in the 3 blanks in Figure 1.1.*

Imagine that you are a pastor who has just received a letter from a dear friend. The friend is a member of a church you started 4 years earlier. When you left the church, it was strong and growing. Now your friend writes that the church is full of problems. There have been several pastors since you left, and members have begun to emphasize the pastors instead of Christ! The result is that the church has moved away from the truth to unbiblical teachings. In time, three members visit you. The church chose these three to bring you a list of problems and questions. Since you were their first pastor, they trust your wisdom and counsel.

The story above is very close to what Paul faced when he wrote 1 Corinthians. Paul started the church at Corinth during his second missionary journey. When he left, the church was healthy and growing. Then, members from Corinth told him about the problems. Many of these problems arose because the Corinthians had followed values and attitudes of the world. They forgot much of what Paul taught. He loved the Corinthians dearly. So he wrote them a letter to help solve their problems and answer their questions.

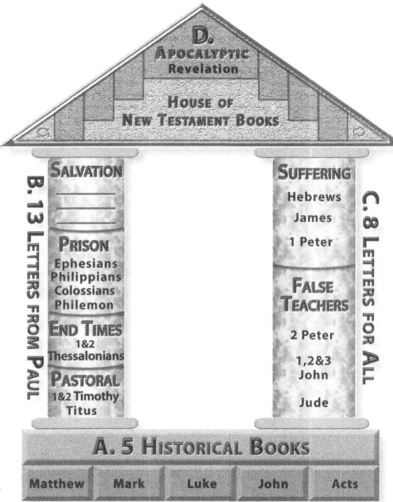

Figure 1.1 House of New Testament Books

Lessons:

Understanding 1 Corinthians
Goal A: *Identify the author and date of 1 Corinthians.*
Goal B: *Summarize the purposes of 1 Corinthians, as you look at its outline.*
Goal C: *Comment on the size, location, and reputation of Corinth.*
Goal D: *Trace the Corinthian church from its beginning to the first letter Paul wrote to its members.*

Paul's Greeting and Thanksgiving (1 Cor. 1:1-9)
Goal A: *Explain why Paul emphasized that he was an apostle.*
Goal B: *Describe 3 types of holiness related to 1 Corinthians 1:2.*
Goal C: *Summarize what 1 Corinthians 1:7 teaches about spiritual gifts*

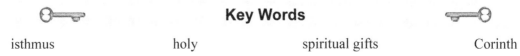

Key Words

isthmus   holy   spiritual gifts   Corinth

Understanding 1 Corinthians

Lesson 1

Goal A: *Identify the author and date of 1 Corinthians.*
Goal B: *Summarize the purposes of 1 Corinthians, as you look at its outline.*
Goal C: *Comment on the size, location, and reputation of Corinth.*
Goal D: *Trace the Corinthian church from its beginning to the first letter Paul wrote to its members.*

Setting

Group	Book Title	Book Sub-group	Date A.D†	Author
1. Historical Books (5)	Matthew	Synoptic Gospels	55-70	Matthew
	Mark		50-68	Mark
	Luke		60	Luke
	John		85-95	John
	Acts		62	Luke
2. Paul's Epistles (13)	Romans	Salvation Epistles	55-56	Paul
	1 Corinthians		55	
	2 Corinthians		56	
	Galatians		48-49	
	Ephesians	Prison Epistles	60-61	
	Philippians		61	
	Colossians		60-61	
	Philemon		60-61	
	1 Thessalonians	Epistles about the future	50-51	
	2 Thessalonians		51	
	1 Timothy	Pastoral Epistles	63	
	2 Timothy		67	
	Titus		65	
3. Hebrews and the General Epistles (8)	Hebrews	Epistles to suffering believers	65-70	Unknown
	James		45-49	James
	1 Peter		63-65	Peter
	2 Peter	Epistles to correct false teachings	65-67	Peter
	1 John		85-90	John
	2 John		85-90	John
	3 John		85-90	John
	Jude		67-80	Jude
4. Prophecy	Revelation	Apocalyptic	90-95	John

Figure 1.2 Groups, sub-groups, dates, and authors of New Testament books

Welcome to our study of 1 and 2 Corinthians. These are two letters that Paul wrote in a group of his letters about salvation (Figure 1.1 and Figure 1.2).

Recall that it is easy to divide Paul's letters into four groups. The first group includes Romans, Galatians, and 1 and 2 Corinthians. These books focus on salvation

Q 2 *What is the theme of the four books of Romans through Galatians?*

---

† Bible scholars differ on the exact dates of New Testament books.

(Soteriology). Paul often uses the words *"in Christ"* to emphasize our relationship with Jesus—our Savior and Lord.

A. Author and date of 1 Corinthians

Date (A.D.)	Event	Scriptures
52	Paul evangelized Corinth on his second missionary trip. Some Jews there accused him. Gallio threw Paul's case out of the Roman court.	Acts 18:1-17
Spring, 55-56	Paul traveled from Antioch, Syria, to Ephesus on his third missionary trip. He ministered in Ephesus for 3 years. During this time, he wrote 1 Corinthians. Timothy carried the letter to the church.[1]	Acts 18:23–21:26; 1 Cor. 16:5-8
Fall, 55-56	Paul traveled from Ephesus up to Troas after the Feast of Pentecost. Titus had agreed to meet him there, but was late with the report on Corinth.[2] So Paul continued to Macedonia on his third missionary trip. There he met Titus. Paul then wrote 2 Corinthians. Afterward, Paul went to see the Corinthians for the third time.	2 Cor. 2:13; 7:5-7; 12:14; 13:1

Figure 1.3 Dates and events related to 1 and 2 Corinthians

Q 3 *Which direction is Corinth from Ephesus? About how far are these cities apart?*

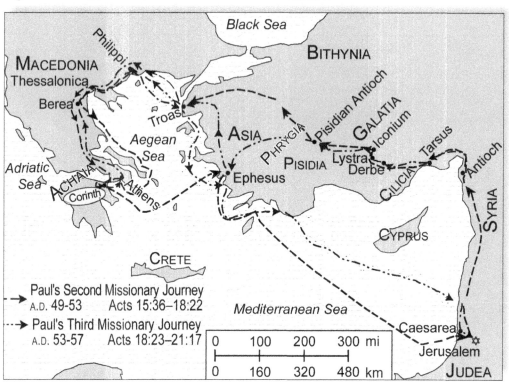

Figure 1.4 Corinth was located in a great place for business. It connected the Aegean and Adriatic Seas.

Author. The letter of 1 Corinthians tells us that Paul wrote it (1 Cor. 1:1-2; 16:21). Likewise, the early church fathers, such as Clement, recorded that Paul wrote 1 Corinthians.

Q 4 *When did Paul write 1 Corinthians? Where was he?*

Date. Paul wrote 1 Corinthians about A.D. 55 from Ephesus, near the end of his third journey (Acts 19:1-41; 20:31; 1 Cor. 16:7-9).

B. Purposes of 1 Corinthians

Q 5 *According to the outline, what were 2 reasons why Paul wrote 1 Corinthians?*

Paul wrote for two reasons.
- *First,* to correct the problems. Someone from the house of Chloe reported problems in Corinth (1 Cor. 1:11). Our outline shows that these problems included division, lawsuits, and sexual sins (1 Cor. 1–6).

Q 6 *How did Paul know about problems in Corinth?*

- *Second,* Paul wrote to answer questions. He received a letter from the Corinthian church elders. They asked questions about some issues. Paul wrote to give them answers.

Introduction to First Corinthians

C. Outline of 1 Corinthians

Our outline shows that Paul wrote about questions on marriage, head coverings, communion, *spiritual gifts, the resurrection, and giving (1 Cor. 7–15).

> I. **Paul wrote 1 Corinthians to solve problems (1 Cor. 1–6).**
>   A. Introduction (1:1-9)
>   B. The problem of divisions (1:10–4:21)
>   C. The problem of the immoral brother (5:1-13)
>   D. The problem of lawsuits (6:1-11)
>   E. The problem of sexual immorality (6:12-20)
>
> II. **Paul wrote 1 Corinthians to answer questions (1 Cor. 7–16).**
>   A. Questions about marriage (7:1-40)
>   B. Questions about conscience (8:1–10:33)
>   C. Questions about head coverings (11:1-16)
>   D. Questions about communion (11:17-34)
>   E. Questions about spiritual gifts (12:1–14:40)
>   F. Questions about the resurrection of the dead (15:1-58)
>   G. Questions about giving (16:1-4)
>   H. Conclusion (16:5-24)

Figure 1.5 Outline of 1 Corinthians

Q 7 Identify 4 problems in 1 Corinthians 1–6.

Q 8 Do being born again and being filled with the Spirit get rid of all of our problems at once? Explain.

The Corinthians were new believers in Christ, but they had many problems! Can you imagine a church with no problems? Such a church does not exist on earth. Churches are for people, and people are not perfect. Corinth was a church that was rich in spiritual gifts (1 Cor. 1:7). Still, it had many problems. One of the biggest problems was division (1 Cor. 1–4). Other problems were sexual sins (1 Cor. 5; 6:12-20), believers fighting each other in court (1 Cor. 6:1-11), and confusion during church services (1 Cor. 11–14).

First Corinthians emphasizes that God is patient with believers. No matter how bad the problems are in a church, God has solutions. Corinth was one of the darkest, most sinful cities of Paul's day. There, the gospel light shone brightly. And those who were saved learned to grow in grace and follow Christ.

D. Corinth: The city and its people

1. Corinth was a big city. Athens may have had a population of less than 10,000.[3] But Corinth was much larger. Estimates range from 100,000 to several hundred thousand people.[4] Scholars of the NIV Study Bible think Corinth may have had 250,000 free people and as many as 400,000 slaves.[5] Most scholars agree that the most populated city of Paul's day was Rome, followed by Alexandria, and then Antioch. But cities like Ephesus, Philippi, and Corinth were also large.

Figure 1.6 The Acrocorinth, or hill of Corinth, stood behind the city. A great temple to Aphrodite stood on top of the mountain. (Ruins of Corinth in the front)

Q 9 Did Athens and Corinth have the same number of people? Explain.

Large cities are more common today. Now, there are over 400 cities with more than a million people.[6] Over half the world lives in big cities. But there have not always been so many large cities. In 1850, there were only four cities in the world with populations over one million.[7] Corinth was a big city in its day! And big cities were Paul's favorite targets for the gospel.

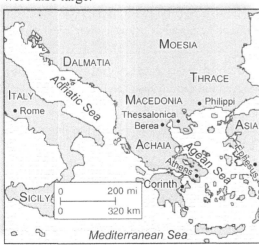

Figure 1.7 Corinth connected the Aegean and Adriatic Seas.

2. Corinth was famous for business. Locate Corinth on the map. This huge city was 50 miles (80 km) west of Athens. Paul walked on a short neck of land from Athens to Corinth.

Q 10 How far was Athens from Corinth?

Q 11 What did this proverb mean: "Act like a Corinthian"?

Sailors dragged smaller ships four miles over this neck or *isthmus. It connected the Aegean and Adriatic Seas. Crossing these 4 miles over land saved them days of sailing 200 miles (322 km) around the southern part of Achaia.[8] Ships from the East and the West came to Corinth. The location of Corinth made it a center for business.

3. Corinth was famous for its sin. Sailors worked on the water and played in the temple.[9] Corinth was a city of the world and the flesh. To *act like a Corinthian* meant to commit sexual sins.[10] Behind the city was the Acrocorinth, or hill of Corinth. It stood like a tower, almost 1,500 feet (457 meters) above Corinth. On it was a temple to Aphrodite (Greek name) or Venus (Roman name). Venus was the goddess of love[11] and sex.[12] In this temple about 1,000 female slaves committed sexual sins with those who came to worship. At night, they walked the streets as prostitutes.[13] Paul reminded the Corinthians of their life before they met Jesus.

Figure 1.8 One of the temples of Aphrodite (Venus, the goddess of love and sex). Many female prostitutes "served" there, providing the finances for maintaining the temple. On the back of their sandals were the words, "Follow me."

Q 12 What were the Corinthians like before Jesus changed them?

*[9]Do you not know that the wicked will not inherit the kingdom of God? Do not be deceived: Neither the sexually immoral nor idolaters nor adulterers nor male prostitutes nor homosexual offenders [10]nor thieves nor the greedy nor drunkards nor slanderers nor swindlers will inherit the kingdom of God. [11]**And that is what some of you were.** But you were washed, you were sanctified, you were justified in the name of the Lord Jesus Christ and by the Spirit of our God* (1 Cor. 6:9-11).

Jesus made some big changes in people at Corinth.

E. Paul's ministry to the Corinthians

Q 13 Which chapter in Acts describes Paul's visit to Corinth?

Acts tells us that Paul first visited Corinth during his second journey (Acts 18:1-17). This was about A.D. 52. In Corinth, Paul met Aquila and Priscilla. Like Paul, they were tentmakers. He lived with them while preaching in and around Corinth. They became close friends and ministers. Every Sabbath, Paul entered into discussions in the synagogue trying to persuade Jews and Greeks (Acts 18:4).

While in Corinth, Paul preached first to the Jews. With God's power he told them *"that Jesus was the Christ"* (Acts 18:5). The noun *Christ* means "Messiah." As usual, some Jews became upset with Paul's preaching. They were so abusive that Paul moved next door to the house of Titius Justus and began ministering to the Gentiles (Acts 18:6). Many believed. How inspiring it was that even Crispus, ruler of the synagogue, believed in Christ. He and his household were baptized. Likewise, many other Corinthians believed and were baptized.

Unbelieving Jews at Corinth took Paul to court. They accused him before Gallio, pro-consul (governor) of the big province of Achaia. Gallio was the brother of Seneca, the tutor of Nero, who became the Emperor of Rome![14]

Q 14 Why did Gallio refuse to judge Paul's case in Corinth?

Q 15 How long did Paul stay in Corinth the first time he went there?

Gallio refused to judge the matter. He threw Paul's case out of the Roman court in Corinth. This was a huge decision in favor of Christianity. It showed that the Roman government allowed Jews like Paul to worship God rather than Caesar. Gallio's decision meant that Christianity was protected under the umbrella of Judaism. Gallio ruled that following Jesus did not break Roman law. He said that Christians and Jewish leaders needed to settle their disagreements outside of Roman courts. This prevented the unbelieving Jews from using Roman law against believers. Wow! Gallio's decision helped believers in Corinth, the province of Achaia, and other places. After God encouraged Paul in a vision (Acts 18:9-10), he ministered in Corinth for at least 18 months.

Introduction to First Corinthians

Paul wrote to the Corinthians 3 years after he visited them. He was at Ephesus on his third journey (Acts 19:1-41). At that time, a Corinthian believer from the house of Chloe reported that things were not well in the Corinthian church (1 Cor. 1:11). Paul also received a letter from the church elders at Corinth. They asked questions about some issues and problems. Review the outline of 1 Corinthians to recall the problems and questions about which Paul wrote.

Q 16 *How did Paul learn about problems in Corinth?*

We have reviewed the background and outline of Paul's first letter to the Corinthians. This gives us a good foundation for the lessons to come.

> **Lesson 2**
> **Paul's Greeting and Thanksgiving (1 Cor. 1:1–9)**
> **Goal A:** Explain why Paul emphasized that he was an apostle.
> **Goal B:** Describe 2 types of holiness related to 1 Corinthians 1:2.
> **Goal C:** Summarize what 1 Corinthians 1:7 teaches about spiritual gifts.

Let us look at three principles in 1 Corinthians 1:1-9.

A. As an apostle, Paul wrote with the authority of God (1 Cor. 1:1).

"Paul, called to be an apostle of Christ Jesus by the will of God" (1 Cor. 1:1). As Paul greeted the Corinthians, he reminded them that he was an apostle (1 Cor. 1:1). His greeting showed that the letter of 1 Corinthians was from him. And it reminded the Corinthians that as an apostle, Paul wrote with God's authority. The early church followed the teachings and writings of the apostles (Acts 2:42).

Q 17 *Why did Paul remind the Corinthians that he was an apostle?*

Likewise, today, we treat the Scriptures in a special way. We believe they are inspired by God and have authority over us. People have many ideas. But the apostles wrote the words of God. That is why we place the Bible above all other books. The words, *"Paul, called to be an apostle of Jesus Christ,"* prepare all readers to hear from God. The Church is *"having been built on the foundation of the apostles and prophets, Christ Jesus Himself being the corner stone"* (Eph. 2:20).

Q 18 *Give an example of a practice in your culture that the Bible has changed.*

Historical note: From Ephesus, the apostle Paul wrote to the Corinthians. Sosthenes was with Paul when he wrote (1 Cor. 1:1). This was probably the Sosthenes from Corinth—the ruler of the synagogue when Paul visited Corinth (Acts 18:17). Recall that the Jews beat Sosthenes. Crispus, the previous ruler of the synagogue, believed in the Lord (Acts 18:8). It appears that Sosthenes followed in the footsteps of Crispus and became a believer. The Holy Spirit enabled Paul to guide many leaders to Christ.

B. We are the holy Church of God (1 Cor. 1:2).

To the <u>church of God</u> in Corinth, to those <u>sanctified in Christ Jesus</u> and <u>called</u> [to be] <u>holy</u>, together with all those everywhere who call on the name of our Lord Jesus Christ—their Lord and ours (1 Cor. 1:2).

The word *church* means "the ones called out." Believers are the Church—the ones called out from sin unto Him. He has bought us with the blood of Christ (Eph. 1:7). So, as believers, we no longer belong to ourselves. As Paul tells the Corinthians, *"You are not your own, you were bought with a price. Therefore honor God with your body"* (1 Cor. 6:19-20). The church belongs to God (1 Cor. 1:2).

As members of the Church of God, we are holy *in Christ*. A form of the word *holy* appears twice in 1 Corinthians 1:2.

Q 19 *In 1 Corinthians 1:2, which 2 words are forms of the word "holy"?*

- *Sanctified in Christ* refers to our position or standing. The moment we are born again, in a legal sense, we have perfect holiness in Christ. We are justified and clothed with a righteousness that is not our own (Phil. 3:9-10).
- Likewise, in Christ Jesus we are *holy* (saints). The word *holy* and the word *saints* are the same Greek word (*hagiois*). The *saints* are the *holy* ones—all believers in Christ.

Q 20 *What are 3 things that being "holy" means?*

Q 21 *Who are the saints?*

As a triangle has three sides, there are three aspects of our holiness: our position, our orientation, and our condition. (For more explanations on the three aspects of holiness, see Figure 3.5).

All believers are saints (holy ones). Some spoil the word *saints* by using it as a title for their dead heroes.[15] Paul does not say we become saints or holy ones *after* we die. We are saints now! Paul wrote to the *saints* in Rome (Rom. 1:7), to the *saints* in Ephesus (Eph. 1:1), to the *saints* in Philippi (Phil. 1:1), and even the *saints* in Corinth (1 Cor. 1:2). Some Bibles, like the NIV, have the words *"called to be saints"* (Rom. 1:7; 1 Cor. 1:2). But in the Greek Bible, the words *to be* are not there. We are *saints* or holy ones NOW! Paul does not tell sinners on earth to pray to saints in heaven. He tells *saints* on earth to pray to Jesus in heaven (1 Cor. 1:2).

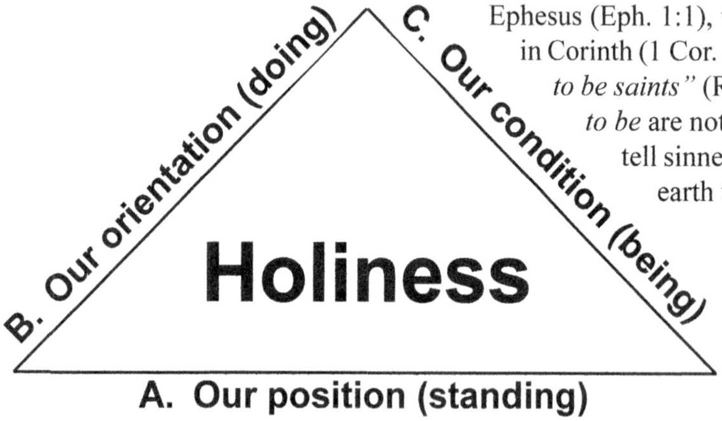

In Jesus Christ, we are saints—holy ones—in three ways.

- *First,* we are holy in our *position*. Holiness of position includes justification and regeneration. The holiness through justification is *imputed holiness*—it is the same for each believer. God credits us with the holiness of Christ, which can never increase. This *imputed* holiness is complete at the moment of conversion.[16] In contrast, the holiness of regeneration is *imparted holiness*—something God gives us. At the new birth God *imparts* holiness to us. We receive God's Spirit, and participate in His holy nature (2 Pet. 1:4). As God's children, we enjoy this exalted position of holiness. The credited, *imputed* holiness of justification is perfect at conversion. But the *imparted* holiness we experience at regeneration is progressive. That is, we grow in holiness. Little by little God conforms us to the likeness of Christ—from the new birth to glorification (Rom. 8:29; 2 Cor. 3:18). In our holiness of position, we are God's justified, holy children.

- *Second,* we are holy in our *orientation*. We are holy because of what Jesus does *through* us, as we separate ourselves from sin to God. This type of holiness is about our lifestyle—we hate what is wrong and love what is right. We offer our bodies as living sacrifices and holy vessels for God to use (Rom. 12:1-2; 2 Tim. 2:21).

- *Third,* we are holy in our *condition*. We are holy because of what Jesus continues to do *in* us. When we were born again, God changed us on the inside. We started to become like God and began to share His divine nature (2 Pet. 1:4). As we grow in grace, this inner holiness grows. Little by little we become more like Christ as we walk in the Spirit (2 Cor. 3:18). This process is called sanctification. Our holiness of condition increases—from regeneration to glorification (Rom. 8:29).

Figure 1.9 Three aspects of holiness
- A. Our position (standing)
- B. Our orientation (doing)
- C. Our condition (being)

Q 22 *Which side of the triangle refers to imputed righteousness? Explain.*

Today, some people like to emphasize part of side A of the holiness triangle. They stress the imputed holiness of justification, saying that is our *only* holiness. Justification is a benefit of positional holiness, and we thank God for it. But it is important to teach that the ministry of Jesus did not end on the cross. He rose from the tomb and *continues* to minister to us today through His Holy Spirit. At justification and regeneration we are holy infants in Christ. But our holiness will increase until we mature and are conformed to the image of Christ (2 Cor. 3:18; Rom. 8:29). We are thankful for holiness of position, side A, which includes justification and regeneration. But we are also thankful for sides B and C—holiness in our orientation and our condition. We rejoice for holiness God gives to us (imparts) in our position, our orientation, and our condition. God imparts holiness to us through the new birth, the baptism in the Spirit, and our fellowship with the Holy Spirit day by day.

Our position in Christ affects our orientation (actions) and our condition (character, values, and attitudes). We are no longer slaves of sin, but we have become the holy servants of righteousness (Rom. 6). So let us always emphasize the three ways we are holy. All of our holiness comes from the life and ministry of Jesus, by the Spirit. And we are holy in our position, our orientation, and our condition.

Throughout our study of 1 and 2 Corinthians, Paul will have a lot to say about holiness. He will emphasize that Jesus is the source of all our holiness, and that all who belong to Christ live holy lives. To study more on the three aspect of holiness, turn to Lesson 9 (1 Cor. 6:9-11).

Q 24 *How should we feel about being called holy? Are you growing in holiness?*

Each believer has three aspects of holiness in Christ.

- *First,* we are holy in our position—our standing in Christ. We are God's justified, holy children.
- *Second,* we practice holiness in our orientation—our actions and choices. We separate ourselves from the unclean and present ourselves to God as His sons and daughters (2 Cor. 6:17–7:1).
- *Third,* through the holiness of our position and our orientation, we grow in the holiness of our condition. We have been born again and changed on the inside. Little by little we become more and more holy. We are being changed into the likeness of Christ, with ever-increasing glory (2 Cor. 3:18). The more we are filled with His Spirit and walk in His Spirit, the more holy we live (Gal. 5:16-26). As God's holy children, we rejoice in what Jesus did for us through the cross and what He continues to do in us by the Spirit (holiness of orientation and condition).

Q 25 *How does being holy affect your lifestyle? How does your lifestyle affect being holy?*

Edgardo was hired to supervise workers in a factory. During the first 2 days, the workers were unhappy about listening to him. On Monday, his first day at work, he greeted each person. But they did not pay much attention to him. On Friday, the owner of the factory introduced Edgardo to the workers and explained his job in the factory. From that moment on, Edgardo noticed a big change in the attitude of those around him. They needed to understand who he was, what role he had, and who commissioned him. So it is with us. Until people get to know us, they may not pay much attention to us. But as our light shines, people understand our position and relationship with the Owner of everything—and what He expects us to be and do. Then we will have more influence on those with whom God has called us to work.

C. God wants all spiritual gifts to be active in the Church until Christ returns (1 Cor. 1:4-7).

⁴I always thank God for you because of his grace given you in Christ Jesus. ⁵For in him you have been enriched in every way—in all your speaking and in all your knowledge— ⁶because our testimony about Christ was confirmed in you. ⁷Therefore you do not lack any spiritual gift as you eagerly wait for our Lord Jesus Christ to be revealed (1 Cor. 1:4-7).

Paul thanked God for giving the Corinthians grace in Jesus Christ (1 Cor. 1:4). This grace included spiritual gifts. Paul introduces the topic of spiritual gifts here, but later in this letter, he writes an entire section on spiritual gifts (1 Cor. 12–14). In the passage at hand, Paul highlights two areas in which the Corinthians received gifts: speech and knowledge (1 Cor. 1:4-7). Greek culture taught people to value speaking and knowing.[17] In 1 Corinthians 1:5, Paul refers to the gifts of speaking and revelation (tongues, interpretation, prophecy, word of knowledge, and word of wisdom—See 1 Cor. 12:8-10). Later in this letter, Paul explains that it is the Holy Spirit who gives spiritual gifts to the body of Christ (1 Cor. 12:4-13). The Greek word for *"spiritual gifts"* (*charismata*) contains the word for *grace* (*charis*).[18] So, spiritual gifts are "grace gifts" from God.

Q 26 *What is the relationship between grace and spiritual gifts?*

Q 27 *Why are some believers called Charismatics?*

Q 28 *When do we need spiritual gifts? Why?*

These gifts were a sign that they had received Paul's testimony about Christ (1 Cor. 1:6). The Corinthians lacked none of the spiritual gifts (1 Cor. 1:7).

Notice the period of time that 1 Corinthians 1:7 emphasizes. It tells us that we need spiritual gifts <u>as we wait for Jesus to return</u>. Some people falsely teach that spiritual gifts are not for today. But the apostle Paul thanked God that the Corinthians did not lack any spiritual gift <u>while they waited for the Second Coming of Christ</u>. When Jesus returns, we will not need spiritual gifts. But while we are waiting for Him, it is God's will for the Church to have all spiritual gifts! Spiritual gifts help keep the Church strong to the end (1 Cor. 1:8-9).

> *⁸He will keep you strong to the end, so that you will be blameless on the day of our Lord Jesus Christ. ⁹God, who has called you into fellowship with his Son Jesus Christ our Lord, is faithful* (1 Cor. 1:8-9).

Q 29 *Have you seen some spiritual gifts in your church? Explain.*

Elena Diaz was a fourth year student at Instituto Biblico Rio de la Plata in Buenos Aires, Argentina. She was teaching on spiritual gifts at a night Bible school. As she taught, she trembled, feeling unqualified, because she was young. Suddenly, a student interrupted her, speaking in a loud voice: "Gloria a Dios por la hermana." (In Spanish this means: "Glory to God for the sister!") Elena was surprised as the student kept repeating the words. Then the class explained to her that the student had been mute. He spoke his first words as she was teaching the class on spiritual gifts. Elena continued to tremble, but this time it was in awe of the presence of God.[19]

In Argentina, lay people from the King of Kings Church went to pray for a boy in a children's hospital. The smell of the tumor on his brain filled the room with stench. But after these believers prayed the prayer of faith, God completely healed the small boy and he went home.[20] We need spiritual gifts to minister for Jesus today, and every day, until He returns!

Introduction to First Corinthians

 Test Yourself: Circle the letter by the *best* completion to each question or statement.

1. The author of 1 Corinthians was
   a) Peter.
   b) Paul.
   c) Luke.
   d) Iranaeus.

2. Which problem did Paul NOT address in 1 Corinthians?
   a) Divisions
   b) Lawsuits
   c) Persecution
   d) Sexual sins

3. First Corinthians was written to answer questions about
   a) the new birth.
   b) the virgin birth.
   c) predestination.
   d) spiritual gifts.

4. Which order of size is correct, from largest to smallest?
   a) Rome, Alexandria, Antioch, Corinth
   b) Rome, Antioch, Athens, Corinth
   c) Rome, Alexandria, Thessalonica, Corinth
   d) Rome, Ephesus, Antioch, Corinth

5. Which 3 seas surrounded Corinth?
   a) Dead Sea, Caspian Sea, Mediterranean Sea
   b) Black Sea, Red Sea, Sea of Galilee
   c) Aegean Sea, Philippian Sea, Berean Sea
   d) Adriatic Sea, Mediterranean Sea, Aegean Sea

6. Which chapter gives us the background of 1 Corinthians?
   a) Acts 16
   b) Acts 17
   c) Acts 18
   d) Acts 19

7. Paul referred to himself as an apostle
   a) to introduce himself to the Corinthians.
   b) to bridge the gap with Roman leaders.
   c) to emphasize his spiritual authority.
   d) to endear himself to his readers.

8. We may refer to holiness *for* us and *in* us as
   a) imputed and imparted.
   b) regeneration and glorification.
   c) adoption and justification.
   d) earthly and heavenly.

9. Holiness that Jesus develops in us is
   a) justification.
   b) sanctification.
   c) adoption.
   d) glorification.

10. First Corinthians 1:7 teaches that
    a) Paul was an apostle, called by God.
    b) divisions in the church are carnal.
    c) spiritual gifts continue until Jesus returns.
    d) each person must stand at the judgment seat.

 Essay Test Topics: Write 50-100 words on each of these goals that you studied in this chapter.

Understanding 1 Corinthians

Goal: *Identify the author and date of 1 Corinthians.*

Goal: *Summarize the purposes of 1 Corinthians, as you look at its outline.*

Goal: *Comment on the size, location, and reputation of Corinth.*

Goal: *Trace the Corinthian church from its beginning to the first letter Paul wrote to its members.*

Paul's Greeting and Thanksgiving (1 Cor. 1:1–9)

Goal: *Explain why Paul emphasized that he was an apostle.*

Goal: *Describe 2 types of holiness related to 1 Corinthians 1:2.*

Goal: *Summarize what 1 Corinthians 1:7 teaches about spiritual gifts.*

Chapter 2:
Christian Preferences
(1 Corinthians 1:10–4:21)

Introduction

A church had the habit of making its new pastor feel small and inferior. Each time a new minister came, he listened to flattering comments about the former pastor. The members said things like: "Are you going to do things this way? Our last pastor had a different method that was very successful!"

Due to this lack of respect, each new pastor suffered a short time, and then left. But as soon as the new pastor arrived, the church began to praise the former pastors.

In truth, no pastor was better than the ones before him. The church members, not the pastors, had a problem. When a pastor was present, these believers criticized his

Figure 2.1 Christians from different cultures and different places prefer to dress in different ways.

weaknesses. They did not appreciate any leader until *after* he left. They were like people who put flowers on a person's casket, but never gave him anything good while he was alive. They were like parents who always criticized one child, but bragged on his brother or sister.

It is easy for us to focus on the negative points of a ministry. But the more we understand people, the more we realize that God created all of His servants with weaknesses and strengths. Some leaders excel at preaching. Others are better teachers. Some build strong relationships. Others have superior gifts to lead and administrate. So wise believers do not measure one pastor by another. Rather, they thank God for all of the leaders He has given to build up and equip the body of Christ.

Lessons:

The Problem and the Contrast (1 Cor. 1:10–2:5)
Goal A: *Explain the problem Paul writes about in 1 Corinthians 1:10-17.*
Goal B: *Summarize 3 illustrations Paul gives that contrast human and divine wisdom (1 Cor. 1:18–2:5).*

Three Types of People (1 Cor. 2:6–3:4)
Goal: *Identify 3 types of people and state characteristics of each (1 Cor. 2:6–3:4).*

Three Examples to Show That the Church Belongs to God (1 Cor. 3:5-23)
Goal A: *Explain each of the 3 illustrations that show that the Church belongs to God (1 Cor. 3:5-17).*
Goal B: *Explain the sense in which all things belong to the saints (1 Cor. 3:18-23).*

Guidelines for the Corinthians and Their Apostle (1 Cor. 4:1-21)
Goal: *Explain a principle about each of these: faithfulness, conscience, God's Word, spiritual children, and God's kingdom.*

Key Word

illumination

Lesson 3: The Problem and the Contrast (1 Cor. 1:10–2:5)

Goal A: *Explain the problem Paul writes about in 1 Corinthians 1:10-17.*
Goal B: *Summarize 3 illustrations Paul gives that contrast human and divine wisdom (1 Cor. 1:18–2:5).*

Setting

Paul greets believers and gives a prayer of thanks for the Corinthians (1 Cor. 1:1-9). Then he goes straight to the first topic—divisions. Even though the believers had been given grace in Christ Jesus (1 Cor. 1:4), they were not a united church. Paul had learned from *"Chloe's people"* that the Corinthian believers were quarreling with one another (1 Cor. 1:11). So he begins with an appeal for unity. He urges them to *"agree with one another"* and *"be perfectly united in mind and thought"* (1 Cor. 1:10). Then there would be no divisions among them.

A. The Problem: Worldly wisdom exalts one leader over another, which brings division (1 Cor. 1:10-17).

One of you says, "I follow Paul"; another, "I follow Apollos"; another, "I follow Cephas"; still another, "I follow Christ" (1 Cor. 1:12).

The world likes to exalt one person above another. People choose their *favorite* actors, singers, writers, athletes, heroes, leaders, teachers, and preachers. Exalting and favoring one person over another is the way of human wisdom.

Following the wisdom of the world, the Corinthians divided themselves into four groups. Each believer chose the leader he or she favored. Some liked Paul best. He was a great apostle and had a heart for the Gentiles. Others liked Peter better than Paul. Peter had a powerful ministry. Acts records that he healed the sick and raised the dead. At times, even his shadow brought healing (Acts 5:15). Still others exalted Apollos. He was highly educated and a great speaker (Acts 18:24-26). A fourth group in Corinth exalted Christ. We should all exalt Jesus. But this fourth group at Corinth may have been *super-spiritual*. We wonder if this group showed a lack of respect to church leaders. Did they say, "We follow Jesus, but not Paul or Peter"?

Q1 *The Corinthian believers were divided into which 4 groups?*

Paul asked them three quick questions:
- *"Is Christ divided?*
- *Was Paul crucified for you?*
- *Were you baptized into the name of Paul?"* (1 Cor. 1:13).

The answer to all these questions is "No!" Perhaps some believers were following the leader who baptized them. This led Paul to say he was glad he had not baptized many of them (1 Cor. 1:14-16).

Q2 *What is the result of exalting one leader over another?*

By exalting one leader over another, the Corinthians divided the body of Christ. These confused believers had wandered off the path. They thought that a leader's style or ministry was more important than the message! And what is the message? The gospel message is that Jesus was crucified on the cross for our sins! Paul's warning is still important today. When we exalt one leader over another, we divide the body of Christ. But a divided house cannot stand (Matt. 12:25).

There is a story about four bulls that were friends. They went everywhere together. They ate and rested together. They always kept close to each other. That way if danger came, they could face it together.

A hungry lion wanted to devour them, but he could never find them separated. He could defeat any one bull, but not all four at once. So, he waited for his opportunity. At times one bull would lag a little bit behind the others as they grazed. Then the lion crept

Q3 *Summarize the lesson of the lion and the four bulls.*

Figure 2.2 *"Be self-controlled and alert. Your enemy the devil prowls around like a roaring lion looking for someone to devour"* (1 Peter 5:8).

near that bull and whispered that the other bulls had been saying unkind things about him. He did this so often that the four friends became uneasy. Each thought the other three were plotting against him. Finally, as there was no trust among them, they went off by themselves. Their friendship had been broken. Once united, they were now divided. This was exactly what the lion wanted. One by one he killed them and enjoyed four good meals.

Division brings deadly results. The Bible says that Satan is like a roaring lion, seeking someone to devour (1 Pet. 5:8). Imagine how alert you would be if you believed there were a hungry lion nearby! Satan's purpose is to divide the Church, Christ's body. Whenever he sees an open door of opportunity, he creeps in and whispers lies. Then he can attack us more easily. United, we will overcome the enemy. Divided, we may be overcome. When believers exalt one leader over another, division comes. Then the local church is open to the deadly attack of our enemy. So we must be careful to remain one body and not divide into groups that oppose each other.

Applications: In the home, division results if children exalt one parent over another, or if parents exalt one child over another. Isaac favored Esau, and Rebekah favored Jacob (Gen. 25:28). This led to a division that has lasted for centuries. Likewise, Jacob exalted Joseph, and this led to division. Parents, be careful not to divide your family by exalting one child over another.

- At work, division results if leaders show favoritism, exalting some workers over others.
- In the church, division results if believers exalt one over another. We must avoid exalting or comparing song leaders, deacons, teachers, or preachers. When people *"measure themselves by themselves and compare themselves with themselves, they are not wise"* (2 Cor. 10:12).

Q 4 *What are some causes and results of divisions you have seen?*

It is easy for us to look down on those of a different race or culture. A different language caused a division in the early church (Acts 6). Believers solved this problem by preferring one another in love.

In many countries, people from one region look down on those from another area. This prejudice causes harsh feelings. More than one country has had a civil war as a result of such divisions. And many churches have split when believers did not guard against division.

B. The Contrast: Human wisdom and God's wisdom (1 Cor. 1:18–2:5)

Q 5 *Which 2 types of wisdom does Paul contrast (1 Cor. 1:18–2:5)?*

The Corinthians were following human wisdom—exalting one person above another. Worldly wisdom taught them to choose heroes such as Paul, Peter, and Apollos. Worldly wisdom is common. Israel liked Saul because he was the tallest. The world favors those who are the strongest, the richest, the smartest, the best speakers, the best singers, the best athletes, the best looking, and the most powerful. But God does not use this standard! Paul gives the Corinthians three examples to remind them that God's wisdom is the opposite of the world's wisdom. Let us look at Paul's **three examples:** 1) the message of the cross, 2) the Corinthians themselves, and 3) Paul's preaching. These three examples contrast worldly wisdom with God's wisdom.

Q 6 *What is Paul's first example in order to contrast human and divine wisdom?*

1. The message of the cross is foolishness to the world, but it is the wisdom of God (1 Cor. 1:18-25).

¹⁸For the message of the cross is foolishness to those who are perishing, but to us who are being saved it is the power of God. ¹⁹For it is written: "I will destroy the wisdom of the wise; the intelligence of the intelligent I will frustrate." ²⁰Where is the wise man? Where is the scholar? Where is the philosopher of this age? Has not God made foolish the wisdom of the world? ²¹For since in the wisdom of

God the world through its wisdom did not know him, God was pleased through the foolishness of what was preached to save those who believe. ²²Jews demand miraculous signs and Greeks look for wisdom, ²³but we preach Christ crucified: a stumbling block to Jews and foolishness to Gentiles, ²⁴but to those whom God has called, both Jews and Greeks, Christ the power of God and the wisdom of God. ²⁵For the foolishness of God is wiser than man's wisdom, and the weakness of God is stronger than man's strength (1 Cor. 1:18-25).

The ancient Greeks loved wisdom. One of the questions Paul asks is, *"Where is the philosopher of this age?"* The word *philosopher* means "lover [*philo*] of wisdom [*sophia*]." The scholars praised those who sought wisdom and truth through the mind and reason. Paul contrasts two kinds of wisdom: the wisdom of the world (or *"this age"*—1 Cor. 1:20) with the wisdom of God (1 Cor. 1:21). Paul presents no common ground between these two types of wisdom. Through the wisdom of the world, people cannot come to know God (1 Cor. 1:22). The wisdom of God does not belong to this age but to a new age that began with the coming of Christ. Now, in the preaching of the gospel, the wisdom of God can be heard in the message of the cross (1 Cor. 1:17-18). Those who belong to this age see only foolishness in the gospel message.

Q 7 *What did the word "philosopher" mean to Paul's readers?*

Paul explains why the message of the cross hides the wisdom of God from both Jews and Greeks.

- Jews seek signs of God's wisdom and power. They find the cross to be foolishness. How could God's Chosen One, the Christ (Greek *Christos*—"Anointed One of God") be the one who is crucified? Such an idea is a stumbling stone to the Jews. Their Scriptures teach them: *"cursed is everyone who hangs on a tree"* (Deut. 21:23; Gal. 3:13).
- Greeks believed that death was only for humans. Their gods did not die. How could the wisdom and power of God (1 Cor. 1:24) be revealed through death?

Remember that the Corinthians were following the wisdom of the world. This caused them to divide into groups. But Paul gives three examples to contrast the wisdom of the world and the wisdom of God. In his first example, Paul states that the message of the cross is God's wisdom, but this gospel message is foolish to worldly Jews and Greeks. Human wisdom teaches us to depend on powerful signs and those who cannot die. In contrast, God's wisdom teaches us to depend on our crucified Savior.

2. The Corinthian believers were a contrast to human wisdom and standards (1 Cor. 1:26-31).

Q 8 *Underline 4 types of people God chooses (1 Cor. 1:26-31).*

²⁶Brothers, think of what you were when you were called. Not many of you were wise by human standards; not many were influential; not many were of noble birth. ²⁷But God chose the foolish things of the world to shame the wise; God chose the weak things of the world to shame the strong. ²⁸He chose the lowly things of this world and the despised things—and the things that are not—to nullify the things that are, ²⁹so that no one may boast before him. ³⁰It is because of him that you are in Christ Jesus, who has become for us wisdom from God—that is, our righteousness, holiness and redemption. ³¹Therefore, as it is written: "Let him who boasts boast in the Lord" (1 Cor. 1:26-31).

Boast in the Lord, not in self—nor in Paul, Peter, Apollos or any other leader!

The world chooses and honors its heroes. In contrast, God chooses common people, like the Corinthians, and like us. This way, the focus is not on humans. Rather, we focus on Jesus Christ who is our wisdom, our righteousness, our holiness, and our redemption (1 Cor. 1:30). The Corinthian believers were Paul's second example that contrasted human and divine wisdom. God did not pick the smartest, richest people He could find. He picked common Corinthians.

Q 9 *Give an example of an average, ordinary person whom God has used to build His kingdom.*

The story of Gideon in the Old Testament sheds light on the method of God's wisdom (Judges 7). Recall that Gideon brought together 32,000 warriors to fight the Midianites. Then God told him that there were too many soldiers. Is there such a possibility in human thinking—too many soldiers? But God told him to send away all the men who were afraid, and 22,000 went home to their families. Next, God had Gideon take the men down to the river to drink water. Out of the 10,000 men who remained, 9,700 got on their hands and knees and drank water. Only 300 men scooped water with their hands into their mouths. These were the ones God chose—only 1 percent of the original 30,000! Yet with this army of 300, God defeated the entire army of the Midianites! God did this so Israel would not boast. He did not want them to think that they saved themselves with their own strength. In His wisdom, he asked Gideon to act in military foolishness. God's wise method caused the praise to shine on Him. God chooses the foolish, the weak, the lowly, and the despised. This way, God gets the credit that only He deserves!

Years ago, leaders decided to close a Bible school. There were not enough students to pay the expenses. Experts could not find ways to increase the income of the school. Many thought it best to sell the school and buy property in a better location. Still, with great passion, the president of the school opposed the decision to close it. So leaders decided to wait 2 years.

To the surprise of everyone—even the president—the number of students grew each year. Some of those new students are now executives in the denomination. Today, that institution is full. Common sense and human reason agreed to close the school. However, the wisdom of God saw the future and knew what no man could know. God's wisdom guided the leaders to the correct decision. The executives of those days became wise in God when they paid attention to the plea of the president.

Samuel journeyed to Bethlehem to anoint a new king. God told Samuel to invite Jesse and his sons and to anoint one of them (1 Sam. 16:4-13). Samuel thought that Eliab looked like the next king of Israel. He was tall and handsome. Yet the Lord told Samuel, *"The Lord does not look at the things man looks at. Man looks at the outward appearance, but the Lord looks at the heart"* (1 Sam. 16:7). God had chosen David, the youngest and least impressive, for God's wisdom is quite different from worldly wisdom.

Q 10 *How did Paul's preaching differ from the great speakers of his day?*

3. Paul's preaching was a contrast to human wisdom (1 Cor. 2:1-5).

¹When I came to you, brothers, I did not come with eloquence or superior wisdom as I proclaimed to you the testimony about God. ²For I resolved to know nothing while I was with you except Jesus Christ and him crucified. ³I came to you in weakness and fear, and with much trembling. ⁴My message and my preaching were not with wise and persuasive words, but with a demonstration of the Spirit's power, ⁵so that your faith might not rest on men's wisdom, but on God's power (1 Cor. 2:1-5).

Paul kept the focus on Christ, not on himself. In contrast, human wisdom exalts great speakers.

Q 11 *Give an example of a preacher today who is like a picture frame that steals attention away from the picture.*

There is something wrong when the picture frame steals the attention away from the picture. The casket should not attract more attention than the person in it. The light is worthy of more praise than the bulb. And electricity deserves more appreciation than the wire that brings it. It is perverse and twisted when we exalt leaders and their gifts instead of God.¹ In 2 Corinthians, Paul reminds us that *"we have this treasure in jars of clay to show that this all-surpassing power is from God and not from us"* (2 Cor. 4:7). It is wrong for any believer to absorb the glory that belongs to God alone!

Q 12 *Which 3 examples does Paul use to contrast human and divine wisdom?*

Conclusion: Human wisdom led the Corinthians to exalt one leader above another. The result was division. But the Church should not follow the wisdom of the world.

Paul gave three examples to contrast the world's wisdom and God's wisdom. His three examples were:
- *First,* the gospel message of Christ crucified. This is foolishness to worldly Jews and Greeks. But it is the wisdom of God for all who will accept it.
- *Second,* the Corinthians themselves were a contrast to human wisdom and standards. Like us, they were common people who put their trust in God's powerful Savior.
- *Third,* Paul's preaching was not powerful or wise by human standards. The power was in the message, not in the style of the preacher.

Paul used these examples and more to help the Corinthians. The Spirit guides us to lift up Jesus, not leaders or their styles. In this way, the body of Christ is united and Jesus is glorified!

William J. Seymour, an African-American, was the son of freed slaves. After a year of Bible school, he became the leader of the Azusa Street Mission in Los Angeles, California, in 1906. He was not a highly trained theologian or a dynamic speaker. But he was a humble man of prayer. People who came into the services were surprised to see him kneel and hide behind the boxes that served as a pulpit on the platform. There he would seek the Lord until he felt he had a message for those present. He taught against racial prejudice, which was common in his day. Many were filled with the Holy Spirit and spoke in tongues at his meetings. He encouraged lay people who were blessed to go out and tell others. People loved, respected, and appreciated him. Many today recognize him as the father of modern Pentecostalism.[2] Would you have chosen him to be the spiritual forefather of half a billion Pentecostals and Charismatics?

Figure 2.3
William J. Seymour

Lesson 4: Three Types of People (1 Cor. 2:6–3:4)[3]

Goal: *Identify 3 types of people and state characteristics of each (1 Cor. 2:6–3:4).*

The big topic of 1 Corinthians 1–4 is division in the church. Human wisdom has led the Corinthian believers astray—guiding them to exalt human leaders. As we have seen, the body of Christ in Corinth was divided into four groups. In 1 Corinthians 2:6–3:4, Paul continues to contrast worldly and godly wisdom. He describes three types of people in this passage. It will not take you long to recognize the level of the Corinthians. Let us take a close look at these three types of people (Figure 2.4). (Note—one pastor illustrated this lesson by putting three chairs on the platform, and asking "Which chair are you sitting in?")

	C. The spiritual—maturing believers in Christ (1 Cor. 2:6, 15; 3:1)
	B. Worldly Christians—people who have been born again, but continue to live as babes in Christ (1 Cor. 3:1-3)
A. The unspiritual—people without the Spirit of God in them (1 Cor. 2:14)	

Figure 2.4 There are three types of people in the world, and each lives on a different level.

A. The unspiritual—people without the Spirit of God in them (1 Cor. 2:14)

The Bible has much to say about the unspiritual (Greek: *psuchikos*). They reject the righteous ways of the Spirit. Paul refers to this type of person as the man without the Spirit. *"The man without the Spirit does not accept the things that come from the Spirit of God, for they are foolishness to him, and he cannot understand them, because they are spiritually discerned"* (1 Cor. 2:14).

All of us were born into this world as unspiritual people. This is why we needed to be born again. But the unspiritual remain unborn spiritually. They are just natural people, unregenerated by the Spirit. These people, like animals, are guided by their natural desires (2 Pet. 2:12). They are under the rule of Satan (John 8:44; Acts 26:18). Unspiritual people do not have the Holy Spirit (Rom. 8:9). And they do not belong to God. The Bible often refers to these unspiritual people as sinners. All of us were once in this group. As Paul wrote to the Ephesians:

> ^{1}*And you were dead in your trespasses and sins, ^{2}in which you formerly walked according to the course of this world, according to the prince of the power of the air, of the spirit that is now working in the sons of disobedience. ^{3}Among them we too all formerly lived in the lusts of our flesh, indulging the desires of the flesh and of the mind, and were by nature children of wrath, even as the rest* (Eph. 2:1-3).

The unspiritual are moving toward God's judgment and eternal hell. God sees the unspiritual as evil and wicked—sinners who refuse to repent and be saved from sin. Paul reminds the Corinthians that they were once in this group of people.

> ^{9}*Do you not know that the wicked will not inherit the kingdom of God? Do not be deceived: Neither the sexually immoral nor idolaters nor adulterers nor male prostitutes nor homosexual offenders ^{10}nor thieves nor the greedy nor drunkards nor slanderers nor swindlers will inherit the kingdom of God. ^{11}And that is what some of you were. But you were washed, you were sanctified, you were justified in the name of the Lord Jesus Christ and by the Spirit of our God* (1 Cor. 6:9-11).

Unspiritual people belong to the world and live by the world's standards and values (James 4:4). The love of God is not in them. John wrote about these people when he said,

> ^{15}*Do not love the world nor the things in the world. If anyone loves the world, the love of the Father is not in him. ^{16}For all that is in the world, the lust of the flesh and the lust of the eyes and the boastful pride of life, is not from the Father, but is from the world* (1 John 2:15-16).

Can unspiritual people understand the Scriptures? Unspiritual people are not able to understand God's Word or His ways well (1 Cor. 2:14). Sometimes non-Christians do not understand the Bible at all. They are ever hearing, but never understanding (Matt. 13:13). They may be always learning, but never able to acknowledge the truth (2 Tim. 3:7). These remind us of the soil beside the path.

> *"When anyone hears the word of the kingdom and does not understand it, the evil one comes and snatches away what has been sown in his heart. This is the one on whom seed was sown beside the road"* (Matt. 13:19).

At other times, non-Christians may understand part of the Bible. They may understand the words, the facts, and some of the truths in Scripture. These may be like the rich ruler who understood the words of Jesus, but went away sad (Matt. 19:22). Or like Felix, they may understand the Word of God and fear the judgment to come (Acts 24:25).

The Holy Spirit enables believers to understand, grasp, and know spiritual truths that are beyond mere human knowledge. That is, He helps us know truths in our hearts and spirits, not just our minds. Theologians refer to this spiritual knowledge as *illumination—the result of the Spirit's revealing a truth within us and our experiencing it. We see God's truth with spiritual eyes, believe it, and are assured of it within our spirit. Paul wrote about this spiritual knowledge that goes beyond human knowledge (Eph. 3:17-19; Phil. 4:6-7). Heaven is an example of truth beyond the human mind. ^{9}*...*"*No eye has seen, no ear has heard, no mind has conceived what God has prepared for those who love him'— ^{10}but God has revealed it to us by his Spirit"* (1 Cor. 2:9-10).

> UNSPIRITUAL PEOPLE ARE NOT ABLE TO UNDERSTAND GOD'S WORD OR HIS WAYS WELL.

Q 13 *Is it possible for unbelievers to understand Scripture? Explain.*

Q 14 *Explain what it means to know truth that is beyond knowledge.*

¹⁸*But <u>the path of the righteous is like the light of dawn</u>, that shines brighter and brighter until the full day.* ¹⁹*<u>The way of the wicked is like darkness</u>; they do not know over what they stumble* (Prov. 4:18-19).

(For more discussion about how the Spirit helps us understand and interpret Scripture, study the final chapter of our *Faith & Action Series* course on *General Principles for Interpreting Scripture—Hermeneutics 1*.)

The Bible has much more to say about the unspiritual—those who are spiritually dead in their relationship to God (1 Cor. 2:6, 14). Most people are in this group and are on the broad road to destruction. In Corinth, unspiritual people were influencing the thinking of believers. So Paul reminded them that unspiritual people think only like the world thinks. They reject the wisdom of God. Now let us look at the second type of people Paul mentioned.

B. Worldly Christians—people who have been born again but continue to live as mere babies in Christ (1 Cor. 3:1-3)

¹*Brothers, I could not address you as spiritual but as worldly—mere infants in Christ.* ²*I gave you milk, not solid food, for you were not yet ready for it. Indeed, you are still not ready.* ³*You are still worldly. For since there is jealousy and quarreling among you, are you not worldly? Are you not acting like mere men?* (1 Cor. 3:1-3).

All people who receive Jesus as Savior are born again. At the moment of the new birth, God forgives our past sins, and the Holy Spirit enters us (Rom. 8:9). At this time of the new birth (regeneration), we become God's children (John 1:12-13).

Q 15 ↗ *How is an unspiritual person different from a worldly Christian?*

As God's new children in Christ, we are spiritual babies—mere infants in Christ. In those early days, we need milk, not meat. Peter tells us to desire the pure milk of the Word so that we will grow (1 Pet. 2:2). All babies are weak and need someone to feed them. It is God's will and plan for babies to grow into mature adults.

But some believers, like those at Corinth, do not grow in grace. Rather, as the years go by, they remain spiritual babies. As Paul said, these believers behave in a worldly manner *"—like mere infants in Christ"* (1 Cor. 3:1). The Greek text refers to worldly living as *fleshly* (*sarkikos*) (1 Cor. 3:1, 3).

The author of Hebrews wrote to believers in this group:

¹¹*Concerning him we have much to say, and it is hard to explain, since you have become dull of hearing.* ¹²*For though by this time you ought to be teachers, you have need again for someone to teach you the elementary principles of the oracles of God, and you have come to need milk and not solid food.* ¹³*For everyone who partakes only of milk is not accustomed to the word of righteousness, for he is an infant.* ¹⁴*But solid food is for the mature, who because of practice have their senses trained to discern good and evil* (Heb. 5:11-14).

At the new birth, we share in the divine nature of God (2 Pet. 1:4). Still, we remain in a body of flesh, and continue to have fleshly desires. In the life of a believer, our spiritual nature wars against our fleshly desires. Galatians describes the works of the flesh (Greek *sarx*, sometimes interpreted as *"the sinful nature"*).

¹⁶*But I say, walk by the Spirit, and you will not carry out the desire of the flesh.* ¹⁷*For the flesh sets its desire against the Spirit, and the Spirit against the flesh; for these are in opposition to one another, so that you may not do the things that you please.* ¹⁸*But if you are led by the Spirit, you are not under the Law.* ¹⁹*Now the deeds of the flesh are evident, which are: immorality, impurity, sensuality,* ²⁰*idolatry, sorcery, enmities, strife, jealousy, outbursts of anger, disputes, dissensions, factions,* ²¹*envying, drunkenness, carousing, and things like these, of*

which I forewarn you, just as I have forewarned you, that those who practice such things will not inherit the kingdom of God (Gal. 5:16-21).

Paul warned Galatian believers that if they followed the desires of their sinful nature (flesh), these desires would lead them away from heaven to hell (Gal. 5:21). In contrast, the Spirit leads us to produce good fruit, such as *"love, joy, peace, patience, kindness, goodness, faithfulness, gentleness, self-control"* (Gal. 5:22-23). Each believer must choose to be led by the flesh or by the Spirit.

In Corinth, at times, some believers were choosing to be led by the flesh. They were not living in complete disobedience to God. But they followed the world, the devil, and the flesh in some areas of their lives. These fleshly believers were living with one foot in the world and the other in the kingdom of God (1 Cor. 10:21; 2 Cor. 6:14-18; 11:3; 13:5). It is important to discern two truths about worldly Christians.

Q 16 *What are some characteristics of worldly believers?*

1. Worldly Christians are not growing in grace. They live like new converts, who do not understand what it means to follow Jesus (1 Cor. 3:1-2). In Corinth, their worldliness appeared in many ways. They had *"jealousy and quarreling"* (1 Cor. 3:3). They allowed sexual sins within the church (1 Cor. 5:1-13; 6:13-20). They were proud and did not respect church leaders, such as Paul (1 Cor. 4:18-19). They were going to courts of law on small matters (1 Cor. 6:8).

Q 17 *What dangers do worldly believers face?*

2. Worldly Christians are in great spiritual danger. In Corinth, worldly Christians were in danger of being led astray from their pure and sincere love for Christ (2 Cor. 11:3). They were in danger of being more and more like the world (2 Cor. 6:14-18). A little water can cause a sack of cement to become as hard as stone. Likewise, the influence of the world can cause a person to become completely worldly. A little leaven (yeast) affects the whole loaf (1 Cor. 5:6-7). Those who rebel against the Lord may be disciplined in this life (1 Cor. 11:30-32). Those who are led by the flesh will not inherit the kingdom of God (1 Cor. 6:9-10; Gal. 5:21).

> WORLDLY CHRISTIANS ARE IN GREAT SPIRITUAL DANGER.

For this you know with certainty, that no immoral or impure person or covetous man, who is an idolater, has an inheritance in the kingdom of Christ and God (Eph. 5:5).

Those who do not grow in grace are in danger of forgetting that they were once cleansed from past sins (2 Pet. 1:9). Then they deny, in words or deeds, the Lord who bought them (2 Pet. 2:1). They leave the straight way and wander off to follow the way of Balaam (2 Pet. 2:15). They become like a dog that returns to its vomit, and a sow that returns to the mud (2 Pet. 2:22).

> ¹⁷*You therefore, beloved, knowing this beforehand, be on your guard so that you are not carried away by the error of unprincipled men and fall from your own steadfastness,* ¹⁸*but grow in the grace and knowledge of our Lord and Savior Jesus Christ To Him be the glory, both now and to the day of eternity. Amen* (2 Pet. 3:17-18).

C. Spiritual Christians—maturing believers in Christ (1 Cor. 2:6, 15; 3:1)

As we have said, all who are born again have received the Holy Spirit (Rom. 8:9). At the moment of the new birth, we become babies in Christ. It is God's will for every spiritual baby to become a mature believer. Paul spoke about God's wisdom among the mature (1 Cor. 2:6). The spiritual understand the mind of Christ on many things.

How would the three types of people evaluate God's call to be a missionary?
- The natural man, not born again, says going to serve the Lord in another culture is foolish. It is a way of wasting years of life in an uncomfortable culture.
- A carnal or worldly believer thinks it is unnecessary for a missionary to leave home. He thinks God will call someone who lives closer to that place.
- The spiritual believer helps the missionary fulfill the call of God on his or her life.

¹⁵*The spiritual man makes judgments about all things, but he himself is not subject to any man's judgment:* ¹⁶ *"For who has known the mind of the Lord that he may instruct him?" But we have the mind of Christ* (1 Cor. 2:15-16).

Paul contrasts the fleshly believers at Corinth with those who are spiritual—more mature:

Q 18 *What are 2 types of believers in 1 Corinthians 3:1?*

¹*Brothers, I could not address you as spiritual but as worldly—mere infants in Christ.* ²*I gave you milk, not solid food, for you were not yet ready for it. Indeed, you are still not ready.* ³*You are still worldly. For since there is jealousy and quarreling among you, are you not worldly? Are you not acting like mere men?* (1 Cor. 3:1-3).

The Corinthians were *"Brothers"* in Christ, but they were baby brothers—mere infants on milk. In contrast, spiritual brothers are mature and can eat spiritual *meat*.

In Galatians, Paul contrasts the spiritual with believers who get trapped, tangled, and caught in the net of sin. *"Brothers, if someone is caught in a sin, you who are spiritual should restore him gently. But watch yourself, or you also may be tempted"* (Gal. 6:1).

Q 19 *Which 2 types of believers does Paul contrast in Galatians 6:1?*

Notice that Paul warns spiritual believers to be gentle, humble, and alert, lest they be tempted by the sins that have trapped others (Gal. 6:1). All believers can be tempted, since even Jesus was tempted (Matt. 4:1-10). Jesus taught us to watch and pray, so that we do not enter into temptation. The spirit part of us is willing, but our flesh is weak (Matt. 26:41). The Spirit guides us to turn away from and go around temptations. We cannot keep a bird from flying over our heads, but we can prevent it from building a nest in our hair. Likewise, we cannot avoid all temptation, but we can avoid entering into it. *"But I say, walk by the Spirit, and you will not carry out the desire of the flesh"* (Gal. 5:16).

There is an old story about a man who had a black dog and a brown dog. He traveled around with the dogs, and some people bought tickets to see the two dogs fight. Sometimes the black dog won, and other times the brown dog won. But the owner always knew which dog would win. A visitor once asked the owner how he could always choose the winner. "It is easy," replied the owner. "The winner will always be the one that I feed that week!" Likewise, in the struggle between the flesh and the spirit, the winner is always the one we feed!

Q 20 *What lesson is in the story of the two dogs?*

Figure 2.5 Living a spiritual, holy life is more like riding a sailboat than rowing a boat with oars. We must depend on the Holy Spirit to enable us to live a holy life.

Hundreds of verses in the New Testament urge us to grow in grace. Such verses emphasize walking in the Spirit, not the flesh, and living a holy life that is worthy of our calling. Here are some qualities and characteristics of mature, spiritual believers in Christ:

Q 21 *What are some characteristics of spiritual, maturing believers?*

- A spiritual person thinks the thoughts of God (1 Cor. 2:11-13). This includes meditating on God's Word.

- A spiritual person depends on, yields to, and is led by the Spirit of God (Rom. 8:4-17; Gal. 5:16-26). We cannot live a holy life in our own strength. But it is as easy for us to live a holy life by the Spirit as it is for a fruit tree to produce good fruit. By living in the Spirit, we overcome the power of our fleshly desires. As the spiritual part of us becomes strong, our sinful nature becomes weak.
- A spiritual person resists evil thoughts, sinful desires, worldly temptations, and sin's rule (Rom. 8:13-14; James 4:7; Matt. 4:1-11; 16:23; Heb. 12:1).
- A spiritual person loves what is right and hates what is wrong (Rom. 12: 9; Heb. 1:9).
- A spiritual person practices denying self daily (Matt. 16:24; Rom. 8:12-13; Tit. 2:12).
- A spiritual person gets rid of *dark* things from the old self, such as lying, stealing, laziness, unhealthy talk, bitterness, rage and anger, brawling, slander, sexual sins, and drunkenness (Eph. 4:22–5:5, 18; Col. 3:5-11); deceit, hypocrisy, and envy (1 Pet. 2:1).
- A spiritual person purifies himself from all that displeases God (Rom. 6:14-16; 1 Cor. 6:9-10; 2 Cor. 6:14-18; Gal. 6:7-9; James 1:12-16).
- A spiritual person makes every effort to put on the *light* things of the new self, such as kindness, compassion, forgiveness (Eph. 4:32); goodness, righteousness, truth, and all that pleases the Lord (Eph. 5:9-10); and humility, gentleness, patience, love, peace, spiritual songs, and holiness (Col. 3:12-17; 1 Pet. 1:13-16; 2 Pet. 1:5-11).
- A spiritual person is filled with the Spirit, again and again, day after day (Eph. 5:18). As we noted, all believers receive the Holy Spirit at the new birth. But after this, believers should seek to be filled with the Spirit, as the apostles and others were filled with the Spirit on the Day of Pentecost (Acts 2:1-4). Being filled with the Spirit for the first time, after salvation, is called the baptism in the Holy Spirit (Acts 1:5). There is one baptism in the Spirit, but there are many fillings of the Spirit (Acts 4:8, 31). All believers should seek to be filled with the presence of God day by day. The more of the Holy Spirit we have, the easier it is to live a holy life. As we noted earlier, living by the Spirit is the key to living a holy, spiritual life (Rom. 8:4-17; Gal. 5:16-26). Yesterday's power is not enough for today's battles. We need daily bread for our physical bodies. And we need daily spiritual bread to be strong in spirit.
- A spiritual person prays often in tongues to edify himself (1 Cor. 14:4, 18; Jude 20).
- A spiritual person learns from the example of the Israelites, whom God destroyed because of sin (1 Cor. 10:5-12).
- A spiritual person discerns that it is impossible to share in the things of God and the things of Satan at the same time (Matt. 6:24; 1 Cor. 10:21; 1 John 1:5-8).
- A spiritual person follows the path of holiness (Heb. 12:14; 1 Pet. 1:15) and perfects holiness (holy living) in respect and reverence for God (2 Cor. 7:1).

Conclusion: We have looked at three types of people: the unspiritual (spiritually unborn), worldly Christians (infants in Christ), and the spiritual (maturing believers). Let us be aware of our Father's plan for His children to grow and mature. Let us realize that it is hard to stand still. Rather, we tend either to go backward or to go forward in our relationship with God. We either become less like Christ or more like Him. Let us study what the Scriptures teach about conforming to Christ, rather than being guided by the world (Rom. 12:1-2). The apostle Peter's words summarize this topic well, which the NIV calls, "Making One's Calling and Election Sure:"

> ³*Seeing that <u>His divine power has granted to us everything pertaining to life and godliness</u>, through the true knowledge of Him who called us by His own glory and excellence.* ⁴*For by these He has granted to us His precious and magnificent promises, <u>so that by them you may become partakers of the divine nature, having escaped the corruption that is in the world by lust.</u>* ⁵*Now for this*

very reason also, <u>applying all diligence</u>, in your faith supply moral excellence, and in your moral excellence, knowledge, ⁶and in your knowledge, self-control, and in your self-control, perseverance, and in your perseverance, godliness, ⁷and in your godliness, brotherly kindness, and in your brotherly kindness, love. ⁸For if these qualities are yours <u>and are increasing</u>, they render you neither useless nor unfruitful in the true knowledge of our Lord Jesus Christ. ⁹For he who lacks these qualities is blind or short-sighted, having forgotten his purification from his former sins. ¹⁰Therefore, brethren, <u>be all the more diligent to make certain about His calling and choosing you</u>; for as long as you practice these things, you will never stumble; ¹¹<u>for in this way the entrance into the eternal kingdom of our Lord and Savior Jesus Christ will be abundantly supplied to you</u> (2 Pet. 1:3-11).

Figure 2.6 Spiritual believers grow in grace by facing the Lord and taking small steps day by day.

Lesson 5: Three Examples to Show That the Church Belongs to God (1 Cor. 3:5-23)

Goal A: *Explain each of the 3 illustrations that show that the Church belongs to God (1 Cor. 3:5-17).*
Goal B: *Explain the sense in which all things belong to the saints (1 Cor. 3:18-23).*

Setting

The wisdom of the world had led Corinthian believers astray. As the world lifts up its heroes, the believers at Corinth were lifting up Paul, Peter, Apollos, and perhaps false apostles (2 Cor. 11). Also, some believers at Corinth were proud and arrogant (1 Cor. 4:18). These self-centered believers were acting like the church belonged to them. So Paul gives three illustrations to remind them that the whole Church, and each local church, belongs to God. Paul compared the church to a field, a building, and a temple. Let us look at each of these three illustrations and consider principles to guide us.⁴

A. We are God's field (1 Cor. 3:5-9).

Consider four truths about believers—God's field.

1. Workers are necessary for a field to be fruitful (1 Cor. 3:5). This is true about a garden, a farm, or a church.

Q 22 What are some things in a local church that depend on the believers in it?

Two friends stood in a garden and talked together. The owner was thankful for all of the ripe tomatoes, onions, cabbage, and potatoes. The visitor smiled and said, "But this is God's garden, and He deserves all the credit." "That is true," said the owner, "but you should have seen it when God had it by Himself, without my help!"

Likewise, each local church is God's field. But God needs pastors, teachers, deacons, and faithful members to work in His field. Otherwise, it will not be fruitful as He intends. God needs a prepared pastor to preach a good sermon. He needs dedicated and prepared teachers to teach good lessons. It takes faithful members to live holy lives, witness, and tithe.

2. The workers in God's field are servants, not heroes (1 Cor. 3:5, 7). The world has heroes, but the Church has only servants.

Q 23 The world has heroes, but the Church has _____ .

What, after all, is Apollos? And what is Paul? <u>Only servants</u>, through whom you came to believe (1 Cor. 3:5).

So neither he who plants nor he who waters is anything, but only God who makes things grow (1 Cor. 3:7).

Jesus reminded His followers to call themselves servants, even when God has blessed their work (Luke 17:10).

3. The servants in God's field have one purpose, but different tasks (1 Cor. 3:8). Paul planted, but Apollos watered.

> *What, after all, is Apollos? And what is Paul? Only servants, through whom you came to believe—as the Lord has assigned <u>to each his task</u>* (1 Cor. 3:5).

Application: It was wrong for the Corinthians to exalt Apollos over Paul. God created both servants for different tasks. Likewise, God has work for each believer in the church. Believers today should not exalt one servant over another.

Paul has more to say about workers and rewards in his second example—*"You are God's field, God's building."*

B. We are God's building (1 Cor. 3:9-15).

These verses contain four principles related to believers—God's building.

1. The foundation of God's building, the Church, is Jesus Christ (1 Cor. 3:10-11). *"For no one can lay any foundation other than the one already laid, which is Jesus Christ"* (1 Cor. 3:11).

The foundation is the most important part of a building. It is built first and must be strong enough to support the whole building. Jesus Christ, the Son of God, is our Rock—the solid foundation on which the Church is built (Matt. 16:16-18).

2. Each believer is either a wise or foolish builder (1 Cor. 3:12). *"If any man builds on this foundation using gold, silver, costly stones, wood, hay or straw…"* (1 Cor. 3:12).

Wise believers build with gold, silver, and costly stones. Foolish believers build with wood, hay, or straw. What does this mean? Notice that Paul contrasts temporary materials (wood, hay, and straw) with permanent materials (gold, silver, and costly stones). In other words, some believers live and work only for the temporary—their life on this earth. These foolish believers work for foolish reasons such as selfish desires or the praise of men. Other believers live and work for eternity. These lay up treasure in heaven and live to please God (Matt. 6:1-24).

3. Fire will test the quality of each man's work (1 Cor. 3:13). Imagine a great fire in front of people at the judgment seat of Christ. All believers will be there and must carry their works into the fire.

> *For we must all appear before the judgment seat of Christ, that each one may receive what is due him for the things done while in the body, whether good or bad* (2 Cor. 5:10).

Note that this is a judgment of rewards for our works. We are saved by grace, not works. But God promises to reward us for our works for Him. God gives us the grace to succeed, and then He rewards us for being good stewards of His grace!

All works must pass through the same fire. This fire acts like a judge, who does not favor one person over another. Rather, it judges all works by the same standard. Believers will walk toward this fire, carrying their works—the good deeds they did on earth. Some will approach the fire with both arms full of good works and come out on the other side with all they expected. These are those who built with permanent materials and pure motives. Others will pass through the fire and come out with little or nothing on the other side. These are the foolish believers who lived only for the passing blessings of earth. How will it be for each of us? Will we bow our heads in shame over wasted years? Or will we rejoice for all of eternity that we lived our lives wisely? Lord, *"Teach us to number our days aright, that we may gain a heart of wisdom"* (Ps. 90:12).

4. God will reward each believer for what passes through the fire (1 Cor. 3:8, 14-15). Works that survive the fire test are the basis of eternal rewards. Passages such as Matthew 19:28-30 and Luke 19:11-27 teach that God will reward those who are faithful in this life.

Q 24 How do the tasks God has given you differ from the tasks of other believers?

Q 25 What do wood and gold each represent?

Q 26 What type of works will pass through the fire unharmed?

Q 27 What promise for workers is in 1 Corinthians 3:8?

Q 28 What does Luke 19:11-27 teach about rewards?

Christian Preferences

C. We are God's temple (1 Cor. 3:16-17).

¹⁶Don't you know that you yourselves are God's temple and that God's Spirit lives in you? ¹⁷If anyone destroys God's temple, God will destroy him; for God's temple is sacred, and you are that temple (1 Cor. 3:16-17).

The word *you* in 1 Corinthians 3:16-17 is plural, referring to all believers together in a group. God's Spirit lives in His body, the Church. Paul warns each person not to destroy God's temple (the Church), or God will destroy him. Believers in Corinth were destroying God's temple by dividing the Church—by exalting one leader over another (1 Cor. 1–4).

Q 29 *Will God destroy _____ for destroying His Church through division (1 Cor. 3:16-17)?*

As a young man, Kevin accepted Christ and received biblical training. People often thanked him for ways he served the church. In Bible school, he became a member of the student council. An official of the denomination talked to him about a small group of people in the mountains. They wanted to form a church and needed a pastor to lead them. But Kevin said he did not feel that was where he should work for the Lord.

In the capital city he, with some of his friends from school, decided to do something great. Why should he waste time with a few people hidden away in a village? So Kevin found a piece of property in a nice part of the city. He told several friends that he was going to do something for all to see. Soon, construction of a great church began. The group was able to build a magnificent building. But it seemed strange that in such a big church, the offerings for missions were small. And there were no appeals to raise funds to open new churches—in the city or the rural areas.

Over time the church had one conflict after another. Attendance decreased until few people attended the large church. Kevin had led the building project with pride and vanity. His desire was not to build God's kingdom, but to build a name for himself. The foundation of that church was neither gold, silver, nor precious stones—it was wood, hay, and straw.

Several years ago, Armando, a youth at church, discovered that some believers were growing slowly. He did not understand that believers grow at different rates. And he did not discern that the church should be patient with all believers. So this young man accused the leadership of being sinful and lukewarm. Then, he called a meeting of all the young people who wanted the church to be more spiritual. As a result the church services became very tense. Finally, the church suffered a division.

In time, many of the young people who paid attention to the murmuring drifted away and lost their faith. Some of them turned to drugs. Now, Armando, the youth who caused the problem, no longer attends any church. And he suffers mental problems, which have separated him from his family.

Meanwhile, the church Armando called unspiritual has multiplied several times. Some of those who had not shown much growth in the beginning have become mature leaders.

D. Conclusion: *"All things are yours"* (1 Cor. 3:18-23).

As we close this lesson, notice that Paul focuses on two things.

First, he tells us to reject worldly wisdom that conflicts with God's wisdom (1 Cor. 3:18-20). God catches the worldly wise, like Haman (Est. 7:9), in their own web.

Second, he says to receive all of God's blessings with a thankful heart (1 Cor. 3:21-23).

²¹So then, no more boasting about men! All things are yours, ²²whether Paul or Apollos or Cephas or the world or life or death or the present or the future—all are yours, ²³and you are of Christ, and Christ is of God (1 Cor. 3:21-23).

Q 30 *What does this mean: "All things are yours"? Give examples.*

Paul counsels believers to see the big picture. Everything around us is ours—everything is a blessing from God to us. All things belong to the saints, for we are joint heirs with Christ (1 Cor. 3:21).

- *Workers* like Paul, Apollos, and Peter are blessings from God. Appreciate all of them, but do not exalt one over another.
- The *world* is a gift from God for us to use, but not abuse—to enjoy as we pass through it (1 Cor. 7:31).
- *Life* is a blessing from God to us. Let us live it wisely.
- *Death* is also a blessing. It is a gate from this life to a better one.
- The *present* is God's gift to us. The past is gone. But the present is here for us to appreciate and use wisely.
- The *future* will bring the coming of Christ, the resurrection of the body, the day of judgment, heaven, and everlasting life.

All of these blessings belong to us, and we belong to Christ, the Son of God (1 Cor. 3:23).

Lesson 6 — Guidelines for the Corinthians and Their Apostle (1 Cor. 4:1-21)

Goal: *Explain a principle about each of these: faithfulness, conscience, God's Word, spiritual children, and God's kingdom.*

Setting

The Corinthians are not only *for* Apollos and Peter, some of them are *against* Paul. The streams of problems at Corinth flow into a river of opposition against Paul.[5] In 1 Corinthians 4, he defends his role as an apostle.

Paul made it clear that he and all believers are servants of Christ. *"So then, men ought to regard us as servants of Christ and as those entrusted with the secret things [mystery] of God"* (1 Cor. 4:1). In 1 Corinthians 4:1, the Greek word for *"secret things"* is *musterion,* often translated "mystery." In other places, Paul explains that the mystery is about our blessings through Jesus Christ.

> *⁴... the mystery of Christ ... ⁶to be specific,[is] that the Gentiles are fellow heirs and fellow members of the body, and fellow partakers of the promise in Christ Jesus through the gospel* (Eph. 3:4, 6).

Q 31 *How are believers like rowers on a boat?*

Let us examine five principles that Paul gives to help members of the body see themselves and their leaders correctly.

A. God does not require us to be successful servants, but He does require us to be faithful (1 Cor. 4:1-2).

¹So then, men ought to regard us as servants of Christ and as those entrusted with the secret things of God. ²Now it is required that those who have been given a trust must prove faithful (1 Cor. 4:1-2).

Paul says God has entrusted the gospel mystery to His servants—the apostles (and all believers). In 1 Corinthians 4:1, the Greek word for *servants* is *huperates*. This word is made up of two words—*hupo* (under) and *eretes* (rower).[6] Roman warships came to Corinth from the seas nearby (Figure 2.8). The lowest level of a warship had rows of benches on both sides of the ship. Rowers sat on these benches and rowed the ship with the oars that went into the water (Figure 2.7).[7] The rowers were under (*hupo*) the captain, who sat a level above them. The task of the rowers was to do exactly as the captain above them said. Their whole job was to obey orders. Likewise, Paul refers to himself and believers as servants (*huperetes*)—rowers under our heavenly Captain. All that He requires of us is to obey Him!

Figure 2.7 In Paul's day, rowers enabled many boats to move forward.

Figure 2.8 Roman warships came to Corinth from three seas: the Adriatic, Mediterranean, and Aegean.

B. God, not conscience, is our final judge (1 Cor. 4:4).

My conscience is clear, but that does not make me innocent. It is the Lord who judges me (1 Cor. 4:4).

The Bible says several things about the conscience.

- Each person has a conscience. Conscience is a gift from God. It is a lesser judge within. It is aware of all the actions, thoughts, and decisions that a person makes. A good conscience testifies that a person has done right. A guilty conscience occurs if a person sins against God or others. Paul said that conscience either accuses or defends a person (Rom. 2:15).

    Q 32 *What is a conscience?*

- It is possible for a person to be sinning and still have a clear conscience. *"Paul looked straight at the Sanhedrin and said, 'Brethren, I have lived my life with a perfectly good conscience before God up to this day'"* (Acts 23:1). This verse includes Paul's life before he was a believer. Remember that he obeyed the Law before receiving Christ. By the Law, Paul was without fault (Phil. 3:6). Some unbelievers may live with a clear conscience.

    Q 33 *How is it possible for some who sin not to have a guilty conscience?*

- A conscience can make mistakes. It acts on the basis of knowledge. Knowledge is information or understanding gotten through experience. But knowledge may be incomplete. Paul's conscience did not accuse him when he rebuked the high priest (Acts 23:1-5). Why? Because Paul did not know he was talking to the high priest. Likewise, Paul once thought it was God's will for him to persecute believers (Acts 26:9; 1 Tim. 1:13). He did not know that he was doing the opposite of God's will. The conscience does not condemn a person for things it does not know are wrong. Likewise, some consciences do not condemn because they have been seared—ignored and opposed until they are ruined (1 Tim. 4:2).

Application. Knowledge may be true or false. People know what they have learned. But there are true teachings and false teachings. Some cultures approve things that God forbids. These sins may include lying, having many wives, having sex outside of marriage, stealing, killing unborn babies, bribing, drunkenness, gossip, selfishness, and so on. It is sad when culture opposes God and truth. Then people live by standards that are false; the light that is in them is darkness (Matt. 6:23).

Q 34 *Is all knowledge true? Explain.*

Conscience judges only on the basis of what it knows. Paul writes of those who have a weak conscience. He says these have a weak conscience because they lack true knowledge (1 Cor. 8:7). The consciences of many people are not accurate. Why? Because they have not been taught what God says is right and wrong. Many do what is right in their own eyes (Judges 17:6). But they are wrong in God's eyes.

Some believers live with false knowledge. They are true to what they believe. But what they believe is not true. They grow up under false teachings in the world or the

Q 35 *What are some examples of sincere people living with false knowledge?*

church. These false teachings include things like false security, false apostles, purgatory, salvation by works, living unholy lives, worshiping ancestors, and doubting the value of education, medicine, or technology.

Q 36 *How can a person have a conscience that prepares him to stand before God?*

A conscience can be renewed and enlightened. The Scriptures make a person's conscience more reliable. Paul explains that a person may not recognize some sins without Scripture (Rom. 7:7). God's Word is a light to our paths and our conscience (Ps. 119:105). The Scriptures and the Holy Spirit enlighten the conscience—they guide it to judge by God's standards of truth, rather than the standards of the world.

(For more about conscience, see the *Faith & Action* course *Acts of the Holy Spirit*, chapter 13, Lesson 38, points A and B.)

C. God's Word, not church leaders, is the basis of our faith (1 Cor. 4:6).

"Do not go beyond what is written." Then you will not take pride in one man over against another (1 Cor. 4:6).

Q 37 *Is it always wise to follow church leaders? Explain.*

Believers at Corinth were being guided by human wisdom and human talent rather than the Scriptures. Is it always wise to follow church leaders? No! We should only follow church leaders as they walk in the light of Scriptures. About A.D. 50 the Galatian believers made the same type of mistake the Corinthians were making in about A.D. 55. They left the path of gospel truth to follow false teachers. Paul wrote to the Galatians:

> ⁶*I am amazed that you are so quickly deserting Him who called you by the grace of Christ, for a different gospel;* ⁷*which is really not another; only there are some who are disturbing you and want to distort the gospel of Christ.* ⁸*But even if we, or an angel from heaven, should preach to you a gospel contrary to what we have preached to you, he is to be accursed!* ⁹*As we have said before, so I say again now, if any man is preaching to you a gospel contrary to what you received, he is to be accursed!* (Gal. 1:6-9).

Do not be foolish like some were in Galatia and in Corinth. Those who follow false teachers are not innocent. God will not excuse lazy believers who refused to search the Scriptures. God will not excuse weak believers who were afraid to stand up for the truth. If your pastor or church leader preaches false doctrines, turn away from him. Follow the truth, and lead your family and friends on the path of biblical teaching.

Sometimes, those who preach mix truth and error. We should turn away from these false teachings and base our faith on the Bible. What answers do the Scriptures give on these topics:

Q 38 *Answer the 10 questions on modern topics.*

- Is it right to baptize babies?
- Did miracles cease with the apostles, or are they still for today?
- Is it God's will for all believers to speak in tongues?
- Should every believer seek to live a life of victory over sin?
- Is it possible to fall from grace and be lost?
- Who should win the most people to Christ, pastors or lay people?
- Can believers who are following Jesus be possessed by demons?
- Is it God's will for all believers to be wealthy?
- Should we pray to Mary or believers who have died?
- What are the characteristics and signs of a true apostle?

Q 39 *What are some teachings your culture accepts that the Bible forbids?*

The Jews at Berea were more noble than the Jews at Thessalonica. They searched the Scriptures to see what was true (Acts 17:11). Let us not be content to approve what preachers say, until we search the Scriptures and confirm the truth.

D. God's most spiritual children may not be the richest or the safest (1 Cor. 4:8-13).

In his second letter to the Corinthians, Paul will have a lot to say about false apostles. But First Corinthians reveals that some were claiming to be more spiritual

Christian Preferences 43

than Paul. The wisdom of the world led some believers to a false conclusion. They thought that the more spiritual a person is, the wealthier he is. Paul rebukes this foolish thinking.

> *⁸Already you have all you want! Already you have become rich! You have become kings—and that without us! How I wish that you really had become kings so that we might be kings with you! ⁹**For it seems to me that God has put us apostles on display at the end of the procession,** like men condemned to die in the arena. We have been made a spectacle to the whole universe, to angels as well as to men. ¹⁰We are fools for Christ, but you are so wise in Christ! We are weak, but you are strong! You are honored, we are dishonored! ¹¹To this very hour we go hungry and thirsty, we are in rags, we are brutally treated, we are homeless. ¹²We work hard with our own hands. When we are cursed, we bless; when we are persecuted, we endure it; ¹³when we are slandered, we answer kindly. Up to this moment we have become the scum of the earth, the refuse of the world* (1 Cor. 4:8-13).

Q 40 *Underline 10 characteristics of Paul, a great spiritual leader (1 Cor. 4:8-13).*

Q 41 *How did Paul differ from some who call themselves apostles today?*

Q 42 *Can we measure a person's spirituality by his wealth? Explain.*

E. God's kingdom is not a matter of talk, but of power (1 Cor. 4:14-20).

For the kingdom of God is not a matter of talk but of power (1 Cor. 4:20).

Some people at Corinth had become proud (1 Cor. 4:18). These were attacking Paul and exalting themselves. Paul will write a lot about haughty believers and super apostles later (see 2 Cor. 10–13). Paul assures believers that when he comes to Corinth, he will come with the power of an apostle (1 Cor. 4:18-21; 2 Cor. 13:2-4).

Q 43 *Do some people today claim the title and honor of "apostle," but lack the power? Explain.*

The kingdom of God is a kingdom of power, not just talk. God's power enables us to be born again. His power frees us from sin at the new birth. Afterward, when He fills us with the Holy Spirit, He gives us power to witness, power to serve, and power to live a holy life. The power of God is present in all of the believers in God's kingdom.

And in the apostles, the power of God is present in a special way. False teachers are often good talkers. They will talk with great authority from sun-up to moon-down. Therefore, God gives apostles special power to establish the kingdom of God. Otherwise, people can be led astray by false teachers.

The power of God was present with Peter when Ananias and Sapphira lied (Acts 5). The young church was growing, and the devil tried to hinder it through lies and hypocrisy. But the power of God flowed through the apostle Peter, and the Holy Spirit struck Ananias and Sapphira dead. The most clever lies are not a match for God's power.

> *⁶When they [Paul and Barnabas] had gone through the whole island as far as Paphos, they found a magician, a Jewish false prophet whose name was Bar-Jesus, ⁷who was with the proconsul, Sergius Paulus, a man of intelligence. This man summoned Barnabas and Saul and sought to hear the word of God. ⁸But Elymas the magician (for so his name is translated) was opposing them, seeking to turn the proconsul away from the faith. ⁹But Saul, who was also known as Paul, filled with the Holy Spirit, fixed his gaze on him, ¹⁰and said, "You who are full of all deceit and fraud, you son of the devil, you enemy of all righteousness, will you not cease to make crooked the straight ways of the Lord? ¹¹Now, behold, the hand of the Lord is upon you, and you will be blind and not see the sun for a time." And immediately a mist and a darkness fell upon him, and he went about seeking those who would lead him by the hand. ¹²Then the proconsul believed when he saw what had happened, being amazed at the teaching of the Lord* (Acts 13:6-12).

Where the power of God is lacking, false teachers and false apostles take turns talking. To establish the church, and keep it on the right path, we must have the power of God today.

Q 44 *What are some ways the Spirit gives us power today?*

In the kingdom of God, a power encounter is often necessary. For God's kingdom to expand, we must conquer areas of the devil's kingdom. So God gives us the power of the Holy Spirit. This power reveals itself in various anointings and spiritual gifts. God's power enables us to preach clearly, refute false teaching, and cast down every thought that exalts itself against the knowledge of Christ (2 Cor. 10). The Holy Spirit empowers us to cast out demons, heal the sick, discern spirits, prophesy the secrets of men's hearts, and make wise decisions beyond our own ability. Today, we are thankful for education, technology, and other modern helps for spreading the gospel. But our great need continues to be for the power of God in our lives. May God help us to avoid the error of the Corinthians, who turned away from God's power to follow charismatic personalities, polished talkers, and talented performers.

Test Yourself: Circle the letter by the *best* completion to each question or statement.

1. Paul refutes which type of worldly wisdom?
   a) Respecting professors
   b) Choosing favorites
   c) Seeking doctors
   d) Obeying officials

2. Which types of wisdom did Paul contrast?
   a) The wisdom of babes and the mature
   b) The wisdom of Jews and Gentiles
   c) The wisdom of parents and children
   d) The wisdom of God and man

3. To illustrate divine wisdom, Paul used
   a) Solomon's temple.
   b) the Jews.
   c) the Corinthians.
   d) the creation.

4. At Corinth, a result of worldly wisdom was
   a) prosperity.
   b) honor.
   c) sickness.
   d) division.

5. To whom does Paul refer as *"infants in Christ"*?
   a) Gentiles
   b) Jews
   c) Worldly believers
   d) The unspiritual

6. Who is in danger of losing salvation?
   a) Unspiritual believers
   b) Worldly believers
   c) Mature believers
   d) All believers

7. Which 3 did Paul use to show that we belong to God?
   a) A field, a building, a temple
   b) A field, a temple, a vineyard
   c) A temple, a household, an army
   d) A building, a temple, a tower

8. In 1 Corinthians 3, Paul specifically taught that
   a) heaven belongs to the saints.
   b) hell belongs to the saints.
   c) Scripture belongs to the saints.
   d) death belongs to the saints.

9. What does God require from His servants?
   a) Faithfulness
   b) Success
   c) Motivation
   d) Creativity

10. In the parade of life, where do apostles walk?
    a) At the front of the line
    b) In the middle of the line
    c) In a line by themselves
    d) At the end of the line

 Essay Test Topics: Write 50-100 words on each of these goals that you studied in this chapter.

The Problem and the Contrast (1 Cor. 1:10–2:5)

Goal: *Explain the problem Paul writes about in 1 Corinthians 1:10-17.*

Goal: *Summarize 3 illustrations Paul gives that contrast human and divine wisdom (1 Cor. 1:18–2:5).*

Three Types of People (1 Cor. 2:6–3:4)

Goal: *Identify 3 types of people and state characteristics of each (1 Cor. 2:6–3:4).*

Three Examples to Show That the Church Belongs to God (1 Cor. 3:5-23)

Goal: *Explain each of the 3 illustrations that show that the Church belongs to God (1 Cor. 3:5-17).*

Goal: *Explain the sense in which all things belong to the saints (1 Cor. 3:18-23).*

Guidelines for the Corinthians and Their Apostle (1 Cor. 4:1-21)

Goal: *Explain a principle about each of these: faithfulness, conscience, God's Word, spiritual children, and God's kingdom.*

Chapter 3:
Christian Choices
(1 Corinthians 5–7)

Introduction

A reporter who worked for a well-known newspaper called me when I was a pastor. "I must talk to you as soon as possible," he said. When he arrived, he accused me and our church of deceiving him. "You raised my hopes to believe that my troubles with my wife and all those at work would end if I accepted Christ as my Savior. But this did not happen. When I told my wife that I had accepted the Lord, fury broke out. My wife cried in anger. The rest of my family said I had brought shame on them. And things have only gotten worse as the days go by."

Figure 3.1
Main street of ancient Corinth, now in ruins. As often happens in seaport cities, Corinth was a center of all kinds of sin—especially sexual immorality. In fact, "to Corinthianize" was a proverb in Paul's time that referred to practicing the worst kind of vileness.

The angry reporter even threatened to take me to court in a lawsuit. I did my best to assure him that the Lord would help him. He just needed to affirm his faith in God and in the Scriptures. But the more I talked, the more upset the reporter became.

Finally, I told him, "Look, sir, we must understand what is going on. God has allowed these fierce trials, but He is in control. The Lord will not permit Satan to destroy our faith. We must stand firm in trials. In a very short time, the powers of the enemy will be defeated."

I felt so sad when the reporter walked out of my house. He said, "Never again will I listen to the promises of the Evangelicals." As he left, I made a vow in my heart. "Never again will I paint a picture of the Christian life without explaining that at times, following Jesus is very difficult." And we always need to have patience and faith when the trials are many.[1]

Lessons:

Choices About Church Discipline (1 Cor. 5:1-13)
Goal: *Summarize 4 principles on discipline in the local church.*

Choices About Legal Disputes (1 Cor. 6:1-8)
Goal: *Summarize 3 reasons why believers should settle disputes in the local church, not in court.*

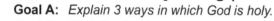
Choices About Holy Living (1 Cor. 6:9-11)
Goal A: *Explain 3 ways in which God is holy.*
Goal B: *Explain what it means to be holy in our position in Christ. Cite Bible references.*
Goal C: *Draw the triangle of holiness, and explain its sides and corners.*
Goal D: *Compare and contrast 3 aspects of holiness. Match Scriptures with each aspect.*

Choices About Sex (1 Cor. 6:12-20)
Goal A: *Explain how sexual sins are against self and God.*
Goal B: *List and explain 4 ways in which to honor God with your body and avoid sexual sins.*

Choices About Marriage (1 Cor. 7:1-40)
Goal: *Explain 4 biblical principles related to marriage.*

 Key Words

discipline   excommunicating

Lesson 7

Choices About Church Discipline (1 Cor. 5:1-13)

Goal: *Summarize 4 principles on discipline in the local church.*

Setting

Among the problems reported to Paul was a shocking case of immorality—a man was living with his father's wife.² We can almost hear Paul gasp. He remarks that this kind of immorality is not even practiced among pagans!³ The Greeks were known for sexual sins, but no Greek city had a worse reputation than Corinth. One Greek writer created a verb: *Korinthiazein*. To *act like a Corinthian* meant to commit fornication.⁴ In Corinth, prostitutes in the pagan temples had sex with those who came to worship. This darkened the city's reputation.⁵

It is not surprising that people raised in Corinth struggled with sexual sins. Still, Paul was shocked that sexual sin existed in the church. And the apostle was amazed that believers tolerated it. Let us look at four principles related to church *discipline.

A. Sin in the church should lead to grief among the members (1 Cor. 5:1-2).

¹It is actually reported that there is sexual immorality among you, and of a kind that does not occur even among pagans: A man has his father's wife. ²And you are proud! Shouldn't you rather have been filled with grief and have put out of your fellowship the man who did this? (1 Cor. 5:1-2).

Q 1 How did believers in Corinth first respond to sexual sin in the church?

The problem. There was sexual sin in the church at Corinth. But their response was not tears of sorrow. Rather, their attitude was to accept, tolerate, and even boast about it.

The roots of the problem. The Corinthians were being influenced by the world again. Like the world, they bragged about the sexual sin among them. Also, some may have accepted the sin because the sinner was close to them. When someone we love sins, there is the temptation to defend the sinner's action or ignore it.

Q 2 Which leader in the Old Testament tolerated the sin of his sons (1 Sam. 2:22-36)? What was the result?

Q 3 What warning did the Lord give the church at Thyatira (Rev. 2:20-23)? Why?

The solution. Paul teaches us that sin is sin, whether it is in our home or someone else's. Our response to sin in the church should always be sadness, then action to remove it, and discipline to restore the sinner.

B. Discipline in the church flows from the love members have for a sinning believer (1 Cor. 5:3-5).

Shouldn't you rather have been filled with grief and have put out of your fellowship the man who did this? (1 Cor. 5:2).

Q 4 What is the purpose of church discipline (1 Cor. 5:3-5)?

³Even though I am not physically present, I am with you in spirit. And I have already passed judgment on the one who did this, just as if I were present. ⁴When you are assembled in the name of our Lord Jesus and I am with you in spirit, and the power of our Lord Jesus is present, ⁵hand this man over to Satan, so that the sinful nature [fleshly desires] *may be destroyed and his spirit saved on the day of the Lord* (1 Cor. 5:3-5).

Q 5 According to Hebrews 12:6, whom does our heavenly Father discipline?

Love leads to discipline. The purpose of discipline is not to punish; it is to redeem, restore, and refine. Love guides parents to discipline their children. *"He who withholds his rod hates his son, but he who loves him disciplines him diligently"* (Prov. 13:24). See also Proverbs 22:15; 23:13-14; and 29:15.

Note: For insights on parents' disciplining their children, see the *Faith & Action* book *Marriage & Family*, chapter 10, Lesson 30, "15 Guidelines for Discipline," pages 177-181.

Q 6 *What attitude in the pastor and members helped Sophia?*

Q 7 *What caused a teenager in trouble to leave the church?*

Q 8 *At which times is it necessary to follow Matthew 18:15-20? Explain.*

Q 9 *What type of discipline does Paul command toward those who rebel against Scripture (2 Thess. 3:14-15)?*

Q 10 *How does severe discipline help bring a sinning believer to repentance (1 Cor. 5:3-5)?*

Sophia, a young lady, had been raised in the church. She said she was strong and would never have problems if she went out with her boyfriend. She argued a lot with her parents about the need to accept modern values. But Sophia got pregnant. She stopped going to church. Her parents succeeded in convincing her that she should have a talk with the pastor.

Without condemning her, the pastor asked Sophia whether she wanted to abandon the Lord Jesus. He spoke tenderly and invited her to pray with him. She said that she feared that the church people would treat her as a pagan. But because of the pastor's kind attitude, she agreed to meet with the church elders. In that meeting, they decided that she would be under discipline. She would attend church, but would lack the privileges of a member. After the birth of the baby, the elders would decide how to restore her to church fellowship. She asked all the deacons to pray for her and for the father of the unborn child. Soon after, the baby's father said he would not stay in such a strict church with puritan ways. So he abandoned Sophia.

All the church people showed great love and interest in the young girl. They did much to help her and to get her ready for motherhood. With time, things worked out.

In another church, a teenager in the youth group became pregnant. The pastor announced in the main service that the girl was under discipline. The pastor told her friends in the youth group that they could not associate with her or even talk to her. They were told that she was a fornicator, and, as a result, they would have to ignore her—even if they saw her in a shop. This church discipline lacked love. It was rude and harsh. As a result, the disgraced teenager soon abandoned her faith in Christ.

All discipline for the moment seems not to be joyful, but sorrowful; yet to those who have been trained by it, afterwards it yields the peaceful fruit of righteousness (Heb. 12:11).

Many times, believers may sin or offend in small ways without causing a need for church discipline. Jesus taught that when we offend a brother, we should seek restoration in private (Matt. 18:15-20). Only major problems, which cannot be solved between two believers, should be brought to the church elders. These include sexual sins, child abuse, drug problems, and large financial matters.

Severe discipline is for those who refuse to repent and to submit to Scripture. Paul said believers should not associate with rebels in the church, but we should warn them as brothers (2 Thess. 3:14-15). Severe discipline removes a person from the spiritual shelter of the church. The church is like an umbrella that gives some protection to its members. Satan may rain problems on those not in the church. These problems may be physical, emotional, or mental. All believers face problems, but there is a special protection that God gives to those in the church. To members of the Church, God is faithful and promises to limit our trials (1 Cor. 10:13). But those who are not in a right relationship with God cannot claim His protection.

In Corinth, church members responded to Paul by *excommunicating the man sinning with his father's wife (1 Cor. 5:1-2). The elders put this sinning believer out of the church. Afterward, the man repented. In time, Paul instructed the church to restore the man to fellowship (2 Cor. 2:5-11). Because the church loved this man enough to discipline him, he repented and was not lost forever. Love that confronts rescues many sinners.

C. Discipline helps keep the church pure (1 Cor. 5:6-8).

⁶Your boasting is not good. Don't you know that a little yeast works through the whole batch of dough? ⁷Get rid of the old yeast that you may be a new batch without yeast—as you really are. For Christ, our Passover lamb, has been sacrificed. ⁸Therefore let us keep the Festival, not with the old yeast, the yeast of malice and wickedness, but with bread without yeast, the bread of sincerity and truth (1 Cor. 5:6-8).

Explanation: In Jewish writings, yeast (leaven) was often used to represent the evil influence of sin.⁶ Sin, undisciplined, is like yeast that spreads through the whole batch of dough (1 Cor. 5:6). Paul calls for the discipline of putting the offending brother out of the church (1 Cor. 5:2, 13). This action was to prevent sin from spreading to other members. Sin in a church soon spreads from one person to two, three, and more.

Q 11 How is sin like yeast?

The Jews left Egypt in a hurry (Exod. 11). There was not time for them to bake bread made with yeast. Each year, the Jews celebrated the Passover—the time the death angel passed over their homes. At the celebration, Jews ate the Passover lamb and unleavened bread—flat bread that does not contain yeast. Likewise, Jesus has become our Passover Lamb (1 Cor. 5:7). And we celebrate this by living a life without the yeast of sin in it. Our time on earth is short, compared to eternity. We do not have time to allow the yeast of sin to spread through our lives. Rather, our lives should be like plain bread made with truth and sincerity (1 Cor. 5:8).

Q 12 How should our lives be like unleavened bread?

D. Believers discipline sinners inside the church, but leave those outside to God (1 Cor. 5:9-13).

⁹I have written you in my letter not to associate with sexually immoral people— ¹⁰not at all meaning the people of this world who are immoral, or the greedy and swindlers, or idolaters. In that case you would have to leave this world. ¹¹But now I am writing you that you must not associate with anyone who calls himself a brother but is sexually immoral or greedy, an idolater or a slanderer, a drunkard or a swindler. With such a man do not even eat. ¹²What business is it of mine to judge those outside the church? Are you not to judge those inside? ¹³God will judge those outside. "Expel the wicked man from among you" (1 Cor. 5:9-13).

Q 13 Should the church discipline an outsider who sins against a believer?

Q 14 Whom does the church judge and discipline (1 Cor. 5:9-13)?

We do not judge or discipline those outside the church. God Himself will one day judge all sinners. But God wants the church to discipline members who live in sin. Paul wrote that believers should not even eat with anyone who calls himself a brother but practices sin (1 Cor. 5:11).

We have known people who thought they were in good health but suddenly realized they had a tumor that was cancerous. Doctors recommend that such tumors be removed in haste, although the process is painful. Likewise, removing a sinner from the church, although he has many friends, is the biblical way to save the sinner as well as the believers around him in the body of Christ.

Lesson 8: Choices About Legal Disputes (1 Cor. 6:1-8)

Goal: *Summarize 3 reasons why believers should settle disputes in the local church, not in court.*

Setting

Recall that Corinth, the ancient capital of southern Greece, was very close to Athens, the modern capital of Greece. The believers in Corinth were influenced by their culture, which emphasized worldly wisdom. As the Greeks had their heroes, some in Corinth tried to make heroes out of Peter, Apollos, and Paul (1 Cor. 1–4). Likewise, some believers in Corinth were following the Greek example of going to court (1 Cor. 6).

Figure 3.2 Athens was nearby and had a lot of worldly influence on Corinth.

Q 15 What were 2 ways in which worldly Greek wisdom influenced believers in Corinth (1 Cor. 1–6)?

Q 16 *How did Greeks settle disputes?*

For Greeks, going to court was a common part of life—a privilege they enjoyed. If there was a dispute in Athens, the first step was to choose an arbitrator—a private person to judge. If this attempt to bring peace failed, the matter went to *the Forty,* a group of 40 elders. Part of their task was to choose another judge. All elders of Athens who were at least 60 years old served as private judges. If this effort failed, the matter went to a jury. All citizens served as members of juries. Juries of 1,000 to 6,000 people were common.[7]

Unlike Greeks, the Jews seldom went to court. The elders of the village, town, or synagogue settled the disputes of the local Jews. Jewish laws forbade Jews to go to public court.[8]

We have looked at the background for lawsuits in Corinth. Now, let us study two paragraphs Paul wrote about lawsuits.

A. Legal disputes among believers should be settled in the local church, not in court (1 Cor. 6:1-8).

Unspiritual believers in Corinth saw no problem in taking other believers to court. In contrast, Paul questioned, "How dare you do such a thing?" (1 Cor. 6:1).

If any of you has a dispute with another, dare he take it before the ungodly for judgment instead of before the saints? (1 Cor. 6:1).

Paul wrote three reasons why the church should settle disputes between believers.[9]

Q 17 *Why does it not make sense for believers to go to court?*

1. It does not make sense for believers to go to court (1 Cor. 6:1). Paul refers to those outside the church as unrighteous or unjust (Greek: *adikoi*). It is not wise to seek justice from the unjust!

Believers may seek justice from the courts when the Church does not have the legal power to enforce justice. In such cases, the government is the servant of God.

³For rulers are not a cause of fear for good behavior, but for evil. Do you want to have no fear of authority? Do what is good and you will have praise from the same ⁴for it is a minister of God to you for good. But if you do what is evil, be afraid; for it does not bear the sword for nothing; for it is a minister of God, an avenger who brings wrath on the one who practices evil (Rom. 13:3-4).

Q 18 *What are some examples of when believers can use public court?*

There were times when Paul referred to his rights as a Roman citizen (Acts 16:37) and used those legal rights (Acts 22:25; 25:10-12). Likewise, a believer may go to court on such matters as child rights or spouse support—for matters that only the government can enforce. Note that believers seek justice from the courts only when the other sinning believers have refused guidance from the church.

Q 19 *To which angels does Paul probably refer?*

2. Believers will judge eternal matters for the world and angels, so we should judge lesser matters now (1 Cor. 6:2-6). In 1 Corinthians 6:2, we again see the word *saints* (the Greek word *hagioi,* which was translated as *holy* in 1 Corinthians 1:2). The saints are those whom God has made holy through the cross, the blood, and the Holy Spirit (1 Cor. 6:11). Paul reveals that we, with Christ, will judge the world, and even angels (Matt. 19:28; 2 Tim. 2:12; Rev. 20:4). *Angels* probably refers to fallen angels (2 Pet. 2:4 and Jude 6). Since we, God's holy people, will judge eternal matters, surely we can judge the lesser (trivial) matters of this life.

Q 20 *Paul contrasts the weighty task of judging angels with the light task of _____.*

²Do you not know that the saints will judge the world? And if you are to judge the world, are you not competent to judge trivial cases? ³Do you not know that we will judge angels? How much more the things of this life! (1 Cor. 6:2-3).

¹⁵"If your brother sins, go and show him his fault in private; if he listens to you, you have won your brother. ¹⁶But if he does not listen to you, take one or two more with you, so that BY THE MOUTH OF TWO OR THREE WITNESSES

EVERY FACT MAY BE CONFIRMED. ¹⁷If he refuses to listen to them, tell it to the church; and if he refuses to listen even to the church, let him be to you as a Gentile and a tax collector. ¹⁸Truly I say to you, whatever you bind on earth shall have been bound in heaven; and whatever you loose on earth shall have been loosed in heaven" (Matt. 18:15-18).

Andrew, a believer, gave some money to Simon, a carpenter in his local church. The money was for Simon to buy boards and build a table and chairs for Andrew. But soon, Simon's family became sick, and he spent the money from Andrew on medical bills. Over a period of several weeks, Andrew asked Simon about the table. Simon gave many excuses, and always asked Andrew to be patient. Finally, Andrew took the matter to the church. In the light of Matthew 18:15-20, Andrew and two elders talked with Simon. He repented and built the table and chairs within 2 weeks. Andrew was thankful that he got justice and did not lose his brother (Matt. 18:15-16).

Q 21 *How did Andrew use Matthew 18:15-18 to settle a dispute? Explain.*

Earlier, Paul wrote about the lack of respect the Corinthians showed him as a father. *"I am not writing this to shame you, but to warn you, as my dear children"* (1 Cor. 4:14).

Q 22 *What contrast is there between 1 Corinthians 4:14 and 1 Corinthians 6:5?*

In contrast, Paul wrote about lawsuits among believers to shame the Corinthians. *"I say this to shame you. Is it possible that there is nobody among you wise enough to judge a dispute between believers?"* (1 Cor. 6:5).

The Corinthians claimed to be wise. But choosing an unspiritual person, a judge of the world, to judge spiritual people of the church was foolish. Should those in the kingdom of light seek a judge from the kingdom of darkness? This is shameful! It is better to have a common believer settle a dispute between believers than to seek a pagan judge.

Samuel had a lot of friends in the church. But he had a bad habit of borrowing money and not paying it back. One Sunday, Samuel borrowed money from Amos. Unlike other believers, Amos continued to ask Samuel to repay the money he borrowed. Finally, Amos obeyed the counsel of Matthew 18:15-20 and took the matter to the church. The pastor chose two elders to go with Amos and talk to Samuel. Samuel refused to repent, and he left the church. But after 1 month, he repented and returned. The elders discussed the matter with him and put him under discipline for a time. After they announced the discipline, many believers reported that Samuel had cheated them. The elders helped Samuel create a schedule to repay, little by little, all of the money he had borrowed. Each month, they met with him to review his progress. Some believers did not require Samuel to repay the money. One wealthy believer even helped repay some of the money. After 2 years, he had repaid all of his debts. In this way, the church helped Samuel return to the path of righteousness and regain his dignity and testimony. Church members grew closer together. When believers obey Matthew 18:15-20, the whole church is blessed!

Q 23 *How did the church elders help Samuel and Amos with a dispute?*

3. When believers fight in court, their purpose and witness are defeated (1 Cor. 6:7-8).

⁷The very fact that you have lawsuits among you means you have been completely defeated already. Why not rather be wronged? Why not rather be cheated? ⁸Instead, you yourselves cheat and do wrong, and you do this to your brothers (1 Cor. 6:7-8).

Believers were going to court to win, but Paul said they had already lost. Those having lawsuits were already defeated—regardless of what happened in court.¹⁰ How were they already defeated? Paul believed that those fighting in court lose in three, or perhaps even four, ways.

Q 24 *In what ways were those going to court already defeated, before the pagan judge's decision?*

- ***First,*** the person defending his rights and protecting his property is not following the example of Jesus, who came to give away His rights. When our greatest concern is to protect our rights and property, we are not practicing self-denial, not turning the other cheek, and not remembering that vengeance belongs to God. Thus Paul says, *"Why not rather be cheated?"* (1 Cor. 6:7).

  At times, believers should surrender their rights for the reputation of Christ and His Church. Remember that Jesus did not come to get His rights. Rather, He came to get His wrongs—our sins and weaknesses. And He got them! So we ought to put up with one another in love (Eph. 4:2; Col. 3:13).

- ***Second,*** when believers fight in court, regardless of the court decision, the church loses. It loses its testimony of being loving, giving, and forgiving, and gains the reputation of being people who fight and take.

  Jesus calls us to witness to the lost. He calls us to be the light of the world and the salt of the earth. He said that all will know we are His disciples if we love one another (John 13:35). In contrast, when believers fight in court, they defeat themselves. When believers act the same as unbelievers, it is like turning off the light in the darkness. One proverb says, "When two bulls fight, it is the grass that suffers." Likewise, when believers fight, they lose, and those around them suffer the loss of light in a dark world.

Figure 3.3   When two bulls fight, it is the grass that suffers the most.

  A farmer refused to attend church because he felt one of the members was a hypocrite. One day, the pastor came to buy a cow from the farmer. After looking at all the fine animals, he selected a weak, sickly cow. "Oh, Pastor, you don't want that one," the farmer said. But the pastor insisted. After the purchase, the pastor said, "Now I'm going to show this weak, skinny, sick cow all over town and tell everyone that this is the type of cow you raise." "But Pastor, that's not fair!" said the farmer. "One poor cow does not represent the whole herd!" "Oh?" the pastor replied. "I'm only following your example. You condemn the whole church because of one weak member." The farmer got the point and attended church after that! Nevertheless, many people will stumble over the bad example of one church member.

- ***Third,*** when believers go to court, the church has given up its freedom to solve its own problems. An indigenous church governs itself. But when believers go to court, they ask the pagans to govern them. This is a great defeat, since we preach that we have the answers to the problems of life.

- ***Fourth,*** Paul warns that no matter what happens in court, those who cheat and swindle are in danger of losing their eternal inheritance. It is unfortunate that the NIV begins a new paragraph at 1 Corinthians 6:9. For in these verses, Paul is warning those who once believed but were returning to their old ways of cheating. In 1 Corinthians 6, note the connection between cheating and doing wrong (1 Cor. 6:7-8) with greed, thievery, and swindling (1 Cor. 6:10). Paul

Christian Choices

warns that the wicked will have no inheritance in the kingdom of God. When a believer loses his inheritance, this is the greatest defeat of all.[11]

> **Lesson 9**
>
> **Choices About Holy Living (1 Cor. 6:9-11)**
> **Goal A:** *Explain 3 ways in which God is holy.*
> **Goal B:** *Explain what it means to be holy in our position in Christ. Cite Bible references.*
> **Goal C:** *Draw the triangle of holiness, and explain its sides and corners.*
> **Goal D:** *Compare and contrast 3 aspects of holiness. Match Scriptures with each aspect.*

Background

Those who live like sinners will not inherit the kingdom of God (1 Cor. 6:9-10).

Earlier, in 1 Corinthians 6:1, Paul referred to those outside the church as ungodly—not like God. Now, in 1 Corinthians 6:9, Paul writes that the *adikoi* (Greek for unrighteous, ungodly, and unjust) will not inherit the kingdom of God. He lists ten types of sinners in this *adikoi* group. In 1 Corinthians 5–6, Paul already mentioned six of the ten types of sinners. It is not surprising, due to the reputation of Corinth, that four of the ten types of sinners are those who commit sexual sins. These are not the only sinners who will miss heaven. But Paul emphasizes these sinners to the Corinthians because of their problems.

> ⁹*Do you not know that the wicked will not inherit the kingdom of God? Do not be deceived: Neither the sexually immoral nor idolaters nor adulterers nor male prostitutes nor homosexual offenders* ¹⁰*nor thieves nor the greedy nor drunkards nor slanderers nor swindlers will inherit the kingdom of God* (1 Cor. 6:9-10).

Q 25 *Which of the 10 types of sinners in 1 Corinthians 6:9-11 has Paul already mentioned in 1 Corinthians 5–6?*

Some of the Corinthians were going backward instead of forward. They were returning to their old ways of sexual sins, greed, cheating, and swindling others (1 Cor. 6:8). In the end, sin causes us to lose our inheritance in the kingdom of God. As James wrote: *"and sin, when it is full grown, gives birth to death"*—condemnation and eternal separation from God (James 1:15).

Some in Corinth had once lived ungodly, evil lives. But God washed and sanctified them—He made them holy.

Q 26 *What does 1 John 3:4-6 teach about continuing to sin?*

> ⁹*Do you not know that the wicked will not inherit the kingdom of God? Do not be deceived: Neither the sexually immoral nor idolaters nor adulterers nor male prostitutes nor homosexual offenders* ¹⁰*nor thieves nor the greedy nor drunkards nor slanderers nor swindlers will inherit the kingdom of God.* ¹¹*And that is what some of you were. But you were washed, you were sanctified, you were justified in the name of the Lord Jesus Christ and by the Spirit of our God* (1 Cor. 6:9-11).

Q 27 *How can we discern a child of God from a child of the devil (1 John 3:9-10)?*

God is holy. Any discussion of holiness should begin with God. He is holy in three ways:

Q 28 *What are 3 ways in which God is holy?*

- **God is holy in His position.** Holy is the opposite of common. We say that God is holy because He is high above all else. He is holy because there is none like Him. In His position, God is holy—divine, supreme, exalted, glorious above all of creation. God's holiness is His might that makes people tremble and nations dread (Exod. 15:11-18; 1 Sam. 6:20; Ps. 68:35).[12] In His position above all, God alone is holy, for He alone is God (Rev. 15:4)!

Q 29 *What are some characteristics linked to God's holiness in Revelation 15:3-4?*

- **God is holy in His actions**—holy in all He does. His decrees and conduct are completely holy—altogether just, righteous, and true.

- **God is holy in His nature.** He is light, in whom there is no darkness. His character is 100 percent pure, unmixed with any trace of evil.

Q 30 *What makes an object or person holy? Give an example.*

Throughout the New Testament, the many references to the Holy Spirit emphasize that God is holy.

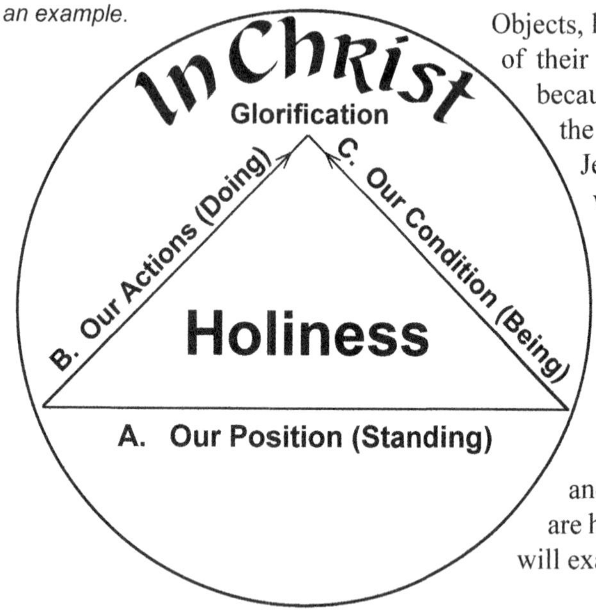

Objects, humans, and angels have a derived holiness—a holiness because of their relationship to God. The ground Moses walked on was holy because the holy God was there (Exod. 3:5). The dishes and objects in the temple were holy because they were related to the holy God. The Jerusalem on earth is called the holy city because it is the city where Jesus ministered, died for us, and rose from the dead (Matt. 4:5). Likewise, the heavenly Jerusalem is called holy because it is associated with the holy God (Rev. 21:2). The New Testament explains that we participate in the divine nature (2 Pet. 1:4)—we share in God's holiness (Heb. 12:10). Nothing is holy in itself besides God, but it becomes holy, sacred, and uncommon when it is related to God.[13]

Paul reminded Corinthian believers that they had been washed and sanctified—made holy. As God is holy in three ways, believers are holy in the same three ways as we relate to Him. In this lesson, we will examine three aspects of our holiness or sanctification (Figure 3.4).

Figure 3.4 There are three aspects or sides of holiness in Christ.

Aspect of Holiness	Explanation	Scriptures
A. Our Position (Where we stand in Christ)	The cross is the key to our positional sanctification.[14]	1 Cor. 1:30 *You are in Christ Jesus, who has become for us wisdom from God—that is, our righteousness, holiness and redemption.*
B. Our Orientation (What we do)	Holiness means living separated *from* sin *to* God.	2 Cor. 7:1 *Let us purify ourselves from everything that contaminates body and spirit, perfecting holiness out of reverence for God.* 1 Pet. 1:15-16 *Be holy in all you do.*
C. Our Condition (What we are)	This aspect of holiness focuses on our purity and character. Christ imparts this holiness to us by the Spirit. This is holiness we experience. It increases in us from the new birth to the new body, from regeneration to glorification.	1 Thess. 5:23 *Now may God of peace Himself sanctify you entirely.* 2 Cor. 3:18 *And we, who with unveiled faces all reflect the Lord's glory, are being transformed into his likeness with ever-increasing glory, which comes from the Lord, who is the Spirit.*

Figure 3.5 Holiness (sanctification) includes three aspects: our position, our orientation, and our condition.

Q 31 *What are 3 aspects or sides of holiness in Christ?*

We want to practice good hermeneutics—interpreting the Bible correctly. So when we refer to Scriptures on holiness, we should be aware of which aspect or aspects of holiness a verse emphasizes. For example, if we want to emphasize our position in Christ, we should not quote verses that are about our condition.[15] Still, as we study the three aspects of holiness, we will apply some verses to more than one aspect of holiness. Also, we will discover that the aspects of holiness affect one another. For example, our orientation affects our condition—what we do affects what we are. Now, let us take a closer look at the three aspects of holiness.

Q 32 *What does it mean to be holy in our position?*

A. We are holy in our position—where we stand in Christ.

Dr. Stanley M. Horton wrote, "Positional sanctification is necessary before we can begin to live a holy life."[16] To begin to live a holy life, we must enter into a relationship with the holy God. Through the cross, God makes this position of holiness possible. Without Christ's sacrifice on the cross, we would be separated from God's presence and separated from the divine power we need to live a holy life. So positional holiness makes possible the other aspects of holiness.

Holiness of position includes justification and regeneration. The holiness through justification is *imputed* holiness. God credits us with the holiness of Christ, which can never increase. This *imputed* holiness is complete at the moment of conversion.[17] In contrast, the holiness of regeneration is *imparted* holiness. At the new birth God *imparts* holiness to us. We receive God's Spirit, and participate in His holy nature (2 Pet. 1:4). As God's children, we enjoy this exalted position of holiness. The credited, *imputed* holiness of justification is perfect at conversion. But the *imparted* holiness we experience at regeneration is progressive. That is, we grow in holiness. Little by little God conforms us to the likeness of Christ—from the new birth to glorification (Rom. 8:29; 2 Cor. 3:18). In our holiness of position, we are God's justified, holy children.

Through Calvary, we have a new standing, a new position in Christ:
- *"To those sanctified in Christ Jesus and called [to be] holy"* (1 Cor. 1:2).
- *"And this is what some of you were. But you were washed, you were sanctified, you were justified in the name of the Lord Jesus Christ and by the Spirit of our God"* (1 Cor. 6:11).
- *"By this will we have been sanctified through the offering of the body of Jesus Christ once for all"* (Heb. 10:10).

B. We are holy in our orientation—what we do as we serve Christ and others.

> HOLINESS OF ORIENTATION IS BEING SEPARATED *FROM* EVIL AND DEDICATED *TO* GOD.

Holiness of orientation is being separated *from* evil and dedicated *to* God. Being holy in our orientation includes our choices, ethics, values, attitudes, lifestyle, and service. As *holy* people we hate and turn from what is wrong; we choose to love, embrace, and practice what is right. Thus we fellowship with the holy God and are able to serve others.

Q 33 *What does it mean to be holy in our orientation?*

Positional holiness focuses on our standing. But orientational holiness emphasizes the way we live, as we consecrate our lives to Him. Our holy attitudes and actions grow as we study and meditate on God's Word. Our holiness grows as we fellowship with the holy God. Our holy actions and attitudes increase as we are filled with the Holy Spirit, and walk in the Spirit.

Q 34 *How does holiness in position differ from holiness in orientation?*

Positional holiness is God's gift to us through Christ. But as one writer notes, the gift becomes the task![18] God gives us holiness but commands us to practice holy living. Orientational holiness is our response to God as we yield to and depend on His gracious Spirit in us. To be holy means to *"present [our] bodies a living and holy sacrifice,"* and *"do not be conformed to this world, but be transformed by the renewing of [our] mind."* This holy lifestyle is our gift to God. It is our spiritual worship, and proper response to God's gift of positional holiness to us (Rom. 12:1-2).

Our position of holiness begins in a moment at conversion. But holiness is not just a fact or an event—it is a way of life. Those who are holy in position are those, and only those, who are holy in their orientation and condition. Those who are washed and sanctified are those who practice resisting the desires of the flesh and submitting to the leadership of the Spirit. It is true that we are *dead to sin* (Rom. 6) only when we refuse lower desires and are obedient to a higher power. So Christianity is always a combination of gift and task. In the triangle of holiness, our position is connected to both our orientation and our condition. In our relationship to God, to be holy in our position, we must be holy in our orientation, which results in holiness of condition. Paul emphasized to the Corinthians that holy people live holy lives!

Q 35 *In the triangle of holiness, what do the bottom two corners emphasize?*

Q 36 *How do Paul's words in 1 Corinthians 6:9-10 compare with Spurgeon's preaching on Hebrews 12:14?*

Charles Spurgeon, a famous preacher in London who lived from 1834 to 1892, preached on Hebrews 12:14—*"Pursue peace with all men, and the sanctification without which no one will see the Lord."* He said that if you get drunk, or if you swear, or cheat at business, do *not* talk about being a Christian. You are on the same road as Judas Iscariot. For those without holiness (and much more those without morality) should not expect to see the face of God and be accepted by Him.[19] Beware lest you be among those who claim to know God, but deny Him by their actions (Titus 1:16). In contrast to the unholy, *"Blessed are the pure in heart, for they will see God"* (Matt. 5:8).

Here are some verses about being holy in our orientation—in our attitudes and actions. (Note that none of these verses refer to our position.)

- *"Let us purify ourselves from everything that contaminates body and spirit, perfecting holiness out of reverence for God"* (2 Cor. 7:1).
- *"...present your bodies a living and holy sacrifice, acceptable to God, which is your spiritual service of worship"* (Rom. 12:1).
- *"Follow after holiness..."* (Heb. 12:14 KJV).
- *"...be holy yourselves also in all your behavior"* (1 Pet. 1:15).
- *"Therefore, if anyone cleanses himself from these things, he will be a vessel for honor, sanctified, useful to the Master, prepared for every good work"* (2 Tim. 2:21).

Q 37 *How would you respond to a person who said: "Holiness in me is God's responsibility, not mine"?*

All of these five verses on holiness refer to our orientation—our responsibility and response to turn away from what is wrong, turn toward what is right, and present ourselves as living sacrifices, *holy* and pleasing to God (Rom. 12:1). Our holiness does not just depend on what Jesus did *for* us on the cross, but what we allow Him to do *in* us, enabling us to make right choices and have right attitudes.

Sin is the *antithesis or opposite of holiness. The holy are those like God, but the sinful are like the devil. Understanding what sin does guides us to holiness. Sin destroys all of our senses. Sin decreases sight and pulls toward blindness. Sin numbs hearing and makes men deaf. Sin perverts the taste, causing men to confuse the sweet with the bitter. Sin hardens the touch and leads us to being "past feeling." All of these are biblical comparisons. Sin blocks and chokes the senses of the spirit. Sin causes us to be insensitive and unable to fellowship with God. Sin creates calluses and makes us unaware of our dangerous condition.[20]

Q 38 *Contrast the way sin and holiness affect us.*

Holiness does the opposite of what sin does. Holiness enhances all of our senses. It enables us to see, hear, and taste accurately. Holiness enables us to feel the leading of God's Spirit. Holiness opens the senses of the spirit. It makes it possible for us to discern right from wrong and live close to God.

C. We are holy in our condition—what we are in Christ.

Q 39 *How does holiness of position differ from holiness of condition?*

The holiness of our position emphasizes the basis of our salvation. This focuses on words like regeneration and justification In contrast, the holiness of our *condition* is about what God continues to do in us. Being holy in our condition means conforming to God's nature.[21] John Wesley wrote a lot about entire sanctification (also called perfect holiness, complete holiness, and Christian perfection). Wesley taught that perfect holiness is possible on earth, instantaneously, through an experience with God after being born again. In contrast, we believe that the holiness of our condition is progressive, not instantaneous. We are changed into the likeness of Christ little by little on earth, not all at once (2 Cor. 3:18). Although we do not agree with John Wesley on the timing of perfect holiness, his descriptions of holiness are helpful. Wesley taught that when we are completely holy, the *quality* of our love for God and man will not increase. If a person is completely holy, every thought, word, and deed is guided by pure love. Wesley helps us understand that being holy in our condition refers to the quality of our love and character.

What is a holy person like within? When we say that we are holy in our condition, we mean that our hearts are pure; we mean that our nature is like God's nature. To be holy means to have motives and desires that are unselfish, pure, and unmixed. When we pray, "Father, help me to be more like you," we are asking God to make us holier. Thus we say that holiness is conformity to God's nature.

Men refine metals like gold and silver to purify them. For example, gold, in its natural state, is mixed with rock that has no value. To refine gold, workers put it in big metal pots and build a hot fire under it. As the fire melts the gold, impurities rise to the top, and they skim them off. The metal that results from this process is *pure* gold, of great value. Trials refine our faith as fire refines gold (1 Pet. 1:7). And God refines our holiness through the trials of life and through discipline or training (Heb. 12:10). He also makes us holier as we study and meditate on the Bible, pray, worship, and fellowship with other believers. The more time a person spends in a garden of flowers, the more he or she smells like flowers. And the more time we spend in God's presence, the holier we become like Him.

As a condition, holiness is the opposite of sinfulness. As darkness represents sinfulness, light represents holiness. God is holy—He is light, and there is no darkness in Him at all. At conversion, God delivered us from the kingdom of darkness and brought us into the kingdom of light. As God's children, we are in His kingdom of light and holiness. But like all healthy children, we will grow.

The holiness of our *condition* is progressive—it grows. Our holiness does not end at the new birth—it only begins there! The Corinthians had been sanctified at the new birth when they were justified. In their position, in Christ, they had perfect holiness. But Paul called the Corinthians mere infants in Christ. That is, their *condition* did not match their *position*.²² They needed to grow and mature in grace and holiness. In heaven, when our holiness is complete and entire, pure love will govern all of our thoughts, words, motives, and deeds. We look forward to the day when our love for God and mankind will be completely holy, unmixed with selfish desires. Meanwhile, as we walk in the Spirit and submit to Him, He enables us to please God and become holier, like Jesus (2 Cor. 3:18).

In the triangle of holiness, two sides join together at the top. This reminds us that there is a close relationship to our holiness of orientation and our holiness of condition. Orientational holiness affects our condition. What we *do* affects what we *are*. Holy choices and holy living shape our hearts and character. For example, 2 Corinthians 7:1 tells us to *"perfect holiness."* This verse refers to our attitudes and actions. It teaches us to separate ourselves from evil and purify ourselves from all that contaminates body and spirit. This continued "self-consecration"²³ improves our *condition* of holiness.

Holiness of orientation and condition are not options for Christians. We know a tree by its fruit. As P. C. Nelson said, holiness of *condition* is the fruit or result of our *position* in Christ.²⁴ In contrast to the holy, Paul warned that the wicked—those who rebel like the devil— *"will not inherit the kingdom of God"* (1 Cor. 6:9). Therefore, we must cooperate with the Holy Spirit and *"pursue peace ...and sanctification"* (Heb. 12:14).

Q 40 *Describe the heart of a holy person.*

Q 41 *How does God purify us to be holier?*

Q 42 *As a condition, holiness is the opposite of _____, as _____ is the opposite of _____.*

Q 43 *Which aspect of our holiness is perfect and will never increase?*

Q 44 *Which 2 aspects of our holiness increase as we grow in grace?*

Q 45 *What does the top corner of the triangle of holiness emphasize? Explain and illustrate this truth.*

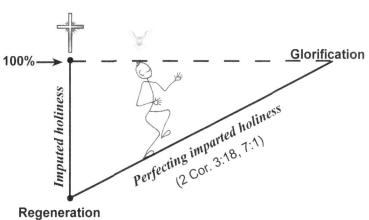

Figure 3.6 The process of sanctification (holiness) begins at regeneration (the new birth) and reaches its highest level at glorification (the new body). In between the new birth and the new body, we perfect holiness; that is, we mature in our separation from sin and our commitment to God. This growth or perfecting holiness involves our attitudes, choices, and actions, which affect our condition. Right attitudes and actions strengthen and increase holy character.

- *"And we, who with unveiled faces all reflect the Lord's glory, are being transformed into his likeness with ever-increasing glory, which comes from the Lord, who is the Spirit"* (2 Cor. 3:18).
- *"God disciplines us for our good, so that we may share in His holiness"* [of orientation and condition] (Heb. 12:10).

Q 46 How do our position, orientation, and condition affect each other?

Being is more important than *doing*. Our condition of holiness is more vital than witnessing, evangelizing, giving, and every other form of Christian service. God wants us to *be* holy, not just *do* good deeds. "For only as we become like Jesus, can what we do be effective and bring glory to God."[25]

According to the New Testament, holiness in our condition is an important work of the Holy Spirit.

Q 47 Beside each statement in Figure 3.7, put the letter or letters (A, B, C) for the holiness described.

(**Suggestion:** Ask yourself, "Does this statement refer to my position? My orientation? My condition?")

Statements About Holiness	Aspects of Holiness
1. "My holiness is complete and perfect; it will never improve."	A
2. *Now may the God of peace Himself sanctify you entirely* (1 Thess. 5:23).	
3. *Be holy yourselves also in all your behavior* (1 Pet. 1:15).	
4. *Let the one who <u>does</u> wrong, still do wrong; and the one who <u>is</u> filthy, still be filthy; and let the one who <u>is</u> righteous, still practice righteousness; and the one who <u>is</u> holy, still keep himself holy* (Rev. 22:11).	
5. *To those sanctified in Christ Jesus and called to be holy* (1 Cor. 1:2).	
6. *Present your bodies a living and holy sacrifice, acceptable to God* (Rom. 12:1).	
7. "My holiness depends completely on Jesus and not on me."	
8. *We….are being transformed into his likeness with ever-increasing glory* (2 Cor. 3:18).	
9. *You are in Christ Jesus, who has become for us wisdom from God—that is, our righteousness, holiness and redemption* (1 Cor. 1:30).	
10. *Just as He chose us in Him before the foundation of the world that we would be holy and blameless before Him* (Eph. 1:4). Note: This holiness will be fulfilled in part C, in heaven.	A, B, C
11. "I am holy, set apart for the Master to use, as I choose to separate myself from the sinfulness of the world" [see 2 Tim. 2:21].	
12. Spurgeon said that if he could choose from all the blessings, he would choose perfect conformity to the Lord Jesus, or, in one word, holiness.[26]	
13. *We have been made holy through the sacrifice of the body of Jesus Christ once for all* (Heb. 10:10).	
14. *Let us purify ourselves from everything that contaminates body and spirit, perfecting holiness out of reverence for God* (2 Cor. 7:1).	A, B
15. "Holiness is better than morality. It goes beyond it. Holiness affects the heart."[27]	
16. Perfect holiness is the aim of saints on earth and the reward of saints in heaven.[28]	
17. Of Hebrews 12:14, Spurgeon said: "You will not gain holiness by standing still. Nobody ever grew holy without consenting, desiring, and agonizing to be holy. Sin will grow without sowing, but holiness needs cultivation [hoeing]. Follow it; it will not run after you. You must pursue it with determination, with eagerness, with perseverance, as a hunter pursues his prey."[29]	
18. Tozer: "A holy man is not one who cannot sin. A holy man is one who will not sin."[30]	
19. *Blessed are the pure in heart, for they will see God* (Matt. 5:8).	
20. *³For this is the will of God, your sanctification; that is, that you abstain from sexual immorality; ⁴that each of you know how to possess his own vessel in sanctification and honor* (1 Thess. 4:3-4).	
21. "The whole purpose of God in redemption is to make us holy and to restore us to the image of God."[31]	
22. *And nothing unclean and no one who practices abomination and lying…* (Rev. 21:27).	

Figure 3.7 Practice identifying three aspects of holiness—A: Our Position, B: Our Orientation, C: Our Condition

Christian Choices 59

Summary: God is holy in three ways. *First,* He is holy in His position. He is the holy God, high above His creation. *Second,* He is holy in all His ways. And *third,* He is holy in His nature. Likewise, we are holy as we belong to Him and relate to Him. Like God, we are holy in our position, orientation, and condition. As the three sides of a triangle are joined together, the three aspects of our holiness are joined together.

Q 48 *In 1 Corinthians 6:9-11, what is the key to inheriting the Kingdom? Explain.*

Through His Word, His Spirit, and the ministry of His body (the Church), God lifts us into fellowship with Him and gives Himself to us. As a result, we grow in holiness, in His likeness (Eph. 4:15; 2 Cor. 3:18).[32]

We have studied three aspects of holiness. Together, these three aspects give us a balanced understanding of what it means to be sanctified and holy. May God help us to learn well the lesson Paul wrote in 1 Corinthians 6:9-11. To inherit the kingdom of God, we must live in a holy relationship to the holy King.

Lesson 10: Choices About Sex (1 Cor. 6:12-20)

Goal A: Explain how sexual sins are against self and God.
Goal B: List and explain 4 ways in which to honor God with your body and avoid sexual sins.

1 Cor.	Proverb of sinning Corinthians	Response from Paul
6:12;	Everything is permissible for me.	But not everything is beneficial.
10:23	Everything is permissible for me.	But I will not be mastered by anything.
6:13-14	Food for the stomach and the stomach for food	Agreed: Food and the stomach will perish with the earth.
	Application: Sex is for the body and the body is for sex with prostitutes.	The body is for the Lord, and the Lord for the body. God will resurrect the body.

Figure 3.8 First Corinthians 6:12-14 is a mixture of Corinthian proverbs and Paul's responses.

[12]*"Everything is permissible for me"—but not everything is beneficial. "Everything is permissible for me"—but I will not be mastered by anything.* [13]*"Food for the stomach and the stomach for food"—but God will destroy them both. The body is not meant for sexual immorality, but for the Lord, and the Lord for the body.* [14]*By his power God raised the Lord from the dead, and he will raise us also* (1 Cor. 6:12-14).

A common proverb at Corinth was, "All things are permissible for me." Some believers at Corinth were quoting this proverb—saying it was okay to have sex with prostitutes. These were trying to use grace as a coat to cover their sins (Rom. 6:1). Perhaps they wrote foolish songs that said they were still sinners covered by the blood of Jesus. But the New Testament does not emphasize that the blood *covers* our sins. Rather, it teaches often that the blood *washes* us and *cleanses* us from our sins so that we are holy, not sinful (1 Cor. 6:11).

Q 49 *Does the blood of Jesus cover our sins (1 Cor. 6:11)?*

Q 50 *Does the blood of Jesus cleanse us if we walk in darkness (1 John 1:7)?*

The blood of Jesus is more than a covering; it is a cleanser. Likewise, grace is *not* a clean coat to wear over a dirty shirt. Grace is a teacher!

Q 51 *What do students of Professor Grace learn?*

[11]*For the grace of God has appeared, bringing salvation to all men,* [12]*instructing us to deny ungodliness and worldly desires and to live sensibly, righteously and godly in the present age* (Tit. 2:11-12).

Paul quotes and refutes the evil proverb of the Corinthians. They claimed great freedom, saying, *"Everything is permissible for me."* Paul replied, *"But not everything is beneficial."* Some Corinthians said, *"Everything is permissible for me."* Paul responded, *"But I will not be mastered by anything"* (1 Cor. 6:12).

Q 52 *What was Paul's response to the Corinthian claims about freedom?*

The Bible compares all of us to slaves. Our master is *either* sin or righteousness. We cannot serve both sin and Christ, for no man can serve two masters (Matt. 6:24). So we must choose which master we want. We are slaves of the master to whom we yield ourselves (John 8:34; Rom. 6:16-18). Those who sin sexually are serving Satan. This is permissible; that is, God permits people to choose to serve sin. But choosing sin does not benefit. Rather, it results in slavery to sin (1 Cor. 6:12).

Samson was a free man who made bad choices. He was chosen by God, anointed by the Spirit, bold, and powerful. His parents counseled him to choose a wife from among the Israelites—a godly woman of his own faith. But fleshly lusts led Samson to the lap of Delilah, a beautiful prostitute. In the early days, this sinful relationship was exciting and fun. But in the end, it cost him his calling, his eyes, and his life. Following lust, he traded his freedom to become a slave of sin and the Philistines. God permitted him to choose Delilah, but his choices did not benefit him—they changed a free man into a slave (Judges 14–16).

Let us look at two reasons why all believers must choose to be holy and avoid sexual sins.

A. Sexual sins are against self (1 Cor. 6:15-18).

15Do you not know that your bodies are members of Christ himself? Shall I then take the members of Christ and unite them with a prostitute? Never! 16Do you not know that he who unites himself with a prostitute is one with her in body? For it is said, "The two will become one flesh." 17But he who unites himself with the Lord is one with him in spirit. 18Flee from sexual immorality. All other sins a man commits are outside his body, but <u>he who sins sexually sins against his own body</u> (1 Cor. 6:15-18).

The Bible teaches that some sins are worse than others. For example, Caiaphas's sin of rejecting the Messiah was greater than Pilate's sin of yielding to the crowd.[33]

Jesus answered, "You would have no authority over Me, unless it had been given you from above; for this reason he who delivered Me to you has the greater sin" (John 19:11).

This photo of Corinth shows the ruins of the temple of Aphrodite (goddess of love). Men came to worship in this pagan temple and have sex with the prostitutes in it. Paul taught that sexual sins are among the worst sins people can commit. No one who practices sexual sins has any inheritance in the kingdom of God.

Paul taught that sexual sins are among the worst sins.

Paul teaches that those who commit sexual sins sin against themselves in two ways.

Q 53 *Are some sins worse than others? Explain.*

Q 54 *How do sexual sins harm a person in a non-physical way?*

1. Sexual sins are against self in a non-physical way. Those who commit sexual sins harm themselves emotionally, mentally, and spiritually. Paul speaks strongly against sexual sins, because they are so harmful and evil. Some falsely refer to sexual sins as "casual sex." The word *casual* means "unimportant, relaxed, and of little meaning." But some things are never casual. There is no such thing as casual blasphemy, casual murder, or casual sex. The act of sexual union unites two people as one flesh. This sexual union is not casual; it is deep and profound. Paul even compares the sexual union—becoming one flesh—to the profound mystery of Christ and His Church (Eph. 6:31-32). Those who commit sexual sins violate and rebel against God's law and decree, for sex unites two people as one flesh for all of life. Those who commit sexual sins sin against themselves, for they unite themselves with the sinful (1 Cor. 6:18; Prov. 6:32).

To show that sexual sins are a sin against self, a pastor used two photos—one of a man, and the other of a woman. He put glue on each photo and pressed them together. Later, after they dried, he asked a young man to try to pull them apart. When he tried to separate them, a part of each photo stuck to the other. Likewise, when two people have sex, their bodies, souls, and emotions unite. If they separate, each will lose a part of himself and keep a part of the other person. The sexual union is deep and profound, affecting the mind, soul, emotions, and spirit.

Christian Choices

2. Sexual sins are against self physically.

Sexually Transmitted Diseases (STDs)	Linked to Cancer?	Deadly?
1. HIV/AIDS	Yes	Yes
2. Chancroid	No	No
3. Chlamydia	No	Yes (in women)
4. Gonorrhea	No	Yes
5. Hepatitis A	No	No
6. Hepatitis B	Yes	Yes
7. Hepatitis C	Yes	Yes
8. Herpes	No	No
9. HPV	Yes	Yes
10. HTLV-I	Yes	Yes
11. HTLV-II	Unknown	No
12. Lice	No	No
13. LGV	No	No
14. Molluscum	No	No
15. Scabies	No	No
16. Syphilis	No	Yes
17. Trichomonas	No	No
18. Yeast infection	No	No

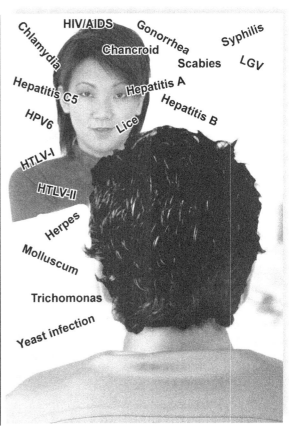

Figure 3.10   Some people, like prostitutes, spread as many as 18 sexual diseases. One study traced the deaths of 300 men by HIV/AIDS to one woman who worked for an airline. Samson killed a thousand men with the jawbone of a donkey. But one prostitute can kill a thousand men with her own body. Note: Sexual diseases are not limited to prostitutes.

More than 18 diseases are passed through sexual relationships. Those who practice sexual sins often get deadly diseases, such as chlamydia, syphilis, gonorrhea, and HIV/AIDS. Many discover that the wages of sexual sin is death. And even the sexual diseases that do not kill are often painful, unsightly, inconvenient, and embarrassing. Deadly and painful diseases punish those who commit sexual sins. This reminds us that sexual sins are among the worst sins. Those who commit sexual sins sin against themselves by contacting painful and fatal diseases.

Q 55   Do you know anyone with a sexual disease?

Q 56   What are some symptoms of sexual diseases?

Q 57   What warning did Frank's pastor give him?

Frank a believer, sat in the pastor's office. "Pastor, I have met a woman who is very beautiful. She makes me feel so alive. If I divorce my wife and leave my children, will God forgive me?" The question was like a coiled snake on the table. The wise pastor thought for a moment and then said, "God is willing to forgive almost every sin. So the problem of receiving forgiveness is not with God. The problem is that sin hardens. That is why the author of Hebrews writes, [12]*"Take care, brethren, that there not be in any one of you an evil, unbelieving heart that falls away from the living God.* [13]*But encourage one another day after day, as long as it is still called 'Today,' so that none of you will be hardened by the deceitfulness of sin"* (Heb. 3:12-13).

The pastor continued, "There are some believers, such as David, who committed sexual sins and were forgiven. But history tells of many who knew God, chose to turn away from Him, dishonored the Holy Spirit, trampled the blood of Jesus under their feet, and never returned. God would have taken them back, but sin hardened their hearts, and they did not want to repent."

Sexually Transmitted Diseases (STDs)	Deadly
HIV/AIDS	Yes
Chlamydia	Yes (in women)
Gonorrhea	Yes
Hepatitis B	Yes
Hepatitis C5	Yes
HPV6	Yes
HTLV-I	Yes
Syphilis	Yes

Figure 3.11   At least eight of the diseases spread through sexual sins can kill you.[34]

Q 58 *The Corinthians claimed to be wise. But in 1 Corinthians 6, how many times does Paul say to them, "Do you not know"?*

Q 59 *Why is the body of a believer holy?*

Q 60 *Explain: Sexual sins of believers are spiritual adultery.*

Q 61 *In the last days, whom did Paul say people would love instead of God?*

B. Sexual sins are against God (1 Cor. 6:19-20).

¹⁹*Do you not know that your body is a temple of the Holy Spirit, who is in you, whom you have received from God? You are not your own;* ²⁰*you were bought at a price. Therefore honor God with your body* (1 Cor. 6:19-20).

> THE BODY OF A BELIEVER BELONGS TO CHRIST. JESUS BOUGHT US WITH A GREAT PRICE—
> **HIS BLOOD.**

The body of a believer belongs to Christ. Jesus bought us with a great price—His blood (1 Cor. 6:20; Eph. 1:7). Earlier, Paul wrote that *all believers together* are the temple of God (1 Cor. 3:16-17). But in 1 Corinthians 6:19, Paul writes that *each* believer is the temple of the Holy Spirit. The body of a believer belongs to God, so it is holy. (Recall that anything that belongs to God is no longer common, but sacred and holy).

When a believer joins his body to another outside of marriage, he removes his holy body from union with Christ and unites it to sinful flesh. Sexual sins of a believer are spiritual adultery against God. Those who commit sexual sins are walking away from God and away from their inheritance God has planned. Esau traded his birthright for a bowl of soup. A few hours later, he was hungry and sorry. Likewise, those who are foolish trade their eternal inheritance for a few moments of sinful pleasure, followed by sorrow (1 Cor. 6:9-10).

Paul wrote to Timothy, ¹*"But realize this, that in the last days difficult times will come.* ²*For men will be lovers of self…* ⁴*…lovers of pleasure rather than lovers of God,* ⁵*holding to a form of godliness, although they have denied its power;* [to save from sins] *avoid such men as these"* (2 Tim. 3:1-2, 4-5).

We are living in the days Paul warned about. The world is filled with people who love pleasure instead of God. Millions on earth are slaves of sexual sins. Multitudes of youth and adults are addicted to pornography. Half of husbands and wives are unfaithful to their marriage vows and their families. People have fallen in love with themselves (2 Tim. 3:2).

The pages of the Bible and the pages of history contain many examples of free people whose choices made them slaves of sin and shame. A few examples of people who made bad choices are Adam and Eve, Cain, Noah, and the whole society of sinners who perished in the flood. Paul will return to this topic in 1 Corinthians 9–10. There, he will give a million examples of free people who made bad choices. And all of these Israelites died in the wilderness, without inheriting the land God had promised to give them. Christian, beware how you use your freedom to choose! Do not sin against yourself and your God!

C. Four ways to avoid sexual sins (1 Cor. 6:19-20)

News of sexual sins is no longer new or surprising—it is common. Priests, pastors, government officials, and lay people are falling into sin all around us. Still, Jesus has promised to save from sin those who follow Him. Here are four keys to honoring God with your body. Note that three are for *defense* (defending), and one is for *offense* (moving forward).

Q 62 *Who overcame sexual sins by running from them?*

Q 63 *What is your method of dealing with sexual temptation?*

1. (Defense) ***Run from sexual sins*** **(1 Cor. 6:18).** More than 4,000 years ago, Joseph overcame sexual temptation with a method that still works today: he ran from sin (Gen. 39:6-12). This method is the one Paul gives us. *"Flee from sexual immorality"* (1 Cor. 6:18). Do not pick up magazines filled with pornography—run from them. Do not shop the Internet to find sexual sins—run from pornography sites. Run from sinful friends and sinful situations that seduce you. Would you pick up a poisonous snake and play with it? Run from sin as you would run from a serpent. Do not turn sinful thoughts over and over in your mind as you turn a piece of candy over in your mouth (See the lesson on 2 Corinthians 10:1-6 in this book). Run from sin. This is the only solution you need if you will use it.

Sin is not like a bad dog that chases people; it is like a fire that burns those who embrace it. Concerning sexual sins, Solomon wrote, *"Can a man take fire in his bosom and his clothes not be burned?"* (Prov. 6:27). If you run from sin, you will escape from it. In contrast, sin defeats all who run to it, pick it up, or continue to look at it. You do not need a ring full of keys to unlock your front door. Likewise, you do not need a collection of keys to overcome sexual sins. Run from sin. This one key will enable you to overcome every sexual temptation. Use it, as Scripture commands, or you will lose the battle. Make up your mind now, before temptations come. Choose *running* as your plan, and follow it on the days when God enables you to breathe.

2. (Defense) Count the cost. Sin is not cheap; it is expensive. The devil offers no bargains. If you accept the sexual temptations Satan offers you, it will cost you your health, peace of mind, reputation, respect, relationship with God, and more. Before you add your name to the list of fools who accepted the devil's temptations, remember others on that list—Adam and Eve, Balaam, Achan, Samson, David, Judas, and a thousand television stars. Sin will take you further than you want to go, keep you longer than you want to stay, and charge you more than you want to pay.

Q 64 *What does sin cost those who buy it?*

Before deciding to buy, a wise person always asks, "What is the price?"
- Would Adam and Eve have bought the forbidden fruit *if they had asked the price?*
- Would David have bought Bathsheeba *if he had asked the price?* What did she cost him?

3. (Defense) Be accountable to others. Sin grows in the dark, but dies in the light. Talk with your spouse or a close friend about your spiritual life, temptations, and victories. Invite this person to ask you questions about your thoughts. *"And if one can overpower him who is alone, two can resist him. A cord of three strands is not quickly torn apart"* (Eccl. 4:12).

Q 65 *How can friends help each other overcome temptations?*

Figure 3.12 Sabio says, "Fighting temptations alone is as unnecessary as carrying your donkey. Fight smarter, not harder."

It is God's plan for believers to help each other. Fighting your battles of temptation alone is *quite unnecessary.* Work smarter, not harder. Talk with a friend about how you are overcoming temptations. Pray with someone about sexual temptations, which are common. Compare ways in which you can overcome sin.

4. (Offense) Glorify God with your body (1 Cor. 6:20). The best defense is a good offense. Do not just run from sin; run toward God and those to whom He guides you. Use your body to thank Jesus for hanging on the cross for you. Use your body to pray, study the Bible, attend church, do good deeds, enjoy life with spiritual friends, witness to the lost, encourage the weak, and worship the Lord. If we walk in the Spirit, we will not fulfill the sinful desires of the flesh (Gal. 5:16). Live to enjoy a wonderful life of fellowship with God *and* eternity in paradise.

Q 66 *What are some ways to overcome sexual sins by offense?*

Love God with all your heart, soul, mind, and strength. There is an American proverb that says, "An idle mind is the devil's workshop." Be like Thomas Edison, who created more than 1,000 inventions. (These include the light bulb and the phonograph, which led the way to modern music players.) When asked whether he was tempted to sin, Edison said he was so busy doing good things that he did not have time for temptations. *"Do not be overcome by evil, but overcome evil with good"* (Rom. 12:21).

Note: There are many books and articles on the problems and solutions of sexual sins. Two resources are:
- The *Faith & Action* book *Marriage & Family,* chapter 11, Lesson 32. It explains and illustrates 11 principles for overcoming the threat of sexual sins.
- *Why Great Men Fall* by Wayde Goodall, chapter 6, pages 55-64.

Lesson 11: Choices About Marriage (1 Cor. 7:1-40)

Goal: Explain 4 biblical principles related to marriage.

Setting

In this lesson, we will study four principles related to marriage.

A. God's plan to fulfill sexual desires is through marriage (1 Cor. 7:1-6).

Greek philosophy linked the world with evil and looked down on the physical body. This led to two opposite views.

Q 67 *What did the Greek view of sexual liberty teach?*

- One view said that the body and its desires did not matter. This view falsely taught that a person could do whatever the body desired—that deeds of the body did not affect the spirit. This view was called *libertinism,* because it allowed *liberty,* or total freedom, to satisfy appetites of the body.

Q 68 *What error did those who denied the body's needs commit?*

- The opposite view was called *asceticism*—denying the desires of the body for religious reasons. Ascetics, like later monks who lived apart from society, saw the body and its desires as something to master. This required strict discipline and self-denial—included fasting and abstaining from sexual relations. Some in Corinth had accepted this view. So Paul responds to those who had written, asking, "Is it best not to touch a woman?"³⁵

The expression translated *"not to marry"* is used in Greek literature as a polite way of referring to sexual intercourse. Some may have thought that *celibacy was more spiritual than marriage. Perhaps these misunderstood Luke 20:34-35 and thought that believers should live without sexual relations, like the angels.³⁶

Q 69 *What shows that two souls are united?*

Paul said that because of our sexual desires, it is good to marry. But Paul is not just saying that marriage is a wise way to avoid immorality and fulfill sexual desires. He is stating God's plan for humanity. God made men and women sexual beings, and created marriage as the context in which we would experience and enjoy sexual fulfillment. Through sex, a husband and wife unite their bodies and souls. They renew their love and commitment to each other. God created sex to be fun, exciting, and renewing in marriage. If sex were just for creating children, God would have wanted us to have sex only once a year! It is true that children come through sex. But the main purpose of sex, the rest of the year, is that a husband and wife love each other. If the main purpose of sex were to create one child, why would God create us to have sex 100 or more times each year? And why would women continue to have sexual desires long after they are able to bear children?

Q 70 *Is sex between a husband and wife a necessary evil, or something God planned for our enjoyment?*

Note: For a thorough discussion of sex in marriage, see the *Faith & Action* book *Marriage & Family,* chapter 5.

B. God gives most people the gift of marriage, and a few the gift of singleness (1 Cor. 7:7-9).

⁷I wish that all men were as I am. But each man has his own gift from God; one has this gift, another has that. ⁸Now to the unmarried and the widows I say: It is good for them to stay unmarried, as I am. ⁹But if they cannot control themselves, they should marry, for it is better to marry than to burn with passion (1 Cor. 7:7-9).

Paul saw some advantages to remaining single. The unmarried may focus on the Lord without the concerns of a family (1 Cor. 7:32-35). Centuries of history reveal that a small percentage of people remain single and serve the Lord.

On the other hand, some of us men who are married see many advantages in having a wife. Besides sexual fulfillment, which 1 Corinthians 7:9 mentions, marriage enables two people to share the work of life. A single man or woman faces the normal tasks of life alone, including working, buying food, cooking, washing dishes, washing clothes, paying bills, and encouraging himself.

Also, most men can testify that living with a wife helps them relate better to people, make wiser decisions, be more honest, be kinder, and develop the closest friendship of life. Perhaps the many blessings of being married help us understand the reason why God said, *"It is not good for man to be alone"* (Gen. 2:18) and why God gives very few the gift of living alone, like Paul.

Q 71 *What are 2 reasons why God gives few people the gift of living alone?*

Whether a person marries or remains single depends on the gift God gives that person.[37] Jesus told the disciples that God does not approve of divorce for most reasons. They responded:

Q 72 *How can a believer know whether or not to marry?*

10The disciples said to Him, "If the relationship of the man with his wife is like this, it is better not to marry." 11But He said to them, "Not all men can accept this statement, but only those to whom it has been given. 12"For there are eunuchs who were born that way from their mother's womb; and there are eunuchs who were made eunuchs by men; and there are also eunuchs who made themselves eunuchs for the sake of the kingdom of heaven. He who is able to accept this, let him accept it" (Matt. 19:10-12).

To summarize, we can say that if a person has a strong desire to marry, this desire is from God. And if a believer does not desire to marry, this attitude is also a gift from God.

Some have remained single when it was not their gift. Many of these have brought shame on the Lord's name. In the USA alone, more than 1,300 priests have been accused of abusing children since the 1950's.[38] Although all of these priests remained single, perhaps many of them did not have the gift of celibacy.

Q 73 *What happens when some try to live alone without the gift of celibacy or singleness?*

God does not want us to make an agony out of Christianity. It is the devil who comes to steal, kill, and destroy. Jesus came so that we may have life, and have it to the full (John 10:10). So live life in harmony with the gift God has given you—whether it is being married or single.

C. God wants us to serve Him in the situation in which He saves us (1 Cor. 7:10-24).

Christianity does not lead a person to rebel against the structure of society. Paul says, "When you meet Jesus and begin to follow Him, be a Christian where you are."[39] Paul gives three examples of one principle: Serve God where you are when you are called to follow Jesus.[40] Let us look at these three examples.

Q 74 *In 1 Corinthians 7:10-24, which 3 examples teach us to serve God as we are when we are saved?*

1. First example—Marriage: If you are married when you become a believer, stay married and serve God (1 Cor. 7:12-16).

12To the rest I say this (I, not the Lord): If any brother has a wife who is not a believer and she is willing to live with him, he must not divorce her. 13And if a woman has a husband who is not a believer and he is willing to live with her, she must not divorce him. 14For the unbelieving husband has been sanctified through his wife, and the unbelieving wife has been sanctified through her believing husband. Otherwise your children would be unclean, but as it is, they are holy. 15But if the unbeliever leaves, let him do so. A believing man or woman is not bound in such circumstances; God has called us to live in peace. 16How do you

Q 75 *In what way does a godly parent sanctify a mate or child in a family?*

know, wife, whether you will save your husband? Or, how do you know, husband, whether you will save your wife (1 Cor. 7:12-16).

This passages teaches that one believing parent in a family has a holy, sanctifying influence on all. For example, suppose two sinners marry and have children. Later, the wife becomes a believer. Paul says that this godly wife will sanctify her husband—that is, she will have a holy influence on him (1 Cor. 7:13). Likewise, as she lives a godly life, takes the children to church, and teaches them about God day by day, this mother has a holy influence on her children. And in time, each of them may choose to follow Christ.[41]

2. Second example—Nationality (Jew or Gentile): Remain in the nation where you are born again and serve God there (1 Cor. 7:17-20).

[17]Nevertheless, each one should retain the place in life that the Lord assigned to him and to which God has called him. This is the rule I lay down in all the churches. [18]Was a man already circumcised when he was called? He should not become uncircumcised. Was a man uncircumcised when he was called? He should not be circumcised. [19]Circumcision is nothing and uncircumcision is nothing. Keeping God's commands is what counts. [20]Each one should remain in the situation which he was in when God called him (1 Cor. 7:17-20).

Q 76 *Why does God want most believers to remain in the nation where they discover Christ?*

Bloom where you are planted. Some try to migrate when they become believers. Perhaps they want to move to a place where there are more believers, a better economy, less persecution, or easier circumstances. But if believers move away from unbelievers, there will be no light in the darkness. There are times when God guides people to move, as in times of war, persecution, or famine. But Paul reminds us to follow the leading of the Spirit and not the leading of our own desires.

One man was filled with a legion of demons. When Jesus set him free, the man wanted to follow Jesus. But the Lord told Him, *"Go home to your people and report to them what great things the Lord has done for you, and how He had mercy on you"* (Mark 5:19). God calls some to leave their families and preach the gospel in new places. But His will for most people who become believers is to remain in the situation in which they were when He called them (1 Cor. 1:20).

3. Third example—Slavery: If you are saved when you are a slave and you cannot be freed, do not run away—serve God as a slave (1 Cor. 7:21-24).

[21]Were you a slave when you were called? Don't let it trouble you—although if you can gain your freedom, do so. [22]For he who was a slave when he was called by the Lord is the Lord's freedman; similarly, he who was a free man when he was called is Christ's slave. [23]You were bought at a price; do not become slaves of men. [24]Brothers, each man, as responsible to God, should remain in the situation God called him to (1 Cor. 7:21-24).

Paul was not in favor of slavery. But he knew that change takes place slowly. If Christianity tried to change society suddenly, it would give the gospel a bad name and turn the government against the Church.

Q 77 *Why did Paul send Onesimus back to his master?*

Onesimus, a runaway slave, was saved under Paul's ministry. Paul sent him home, suggesting, but not demanding, that Philemon, his master, receive Onesimus *"no longer as a slave, but better than a slave, as a dear brother"* (Phm. 16). Likewise today, believers must be wise and patient to help change society in God's timing.

Applications. Here are some questions and situations to discuss:
- Suppose a woman, who is one of four wives married to an unbeliever, gets saved. Does Christianity teach her to take her children and leave her husband?
- Should a person who becomes a believer seek a new job if his boss is dishonest or if other workers are sinful?
- Suppose a rich man's mistress accepts Christ. If she leaves him, how will she support her children?

Christian Choices

- Should a woman living in a "common law" marriage agree to marry after she is saved?
- Does Christianity encourage a prostitute to leave her life of immorality?
- If people get saved in an evangelistic meeting, should they return to churches that do not preach the full truth of the Bible?

D. Serving God should be the center of our focus (1 Cor. 7:25-38).

Perhaps there was a crisis in Paul's day that made it unwise to marry. We know that believers faced persecution from unbelieving Jews, pagans, and at times the government. Paul wrote 1 Corinthians about A.D. 55 to 56. This was after Stephen had been stoned and believers had fled from Jerusalem. At that time, they lost most or all of their possessions. Paul himself had put many believers in prison before he met Jesus. Also, the letter to the Hebrews (written sometime before the destruction of the temple in A.D. 70) refers to *"former days"* of much persecution.

Q 78 *Read 1 Corinthians 7:25-38. What crisis in Paul's day do you think affected marriage plans?*

32But remember the former days, when, after being enlightened, you endured a great conflict of sufferings, 33partly by being made a public spectacle through reproaches and tribulations, and partly by becoming sharers with those who were so treated. 34For you showed sympathy to the prisoners and accepted joyfully the seizure of your property, knowing that you have for yourselves a better possession and a lasting one (Heb. 10:32-34).

So Paul's words, *"this present crisis"* (1 Cor. 7:26), may have referred to a crisis of persecution at that time. His words remind us that marriage plans should match circumstances. For example, it might be unwise to marry in the midst of a war or famine. *"There is an appointed time for everything"* (Eccl. 3:1).

On the other hand, Paul emphasizes that our time on earth is short. We should keep our focus on serving the Lord at *all* times.

Q 79 *What principle does 1 Corinthians 7:29-31 emphasize?*

29What I mean, brothers, is that the time is short. From now on those who have wives should live as if they had none; 30those who mourn, as if they did not; those who are happy, as if they were not; those who buy something, as if it were not theirs to keep; 31those who use the things of the world, as if not engrossed in them. For this world in its present form is passing away (1 Cor. 7:29-31).

Keep one eye on what you are doing and the other on Jesus.

"This present crisis" may be Paul's reminder that our time on earth is short and Jesus is coming soon. As Scripture says: *"FOR YET IN A VERY LITTLE WHILE, 'HE WHO IS COMING WILL COME AND WILL NOT DELAY'"* (Heb. 10:37).

Keep your priorities in order. Ask yourself these questions:
- How does single life affect my relationship with God?
- How does marriage affect my relationship with God?
- How does grief or joy affect my relationship with God?
- How does the "good life" affect my relationship with God?

Q 80 *Complete Figure 3.13.*

Bible Verse	Summary of verse (in your own words)
Matt. 13:22	
Matt. 24:42	
2 Cor. 4:17	
2 Tim. 2:4	
1 Pet. 5:8	
1 John 2:15-16	

Figure 3.13 Practice summarizing verses related to our priorities and focus

May these four principles in A–D above related to marriage guide us to live wisely.

Test Yourself: Circle the letter by the *best* completion to each question or statement.

1. The purpose of discipline is to
   a) punish the sinner.
   b) redeem the sinner.
   c) make an example of the sinner.
   d) excommunicate the sinner.

2. When believers fight in court,
   a) God brings righteousness through sinners.
   b) the world gains respect for justice.
   c) those doing wrong learn to do right.
   d) even those who win are defeated.

3. *God is holy in His position* means that
   a) He is high above all of creation.
   b) He is righteous in all His acts.
   c) He is pure light, without any darkness.
   d) He is omnipotent and omniscient.

4. *Holiness in our position* refers to
   a) the choices we make about right and wrong.
   b) the change Jesus makes in us, by His Spirit.
   c) the status we have through Christ's sacrifice.
   d) the way in which we relate to saints and sinners.

5. The right side of the triangle of holiness is
   a) our position.
   b) our condition.
   c) our transition.
   d) our orientation.

6. Which aspect of our holiness will never grow?
   a) Our position
   b) Our condition
   c) Our transition
   d) Our orientation

7. How are sexual sins against self?
   a) They cause guilt.
   b) They are spiritual adultery.
   c) They bring shame on children.
   d) They break the marriage covenant.

8. Why is the body of a believer holy?
   a) It belongs to God.
   b) It was created in God's image.
   c) It is eternal.
   d) It belongs to a spouse.

9. Through offense, you overcome sexual sin by
   a) running from it (1 Cor. 6:18).
   b) counting the cost.
   c) being accountable to others.
   d) glorifying God with your body.

10. Which of these is TRUE about sex?
    a) Its main purpose is to create children.
    b) It is a duty, but not a pleasure.
    c) God wants it to be fun in marriage.
    d) It is the center of a godly marriage.

Christian Choices

 Essay Test Topics: Write 50-100 words on each of these goals that you studied in this chapter.

Choices About Church Discipline (1 Cor. 5:1-13)

Goal: *Summarize 4 principles on discipline in the local church.*

Choices About Legal Disputes (1 Cor. 6:1-8)

Goal: *Summarize 3 reasons why believers should settle disputes in the local church, not in court.*

Choices About Holy Living (1 Cor. 6:9-11)

Goal: *Explain 3 ways in which God is holy.*

Goal: *Explain what it means to be holy in our position in Christ. Cite Bible references.*

Goal: *Draw the triangle of holiness and explain its sides and corners.*

Goal: *Compare and contrast 3 aspects of holiness. Match Scriptures with each aspect.*

Choices About Sex (1 Cor. 6:12-20)

Goal: *Explain how sexual sins are against self and God.*

Goal: *List and explain 4 ways to honor God with your body and avoid sexual sins.*

Choices About Marriage (1 Cor. 7:1-40)

Goal: *Explain 4 biblical principles related to marriage.*

Chapter 4:
Christian Rights
(1 Corinthians 8–11:1)

Introduction

Question: What do these topics have in common: Eating meat sacrificed to idols, drinking wine, dancing, attending a theatre, wearing a woman's head covering, wearing cosmetics, and attending an athletic event?

Answer: Each of the above topics has to do with deciding what is right or wrong.

Believers serve the same God, love the same Savior, and read the same Bible. But they do not have the same opinions about what is right and wrong. Here are some examples:

Figure 4.1
Restored "meat shop," like one in Paul's day. Paul dealt with a problem at Corinth. Should believers eat meat which was offered to a god?

- In Corinth 2,000 years ago, some believers said it was right to eat meat offered to idols. Others said this was a sin.
- In many nations, Christians believe it is a sin to drink wine or beer. But in some countries, such as in Europe, some Pentecostal believers drink wine and beer.
- In some countries today, Christian athletes have great influence and bring many people to Christ. In other nations, the church teaches that all athletic contests are sinful.
- There was a time in America when some believers felt no shame in owning slaves. Other believers felt this was wrong. The conflict in the nation became so strong that it led to civil war.
- Some today teach that it is wrong to attend a theater to watch a movie. Others feel no guilt when they watch a (decent) movie in a theater.
- Some churches teach that women must have long hair, avoid using cosmetics, wear no jewelry, and wear skirts or dresses rather than pants. Other churches believe that women are free to choose their own styles of hair and dress and are free to wear make-up and jewelry.

How do we explain these differences among believers who worship the same God, love the same Lord, and read the same Bible? Once we understand the differences in opinions, how do we decide what is right and wrong where we live? In 1 Corinthians 8–10, we will explore principles that guide us to answer these questions.

Lessons:

Love and Rights (1 Cor. 8:1-13)

Goal A: *State and illustrate 2 principles about conscience.*
Goal B: *Explain the proper relationship between knowledge and love.*
Goal C: *Analyze the balance between personal freedom and concern for others.*

Giving Up Rights: Paul's Example (1 Cor. 9:1-27)

Goal A: *Summarize 4 reasons why Paul had the right to be paid at Corinth.*
Goal B: *Explain and illustrate 3 principles about giving up some of our rights.*

Abusing Rights: The Israelites' Example (1 Cor. 10:1–11:1)

Goal A: *Identify 5 warnings from Israel's history. Apply these to us.*
Goal B: *Summarize 3 keys to overcoming temptations and trials.*
Goal C: *Explain why it was wrong for the Corinthians to eat meat at pagan feasts. Apply this to us.*

Key Words

rightsconscience
*koinonia*sacraments

 Lesson 12: Love and Rights (1 Cor. 8:1-13)
Goal A: State and illustrate 2 principles about conscience.
Goal B: Explain the proper relationship between knowledge and love.
Goal C: Analyze the balance between personal freedom and concern for others.

Setting

In Chapters 8–10, Paul answers the second question from the Corinthians. The first question was about marriage (1 Cor. 7). The second question is, "Is it all right to eat meat offered to idols?" Paul answers this one question in three chapters:

- In 1 Corinthians 8, the answer is "Do not eat meat offered to idols if you offend your *conscience, or if you offend your brother's conscience.
- In 1 Corinthians 9, Paul uses himself as an example. He gave up his *rights for several reasons.
- In 1 Corinthians 10, Paul uses Israel as an example, showing that freedom can lead to destruction.

Q 1 *What question is Paul answering in 1 Corinthians 8–10?*

Meat sacrificed to idols was a common part of life in Paul's day. Pagans thought eating meat sacrificed to idols was a way to fellowship with a god. Only a small part of the sacrifice was dedicated to the god. The rest was given to the priest and worshiper. Often this meat went to a banquet or was sold to the meat shops nearby.[1] Some believers thought it was all right to eat this type of meat. But others felt it was wrong to eat meat that had been sacrificed to an idol.

Q 2 *How was meat related to idols at Corinth?*

Here are some examples of how meat sacrificed to idols affected daily life in Corinth:
- The meat sacrificed to idols was sold in shops near the temple. Per pound, this meat from the temple was half the price of meat sold in shops nearby.
- Suppose a believer in Corinth was invited to dinner at the home of an unbeliever. Perhaps the meat on the table came from the temple. Should the believer eat this meat?
- Suppose there was a public meeting with food. Perhaps the city council was meeting or the place where a believer worked cooked food for a meeting. It is likely that the meat came from the temple. Should a believer eat this meat?

Q 3 *Why do you think meat sacrificed to idols was cheap?*

These are the tough situations believers at Corinth faced about meat offered to idols. Read 1 Corinthians 8:1-13. Then we will examine four principles that Paul gives believers in 1 Corinthians 8. We can use these same principles to answer the questions we face today about our rights.

A. Principle 1:
Consciences vary—what one conscience allows, another condemns.

Conscience is an inner voice from God that either approves or condemns our actions. We should pay attention to our consciences and live in harmony with these inner judges. Likewise, we should show respect for the consciences of others. Having a good conscience is a key to salvation (Acts 24:16). Those who rebel against conscience may shipwreck their faith and be lost in a sea of knowledge, with no one to guide them (1 Tim. 1:19). Even those without the Law or gospel will be condemned by their consciences (Rom. 2:15).

Q 4 *What is conscience?*

Q 5 *How did consciences vary at Corinth in relation to eating meat?*

Figure 4.2
Ruins of the temple of Apollo

What one conscience allows, another condemns. So what is safe for one believer may not be safe for another. Strong, educated believers at Corinth ate meat sacrificed to idols. They realized that an idol was not a god—just something humans created. When these strong believers ate meat from heathen temples, their consciences did not accuse them.

In contrast, some believers at Corinth felt that it was wrong to eat meat offered to idols. Years earlier, the Jewish Council at Jerusalem asked Gentiles to *"abstain from food sacrificed to idols"* (Acts 15:29). The main purpose of this request was to build relationships between Jews and Gentiles. But it may be that this request was temporary. Weak believers at Corinth knew that idols were just the work of human hands. But before these believers came to Christ, they had experienced the powers of darkness linked to idols. In 1 Corinthians 10:20, Paul emphasizes that idols *represent* the demons behind them.

So we see that the consciences of believers at Corinth varied. Some felt free to eat meat from pagan temples, while others believed this was wrong.

> THE CONSCIENCES OF BELIEVERS VARY TODAY.

Application. The consciences of believers vary today. Review the introduction to this chapter. It mentions many topics on which consciences vary, such as wine, athletic events, movies, clothing styles, hair, and cosmetics. The first step in evaluating what is right and wrong is to recognize that the consciences of people vary. What one person can do on the way to heaven may send another person to hell.

Q 6 *What are some ways in which consciences vary where you live?*

B. Principle 2: Conscience judges by what it knows (1 Cor. 8:4-8).

> *⁴So then, about eating food sacrificed to idols: We know that an idol is nothing at all in the world and that there is no God but one. ⁵For even if there are so-called gods, whether in heaven or on earth (as indeed there are many "gods" and many "lords"), ⁶yet for us there is but one God, the Father, from whom all things came and for whom we live; and there is but one Lord, Jesus Christ, through whom all things came and through whom we live. ⁷But not everyone knows this. Some people are still so accustomed to idols that when they eat such food they think of it as having been sacrificed to an idol, and since their conscience is weak, it is defiled. ⁸But food does not bring us near to God; we are no worse if we do not eat, and no better if we do* (1 Cor. 8:4-8).

Earlier in this book, we emphasized that the conscience judges on the basis of what it knows (chapter 2, Lesson 4, point B). As biblical knowledge increases, it enables the conscience to judge better.

Q 7 *On what basis does conscience judge? Is conscience always right?*

Some believers at Corinth were weak. They lacked basic knowledge. They did not yet understand that the type of food we eat does not matter to God (1 Cor. 8:8). They did not grasp Jesus' teaching that what goes into a man's stomach does not defile him (Mark 7:15-19). Paul had not yet taught them that false teachers ³*"...forbid marriage and advocate abstaining from foods which God has created to be gratefully shared in by those who believe and know the truth. ⁴For everything created by God is good, and nothing is to be rejected if it is received with gratitude; ⁵for it is sanctified by means of the word of God and prayer"* (1 Tim. 4:3-5).

Since they lacked knowledge, the consciences of these weak believers condemned them when they ate meat from the market or at the table of an unbeliever.

Q 8 *Why should each believer always obey conscience?*

Weak believers at Corinth felt it was wrong to eat food sacrificed to idols, even though they knew idols were not gods. Still, if the conscience is weak, it is good to submit to it.

²²...Happy is he who does not condemn himself in what he approves. ²³But he who doubts is condemned if he eats, because his eating is not from faith; and whatever is not from faith is sin (Rom. 14:22-23).

Application.   Conscience is an inner friend that God gives to each person.

We should recognize that conscience judges by what it knows. And we should continue to study Scripture and grow in grace and knowledge. This will enable our consciences to judge better. Likewise, we should disciple others, little by little, so that their consciences will be filled with the knowledge of God's Word and God's will.

Q 9 *How can we enlighten and improve conscience?*

C. Principle 3: Knowledge should be married to love (1 Cor. 8:1-3).

When knowledge lives alone, it is barren. To be fruitful, knowledge must marry love. The words *knowledge* and *know* appear many times in First Corinthians. *"...All possess knowledge"* (1 Cor. 8:1). Yet none of us know as much as we should (1 Cor. 8:2). *"Knowledge puffs up, but love builds up"* (1 Cor. 8:1). Knowledge is never like the person God created to live alone. Knowledge should always marry love!

Knowledge and love should always travel together, and love should do the driving. For knowledge without love leads to pride that destroys. God wants us to speak the truth *"in love"* (Eph. 4:15). *"If I have the gift of prophecy and can fathom all mysteries and all knowledge,...but have not love, I am nothing"* (1 Cor. 13:2). Figure 4.3 contrasts two types of believers—those proud of their knowledge and those known for their love.

Q 10 *What are 2 contrasts between believers who are proud of knowledge and believers who are loving (1 Cor. 8:1-3)?*

1 Cor.	The believer who boasts about knowledge	The believer who loves	1 Cor.
8:1	Is puffed up	Builds up others	8:1
8:2	Knows less than he should	Is known by God	8:3

Figure 4.3   Some believers boast about knowledge, but others have knowledge with love (1 Cor. 8:1-3).

We are glad you are studying this book. And we hope that you will continue your education. On earth, people keep records and transcripts of studies. Still, there is no evidence that God keeps a file in heaven of our studies on earth. Knowledge alone does not impress God. But He keeps a record of those who love. The man who loves is known by God (1 Cor. 8:3). God does not forget the love we show to others (Heb. 6:10). He will reward those who love—even those who give someone a cup of cold water in His name (Matt. 10:42). The judgment of the sheep and the goats will be based on the love we showed or withheld (Matt. 25:31-46). All people know we are Christ's disciples by the love we show (John 13:35).

Q 11 *Which impresses God more, knowledge or love? Explain.*

Q 12 *Which touches sinners more, our knowledge or our love? Explain.*

A father and son watched as Onan worked beside their house. Onan had a mental problem. He worked hard, but he talked funny. He dressed sloppily and had a bad habit of spitting every few seconds. The son laughed as the father imitated the way Onan talked. Just then, the son's mother appeared. She had noticed how much Onan was sweating as he worked in the hot sun. She felt compassion and took him a glass of cold water and a slice of bread with butter. Knowledge looks down, but love builds up.

Some think the most educated are the most spiritual. Many believe those who raise their hands the highest and sing the loudest are the most spiritual. Others think the most important thing about Christianity is memorizing Scripture or knowing correct doctrine. But the Bible says, *"Pure and undefiled religion in the sight of our God and Father is this: to visit orphans and widows in their distress..."* (James 1:27). The one who practices 1 Corinthians 13 is known by God (1 Cor. 8:3).

Q 13 *What does God recognize as pure religion?*

"Look, Daddy, at that funny lady across the street. She is wearing a man's hat." A father had taken his little son to buy a gift for his mother's birthday. The boy was startled to see a lady dressed in many layers of skirts and wearing what appeared to be a man's hat. The dad told him not to point at her, and explained that people from the country may dress differently from those from the city. He also told the young child that pointing at

Q 14 *As you study, are you maintaining the balance between knowledge and love?*

people is not polite, for it can embarrass those being watched. Love is never rude (1 Cor. 13:5).

D. We must sacrifice personal rights if they cause weak believers to stumble (1 Cor. 8:9-13).

Q 15 *How do we know when to sacrifice freedom, and when to defend it? Explain.*

⁹Be careful, however, that the exercise of your freedom does not become a stumbling block to the weak. ¹⁰For if anyone with a weak conscience sees you who have this knowledge eating in an idol's temple, won't he be emboldened to eat what has been sacrificed to idols? ¹¹So this weak brother, for whom Christ died, is destroyed by your knowledge. ¹²When you sin against your brothers in this way and wound their weak conscience, you sin against Christ. ¹³Therefore, if what I eat causes my brother to fall into sin, I will never eat meat again, so that I will not cause him to fall (1 Cor. 8:9-13).

Here is the problem: The strong believers ate meat, and their consciences did not accuse them. Meanwhile, the weak believers watched the strong, followed their example, and felt guilty. They remind us of the boy who was following his big brother. The taller boy jumped easily over a ditch. But when the younger boy tried, he fell and hurt his leg.

So Paul told the strong to *"be careful"* so that the exercise of their freedom did not become *"a stumbling block to the weak"* (1 Cor. 8:9). Paul warned that we must be careful not to destroy the brother for whom Christ died (1 Cor. 8:11). This verse echoes Romans 14:20, *"Do not tear down the work of God for the sake of food."* Can you imagine someone who loves a bite of meat, a drink of wine, or an event more than a person?

Q 16 *Why did the former Muslim refuse to eat a ham sandwich?*

A former Muslim from India was the head of a tea business. He had come to know the Lord. At a Sunday school dinner, a young girl came by passing out sandwiches. She said to the former Muslim, "Will you have sandwich?" "What kind are they?" he asked. "Fresh pork or ham." "Do you have any beef, lamb, or chicken?" he asked. "No, I don't," she answered. "Thank you, he said, "But I won't have any today." Laughing, she replied, "Are you so under the law that you don't eat pork? Don't you know that a Christian is at liberty to eat any kind of meat?" "I am at liberty," he responded, "but I am also at liberty to let it alone. I was brought up a strict Muslim. My old father, nearly 80 years of age, is still a Muslim. Every 3 years I go back to India to give an account of the tea business, of which he is the head. When I get home, I always know how he will greet me. My father will say to me, 'Have those infidels taught you yet to eat that filthy meat?' And I will say to him, 'No, father. Pork has never passed my lips.' Then I can have the opportunity to share Christ with him. But if I took one of your sandwiches, my father would not let me in the house the next time I went home—and I could not preach Christ to him."²

The young lady understood, and we all understand this story. The former Muslim was obeying what the apostle Paul wrote. We have freedom to refrain from things that trouble others. In all situations, love becomes our main motive. *"Therefore, if what I eat causes my brother to fall into sin, I will never eat meat again, so that I will not cause him to fall"* (1 Cor. 8:9-13). True Christian freedom values others more than our rights, and unites knowledge with love!

Paul does not say, "Always sacrifice your freedom." Instead, he says *"Be careful"* with your freedom (1 Cor. 8:9). There are times when we should use our knowledge to increase the knowledge and freedom of others. Recall that Paul used his freedom to defend the freedom of the Gentiles and to increase Peter's freedom. Paul knew that Peter did not eat with Gentiles. Peter's conscience accused him, for the Law taught Jews to avoid eating some foods and eating with Gentiles. Likewise, the Judaizers taught that

Gentiles must avoid certain foods. But Paul knew that Jesus gave us freedom to eat all foods. So he did not give in to the way Peter refused to eat with Gentiles. Rather, Paul emphasized that in Christ, we are free to eat all foods with all people, and our salvation is not based on what we eat. So Paul stood up to Peter about the menu (Gal. 2:11).

Juan and Julio stopped at a café to eat lunch. Julio was shocked when his friend ordered ham. "I do not eat pork," said Julio, "because when Jesus cast out the demons they went into the pigs" (Matt. 8:32). Juan nodded and asked, "And where did the pigs with the demons go?" "Into the water," replied Julio. "So do you drink water?" asked Juan with a smile.

The people in the country where Edgardo lived for 12 years had strong feelings about the way a person must take care of himself when he gets a cold. No student in the Bible institute would shave if he had a cold.

One time, Edgardo caught a cold, but he had been taught that you feel better if you clean up and shave. Students were horrified when he came to class, still afflicted with a cold, but clean shaven. He told them that where he grew up, men had the custom of shaving, even if they had a cold. He had never heard of anyone dying because he shaved. So Edgardo paid no attention to the local idea that you could die if you shaved while suffering from a cold. Many watched to see whether he would die!

Q 17 Did Edgardo offend others with his freedom? Explain.

Application.

Hair styles	Relating to divorce	Places people go to eat	Sports events
Clothing styles	Bible versions	Television/Internet	Carnal Christians
Dancing in church	Women in ministry	How people are baptized	Entertainment
Worship styles	Legalism	Using birth control	Music styles
Traditions	Food and drink	Speaking in tongues	The place of work

Figure 4.4 A list of things that may cause people to stumble

Q 18 In your society, what things cause believers to stumble? Explain.

Q 19 Do youth stumble over the same things that older believers stumble over? Explain.

Paul describes several ways a strong believer may harm a weak believer (1 Cor. 8:8-13).
- My example may cause the conscience of a weaker believer to be *defiled* (1 Cor. 8:7).
- My example may cause someone to *stumble* (1 Cor. 8:9).
- My example may *wound* the weak conscience of another (1 Cor. 8:12).
- Worst of all, my example may become a *snare* to another (1 Cor. 8:13). The NIV phrase *fall into sin* is based on the Greek word *scandalon*—which means "scandal." But in Greek, a *scandalon* was a stick, which was the trigger of a trap. To catch a bird or animal, people often use traps. And every trap has a trigger. When the bird or animal touches the *scandalon* (trigger), the trap snaps and snares the victim. Paul warns: "Christian, do not let your freedom be the trigger of the trap that snares your brother."[3]

Figure 4.5
Every trap depends on a trigger. Be careful that your freedom does not push your brother into a trap.

Lesson 13 Giving Up Rights: Paul's Example (1 Cor. 9:1-27)

Goal A: *Summarize 4 reasons why Paul had the right to be paid at Corinth.*
Goal B: *Explain and illustrate 3 principles about giving up some of our rights.*

Setting

Recall that chapters 8–10 are a unit or block in 1 Corinthians. The theme of chapters 8–10 is Christian rights. At Corinth, believers were divided over the topic of eating meat offered to idols. Strong believers felt they had the right to eat this cheap meat. But weak believers felt it was wrong to eat meat sacrificed to idols.
- In 1 Corinthians 8, Paul emphasized that love guides us to give up our rights if they are a stumbling block to others.

Q 20 In 1 Corinthians, which chapters are a unit of thought on rights?

- In 1 Corinthians 9, Paul uses himself as an example of giving up rights. The question in the background is still whether or not to eat meat sacrificed to idols. But Paul teaches principles we can apply to many topics.

One sermon title on 1 Corinthians 9 was "What about my rights?"[4] We will divide this lesson into four parts: the foundation, and three principles about limiting our rights.

A. Foundation: Paul had the right to be paid at Corinth.

As a foundation, Paul emphasizes that he had the right to be paid by the Corinthians (1 Cor. 9:1-14). This was a sensitive issue. Later, in 2 Corinthians, we will see that false teachers claimed that Paul did not deserve pay (2 Cor. 11:7-15). And even when Paul wrote 1 Corinthians, some in Corinth did not believe he had the right to receive financial help for his ministry. So, he uses 14 verses to prove that he is worthy of financial help from the Corinthians. Figure 4.7 lists four reasons why Paul had the right to paid by those he evangelized and discipled at Corinth.

Figure 4.6 An ox that treads grain deserves to eat some of it.

Q 21 *Read 1 Corinthians 9:1-6. What is the first reason Paul used to prove his right to receive financial support at Corinth?*

Four Reasons Why Paul Had the Right to Be Paid by the Corinthians	1 Cor.
1. **Apostles** are paid by those whom they serve.	9:1-6
2. **Society** teaches that workers deserve pay for their labors. • Soldiers who serve are paid by the government. • Workers who plant a vineyard eat some of its grapes. • Shepherds who tend a flock drink some of the milk.	9:7
3. **Old Testament Law** taught the principle that ministers eat from the offerings of those they serve. • Oxen that plow and grind deserve some of the grain (Deut. 25:4). • People who plow and thresh share in the harvest. Since Paul sowed spiritual seed among the Corinthians, he had the right to material harvest. Paul had more of a right to receive support than others whom the Corinthians supported. • The Law taught that priests get their food from the temple where they work (Lev. 6:16, 26; Deut. 18:1).	9:8-13
4. **New Testament teaching.** Jesus commanded that those who preach the gospel should live by the gospel (Matt. 10:10-16; Luke 10:7).	9:14

Figure 4.7 Four reasons why Paul had the right to receive financial support from the Corinthians (1 Cor. 9:1-14)

Comments on Figure 4.7, Four reasons why Paul had the right to receive financial support from the Corinthians

Q 22 *What are at least 3 biblical qualifications of an apostle (1 Cor. 9:1-3; 2 Cor. 12:11)?*

Q 23 *Does anyone you know qualify to be called an apostle? Explain.*

1. Apostles are paid by those they serve. Paul fulfilled the many qualifications of being an apostle. He had seen Jesus (1 Cor. 9:1; Acts 9:1-6). And Jesus Christ chose and commissioned Paul to be an apostle to the Gentiles (Acts 9:15; 1 Cor. 1:1). The things that mark an apostle—signs, wonders, and miracles—were done at Corinth by Paul (2 Cor. 12:11). The Corinthians themselves were the seal or official proof that Paul was an apostle (1 Cor. 9:2). Through Paul's ministry, the Corinthian church was born. Paul fulfilled all the qualifications of an apostle. So he had the right to be paid, like the other apostles were paid.

Q 24 *Was it common for apostles to marry? Explain.*

Some today falsely teach that the apostles did not marry. But it was common for apostles to marry. Paul states that he could have traveled with a wife, like the other apostles did, including the Lord's brothers, and even Peter (1 Cor. 9:5). And if an apostle traveled with his wife, he had the right for his and her food expenses to be provided. But as we know, Paul did not marry. Unlike the other apostles, God led him to give up this right.

Q 25 *Does your society teach that workers deserve to be paid? Give examples.*

2. Society teaches that workers deserve pay for their labor. This principle of human experience is true for soldiers, workers in a field, and shepherds. But it is also true for apostles, pastors, teachers, and all other employees of society. So like any other worker, Paul had the right (the Greek word *exousia,* means "right or authority.") Still, he did not use the right. Paul's rights were often like a check he never cashed.

Q 26 How did Paul use Old Testament Law to prove his right to payment (Figure 4.7)? Explain 2 illustrations.

3. The Old Testament Law taught that workers deserve payment. Paul gave two examples of this principle from the Law. *First,* he referred to oxen. Deuteronomy 25:4 forbids muzzling the ox that treads grain. A muzzle was cloth or leather fastened around an animal's mouth to keep it shut. So an ox with a muzzle could not open its mouth to eat grain. As the ox worked to thresh the grain, it smelled it.⁵ God's Law allowed the ox to eat some of the grain that it ground. Some pastors use this verse to demand all of the church offerings for themselves. However, the Law did not say oxen should eat *all* of the grain, but only a part of it. Even so, Paul chose not to receive *any* offerings from the Corinthians.

Second, the Law taught that priests eat from the offerings of the people. Likewise, Paul had the right to be blessed by the people he served at Corinth. But he left this food on the plate and refused to eat it.

4. In the New Testament, Jesus taught that those who preach the gospel should live by the gospel. He said that when His disciples ministered in a home, they should *"stay in that house, eating and drinking whatever they give you, for the laborer is worthy of his wages"* (Luke 10:7).

Figure 4.8 Oxen pulled a threshing sledge to separate the stalks and chaff from the wheat. God's law forbade muzzling an ox as it worked (Deut. 25:4; 1 Cor. 9:9). The ox deserved some grain as wages. Paul used this example to show that ministers have the right to be paid by those they serve.

Paul had the right (Greek: *exousia*) to be paid. And yet, this great apostle gave up his right to be paid at Corinth for three reasons (B–D). Let us examine these one by one.

Q 27 What did our Lord teach about a minister's right to be paid?

B. Principle: We should give up some rights so others will not stumble (1 Cor. 9:15-23).

¹⁵But I have not used any of these rights. And I am not writing this in the hope that you will do such things for me. I would rather die than have anyone deprive me of this boast. ¹⁶Yet when I preach the gospel, I cannot boast, for I am compelled to preach. Woe to me if I do not preach the gospel! ¹⁷If I preach voluntarily, I have a reward; if not voluntarily, I am simply discharging the trust committed to me. ¹⁸What then is my reward? Just this: that in preaching the gospel I may offer it <u>free of charge</u>, and so not make use of my rights in preaching it (1 Cor. 9:15-18).

In Paul's day, like today, many used religion to gain money. So often, unbelievers believe that people use spiritual matters to get rich.

Q 28 In Paul's day, what were some examples of using religion as a business?

- In *Jerusalem,* the family of the high priest was wealthy from cheating the people. Jesus drove some of these thieves out of the temple (Mt. 21:12-13). And He condemned the Pharisees for using long prayers as a show, meanwhile devouring widows' houses (Matt. 23:14).
- In *Samaria,* Simon the sorcerer gained influence, power, and wealth through the spiritual realm. He offered Peter money, wanting to continue using spiritual power to fill his bank account (Acts 8:9-23).
- In *Philippi,* a girl *"was bringing her masters much profit by fortune-telling"* (Acts 16:16). Likewise, Paul wrote the *Philippians* about those who preach Christ for the wrong reasons (Phil. 1:17).
- In *Ephesus,* Demetrius the silversmith sold idols for great profits (Acts 19:23-27).

- In *Crete,* Titus was warned about false teachers who ruin families for dishonest profit (Tit. 1:11-12).
- And in *Corinth,* Paul wrote about false apostles who enslave, exploit, and take advantage of the bride of Christ (2 Cor. 11:20).

Everywhere, many made up stories to exploit those in need (2 Pet. 2:3). And false teachers today continue to make up stories to cheat believers. Deceivers have always used people's hunger for God as a way to steal their money. *"For the love of money is a root of all sorts of evil"* (1 Tim. 6:10). Religion has always been a big business for greedy men.

Therefore, Paul chose to preach the gospel *free of charge* in Corinth (1 Cor. 9:18). His ministry reflected the teaching of Jesus, *"freely you have received, freely give"* (Matt. 10:8). However, he did accept some offerings from churches in other places (2 Cor. 11:8; 12:13).

Thieves dressed as preachers were stumbling blocks to sinners. These bandits behind pulpits caused sinners to be skeptical. Paul wanted to open people's hearts to the gospel. So it appears that he did not accept offerings from those in a city where he was planting a new church. Thus, in Corinth, he gave up the right to be paid by his converts.

Because Paul gave up his right to be paid, sinners might say, "Hey, this man is not trying to get our money. Let's listen to what he says."

Figure 4.9
Some pastors hammer on tithing and giving like a woodpecker hammers on a dead tree.

Q 29 *How do greedy preachers give the gospel a bad name today? Give examples.*

Application. It is sad today that preachers talk so much about money, and that some live on a level above most of the people they serve. Some pastors hammer on tithing and giving like a *woodpecker hammers on a dead tree. Likewise, it is a stumbling block to the lost that some preachers sell religious services and items. Even when it comes to books and CDs, the main motive of some seems to be money, not ministry. In contrast, Paul did not peddle the gospel (2 Cor. 2:17).

Religion continues to be a big business today. Many preachers promise that God will bless you when you send in an offering. Others sell prayer cloths, anointing oil, and religious items. Some sell religious degrees that are fake, offering honor to those who do not deserve it. One bishop preached a sermon on spiritual warfare, and then sold small swords for people to carry. Even though the sword was useless against spiritual forces, the preacher made a lot of money selling the swords. Some sell prayers, promising to release loved ones from purgatory, which does not exist! Meanwhile, millions of sinners stumble into hell, while false preachers and hirelings grab all the money they can get! In contrast, it is encouraging to see preachers like Paul, with a pure heart and a godly attitude toward money.

As we leave this point, note another important principle: Our attitude, in whatever we give or give up, determines our reward (1 Cor. 9:17). We will study this principle when we come to *"God loves [blesses] a cheerful giver"* (2 Cor. 9:7). Whatever we do, let us do it with a cheerful heart as an offering to God. Giving with a wrong attitude poisons the seed we sow.

Samson's passion was pleasure; Alexander the Great had a passion for power; Pilate's passion was politics; Judas had a passion for money; may we, like Jesus and Paul, have a passion for the souls of men.

C. Principle: We should give up some rights to build bridges to the lost (1 Cor. 9:15-23).

[19]Though I am free and belong to no man, I make myself a slave to everyone, to win as many as possible. [20]To the Jews I became like a Jew, to win the Jews. To those under the law I became like one under the law (though I myself am not under the law), so as to win those under the law. [21]To those not having the law I

became like one not having the law (though I am not free from God's law but am under Christ's law), so as to win those not having the law. ²²To the weak I became weak, to win the weak. I have become all things to all men so that by all possible means I might save some. ²³I do all this for the sake of the gospel, that I may share in its blessings (1 Cor. 9:19-23).

Paul amazes us. All of us would like to see slaves become free. But how many of us want to see free men become slaves? And yet Paul, a free man, made himself *"a slave to everyone,"* especially the lost (1 Cor. 9:19)! This type of behavior is not human. It is supernatural.

Q 30 *Was Paul's attitude about rights normal? Explain.*

Our human flesh grasps for all the rights and privileges it can get. As humans, we tend to want the highest wages we can get. We want the clothes we like, the food we like, and the houses we like. We want the best education, the best transportation, and the best medication and health care. We want to be with the people we love most. We want to talk about our favorite topics. We want to be loved and respected. We want, we want, we want. This is human nature. In contrast, Paul went through life guided by one want. He wanted to win the lost so they could go to heaven with him, and not hell.

Q 31 *What are some rights that most people you know seek?*

We have only as much influence as we have relationship. Paul knew this great secret of persuading people. Influence increases as a relationship increases. To guide people to Christ, we must build bridges so we can move close to them. So Paul's strategy was to look for common ground. Paul was always asking questions such as: "What can I do to become a friend to this sinner? What can we talk about that will bring us closer together? What does life look like through his or her eyes?"

Q 32 *What is a key to influencing others?*

Paul practiced the skill of seeing life through the eyes of others. If the sinner was a Jew under Law, Paul talked from the Jewish point of view. If the sinner was Gentile, Paul did not talk about circumcision and animal sacrifices. For example, to the Gentiles in Athens, he noticed that they had an altar to an unknown God. So he used that link to talk to them about the God they did not know (Acts 17). Why? He gave up his rights in order to build bridges to the lost. To the weak he became weak. For example, if someone stumbled over eating meat sacrificed to idols or drinking wine, Paul said, "I am with you friend. Let's leave the meat and wine behind and walk together toward Christ." If a sinner said, "All preachers are after money," Paul said, "There is too much truth in that, friend. But I preach for free. I am the preacher you are looking for, with the message you have been waiting for." So Paul could say, *"What I want is not your possessions but you"* (2 Cor. 12:14). To Paul, personal rights were like money in his pocket—to spend on someone else. Unbelievable! Here was a man truly under Christ's law and rule (1 Cor. 9:21)—the law of love that seeks to serve others. Oh God, open our hearts to be like Jesus, and like Paul!

Q 33 *What skill did Paul practice to win the lost? Give examples.*

Thomas, a believer, noticed that his neighbor, Chris, never went to church. Chris had three dogs that barked a lot at night. Thomas felt like he had the right to a good night's sleep. But his heart was drawn to help Chris find a good eternity. So he walked across the street to visit Chris. In Chris's garage were many pictures of sexy women. Thomas turned away from these as he talked to Chris, who was drinking a can of beer. Thomas was praying about a bridge so he could move closer to Chris. So he asked, "What do you like to do on your day off from work?" Chris answered, "I like to go fishing!" It was clear that fishing meant a lot to Chris. So Thomas asked questions such as, "What kind of fish do you like to catch? Where do you like to go? What is the best way to catch fish?" Two hours later, Chris was still talking about fish! And Thomas and Chris had taken steps toward becoming friends. One year later, after Chris and his wife had eaten twice in Thomas's home, after Thomas had learned the names and ages of Chris's three dogs, after Thomas knew the names and problems of Chris's two children, after they had talked about fishing many, many hours, Chris asked Jesus to come into his heart! And

Q 34 *What rights did Thomas surrender to reach Chris?*

today, 15 years later, Chris and his family are faithful believers, serving God in an Assemblies of God church. Why? Because Thomas gave up his right to a good night's sleep. Because Thomas gave up his right to talk, and chose to listen. Because Thomas gave up his right to enjoy his free time, and gave it to help Chris. Mature, spiritual believers give up their rights both to win the lost *and* to keep the saved from being lost.

Some church members give up many rights to build bridges toward the lost. They help sinners clean up their yards. They cook meals and invites sinners to eat for free. In some churches, carpenters repair homes for free on their day off, mechanics help the poor, a group of believers volunteers to paint a school in the community, and women bake cakes and cookies and give them to visitors who attend the church. Some give up their time and pray for the lost. Some visit hospitals and prisons to pray for people and encourage them.

Q 35 *What rights are you and your church giving up to reach the lost?*

In Corinth, some were focused on enjoying their rights. Paul used himself as an example to turn their thoughts from self to others. To follow Christ, we must practice self-denial and become slaves to win the lost. We must give up some of our rights so we can build bridges to the lost.

D. Principle: We should give up some rights for our own benefit (1 Cor. 9:24-27).

²⁴Do you not know that in a race all the runners run, but only one gets the prize? Run in such a way as to get the prize. ²⁵Everyone who competes in the games goes into strict training [discipline]. *They do it to get a crown that will not last; but we do it to get a crown that will last forever. ²⁶Therefore I do not run like a man running aimlessly; I do not fight like a man beating the air. ²⁷No, I beat my body and make it my slave so that after I have preached to others, I myself will not be disqualified for the prize* (1 Cor. 9:24-27).

Figure 4.10 Corinth was famous for the Isthmian Games in which runners ran for an earthly crown. The games were named for an isthmus— a narrow neck of land.⁶

Paul liked to use athletic events as illustrations. The Greeks enjoyed the Olympic games. And the Corinthians were famous for the Isthmian races and other athletic contests.

Paul compared heaven to the prize at the end of a runner's race. On earth, athletes compete for a crown that perishes; but we seek a crown that will last forever—an *eschatological victory.⁷

Q 36 *How do athletes discipline themselves to run a race?*

Winning requires discipline. To win a race, even the best athletes must practice self-control. Athletes discipline themselves in the choices they make. They refuse foods that will make them fat and choose foods that will make their muscles strong. They choose to go to bed early so they will get plenty of sleep to be strong for the race. While others relax in comfort, athletes who win train by running to be in top condition.

Q 37 *In what ways do you think Paul limited the desires of his body? Explain.*

Paul was like an athlete. He did not give his body all of the things it desired. Paul was not a slave to his fleshly desires. Rather, his body was a slave to God's Spirit within. So Paul said, *"I beat my body and make it my slave"* (1 Cor. 9:27). Why?

Q 38 *How is giving up rights related to self-discipline? Give examples.*

Self-discipline is just another way of saying "giving up some rights." Why did Paul refuse to give his body and soul all they wanted? Why did he refuse to indulge himself? Why did he treat his body like a slave, instead of a master? Why did Paul practice self-discipline? The answer is: *"So that after I have preached to others, I myself will not be disqualified for the prize"* (1 Cor. 9:27).

In Paul's day, if an athlete broke the rules, the judges would disqualify him from the race. Likewise, today, runners must play by rules such as starting on time, staying in bounds, treating other players fairly, and avoiding drugs like *steroids. Athletes who break the rules are disqualified and receive no reward.

Today, as in Paul's day, the goal to reach heaven is like running a spiritual race. Many who begin the race will be disqualified and will miss the prize of heaven.

Sadly, some scholars teach that it is impossible for a believer to backslide and be lost. These think that all who begin the race win it. They teach that Paul's prize was to win others to Christ. But throughout Corinthians and all of Paul's letters, the greatest prize for believers is heaven. For example, in Philippians 3, Paul compares himself to a runner in a race. With all his strength and focus he strains for the goal—to gain Christ forever and attain the resurrection (Phil. 3:8-11). Likewise, the letter to the Hebrews compares us to those in a race, fixing our eyes on Jesus, and running toward the prize of heaven (Heb. 12:1-2).

Q 39 *Was it possible for an apostle to lose his salvation? Explain.*

Paul needed self-discipline for his mission and his salvation.[8] One commentary covers 1 Corinthians 8–10 in a strange order. It treats 1 Corinthians 8, then 1 Corinthians 10, and then 1 Corinthians 9.[9] Using this unorthodox, unnatural approach, Warren Wiersbe claims that Paul did not think it was possible to be lost. He notes that even a runner who was disqualified from the race was still a citizen. We are thankful for the many helpful insights that brother Wiersbe gives. But proper hermeneutics guides us to recognize the relationship between 1 Corinthians 9 and 10. *"Castaway"* (1 Cor. 9:27, KJV) is just *a verse away* from 1 Corinthians 10:1. Chapter 9 ends with the reason why Paul practices self-discipline: *"So that after I have preached to others, I myself will not be disqualified for the prize"* (1 Cor. 9:27). And notice that 1 Corinthians 9:27 is connected to 1 Corinthians 10:1 by the Greek word *gar,* which means "for." As we will see in the next lesson, Paul uses the illustration of Israel to explain what he means by *"disqualified for the prize"* (1 Cor. 9:27). Israel longed for the food of Egypt. The Israelites did not discipline this fleshly desire. Next, it led them to the feasts of their pagan neighbors. And eating at the pagan feasts led Israel into idolatry and immorality. They had the right to attend the feasts and do whatever they desired. It was permissible, but not beneficial. The final result of Israel's lack of discipline was terrible. They broke their covenant, lost their relationship with God, and forfeited their inheritance. God was not pleased with most of them; their bodies were scattered over the desert (1 Cor. 10:5). God vowed, *"They shall never enter my rest"* (Heb. 3:11; 4:3). Likewise, Paul knows that eating meat sacrificed to idols leads to eating at pagan feasts in Corinth. So it is necessary to give up the right to eat meat—for your brother, and for your own good. Self-discipline—limiting some rights—is a key to reaching heaven. Even an apostle can lose his salvation. Ask Judas.

Q 40 *What is the relationship between 1 Corinthians 9:27 and 10:1-5?*

Application. Freedom, rights, and privileges surround us. But many rights in life are on a border—just a step away from sin and bondage. In Corinth, eating meat sacrificed to idols was just a step away from kneeling to an idol or having sex with a prostitute at a pagan temple.

As knowledge must be married to love, rights must be married to self-discipline. Self-control or self-discipline is a fruit of the Holy Spirit (Gal. 5:22-23). As we walk in the Spirit and submit our will to Him, He will guide us to be the masters of our bodies. Let us cooperate with the Holy Spirit to practice self-discipline in these seven areas:

- **Time.** Go to bed early enough that you can get up early enough for devotions. Take time to exercise, study your Bible, and be with family members. Limit the time you spend on entertainment, such as television and games. Too much entertainment strengthens the body and weakens the spirit. As a sweet before dinner dulls the appetite, too much entertainment causes us to lose our appetite for spiritual things.
- **Money.** Seek daily to find the balance between spending money on self and spending money on others. Learn to be a good steward of all God gives you.

Q 41 *In which of these 7 areas do people in your culture need the most self-discipline? Explain.*

Remember, there is no verse that says, *To whom much is given, 10 percent will be required.* Practice Matthew 6:33.
- **Talking.** Limit your words. Put a bridle on your tongue (James 1:26). Practice listening twice as much as you talk. We gain influence with others as we take time to listen to them.
- **Food.** Be careful what you eat. Refuse to eat too much of foods that will make your body fat and sloppy. Offer God a body that is fit and in shape so you can be alert and be a good example.
- **Thoughts.** Let the Spirit train you to love what is right and hate what is wrong. Turn away from evil thoughts of profanity, nudity, and pornography. Turn toward thoughts that honor God. Run from evil thoughts as you would run from an angry lion. Live the prayer: *"Let the words of my mouth and the meditation of my heart be acceptable in Your sight"* (Ps. 19:14). Have integrity and purity in what you think about in private, and God will bless you in public.
- **Sex.** Enjoy sex only within marriage, with your spouse. Before marriage, stay a distance away from relationships that dishonor God, the church, and your family. After marriage, be as faithful to your spouse in private as you are in public. Do not be like Adam or Eve, who longed for what God forbade. Be content with God's sexual plan for your life. Be accountable to a mentor or friend.
- **Success.** Beware of pride when you succeed. Limit the amount of credit and praise you receive. Instead of bragging about success, discipline yourself to remain humble and give God the glory. Pass it up.

Q 42 — Identify and explain 5 places in 1 Corinthians that Paul writes about giving up our rights for others.

Conclusion. Earlier in Corinthians, Paul taught about the need to limit our rights. If we insist on our right to exalt our favorite leader, this leads to division in the church (1 Cor. 1–4). If we use our freedom to practice sexual sins, this will destroy the body of Christ (1 Cor. 5). If we insist on our rights in court, we may discredit our testimony to the lost around us (1 Cor. 6:1-11). If we refuse to discipline our fleshly appetites, and return to our old ways of sin, we have no inheritance in God's kingdom (1 Cor. 6:9-11). Paul will continue to emphasize the need to think about others in 1 Corinthians 12–14. Limiting our rights—practicing self-discipline like an athlete—is necessary to serve others and to reach heaven. In a race of athletes, only one wins. In contrast, in our race to heaven, all can win. Still, the prize is not for those who begin the race, but only for those who finish it. *"So run in such a way as to get the prize"* (1 Cor. 9:24). Limit your rights. Practice self-discipline—for others and for self.

Live to win the long run. Missionary Jim Elliot had a good view of giving up freedom and rights. He wrote: "He is no fool who gives what he cannot keep to gain what he cannot lose."[10]

Abusing Rights: The Israelites' Example (1 Cor. 10:1–11:1)

Goal A: *Identify 5 warnings from Israel's history. Apply these to us.*
Goal B: *Summarize 3 keys to overcoming temptations and trials.*
Goal C: *Explain why it was wrong for the Corinthians to eat meat at pagan feasts. Apply this to us.*

Setting

1 Cor.	Theme
8	Practice love. Do not use your freedom in a way that causes others to stumble.
9	Be like Paul. Give up your rights for others and for self.
10	Do not be like Israel. Limit your freedom—discipline yourself—so you do not fall away. (Stay away from the pagan feasts, for they are a form of idolatry.)[11]

Figure 4.11 The themes of 1 Corinthians 8–10 in relation to rights and freedom

Recall that 1 Corinthians 8–10 is one unit of thought. The big question is: "What about my rights?" Some Corinthians felt that they had the right to attend pagan temples and eat the meat offered to idols. In 1 Corinthians 8, Paul began talking about weak believers. He counseled the strong not to do anything to cause the weak to stumble. Then, in 1 Corinthians 9, Paul used his own life as an example of giving up rights for others.

In 1 Corinthians 10, Paul becomes very bold. We will study this chapter in four parts:

- **Warnings.** In 1 Corinthians 10:1-10, the apostle gives severe warnings from the Old Testament.
- **Encouragement.** In 1 Corinthians 10:11-13, Paul gives three keys to help us finish the race.
- **Final warning.** In 1 Corinthians 10:14-22, Paul teaches that eating at a spiritual table includes having fellowship with a spiritual power.
- **Conclusion.** In 1 Corinthians 10:23–11:1, Paul summarizes several principles on using our rights.

Let us take a closer look at these four parts.

A. Warning: Past rights and privileges do not guarantee future success (1 Cor. 10:1-10).

Figure 4.12 contains five warnings. Take a moment to read the chart. Then we will briefly study each of the warnings.

Warnings	Explanation	Scriptures
1. *I do not want you to be ignorant of the fact....*	The Israelites were delivered from the bondage of Egypt and promised Canaan. But they died in the desert.	1 Cor. 10:1-5
2. *Do not be idolaters,*	Wild eating, drinking, and pagan parties are a form of idolatry—a way of bowing down to worldly values and gods.	1 Cor. 10:7; Exod. 32:4-6, 19
3. *We should not commit sexual immorality,*	The next step after the pagan party was sexual sin. Then came God's judgment, and 23,000 died in one day.	1 Cor. 10:8; Num. 25:1-9
4. *We should not test the Lord,* [not provoke Him to anger]	The Israelites spoke against Moses. Some were killed by snakes.	1 Cor. 10:9, 21-22; Num. 21:4-6
5. *Do not grumble, as some of them did.*	Some were killed by the destroying angel when they grumbled over Korah's judgment.	1 Cor. 10:10; Num. 16:41, 49; 17:5, 10

Figure 4.12 Five warnings from Israel's past sins (1 Cor. 10:1-10)

Comments on the five warnings of Figure 4.12 (1 Cor. 10:1-10)

Warning 1. Past rights and privileges do not guarantee future success. *"I do not want you to be ignorant of the fact brothers, that our forefathers..."* had rights and privileges like ours. They even had a form of the *sacraments of water baptism and communion (1 Cor. 10:1-5).

Q 43 *What was Israel's form of water baptism, after deliverance from bondage?*

- **The Israelites had a form of baptism, as we do.** Paul uses Israel as an example for believers. God delivered them from the bondage of Egypt. Then, they had a form or type of baptism. *"All were baptized into Moses in the cloud and in the sea"* (1 Cor. 10:1-2; Exod. 13:21-22; 14:31). Note the comparison. Believers follow Jesus and are baptized. The Israelites followed Moses and had a form of baptism as the water of the Red Sea and the cloud surrounded them.

- **The Israelites had a form of communion, as we do.** In his second comparison, Paul mentions Israel's communion. Believers celebrate communion or the Lord's Supper as we take bread and grape juice. Likewise, Israel had a form of communion—manna and water. The Israelites *"all ate the same spiritual food and drank the same spiritual drink; for they drank from the spiritual rock*

Q 44 *What was Israel's form of communion?*

that accompanied them, and that rock was Christ" (1 Cor. 10:3-4; Exod. 16:14-16). Note that Paul refers to Christ as a spiritual rock that was with Israel. This is another way of saying that Jesus was their source—He was with them and provided for their needs.

- **The Israelites sinned and fell from God's favor.** Shall we do this? Israel, after their deliverance, baptism, and communion, fell from grace. They had great rights and privileges. *"Nevertheless ... most of their bodies were scattered over the desert"* (1 Cor. 10:5; Num. 14:22-24; 28-35; Heb. 3:17). Instead of enjoying the land of Canaan, their graves littered the desert.

Q 45 *What happened to Israel even though they had forms of the sacraments?*

Q 46 *Beginning in Genesis, name 5 people who used their rights unwisely and faced judgment.*

In passages like 1 Corinthians 10:1-5, the types of the Old Testament amaze us, such as baptism in the Red Sea, manna, and water from the spiritual Rock, Christ. It is good to study and enjoy these types. But let us be careful not to miss the point. A generation of Israelites had great rights and privileges. Of this multitude of a million or more, all but two, Joshua and Caleb, fell from favor and grace with God. Why? They failed to use their freedom and privileges wisely. That is why Paul limited his rights. He controlled his desires and made his body a slave—so he would not be disqualified (1 Cor. 9:27). God did not tolerate the idolatry of Israel. Paul warned that He would not tolerate the idolatry of the Corinthians. And He will not tolerate our idolatry today, in any form, such as being greedy or bowing down to the sinful pleasures of the world today.[12]

Q 47 *What is Paul's point in 1 Corinthians 10:1-5? Apply this.*

Q 48 *What is the main reason Paul gives the five examples (1 Cor. 10:1-10)?*

Q 49 *Which warning was from Moab?*

Warnings 2–5 (Figure 4.12). Those who use their freedom to set their hearts *"on evil things"* will be judged (1 Cor. 10:6-11). Paul's first example was 1 Corinthians 10:1-5. Then he gives four more examples. Take time to read all five of the examples (1 Cor. 10:1-11). Also, review them in Figure 4.12. And notice that the big reason these examples are in our Bibles is *"To keep us from setting our hearts on evil things"* (1 Cor. 10:6, 11).

- **Warning 2.** At Sinai, the Israelites committed idolatry, like some of the Corinthians were doing (Exod. 32). The Israelites worshiped the golden calf and then committed sexual sins (1 Cor. 10:7; Exod. 32:6). <u>They set their hearts on evil things</u>.
- **Warning 3.** At Moab, men of Israel went with pagans to sacrifice animals to pagan gods and commit sexual sins (Num. 25). Like the Corinthians who attended pagan feasts, <u>they set their hearts on evil things</u>.
- **Warning 4.** In the wilderness, the Israelites murmured against Moses, because they had to eat manna instead of ordinary food. Likewise, the Corinthians spoke against Paul, because they wanted to eat meat at pagan feasts. <u>They set their hearts on evil things</u>.
- **Warning 5.** Like example 4, the Israelites refused to be content with God and His leader, Moses. Like the Corinthians, they chose to complain and grumble. Instead of resting in God's leader, plan, and provision, <u>they set their hearts on evil things</u>.

Q 50 *Has God given you as many rights as He gave Israel (Rom. 9:4-5)?*

All of Paul's five examples are about the choices people make. God gives us the right and privilege to choose. Those who set their hearts on evil things, as the Israelites did, prefer to love the world more than they love God. This is idolatry. Consider Paul's warnings about freedom. The frightening truth is, **God will give us what we choose**—whether evil things of earth, or our eternal relationship with Him! But we win or lose by the way we choose.

Q 51 *Who are some people you know who have lost their relationship with God?*

Let us beware of Paul's stern warnings about Israel. We must not abuse our right to choose. Today's rights do not guarantee tomorrow's success. Remember Adam and Eve, Cain, Noah, Lot, Lot's wife, Esau, Balaam, the Israelites, Achan, Samson, David, the rich ruler, Judas, and more.

Christian Rights

B. Encouragement: Three keys to avoid falling from favor to judgment (1 Cor. 10:11-13)

Paul has given the Corinthians and us five warnings. And in the rest of the chapter, he will make it clearer that we must separate ourselves from the tables of demons and the world. But before he continues, the Spirit leads him to give encouragement. Peter gave us keys so we would never fall but make our calling and election sure (2 Pet. 1:10). Likewise, Paul gives us keys. Let us look briefly at three ways to stay on the narrow road that leads up to heaven.

1. Be a learner. *"These things happened to them as examples and were written down as warnings for us, on whom the fulfillment of the ages has come"* (1 Cor. 10:11). After the first warning, Paul wrote that this example should *"keep us from setting our hearts on evil things, as they did"* (1 Cor. 10:6). Likewise, after examples 2–5, he says that we should learn from Israel's mistakes.

Q 52 *Complete Figure 4.13 on learning from the Scriptures.*

Things written down as warnings for us	Summary in your own words
Heb. 2:1	
2 Pet. 1:19	
1 Cor. 10:1-5	
1 Cor. 10:7-10	

Figure 4.13 Practice summarizing warnings from which we should learn

Some learn from the mistakes of others, while others repeat the mistakes.

- A herd of animals walked together toward some grain in a field. A hunter shot one of them, so the others ran away. They learned from the death of their friend.
- Two mice walked toward some cheese. When one mouse ate a bite, he was caught in a trap. The other mouse ran away, but later came back. Soon, he was also caught in a trap.
- A multitude of people suffer from sexual diseases. Some learn from this, while others do not.
- One son suffered greatly because his father was an alcoholic. As a result, the son chose never to taste wine or beer.

Those alive today are the ones *"on whom the fulfillment of the ages has come"* (1 Cor. 10:11). The death and resurrection of Christ marks the beginning of the end—the old is passing and the new is coming. May we learn from the mistakes of others, remain the people of God, and enjoy His eternal plan for the redeemed.

2. Be careful. *"If you think you are standing firm, be careful that you don't fall!"* (1 Cor. 10:12). Paul wrote these words to the Corinthians, who enjoyed a relationship with God. They had the sacraments of baptism and communion. But Israel had similar sacraments and lost their inheritance. So let us not be presumptuous, proud, or overconfident. Paul warns that we can fall just as Israel fell.

Q 53 *Complete Figure 4.14 on stating principles we should learn about being careful.*

Scripture	Principle for us
Prov. 16:18	
Dan. 4	
Matt. 24:45-51	

Figure 4.14 Practice stating principles about being careful

3. Be assured. *"No temptation has seized you except what is common to man. God is faithful; he will not let you be tempted beyond what you can bear. But when you*

are tempted, he will also provide a way out so that you can stand up under it" (1 Cor. 10:13).

This amazing verse concerns several insights about temptations we face.[13]

First, all temptations are common. *"No temptation has seized you except what is common to man"* (1 Cor. 10:13). The Greek word *peirasmos* can mean "temptation to sin" or "trial (test)," which can lead to sin if we do not bear up under it.[14] Satan may try to make us think our temptations and trials are unique or unusual—or, as Elijah thought, that we are alone in our struggles (1 Kings 19:10). But temptations are as ordinary as hooks for fishing. Satan tempts one and all. Temptation is as old as Eden. The lust of the flesh, the lust of the eyes, and the pride of life—these are as normal as skin to humans. When tempted, you are not a lone traveler on a path with no footprints. You are with billions of people who face common temptations. The temptations you have to endure are the very same that the saints in heaven once faced.

The world offers the same types of sins to every generation. Common temptations include sex, money, time, power, position, praise, drugs, success, excess (eating too much, talking too much, wanting too much, resting too much, working too much, playing too much), complaining, not believing, and quitting. The form of each temptation may vary, but the topics are common. As Solomon said, *"there is nothing new under the sun."* The devil has many recipes, but he cooks with the same ingredients.

Q 54 *Explain: "The devil has many recipes, but he cooks with the same ingredients."*

Q 55 *Which words in 1 Peter 5:8-9 remind us that trials are common?*

So what? Stiffen up and stand firm. Be tough and alert. You are in a war for your soul. Satan seeks to destroy every person on earth through temptations and trials. Do not despair if you are tempted like those before you, around you, and after you. Even Jesus was tempted. There is no sin in being tempted. The sin is in the tempter, not in the temptation or the tempted.

> ⁸*Be of sober spirit, be on the alert. Your adversary, the devil, prowls around like a roaring lion, seeking someone to devour.* ⁹*But resist him, firm in your faith, knowing that the same experiences of suffering are being accomplished by your brethren who are in the world* (1 Pet. 5:8-9).

Q 56 *How can we apply Job 38:11 to our temptations?*

Second, all temptations are limited. God is faithful; He will not let you be tempted beyond what you can bear. God matches our trials to our strength. Few suffer like Job, Paul, or Jesus. Weaker believers face lesser trials. Strong believers may face greater trials and temptations. God *"knows our frame; He is mindful that we are but dust"* (Ps. 103:14). God is sovereign over Satan. The dog of hell cannot even bark at us without God's permission. Our heavenly Father is in control, and He is faithful. The tide of temptation may rise. But God will say, *"Thus far you shall come, but no farther; and here shall your proud waves stop"* (Job 38:11). The enemy of our souls is evil, but the Shepherd of our souls is faithful (1 Pet. 2:25).

Q 57 *Contrast the dangerous attitude in 1 Corinthians 10:12 with the safe attitude of 10:13.*

Third, in all temptations God will make *"a way out." "But when you are tempted, he will also provide a way out so that you can stand up under it"* (1 Cor. 10:13). There may be ten ways out of temptations and trials. But the right way out is the way God provides. For example, one man faced a financial trial. He chose the wrong way out when he misused funds that others had entrusted to him. Notice the promise in our text: *"God is faithful... he will also provide a way out"* (1 Cor. 10:13).

The Greek words for *"a way out"* relate to the picture of a mountain pass. When an army or enemies surround a believer, God will show a way to escape through a pass in the mountains. Are you facing financial trials? God will provide a way out. Are you struggling with a trial of sickness, pain, or suffering? God will provide a way out. Have you lost a loved one, lost hope, and are drowning in sorrow? God will provide a way out. Are the tests and challenges you face too great for you? **God** will provide a way out.

Q 58 *Where are some places "the way out" may take believers?*

The way out may take many routes.

- The *way out* may pass through the Red Sea, after obeying the promise, *"Stand firm and you will see the deliverance the Lord will bring this day"* (Exod. 14:13).
- The *way out* may pass through Smyrna, where believers were called on to be faithful in poverty and prison (Rev. 2).
- The *way out* may pass through Philippi, where iron gates open as beaten believers sing praise at midnight (Acts 16:25-26).
- The *way out* may pass through the cemetery, after we overcome by the blood of the Lamb and the word of our testimony, and love not our lives unto the death (Rev. 12:11).

The way out is always by faith, as the believers of Hebrews 11 testify. And the way out is always toward God, not away from Him.

The Corinthians were facing a particular trial. They were being tempted to enter pagan temples and eat meat offered to idols. If they took that step toward sin, the next temptation would be sexual sins in the temples. So for the Corinthians, God's way out was to flee from idolatry (1 Cor. 10:14). Likewise, God's way of escape for us is running from, not toward, sinful desires of the world and the flesh. Like Joseph, we should flee from temptation. Like Timothy, we should flee youthful lusts (2 Tim. 2:22). Like the Corinthians, we should flee from sinful situations. The way out is for those who seek it, not for those looking for a way in.[15] We will study more about this in point C. The way out is always away from sin, and never toward it.

Q 59 *Does God promise a way out to those looking for a way in? Explain.*

Consider these illustrations about temptation.

- *"Keep watching and praying"* so that you will not fall into temptation. The spirit is willing, but the body is weak (Matt. 26:41).
- Reject temptation when it first knocks. For the desire for evil is like the desire for God: the more you feed it, the stronger it grows.
- The matador plant in South America is a vine that appears harmless when it is small. It begins at the base of a tree and slowly climbs up. Little by little it kills the tree, and finally produces a flower at the top to crown itself.
- When lesser birds attack a hawk, it does not stand and fight. Rather, it soars higher with wide circles, until its tormentors leave it alone.
- A colorful spider lives on the banks of the Amazon. It spreads out to look like a beautiful flower. Bees and other insects come to it, expecting honey. Instead, the spider gives them poison and death.
- Temptation, if not resisted, becomes irresistible.
- The time to set a record for fast running is when fleeing from temptation.
- Half the trouble in life is from saying *yes* too quickly and *no* too slowly.
- It is easier to refuse the first desire than to satisfy all that follow it when you open the door.[16]

Q 60 *Which of these illustrations do you like best? Explain.*

C. Final Warning: Eating at a spiritual table includes having fellowship with a spiritual power (1 Cor. 10:14-22).

In 1 Corinthians 10:14, Paul begins to close the long discussion that started in 8:1. These three chapters have been on using rights—and specifically on the right to eat meat at pagan feasts. In these final verses, Paul illustrates one principle three times. The principle is this: **Eating at a spiritual table includes having fellowship with a spiritual power.** Let us look at Paul's three examples.

Q 61 *Why would it be good to preach one message on 1 Corinthians 10:1-13 and another message on 1 Corinthians 10:14–11:1? Explain.*

Q 62 *Which principle does Paul illustrate 3 times in 1 Corinthians 10:14-22?*

1. First example: Eating at the Lord's table includes fellowshipping with the Lord (1 Cor. 10:14-17, 21).

Is not the cup of thanksgiving for which we give thanks a participation in the blood of Christ? And is not the bread that we break a participation in the body of Christ? (1 Cor. 10:16).

Q 63 *Which is not an illustration in 1 Corinthians 10:14-22: a) communion, b) Old Testament sacrifices, c) pagan feasts, d) Passover?*

In 1 Corinthians 10:16, the word *participation* is a translation of the Greek word *koinonia*—which means "fellowship" or "sharing with someone." In the early years of the Church, believers celebrated the Lord's Supper at a communion meal. At this meal, they drank from the cup and ate the bread. Paul explains that as we participate in the Lord's Supper, during this worship we have fellowship with the Lord. Jesus is present where two or three gather in His name (Matt. 18:20). The Lord is present at the Lord's Supper. Those who eat the bread and juice have fellowship with Jesus Christ.

Q 64 *What 2 things does the one loaf represent (1 Cor.10:17)? Explain.*

The figurative language of 1 Corinthians 10:17 was probably clearer to the first readers. It seems to be a *metonomy. In a metonomy, one word represents another. For example, in *"Give us today our daily bread,"* the bread represents all of our needs (Matt. 6:11). Likewise, in 1 Corinthians 10:17, the loaf represents both the physical body of Christ and His spiritual body of all believers. As there is one loaf at the Lord's table, believers form one body and should all honor the Lord.[17] Likewise, Paul again uses metonomy in the next verse, for the altar represents both the sacrifice on it and the Lord near it (1 Cor. 10:18).

Q 65 *What 2 things does the altar represent (1 Cor.10:18)? Explain.*

Figure 4.15
At the Lord's table, we fellowship with the Lord Himself.

2. Second example: Eating meat from the altar includes fellowshipping with the God of the altar (1 Cor. 10:18). *"Consider the people of Israel: Do not those who eat the sacrifices participate in the altar?"* (1 Cor. 10:18). Paul is still illustrating the principle that eating at a spiritual table includes having fellowship with a spiritual power. In the Old Testament, people sacrificed animals on altars to God. Once sacrificed, the animal belonged to God. But God was gracious and invited those who worshiped to share part of the meat from the altar. Paul emphasizes the connection of the meat to the altar and the spiritual power present at the altar. Those who ate meat sacrificed to God were having fellowship with God—for the altar was the meeting place for God and man.

3. Third example: Eating meat sacrificed to idols includes having fellowship with demons (1 Cor. 10:19-22).

[19]*Do I mean then that a sacrifice offered to an idol is anything, or that an idol is anything?* [20]*No, but the sacrifices of pagans are offered to demons, not to God, and I do not want you to be participants with demons* (1 Cor. 10:19-20).

Earlier, Paul wrote that an idol is nothing and that there is only one God (1 Cor. 8:4-5). Still, there are demons behind the idols people create (1 Cor. 10:20). And Paul did not want the Corinthians to fellowship with demons.

Q 66 *How was the mistake of the Corinthians like that of Israel in Deuteronomy 32:21?*

Paul's point is clear. The meals at pagan feasts were sacrifices to demons. Eating at these meals was a form of idolatry and worshiping demons. Believers are bound to the Lord, to one another, and to the Lord's Table. Therefore, God forbids us to have fellowship with demons. Those who rebel and fellowship with demons are provoking the Lord to jealousy and anger (1 Cor. 10:22). This was the same mistake Israel made: *"They have made Me jealous with what is not God; they have provoked Me to anger with their idols"* (Deut. 32:21). Christianity has some absolutes, such as: Believers must never bow down to idols. We must never fellowship with demons. We cannot serve God and money. We cannot fellowship with God and demons.

Application. A table is a place where people meet for fellowship. The word *table* may represent anyplace we fellowship with God. The Lord invites us to fellowship with Him at *"tables"* such as the Lord's Supper, church services, meetings in homes, Bible studies, Christian concerts, and other Christian events. It pleases God when we attend places and events to fellowship with Him and His people. Likewise, attending weddings, funerals, and baby dedications in the Lord's name is a way to fellowship with God and believers.

Figure 4.16
Through an animal sacrifice on an altar, the Israelites sought fellowship with God.

In contrast, the devil and his demons invite people to various *tables*. People fellowship with demons through sexual sins, pornography, killing, lying, coveting, cheating, stealing, gossiping, and idolatry (putting anything in the place where only God should be).

The error of some at Corinth was thinking they could drink from the cup of Christ *and* the cup of demons (1 Cor. 10:21). These people wanted to mix righteousness and unrighteousness. They wanted the holy and the unholy. From the menu of life, they chose what is of Christ and what is of the devil. They did not understand God's holy jealousy (1 Cor. 10:22; Exod. 20:5; Deut. 4:24; Josh. 24:19). They did not discern that friends of the world are enemies of God (1 John 2:15-17). Jesus Himself taught on this fatal mistake: *"No one can serve two masters"* (Matt. 6:24).[18] Likewise, as believers today, we must separate ourselves from evil. As Paul wrote to the Corinthians, *"Since we have these promises, dear friends, let us purify ourselves from everything that contaminates body and spirit, perfecting holiness out of reverence for God"* (2 Cor. 7:1). The holy, not the wicked, will inherit God's kingdom (1 Cor. 6:9). Most of life is an invitation to two tables—a place to fellowship with God or Satan.

Q 67 *How do some today repeat the error of 1 Corinthians 10:21? Give examples.*

A great carver created a statue of Christ. This man was offered a large amount of money to carve a statue of the goddess Venus. His answer was, "The hands that carved the form of Christ can never carve the form of a heathen goddess." Likewise, hands that receive from the table of the Lord should never take things from the table of demons. It was true in Corinth, and it is true today. The person who has handled the holy things of Christ must never dirty his hands with evil things of the world.[19]

D. Conclusion (1 Cor. 10:23–11:1)

In these verses, Paul concludes his discussion on personal rights (1 Cor. 8–10). But notice that he goes all the way back to a verse he wrote in 1 Corinthians 6:12. The apostle has taken a lot of time and space to rebuke sexual sins and idolatry—linked to the pagan feasts. The Corinthians were basing their choices on knowledge and personal freedom. In contrast, Paul taught that we should base our choices on love—love for God and others.

Q 68 *What is your favorite principle in Section D? Explain.*

In these final verses of the section, Paul emphasizes several principles to guide us in choices about our rights:

- **Make choices that benefit and edify self and others (1 Cor. 10:23).** Remember the poor choices Israel made that led to destruction and the loss of their inheritance.
- **Seek what is best for others (1 Cor. 10:24).** Be your brother's keeper.
- **"Meat is meat; buy and eat"**[20] **(1 Cor. 10:25-27).** Paul teaches us not to make an issue out of good things sold in public places. God is the source of all meat. *"For the earth is the Lord's, and everything in it"* (1 Cor. 10:26; Ps. 24:1). So there is no need to ask questions about who butchered meat or where it came from. In contrast, tradition required Jews to ask where the meat came from. But Paul takes a broader view. On things sold in public, for the sake of our conscience, and the consciences of others, it is better not to dig into the background of the product. For example, today, when we buy good things at a store, it is better not to ask whether these things were made by sinful people.
- **Do not cause anyone to stumble (1 Cor. 10:32).** If something troubles the conscience of another, avoid it (1 Cor. 10:27-28).
- ***"Whatever you do, do it all for the glory of God"*** **(1 Cor. 10:31).** Our main task in life is to please God and honor Him. At Corinth, this excluded attending pagan feasts. Today, it excludes watching evil television, evil Internet, or evil movies. As believers, we must set high standards. We should refuse to sit at any table that does not honor Jesus. What we cannot do to glorify God, we should not do at all. Let

this question be a guide and test of our thoughts and actions: "Does this glorify my Savior and Lord?"

- **Set an example for others to follow by following Christ, as Paul did (1 Cor. 10:33).** Jesus made it a habit always to do what pleased the Father (John 8:29). Our love for God and others must guide our choices, thoughts, and steps. For more on this verse, see the *Full Life Study Bible* (also called the *Life in the Spirit Study Bible*) note on 1 Corinthians 10:33.

Type of Table	Explanation of Tables	Counsel from Paul
1. New Testament Table of the Lord (1 Cor. 10:14-17, 21)	Tables for taking the bread and the cup of Christ in a holy setting	Yes, go ahead. Fellowship with God as you celebrate the Lord's Supper.
2. Old Testament Table of the altar (1 Cor. 10:18; Lev. 10:12-15; 1 Sam. 9:10-24)	The priests and worshipers ate part of the meat from the altar.	Discern that those who ate the meat from the altar were fellowshipping with the God of the altar.
3. Table of demons (1 Cor. 10:19-22)	Tables for pagan feasts in their temples	No, stop. Eating from this table includes having fellowship with demons.
4. Table of common people (1 Cor. 10:27-30)	Tables for food in public or in a home	Maybe, but be cautious. Believers may eat at this table, unless someone says the meat was sacrificed to demons.

Figure 4.17 Four types of tables in 1 Corinthians 10:14–11:1

In cities of the world, there are *signal lights at street intersections. These lights guide those who drive cars, motorcycles, and bicycles so they will know when it is safe to go forward. A green light means go ahead—it is safe to drive through the intersection. After the green light, a yellow light appears briefly, meaning caution—watch out, it is time to slow down or stop. A red light means stop—do not go ahead or you will harm someone. Likewise, God gives us lights in life. He gives us red lights—warnings to stop so that we do not hurt ourselves or others. For example, He tells us to flee from things such as idols, adultery, stealing, and lying. In contrast, God gives us green lights—go ahead signs for things that bring glory and praise to Him. And God gives us yellow lights—warnings to slow down and be sure that our choices do not hurt self or others.[21]

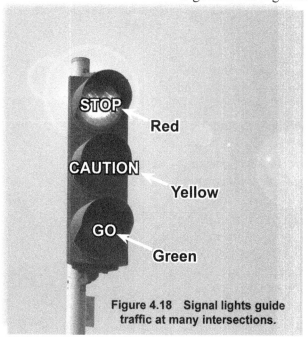

Figure 4.18 Signal lights guide traffic at many intersections.

Test Yourself: Circle the letter by the *best* completion to each question or statement.

1. Which of these is TRUE about consciences?
a) Consciences judge by the same standards.
b) Consciences vary from person to person.
c) Consciences are based mostly on the Bible.
d) Consciences will not excuse the guilty.

2. Paul taught that knowledge should marry
a) wisdom.
b) grace.
c) prudence.
d) love.

3. We should sacrifice personal rights
a) if the consciences of some are offended.
b) if other believers have opinions that differ.
c) if our actions cause others to stumble and fall.
d) if we have the opportunity to deny ourselves.

4. Paul had the right to be paid by the Corinthians,
a) for he was the first apostle God sent to them.
b) for he was the first apostle who wrote to them.
c) for he was greater than all apostles they knew.
d) for he was the last apostle who wrote to them.

5. Which illustration does Paul use in 1 Corinthians?
a) Carpenters are paid for the houses they build.
b) Oxen deserve some of the grain they thresh.
c) Landowners collect rent from their tenants.
d) God pays wages to all who work for Him.

6. A principle in 1 Corinthians 9 is that we should
a) use our rights as citizens to protect ourselves.
b) beware of rights that come without a price.
c) give up most of our rights for other believers.
d) give up some rights for our own good.

7. How many warnings are in 1 Corinthians 10:1-11?
a) 5
b) 4
c) 3
d) 2

8. How does 1 Corinthians 10:1-11 relate to 1 Corinthians 9:27?
a) 1 Cor. 10:1-11 has no relationship to 1 Cor. 9:27.
b) 1 Cor. 10:1-11 is a contrast to 1 Cor. 9:27.
c) 1 Cor. 10:1-11 illustrates 1 Cor. 9:27.
d) 1 Cor. 10:1-11 begins a new topic.

9. Concerning temptations and trials, Paul says:
a) Some are more common than others.
b) God will provide a way out.
c) Satan is the source of both.
d) There is no limit to God's grace.

10. When is it wrong to eat meat offered to idols?
a) Whenever and wherever it is offered
b) When the meat is in a pagan temple
c) When the meat is at an unbeliever's home
d) When there is no prayer of thanksgiving

Essay Test Topics: Write 50-100 words on each of these goals that you studied in this chapter.

Love and Rights (1 Cor. 8:1-13)

Goal: *State and illustrate 2 principles about conscience.*

Goal: *Explain the proper relationship between knowledge and love.*

Goal: *Analyze the balance between personal freedom and concern for others.*

Giving Up Rights: Paul's Example (1 Cor. 9:1-27)

Goal: *Summarize 4 reasons why Paul had the right to be paid at Corinth.*

Goal: *Explain and illustrate 3 principles about giving up some of our rights.*

Abusing Rights: The Israelites' Example (1 Cor. 10:1–11:1)

Goal: *Identify 5 warnings from Israel's history. Apply these to us.*

Goal: *Summarize 3 keys to overcoming temptations and trials.*

Goal: *Explain why it was wrong for the Corinthians to eat meat at pagan feasts. Apply this to us.*

Unit Two: Guidelines for Worship (1 Cor. 11–16)

Chapter 5 focuses on the important topic of relationships in worship (1 Cor. 11:2-34). In this chapter you will learn to:
- *Summarize how Christianity lifted the status of women in the early church.*
- *Explain three reasons why women wore veils at Corinth (1 Cor. 11:1-17). Apply these to today.*
- *Contrast celebrating communion in the early church and in the church today.*
- *Explain four directions in which Paul teaches us to look at the Lord's Supper.*

Chapter 6 explores spiritual gifts in worship (1 Cor. 12:1-11). We will guide you to:
- *Identify four types of spiritual gifts, and give examples of each.*
- *Expose six reasons why believers do not receive spiritual gifts.*
- *Define the spiritual gift of a word of wisdom.*
- *Give examples of a word of wisdom in the ministry of apostles, church leaders, and common believers.*
- *Define the spiritual gift of a word of knowledge.*
- *Give examples of a word of knowledge in the ministry of preachers, teachers, and common believers.*
- *Explain what the spiritual gift of faith is not and is. Give examples.*
- *Compare and contrast a gift of healing and a miracle. Illustrate each.*
- *Give examples of how spiritual gifts may overlap.*
- *Identify three spiritual sources, and give examples of what each produces.*

Chapter 7 is about ministries and love in worship (1 Cor. 12:12–13:13). In this chapter we study how to:
- *Explain some ways in which the Spirit unites us, yet makes us different.*
- *Identify and illustrate ways that believers depend on one another.*
- *Give examples of spiritual gifts that various ministries need.*
- *Explain what 1 Corinthians 12:29 does and does not teach about tongues.*
- *Explain the necessity of love as the path of spiritual gifts.*
- *Explain and illustrate ten characteristics of love.*
- *Analyze the contrast in 1 Corinthians 13:8-13.*

Chapter 8 emphasizes edification in worship (1 Cor. 14). As you master this chapter, you will be able to:
- *Explain what speaking in tongues is not and is.*
- *Explain what the spiritual gift of prophecy is not and is.*
- *Explain four principles for tongues, interpretation, and prophecy in a service.*
- *Explain six guidelines for maintaining order as believers manifest spiritual gifts in a service.*

Chapter 9 analyzes the relationship of doctrine and worship (1 Cor. 15–16). The lessons in this chapter equip you to:
- *Explain why we must believe in the resurrection of Christ.*
- *Analyze why the gospel is bad news if Christ was not raised from the dead.*
- *Relate the resurrection of Christ to the firstfruits and the first Adam.*
- *Explain how the doctrine of the Resurrection affects the daily living of believers.*
- *Summarize five truths about the resurrection body.*
- *Summarize six ways in which we should be stewards of the wealth God entrusts to us.*
- *Explain two ways in which we should be stewards of the opportunities God gives us.*
- *Analyze the importance of being stewards of relationships in the church.*
- *Define "anathema" and "maranatha" in your own words.*

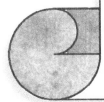

Chapter 5:
Christian Worship
(1 Corinthians 11:2-34)

Introduction

Priscilla's heart contained a mixture of emotions. One Saturday, she was baptized in the Holy Spirit and experienced the joy of praying in tongues as God's love overflowed in her. For months, she prayed in tongues and prayed in her native language that her husband, Cleophas, would be saved—and not bring a second wife home. Then, one evening he said, "Tomorrow I will walk 7 miles to bring Kijakazi, my second wife, home. You have been submissive to me and not fought me on this matter, like other wives. So please come with me to bring her home." Telling this story, Priscilla says that God spoke to her and said, "Go with him, and also take the money you make by selling eggs and buy him a new shirt. Press his pants, be kind to him, and trust Me." The next morning, Cleophas was amazed when he saw her goodness to him. They took the long walk, and she waited outside the village under a tree. When he reached the village, an elder told him that Kijakazi did not want to marry him. She was in secondary school and wanted to marry a young man she knew there. Priscilla saw him coming back. His head was down and his shoulders stooped. Her husband approached her very

Figure 5.1 First Corinthians 11 describes the biblical relationship of a husband and wife in Christ as they worship and serve together and honor each other.

slowly. He asked, "What am I going to do, Priscilla? I have lost face. She refused me for a younger man." Priscilla said, "Cleophas, you could kneel now and give your heart to Jesus. Then He will help you through this shame." He agreed and fell on his knees. She took off her best white sweater and put it on the ground for him to kneel on with his best pants. There, under a tree, he received Jesus into his heart. Later, he was baptized in the Holy Spirit, and God called him to preach. Priscilla went on to become the National Women's Leader of the Kenya Assemblies of God. Cleophas grew in Christ and became the Assemblies of God Superintendent of his district. Through submitting to her husband and praying in the Spirit, one woman affected hundreds of families.[1]

Lessons:

Instructions on Headship in Worship (1 Cor. 11:2-16)
Goal A: *Summarize how Christianity lifted the status of women in the early church.*
Goal B: *Explain 3 reasons why women wore veils in Corinth (1 Cor. 11:1-17). Apply these to today.*

Instruction on the Lord's Supper in Worship (1 Cor. 11:17-34)
Goal A: *Contrast celebrating communion in the early church and in the church today.*
Goal B: *Explain 4 directions in which Paul teaches us to look at the Lord's Supper.*

 Key Words

head   head covering   communion/Lord's Supper   love feast

Lesson 15: Instructions on Headship in Worship (1 Cor. 11:2-16)

Goal A: *Summarize how Christianity lifted the status of women in the early church.*
Goal B: *Explain 3 reasons why women wore veils in Corinth (1 Cor. 11:1-17). Apply these to today.*

A. Setting and background

Corinthians is a letter about problems and questions.

- The *problems* include divisions (1 Cor. 1–4), tolerating sexual sin in the church (1 Cor. 5), lawsuits among believers (1 Cor. 6), and unholy living (1 Cor. 6).
- The *questions* are on marriage (1 Cor. 7), rights (1 Cor. 8–10), public worship (1 Cor. 11–14), the resurrection (1 Cor. 15), and the offering for poor believers in Jerusalem (1 Cor. 16).

At Corinth, a question arose about worship: Should women wear a *head covering while praying or prophesying in church (1 Cor. 11:2-16)? A head covering on a woman was a *veil. Some veils covered only the hair, while others covered the face and shoulders. In New Testament times, a Jewish woman wore a veil on her head in public.[2] The veil showed that she was under the authority of her husband, her *head. This was a Jewish custom. Likewise, respectable Greek and Roman women wore veils in public.[3] In contrast, rebellious women, such as prostitutes, did not wear veils.

Q 1 *What did a woman's veil show in Corinth?*

Figure 5.2 In some countries today, women wear veils or head coverings to honor their husbands.

Christianity brought new freedom to women. Did this new freedom in Christ give women the right to remove their veils in public? Before we study Paul's answer in 1 Corinthians 11:2-16, let us look at four factors behind this question.[4]

Q 2 *Why did some women in the Corinthian church consider removing their veils?*

1. Jewish culture and women in New Testament times.

In Jewish culture of the first century, women had few rights. They were viewed as the possessions of their fathers or husbands. Culture forbade Jewish women to study the Law or to take part in the local synagogue services. A man who came to the synagogue worshiped and learned. But a woman who came to the synagogue sat at the back to watch and listen. And in the temple at Jerusalem, women could pass through an area for the Gentiles into a place called *the court of women*. But beyond that, only men were allowed to enter the main part of the temple, called the *temple proper*.[5]

Q 3 *In Paul's time, in what ways was a woman's status below a man's?*

Jewish society did not allow a woman to teach—not even the youngest children in school. A strict rabbi would not greet a woman on the street. One rabbi said that a woman's work was to send her children to the synagogue, to enable her husband to study, and to keep house for him until he returned. Each morning, a Jewish man thanked God that he was not a Gentile, a slave, or a woman.[6] In the days of Jesus, women lived on a level far below men.

2. Jesus and women.

Jesus lifted women to a new level in society. He could have entered the world in many ways, but He chose to be born of a woman (Gal. 4:4). Jewish genealogies listed only the names of men. But the genealogy of Jesus contains the names of five women! Likewise, Jesus broke tradition by talking to women in public. This

Q 4 *What were some ways in which Jesus lifted women in society?*

was something a respected rabbi did not do! Yet our Lord talked to the woman at the well (John 4), forgave the sinful woman in public (Luke 7:36-50; John 8), praised the insights of Mary, the sister of Lazarus (John 12), and honored His mother from the cross (Matt. 26). Our Lord praised Mary for sitting at His feet to learn (Luke 10:38-42). He commended the faith of women (Matt. 9 and 16). Jewish men divorced their wives for the smallest reasons. But Jesus emphasized that women have rights and that the Law allowed a man to divorce his wife only for the reason of adultery (Matt. 5:31-32). Jesus died for all people. And when Jesus rose from the dead, He honored women by appearing to them first and commissioning them to go and tell others. Jesus lifted women to a new level.

Jesus said there will be no marriages in heaven (Matt. 22:30). One preacher smiled and explained: "Perhaps the reason why there will not be marriages in heaven is because there will not be enough men there!"

Q 5 *How did the Holy Spirit raise the level of women?*

3. The Holy Spirit and women. The ladies in Corinth could point to the fact that women were filled with the Spirit. At Pentecost, the women were present with men, not just to cook, but to receive the Spirit! Peter quoted God's promise to pour out the Spirit on men and women (Acts 2:18; Joel 2:29).

The Spirit gifted women to minister. Under the Old Testament, the Holy Spirit anointed women like Deborah to be a judge (Judges 4). In the New Testament, there are several other examples. Anna, Elizabeth, and Mary all prophesied before Pentecost (Luke 2). Philip had four daughters who prophesied (Acts 21). In Corinth, women prayed and prophesied—that is, they manifested the spiritual gift of prophecy (1 Cor. 11:5; 12–14). A woman named Priscilla taught with her husband, Aquilla. Luke mentions them six times. Of these, Priscilla's name appears first four times. So it seems that she was a more notable teacher than her husband. The Holy Spirit anoints men *and* women to serve the Church.

Q 6 *How did Paul lift women to a new level?*

4. Paul and women. What Jesus taught about women, and what the Holy Spirit confirmed about women, Paul emphasized and expanded. In Romans 16:1-15, Paul wrote 28 names of outstanding servants in the church, and 8 of these were names of women. In Philippians, Paul's calls two women, Euodia and Syntyche, co-workers, not sub-workers! And in Galatians, which Paul wrote several years before his letters to the Corinthians, he taught that *"There is neither Jew nor Greek, there is neither slave nor free man, there is neither male nor female"* (Gal. 3:28). Likewise, Paul taught husbands to love their wives as they love themselves (Eph. 5:25).

Q 7 *In what ways has Christianity raised the level of women in your culture?*

We have looked at the background of 1 Corinthians 11:2-16. Christianity raised the level of women in Jewish society. Jesus, the Holy Spirit, and Paul treated women with new dignity and respect. These factors raised the question in Corinth, "Should a Christian woman wear a veil when she prays or prophesies in church?" Wearing a veil showed that a woman was in submission to her husband, the head or authority God had placed over her. So the question in Corinth of the veil was on the topic of headship. Paul gave four reasons why women in Corinth should wear veils in public.

B. Three reasons for a woman to wear a veil in Corinth (1 Cor. 11:2-16)

1. Headship is a part of God's design for heaven and earth (1 Cor. 11:3).

Q 8 *Underline the word "head" the 3 times it appears in 1 Corinthians 11:3.*

Now I want you to realize that the head of every man is Christ, and the head of the woman is man, and the head of Christ is God (1 Cor. 11:3).

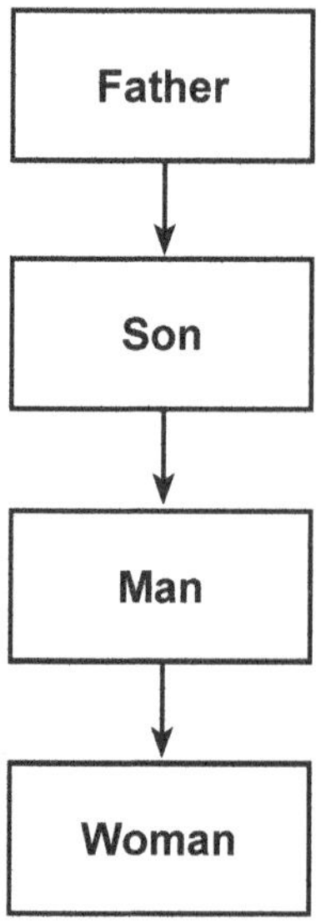

Figure 5.3 Headship is a part of God's design for heaven and earth.

The Greek word for head, *kephale*, appears nine times in 1 Corinthians 11:3-10. *Head* occurs three times in 1 Corinthians 11:3. Hermeneutics, the study of interpreting Scripture, teaches us that if a word appears several times in a verse, we should try to interpret it the same way each time. So in a verse like 1 Corinthians 11:3, we should interpret the meaning of *"head"* the same way all three times, if possible. In this verse, the word *head* expresses authority and divine order.[7]

Headship is not just a teaching for women to learn. There is a head or authority over all of these: men, women, children, employees, citizens, angels, and even Jesus Christ. Everywhere, in the realm of the Godhead and creation, headship and submission exist. In pairs or groups of animals, birds, and fish, one of them is the head. And in the relationship between different kinds of animals, there is submission and headship. The lion is often called "the king of beasts." Wherever there is more than one of something, headship and submission must exist for order. As long as the earth exists, there must be headship and submission on it. And as long as heaven exists, there must be headship and submission in it. This is God's design and plan.

"...the head of every man is Christ" (1 Cor. 11:3). Man is not the top head or authority. Every man, whether Christian or non-Christian, has lesser and greater authorities over him. Lesser authorities over men may include government (national, state, and local), church leaders, employers, bosses, parents, various elders, and teachers. But the top authority over every man, both Christian and non-Christian, is Jesus Christ. Some men submit to Christ and thus receive the blessings God intends. Other men refuse to submit to Christ now. But the time will come when every man will kneel and confess that Jesus is Lord (Phil. 2:10-11). Afterward, Christ, the Head of all men, will judge them.

"...the head of the woman is man" (1 Cor. 11:3). As Christ is the head of man, man is the head of woman. This is God's plan for order and responsibility.

Application. Headship for a man brings order and honor, but also great responsibilities. God commands each husband, as the head, to love his wife as Christ loved the Church (Eph. 5:25-33).

> [25]*Husbands, love your wives, just as Christ also loved the church and gave Himself up for her,* [26]*so that He might sanctify her, having cleansed her by the washing of water with the word,* [27]*that He might present to Himself the church in all her glory, having no spot or wrinkle or any such thing; but that she would be holy and blameless.* [28]*So husbands ought also to love their own wives as their own bodies. He who loves his own wife loves himself;* [29]*for no one ever hated his own flesh, but nourishes and cherishes it, just as Christ also does the church,* [30]*because we are members of His body.* [31]*FOR THIS REASON A MAN SHALL LEAVE HIS FATHER AND MOTHER AND SHALL BE JOINED TO HIS WIFE, AND THE TWO SHALL BECOME ONE FLESH.* [32]*This mystery is great; but I am speaking with reference to Christ and the church.* [33]*Nevertheless, each individual among you also is to love his own wife even as himself, and the wife must see to it that she respects her husband* (Eph. 5:25-33).

Wow! What a responsibility. Read Ephesians 5:25-33 and consider five things it means for a husband to love his wife as Christ loved the Church:

- **A husband's love should sacrifice for his wife (Eph. 5:25).** Jesus *"gave Himself up for"* the Church (Eph. 5:25). Husband, sacrifice some of your time to meet your wife's needs. Take time to listen to her, and talk with her. Help do some of her work. Sacrifice some of your will and seek what pleases her. Be a living sacrifice for your wife.
- **A husband's love should make his wife better (Eph. 5:26-27).** Jesus' love for His bride led him to *"sanctify her, having cleansed her..."* The love of Jesus made His bride purer. Wives need to see a pure husband—not one who is a slave

---

Q 9 *What are some examples of headship and submission in society?*

Q 10 *Is Christ the head of every man, or just Christian men? Explain.*

Q 11 *What are 5 responsibilities that headship brings to a man? Illustrate each.*

Q 12 *How does a husband follow the example of Christ's sacrifice?*

to pornography, immorality, dishonesty, or other forms of sin (Eph. 5:26-27). A husband should set a holy standard in the home.

If a husband has a wife who is not a Christian, he is to live the Christian life in front of her. He should pray for her and do all he can to show the love of God to her. At times, some Christians feel that they can divorce a spouse because he or she is not a Christian. The Bible forbids this and tells us; *"If any brother has a wife who is not a believer and she is willing to live with him, he must not divorce her"* (1 Cor. 7:12).

A husband's love should help enrich his wife's mind. How a husband does this will vary from country to country. In some countries like Bangladesh and Pakistan, up to 85 percent of the women cannot read. In many African countries, about 50 percent of the women do not read. In such situations, a husband's love should lead him to help his wife learn to read. In countries where there is a higher standard of education, a husband's love might help his wife study or learn a skill, such as sewing, being a secretary, or nursing. A husband's love should make his wife better.

- **A husband's love should care for and nurture his wife (Eph. 5:28-29).** A husband is the shepherd of his home. It is his job to care for the needs of each sheep in his little flock. Husband, where does your wife fit into your daily priorities? After your relationship with God, she is next. You are to care for your wife more than your job or ministry (Eph. 5:29). You are to love your wife as yourself.

A man's role is not to rule over his wife. The Bible says that a husband should love his wife as Christ loves the Church. This means that as husbands, we must care for our wives as Jesus cares for the needs of the Church.

- **A husband's love should unite him to his wife (Eph. 5:30-31).** Jesus is one with His Church. We are members of His body (Eph. 5:30). Nothing can separate us from the love of Christ (Rom. 8:35-39). Likewise, a husband and wife are one flesh (Eph. 5:31).

It is strange to see that some couples live together, sleep together, and raise children together, yet are emotional strangers to each other. They are legally married, yet without the bond of deep love. In contrast, a husband's love should cause him to be close to his wife. He should seek to understand her feelings and emotions. Jesus cares about His bride. He knows the number of hairs on each head. He cares about the little things of life. Likewise, a husband should become very close to his wife.

Husband, how well do you know your wife? Do you know her favorite food? Would she rate your marriage as an A, B, C, D, or F? What part of her day does she like the most and the least? Is she your best friend? What does she like most about you? In which area would she like you to improve a little?

Q 13 *What are some ways in which a husband must be faithful to his wife?*

- **A husband's love should be faithful to his wife until death (Eph. 5:25-33).** Jesus was and is faithful to His bride, the Church. He came to die for us, and He was faithful. With His last words, He said, *"It is finished"* (John 19:30). He was faithful unto death. Likewise, a husband's love causes him to be faithful to his wife. A loving husband guards his emotions. He refuses to love other women (outside his family) or become emotionally close to them. In business or friendship, he is faithful to his wife with his words, actions, and private thoughts.

The man is the head of his wife, but this brings many responsibilities! And all the women said "Amen!" For more teaching on "How to be a loving husband," see the *Faith & Action* book *Marriage & Family,* chapter 7.

Some women in Corinth were choosing not to cover their heads during public worship. In Corinth, a veil on a woman showed that she recognized her husband as her head and she was in submission to him. Woman believers realized that they were new creatures in Christ (2 Cor. 5:16-18). They knew that they were co-heirs with their husbands (1 Pet. 3:7). So some ladies thought they could stop using the veil. But Paul's first reason for women in Corinth to wear a veil was that submission to headship is a part of God's plan. And in Corinth, wearing the veil showed submission to headship.

Application. Submission to headship often takes place among equals. Submission does not show that one person is inferior or worth less than another. A person may submit to another when both are equal. For example, the Bible teaches that God is a Trinity—Father, Son, and Holy Spirit. These three persons are eternal and equal. Yet, *"the **head** of Christ is God"* (1 Cor. 11:3). Together, they agreed on a plan to redeem fallen humanity and all of creation. The Son submitted to the Father and came to die on the cross. After the cross, Jesus rose from the dead and ascended to a throne at the right hand of the Father. In time He will return, rule for a thousand years on earth, and judge all His enemies. Then, Christ will submit to the Father forever:

> [24]*Then the end will come, when He hands over the kingdom to God the Father after He has destroyed all dominion, authority and power.* [25]*For he must reign until he has put all his enemies under his feet.* [26]*The last enemy to be destroyed is death.* [27]*For he "has put everything under his feet." Now when it says that "everything" has been put under him, it is clear that this does not include God himself, who put everything under Christ.* [28]*When he has done this, then the Son himself will be made subject to him who put everything under him, so that God may be all in all* (1 Cor. 15:24-28).

Likewise, in Christ, a husband and wife are equal. They are joint heirs of the grace of life (1 Pet 3:7). And in Christ, there is neither male nor female (Gal. 3:28). First Corinthians 11:3-16 and other passages teach that a wife should submit to her husband (Eph. 5:24; Col. 3:18; Titus 2:5; 1 Pet. 3:1).[8] But let every husband remember that in the eyes of Christ, his wife is his equal. Headship is a part of God's design, but so is equality among people. In God's eyes, all people are equal in worth. Great and small, old and young, male and female, Jew and Gentile, educated and illiterate, rich and poor, black and white, slave and free—each of these has the same value to the Almighty. God does not show favoritism to anyone (Acts 10:34-35; Rom. 2:11; Gal. 2:6; James 2:1).

2. Our testimony depends on how we relate to our culture (1 Cor. 11:4-6; 13-16).

> [4]*Every man who prays or prophesies with his head covered dishonors his head.* [5]*And every woman who prays or prophesies with her head uncovered dishonors her head—it is just as though her head were shaved.* [6]*If a woman does not cover her head, she should have her hair cut off; and if it is a disgrace for a woman to have her hair cut or shaved off, she should cover her head* (1 Cor. 11:4-6).

Culture includes the values and practices of a group of people. If culture conflicts with the Bible or with conscience, we should not submit to it. For example, in Corinth, the culture encouraged eating meat sacrificed to idols and having sex with prostitutes at the temple. Paul wrote that believers must abstain from sinful practices such as these (1 Cor. 6:9-10; 10:8-10).

Respect for headship and culture must not contradict submission to God. Peter and John did not submit to the authority of the Sanhedrin and refuse to preach Christ. We ought to obey God rather than man (Acts 4:18-22). Sapphira should not have submitted to her husband Ananias and lied. Her submission and partnership in sin led to her judgment. No believer should submit to something that violates Scripture or conscience.

But in many cases, the beliefs and practices of culture do not conflict with the Bible. For example, in some countries, it is a custom for men to stand and remove their hats when they hear the national anthem. Standing or removing a hat for a song does not conflict

Q 14 Does submission mean one person is inferior to another? Explain.

> OUR TESTIMONY DEPENDS ON HOW WE RELATE TO OUR CULTURE.

Q 15 What is culture? How did culture conflict with Scripture in Corinth?

Q 16 *Why is it good to honor culture when possible?*

with Scripture. So believers in such a culture should follow this custom. Otherwise, if they sit or leave their hats on during the national song, this will be a stumbling block to those around them—and will give the gospel a bad reputation.

In Corinth it was a disgrace for a woman to appear in public without a veil.[9] Paul asked the Corinthians to judge this matter, based on their own insights and experience (1 Cor. 11:13-16). Most women without veils in Corinth were prostitutes and adulterers. So when women took off their veils in church, it sent a bad message to the community. In Corinth, a woman without a veil was a woman who did not respect her husband or the sexual guidelines of society. Prostitutes in the pagan temples in Corinth wore no veils. Likewise, the shaved head revealed a woman was either shamed in public, or was showing her independence to authority.[10] Therefore, Paul said that if a woman was going to take off her veil and thus appear to be immoral, she should also cut her hair.

In contrast, when women wore their veils in public, it showed that they respected their husbands and their culture. Freedom in Christ should not oppose culture and society without a biblical reason. Jesus paid taxes He did not owe to avoid offending citizens (Matt. 17:24-27). Paul did his best not to offend anyone so he could win as many as possible (1 Cor. 9:12, 19-22). Our influence depends on our relationship to our culture. So we should guard our testimony by showing respect for people and customs when we can do so with a good conscience. Paul said that people should not argue or be contentious about woman wearing a veil in Corinth. This was the way to honor culture, have harmony, and have a good testimony. All of the churches agreed with Paul on this matter (1 Cor. 11:16). Only a rebellious and stubborn person would disagree about wearing a veil in Corinth.

Q 17 *In your culture, what are some ways in which a wife shows respect for her husband?*

The way a woman honors her husband depends on the culture. In Corinth, a woman honored her husband by covering her head with a veil in public. But around the world, women show submission in various ways. In many places, if a wife wore a veil today, the community would laugh at her. This would bring dishonor on her husband and would embarrass the church. So it is important for a woman to show respect in a way that pleases her husband and her community.

3. The creation account reveals that woman is man's glory and helper (1 Cor. 11:7-12).

Q 18 *What are some characteristics of a wife who is a glory to her husband?*

Paul reminds us that in the beginning, God created man first and then created woman. This order emphasizes that man is the head of woman. Furthermore, Genesis states that woman is man's helper. And Paul teaches that the woman is man's glory. A husband rejoices in the faith, purity, character, and beauty of his wife. Proverbs 31 exalts and praises the godly woman and her relationship to her husband and family. Paul intends for these verses to emphasize the divine order and purpose. Thus, it was fitting for a woman to show proper cultural signs of authority as a sign of submission to the husband she helped and complemented. Paul mentions that the angels notice a woman's attitude toward her husband (1 Cor. 11:10). Angels are above us, for now, in authority, although we will one day judge them (1 Cor. 6:3). Angels are often present as God's servants and representatives. Paul wrote that the angels watch humans (Eph. 3:10). An angel struck down King Herod because he did not glorify God (Acts 12:21-23). No doubt the angels are often present when believers gather for public worship. Out of respect for these heavenly messengers, we should honor God's plan for headship. In Corinth, this meant that women should wear veils in public.

Q 19 *Why does a wife deserve the same dignity and respect as her husband?*

Paul has two concerns. *First,* he gives a forceful teaching that the man is the head of the woman. But *second,* he does not want Christianity to be an excuse for abuse. So Paul reminds his readers that **"in the Lord,"** and in nature, man and woman depend on each other. In the flesh, woman came from man in Eden, but since then, men come from women. All men have mothers! Above all of these discussions about who depends on whom, there is the truth that *"everything comes from God"* (1 Cor. 11:12). Both men and women are created in the image of God. Although a wife is submissive to her husband, she deserves the same dignity as her husband. In Christ, there is neither male nor female. So, *in the Lord* a husband should respect his wife who submits to him.[11]

Godly submission to headship is a matter of choice, because of respect for God, not force (1 Cor. 11:3). God does not force Jesus to submit. Jesus does not force man to submit. A man should not force his wife to submit. Jesus attracts us to submit to Him through love and gentleness, not force. He is so gentle that He will not break a bruised reed, or quench a smoking candle wick (Matt. 12:20). We choose to submit to Him because He loves and cares for us so much. In contrast, dictators force their authority on people, but the people will rebel when they know they can succeed. Gentleness and love succeed where force fails.

Conclusion: Headship and submission result in many blessings.

- **Submission to headship brings order.** Without submission, there is chaos in society. The Bible mentions many rebellions, such as the rebellions of Korah (Num. 16), Theudas (Acts 5:36), Barabbas (Matt. 27:15-18, 20-21), and the Zealots (Matt. 10:4). But Paul tell us to honor leaders so that peace will prevail in our nations (1 Tim. 2:1-2). God's plan calls for submission in many areas so there can be order. Therefore, children submit to parents, wives submit to their husbands, husbands submit to Christ, workers submit to employers, students submit to teachers, and all believers submit to government. Even though all people are of equal value and worth in God's eyes, submission is necessary for order. Too many cooks spoil the soup. Too many chiefs and too few workers means too little progress.

Q 20 *What happens when people rebel against headship? Give examples.*

- **Submission to headship brings blessings.** For example, submission to headship enables God to share His glory. This is an amazing truth. An evangelist once erred by saying that God will not share His glory with anyone. But the Bible says that God delights to share His glory with us, as we submit to Him. The Godhead shares glory among it members through headship and submission. Jesus brought glory to God by submitting to be our Savior. Then God glorified the Son by accepting His sacrifice, raising Him from the dead, and exalting Him to heaven. [4]*"I glorified You on the earth, having accomplished the work which You have given Me to do.* [5]*Now, Father, glorify Me together with Yourself, with the glory which I had with You before the world was"* (John 17:4-5). Furthermore, Jesus shared His glory with His disciples. [22]*"The glory which You have given Me I have given to them, that they may be one, just as We are one;* [23]*I in them and You in Me, that they may be perfected in unity, so that the world may know that You sent Me, and loved them, even as You have loved Me"* (John 17:22-23). Many verses reveal that as we submit to God's plan, He shares His glory with us (Rom. 8:18; 1 Cor. 2:7; 15:43; 2 Cor. 3:18; 4:17). As children submit to the headship of parents, all the blessings that a father and mother want to share come upon their children. Likewise, throughout the earth, as we submit to headship, the blessings of the Creator come upon mankind.

Q 21 *How does submission to headship enable God to share His glory? Give examples.*

 Lesson 16 Instruction on the Lord's Supper in Worship (1 Cor. 11:17-34)

Goal A: *Contrast celebrating communion in the early church and in the church today.*
Goal B: *Explain 4 directions in which Paul teaches us to look at the Lord's Supper.*

Setting

Today, *communion follows a message. In the early church communion followed a meal.[12] In 1 Corinthians 11:20, communion is called *"the *Lord's Supper."* The early church celebrated it after they had eaten together at a *love feast. Recall that Jesus first celebrated the Lord's

Figure 5.4 The Last Supper

Supper after the Passover meal (Matt. 26). Following His example, the early church ate a meal together and then received the holy bread and wine of communion.

But in Corinth, the focus had shifted from the Lord's Supper to selfish, personal desires. People were more concerned about their appetites than either the Lord or their brothers. In 1 Corinthians 11:2, Paul praised the Corinthians: *"I praise you for remembering me in everything and for holding to the teachings, just as I passed them on to you."* But Paul had no praise for them in regard to their abuse of the Lord's Supper: *"In the following directives I have no praise for you, for your meetings do more harm than good"* (1 Cor. 11:17).

In New Testament times, supper was the big meal. People ate a small breakfast—perhaps a piece of bread dipped in olive oil or wine. And lunch was also a light meal. But supper was the one meal of the day when the family sat together. So the evening meal was for food and fellowship. In this context, the Corinthians were eating supper together, celebrating communion after the meal. God's apostle wrote to correct their selfish behavior at communion and to give guidelines for all to celebrate the Lord's Supper.

Q 22 *How do we celebrate communion differently than the early church did?*

Application. Through years and centuries of practice, the Lord's Table has been separated from eating it after a supper. But we can recover this from the early church and from the first letter to the Corinthians. After a group of believers eat supper together in a home, they can take communion together. Neither First Corinthians, nor any other passage in the New Testament, teaches that it is necessary to have an ordained minister present. And the Bible does not tell us any particular directions we must follow for the Lord's Supper, or that it must be in a church building. Rather, it appears that the Corinthians celebrated communion in a home. So, let us continue to celebrate communion together in a church setting, perhaps once a month. But also, in small groups in our homes, let us receive communion together after a supper. As we recover this practice of the early church, it will strengthen our relationships and increase a holy awareness of God's presence among us.[13]

Next, Paul teaches us to look in four directions whenever we come to the Lord's Table.

A. Look around: At the Lord's Supper, believers should look around and discern the spiritual body of Christ (1 Cor. 11:17-22, 33-34).

Q 23 *What error were believers making at communion in Corinth?*

[17]*In the following directives I have no praise for you, for your meetings do more harm than good.* [18]*In the first place, I hear that when you come together as a church, there are divisions among you, and to some extent I believe it.* [19]*No doubt there have to be differences among you to show which of you have God's approval.* [20]*When you come together, it is not the Lord's Supper you eat,* [21]*for as you eat, each of you goes ahead without waiting for anybody else. One remains hungry, another gets drunk.* [22]*Don't you have homes to eat and drink in? Or do you despise the church of God and humiliate those who have nothing? What shall I say to you? Shall I praise you for this? Certainly not!* (1 Cor. 11:17-22).

[33]*So then, my brothers, when you come together to eat, wait for each other.* [34]*If anyone is hungry, he should eat at home, so that when you meet together it may not result in judgment. And when I come I will give further directions* (1 Cor. 11:33-34).

People go to a church service to worship, fellowship, and receive spiritual strength. But imagine a church service that did *"more harm than good"* (1 Cor. 11:17). The words in one spiritual song are, "You won't leave here like you came, in Jesus' name." The song promises that people will be better after attending church. At Corinth, it was true that people did not leave a communion service like they came—they left worse than they came! Imagine people leaving a church service saying, "That tore me down more than it built me up!" Communion at Corinth was chaos.

Paul heard that there were divisions in the communion service in Corinth (1 Cor. 11:18). Earlier in First Corinthians, Paul wrote to correct divisions over leaders—Paul, Apollos, Cephas, and Christ (1 Cor. 1–4). But in 1 Corinthians 11, Paul is writing about the division between the rich and the poor.

At a private supper, people invite whomever they want to come. Close friends sit and fellowship together. But at the Lord's Table, God invites the guests, and He invites all believers to come. The Corinthians had forgotten this. They were thinking it was their table, rather than the Lord's Table. Perhaps the rich came early and brought lots of food, and the poor, such as slaves, came late and brought little food. The rich sat together to eat and drink all they could hold. But the poor were left alone, with little to eat. The Corinthians came to the Lord's Supper to grab all the food they could get. Eye doctors call perfect vision 20/20. But we may refer to the distorted vision of 1 Corinthians 11:20-22 as 20/22 vision. Read these verses. Believers were not looking around to discern their brothers and sisters. They were thinking only of themselves. And the rich were looking down on the poor. They had lost sight of the fact that communion was not the meal itself, but only the bite of bread and taste of juice after the meal.

Q 24 *What is the meaning of 20/22 vision?*

A wise man once said that the ground is level at the foot of the cross. In Christ, the rich and the poor celebrate new life together. Communion is not just an individual, personal party. Communion is not just about what Christ did for *me*. It is a group activity—a celebration of what God has done for *us*. Believers at Corinth did not recognize that the *spiritual body* of Christ is made up of all believers.

Q 25 *What are some various types of people who receive communion in your church?*

Application. When we gather to receive the Lord's Supper, let us discern the presence of Christ in our brothers and sisters. As we wait for each other, until all have been served, let us give thanks for what Jesus has done for all of us. And let us remember that our brothers and sisters, though different from us in many ways, are beside us, not below us.

A pastor who was traveling attended a church of another denomination. At the close of the service, they refused to let him take communion. A deacon explained, "We practice closed communion; that is, only the members of this denomination may receive communion." In contrast, at another church, a pastor announced, "We practice open communion here. That is, all who love and obey the Lord Jesus Christ may receive communion. This is not the table of First Assembly; rather, it is the Table of the Lord!"[14]

Q 26 *Should your church practice open or closed communion? Explain.*

B. Look back: At the Lord's Supper, believers should look back to Calvary (1 Cor. 11:23-26a).

[23]*For I received from the Lord what I also passed on to you: The Lord Jesus, on the night he was betrayed, took bread,* [24]*and when he had given thanks, he broke it and said, "This is my body, which is for you; do this in remembrance of me."* [25]*In the same way, after supper he took the cup, saying, "This cup is the new covenant in my blood; do this, whenever you drink it, in remembrance of me."* [26]*For whenever you eat this bread and drink this cup, you proclaim the Lord's death until he comes* (1 Cor. 11:23-26).

Paul turns from the problem to the solution. He shifts from the wrong way to the right way to receive the Lord's Supper. Note his words, *"For I received from the Lord what I also passed on to you"* (1 Cor. 11:23). Paul was not present with Jesus at the first communion. In fact, he was called Saul at that time and was not a follower of Jesus.

But after Saul's conversion, Jesus taught him about the Lord's Supper. What Paul knew about communion, he learned through direct revelation from God.

As we look back to the first communion service, we remember that it was in an upper room—just hours before the cross. Jesus and His disciples had gathered to celebrate the Jewish Passover. Recall that the Jews celebrated the first Passover as slaves in Egypt (1 Cor. 5:7). They killed the Passover lamb and put the blood on their door posts so the death angel would pass by (Exod. 12). Throughout their history, every year for about 1,500 years, the Jews celebrated the Passover. This great event reminded them through the death of the Passover lamb that God freed them from the bondage of Egypt. On the night of the Passover, God sent the tenth and final plague and delivered the Israelites from slavery. Jesus chose the night of the Passover to begin the Lord's Supper. Why? Because He came to fulfill the prophetic event of the Passover in Egypt. The first Passover in Egypt was only a shadow of the final Passover in Jerusalem.

Q 27 *In what way did Jesus change Passover? How?*

Jesus changed the meaning of Passover—He became our Passover Lamb. As Paul wrote earlier in 1 Corinthians, *"Christ, our Passover lamb, has been sacrificed"* (1 Cor. 5:7).

Q 28 *At communion, what does it mean to look back?*

One writer notes three things about looking back. We should remember *that* He died. We should remember *why* He died. And we should remember *how* He died.[15] Look back to Calvary and behold *"The Lamb of God, who takes away the sin of the world"* (John 1:29)! Look back to Calvary and behold your substitute—the One who died on a rugged cross to take our place. Darkness covered the earth, and the Father turned away as *"God made Him who had no sin to be sin for us, so that in him we might become the righteousness of God"* (2 Cor. 5:21).

At communion, we look back to the cross. The bread reminds us of His body, broken for us. And the juice helps us recall His blood, which He shed to initiate the new covenant. "The world drinks to forget, but we drink to remember."[16]

As we celebrate communion, we look back and thank God for Calvary. As one song states, "When He was on the cross, I was on His mind."[17]

C. Look ahead: At the Lord's Supper, believers should look forward to the Second Coming (1 Cor. 11:26).

"For whenever you eat this bread and drink this cup, you proclaim the Lord's death until he comes" (1 Cor. 11:26).

Communion is a proclamation (1 Cor. 11:26). When we celebrate the Lord's Supper, we are making a statement—a declaration of faith.

Q 29 *What sermon do we proclaim at communion?*

Most believers have never preached a sermon from behind a pulpit. But whenever we take the bread and the cup, we are preaching—proclaiming our faith in Christ. Communion in Corinth did not preach Jesus, for their practice was self-centered rather than Christ-centered. But when we take communion in a biblical way, we preach Christ. We declare, in taking the bread and the cup, "Jesus pardons. Jesus died in my place. Jesus bore my sins. His new creation is taking place in me. This bread represents His body. This cup represents the blood of His covenant." We are preaching when we receive the Lord's Supper. Communion is a sermon that we act out.

Q 30 *To whom do we preach at the Lord's Supper?*

To whom are we preaching at communion? When we take the Lord's Supper, we are declaring to the Lord that we are His. We are reminding ourselves that He bought us. We are proclaiming to believers and unbelievers around us that we participate in the death of Christ. We are announcing to principalities, powers, and the forces of evil that we belong to Jesus Christ. We proclaim to angels who are present that we are God's children through Jesus Christ.

Although we look back at communion, we also look forward. For as Paul says, at this celebration we proclaim His death *until* He comes (1 Cor. 11:26). So at communion, we look forward and upward, for the completion of our salvation is near. *"He who testifies to these things says, 'Yes, I am coming quickly.' Amen Come, Lord Jesus"* (Rev. 22:20).

D. Look within: At the Lord's Supper, believers should look within and repent of any attitudes that are uncaring, selfish, or unholy (1 Cor. 11:26-32).

²⁶For whenever you eat this bread and drink this cup, you proclaim the Lord's death until he comes. ²⁷Therefore, whoever eats the bread or drinks the cup of the Lord in an unworthy manner will be guilty of sinning against the body and blood of the Lord. ²⁸A man ought to examine himself before he eats of the bread and drinks of the cup. ²⁹For anyone who eats and drinks without recognizing the body of the Lord eats and drinks judgment on himself. ³⁰That is why many among you are weak and sick, and a number of you have fallen asleep. ³¹But if we judged ourselves, we would not come under judgment. ³²When we are judged by the Lord, we are being disciplined so that we will not be condemned with the world (1 Cor. 11:26-32).

Paul concludes by warning the Corinthians not to take communion in an *"unworthy manner"* (1 Cor. 11:27). By this Paul means that believers should have the right attitude as we approach the Lord's Supper. We should recognize the body of Christ in two ways. *First,* the believers around us are holy, for they are a part of the Lord's body. *Likewise,* the bread and wine are not common. Rather, they represent the holy, physical body and blood of Jesus Christ.¹⁸ To take communion in an unworthy, unholy, undiscerning manner invites the discipline and judgment of God (1 Cor. 11:28-32). To avoid this judgment, we believers should examine ourselves—our attitudes toward God and others—as we approach the Lord's Table. We should discern whether there is any need to repent.

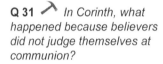 **Q 31** *In Corinth, what happened because believers did not judge themselves at communion?*

When we get up in the morning, we need a mirror to look into to adjust ourselves for the day. Without using a mirror, our hair might look funny. In a similar way, communion is like a mirror in which we examine our relationship with the Lord and with others. If we are mistreating other believers, as the Corinthians were doing, Paul says we are sinning against the body and blood of Christ—sinning against the Lord and His people.

At the first Lord's Supper, Jesus began by correcting relationships at the table. He took a towel and washed their feet, because they were arguing about which of them was the greatest—man-centered worship. That same problem that Jesus corrected at the first Lord's Supper, Paul corrected at Corinth. And we must correct it again wherever it occurs in our own lives. So God calls us to examine ourselves lest we fall into judgment. Paul says that this is why many in the Corinthian church have fallen sick and some have even died prematurely—before it was God's will for them to die (1 Cor. 11:30). Failure to examine ourselves leads to God's judgment and even early death.

Rafael refused to take communion in church. Later, the pastor asked why. Rafael said that he did not take communion because he had a bitter attitude toward another person in the church. The pastor explained that communion is a good time to repent, receive forgiveness, and celebrate a right relationship with God. The pastor rejoiced when Rafael received communion at the next opportunity. The apostle Peter once made a mistake like Rafael. He told the Lord, *"Go away from me, Lord; for I am a sinful*

 Q 32 *What should a sinning believer do instead of avoiding communion? Why?*

man!" (Luke 5:8). God's will is not to *go away from* sinners, or for sinners *to go away from* Him. The solution for sin in our lives is not to avoid communion. For many verses of Scripture teach that when believers sin, God will discipline us—whether we take communion or not. The Father disciplines every one of His children so that we may partake of His holiness (Heb. 12:10). When we become aware of our sins, we should move *toward* God, not away from Him. The Table of the Lord is God's invitation for us to repent, receive forgiveness, and celebrate the love God offers us in Jesus Christ. Whenever there is communion, let us never miss the opportunity to repent of any known sin and embrace anew the Savior who died to save us from our sins. Communion teaches us to look in four directions: around, back, forward, and inward.

One preacher guided His flock to remember three rooms when they celebrate the Lord's Supper.

The ***first room*** is the room in which the Lord's Supper first happened. Picture yourself in that upper room in Jerusalem. Imagine yourself, as a believer in Christ, slipping into the room with Peter, James, John, the other disciples, and Jesus. Smell the unleavened bread and the roasted Passover lamb. Thus you can remember that first night when Jesus started the Lord's Supper.

The **second room** is the one where we celebrate communion now. Look around and see people you know—from close friends to strangers. In this room, at this time in God's kingdom, we share this moment together. Recognize that some people are not here this year who were here last year. The nature of this body changes. So this moment is precious. We share it together as a group of people traveling from earth to heaven.

Q 33 *Does the illustration of the three rooms help you? Explain.*

The **third room** to think about is in heaven. We celebrate communion on earth until He comes. Then we will sit and drink the cup anew with Him in the kingdom of God. Imagine that huge heavenly room, with so many people you cannot count them. The whole church of Jesus Christ will gather from every age, from every nation, from every ethnic group. And we will all sit with Christ at a great banquet. And at that great table, He will lift the cup to celebrate our eternity with Him.[19] This third room inspires us to sing the Hallelujah Chorus!

Figure 5.5 The Greatest Communion Service will be in a big, upper room in heaven.

Test Yourself: Circle the letter by the *best* completion to each question or statement.

1. How did Jesus lift the level of women?
a) He taught them in the synagogue.
b) He changed their place in the temple.
c) He talked to them in public.
d) He chose two as apostles.

2. Which teaching of Paul lifted women?
a) Wife, be submissive to your husbands.
b) Wife, remove your veils in the church.
c) Husband, love your wife as yourself.
d) Husband, remember that your wife is weaker.

3. What does 1 Corinthians 11 teach on headship?
a) The head of children is parents.
b) The head of Christ is God.
c) The head of men is the Church.
d) The head of unbelievers is government.

4. Why did women in Corinth wear veils?
a) To show that they were old enough to marry
b) To acknowledge that men were superior
c) To prevent men from feeling lust
d) To show respect for their husbands

5. In 1 Corinthians 11, Paul says creation teaches
a) that men are superior to women.
b) that women are made in God's image.
c) that women are the glory of men.
d) that men and women are equal.

6. In the early church, communion
a) took place in the temple.
b) came after a meal.
c) was served in the synagogue.
d) followed a sermon.

7. What error did believers make in Corinth?
a) They focused on themselves at communion.
b) They used leavened bread and fermented wine.
c) They celebrated communion too often.
d) They neglected to take the Lord's Supper.

8. Looking back at the Lord's Supper, we see that
a) Jesus became our Passover Lamb.
b) only the leader drank from the cup.
c) the wine was turned to blood.
d) the Jewish Passover remains the same for us.

9. Which statement is TRUE about communion?
a) It is only for members of a local church.
b) It is a sermon that all believers proclaim.
c) It is the same in both testaments.
d) It is a proclamation to every city.

10. At communion, a sinning believer should
a) be wise and avoid the bread and cup.
b) pray, but not accept the bread and cup.
c) accept the bread and cup by faith.
d) repent and receive the bread and cup.

 Essay Test Topics: Write 50-100 words on each of these goals that you studied in this chapter.

Instructions on Headship in Worship (1 Cor. 11:2-16)

Goal: *Summarize how Christianity lifted the status of women in the early church.*

Goal: *Explain 3 reasons why women wore veils in Corinth (1 Cor. 11:1-17). Apply these to today.*

Instruction on the Lord's Supper in Worship (1 Cor. 11:17-34)

Goal: *Contrast celebrating communion in the early church and in the church today.*

Goal: *Explain 4 directions in which Paul teaches us to look at the Lord's Supper.*

Chapter 6:
Spiritual Gifts in Worship
1 Corinthians 12:1-11

Introduction

A teacher of biblical studies stood in front of his students. He had given them the task of memorizing the Apostles' Creed. Since it was long, he did not require each student to memorize the entire creed. Instead, each student had a small part to memorize and recite.

The first student began, "I believe in God, the Father Almighty, maker of heaven and earth."

The second student said, "And I believe in Jesus Christ, His only Son, our Lord."

Student by student, they continued. All went well until a student said, "He ascended into heaven and sits at the right hand of God the Father. From thence He will come to judge the living and the dead."

Then, there was a long silence. Something was wrong. Finally, one of the students spoke up: "The boy who believes in the Holy Spirit is absent today!"[1]

In the first lesson of this chapter, we will study six sad reasons why believers do not receive spiritual gifts. One of these reasons is that many do not believe in the Holy Spirit the way the early church believed. May the Lord use this chapter to increase our faith so that we may receive the gifts our Father desires to give us.

Figure 6.1
God desires to give us spiritual gifts as we worship and walk in His presence.

Lessons:

Six Sad Reasons Why Believers Do Not Receive Spiritual Gifts (1 Cor. 12:1-7)

Goal A: *Identify 4 types of spiritual gifts and give examples of each.*
Goal B: *Expose 6 reasons why believers do not receive spiritual gifts.*

Gifts of Wisdom and Knowledge (1 Cor. 12:1-8)
Goal A: *Define the spiritual gift of a word of wisdom.*

Goal B: *Give examples of a word of wisdom in the ministry of apostles, church leaders, and common believers.*
Goal C: *Define the spiritual gift of a word of knowledge.*
Goal D: *Give examples of a word of knowledge in the ministry of preachers, teachers, and common believers.*

Gifts of Faith, Healing, and Miracles (1 Cor. 12:9-10)

Goal A: *Explain what the spiritual gift of faith is not and is. Give examples.*
Goal B: *Compare and contrast a gift of healing and a miracle. Illustrate each.*
Goal C: *Give examples of how spiritual gifts may overlap.*

Gift of Discerning of Spirits (1 Cor. 12:10)
Goal: *Identify 3 spiritual sources, and give examples of what each produces.*

 Key Words

manifestation   spiritual gifts

Lesson 17: Six Sad Reasons Why Believers Do Not Receive Spiritual Gifts (1 Cor. 12:1-7)

Goal A: *Identify 4 types of spiritual gifts and give examples of each.*
Goal B: *Expose 6 reasons why believers do not receive spiritual gifts.*

Setting

Another question in Corinth was on the use of "spiritual gifts." The Greek word *charismata* refers to spiritual gifts God gives to the Church through the Holy Spirit (1 Cor. 12:4).

The Bible has much to say about the *gifts* God wants to give us. Take a few minutes to study four types of gifts (Figure 6.2). God is generous and has many gifts to give the Church.

Q 1 *What are 4 types of spiritual gifts?*

Q 2 *What are some spiritual gifts for every believer?*

Q 3 *What types of gifts does Paul mention in Ephesians 4:11-12? Are you one of these gifts?*

Q 4 *Which gifts does Romans 12:3-8 list? What are your spiritual gifts?*

Q 5 *Which gifts in 1 Corinthians 12:7-11 have you received, or are seeking?*

Q 6 *Where do you think the 2 types of gifts in 1 Peter 4:10-11 fit on the chart?*

Type of Gifts	Examples of Spiritual Gifts	Time/Purpose
1. Personal gifts—for each believer	**Eternal life:** *"For the wages of sin is death, but the free gift of God is eternal life in Christ Jesus our Lord"* (Rom. 6:23).	A person receives this gift when he or she is born again. Its purpose is to impart spiritual life to those who were dead in sins (Eph. 2:1-5).
	Baptism in the Holy Spirit: *⁴"Gathering them together, He commanded them not to leave Jerusalem, but to wait for what the Father had promised, 'Which,' He said, 'you heard of from Me; ⁵for John baptized with water, but you will be baptized with the Holy Spirit not many days from now'"* (Acts 1:4-5). Note that Luke refers seven times to the fullness of the Holy Spirit as a gift our Heavenly Father gives (Luke 11:13; Acts 1:4; 2:38-39; 8:20; 10:45; 11:17; 15:8).	A person usually receives this gift after being born again. The purposes are to help each believer to be a powerful witness (Acts 1:8) and to live a victorious life (Gal. 5:16). See also Matthew 3:11; Acts 2:1-4; 8:14-19; 9:17-19; 10:44-46; 19:1-7.
	Speaking in tongues (private): *"He who speaks in a tongue edifies himself, but he who prophesies edifies the church"* (1 Cor. 14:4, 28).	The Spirit enables a believer to pray in tongues at the time of being baptized in the Spirit. Afterward, a believer should, like Paul, pray in tongues often to build himself up spiritually (1 Cor. 14; 18; Jude 20).
	Wisdom: *"But if any of you lacks wisdom, let him ask of God, who gives to all generously and without reproach, and it will be given to him"* (James 1:5).	God gives us wisdom as we seek Him so that we can make wise decisions.
	Other gifts: *"Every good thing given and every perfect gift is from above, coming down from the Father of lights, with whom there is no variation or shifting shadow"* (James 1:17).	God gives many, many gifts to us day by day, because He loves us and cares about us.
2. Ministry gifts—for leaders of the body (Offices)	*"And He gave some as apostles, and some as prophets, and some as evangelists, and some as pastors and teachers"* (Eph. 4:11). (Note that these gifts are people who serve day by day.)	These "people gifts" are to establish the Church and *"to prepare God's people for works of service so that the body of Christ may be built up"* (Eph. 4:12).
3. Ministry gifts—for helpers in the body (Assistance)	*⁵"So we, who are many, are one body in Christ, and individually members one of another. ⁶Since we have gifts that differ according to the grace given to us,... prophecy,... service,... teaching;... exhortation;... gives, with liberality;...leads, with diligence;... mercy, with cheerfulness"* (Rom. 12:5-8).	God may give these gifts to a person at any time. Timothy received a gift through the laying on of hands (1 Tim. 4:14). These gifts seem to be frequent or continuous, much like those of Ephesians 4:11.

Continued on next page

Type of Gifts	Examples of Spiritual Gifts	Time/Purpose
4. Ministry gifts—*manifestations for the body (Dramatic/sudden/charismatic)	"Now to each one the manifestation of the Spirit is given for the common good…" wisdom, knowledge, faith, healing, miracles, prophecy, discerning of spirits, tongues, interpretation (1 Cor. 12:7-11). (Note that these gifts are sudden, brief flashes—manifestations of the Spirit in the church.)	Christ gives these gifts as we desire and seek them, to meet the needs of the church (1 Cor. 12:3, 11; 14:1). Unlike the gifts of Ephesians 4:11 and Romans 12:3-8, these gifts are brief signs of the Spirit's presence.

Figure 6.2 God gives some spiritual gifts to help each person and some gifts to edify the whole body.

God has many gifts to give us. But why do believers receive some gifts, yet refuse other *spiritual gifts God desires to give us? Let us examine six reasons why we, as God's children, may fail to receive spiritual gifts from our gracious heavenly Father.

A. Unbelief: Some do not receive spiritual gifts because they think these gifts have ceased (1 Cor. 12:1).

Q 7 *Did spiritual gifts like healings, miracles, and speaking in tongues die with the apostles? Explain.*

Some falsely teach that spiritual gifts died with the apostles. Review Figure 6.2, which lists the many kinds of spiritual gifts God gives. Note that if spiritual gifts died with the apostles, we cannot receive eternal life today, because this is a spiritual gift! And if spiritual gifts were buried with the apostles, then there are no pastors today, because pastors are spiritual gifts to the Church! However, we are thankful that the gift of eternal life is still available, the Church is still alive, and spiritual gifts are still here for those who seek them by faith. No Scriptures teach that spiritual gifts have ceased. And Church history reveals that spiritual gifts are received whenever the Church moves close to God.

> SOME FALSELY TEACH THAT SPIRITUAL GIFTS DIED WITH THE APOSTLES.

Q 8 *What perfection is Paul writing about in 1 Corinthians 13:10?*

Q 9 *Does the Bible fulfill our need for spiritual gifts (1 Cor. 13:10)? Explain.*

Others teach that spiritual gifts lived on after the apostles, but died when the Bible was complete. They base this false teaching on a true passage, but misinterpret it. Take a minute to read 1 Corinthians 13:8-12. It says that when the perfect comes, the imperfect will cease. But has the perfect already come?

> *⁸Love never fails. But where there are prophecies, they will cease; where there are tongues, they will be stilled; where there is knowledge, it will pass away. ⁹For we know in part and we prophesy in part, ¹⁰but when perfection comes, the imperfect disappears. ¹¹When I was a child, I talked like a child, I thought like a child, I reasoned like a child. When I became a man, I put childish ways behind me. ¹²Now we see but a poor reflection as in a mirror; then we shall see face to face. Now I know in part; then I shall know fully, even as I am fully known* (1 Cor. 13:8-12).

We can all agree that the Bible is perfect. But this passage is not talking about the Bible—it is the Bible talking! First Corinthians 13:8-12 contrasts two times: *now* and *then*—the present and the future, the imperfect and the perfect. We will study this passage in chapter 7 of this book. For a brief overview, see Figure 7.13, which contrasts the now and then of 1 Corinthians 13 and 15.

Q 10 *Did Paul say to seek spiritual gifts until the Bible comes (1 Cor. 1:7)?*

How long do we need spiritual gifts? Until Jesus returns. Some have said that we do not need spiritual gifts, because the Bible has come, and the Bible is perfect. But it is the Bible that tells us to *"eagerly desire spiritual gifts"* (1 Cor. 14:1)! How long did Paul want the Corinthians to have spiritual gifts? Read 1 Corinthians 1:7 for a clear answer. *"Therefore you do not lack any spiritual gift as you eagerly wait for our Lord Jesus Christ to be revealed."* We need spiritual gifts until Jesus is revealed at His second coming (1 Cor. 1:7).

B. Carnality: Some do not receive spiritual gifts because their hands are full of earthly things.

Some in Corinth did not receive spiritual gifts because they were carnal. They spent their time arguing, bringing division, swindling and suing other believers, eating at pagan feasts, or committing sexual sins.

John Wesley disagreed with those who said spiritual gifts disappeared because there was no need for them. Wesley said the real reason people did not receive spiritual gifts was worldliness. He said that the love of many and most called Christians had become cold. Wesley was referring to the state of the Church under the Roman Emperor, Constantine, from A.D. 306–334. During that time, Christianity became the state religion. Most everyone claimed to be "Christian." But as Wesley wrote, these people calling themselves "Christians" had no more of the Spirit of Christ than the other heathens. So when Christ examined the Church in those days, He found only a dead form left.[2] Yet Wesley believed the Church could recover spiritual gifts through holiness and faith. And his diary records more than 200 healings that occurred in his ministry.

Q 11 What explanation did Wesley give for people missing spiritual gifts?

Carnality means "worldly, fleshly living." Some believers are carnal, yet do not commit such sins as murder, theft, lying, or sexual sins. Rather, these weak believers are worldly because their hearts are set on earthly things. They remind us of the seed in the parable of the sower that was never fruitful because of the cares of life and the deceitfulness of riches (Matt. 13:22). If we eat too many sweets, we may not want to eat healthy things like vegetables. Likewise, too much concern for the things of the world kills our appetite for spiritual matters. To receive spiritual gifts from God, we must take time for God and come to Him with empty, holy hands.

Q 12 What are some things we must put down to pick up spiritual gifts?

C. Lack of balance: Some do not receive spiritual gifts because they emphasize only spiritual fruit.

This reminds us of the man who did not eat potatoes because he ate bananas. Shall we choose between healing and gentleness, or shall we desire both? Shall we choose between the gifts of the Spirit and the fruit of the Spirit? Never! The Scriptures teach us to seek both.

Q 13 How would you respond to someone who wants fruit, not gifts?

Perhaps some have been guilty of *charismania*—emphasizing the gifts too much, if this is possible. When people discover something new and wonderful, this affects their conversation. Pentecostals and Charismatics talk a lot about spiritual gifts because they are wonderful. Can you imagine the blind man Jesus healed remaining silent (John. 9)? Do you think Peter told anyone about the fish with the gold coin in its mouth (Matt. 17)? Springs bubble water, and those filled with the Spirit testify about the river flowing out of them. All believers should value the fruit of the Spirit (Gal. 5:22-23). But let us also seek spiritual gifts. In 1 Corinthians 13, Paul does not guide us to choose between love and spiritual gifts. Rather, love is the path for us to walk on as we use the spiritual gifts Christ gives us to edify His body. Shall we choose between a left shoe and a right shoe? Between sunshine and rain? Between being and doing? We need the fruit *and* the gifts of the Spirit! A church without the fruit of the Spirit is as useless as a barren fig tree. And a church without the gifts of the Spirit is as powerless as Samson without his strength.

D. Self-confidence: Some do not receive spiritual gifts because they depend on natural gifts.

We live in an age in which humans have accomplished great things. Mankind has invented electricity, solar energy, and atomic energy; radio, television, and the Internet; automobiles, trains, and airplanes; photographs, photocopies, and color printers; computers, cell phones, and MP3 players; and vaccinations, antibiotics, and laser surgery. These are just a few of the things on the list of man's success.

Q 14 Give examples of spiritual gifts that helped the Church.

Q 15 *What evidence proves our need for spiritual gifts?*

But before we pat ourselves on the back, and boast that we do not need spiritual gifts, there are some things we should remember:
- A child dies of hunger every 3.5 seconds—25,000 children will starve to death today.
- A third of the people on earth cannot read or sign their names.
- Half of the world has not yet heard the gospel.
- The divorce rate is increasing, and the discipleship rate is decreasing.
- Unless we have great revivals in the major cities of the earth, soon, more people will go to hell in this generation than in all the previous generations added together.
- Many nations on earth are 99 percent Muslim.

Q 16 *What are some examples showing that spiritual gifts help the church?*

Human abilities cannot solve the spiritual challenges that we face. Never in the history of the Church has there been a greater need for spiritual power and spiritual gifts. Daniel's spiritual gifts gave him great influence with three kings. One healing or miracle can lead to hundreds of conversions. When the first believers were filled with the Spirit and Peter prophesied, three thousand people came to Christ in one day (Acts 2:41). When Peter and John healed the crippled beggar, everyone in Jerusalem heard about the miracle (Acts 4:16). When Philip preached with signs and wonders, the whole city of Samaria was shaken for Christ (Acts 8). When Peter healed Aeneas, who had been paralyzed, *"all who lived at Lydda and Sharon saw him, and they turned to the Lord"* (Acts 9:35). "Rise up, O saints of God! The church for you does wait. Her strength unequal to her task; rise up and make her great!"³ It is still God's plan to confirm the gospel with signs and wonders. All over the world today, God continues to give spiritual gifts to expand and strengthen the Church. Let us walk in the Spirit and keep in step with what God desires to do in these last days.

This fourth reason for not receiving spiritual gifts reminds us of the church at Laodicea. Jesus told them:

> ¹⁵*"I know your deeds, that you are neither cold nor hot; I wish that you were cold or hot.* ¹⁶*So because you are lukewarm, and neither hot nor cold, I will spit you out of My mouth.* ¹⁷*Because you say, 'I am rich, and have become wealthy, and have need of nothing,' and you do not know that you are wretched and miserable and poor and blind and naked"* (Rev. 3:15-17).

PRAYER:

OH LORD, WE ARE DESPERATE FOR MORE OF YOUR SPIRIT.

Prayer: Oh Lord, we are desperate for more of Your Spirit. Needs surround us on every side. Enemies of the Church taunt us, as the Philistines ridiculed Samson, and mock Your name. The lost are dying by the millions and will fill the lake of fire. Hungry people visit our churches and go home empty and unchanged. Families are falling apart. The lost work beside us, unconvicted of their sins. Our hearts cry out to You for help. Pour out Your Spirit upon us afresh and anew. Cleanse us and fill us with new power and spiritual gifts. Empower us so that we may glorify Your name and give You a reward for the blood You have already shed.

E. *"Charisphobia:" Some do not receive spiritual gifts because of fear.

Q 17 *What is "charisphobia"? Give some common examples.*

People fear different things.
- Some fear the unknown. These timid souls do not seek spiritual gifts because they are not sure what will happen if they receive them. But is it not enough for us to know the heavenly Father who gives the gifts? Can we trust the God who gave us His only Son to give us the gifts that will help us and others?
- Some have a fear of man. These are afraid that spiritual gifts will make them look foolish. They recall that sinners in Jerusalem made jokes about the 120 who were filled with the Spirit on the Day of Pentecost. Back then, sinners accused the saints

of being drunk (Acts 2). Likewise, some today ridicule and mock those with spiritual gifts. And it is true that some Pentecostals and Charismatics pray out loud and raise their hands in church. This frightens some and looks foolish to others.

God does not embarrass His children. He is the God of order, love, and wisdom. But this type of fear reminds us of Naaman the leper, captain of the Syrian army. At first, when the prophet Elijah told him to dip in the Jordan, he refused. The Jordan was a dirty river. Dipping in it made the great captain feel foolish and embarrassed. But when he humbled himself, he received the spiritual gift of healing that changed his life.

For sure, some who receive spiritual gifts respond in unusual, immature, and unwise ways. For example, some believers in Corinth received the gift of speaking in tongues and caused confusion in the church services. This made them look foolish in the eyes of many. So Paul taught them to respond more wisely to the spiritual gifts God gives. All believers must learn how to respond to the spiritual gifts God gives, for spiritual gifts are developmental. They do not come to us full grown. Just as we grow and learn in all other areas, we must mature in our use of spiritual gifts. But the most important thing is not our self image, our self respect, our pride, or our dignity. People need help from God. And our heavenly Father wants to help us. So let us humble ourselves and seek the gifts He desires to give.

Consider the folly of avoiding areas that might make us look foolish. Shall we avoid using money because some print counterfeit money? Shall we avoid driving because some have accidents? Shall we avoid talking because some pronounce words in the wrong way? Shall we avoid cooking because some make funny mistakes learning to cook? Shall children avoid learning to walk because they look funny falling? Shall students refuse to preach because of the humorous things that happen when beginners speak in public? Is there any new skill or new ministry where we are safe from mistakes? In any area, there is risk on the path to success. Let us count the cost and move forward by faith.

Q 18 *Do you agree with this: "There is always risk on the path to success"? Explain.*

F. Lack of understanding (ignorance): Some do not receive spiritual gifts because the local church does not teach about them.

Now about spiritual gifts, brothers, I do not want you to be ignorant (1 Cor. 12:1).

It is possible to be ignorant—to lack understanding—about spiritual gifts. In fact, it is not only possible, but it is also common for people to be "in the dark" concerning spiritual gifts.

We have mentioned five reasons why people do not receive spiritual gifts (A–E). Each of these reasons concerns an area in which people lack knowledge about spiritual gifts. And in this sixth reason—lack of understanding—we have put several more reasons in one group. Consider these example on the lack of understanding:

- Some people think that God should initiate the gifts. These believers fold their arms and say, "If God wants me to have a spiritual gift, He will give it to me." So they do not seek spiritual gifts. They do not obey Paul's command, *"Earnestly desire spiritual gifts."* Rather, they put all of the responsibility on God, and none on themselves. They do not obey the Lord's command to *ask, seek, knock*. When they need money, do they think God will put it in their pocket?

Q 19 *What are some examples of spiritual ignorance?*

- Some people think that spiritual gifts are only for apostles. These do not discern that spiritual gifts are for common believers in daily life. It is true that the apostles were in the upper room when God poured out the gift of the Holy Spirit. But there were only 12 apostles in the upper room, and the total number there was 120. Only one in 10 (1/10) was an apostle. And throughout Acts, we see lay people spreading the gospel. Stephen had a great ministry in Jerusalem (Acts 6–7). It was Philip who went to Samaria (Acts 8). Common believers spread the gospel while the apostles

Q 20 *Define the "priesthood of each believer." How does this relate to spiritual gifts?*

remained in Jerusalem (Acts 8:4). It was Ananias, a layman, who prayed for Paul to be healed—to receive his sight (Act 9). We thank God for leaders in the Church and the spiritual gifts God gives them. But as the early church believed, and the Reformation emphasized, we believe in the priesthood of every believer. That is, every believer is a type of priest who has a spiritual ministry. God has work for all of us to do, and we need spiritual tools to work. We need tools to match each task. A hammer is good for some jobs, but it will not paint a wall. Tools are not honor badges. No carpenter hangs a hammer around his neck to show it off. Tools are for working. And it is the Holy Spirit's desire to spread many different spiritual gifts throughout the body for spiritual work and warfare (1 Cor. 12).

- Some people seek the gifts and not the Giver. This shows a lack of spiritual understanding. In 1 Corinthians 12:1-11, Paul emphasizes eight times that the Holy Spirit is the Giver of spiritual gifts.[4]

Conclusion: There are several reasons why believers do not receive spiritual gifts. Brothers and sisters, let us teach on spiritual gifts for the Church. May each person who studies this book seek and receive spiritual gifts from God. May we always use these gifts for God's glory, and not our own. And may we teach every believer to seek and use spiritual gifts to minister.

Lesson 18

Gifts of Wisdom and Knowledge (1 Cor. 12:1-8)

Goal A: *Define the spiritual gift of a word of wisdom.*
Goal B: *Give examples of a word of wisdom in the ministry of apostles, church leaders, and common believers.*
Goal C: *Define the spiritual gift of a word of knowledge.*
Goal D: *Give examples of a word of knowledge in the ministry of preachers, teachers, and common believers.*

Q 21 What were some reasons why Paul wrote 1 Corinthians 12:3?

Background and Setting

¹Now about spiritual gifts, brothers, I do not want you to be ignorant. ²You know that when you were pagans, somehow or other you were influenced and led astray to mute idols. ³Therefore I tell you that no one who is speaking by the Spirit of God says, "Jesus be cursed," and no one can say, "Jesus is Lord," except by the Holy Spirit (1 Cor. 12:1-3).

Paul insisted that the Spirit does not lead anyone to say "Jesus is cursed" (1 Cor. 12:3). Believers today may wonder why Paul emphasized this truth. But let us keep four things in mind as we study spiritual gifts:

- Demons lead pagans to curse Jesus. The Corinthians knew that, in the past, demons led them and other pagans to worship idols and to say evil things about Jesus and His followers (1 Cor. 12:2). And it is possible that, even in a house-church at Corinth, a demon could lead an unbeliever to shout "Jesus be cursed."
- The Law said that anyone who hung on a tree was accursed. And since Jesus died on a cross, there was a time when He was cursed for us (Gal. 3:13; Deut. 21:33). But *afterward*, at the resurrection, Jesus overcame the cross, death, and the grave—and God exalted Him to be both Lord and Christ (Acts 2:36).
- Jewish unbelievers, like Paul before he knew Jesus as Savior and Lord, pressured Jewish believers to curse Jesus Christ (Acts 26:11).
- Roman Caesars tried to force Christians to curse Jesus and proclaim Caesar as Lord and master.

So we see that both demons and unbelievers cursed Jesus. In contrast, only the Holy Spirit causes people to declare that Jesus is Lord. But note that declaring *Jesus is Lord*

Figure 6.3 At the Resurrection, Jesus overcame the curse of the cross.

Spiritual Gifts in Worship

requires words *and* actions. For there are many who claim, with words only, that Jesus is Lord (Luke 6:46; Matt. 7:21). In contrast, the Holy Spirit enables us believers, with our words and deeds, to declare that Jesus is Lord.

As we noted earlier, 1 Corinthians 12:1-11 emphasizes eight times that the Holy Spirit is the source of spiritual gifts. Spiritual gifts are supernatural—signs of Someone greater than us. Perhaps the Corinthians erred by thinking spiritual gifts were "alone on the table." But all spiritual gifts reveal the presence of God. So as we study these nine spiritual gifts, let us remember that the gifts are ways in which the Holy Spirit *manifests* or reveals Himself. When a person speaks, sings, or claps, we recognize that he is present. Likewise, when we see any spiritual gifts, we should recognize that the Holy Spirit is *expressing* Himself.[5] We should always keep our focus more on the Giver than on the gift. Light from a flashlight only reminds us that there are batteries inside it. Likewise, spiritual gifts reveal the power of the Holy Spirit within us.[6]

We have studied the background and setting of 1 Corinthians 12. Now let us begin our study of the nine spiritual gifts or manifestations of the Holy Spirit.

A. Message or Word of Wisdom. *"To one there is given through the Spirit the message of wisdom"* **(1 Cor. 12:8).**

The phrases *a message of wisdom* and *a word of wisdom* remind us that these gifts are only part of the whole. God Himself is the source of all wisdom. By the Spirit, we receive a word of wisdom from *"...Christ Himself, in whom are hidden all the treasures of wisdom and knowledge"* (Col. 2:2-3).[7]

1. Definition of *a word of wisdom*. It is a gift of the Holy Spirit that applies knowledge from God to a specific problem or situation. This revelation or insight from God enables a person to act wisely.

Q 22 What is "a word of wisdom" (1 Cor. 12:8)?

God's daily wisdom for life is different from the spiritual gift of wisdom in 1 Corinthians 12:8. Both come from God, so there is a sense in which both are spiritual wisdom. God gives us daily light for our path through the Scriptures (Ps. 119:105). But the spiritual gift of wisdom is not common light; it is a flash of light—a supernatural moment of insight to solve a problem.

2. The apostles often preached a supernatural message of wisdom. The Greek word for wisdom is *sophia*. Forms of the word *sophia* occur more than 20 times in 1 Corinthians 1–3.[8] In these chapters, Paul contrasts the wisdom of the world with the wisdom from God (1 Cor. 1:22-24; 1 Cor. 2:1-4).

Paul's message was often the spiritual gift of wisdom. He got it directly from the Holy Spirit (Gal. 1:11-12).

Application: Likewise today, when God's servants preach the Word of God, there are moments when the spiritual gifts shine forth. In these precious times, God enables the preacher to give a message of wisdom, telling people what to do in their situations. We recognize that not all preaching is *a word of wisdom.* But in anointed, Pentecostal ministry, there often comes a flash of insight beyond the preacher's preparation—beyond his education, experience, or knowledge—that makes our hearts burn within us. We should recognize that this is *a message of wisdom* from the Holy Spirit.[9]

Q 23 Have you ever received or heard a word of wisdom? Explain.

3. Church leaders often receive a message of wisdom from the Holy Spirit. James received a message of wisdom from God at a meeting of the apostles in Jerusalem. This word of wisdom showed Jewish believers what to require of Gentiles seeking salvation (Acts 15:13-22).

Application: Today, pastors, evangelists, missionaries, and deacons should pray and expect a message of wisdom from God in some situations.

4. All believers should seek the spiritual gift of wisdom for important decisions and difficult times. Jesus prayed all night before He chose His apostles (Luke 6:12-16). He was always aware of His need for divine wisdom. He showed great wisdom when leaders brought to Him a woman taken in adultery (John 8), when some brought a coin to test Him, and when enemies asked a difficult question about seven brothers (Matt. 22:23-28). Wisdom from God enabled Jesus to make wise decisions and give wise answers.

Q 24 Do you think Jethro had a spiritual gift of wisdom when he counseled Moses (Exod. 18:13-27)?

When we need wisdom to witness, the Spirit will help us as we pray (Luke 12:12; 21:15). Our Father delights to give us the Holy Spirit to meet our needs (Luke 11:7-11). And when we receive the wisdom we pray for, let us acknowledge that the Holy Spirit is revealing Himself to help us.

A woman was walking to church during a time of great persecution. Some enemy soldiers stopper her and asked where she was going. In an inner flash of light, the Holy Spirit gave her wise words to answer. "I am going to hear the reading of my Elder Brother's will." (This was a wise way of saying that she was going to hear the reading of the New Testament or will that Jesus gave us.) Her words satisfied her enemies. They hoped she would receive a large amount through his will.

B. A message or word of knowledge

Q 25 How do a word of knowledge and a word of wisdom differ?

1. Definition of a word of knowledge. Knowledge is the insights or facts that wisdom uses. A gift of knowledge is information that comes directly from the Holy Spirit. Wisdom is discernment to apply knowledge rightly. Wisdom is greater than knowledge, because knowledge alone lacks direction. Without knowledge, wisdom is limited, like a businessman who lacks money. In contrast, some have plenty of knowledge, but lack the wisdom to apply it.¹⁰ So wisdom and knowledge should walk hand in hand. For example, Jesus told Peter to catch a fish with a coin in its mouth and use it to pay their taxes (Matt. 17). This showed supernatural knowledge and wisdom working together.

Q 26 How may a word of knowledge be like a prophetic insight?

2. A word of knowledge is often connected with prophecy that knows secrets of the heart (1 Cor. 14:24-25). All of the treasures of wisdom and knowledge are hidden in Jesus Christ (Col. 1:15). So we understand that *a word of knowledge* is just a part of the whole knowledge of God.

At times, a word of knowledge and the gift of prophecy overlap. Both involve knowledge from the Holy Spirit.
- Through knowledge from the Holy Spirit, Jesus knew that the woman at the well had five husbands (John 4).
- Through knowledge from the Holy Spirit, Peter was aware that Ananias and Sapphira had lied (Acts 5).
- Through knowledge from the Holy Spirit, Ananias knew to pray for Saul to receive his sight and where to find him (Acts 9).

It does not matter whether we call Peter's message to the Sanhedrin in Acts 4 a word of knowledge or a word of prophecy. What matters is that we practice depending on the Holy Spirit and recognize the ways in which He manifests His presence.

Q 27 What spiritual gift should teachers often have? Explain.

3. A word of knowledge may flash forth as a preacher or teacher ministers God's Word. For sure, there is knowledge that ministers gain through study. But most Pentecostals can testify to times when the Holy Spirit has given them a special anointing—a flash of insight or knowledge beyond study or natural ability. In such times, the sheep have heard the voice of the Good Shepherd speaking through human lips.

We discern the Spirit if there are tongues and interpretation. Yet too often, we are unaware of His presence when He gives us a supernatural message of knowledge through anointed teaching. We recognize God in the loud message of tongues. But we

Spiritual Gifts in Worship

may not discern Him in the still, small voice of teaching (1 Kings 19:11-13). We may be tempted to think that speaking in tongues is supernatural, but anointed teaching is natural. Let us praise God for every message in tongues and desire that it occur with the gift of interpretation. Also, let us pray for spiritual discernment to recognize a word of knowledge the Holy Spirit gives through teaching.

It appears that the Corinthians emphasized speaking in tongues too much, because it sounded supernatural. Paul wrote 1 Corinthians 12–14 to emphasize that all gifts are important for the body, and all come from one Spirit.
- We expect apostles to have the signs of apostles—signs, wonders, and miracles (2 Cor. 12:12).
- We expect prophets to have the signs of prophets, that is, to prophesy.
- Likewise, we should expect teachers to have, at times, a supernatural gift of knowledge to enhance and improve their teaching. Surely God desires spiritual gifts in every ministry of His body.[11]

4. A word of knowledge may come through any believer who is filled with the Spirit. Paul said that all may prophesy (1 Cor. 14:5, 24, 31). Likewise, the Spirit desires to give all believers the gift of knowledge as it is needed. So Paul writes that we should eagerly desire the greater gifts (1 Cor. 14:1, 12).

A husband and wife wanted to plant a new church. After much prayer and discussion with church leaders, they chose a town called Idabel. Although they searched the newspaper and talked to many people, it was difficult to find a house to rent. As they drove through a neighborhood in Idabel, they prayed. Suddenly, they felt led to stop in front of a house. There was no sign that it was for sale or rent. Still, the husband felt led to stop and talk to the people in the house. The owner of the house smiled and said: "It was only last night that we decided to rent this house. How did you know?" The young pastor replied, "I did not know for sure, but I felt led to stop and talk to you." So they rented that house and lived in it for 2 years as they planted a new church in Idabel. And they gave thanks for the help of the Holy Spirit.[12]

People need water. They often build towns and cities near lakes and rivers. The water of a stream brings life and blessing as it flows along. Jesus said the Holy Spirit would flow through believers, like a river.

Q 28 *How often should we expect spiritual gifts in our lives? Explain.*

37Now on the last day, the great day of the feast, Jesus stood and cried out, saying, "If anyone is thirsty, let him come to Me and drink. 38He who believes in Me, as the Scripture said, 'From his innermost being will flow rivers of living water.'" 39But this He spoke of the Spirit, whom those who believed in Him were to receive; for the Spirit was not yet given, because Jesus was not yet glorified (John 7:37-39).

Prayer: Our Father in heaven, let your Spirit flow through us, bringing spiritual gifts and spiritual fruit. Without the ministry of the Spirit, the Church and the world are dry places. But the supernatural gifts and fruit of the Spirit bring life, health, and blessings of every kind.

Lesson 19: Gifts of Faith, Healing, and Miracles (1 Cor. 12:9-10)

Goal A: *Explain what the spiritual gift of faith is not and is. Give examples.*
Goal B: *Compare and contrast a gift of healing and a miracle. Illustrate each.*
Goal C: *Give examples of how spiritual gifts may overlap.*

Earlier, we noted that the gifts of knowledge and prophecy may overlap, like the shingles on a roof. Likewise, we see some common ground in the *gifts of power*—faith, healing, and miracles. In Lystra, a man lame from birth listened as Paul preached. Paul discerned that the cripple had faith to be healed (Acts 14:8-9). In this account we see the

Q 29 *What is an example of how spiritual gifts may overlap?*

spiritual gifts of knowledge (in Paul) and faith (in the cripple) working together with the gift of healing. Our goal is not to put each of the spiritual gifts in neat groups or categories. For we realize that sometimes God's gifts overlap. But our purpose is to study the various spiritual gifts, see how they work together, and ask the Holy Spirit to manifest these gifts in our ministries.

Figure 6.4 The gifts of the Spirit may overlap.

Q 30 *What principle does Acts 14:10 emphasize?*

Principle. In Acts 14:8-9, we see three gifts working together. But also notice that in Acts 14:10 Paul acted on the gift of knowledge that God gave him. Remember this principle: Whenever God gives a spiritual gift, we must step forward in faith to manifest the gift. When God gives a gift of knowledge, we must act on that knowledge or the gift is useless. The young pastor received a gift of knowledge about a house to rent. But the gift was of no value until the pastor acted on the knowledge. Likewise, God may give the gift of tongues, interpretation, or prophecy. But what value are these gifts until a believer speaks? With all spiritual gifts, we must step forward into the supernatural realm by faith. God offers believers many spiritual gifts. But to receive these gifts, we must reach out and take them by faith. For the manifestation of spiritual gifts is neither all God's part nor all man's part. Rather, we see spiritual gifts revealed as God and believers each do their part. God gives, and we receive as we step forward in faith. God gave Paul the gift of knowledge to discern that the cripple at Lystra had faith to be healed. But the man would have remained lame unless Paul acted on the spiritual gift God offered him. So let us walk softly with God and close to Him throughout each day. Then we will hear His voice and be ever ready to respond to Him in faith.

Paul told Timothy: *"Kindle afresh the gift of God, which is in you through the laying on of my hands"* (2 Tim. 1:6). This verse reveals that God may impart spiritual gifts as leaders lay hands on and pray for believers (see also Romans 1:11). But the verse also emphasizes that we have a responsibility to stir up the gifts God gives us. All believers with spiritual gifts can testify that these gifts do not operate within us at all times. For example, the Holy Spirit may manifest the gift of healing through an elder who prays for the sick. Yet not all for whom the elders prays are healed. Still, as the elder stirs up the gift through prayer, worship, fasting, and practice, God will heal many. Likewise, we must all stir up our spiritual gifts through godly living and expecting the Holy Spirit to manifest the gifts as we minister.

Q 31 *How do we stir up spiritual gifts that God manifests through us?*

A. The gift of faith enables us to believe God for special things.

Q 32 *What are 4 things that the gift of faith is NOT?*

1. Pre-definition: What the gift of faith is not (1 Cor. 12:9). Before we examine what the gift of faith is, let us first consider what it is not.
- The gift of faith is not mere belief in God, since the demons believe and shudder (James 2:19).
- Neither is the gift of faith the human ability to believe. Biblical faith is never mind over matter or positive thinking—for both of these are counterfeit faith that comes *from the mind.*
- Nor is the gift of faith in 1 Corinthians 12:9 saving faith, which comes *from the heart* (Rom. 10:9). It is true that saving faith is the *gift of God* (Eph. 2:8). Saving faith is biblical faith, and it is glorious faith, but it is not the same as the gift of faith that 1 Corinthians 12:9 mentions. We may describe saving faith as the faith *every believer* needs to receive Christ, follow Christ, and please God (Heb. 11:6). In contrast, the gift of faith in 1 Corinthians 12:9 is only given to *certain members* of the body, to edify the whole body. Just as the human body has different parts, believers in the body of Christ have different spiritual gifts.

Spiritual Gifts in Worship

- The gift of faith in 1 Corinthians 12:9 is not the faith or faithfulness that Paul refers to among the fruit of the Spirit (Gal. 5:22). *All* believers should have all the fruit of the Spirit, whereas the nine spiritual gifts of 1 Corinthians 12 are distributed here and there throughout the body of Christ.

2. Definition of the gift of faith (1 Cor. 12:9). Bible teachers agree that the gift of faith in 1 Corinthians 12:9 is an extraordinary, special ability to believe *God.* Note that faith always has an object. The Bible never speaks of faith in faith, nor faith in ourselves. Rather, the object of biblical faith is always God. The gift of faith is the supernatural surge of certainty that enables us to believe God for things impossible to humans.

Q 33 Is saving faith the faith of 1 Corinthians 12:9? Explain.

Bible teachers agree that the gift of faith in 1 Corinthians 12:9 is special faith, but the difficult question to answer is "How special?" That is, "How special or unusual must an expression of faith be for us to call it 'the gift of faith'?" Scholars, teachers, and preachers do not agree on the answer to this question. Let us consider a few opinions and then try to state a biblical conclusion.

- One outstanding scholar, Dr. Stanley M. Horton, describes the gift of faith as a supernatural gift that increases the ability of a group of people to believe in God. He notes that Paul's faith, after seeing an angel, helped many to believe that God would rescue them from the fierce storm (Acts 27:25).[13]

Many define the gift of faith as "faith that can move mountains." But this puts the gift too high. It is true that faith that can move mountains is a gift of faith (1 Cor. 13:2). But Paul is not defining spiritual gifts in 1 Corinthians 13:1-3. Rather, in these three verses, Paul looks up to the highest forms and levels of spiritual gifts—the superlatives! Yet a person may have spiritual gifts that are below the highest form. We may have the spiritual gift of speaking in tongues, but fall short of the tongues of angels (1 Cor. 13:1). We may have the gifts of prophecy and knowledge, yet be unable to understand *all* mysteries (1 Cor. 13:2). Even with the gift of knowledge, we still know *in part* (1 Cor. 13:9, 12). We may have the gift of faith to move hills, yet lack the faith to move mountains (1 Cor. 13:2). Likewise, we may give some of our wealth to the poor, but not give all of it. In 1 Corinthians 13:1-3, Paul's thoughts rise to the highest, most extreme levels of spiritual gifts, not the lesser levels of spiritual gifts that God often gives to believers. So let us be careful not to place spiritual gifts so high that we cannot reach them in a lifetime. For God desires to bless us with spiritual gifts daily.

Q 34 Can a person have the gift of faith, but be unable to move mountains? Explain.

- Some teach that the gift of faith enables us to do God's will, persevering to overcome doubt, ridicule, and opposition. These cite the heroes of faith in Hebrews 11. Did the gift of faith enable Noah to build the ark on dry ground, laboring for many years while sinners mocked him? Did the gift of faith enable Abraham, as an old man, to believe God for a son and a multitude of children? Did the gift of faith enable Moses to stand boldly before Pharaoh, the ruler of the world, and demand that he free a nation of slaves? Did the gift of faith enable Gideon, a weak and fearful man, to become a mighty warrior and lead a nation to freedom? At what point does the faith God gives become amazing enough or *special enough* to qualify as the gift of faith in 1 Corinthians 12:9? These questions are too hard for this author and too wonderful to argue about. Our purpose in this course is not to separate one gift from another, as a surgeon's knife divides. Rather, our goal is to understand, appreciate, and create a hunger for spiritual gifts. This much we know: Jesus is the Author and the Finisher of our faith (Heb. 12:2). And He wants to give us all the faith we need in every situation. The gift of healing comes in a moment, but the result of that healing may remain until death. Likewise, the faith that comes from one encounter with God may inspire and sustain people for a lifetime. Many missionaries can testify that the certainty of being called by God in a moment enabled them to be faithful for

Q 35 Do you think Abraham had the gift of faith? Explain.

Q 36 When does faith become special enough to be called the gift of faith in 1 Corinthians 12:9?

Q 37 *Summarize the teaching of Figure 6.5.*

decades, in the most severe circumstances. Adoniram Judson labored 7 years in Burma (Myanmar) before he saw the first convert to Christ. The place he worked was filthy, and his Christian friends encouraged him to leave. Yet he was certain that God had called him to Burma. Before he died, he translated the entire Bible into Burmese, saw 7,000 come to Christ, and started 63 churches. Surely this is an example of "special faith."

- Scripture emphasizes that saving faith begins at conversion, but grows and matures to sustain us through great trials (Heb. 10:35-39). So in Figure 6.5, we show that saving faith must mature above the level of faith needed at the new birth. But who can say when faith is tall enough to be called the gift of faith listed in 1 Corinthians 12:9?

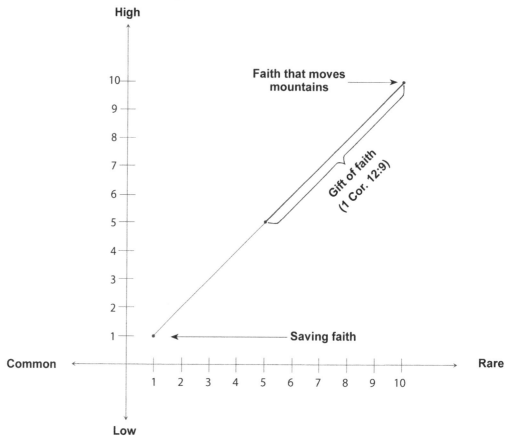

Figure 6.5 Biblical faith ranges from faith in Christ (which results in being born again) to faith that can move mountains.

Q 38 *Do any of the spiritual gifts reside and remain in a person? Explain.*

Q 39 *How might the gift of faith help you in your ministry?*

Conclusion: In contrast to saving faith, which resides and perseveres day by day, it seems that the gift of faith, like all the spiritual gifts, is a flash of intense belief. It is a supernatural surge of confidence in God that enables believers to trust God in a specific situation. The gift of faith is often linked to healings and miracles. Here are some possible examples of the gift of faith:

- A gift of faith enabled Mary to believe that although she was a virgin, she would give birth to the Messiah (Luke 1:34-38).
- A gift of faith enabled a bleeding woman to press through the crowd and touch Jesus for her healing (Matt. 9:20-22).
- A gift of faith enabled Paul to believe that God would save all on the ship, after 2 weeks in a severe storm, and after all hope of being saved was lost (Acts 27:25).
- A gift of faith enabled a pastor to lead his flock to build a new church. Although the cost seemed impossible, the pastor was sure God had spoken to him.

Spiritual Gifts in Worship

- A gift of faith enabled Barnabas to befriend Saul the blasphemer and murderer, who became Paul the apostle.
- A gift of faith enabled a man lame from birth to receive healing (Acts 14:9). This reminds us that the gift of faith often works in harmony with the gift of healing, our next topic.

The gift of faith can enable fathers, mothers, teachers, students, and any other believers to trust God and fulfill His will. So let us walk with God, live in the Word, pray without ceasing, and expect God to give us the faith we need to serve Him well.

Q 40 What examples have you seen of the gift of faith?

B. The gifts of healing. *"To another gifts of healing by that one Spirit"* (1 Cor. 12:9)

We are studying the nine gifts that Paul lists in 1 Corinthians 12:4-11. Our purpose is not to elevate one type of gift over another. James reminds us that every good and perfect gift comes from our heavenly Father (James 1:17). Although we may compare and contrast the gifts that God gives, this is not so we may value one gift above another. It is a wonderful gift when God heals a victim of polio, and a cripple walks. But the vaccination to prevent polio is also a wonderful gift from God that has protected multitudes from this enemy that cripples. It would be unwise to ask which was greater—the healing of a cripple or the polio vaccine. Some of the early missionaries to West Africa died from malaria because they refused the medicine that prevents the deadly disease. These dedicated missionaries meant well. But they placed too high a value on the gift of healing (1 Cor. 12:9) and too low a value on God's gift of medicine (James 1:17). The proper response to God's gifts is to worship Him, not weigh them. In this study we want to understand the gifts of 1 Corinthians 12 in their context—and appreciate, seek, receive, and use these gifts for God's glory.

Q 41 Should we exalt the sudden healing of a cripple above the vaccine for polio? Explain.

A man was trapped in a raging river. He was beginning to drown when a boat passed by and offered to help him. But the man replied, "No, God will save me." He struggled to keep his head above the water as the river swirled around him. Just then, someone on the shore saw him and got a rope to pull him to safety. The person shouted, "Take the rope! I will help you!" But the man answered, "No, God will save me!" Finally, the man drowned and went to heaven. When he saw God, he asked, "God, why didn't you save me when I was drowning?" God replied, "I sent you a boat and then a person with a rope, but you refused help from both of them. What more did you want?"

God has created the human body in such a way that it often heals itself. A cut in our flesh may heal in a few days. Likewise, doctors may heal through medicine or surgery. We thank God for these gifts of healing that God gives, but do not consider them to be examples of the gift of healing that Paul mentions.

1. Definition of the gifts of healing. The Greek text says *gifts of healings*. This emphasizes that there are many types of healings—including those for the body, mind, and emotions. Whatever sickness or disease humans have, God has healings to make us whole. At times, God heals in response to prayer, over a period of time. And we give thanks for all healings from our Father in heaven. The ten lepers were healed on the road to the temple. And a blind man was healed after washing mud from his eyes. Even so, these two healings may have been instantaneous. The healings we read about in the New Testament are sudden, for the most part. So we define the gifts of healings as supernatural blessings received directly from God that restore health in a moment. These divine healings come in the name of Jesus and by the power of the Spirit.

Q 42 Define "gifts of healing" (1 Cor. 12:9).

2. Purposes of the gift of healing. God heals for at least two reasons.

- **God heals to show compassion—because He loves us,** His children. One evening at Peter's home, Jesus healed Peter's mother-in-law, and then healed all

Q 43 What are 2 reasons why God heals?

the sick who came to Him. God is love, and He delights in healing people who are suffering. Jesus rejoices to take away our infirmities and diseases (Matt. 8:17).

- **God heals to show people the right path.** He gives healings, signs, and wonders to confirm the true gospel. When Peter healed a paralyzed man, *"all who lived at Lydda and Sharon saw him, and they turned to the Lord"* (Acts. 9:35). When Jesus sent the 72 out to preach the gospel, He also told them to heal the sick (Luke 10:8-9). Signs and wonders do not replace the preaching of the Word, but they do confirm it.

Q 44 *To whom should we expect God to give gifts of healing?*

3. Agents of the gift of healing: Apostles, evangelists, pastors, deacons and elders, and common believers

- The *apostles* performed many signs and wonders among the people. This helped more and more people to believe in Christ (Acts 5:12-18).
- When Philip evangelized Samaria, the healings and miracles he performed helped the Samaritans believe in Christ (Acts 8:5-8). Likewise, *evangelists*, such as Reinhard Bonnke, are known for the healings and miracles that God enables them to do as they preach the gospel.
- *Pastors* who pray for the sick have seen God heal many in the name of Jesus. Healings confirm the sermon and help persuade people that the gospel is true.
- God enables Spirit-filled *deacons* like Stephen to perform healings, signs, and wonders (Acts 6:8). James tells us that when the *elders* pray in faith, the sick will be healed (James 5:14-15).
- God does not show favoritism (Acts 10:34). When *common believers* pray with faith, God heals the sick (Mark 16:18). God healed Paul's eyes when Ananias, a believer in Damascus, prayed (Acts 9:17-18). We believe in the priesthood and ministry of *all* believers. God has made us *a kingdom of priests* (Rev. 1:6). Smith Wigglesworth was once a plumber, but he became an evangelist as God answered his prayers to heal the sick. All over the world, thousands of believers can testify that the prayer of faith heals the sick, no matter who prays it! Praying for the sick is like kicking to score a goal in soccer. We do not succeed at everything that we try, but we succeed only at what we try. We know that God delights in showing mercy. And we know that He does not show favoritism. Therefore, let us believers pray often for the sick. For God will heal many as we pray.

C. The gift of miracles

Q 45 *Is it acceptable to refer to a sudden healing as a miracle? Explain.*

1. Definition of the gift of miracles. The Greek says *works of power*. In Scripture, a miracle is an act of God that we cannot explain by natural causes.[14] Miracles are evidence of God's power, presence, and purposes. So miracles may include divine healings. God's mighty works of power may have a wide range. A few of the miracles in the Bible are:

> IN SCRIPTURE, A MIRACLE IS AN ACT OF GOD THAT WE CANNOT EXPLAIN BY NATURAL CAUSES.

Q 46 *What are some examples of miracles in the Bible?*

- The creation of the world, and everything in it (Gen. 1–3).
- The ten plagues that God performed through Moses (Exod. 7–11).
- The parting of the Red Sea, provision of manna, and conquest of Canaan.
- The great works of power that God showed through Elijah and Elisha.
- The miracles of Jesus, such as turning water to wine, feeding the multitudes, healing the blind, and raising the dead.
- The miracles of the apostles, such as Peter healing the man at the temple gate, Peter raising Dorcas from the dead, Paul raising Eutychus, and Paul surviving the bite of a viper.

Spiritual Gifts in Worship   123

As Dr. Donald Gee notes, God puts miracles in the middle of the list. This reminds us that one gift of the Spirit is as easy for God as another.[15] Gifts that are supernatural to humans are natural to God. Nothing is too difficult for Him (Num. 11:18-23; Jer. 32:17). So when we pray, let us ask God to meet needs that are great as well as those that are small.

Quentin McGhee tells this story: "My mother, Frances, liked to tell us the account of a miracle God did for her. As a teenager, she suffered from a form of bone cancer called osteomylitis. On x-rays of her leg, a large section of the bone in her thigh appeared black. Her doctor said it was necessary to remove the leg to prevent the disease from spreading. The pain in her leg was so great that when she lay in bed, the slightest movement caused her to cry. Frances had not yet been born again, and neither she nor her mother attended church. Yet in desperation, they decided to ask for prayer. Using the phone book, they located a church and called it. But the pastor said that they did not believe in divine healing. So together, Frances and her mother prayed at home and asked God to help them. At once, the pain stopped, and the rotten bone came out the back of Frances's leg. When they returned to the doctor, he took an x-ray and said that it was a miracle. New bone had replaced the old. For the rest of her life, she walked on two good legs and often told others of this amazing miracle." Read Luke 11:9-13. God is a good God, and He delights to give gifts of the Spirit to those who call on Him.

A Muslim brought his crippled son to a tent revival. The boy was 12 years old, but had never walked. The local pastor laid his hands on the boy and prayed in the name of Jesus. At once, the boy stood to his feet and began walking. The father, his son, and many other Muslims came to Christ through this miracle.[16]

Q 47 *Explain: One miracle is worth a thousand words.*

Lesson 20: Gift of Discerning of Spirits (1 Cor. 12:10)
Goal: *Identify 3 spiritual sources, and give examples of what each produces.*

At the beginning of this chapter, we noted that some spiritual gifts are for personal use. We increase our ability to discern good and evil as we pray, study the Scriptures—led and trained by the Spirit (Heb. 5:14). Likewise, the Bible and God's Spirit within help us to discern the signs of the times (Matt. 16:1-4; 2 Tim. 3:1-4).

The spiritual gift of discerning spirits enables a person to discern among three possible sources: the Holy Spirit, an evil spirit, and a human.[17] There may be times when a believer needs this gift for personal use in daily living. But in 1 Corinthians 12, Paul speaks of this gift to minister to the local church. Let us examine the three sources related to the gift of discernment.

Q 48 *What are 3 spiritual sources of thoughts and actions?*

A. We need to discern when the Holy Spirit is the source.

The problem: Some of the saddest times in the history of the earth are those times when God's people did not recognize His voice or His presence.

- God was speaking words of faith through Caleb. But the Israelites did not discern the Lord's voice to them. As a result, an entire generation fell short of the land of promise (1 Cor. 10:5; Num. 13:30).

Q 49 *What happens when people do not discern God's Spirit? Give examples.*

- [2]*"Listen, O heavens, and hear, O earth; For the LORD speaks, 'Sons I have reared and brought up, But they have revolted against Me.* [3]*An ox knows its owner, and a donkey its master's manger, but Israel does not know, My people do not understand.'* [4]*Alas, sinful nation, people weighed down with iniquity, offspring of evildoers, sons who act corruptly! They have abandoned the LORD, they have despised the Holy One of Israel, they have turned away from Him.* [5]*Where will you be stricken again, as you continue in your rebellion? The whole head is sick and the whole heart is faint.* [6]*From the sole of the foot even to the*

head there is nothing sound in it, only bruises, welts and raw wounds, not pressed out or bandaged, nor softened with oil. ⁷Your land is desolate, your cities are burned with fire, your fields—strangers are devouring them in your presence; it is desolation, as overthrown by strangers. ⁸The daughter of Zion is left like a shelter in a vineyard, like a watchman's hut in a cucumber field, like a besieged city. ⁹Unless the LORD of hosts had left us a few survivors, we would be like Sodom, we would be like Gomorrah"* (Isa. 1:2-9).

- The Pharisees did not discern that the Holy Spirit was working through Christ. ¹⁴*"And He was casting out a demon, and it was mute; when the demon had gone out, the mute man spoke; and the crowds were amazed. ¹⁵But some of them said, 'He casts out demons by Beelzebul, the ruler of the demons'"* (Luke 11:14-15).

- ⁴¹*"When He approached Jerusalem, He saw the city and wept over it, ⁴²saying, 'If you had known in this day, even you, the things which make for peace! But now they have been hidden from your eyes. ⁴³For the days will come upon you when your enemies will throw up a barricade against you, and surround you and hem you in on every side, ⁴⁴and they will level you to the ground and your children within you, and they will not leave in you one stone upon another, because you did not recognize the time of your visitation'"* (Luke 19:41-44).

- ³⁷*"Jerusalem, Jerusalem, who kills the prophets and stones those who are sent to her! How often I wanted to gather your children together, the way a hen gathers her chicks under her wings, and you were unwilling. ³⁸Behold, your house is being left to you desolate! ³⁹For I say to you, from now on you will not see Me until you say, 'BLESSED IS HE WHO COMES IN THE NAME OF THE LORD!'"* (Matt. 23:37-39).

Figure 6.6
"Jerusalem, Jerusalem ..."

Q 50 *What are some reasons why people do not discern God's Spirit?*

The Solution: Paul urges believers to listen carefully for the voice of the Holy Spirit. He says we should examine and weigh carefully what is said or written to the Church (1 Cor. 14:29, 37; 1 Thess. 5:20-21). After the disciples caught a net full of fish, the apostle John recognized that the Lord had spoken (John 21:7). Likewise, we want to discern when Christ is speaking and say, *"It is the Lord"* (John 21:7).

Q 51 *In your church's history, have people rejected leaders God sent? Explain.*

We must beware that we do not reject the leaders God sends us, as Israel rejected the prophets and the Christ. And let us recall that the reasons they rejected them were hardness of heart, fleshly living, pride, jealousy, and new forms of ministry. We must guard against these weaknesses of the flesh. So let us examine ourselves and walk humbly with God—always listening for the gentle voice of the Spirit.

B. We need to discern when an evil spirit is the source.

1. An evil spirit may enable a person to predict the future.

Q 52 *Are there times when evil people can predict the future? Explain.*

¹⁶*It happened that as we were going to the place of prayer, a slave-girl having a spirit of divination met us, who was bringing her masters much profit by fortune-telling. ¹⁷Following after Paul and us, she kept crying out, saying, "These men are bond-servants of the Most High God, who are proclaiming to you the way of salvation." ¹⁸She continued doing this for many days. But Paul was greatly annoyed, and turned and said to the spirit, "I command you in the name of Jesus Christ to come out of her!" And it came out at that very moment* (Acts 16:16-18).

Q 53 *Give an example of false teachings that are leading some astray today.*

2. An evil spirit may be the source of false teachings that lead people astray.

¹*But the Spirit explicitly says that in later times some will fall away from the faith, paying attention to deceitful spirits and doctrines of demons, ²by means*

of the hypocrisy of liars seared in their own conscience as with a branding iron (1 Tim. 4:1-2).

Some believers in Thessalonica were led astray because they did not discern the evil source of a prophecy.

¹Now we request you, brethren, with regard to the coming of our Lord Jesus Christ and our gathering together to Him, ²that you <u>not be quickly shaken from your composure or be disturbed either by a spirit or a message or a letter as if from us</u>, to the effect that the day of the Lord has come. ³Let no one in any way deceive you, for it will not come unless the apostasy comes first, and the man of lawlessness is revealed, the son of destruction, ⁴who opposes and exalts himself above every so-called god or object of worship, so that he takes his seat in the temple of God, displaying himself as being God (2 Thess. 2:1-4).

Beloved, do not believe every spirit, but test the spirits to see whether they are from God, because many false prophets have gone out into the world (1 John 4:1).

Much Mormon doctrine is based on the teachings of Joseph Smith. Many of his teachings are against the light of Scripture. Smith claimed to have a spiritual experience with an angel.¹⁸ But we know that God does not contradict His own Word!

We should always pray for God to help us discern the source of teachings. But the main way we can know that teachings are not from God is if they contradict the Bible. The Spirit will guide us into all truth as we search the Scriptures and pray for discernment.

Q 54 *How can we recognize false teachings?*

3. An evil spirit may possess unbelievers, causing sickness or other physical problems. In some cases, demons may cause insanity (Matt. 8:28-37). At times, evil spirits may cause blindness (Matt. 12:22), seizures, deafness, and muteness (Matt. 17:14-23; Mark 9:14-29; Matt. 9:32).

Q 55 *Are demons the source of any physical problems? Give examples.*

Demons can also cripple.

¹¹And there was a woman who for eighteen years had had a sickness caused by a spirit; and she was bent double, and could not straighten up at all. ¹²When Jesus saw her, He called her over and said to her, "Woman, you are freed from your sickness." ¹³And He laid His hands on her; and immediately she was made erect again and began glorifying God. ¹⁴But the synagogue official, indignant because Jesus had healed on the Sabbath, began saying to the crowd in response, "There are six days in which work should be done; so come during them and get healed, and not on the Sabbath day." ¹⁵But the Lord answered him and said, "You hypocrites, does not each of you on the Sabbath untie his ox or his donkey from the stall and lead him away to water him? ¹⁶And this woman, a daughter of Abraham as she is, whom Satan has bound for eighteen long years, should she not have been released from this bond on the Sabbath day?" (Luke 13:11-16).

4. An evil spirit may oppress or oppose believers. Demons cannot live in Christians. However, these evil spirits oppose us in spiritual warfare.

God allowed an evil spirit to keep a mighty apostle humble.

Q 56 *How did a demon oppress Paul?*

⁷To keep me from becoming conceited because of these surpassingly great revelations, there was given me a thorn in my flesh, a messenger of Satan, to torment me. ⁸Three times I pleaded with the Lord to take it away from me. ⁹But he said to me, "My grace is sufficient for you, for my power is made perfect in weakness." Therefore I will boast all the more gladly about my weaknesses, so that Christ's power may rest on me. ¹⁰That is why, for Christ's sake, I delight in weaknesses, in insults, in hardships, in persecutions, in difficulties. For when I am weak, then I am strong (2 Cor. 12:7-10).

Q 57 *What are some examples of how demons may oppress or oppose believers?*

God may allow evil spirits to fight against the children of God.

For we wanted to come to you—I, Paul, more than once—and yet Satan hindered us (1 Thess. 2:18).

¹⁰Finally, be strong in the Lord and in the strength of His might. ¹¹Put on the full armor of God, so that you will be able to stand firm against the schemes of the devil. ¹²For our struggle is not against flesh and blood, but against the rulers, against the powers, against the world forces of this darkness, against the spiritual forces of wickedness in the heavenly places (Eph. 6:10-12).

⁹And the great dragon was thrown down, the serpent of old who is called the devil and Satan, who deceives the whole world; he was thrown down to the earth, and his angels were thrown down with him. ¹⁰Then I heard a loud voice in heaven, saying, "Now the salvation, and the power, and the kingdom of our God and the authority of His Christ have come, for the accuser of our brethren has been thrown down, he who accuses them before our God day and night. ¹¹And they overcame him because of the blood of the Lamb and because of the word of their testimony, and they did not love their life even when faced with death" (Rev. 12:9-11).

Figure 6.7 *"He was hurled to the earth, and his angels with him"* (Rev. 12:9 NIV).

Q 58 *What are some ways in which demons may tempt believers?*

5. An evil spirit may tempt believers to say wrong things and make wrong decisions.

Then Satan stood up against Israel and moved David to number Israel (1 Chron. 21:1).

But Peter said, "Ananias, why has Satan filled your heart to lie to the Holy Spirit and to keep back some of the price of the land?" (Acts 5:3).

During supper, the devil having already put into the heart of Judas Iscariot, the son of Simon, to betray Him... (John 13:2).

But He turned and said to Peter, "Get behind Me, Satan! You are a stumbling block to Me; for you are not setting your mind on God's interests, but man's" (Matt. 16:23).

Then Jesus was led by the Spirit into the wilderness to be tempted by the devil (Matt. 4:1).

Do not deprive each other except by mutual consent and for a time, so that you may devote yourselves to prayer. Then come together again so that Satan will not tempt you because of your lack of self-control (1 Cor. 7:5).

C. We need to discern when our problems come from a human, not a demon.

Q 59 *Which demon is the hardest to cast out?*

Riddle: Which demon is the hardest to cast out? Jesus gave His followers power to cast out evil spirits (Matt. 10). In time, they found that some demons are harder to cast out than others. Although some came out quickly, others came out only through prayer and strong faith (Matt. 17:20). But the most difficult of all demons to cast out is the one that is not present!

In a Charismatic church, an evangelist once claimed to cast the demon of "sidetrack" out of the local pastor! All of us would like to be free from distractions and be more efficient and fruitful. But the Bible does not teach that distraction is a demon. Allowing our thoughts to turn away from our work, to the left or the right, is a weakness of all humans. But the temptation is not the weakness. The solution to being more fruitful is not casting out a demon that does not exist. Rather, as we get enough sleep, eat the right food, exercise, practice self-control, and walk in the Spirit, God enables us to be alert, focused, fruitful, and more efficient.

1. It is important to discern when the source of a problem is human, not demonic. There are two big reasons why we should not blame a demon for a human problem.

- Saying that someone has a demon will cause that person to feel bad about himself.
- If the source of a problem is not a demon, then blaming a demon will guide a person away from the solution. To solve human problems, we must be responsible. For example, if a person commits sexual sins, he must learn to practice self-control, a fruit of the Spirit. It is not helpful to blame a demon for his behavior. Likewise, it is bad to blame a demon for causing a person to lie, steal, lust, drink alcohol, smoke, or use drugs. Saying "The devil made me do it" shifts the responsibility from a person to an evil spirit. To find solutions to our problems, we must be responsible, admit guilt, repent, seek help, and depend on the Spirit of God to help us.

Q 60 *What are 2 reasons why we should not blame demons for problems that the flesh causes?*

A father blamed the demon of cholera for killing his son. This is very sad, because cholera is a disease, not a demon. The way to prevent cholera is to get an injection (shot) from a doctor. Since the father did not know this, he did not protect his other children from the problem. Soon, more of his children may die from cholera or other diseases. Sometimes God's people are destroyed for lack of knowledge (Hos. 4:6). So it is very important to discern whether the source of a problem is a demon or a human disease.

Q 61 *Do demons cause polio, malaria, or the flu? Explain.*

2. Some false teachings are of human origin, not demonic. We have seen that some false teachers are guided by demons (1 Tim. 4:1). But other false teachers use their own imaginations to make up stories (about miracles, visions, and deliverance) to lead people astray.

Q 62 *Have you known people who were led astray by false stories? Explain.*

> ¹*But false prophets also arose among the people, just as there will also be false teachers among you, who will secretly introduce destructive heresies, even denying the Master who bought them, bringing swift destruction upon themselves.* ²*Many will follow their sensuality, and because of them the way of the truth will be maligned;* ³*and in their greed they will exploit you with false words* (2 Pet. 2:1-3).

One preacher on the radio told an interesting story about a time when he went fishing. He said he was not catching any fish. Then, he remembered that in Genesis, God gave us authority over the animals and the fish. So he commanded the fish to jump into the boat. This preacher claimed that so many fish jumped into the boat that he had to command them to stop, or the boat would have sunk. One listener smiled and asked, "If the fish obey his commands, why does he still beg for offerings?"

A preacher on television told a wild story. He claimed that he was preaching at a revival in Africa. A driver came to pick him up in "the faith wagon"—a car with no brakes. He said they drove with no brakes through many intersections in a big city with thousands of cars and had no accidents. False preachers and teachers like these make up stories to exploit and cheat people. Unfortunately, some people believe every story they hear. These should pay more attention to 2 Peter 2:3 and less attention to liars holding Bibles.

3. Most temptations come from our human, fleshly nature—not demons.

> *But each one is tempted when he is carried away and enticed by his own lust* (James 1:14).

Q 63 *What are some common temptations caused by the flesh?*

⁸And those who are in the flesh cannot please God. ⁹However, you are not in the flesh but in the Spirit, if indeed the Spirit of God dwells in you But if anyone does not have the Spirit of Christ, he does not belong to Him (Rom. 8:8-9).

So I say, walk by the Spirit, and you will not gratify the desires of the flesh (Gal. 5:16).

What is the source of quarrels and conflicts among you? Is not the source your pleasures that wage war in your members? (James 4:1; compare 1 Cor. 3:3).

Q 64 *Did a demon cause Moses to strike the rock, or David to commit adultery with Bathsheba? Explain.*

It was not necessary for a demon to lead King David to commit adultery with Bathsheba. Nor was it necessary for a demon to cause Moses to strike the rock. Sexual sins, like David's, and fits of anger like Moses had are both acts of the fleshly nature (Gal. 5:19-21). All believers must choose to be led by the Spirit or led by their fleshly nature (Rom. 8:1-14; Gal. 5:16-25). Walking is done step by step. If we choose to follow a sinful, fleshly desire, this is a step away from God toward bondage. So we must choose to walk in the Spirit one step at a time, hour by hour. As we make one good choice after another, these choices increase our spiritual strength, maturity, and freedom. The more we walk in the light, the easier it becomes to refuse a step toward the darkness. So let us train ourselves to hate what is wrong and love what is right (Heb. 1:9; Rom. 12:9).

A sincere believer once asked, "What should I do if I cannot discern whether the cause of a problem is a demon or not?" A wise teacher counseled two things:

First, never try to cast a demon out of a believer. It is impossible for a demon to live in the same body in which Jesus Christ lives.

Q 65 *What 2 examples show that demons cannot live in Christians?*

A mole is a small animal that lives underground in total darkness. Asking a demon to live in a Christian is like inviting a mole to live in the light. Jesus has delivered us from the kingdom of darkness and brought us into the kingdom of the light. But moles and demons have not been delivered from darkness, so they refuse the light and choose the darkness. Asking a demon to live in the same body with Jesus is like inviting the worst criminal to share a house with the best policeman. Neither will agree to it!

Q 66 *What are some contrasts in 1 John 4:4?*

As we said earlier, you cannot cast out a demon that is not present. And when someone tries to cast demons out of believers, this confuses, discourages, and causes doubts in believers. Always remember that Christ is in believers, but Satan and demons may be in those who belong to the world (1 John 4:4). *"You are from God, little children, and have overcome them; because greater is He who is in you than he who is in the world"* (1 John 4:4).

Second, when you are praying, plead the blood of Jesus and ask God to bind any powers of Satan that may be hindering. And remember that God does not wait for perfect prayers. If He did, He would not have any prayers to answer! As Paul said, our knowledge on earth is partial (1 Cor. 13:9-12). So we should pray for discernment. But we should not let a lack of knowledge prevent us from praying for help and deliverance. God only has imperfect prayers to answer.

Q 67 *In Luke 9:55, do you think a human spirit or a demon was leading James and John? Explain.*

⁵⁴When His disciples James and John saw this, they said, "Lord, do You want us to command fire to come down from heaven and consume them?" ⁵⁵But He turned and rebuked them, [and said, "You do not know what kind of spirit you are of ⁵⁶for the Son of Man did not come to destroy men's lives, but to save them."] And they went on to another village (Luke 9:54-56).

Spiritual Gifts in Worship

 Test Yourself: Circle the letter by the *best* completion to each question or statement.

1. Which type of gift is eternal life?
   a) A personal gift for each believer
   b) A ministry gift for leaders in the body
   c) A ministry gift for helpers in the body
   d) A ministry gift manifested for the body

2. Some believers do not receive spiritual gifts
   a) because they do not have true faith in Christ.
   b) because they are not favored by God.
   c) because they think the perfect has come.
   d) because they think Jesus has changed.

3. Which gift applies knowledge to a situation?
   a) A word of knowledge
   b) A word of prophecy
   c) A word of enlightenment
   d) A word of wisdom

4. Which gift often helped Paul write letters?
   a) A word of knowledge
   b) A word of prophecy
   c) A word of enlightenment
   d) A word of wisdom

5. The spiritual gift of a word of knowledge
   a) comes through hours of study and research.
   b) is for every believer in the Church.
   c) is information that comes directly from the Holy Spirit.
   d) comes only to mature believers.

6. Which gift should teachers expect often?
   a) The gift of healing
   b) The gift of knowledge
   c) The gift of interpretation of tongues
   d) The gift of wisdom

7. The gift of faith is
   a) positive thinking at its best.
   b) a surge of certainty in God.
   c) saving faith in action.
   d) a fruit of the Spirit.

8. The spiritual gift of healing occurs
   a) as God and doctors work together.
   b) over an extended period of time, by faith.
   c) in a moment of believing.
   d) whenever it is God's will to heal.

9. Which gifts overlapped at Lystra?
   a) Tongues, interpretation, and prophecy
   b) Wisdom, knowledge, and prophecy
   c) Faith, prophecy, and discerning of spirits
   d) Knowledge, faith, and healing

10. What are 3 spiritual sources we studied?
    a) God, Satan, and humans
    b) Witches, spiritists, and fortune-tellers
    c) The Bible, prophets, and teachers
    d) Teachers, prophets, and pastors

 Essay Test Topics: Write 50-100 words on each of these goals that you studied in this chapter.

Six Sad Reasons Why Believers Do Not Receive Spiritual Gifts (1 Cor. 12:1-7)

Goal: *Identify 4 types of spiritual gifts and give examples of each.*

Goal: *Expose 6 reasons why believers do not receive spiritual gifts.*

Gifts of Wisdom and Knowledge (1 Cor. 12:1-8)

Goal: *Define the spiritual gift of a word of wisdom.*

Goal: *Give examples of a word of wisdom in the ministry of apostles, church leaders, and common believers.*

Goal: *Define the spiritual gift of a word of knowledge.*

Goal: *Give examples of a word of knowledge in the ministry of preachers, teachers, and common believers.*

Gifts of Faith, Healing, and Miracles (1 Cor. 12:9-10)

Goal: *Explain what the spiritual gift of faith is not and is. Give examples.*

Goal: *Compare and contrast a gift of healing and a miracle. Illustrate each.*

Goal: *Give examples of how spiritual gifts may overlap.*

Gift of Discerning of Spirits (1 Cor. 12:10)

Goal: *Identify 3 spiritual sources, and give examples of what each produces.*

Chapter 7:
Ministry and Love in Worship
(1 Corinthians 12:12–13:13)

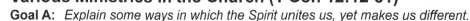

Figure 7.1
As a great mountain stands tall above the earth, our need for love is far above our other needs.

Mt. Aconcagua in Argentina

Introduction

In this chapter, we study the greatest thing in the world—love. First Corinthians 13 is famous, but it is not the only biblical passage on love. *Young's Concordance* lists 500 biblical references on love. Here are a few:

- ⁴³"*You have heard that it was said, 'YOU SHALL LOVE YOUR NEIGHBOR and hate your enemy.' ⁴⁴But I say to you, love your enemies and pray for those who persecute you, ⁴⁵so that you may be sons of your Father who is in heaven; for He causes His sun to rise on the evil and the good, and sends rain on the righteous and the unrighteous. ⁴⁶For if you love those who love you, what reward do you have?"* (Matt. 5:43-46).
- ³⁶"*Teacher, which is the great commandment in the Law?" ³⁷And He said to him, "'YOU SHALL LOVE THE LORD YOUR GOD WITH ALL YOUR HEART, AND WITH ALL YOUR SOUL, AND WITH ALL YOUR MIND.' ³⁸This is the great and foremost commandment. ³⁹The second is like it, 'YOU SHALL LOVE YOUR NEIGHBOR AS YOURSELF.' ⁴⁰On these two commandments depend the whole Law and the Prophets"* (Matt. 22:36-40; Jesus quoted Deut. 6:5).
- "*Love does no wrong to its neighbor; therefore love is the fulfillment of the law*" (Rom. 13:10).
- "*Beyond all these things put on love, which is the perfect bond of unity*" (Col. 3:14).
- "*Above all, keep fervent in your love for one another, because love covers over a multitude of sins*" (1 Pet. 4:8)
- "*...God is love, the one who abides in love abides in God, and God in abides in him*" (1 John 4:16).

Love is a popular word and a biblical concept. But love is not always natural. Even the apostles had to learn to love. James and John wanted to call fire down from heaven on the Samaritans—people of another ethnic group. Matthew's natural desires led him to betray his fellow Jews and steal tax money for the Romans. Simon the Zealot had to overcome his desire to kill Romans. Judas sold Christ for 30 pieces of silver. And Saul thought he was serving God by forcing Christians to blaspheme and putting them in prison. Our natural desires are seldom loving desires.

Most agree that love is the greatest virtue. But like the apostles and the Corinthians, we must often repent for our lack of love, accept God's forgiveness, and daily ask the Spirit to produce the fruit of love in us. For love is the heart and soul of the Christian life. It is the rule that enables us to fulfill all other rules—the new commandment for keeping all the old ones.¹ As a battery powers a flashlight, love gives us energy to follow Christ. However, Jesus prophesied that in the last days, the love of most would grow cold (Matt. 24:12).

Lessons:

Various Ministries in the Church (1 Cor. 12:12-31)

Goal A: *Explain some ways in which the Spirit unites us, yet makes us different.*
Goal B: *Identify and illustrate ways in which believers depend on one another.*
Goal C: *Give examples of spiritual gifts that various ministries need.*
Goal D: *Explain what 1 Corinthians 12:29 does and does not teach about tongues.*

Love: The Path of Spiritual Gifts (1 Cor. 13:1-13)

Goal A: *Explain the necessity of love as the path of spiritual gifts.*
Goal B: *Explain and illustrate 10 characteristics of love.*
Goal C: *Analyze the contrast in 1 Corinthians 13:8-13.*

Key Word

chiasm

Various Ministries in the Church (1 Cor. 12:12-31)

Lesson 21

Goal A: *Explain some ways in which the Spirit unites us, yet makes us different.*
Goal B: *Identify and illustrate ways in which believers depend on one another.*
Goal C: *Give examples of spiritual gifts that various ministries need.*
Goal D: *Explain what 1 Corinthians 12:29 does and does not teach about tongues.*

Setting

We have studied six of the nine spiritual gifts Paul lists in 1 Corinthians 12. The three gifts that remain for us to examine are the spiritual gifts of tongues, interpretation, and prophecy. We will explore these in chapter 8 of this course, which deals with 1 Corinthians 14. For now, let us continue with 1 Corinthians 12 and look at three key principles about spiritual gifts in the Church, the body of Christ.

A. The body of Christ is united, although its members have different gifts (1 Cor. 12:12-14).

¹²The body is a unit, though it is made up of many parts; and though all its parts are many, they form one body. So it is with Christ. ¹³For we were all baptized by one Spirit into one body—whether Jews or Greeks, slave or free—and we were all given the one Spirit to drink (1 Cor. 12:12-13).

First Corinthians 12:12 is a *chiasm (pronounced KY-a-zum). A *chiasm* gets its name from the Greek letter "X" (*chi*, pronounced *kee*). Note that the intersection or center of the Greek letter X divides it into four parts. Likewise, there are four parts of a basic chiasm: A, B, and B¹, A¹ (Figure 7.2). Writers of the Old and New Testaments often used chiasms. Writers build up to their main point (A—>B) and then state the point in reverse order (B¹—>A¹). Note the four parts of the chiasm in 1 Corinthians 12:12.

Q1 *In what sense do we 'drink' of the Spirit?*

As the lines in the letter X cross, the lines of thought in a chiasm cross. A and A¹ may help explain each other, since they are often parallel thoughts. Likewise, B and B¹ shine light on each other.

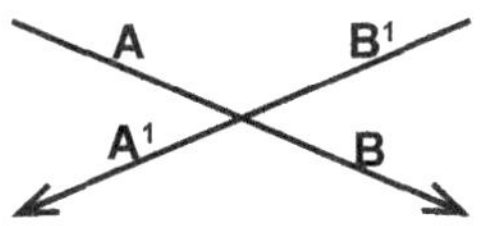

A: The body is a unit,
    B: though it is made up of many parts;
    B¹: though all its parts are many,
A¹: they form one body.

Figure 7.2 There are many chiasms in Scripture, such as in 1 Corinthians 12:12.

Q2 *Complete Figure 7.3.*

1 Cor.	A	B	B¹	A¹
12:12	The body is a unit	though it is made up of many parts	though all its parts are many	
1:19	I will destroy			
6:13	food			
13:7	(love) always protects			

Figure 7.3 Practice identifying chiasms in 1 Corinthians

Paul uses the illustration of a human body to explain the relationship of believers with spiritual gifts. As a physical body has many parts with different purposes, so the body of Christ has many members with different gifts.

As God designed the human body, He also designed the Church, a spiritual body. The Spirit baptizes us into the body of Christ. This spiritual baptism occurs when we are born again (1 Cor. 12:13). Also, at the new birth, we *drink* (receive) of the one Spirit. Paul emphasizes that although there are many believers in the body of Christ, there is

Q3 *Explain: The Spirit baptizes us into one body (1 Cor. 12:13).*

Q 4 *What are at least 2 things all believers have in common?*

only one Holy Spirit who puts us in the body, and we all receive that same Holy Spirit at the new birth.

Earlier, in 1 Corinthians 12:4-6, Paul wrote:
- *"There are different gifts, but the same Spirit."*
- *"There are different kinds of service, but the same Lord."*
- *"There are different kinds of workings, but the same God..."*

So even though believers have different gifts, the Church is united with one Lord, one God, and one Spirit. There is unity and *diversity in the body of Christ. Paul lists nine spiritual gifts in 1 Corinthians 12:7-11 and mentions several other gifts in 12:27-28. The human body has many parts—each with a different place and purpose. Likewise, the body of Christ has many members who have a wide variety of gifts and services.

Q 5 *What are some of the gifts and ministries in your church?*

Application. As believers, we should recognize that each of us has different gifts and different areas of service. Some sing in the choir. Others help repair the church building. Some teach adults. Others teach children. Some visit the elderly and the sick. Others cook for special occasions. Some draw pictures, plan skits, or help advertise the church on the internet. Others greet visitors. There are some areas of ministry that are common to all believers. But there are also areas of ministry in which each believer is unique. The church should accept the differences in believers and not try to squeeze everyone into the same type of service. A wise pastor will help each believer find his or her area of ministry (Figure 7.4).

Some Ministries That a Church Can Have	
Community service	Missionettes—girls program
Ministry to the poor (food, clothes)	Royal Rangers—boys program
Home for abused women	College students (campus and church)
Crisis telephone line	Young adult ministry (younger)
Literacy—reading classes for the illiterate	Single adult ministry (older)
Skills (for jobs, marriage, society, and such)	Single mothers ministry (help and fellowship)
Prison ministry	Senior adult ministry
Recovery Through Christ—addictions	Women's Ministry
Deaf culture ministry	Men's Ministry (includes Honor Bound—Men of Promise)
Soul winning—training and practice	Student ministries—evangelism and discipleship
Street evangelism—special events and tracts	Youth Alive—secondary school program
Athletes ministry—outreach and discipleship	Youth discipleship
Adopt-an-Area—praying for and visiting every home	Youth Bible Quiz
Ministry to the handicapped	Youth drama
Ministry to the terminally ill	Youth choir
Hospital visitation ministry	Speed the Light—youth missions fundraising
Comforting Touch ministry (funerals, sickness, and such)	Youth leadership training
Counseling ministry	Master's Commission—1-2 year training program
Widows ministry	Adult choir
Foreign language ministry	Orchestra
Health ministry—Basic health teachings and clinics	Worship team
Sidewalk Sunday School (Saturday outreach)	Evangelistic music—outreach team
Children's meeting or rally—for children outside the church	Adult drama—acting, costumes, and support
Camps for children and youth	Special events/productions—holiday and evangelistic
Sunday School for all ages	Illustrated sermons
Children's Church—for church children	Fine Arts—using art talents to bless others
Children's choir	Art and design for church needs

Continued on next page

Ministry and Love in Worship

Continued from previous page	
Junior Bible Quiz (children)	Helping hands ministry for church tasks
Weddings—coordinating	Small groups—home fellowships; Bible studies
Welcome center ministry	Prayer ministries (including prayer chain)
Communion—prepare and clean up	Marriage ministries
Church bookstore	Pre-marriage mentoring to prepare couples for marriage
Greeters and ushers	Leadership School
Visitation—visiting new families and visitors	Financial principles training classes
Deacon Ministry—responsible for assigned members	World Missions—praying, giving, and going

Figure 7.4 Some churches have as many as 200 different ministries that church members are doing![2]

B. Members of the body depend on one another (1 Cor. 12:15-26).

¹⁵If the foot should say, "Because I am not a hand, I do not belong to the body," it would not for that reason cease to be part of the body. ¹⁶And if the ear should say, "Because I am not an eye, I do not belong to the body," it would not for that reason cease to be part of the body. ¹⁷If the whole body were an eye, where would the sense of hearing be? If the whole body were an ear, where would the sense of smell be? ¹⁸But in fact God has arranged the parts in the body, every one of them, just as he wanted them to be. ¹⁹If they were all one part, where would the body be? ²⁰As it is, there are many parts, but one body. ²¹The eye cannot say to the hand, "I don't need you!" And the head cannot say to the feet, "I don't need you!" ²²On the contrary, those parts of the body that seem to be weaker are indispensable, ²³and the parts that we think are less honorable we treat with special honor. And the parts that are unpresentable [private] are treated with special modesty, ²⁴while our presentable parts need no special treatment. But God has combined the members of the body and has given greater honor to the parts that lacked it, ²⁵so that there should be no division in the body, but that its parts should have equal concern for each other. ²⁶If one part suffers, every part suffers with it; if one part is honored, every part rejoices with it (1 Cor. 12:15-26).

Consider the wisdom in how God designed the human body. Each part of the body has a *place*. Imagine the body if God had exchanged the places of the ears and the feet. It would hurt to walk on our ears! And if our ears were in our shoes, they would be covered and turned away from sound. And feet would look very funny on the sides of our heads! So God put every part of the body in the place that was best.

Q 6 What are 2 ways in which the design of the human body reveals God's wisdom? Explain.

Likewise, in His wisdom, God created each part of the body with a *purpose*. We cannot pick up things with our eyes, but the hands lift well. We cannot see with our hands, but our eyes enable sight. Each part of the body fulfills the task our Creator ordained.

Members of the human body need one another. And as Paul told the Corinthians, we should recognize that each of us has a gift to help the body of Christ (1 Cor. 12:15-26). God is the One who plans His body and distributes His gifts (1 Cor. 12:18). So no one should feel inferior or jealous (1 Cor. 12:15). Neither should anyone feel proud or superior (1 Cor. 12:21). We all depend on one another. The head needs the feet, and the eye needs the hand.

Q 7 How are church members like members of a soccer team?

Because a man's eyes were weak, he had to wear glasses. But his nose became tired of holding up the glasses every day. One day, the nose said to the man, "You have 2 weeks to find another way to hold up the lenses for your eyes. Otherwise, I will throw the glasses on the rocks!" Days came and went—but the man could find no other plan to hold up his glasses in front of his eyes. Then, on the night of the 14th day, the man was walking home from work. Suddenly, the nose sneezed, and the glasses were lost in the dark. The nose was pleased with himself for getting rid of the glasses. The next

Q 8 What does the story about the nose and eyeglasses illustrate?

morning, the man started walking to work. But without his glasses, he could not see well. He had not walked far when—SPLAT!!! He tripped and fell on his face. What part of his face smashed into the ground? You guessed it! The selfish nose received the force of the blow.³

C. Members of the body need spiritual gifts to match their ministries (1 Cor. 12:27-28).

²⁷Now you are the body of Christ, and each one of you is a part of it. ²⁸And in the church God has appointed first of all apostles, second prophets, third teachers, then workers of miracles, also those having gifts of healing, those able to help others, those with gifts of administration, and those speaking in different kinds of tongues. ²⁹Are all apostles? Are all prophets? Are all teachers? Do all work miracles? ³⁰Do all have gifts of healing? Do all speak in tongues? Do all interpret? (1 Cor. 12:27-30).

Q 9 *Complete Figure 7.5, matching ministries with gifts.*

Ministers	Spiritual gifts needed
Missionaries/evangelists	
Pastors	
Teachers	
Church leaders	
Church members	
Family members	

Figure 7.5 Practice identifying the spiritual gifts that various ministers need

Q 10 *What gifts do you recognize in ministers you know?*

Each type of ministry calls for certain gifts.

- **Missionaries and evangelists** needs signs and wonders.

    When the crowds heard Philip and saw the miraculous signs he did, they all paid close attention to what he said (Acts 8:6). Peter also had this gift.

    ³²Now as Peter was traveling through all those regions, he came down also to the saints who lived at Lydda. ³³There he found a man named Aeneas, who had been bedridden eight years, for he was paralyzed. ³⁴Peter said to him, "Aeneas, Jesus Christ heals you; get up and make your bed." Immediately he got up. ³⁵And all who lived at Lydda and Sharon saw him, and they turned to the Lord (Acts 9:32-35).

    Wherever believers preach the gospel, signs and wonders often confirm our message and help people believe (Matt. 10:1; Heb. 2:3-4).

- **Pastors** need gifts of prophecy, knowledge, and wisdom to minister. They also need the gifts of faith, discerning spirits, and healing. God calls pastors to a spiritual, supernatural ministry. He does not expect them to depend on themselves. Rather, God delights to give them the gifts they need to build His Church. So pastor, pray for the spiritual gifts you need and expect them day by day.

- **Teachers** need wisdom and knowledge. Paul told Timothy to study so that God would approve him (2 Tim. 2:15). God does not approve of laziness. He expects us to study. Even a great spiritual man like Daniel gained insight as he studied the writings of another spiritual man, Jeremiah (Dan. 9:1-2). God requires every pastor and teacher to study. But let us pray as much as we study and while we study! For no amount of study replaces our need for spiritual gifts. The best teachers are known for their research *and* for the insights that the Holy Spirit gives them through gifts of prophecy, wisdom, and knowledge.

- **Church leaders** need gifts of administration (1 Cor. 12:28). Sometimes the church is weakest in the area of management and administration. Administrators supervise, manage, organize, and govern. A leader may have a vision to build a great church. But an administrator will have a strategy and a plan—and will pay careful attention to the project from beginning to end. We Pentecostals should pray more for gifts of administration. For too often, we have signs and wonders to help plant churches, but we do not plan well for discipleship. We have Bible schools, but we do not print books for our students. We teach students well at our Bible schools, but we do not have a plan to help them plant churches in cities. We have a vision to build churches in the cities, but we lack the plan and management to succeed. We have literacy tools, but we do not teach the illiterate to read. May God help us to value more the gifts of administration! Without a vision, the people perish. But they also perish if there is vision without administration.

- **Church members** in every local church need all of the gifts to build up the body and minister to the community. Each local church needs all of the nine gifts Paul lists in 1 Corinthians 12. And believers also need many other gifts to reach their neighbors. (Review Figure 7.4.)
- **Family members.** Parents and children need spiritual gifts at home. All believers need to pray in tongues to build themselves up at home. If we do not take the smaller step of praying in tongues in private, will we have the faith to take the greater step of sharing a gift of tongues in public? If we cannot receive a gift of healing for our own children, shall we expect gifts of healing for neighbors and strangers? Likewise, at various times, we believers may need each of the spiritual gifts in our personal lives. Let us practice receiving and using the gifts in the small circles of our daily lives. As we do this, it will prepare us to minister the gifts in larger circles—in public. Husband, have you received a revelation? Practice sharing it with your wife before you share it with the whole church. Singer, practice your song at home before you stand in front of the whole church. Deacon, do a good job leading your family before you try to help manage the church. Most pastors can testify that only those who use spiritual gifts well in their own affairs use them well in public.

Should all speak in tongues? Let us pay attention to the context of 1 Corinthians 12:29. Paul is teaching about spiritual gifts when the whole body of Christ comes together (1 Cor. 12–14). He has made the point that we have different ministries in public when the church meets. Not all are apostles. Not all are teachers in the church. Few give a message in tongues in church. Let us affirm what Paul teaches about *public* ministry. Gifts vary. But let us also affirm what Paul and other biblical writers teach about ministry that is more *private*.

Q 11 *Does 1 Corinthians 12:30 teach that some believers should not speak in tongues? Explain.*

God has chosen speaking in tongues as an outward sign when a believer is first filled with the Spirit. On the Day of Pentecost, *all* of the 120 believers spoke in tongues (Acts 2:4). As Luke wrote Acts, he did not contradict Paul. But he wrote for a different purpose and in a different context. Luke records that speaking in tongues was the sign that believers were filled with the Spirit in Jerusalem, in Caesarea (Acts 10:44-46; 11:17), and in Ephesus (Acts 19:6). And Paul probably began speaking in tongues when he was first filled with the Spirit (Acts 9:17). Although we have no record that Paul spoke in tongues in public, Paul testified that he spoke in tongues often in private (1 Cor. 14:18). In public, few speak in tongues as a gift for the whole church. But as we compare Scripture with Scripture, we find that all speak in tongues as a sign that they are filled with the Spirit.

As we seek to stay filled with the Spirit, be refilled with the Spirit, and walk in the Spirit, let us pray in tongues every day. For praying in tongues privately is spiritual practice, edification, and preparation for exercising spiritual gifts publicly. Praying in tongues is a spiritual exercise. When a person prays in tongues, his spirit is praying (1 Cor. 14:14). Pentecostal teachers agree that the essence or nature of the gift of speaking in tongues, in public or in private, is the same. But the purpose of speaking in tongues varies. In public, the purpose of speaking in tongues is to edify a group of believers. In private, praying in tongues is to build up the believer who is praying.

Most parents do not teach *in public,* but all parents should teach *in their homes.* And though few men are administrators in the church, all must manage their own homes. Few speak in tongues in public, but let us all pray in tongues in private. For as we have stated above, some need spiritual gifts in the larger circles of society, but we all need spiritual gifts in the smaller circles of our lives. And the spirituality of the church, when we meet together, depends on the spiritual condition of each believer. A chain is only as strong as its weakest link.

A believer named James was praying to be baptized in the Spirit and to receive the gift of praying in tongues. He moaned and groaned in prayer, as if he were begging God. Another believer nearby spoke softly to James. He suggested that we do not need to beg God for a gift. Rather, in His love, God is eager to give good gifts to His children and is already reaching out His hand with the gift. So we do not need to beg, and we should not reach past the gift, for God is very close to us. James paused and thought about this for a short time. He stopped pleading and begging, and began to praise God. In only a moment, He was filled with the Spirit and began to speak in other tongues. Sometimes we reach past the gifts. That is, we try too hard to reach them, instead of just receiving them. Other times, we over-spiritualize the gifts—waiting for a church service, a vision, or a mystical experience. Rather, let us expect to receive spiritual gifts day by day as we walk in the Spirit and commune with God.

Conclusion. *"But eagerly desire the greater gifts. And now I will show you the most excellent way"*—the path to walk on with spiritual gifts (1 Cor. 12:31).

The *"greater gifts"* are those gifts that edify the body through words and deeds that all can understand.[4] Paul will teach much on this topic in 1 Corinthians 14.

Lesson 22: Love: The Path of Spiritual Gifts (1 Cor. 13:1-13)

Goal A: *Explain the necessity of love as the path of spiritual gifts.*
Goal B: *Explain and illustrate 10 characteristics of love.*
Goal C: *Analyze the contrast in 1 Corinthians 13:8-13.*

Q 12 *What are the 3 parts of our outline for 1 Corinthians 13?*

We may divide "the love chapter" into three parts:
- 20%—The necessity of love (1 Cor. 13:1-3),
- 70%—The characteristics of love (1 Cor. 13:4-7), and
- 10%—The permanence of love (1 Cor. 13:8-13).

A. The necessity of love: Love is the path we must walk on with spiritual gifts (1 Cor. 13:1-3).

Q 13 *What is the relationship of love to spiritual gifts?*

Paul introduces love as the *"most excellent way"* or "the best path" (1 Cor. 12:31). Paul is not saying that love replaces the gifts. He does not want us to choose between love and spiritual gifts. Rather, Paul presents love as the path to walk on as we express and use gifts.

Q 14 *Why is it foolish to choose between love and spiritual gifts?*

Imagine the folly of saying, "I choose love *instead* of spiritual gifts." This would be like saying, "I love you, but I will not seek to bring you the gift of healing when you are sick." In contrast, love seeks to help others with their needs. The apostle John reminds us that if we see a brother lacking clothes and food and do not try to help him, the love of God is not in us (1 John 3:17). Likewise, when God's love is in us, we seek spiritual gifts so that we can love those in need. For love is more than a feeling—it includes actions of compassion! Love gives. It is possible to give without loving. But it is not possible to love without giving. Recall John 3:16.

God gives gifts to show His love for us. We give good gifts to our children because we love them. And our heavenly Father, who loves much more than we do, gives the Holy Spirit to those who ask Him (Luke 11:11-13). Spiritual gifts are manifestations of the Holy Spirit God gives. So we do not choose between love and spiritual gifts. Rather, we recognize that spiritual gifts are forms of God's love to and through us.

God is love, so love is the *source* of spiritual gifts. Likewise, Paul emphasizes that love is the path for spiritual gifts (1 Cor. 12:31–13:3). As a signature validates a check, love validates spiritual gifts. Paul warns that if we have the greatest spiritual gifts *without love*, we are empty, unprofitable, and useless.

Figure 7.6 A gong gives a sober announcement that alarms the ears. Likewise, tongues without love announce emptiness.

> ¹*If I speak in the tongues of men and of angels, but have not love, I am only a resounding gong or a clanging cymbal.* ²*If I have the gift of prophecy and can fathom all mysteries and all knowledge, and if I have a faith that can move mountains, but have not love, I am nothing.* ³*If I give all I possess to the poor and surrender my body to the flames, but have not love, I gain nothing* (1 Cor. 13:1-3).

Paul mentions four ministries of spiritual gifts that are useless without love. Notice that he begins each warning with *"If I..."*. Our main concern should always be to examine ourselves rather than others.

Q 15 Why does Paul introduce each category of spiritual gifts with "If I..."?

1. If I speak beautiful spiritual languages without love, these are like the harsh noise of a gong or cymbal. The Corinthians were doing a lot of praying in tongues. But some of it was a waste of time. Pentecostals and Charismatics, let us beware! Do we speak in tongues to show off—to prove that we are spiritual? Or do we speak in tongues because we love to worship God? Do we speak often in tongues to build ourselves up, so that we can be a blessing to others? Do we give a message in tongues in the church to edify others? Would it matter if we wore a hood and no one knew who we were? Let us be careful to pray in tongues for the right reasons. Speaking in tongues without love is just making noise.

Q 16 Create your own example. Having tongues without love is like _____.

2. If I have the spiritual gifts of prophecy and knowledge, so great that I can understand every mystery and answer every question, but do not have love, I am nothing. Balaam was a man who prophesied for money, not for love. His life was a total loss. And Jonah was a loveless prophet. He became upset when God did not destroy Nineveh. In contrast, Jeremiah prophesied out of a heart of love. As the Spirit of God filled him with compassion, he wrote, *"Oh, that my head were waters and my eyes a fountain of tears, that I might weep day and night for the slain of the daughter of my people"* (Jer. 9:1). Likewise, Jesus wept as he prophesied the destruction of Jerusalem (Luke 19:41-44). And Paul ministered with tears (Acts 20:19) and loved the Jews so much that he was willing to be cursed so that they could be saved (Rom. 9:1). When Paul spoke and when he wrote, his words were inspired by love and were wet with tears (2 Cor. 2:4). As we seek the gift of prophecy, let us always ask God to fill us with love. Otherwise, we will be like the preacher who spoke cold truth without love. Some said he preached looking through a rifle scope. But let us speak the truth in love (Eph. 4:15).

Q 17 Who were some prophets without love?

Q 18 Which prophets were known for love?

Q 19 Is your favorite teacher the one who knows the most? Explain.

If I memorize every verse of the Bible, and can relate a chapter and verse to every question people ask, *but lack love,* I am nothing. Without love, my spiritual weight is less than the smallest baby's, and my spiritual height is below that of the shortest child.

3. If I have faith that can move mountains, but do not love, I weigh nothing on the scales of heaven. Faith for great projects, great ministries, and great success, without the self-sacrifice of love, is like smoke in the wind.

Q 20 What are the great ministries near you known for?

4. If I give every penny I own to the poor, but do not have love, my eternal reward is nothing. In the books of heaven, God does not even write down deeds of charity

Q 21 Give examples of giving without loving.

that are not from hearts of love. Many give for the wrong reasons. Some toss coins to beggars, but not for love. They do it to soothe the conscience or to make the beggar move on. If they loved, they would either give more or less. Jesus warned of those who give to be seen (Matt. 6). He said they have full reward the moment people clap for them. Hindus torture themselves to please their gods. But is this for love? Muslims give alms, but is this for love? or for religion? And some who call themselves Christians give large amounts of money to charity, but their hearts are cold. They give for the wrong reasons, desiring recognition or other benefits rather than caring for the needy.

The church in Ephesus had good deeds, but they had left their first love (Rev. 2:4). Jesus warned believers there to repent and return to love. Otherwise, their relationship with Him would end in disaster—He would remove their candlestick. For in any city, it is better to have an empty church than to have a church filled with empty people!

5. If I give my life and become a martyr, but the reason is not love, I lose everything for nothing. Radical Muslims strap bombs to themselves and become martyrs. Is this for love or for hate? Is it for others or for self—that they hope to be among the righteous men surrounded by virgins in heaven?[5] In the early centuries of Christianity, some became martyrs to become famous. What a pity! If we give our lives for a cause, let us be sure the cause is nothing less than love for God and others. All of the apostles became martyrs. They loved Christ, the Church, and the lost so much that they gave their lives. Great is their reward in heaven.

Q 22 *Rate these illustrations from best to worst: Livingstone, 13th floor, Paul, spiritual zero.*

David Livingstone was a famous missionary doctor in Africa. Wherever he went, people felt his love and compassion. Even those who could not understand his words understood his actions.[6] Long before a missionary can speak a native language, the local people can understand the language of love that pours forth from the heart. For love is a universal language that even the deaf can hear.

In many tall buildings, there is no 13th floor. There is a 12th floor, and a 14th, but the 13th floor is missing. This is due to a silly superstition that the number 13 brings bad luck. We may smile at the absence of the 13th floor in a tall hotel. But let us cry if the 13th chapter of Corinthians is missing in our lives!

EVERYTHING MINUS LOVE EQUALS NOTHING.

It is a tribute to Christ that Paul wrote *the love chapter*. For before Paul met Jesus, he was full of hate and was *"breathing threats and murder against the disciples of the Lord"* (Acts 9:1). Paul's hands were stained with the blood of Christians. But Jesus changed Paul from a slave of hate to a servant of love. And if the Lord could change Paul, there is hope that He can do the same to you and me.

Without love, it does not matter how much good we do. Without love, it does not make any difference how many talents we have—or what gifts we possess. Our popularity is not important if we lack love. It does not matter how much influence we have with people if we lack love. For if love does not motivate and guide us, we are a spiritual zero. Without love, whatever we do does not matter.[7] Everything minus love equals nothing.[8]

B. The nature of love: Paul lists ten characteristics of love (1 Cor. 13:4-7).

Q 23 *Why do some refer to the Corinthians as loveless Charismatics?*

The Corinthian church was not walking in the Spirit. They did not yield to the Spirit or come under the Spirit's control and guidance. So they lacked the Spirit's fruit of love. Instead, much of the time they were selfish—doing everything they could to feed their own desires.

Q 24 *In Figure 7.7, how does column 3 relate to column 1?*

Too many of the Corinthians were loveless Charismatics. These fleshly believers did not care what others needed. They grabbed all they could get for themselves. Their actions showed selfishness, pride, jealousy, discord, and disunity.[9] We wish we could give examples of how the Corinthians showed love. But unfortunately, they were known for their *lack* of love. Figure 7.7 contrasts the characteristics of love with the characteristics of some Corinthians.

Characteristic of love	1 Cor. 13	Characteristics of Corinthians who were low on love (1 & 2 Cor.)
1. Patience	Love is patient (13:4).	Some did not wait their turn to minister spiritual gifts in the church (1 Cor. 14:29-33).
2. Kindness	Love is kind (13:4).	Some were tempted to be stingy. "Whoever sows sparingly will reap sparingly" (2 Cor. 9:6).
3. Contentment	It does not envy (13:4).	The foot envied the hand (1 Cor. 12:15).
4. Humility	It does not boast; it is not proud; love doesn't strut (13:5, the Message).	Some boasted of worldly wisdom rather than boasting only of Christ (1 Cor. 1:18-31). Some were proud of prosperity (1 Cor. 4:8-21). Some were proud of their spiritual gifts and forgot they were part of the body (1 Cor. 12).
5. Courtesy	It is not rude (13:5).	Some ignored the poor at Communion and *rushed to feed themselves*[10] (1 Cor. 11:21-22).
6. Unselfishness	It is not self-seeking (13:5).	Some exalted their favorite leaders (1 Cor. 1–4). Some ate meat offered to idols and caused the weak to stumble (1 Cor. 8–10). Some removed their veils in public, which gave the church a bad name (1 Cor. 11:2-16).
7. Self-control	It is not easily angered (13:5).	Some had outbursts of anger (2 Cor. 12:20).
8. Forgiveness	It keeps no record of wrongs (13:5).	Some sued other believers in court (1 Cor. 6:1-8).
9. Spouse of truth	Love does not delight in evil, but rejoices in the truth (13:6).	Some delighted in sexual sin (1 Cor. 5:1-2). Some followed false apostles (2 Cor. 10–12).
10. Perseverance	Love always puts up with anything; Always trusts God; Always hopes for the best (The Message); Bears all things (NASB); There is nothing love cannot face (NEB); Always perseveres (NIV 13:7).	Some gave up their hope in the Resurrection (1 Cor. 15:1-2, 12).

Figure 7.7 Ten characteristics of love in 1 Corinthians 13:4-7

The Spirit inspired Paul to write 1 Corinthians 13. For love is the only way that spiritual gifts have value and meaning. And walking on the path of love is the only way to stop envy, jealousy, pride, and boasting. Love enables us to paint a portrait of Christ so the world can see what He looks like.[11]

What is love? The world uses the word *love* in many ways. We say we love people, but we also say we love food, clothes, music, and even pets. In common language, *love* means to enjoy and delight in things that attract us. This love of the world is based on feelings. With worldly love, we love when we *feel* like loving. But when we do not *feel* like loving, we do not love. So what the world calls love is a *feeling* of strong desire or attraction—a feeling that can change like the wind.

Q 25 *What does the world mean by the word "love"?*

Two people *fell* in love. Their feelings and attraction for each other were strong, in the beginning. Then the wife was in a car accident. Her face was cut with glass, which left ugly scars. So she was not beautiful to look at like she had once been. Soon, her husband decided he did not love her any more. He felt no strong feelings of attraction to her. Love of the world is based on feelings. It can change overnight, or even in a moment.

How does the Bible define and describe love? What does love look like? The New Testament uses the Greek word *agape* for what God calls love. In contrast to worldly love, biblical love is rooted in the will. With biblical love, we choose to love, even when we do not feel like it. Biblical love includes a decision and a commitment. Still, this

Q 26 *How does biblical love differ from what the world calls love?*

agape love has deep emotions and feelings at times. We will study ten characteristics of biblical love in 1 Corinthians 13:4-7.

Since all people are created in the image of God, it is possible to see traces of the love of God in anyone. We may see the love of God in a mother who cares for her new baby. We may see the love of God in a soldier who gives his life for others. But at best, the love in people without Christ is weak and inconsistent. *Without Christ,* no one can love the way 1 Corinthians 13 describes.

However, when we are born again, we are renewed in the image of God. At this new birth, the Holy Spirit comes to live within us. He begins to produce the fruit of love in us. This enables us to love like God loves. And as we grow in grace and submit to the Spirit, we love more and more like God loves.

 Q 27 *How can we compare love to a rainbow?*

First Corinthians 13 is famous for the way it defines and describes love. As a rainbow has many colors, love has many beautiful characteristics. Let us examine ten qualities of biblical love in *the love chapter.*

> THE QUALITIES OF LOVE ARE AS BEAUTIFUL AS THE COLORS OF A RAINBOW.

1. "Love is patient" (1 Cor. 13:4). The word *patient* is a form of the Greek word *makrothumia.* It means to be tolerant, unwearied, and long-suffering *with people.* The tenth characteristic of love is perseverance—which is for circumstances. But patience is for people.

 Q 28 *How is love like a sponge rather than a mirror?*

Love is patient. This quality of love describes the way love *responds* to others. Love is not like a mirror, a hard surface that reflects. Love does not return evil for evil, or insult for insult. Rather, love is like a soft sponge—it absorbs insults, harsh words, and offenses. Love is patient with people. Instead of striking back, it turns the other cheek.

Forms of explosives often have a fuse. Perhaps you have seen a firecracker that has a short fuse. Or you may have seen a stick of dynamite that has a longer fuse. People light the fuse with a match. The fuse gives them time to run away before the explosion occurs. Paul teaches that love has a long fuse. In contrast, we say a person without love has a *short fuse.* He can become angry and provoked quickly. Unlike a good deacon, a short fuse lacks self-control. He may be violent; not gentle, but quarrelsome (1 Tim. 3:2-3).

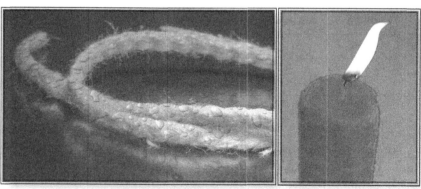

Figure 7.8 Love has a long, wet fuse, not a short, dry fuse. It has a long temper, not a short one.

 Q 29 *Give some examples of those who lacked patience.*

The Bible gives many examples of impatience. James and John lacked love. They were impatient, and wanted to call down fire from heaven on the Samaritans who rejected Jesus. But the Master rebuked James and John, and called them *"Sons of thunder"* (Mark 3:17; Luke 9:54-55). Earlier, we said that Balaam had the spiritual gift of prophecy but lacked love. Likewise, he lacked patience, for he struck his donkey with a stick when it saved him from the angel (Num. 22). And the unmerciful servant was also the impatient servant. The master forgave his debt. Then his fellow servant begged him, *"Have patience with me, and I will repay you. But he was unwilling"* (Matt. 18:29-30). A lack of patience reveals a lack of love.

The Bible lists many examples of patience. At the top of the list is God. He was patient with the Israelites, year after year, as they worshiped idols and rejected the prophets, God's messengers. Even today, God continues to be patient. He delays His wrath and judgment, not wanting anyone to perish (2 Pet. 3:9). And like His Father, Jesus is patient. Recall the many times Jesus was patient with His disciples, who were slow learners, like us (Matt. 16:9; 17:17). And on the cross He was patient with His killers. He prayed, *"Father forgive them; for they do not know what they are doing"* (Luke 23:34). Further down the list of patient people in the Bible we find Stephen, who did not seek revenge (Acts 7:59-60), and Barnabas, who was patient with John Mark (Acts 15:36-40). To be godly (like God), and to be Christian (like Christ), we must be patient.

Q 30 *What are your favorite examples of the patience that love shows?*

An atheist gave a speech to prove there was no God. Then he took out his watch in public and declared, "God, if you exist, I will give you 5 minutes to strike me dead." One wise teacher later heard this and said, "Did the atheist think that a patient God would only wait 5 minutes?"

Figure 7.9 Abraham Lincoln was a president known for patience. His image is on the American penny. Patience should be as common among Christians as pennies in society.

Abraham Lincoln, the American president known for freeing the slaves, was famous for his patience. Before he became president, Lincoln had an opponent named Stanton. Both men wanted to be president, and often debated. Stanton was rude. He ridiculed Lincoln's appearance. Stanton said Lincoln, with his big beard, looked like "the original gorilla." He said they should put Lincoln in the zoo. Lincoln did not reply to these hateful comments. But after Lincoln became president, he chose Stanton to serve in a high position in the government. At Lincoln's death, Stanton referred to him as one of the greatest leaders the world had ever known.[12] Love is patient, and it can turn an enemy into a friend.

Q 31 *How did Lincoln turn Stanton from an enemy to a friend?*

2. *"Love is kind"* (1 Cor. 13:4). Someone has said that patience and kindness are like two sides of a coin. Patience is love's response to those who are offensive, annoying, or wearisome. Kindness is love's action to all—enemies, strangers, and friends. In 1 Corinthians 13:4, in the Greek, *kindness* is a verb—an action.[13] Paul is emphasizing that love is not just a *sweet attitude*. Love does not just *feel good toward people. Love is practical!* It speaks kind words and does kind, useful deeds. Love inspires children to do kind deeds for their brothers and sisters, parents, teachers, friends, and even strangers. Love transforms husbands from being selfish and harsh to being kind at home. Love fills the hearts of mothers so that they can speak and act in kind ways.

Q 32 *How are patience and kindness like 2 sides of a coin?*

Scripture guides us to imitate God. He is kind. God showed His kindness in the *greatest* way when He sent Jesus to save us (Tit. 3:4). And God is kind to us in a million *lesser* ways. He sends His Spirit to live within us, to teach, comfort, counsel, and guide us. He plans families for protection, fellowship, and nurture. He gives us our daily bread, clothing, and a place we call home. These are only a few of the many blessings that God gives us. So let us follow the example that the Father, the Son, and the Spirit set for us. Sinners may be known for being mean and stingy. But let us, the children of our kind heavenly Father, be known for kind words of encouragement, generosity, and kind deeds of mercy, compassion, and thoughtfulness.

Q 33 *What are some examples of how love is kind?*

Remember that Paul was writing to the Corinthians. Many of them were proud, sinful, fleshly, selfish, childish believers. So Paul lifted up the qualities of love in front of them. Love is not just for the easy times and the nice places. Love is for Corinth. Love is kind to the hateful and the harmful. God loved us while we were still sinners. And He calls on us to love those who need it the most and the least. Love is kind—it shares its time, talent, and treasure with others in useful ways.

James reminds us that the type of love that pleases God is kind. It takes care of orphans and widows (James 1:27). Likewise, John wrote that if God's love is in us, we help feed and clothe the hungry (1 John 3:16-18). At the end of our days, one of the reasons why God will recognize us as His children is that we did kind deeds. We visited believers in prison, gave clothes to the naked and cold, and shared our food with the hungry (Matt. 25:35-40).

Abigail was kind to David and his soldiers. The food she sent renewed their strength (2 Sam. 25:18). And today, soldiers appreciate the kind deeds we do for them.

Tabitha (also called Dorcas) was a disciple of Christ *"was abounding with deeds of kindness and charity which she continually did"* (Acts 9:36). She was known for her kind deeds. At her death, *"all the widows stood beside him [Peter], weeping and showing all the tunics and garments that Dorcas used to make while she was with them"* (Acts 9:39).

The Good Samaritan was known for his kindness to his neighbor—a stranger from another culture and ethnic group (Luke 10:25-27). Jesus gave this example to enlighten and guide all of us.

Are you known for kindness? What kind words and deeds are you known for at home, at school, at work, and in the neighborhood and community? What kindness do you show through giving and praying for missions? Can people testify of kind things that you have done for them? We only go through life once. As we pray and ask God to lead us, let us reflect as much kindness as we can.

Q 34 *What is envy? Give illustrations.*

3. *"Love does not envy"* (1 Cor. 13:4). Paul begins with two positive things that love does: it shows patience and kindness. Then Paul lists seven negative things that love does not do. Envy is the first negative quality. It is the first cousin of hate, but is not related to love. Synonyms of envy are jealousy and covetousness. Envy is a feeling of ill-will and bitterness toward others. It is a mood or attitude, a desire of the heart. Envy is leprosy of the soul. It soils and spoils—slowly killing all that is good and beautiful within. In 2 Corinthians 11:2 we will study about a godly jealousy that protects and longs for what is right. But in 1 Corinthians 13:4, Paul refers to sinful envy or jealousy that shows greed and selfishness. In Corinth, the foot envied the hand (1 Cor. 12). Envy is a common sin recorded in Scripture:

- **Eve** envied the knowledge of good and evil that God had (Gen. 3:6).
- **Cain** envied the favor that God showed Abel (Gen. 4:5).
- **The brothers of Joseph** envied the favor that his father, Jacob, showed him (Gen. 37).
- **David** envied Bathsheba, the wife of Uriah. When David did not resist this envy, it led him to commit adultery with Bathsheba and murder Uriah (2 Sam. 11).
- **King Ahab** envied the vineyard of Naboth, and murdered him to get it (1 Kings 21).
- **Jewish leaders** envied Jesus for His grace, prominence, and popularity among the people. Pilate discerned that envy was the reason they wanted to crucify the King of the common people (Matt. 27:18).

Wrath is fierce and anger is a flood, but who can stand before jealousy? (Prov. 27:4).

In contrast to those who sinned through envy, John the Baptist showed a heart of love. When the multitudes left John and followed Jesus, John replied, *"A man can receive nothing unless it has been given him from heaven"* (John 3:27). Love is content and thankful for what God gives. It avoids the sin of envy—coveting what others have.

Q 35 *What are some things that believers may be tempted to envy?*

Envy is a great temptation. But the cure for envy is love, a fruit that only the Holy Spirit can produce in our lives (Gal. 5:22). Love does not envy.

Ministry and Love in Worship

Figure 7.10 Three birds are known for their pride: roosters, turkeys, and peacocks.

Q 36 *Which 3 birds is love not like?*

4. *"Love does not boast; it is not proud"* (1 Cor. 13:4). Love may be as patient as a turtle. But it never crows like a rooster, struts like a turkey, or parades like a peacock. Some Corinthians boasted of their worldly wisdom (1 Cor. 1:18-31), prosperity (1 Cor. 4:18-21), spiritual freedom (1 Cor. 8), and spiritual gifts (1 Cor. 12). All this boasting revealed a lack of love, for love does not brag. When we brag on ourselves, it is like holding up a sign that says, "I lack love" or "I am a turkey." A proud person talks much and listens little. Sometimes pride displays itself by criticizing others. Proud people may do this, trying to make themselves look better. But those who throw mud have dirty hands.

Figure 7.11
A puffer fish expands several times its normal size and is filled with poison.[14] In contrast, love is not puffed up or proud.

Favorite verses of love are:
- *"Let another praise you, and not your own mouth; a stranger, and not your own lips"* (Prov. 27:2).
- *"Let him who boasts boast in the Lord"* (1 Cor. 1:31).
- *"Knowledge puffs up, but love builds up"* (1 Cor. 8:1).

5. *"Love is not rude"* (1 Cor. 13:5). False apostles in Corinth slapped the bride of Christ in the face (2 Cor. 11:20). This is a way of saying they were rude. Others at Corinth were rude, impolite, and unthoughtful at the Lord's Supper. They rushed ahead to feed themselves and ignored the poor among them (1 Cor. 11:21-22).

Q 37 *What are some examples of rudeness in your culture?*

Rudeness is a common sin of society. Some are rude in public. They may crowd in front of others, say things that are not polite, and dress or act in ways that offend. But most often, if we are rude, it is at home. We may say harsh words to family members or do things that show a lack of respect.

In contrast, love is courteous. It tries not to embarrass others or hurt their feelings. Love has good manners—even at home! And in public, love shows respect for the values of culture.

Q 38 *What are some good manners that love practices?*

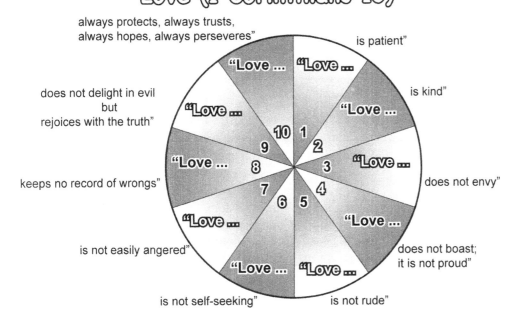

Figure 7.12
Paul mentions at least ten characteristics of love.

Q 39 *Answer the questions to test whether you are selfish.*

6. "Love is not self-seeking" (1 Cor. 13:5). Lust grabs all it can get, but love is not selfish. Here is a short test to see whether you are a selfish person. Answer these questions (when no one is listening):
- Do I get upset when things do not go my way?
- Would the people who know me best say I am difficult to live with?
- Do I dislike spending money on others?
- Am I a poor loser?
- Do I get angry with God when life does not go the way I think it should?
- Does it bother me to help others when I have my own plans?
- Do I persist in doing anything that I know irritates or hurts someone close to me?
- Am I set in my ways; do I refuse to change?
- Do I get upset if I do not get my share of bread, vegetables, fruit, meat, pie, or cake?
- Do I tend to defend myself or argue when someone criticizes me?
- Do I complain and grumble much?[15]

Q 40 *How are mature believers different from childish believers?*

The bad news is that all of us are selfish at times, because we are "selfs". The good news is that Paul wrote 1 Corinthians 13 not to condemn us, but to help us. Small children think mostly of themselves. That is why Paul told the Corinthians, *"Stop thinking like children…in your thinking be adults"* (1 Cor. 14:20). A child's thoughts center on self. But as we mature in Christ, we learn to deny ourselves and practice loving others as we love ourselves. Love is not selfish—it does not think only of self. Love follows in the steps of Jesus, who became poor for a little while, so we could become rich forever (2 Cor. 8:9).

7. "Love is not easily angered" (1 Cor. 13:5). Love is not easily provoked. It is not touchy. Paul began the list of qualities with *"love is patient"* (1 Cor. 13:4). Here, in 13:5, he adds a further explanation about the patience of love. The person who loves is patient with people and does not become angry in a hurry.

Now Eliab his oldest brother heard when he spoke to the men; and Eliab's anger burned against David and he said, "Why have you come down? And with whom have you left those few sheep in the wilderness? I know your insolence and the wickedness of your heart; for you have come down in order to see the battle" (1 Sam. 17:28).

Q 41 *What did the quick anger and harsh words of Eliab reveal?*

Q 42 *Which 2 aspects of God are linked in Nehemiah 9:17-18?*

[17]*"They refused to listen, and did not remember Your wondrous deeds which You had performed among them; so they became stubborn and appointed a leader to return to their slavery in Egypt but You are a God of forgiveness, gracious and compassionate, slow to anger and abounding in lovingkindness; and You did not forsake them.* [18]*Even when they made for themselves a calf of molten metal and said, 'This is your God who brought you up from Egypt,' and committed great blasphemies"* (Neh. 9:17-18).

Q 43 *Has Jesus changed you as much as he changed John? Explain.*

When he first began to follow Jesus, the apostle John had a hot temper. When the Samaritans rejected Jesus, John's quick response was to offer to call down fire and destroy them. But as the years passed, Jesus changed John from a Son of Thunder to an apostle of love. Read 3 John. Diotrephes was a proud, fleshly person in the church who loved *to be first.* He rejected John and spread evil rumors and gossip about the old apostle. Diotrephes refused to help ministers John commended, and put those who obeyed John out of the church. Still, John's response to these insults was kind. He did not become angry, but thanked others for showing love (3 John 6) and encouraged them to practice what is good and kind. Wow! What a difference Jesus made in John's life. And the more we submit to the Holy Spirit and follow in the footsteps of Jesus, the more slowly we become angry, and the longer we are patient.

Ministry and Love in Worship

8. ***"Love keeps no record of wrongs"*** **(1 Cor. 13:5).** In Christ, God forgives our sins and does not hold them against us (2 Cor. 5:19). David wrote, *"As far as the east is from the west, so far has He removed our transgressions from us"* (Ps. 103:12). And about the new covenant that God promised, we read: *"AND THEIR SINS AND LAWLESS DEEDS I WILL REMEMBER NO MORE"* (Heb. 10:17).

Likewise, those who love others forgive and do not keep a list of the past. The one who loves does not remind others of the times they offended, sinned, or erred. For the unforgiving are the unloving (Matt. 18:21-35).

A husband and wife were quarreling. In anger, the husband reminded his wife of a past sin. The husband's words were not loving, and they were not fair. For when we forgive, we should bury sins of the past and never lift them out of the grave.

A small boy had a dog that was dear. When the dog died, the boy buried it, but left the tail sticking up out of the ground. Every few days, the boy went to the grave, grabbed the tail, and pulled the dead dog out to look at. The odor was awful, and the sight was ugly! Then, the boy re-buried the dog, except for the tail. Finally, the Dad smelled the odor on the boy's hand. He helped the boy bury *all* of the dog. And he stopped him from ever digging it up again.[16] Likewise, those who love must forgive *completely*. Digging up the past sins of others causes a bad smell. Arguments may come. But one of the rules of a "fair fight" is to never dig up the past sins of others. *"Love keeps no record of wrongs"* (1 Cor. 13:5).

Q 44 *What lesson does the boy and his dog illustrate?*

9. ***"Love does not delight in evil but rejoices with the truth"*** **(1 Cor. 13:6).**

The negative: Love does not rejoice in evil (unrighteousness). Recall that the Corinthians were bragging about sin among them. They rejoiced when a man in their church committed sexual sin with his father's wife (1 Cor. 5:1-6). This delight in sin showed a lack of love for God and what is right. The Corinthians loved what was wrong. In contrast, Scripture teaches us to love what is right and hate what is wrong. Here are some examples of delighting in evil—**loving what is wrong:**

Q 45 *What are some examples of delighting in evil?*

- It is wrong to rejoice when another person falls or fails. Children often try to get each other in trouble. They may laugh when a brother or sister receives discipline. This reveals a lack of love.
- Adults often gossip. They delight to hear and to tell the sins of others. But Paul says it is a shame even to mention what the disobedient do in secret (Eph. 5:12). When gossip is present, love is absent.
- A wife was not happy in her marriage. She knew that the Bible allows divorce for adultery. When her husband committed adultery, she was glad. Was she delighting in evil?
- Some believers, like the Corinthians, delighted in false teachings. Perhaps these teachings fed their desires for prosperity, success, and happy living. But it is foolish to follow teachings that are wrong. Paul warned that in the last days, men would be *"lovers of self, lovers of money... unloving... haters of good... lovers of pleasure rather than lovers of God"* (2 Tim. 3:1-4). Likewise, Paul warned:

...³men who forbid marriage and advocate abstaining from foods which God has created to be gratefully shared in by those who believe and know the truth. ⁴For everything created by God is good, and nothing is to be rejected if it is received with gratitude (1 Tim. 4:3-4).

Love does not rejoice in evil—what harms others, what pleases Satan, or what offends God.

The positive: Love rejoices in the truth. Love cheers when truth prevails. Satan is the father of lies and liars (John 8:44). But Jesus is the truth (John 14:6) and the Savior of those who love truth. By *truth*, Paul means "the teachings of Scripture." The Word

Q 46 *What does Paul mean by truth?*

Q 47 How can we recognize one who loves the truth?

Q 48 How many times does 2 John 1-3 connect truth and love?

of God is our standard for truth. Without the Bible, people can only guess at what truth is. But God has revealed the truth to us through the Bible. As Jesus said, *"Your word is truth"* (John 17:17). Likewise, Paul's writings refer to the gospel as the truth (2 Cor. 13:8), the truth of the gospel (Gal. 2:5), the word of truth (Eph. 1:13), and truth that is in Jesus (Eph. 4:21).

Truth and love were married in heaven, and we should never separate them on earth. Many verses in the Bible link love and truth:

- *"And this is love: that we walk in accordance to his commandments"* [which are the truth revealed] (2 John 6).
- ¹*"The elder to the chosen lady and her children, whom I love in truth; and not only I, but also all who know the truth, ²for the sake of the truth which abides in us and will be with us forever: ³Grace, mercy and peace will be with us, from God the Father and from Jesus Christ, the Son of the Father, in truth and love"* (2 John 1-3).
- *"But, speaking the truth in love, we are to grow up in all aspects into Him who is the head, even Christ"* (Eph. 4:15).
- ⁹*"The one whose coming is in accord with the activity of Satan, with all power and signs and false wonders, ¹⁰and with all the deception of wickedness for those who perish, because they did not receive the love of the truth so as to be saved"* (2 Thess. 2:9-10).

Some religious leaders encourage unity and fellowship among denominations and world religions, regardless of doctrine. In contrast, Martin Luther said, "Peace if possible, but truth at any price."[17] Truth is the only foundation worth building on. So as believers, we rejoice in true doctrine and actions that are in harmony with the truth. That which is not built on the truth will one day be like a house that falls to the ground (Matt. 7:24-27). Those who say they love God but do not submit to the truth deceive themselves. For love guides us to never delight in evil, but to rejoice, celebrate, live, and die in the light of truth.

Q 49 Which theme does the chiasm of 1 Corinthians 13:7 emphasize?

10. *"Love always protects, always trusts, always hopes, always perseveres"* (1 Cor. 13:7). In this verse, the NIV uses the word *always*, whereas other translations use *all things*, which is in the Greek text. Comparing translations may help us understand a verse. The NASB has, *"Love bears all things, believes all things, hopes all things, endures all things"* (1 Cor. 13:7, NASB). Thus, *all things* means "in everything" or "always." Fee notes that 1 Corinthians 13:7 appears to be a chiasm:

A: *Bears all things,*

    B: *Believes all things,*

    B¹: *Hopes all things,*

A¹: *Endures all things.*[18]

Note that the first and last lines of the chiasm are parallel, emphasizing one truth: enduring, no matter what comes. Likewise, the middle two lines of the chiasm emphasize enduring through trusting God in all things. So all four lines of the chiasm emphasize that love endures all things.

The New English Bible captures the meaning: *"There is nothing love cannot face"* (1 Cor. 13:7). Love endures all things—it never stops believing in God. As we began studying the ten qualities of love, we noted that love is patient, and patience is for people. Paul closes the list saying that love endures, and endurance is for circumstances. Love never quits—at 15, 25, 65, or 85 years of age. It keeps on trusting, obeying, and serving God. The roots of love go down deep into God (Eph. 3:16-19). These roots in love enable us to believe and hope in all situations (1 Cor. 13:7). Patience and endurance are like two brackets around the ten qualities of love.

Ministry and Love in Worship

In the middle two lines of the chiasm (B and B¹⁾), Paul does not mean that love believes everything or everyone. Love is not foolish; it does not believe lies or hope in false teachers. Paul has just said that love rejoices in the truth. What Paul means is that love always has faith and hope ***in God.*** In sunshine and in rain, in comfort and in pain, whatever comes, love keeps on believing and hoping in God. Love bears all things, believes in all things, hopes in all things, and endures all things. *"Love never fails"* (1 Cor. 13:8).

Q 50 *Does love believe everything and everyone? Explain.*

Love is powerful and steadfast. It endures all things. It keeps on believing and hoping in God, no matter what.

- **The love of Jesus** enabled Him to endure the cross and trust God to the end. He entrusted His spirit to God as He was dying.
- **The love of Stephen** gave him strength to endure being stoned and forgive those who murdered him.
- **The love of Paul** empowered him to preach the gospel and persevere through a lifetime of trials and troubles. Second Corinthians 11:16–12:10 lists some of the mountains and valleys that love enabled Paul to climb. When love grows cold, people quit and abandon the faith (Matt. 24:12). But when love remains, we keep on believing and endure to the end. So as we said at the beginning of this lesson, our greatest need is for love. It is the key to following Jesus from earth to heaven. Love is essential.

Q 51 *What are some examples showing that love endures all things?*

Application: Many have noted that the ten qualities of love in 1 Corinthians 13:4-7 are best seen in the life and ministry of Jesus. So we could substitute the name *Jesus* for the word *love* in these verses. We could say, "Jesus is patient. Jesus is kind." But the lesson Paul wants to teach is that love transforms those who follow Jesus. So let us each substitute our own name for the word *love* in these ten characteristics. Let us repent when we do not show love, receive God's forgiveness, and ever seek to be filled and guided by love. Let us hold these verses before us like a mirror and submit to the Holy Spirit. Then, God will produce the fruit of love in us. He will transform us into the image of Christ (2 Cor. 3:18). And more and more, like Jesus, we will show these ten qualities of love.

Q 52 *Whose name should you often substitute for the word "love" in 1 Corinthians 13:4-7?*

C. The permanence of love: its relation to spiritual gifts (1 Cor. 13:8-13)

⁸*Love never fails. But where there are prophecies, they will cease; where there are tongues, they will be stilled; where there is knowledge, it will pass away.* ⁹*For we know in part and we prophesy in part,* ¹⁰*but when perfection comes, the imperfect disappears.* ¹¹*When I was a child, I talked like a child, I thought like a child, I reasoned like a child. When I became a man, I put childish ways behind me.* ¹²**Now** *we see but a poor reflection as in a mirror;* **then** *we shall see face to face. Now I know in part; then I shall know fully, even as I am fully known.* ¹³*And now these three remain: faith, hope and love. But the greatest of these is love* (1 Cor. 13:8-13).

LOVE *"NEVER FAILS."*

Love *"never fails."* That is, love, unlike spiritual gifts, is permanent. Spiritual gifts belong to our time on earth. But love is eternal—for now and forever. Love is the greatest, because it lasts the longest.

Q 53 *How is love so different from spiritual gifts, faith, and hope?*

Recall that 1 Corinthians 13, the love chapter, is in the middle of a section on spiritual gifts (1 Cor. 12–14). The Corinthians were focusing on spiritual gifts but neglecting love. Paul does not want them to turn away from spiritual gifts. But he does want them to walk on the path of love as they manifest the gifts of the Spirit. He has emphasized that love is absolutely necessary. Without love, the gifts lose their value (1 Cor. 13:1-3). And Paul has written about ten qualities of love so that the Corinthians and we will be able

Q 54 *What great event divides the "now" and "then" of 1 Corinthians 13:8-12?*

to identify and practice love. Now, as he closes the love chapter, Paul concludes with a final perspective. He contrasts time before and after Jesus returns.

The Second Coming of Christ divides life into two parts: now and then. *Now,* until Jesus returns, we need spiritual gifts, with love. These gifts give the Church power to evangelize, disciple, and live a victorious Christian life. But someday, Jesus will return, as He has promised. *Then,* most everything will change. Read 1 Corinthians 13:8-13 again. It contrasts several things in the light of the Second Coming of Jesus Christ.

Q 55 *What will life be like when perfection comes?*

- *Now,* we have a great need for spiritual gifts and power. *Then,* we will not need spiritual gifts.
- *Now,* we live in an imperfect time. But *then,* when Jesus returns, perfection will come.
- *Now,* we do not see well—just a poor reflection as in a mirror. But *then,* when Jesus comes, we will see face to face.
- *Now,* we do not understand well—we know in part. But *then,* we will know as we are known.
- *Now,* we live in imperfect bodies. But *then,* we will have perfect bodies (1 Cor. 15).
- *Now,* we live in an imperfect world. But the perfect time is coming, as Jesus prophesied: *"Behold, I am making all things new"* (Rev. 21:5). In that day, when the perfect Savior comes, He will give us new bodies and create a new heaven and new earth. *Then,* and only then, will we outgrow our need for spiritual gifts!

Figure 7.13 contrasts the *now* and *then* times related to the Second Coming of Christ.

Now (The Imperfect Is Here)		Then (The Perfect Comes)	
We need prophecy, tongues, and knowledge.	1 Cor. 13:8-9	We shall not need spiritual gifts.	1 Cor. 13:10
We talk, think, and reason like children.	1 Cor. 13:11	We shall put childish ways behind us.	1 Cor. 13:11
We see but a poor reflection, as in a mirror.	1 Cor. 13:12	We shall see face to face.	1 Cor. 13:12
We know in part.	1 Cor. 13:12	We shall know fully, as we are known.	1 Cor. 13:12
We each live in a physical body.	1 Cor. 15:44	We shall each live in a spiritual body.	1 Cor. 15:44
We are waiting for the trumpet.	1 Cor. 15:52	We shall hear the trumpet sound.	1 Cor. 15:52
We can die.	1 Cor. 15:53	We shall never die.	1 Cor. 15:53

Figure 7.13   First Corinthians 13 and 15 contrast *now* and *then*; they contrast time on earth, as we wait for Jesus, and the time when He returns.

Q 56 *In what sense are all believers like children now?*

Now, we are like children. But when Christ returns, we will be like full adults, who have grown and been perfected to be like Him. Now, we need spiritual gifts, faith, hope, and love. But then, when Christ returns, we will outgrow our need for gifts, faith, and hope. Then, we will be perfected in love and live in the love and light of God forever.

Paul has guided us to the top of love mountain. From 1 Corinthians 13:8-13, we can see into eternity. But in 1 Corinthians 14, we will climb back down the mountain into the local church. And there, we will continue to see how love guides us in the use of spiritual gifts.

Q 57 *Complete Figure 7.14 on the 10 qualities of love.*

Ministry and Love in Worship 149

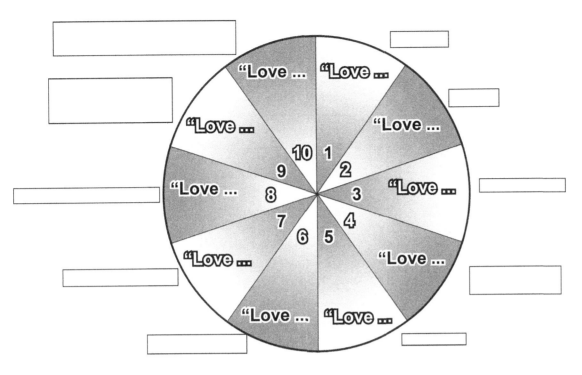

Figure 7.14 Practice pie chart on ten qualities of love

Test Yourself: Circle the letter by the *best* completion to each question or statement.

1. When does the Spirit baptize us into one body?
a) At conversion
b) At water baptism
c) At the baptism in the Spirit
d) At the Second Coming

2. Paul illustrates our need for one another with
a) soldiers in a battle together.
b) the example of the human body.
c) members of an athletic team.
d) believers rowing a boat to shore.

3. Which gift does a teacher need most?
a) The gift of healing
b) The gift of discernment
c) The gift of faith
d) The gifts of knowledge

4. *"Do all speak in tongues?"* refers to
a) private worship and prayer.
b) group meetings of believers.
c) evangelism of lost tribes.
d) the multitude at Pentecost.

5. What does Paul emphasize in 1 Corinthians 13:1-3?
a) I should choose love above spiritual gifts.
b) I want fewer gifts and more love.
c) I need love with my spiritual gifts.
d) I know the gifts will cease, but love endures.

6. Which quality of love is closest to patience?
a) Kindness
b) Mercy
c) Humility
d) Perseverance

7. Which qualities of love does Paul mention in 1 Corinthians 13?
a) Patience, fruitfulness, and faithfulness
b) Patience, kindness, and gentleness
c) Goodness, mercy, and compassion
d) Kindness, love for truth, and perseverance

8. Which 2 qualities should always be together?
a) Love and understanding
b) Love and charity
c) Love and truth
d) Love and unity

9. Whose name should you think of in 1 Corinthians 13?
a) Jesus' name
b) Paul's name
c) Your pastor's name
d) Your own name

10. What separates the *now* and *then* of 1 Corinthians 13?
a) The birth of Christ
b) The resurrection of Christ
c) The ascension of Christ
d) The Second Coming of Christ

Essay Test Topics: Write 50-100 words on each of these goals that you studied in this chapter.

Various Ministries in the Church (1 Cor. 12:12-31)

Goal: Explain some ways the Spirit unites us, and yet makes us different.

Goal: Identify and illustrate ways that believers depend on each other.

Goal: Give examples of spiritual gifts that various ministries need.

Goal: Explain what 1 Corinthians 12:29 does and does not teach about tongues.

Love: The Path of Spiritual Gifts (1 Cor. 13:1-13)

Goal: Explain the necessity of love as the path of spiritual gifts.

Goal: Explain and illustrate 10 characteristics of love.

Goal: Analyze the contrast in 1 Corinthians 13:8-13.

Chapter 8:
Christian Edification and Spiritual Gifts
(1 Corinthians 14)

Introduction

They were new believers—two young men in their first year of Bible school. Both wanted more of the Spirit of God in their lives. They had gone to a rural area to proclaim the good news of salvation. A small group gathered in the home of an interested family. With enthusiasm, all began to pray and expect great things from God. Perspiring, the two young men began to shout. One of them grabbed a new chair the farmer had just purchased. With great strength, he threw it against the wall. The chair fell apart. Angry, the man of the house told the students to leave at once. As they left, they said they would continue in prayer at the Bible school. Soon they were throwing chairs in the dining room of the Bible school as they prayed in loud voices. The director of the school told them, "You are out of order. The Spirit of God does not act like this."

The students answered, "We are yielding to the Spirit. We will not obey you."

The director replied, "With your own words you are proving that you are not in the Spirit. The Bible says to respect authority. Now go to your rooms."

In a few days, the boys left the school. Sadly, they left without learning many basic lessons, such as *"For God is not a God of disorder but of peace"* (1 Cor. 14:33).

Figure 8.1
The gifts of the Spirit increase peace, not confusion, on earth.

Lessons:

The Gifts of Tongues and Interpretation (1 Cor. 14:1-25)
Goal: *Explain what speaking in tongues is not and is.*

The Gift of Prophecy (1 Cor. 14:1-32)
Goal: *Explain what the spiritual gift of prophecy is not and is.*

Principles for Using Spiritual Gifts in Ministry (1 Cor. 14:1-26)
Goal: *Explain 4 principles for tongues, interpretation, and prophecy in a service.*

Guidelines for Order With Spiritual Gifts (1 Cor. 14:26-40)
Goal: *Explain 6 guidelines for maintaining order as believers manifest spiritual gifts in a service.*

 Key Words

tongues   interpretation   prophecy

Lesson 23: The Gifts of Tongues and Interpretation (1 Cor. 14:1-25)

Goal: *Explain what speaking in tongues is not and is.*

In 1 Corinthians 11, we saw that submission to headship brings order. In 1 Corinthians 14, Paul continues to teach about submission and order in the context of spiritual gifts. In the church, if two speak aloud in *tongues at the same time, this creates confusion. One must submit to the other. And when believers sing, teach, or prophesy, they must take turns—being submissive to one another for the sake of order and good doctrine (1 Cor. 14:32).

The words *"follow the way of love"* (1 Cor. 14:1) link all of 1 Corinthians 13 to spiritual gifts. The Corinthians needed special instruction on two gifts: tongues and *prophecy. The Greek culture in Corinth placed great value on the skill of speaking. This guided the Corinthians to boast about speaking in tongues. But love does not boast! Love seeks to edify others rather than just thinking of self (1 Cor. 14:4, 5, 12; 12:7).

Q 1 *Why did the Corinthians need a special emphasis on love?*

Paul compares the two gifts—tongues and prophecy—and their value to edify. In a church setting, Paul prefers prophecy over speaking in tongues. This is because prophecy edifies the church, whereas tongues (unless they are interpreted) edify only the speaker. When tongues are interpreted, their value is equal to prophecy (1 Cor. 14:4-5).[1]

This lesson has two parts:
- Explanations: What the gift of tongues is not and is.
- Explanations: What the gift of prophecy is not and is.

A. The gift of speaking in tongues <u>is not</u> a language the speaker has learned.

Many commentators depart from what Paul means by *speaking in tongues*. For example, Henry Drummond, an outstanding preacher, refers to the gift of tongues as polished speech—the ability to persuade listeners.[2] And John MacArthur is a beloved brother whose expositions are often helpful. But he illustrates tongues by referring to Jonathan Edwards, whose sermons had great influence. After Edwards preached, people were often lying on the ground, praying for mercy.[3] No doubt Edwards preached with a powerful anointing. But in 1 Corinthians 12–14, Paul is not writing about tongues that the speaker or the hearers understand. Describing the gift of tongues as grand speech that the speaker and hearers understand is the opposite of what Paul talks about in 1 Corinthians 12–14!

Q 2 *In 1 Corinthians 14, does speaking in tongues refer to a sermon or speech? Explain.*

Rather, the gift of tongues <u>is</u> a language the speaker has not learned and does not understand. Paul writes, *"For anyone who speaks in a tongue does not speak to men but to God. Indeed, no one understands him; he utters mysteries with his spirit"* (1 Cor. 14:2). The main point of 1 Corinthians 14:6-11 is that there is no profit in speaking to people in tongues, because they do not understand what is being said. Speaking in tongues to people, without an *interpretation, is worse than useless. It is like playing a flute or harp with blurred notes; like blowing an unclear tune with a trumpet; like speaking in a foreign language that the hearers do not know (1 Cor. 14:6-11).

Q 3 *When a person speaks in tongues, is it common for others to understand the language? Explain.*

On the Day of Pentecost, people from many nations were present. When the Holy Spirit filled believers, they spoke in various languages. They did not speak languages they knew. Rather, Acts 2:4 records: *"They were all filled with the Holy Spirit and **began to speak with other tongues**, as the Spirit was giving them utterance."* Here and there in the crowd, people understood a speaker, for they heard their own language (Acts 2:6). But others thought the speakers were drunk because believers spoke in a language that the hearers did not understand (Act 2:13). Throughout the rest of the New Testament,

Figure 8.2 The coming of the Spirit at Pentecost

there are NO other cases of people understanding a person who *speaks in tongues*. And as we have noted in the Corinthian context, when a person speaks in tongues, *no one understands him*—except God (1 Cor. 14:2). Tongues are usually languages that neither the speaker nor the hearers understand.

B. The gift of tongues is not *gibberish—syllables without meaning that a person makes up.

Once in Scripture, people spoke in tongues they did not learn but others understood (Acts 2). So as a rule, neither the speaker nor the hearers understand what is being said. Still, this spiritual gift is not gibberish—foolish or childish syllables the speaker creates.

Rather, the gift of tongues is a language—unknown by the speaker, yet enabled by the Holy Spirit. In Acts and 1 Corinthians 12–14, the Greek word for tongues is *glossai*. Speaking in tongues is often referred to as *glossalalia*, which does not appear in the New Testament, but is formed from the Greek words *glossai* (tongues) and *laleo* (I speak).[4] Paul refers to speaking in tongues (languages) of men and angels (1 Cor. 13:1).

Q 4 *In 1 Corinthians 13, do tongues refer to languages? Explain.*

On earth today, there are more than 6,500 tongues or languages.[5] In addition to these, there are dead languages that were on earth in the past but are no longer spoken today. And Paul mentions the *tongues of angels,* which seem to be heavenly languages (1 Cor. 13:2). Occasionally, Pentecostals and Charismatics speak in a tongue they do not know, yet someone present understands.[6] Many missionaries have understood a language when believers filled with the Spirit spoke in a tongue they never learned.

Paul teaches that *"if I pray in a tongue, my spirit prays, but my mind is unfruitful"* (1 Cor. 14:14). Speaking in tongues involves the human spirit and the Holy Spirit, mingling together and cooperating so that believers communicate directly with God in prayer, praise, worship, or thanksgiving. As Paul says, *"he utters mysteries with his spirit"* (1 Cor. 14:2). Speaking in tongues is a spiritual exercise for self or others, under the influence of the Holy Spirit—apart from the control or direction of the mind (1 Cor. 14:14).[7]

Jack Hayford wrote about meeting a person on an airplane. As they talked, the topic of tongues came up, and the person asked Pastor Hayford many questions. In time, the Spirit led Hayford to pray quietly in a tongue unknown to him. The stranger was amazed, for he recognized and understood the language.

C. The gift of tongues is not a means of preaching the gospel to the lost.

Acts 2 records that believers spoke in tongues and unbelievers understood. But there are no more cases of this in the New Testament. We do not want to limit God or state what He is able to do, for with God, all things are possible. But as far as we know, He does not use tongues as a means of evangelism. To put it another way, speaking in tongues is not a substitute for learning a language in which we want to preach.

Q 5 *What has been the result when people have tried to use tongues to evangelize?*

Professor Gary McGee reports that some early Pentecostal missionaries thought tongues were to evangelize the lost. Some of these left America and traveled to foreign countries to preach the gospel. But they were disappointed to discover that the local people could not understand them. The Holy Spirit does help those who spend hundreds of hours to learn a new language. But speaking in tongues is not a substitute for language school.

Q 6 *Why should believers pray often in tongues in private?*

The gift of tongues, in private, is a means of personal edification. *"He who speaks in a tongue edifies himself"* (1 Cor. 14:4). It is true that Paul wrote to correct the problem of speaking in tongues in church without an interpretation. Still, Paul encouraged believers to pray in tongues in private to edify themselves. Tongues was not a gift that embarrassed the apostle Paul. Rather, he said, *"I thank God that I speak in tongues more than all of you"* (1 Cor. 14:18). Paul and all of the apostles spoke in tongues. This was a common experience of believers in the early church. It is likely that Jude referred to praying in tongues when he told believers, *"But you, beloved, building yourselves up on your most holy faith, praying in the Holy Spirit"* (Jude 20). Likewise, Paul includes praying in tongues when he tells us, *"With all prayer and petition pray at all times in the Spirit"* (Eph. 6:18).

D. Tongues is not ecstatic speech—speaking when in a trance or out of control.

One Greek scholar says that tongues refers to the speech of those *overcome by strong religious emotion.*[8] But this statement is unbiblical, since Paul emphasizes that the believer may remain silent. Imagine a person *overcome with emotion* remaining silent, or speaking to self and to God! Impossible! Rather, praying in tongues, like other forms of prayer, may be done with varying degrees of emotion. And God does not *overcome* us with emotion. When we are full of the Spirit, we are able to control our emotions, speech, and actions.

Q 7 *Are those who pray in tongues unable to control themselves? Explain.*

Illustrations and applications. People have done unusual things in supernatural moments. Some of these responses have been guided by the Spirit, and other responses have been guided by humans.

Q 8 *What are some unusual ways in which the Spirit has guided believers to act?*

- The Spirit guided an entire nation to march in silence around Jericho for 7 days and then blow trumpets and shout (Josh. 6:1-5).
- The Spirit came on Elijah, and he ran for miles, faster than the horses of King Ahab (1 Kings 18:46). Did God want the prophet to respond in this way?
- [23]*"He proceeded there to Naioth in Ramah; and the Spirit of God came upon him also, so that he went along prophesying continually until he came to Naioth in Ramah.* [24]*He also stripped off his clothes, and he too prophesied before Samuel and lay down naked all that day and all that night Therefore they say, 'Is Saul also among the prophets?'"* (1 Sam. 19:23-24). Was it common for prophets to lie on the ground and prophesy?
- Daniel saw an angel and fell down. The prophet had been fasting for 3 weeks. Yet the reason why he became weak and had no strength to stand was the powerful angel before him (Dan. 10:4-19).
- Peter felt the presence of God and saw Jesus transformed with Moses and Elijah. But Peter quickly responded in the wrong way (Matt. 17:4). God rejected Peter's idea to build three booths!
- John fell and became like a dead man when he received a vision of the glorified Christ (Rev. 1:17).
- In the revivals of John Wesley, some sensed the presence of God, got down on their knees, and began barking in an effort to "tree the devil" (make him climb a tree). Were these fleshly responses to the Spirit's presence a stumbling block to many who needed Christ?
- Others, sensing God's presence, have responded in unusual ways, such as shaking, running, yelling, laughing (as if unable to stop), or falling down.

It is possible for God to cause someone to fall. The New Testament is our guide for faith and practice. It records only four times that people fell because of the power of God. Peter once fell into a trance and God told him, *"Get up, Peter, kill and eat"* (Acts 10:9-13). Likewise, the apostle John fell when he saw a vision of the glorified Christ (Rev. 1:17). Soldiers fell in the Garden when they came to arrest Jesus (John 18:6). And Saul fell on the road to Damascus (Acts 9:4). The authors of this course know of cases when believers fell under the Spirit's power. One man was healed of ulcers in a prayer

Q 9 *When someone falls in a service, what are some possible explanations?*

Q 10 *Sabio asks: "If someone falls under the power of God Almighty, after a minute or two, will that person stand and walk off as if nothing happened?" Explain.*

Q 11 *How should believers respond if a minister tries to "push them down" in a prayer line?*

Q 12 *What are some ignorant, immature ways in which believers have responded to God's presence?*

line as he fell under the Spirit's power. And a well-known Methodist minister fell at a large, public meeting when he was filled with the Spirit and spoke in tongues.

However, throughout the New Testament, many experienced miracles and the power of God without falling. And throughout the centuries, millions have experienced God's presence without falling. Most of the time, God gives us power to stand and to walk in the Spirit, not to fall on the floor.

We want all believers to respond to God in the way that the Scriptures and the Spirit guide. So if some fall in God's presence, let us not be critical or judgmental. However, let us not "fall" because we are imitating others. And let us not "fall" to perform "courtesy drops"—to fulfill the expectations of others. When we see the hundreds of people who *fall,* but get up and walk off a minute later, it makes us wonder how much of God's power they experienced.

Sandor was a minister who developed the bad habit of trying to push people down when he prayed for them. A man named Michael went forward, seeking prayer for healing of his back. Sandor laid hands on him, pressing down hard, as if suggesting that Michael should fall. But Michael was seeking the *real* power of God. Sandor continued to press down hard and said, "Submit to God." Michael felt submitted to God, but he refused to pretend that the power of God had caused him to fall. Pastor, remember this: If God wants to cause someone to fall, He does not need you to help push the person down.

We should neither credit nor blame the Holy Spirit for many human responses. On the one hand, we want to encourage people to respond wisely to the Spirit. On the other hand, let us all recall Paul's counsel to the Corinthians: *"Brothers, stop thinking like children"* (1 Cor. 14:20). For God is not the author of confusion or disorder (1 Cor. 14:33).

> WE SHOULD NEITHER CREDIT NOR BLAME THE HOLY SPIRIT FOR MANY HUMAN RESPONSES.

Rather, the gift of tongues (as well as other supernatural gifts) is under the control of the speaker. Many unusual forms of behavior occur because people have not learned how to respond to the presence of God. But as Paul said at the beginning of this section, God does not want us to be *"ignorant* [unlearned or untaught] *about spiritual gifts"* (1 Cor. 12:1). We are all ignorant about some things, for we only know what we have been taught. So Paul takes time to teach the Corinthians, and us, to respond to the Spirit in an orderly way that edifies others. Paul teaches that a person speaking in tongues may choose to be silent, or pray quietly, for personal edification (1 Cor. 14:28, 32-33). Speaking, whether in tongues or our native language, is under the control and free will of each person.

Let us respond to God's Spirit in ways that bless others. When the Spirit of the Lord filled Elizabeth, she prophesied and encouraged Mary (Luke 1:39-45). When the Spirit of the Lord filled Mary, she sang supernatural words that bless every believer who hears or reads them (Luke 1:46-56). When the Spirit of the Lord came upon Philip, he preached the gospel with signs and wonders—and led a new ethnic group to Christ (Acts 8). When the Spirit of the Lord came upon Jesus, He ministered to the poor:

> [18]*"THE SPIRIT OF THE LORD IS UPON ME, BECAUSE HE ANOINTED ME TO PREACH THE GOSPEL TO THE POOR. HE HAS SENT ME TO PROCLAIM RELEASE TO THE CAPTIVES, AND RECOVERY OF SIGHT TO THE BLIND, TO SET FREE THOSE WHO ARE OPPRESSED,* [19]*TO PROCLAIM THE FAVORABLE YEAR OF THE LORD"* (Luke 4:18-19).

When the Spirit of the Lord comes on you, do not waste the opportunity. Respond in a way that blesses others. Paul's big theme in 1 Corinthians 14 is responding to the Spirit in ways that edify others.

Q 13 *In 1 Corinthians 14, what theme does Paul say should guide our responses to the Spirit?*

Lesson 24: The Gift of Prophecy (1 Cor. 14:1-32)

Goal: *Explain what the spiritual gift of prophecy is not and is.*

A. The gift of prophecy <u>is not</u> the same as the office of a prophet.

In Ephesians, Paul mentions the prophet as a gift to build the Church (Eph. 4:11-12). And in 1 Corinthians, Paul explains that the Church is like a body.

²⁷Now you are the body of Christ, and each one of you is a part of it. ²⁸And in the church God has appointed first of all apostles, second prophets, third teachers, then workers of miracles, also those having gifts of healing, those able to help others, those with gifts of administration, and those speaking in different kinds of tongues. ²⁹Are all apostles? Are all prophets? (1 Cor. 12:27-29).

Q 14 *How does the gift of prophecy differ from the office of a prophet?*

Prophets, like apostles, were gifts God gave to build the Church. We believe God that gave the four gifts of Ephesians 4 (apostles, prophets, evangelists, and pastors/teachers) to the Church and that none of the gifts has been removed. Yet we do not believe that it is necessary to use the titles of apostles and prophets for these ministries to be active in the Church today.⁹

The New Testament never describes prophets as holding an office or position. In contrast, the New Testament explains the qualifications and guidelines for those who desire the office or position of a pastor/teacher (1 Tim. 3; Tit. 1). Titles do not accredit ministry. Rather, the spiritual gifts of a person cause others to recognize his or her ministry. We affirm that some missionaries, like the apostles, plant churches in new places. And we believe that many believers, like prophets, speak a message directly from God. Still, we think it best to avoid using the titles of apostles and prophets. For as Jesus said, the top titles, such as *Rabbi* in his day, tend to puff people up as mere air inflates a tire (Matt. 23:5-12). Jesus rebuked the proud Pharisees because they loved titles in front of their names. And some today use a title like a trumpet to announce their presence; like a flag they wave to attract attention to themselves. Rather, let us practice humility. May our favorite title always be *Unworthy Servant* (Matt. 23:11; Luke 17:7-10)! All are not prophets (and none should seek titles), but *"all may prophesy"* (1 Cor. 14:5, 31). Sabio says: "A wise person takes a back seat at the feasts of earth" (Luke 14:7-14).

Q 15 *Why is it wise to avoid calling a person an apostle or prophet today?*

The gift of prophecy <u>is</u> a sudden, supernatural message from the Spirit through a believer. Under the old covenant, prophets stood between God and the common people. Prophets came near to God, heard His voice, and revealed God's will to others—who knew God from a distance. The prophets often helped kings make decisions about battle (1 Kings 22; 2 Chron. 20). In contrast, under the New Testament, believers never used prophecy to guide personal decisions. (See Stamps, *Full Life Study Bible* [also *Life in the Spirit Study Bible*], Acts 21:10 note.) Why? Because under the new covenant, the gap between God and man disappears. Through Christ, God pours out His Spirit on common people. *All* may come close to Him. *All* may know Him in a personal way (Heb. 8:10-13). And as Paul says, *all* may prophesy.

Q 16 *Under the New Testament, why is prophecy never used for personal guidance?*

Under the old covenant, the people of God needed prophets to know God's will. But under the new covenant, all believers know God, and all may prophesy. Joel prophesied about a period of time that would last from Pentecost until the Lord's return. We are living in this era, when all of us may prophesy:

17 "AND IT SHALL BE IN THE LAST DAYS," God says, "THAT I WILL POUR FORTH OF MY SPIRIT ON ALL MANKIND; AND YOUR SONS AND YOUR DAUGHTERS SHALL PROPHESY, AND YOUR YOUNG MEN SHALL SEE VISIONS, AND YOUR OLD MEN SHALL DREAM DREAMS; 18EVEN ON MY BONDSLAVES, BOTH MEN AND WOMEN, I WILL IN THOSE DAYS POUR FORTH OF MY SPIRIT. And they shall prophesy" (Acts 2:17-18).

Q 17   What are 2 insights related to Philip's four daughters?

Luke notes that Philip, one of the seven deacons in the early church, *"had four virgin daughters who were prophetesses"* (Acts 21:9). The Greek text does not call them prophetesses. But it emphasizes that they were known for the ministry of prophesying. Eusebius, a church historian, said that they moved to Asia, lived long lives, and continued to minister in the early church.[10] Like Philip's daughters, all of us believers may prophesy as the Spirit fills and enables us.

B. The gift of prophecy is not a sermon that results from study and human ability.

Q 18   Is prophecy the result of human study or human ability? Explain.

Prophecy is not a product of the human mind. Concerning prophecy in Scripture, Peter wrote, *"For no prophecy was ever made by an act of human will, but men moved by the Holy Spirit spoke from God"* (2 Pet. 1:21). The prophetic Scriptures have a level of authority above all spiritual gifts. But neither the prophecy in Scripture nor the gift of prophecy has its roots in human talent.

Q 19   Is it possible for sermons to include flashes of the gift of prophecy? Explain.

The gift of prophecy is a sudden, supernatural message from the Spirit through a believer. However, we do not limit any of the spiritual gifts to the time when and place where a local church meets. Rather, as a believer spends time in God's presence, a spiritual gift may come at any time, and at any place. For example, as a pastor prays and prepares a sermon, the Holy Spirit may give a gift of prophecy. And the pastor may write that message down as a part of the sermon. Or while preaching, a pastor may speak insights from the Spirit that are above and beyond his preparation. Thus an anointed sermon may contain flashes of the gift of prophecy. Likewise, a lay person may receive a message of prophecy during the week and share this message when believers meet. Still, we must insist that no prophecy has its origin in the human mind. This spiritual gift is a sudden inspiration directly from the Holy Spirit whenever it comes.

Q 20   Does most preaching fall short of the gift of prophecy? Explain.

An anointed sermon may contain flashes of the gift of prophecy, mixed with thoughts influenced by the Spirit. Thus some preaching may contain the spiritual insights of prophecy—like diamonds set in a ring. However, most preaching falls short of the supernatural gift of prophecy.

Q 21   What are 3 keys to help all believers prophesy more?

Prophecy today is always partial, not complete (1 Cor. 13:9). Paul says, *"We prophesy in part."* Still, partial prophecy does not mean partial inspiration. For the gift of prophecy is 100 percent from God and 0 percent rooted in human reasoning. But let us remember three things Paul tells us about our speech:

- *"Let the word of Christ richly dwell within you"* (Col. 3:16).

- *"Let no unwholesome word proceed from your mouth, but only such a word as is good for edification according to the need of the moment, so that it will give grace to those who hear"* (Eph. 4:29).

- *"Let your speech always be with grace, as though seasoned with salt"* (Col. 4:6).

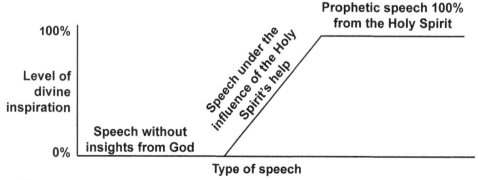

Figure 8.3   Human speech may vary in its level of inspiration from 0% to 100%.

As we practice these three guidelines Paul gave, much of our speech will be *under the influence* of the Holy Spirit. Thus, like prophecy, it will strengthen, encourage, comfort, and instruct others (Figure 8.3, middle). And among our prayerful words, there will often be flashes of the gift of prophecy.

C. The gift of prophecy is not always a message about the future.

Prophecy is not some spooky, mystical, abstract prediction about the end times. Unfortunately, some believers misunderstand the nature of prophecy, thinking it is only about *eschatology*—the last days.

Prophecy is a message by the Spirit to strengthen, encourage, comfort, or instruct (1 Cor. 14:3, 31). The purpose of the gift of prophecy, like all of the gifts of the Spirit, is to edify and build up the body of Christ through encouragement, comfort, correction, or instruction.[11] In 1 Corinthians 14, the Greek word *encouragement* is *paraklesin*. The related Greek verb, *parakaleo*, appears over 100 times in the New Testament. It has a wide range of meanings, including "to exhort." Common *exhortations* in Corinthians and throughout the New Testament encourage people to participate in the salvation process. How? By accepting God's grace, resisting sin, and so cooperating with the Holy Spirit as He leads us in holiness.[12] When prophecy encourages, it may exhort us to moral duty and build up character.[13] Encouragement is often more than a pat on the back or a cheerful word. It may be a loving urge to live in holiness as we depend on the grace of God.

Prophecy may come in at least three forms:

- **Forth-telling**—declaring the terms of the covenant. Prophets of the old covenant announced God's demands and promises to Israel. This was the main work of the Old Testament prophets—enforcing and reinforcing the terms and blessings of the covenant. Likewise, believers who prophesy today may proclaim the requirements and blessings of the new covenant. These are the teachings of Christ and the apostles that all need to obey *right now*.

    Prophetic forth-telling includes emphasizing such *requirements* as repenting, turning away from sin, believing in Christ, accepting forgiveness, forgiving others, being baptized, praying, studying the Scriptures, abiding in Christ, and being led by the Spirit.

    Likewise, *prophetic forth-telling* may emphasize the *promises* of the Second Coming, the resurrection, a new body, and an eternal heaven with God.

    Note that by prophesying, we do not mean preparing and preaching sermons. Rather, we are still talking about the gift of prophecy, whereby the Spirit directs a believer to declare God's truth.

- **Foretelling**—announcing things that will happen *in the future*. Talking about the future may be a lesser part of the gift of prophecy, but this *foretelling* is a vital part of prophecy.

    Ananias received a prophetic insight about the future ministry of Saul, who became Paul:

    > [15]*But the Lord said to him, "Go, for he is a chosen instrument of Mine, to bear My name before the Gentiles and kings and the sons of Israel;* [16]*for I will show him how much he must suffer for My name's sake"* (Acts 9:15-16).

    Agabus spoke a prophecy about a future famine. This *encouraged* believers to send offerings to Judea to help believers (Acts 11:27-28).

    Agabus prophesied that the Jews of Jerusalem would bind Paul (Acts 21:10-12). This did not direct Paul, but it confirmed what he already knew (Acts

Q 28 *What is an example of prophecy that is "heart-telling"?*

Figure 8.4 *The prophecy of Agabus, a painting by Louis Cheron (1660–1713)*[14]

20:22-23). Also, the prophecy strengthened and encouraged believers not to lose heart when they heard about Paul's fate.

Jesus prophesied many times about the future. He often spoke of His future death and resurrection (Matt. 16:21-22). And He foretold the destruction of Jerusalem, the conditions of future centuries, and His Second Coming (Matt. 24).

- **Heart-telling**—revealing secrets of a person's life (1 Cor. 14:25). Earlier, in 1 Corinthians 13:2, Paul mentions the highest possible form of the gift of prophecy—which understands *"all mysteries and all knowledge"* (1 Cor. 13:2). We have seen that spiritual gifts, such as prophecy and knowledge, may overlap. Prophetic insight that fathoms *all mysteries and knowledge* includes understanding God's plans for the last days and beyond.[15] Through the gift of prophecy, God gives believers *knowledge they could never learn* by themselves.[16] Some of these prophetic insights are the secrets that sinners hide in their hearts.

Let us look at some examples of how prophecy may lay bare the secrets of the heart (1 Cor. 14:25).

 Nathan, through prophetic insight, became aware of the adultery and murder of King David (2 Sam. 12).

 King David, through the gift of prophecy, discerned the hidden plan of a messenger that Joab sent (2 Sam. 14:17-19). Thus the woman said, *"But my lord is wise, like the wisdom of the angel of God, to know all that is in the earth"* (2 Sam. 14:20).

 Elijah, through the eyes of a prophet, saw that Gehazi had lied to gain wealth (1 Kings 5:19-27).

 Elijah, through prophetic knowledge, knew that Ahab planned the secret murder of Naboth and stole his vineyard (1 Kings 21).

 Elisha, through prophetic knowledge from God, knew the secrets of foreign kings. The king of Aram thought there was a spy in his castle. When he tried to find the traitor, a servant said, *"No, my lord, O king; but Elisha, the prophet who is in Israel, tells the king of Israel the words that you speak in your bedroom"* (2 Kings 6:12). A characteristic of prophecy, which is neither foretelling nor forth-telling, is heart-telling.

 Jesus, through prophetic insights, often revealed hidden secrets of the heart. He told the woman at the well that she had five husbands in her past and was living with yet another man. When the Lord revealed the secrets of her heart and life, she perceived that He was a prophet (John 4:16-19). But note the love Jesus communicated for this woman. His prophetic insights did not condemn or drive her away. Rather, they drew her closer to the Savior.

 Through prophetic insight, **Jesus** knew Peter's question about taxes *before* Peter spoke (Matt. 17:24-27). Our Lord discerned the thoughts of the teachers of the Law. Although they said nothing, He knew they thought He blasphemed by forgiving the sins of a paralytic (Matt. 9:2-4). And God revealed to Jesus the secret sin in the heart of Judas (Matt. 26:20-25).

 In Samaria, Simon the Sorcerer believed and was baptized (Acts 8:13). But within a few days, he was bitter about losing his influence. Simon offered Peter money for power to impart the Holy Spirit to others. These words revealed that Simon's heart was not right. But Peter's prophetic insights went beyond Simon's words. For like a prophet, **Peter** perceived the hidden condition of Simon's heart and said, *"For I see that you are in the gall of bitterness and in the bondage of iniquity"* (Acts 8:23). Then, Peter *encouraged* and *exhorted* Simon to repent, and he did. Some of Peter's words may seem harsh on the surface. And yet, whenever the Spirit gives the gift of prophecy, the purpose is never to condemn, but always to lead us closer to the Savior. For God is not willing that any should perish, but that all should come to repentance (2 Pet. 3:9). And even when the gift of prophecy enabled Peter to expose the sinful hearts of Ananias and Sapphira, God's larger purpose was to protect the Church from hypocrisy (Acts 5).

Prophecy does not necessarily reveal the *specific* details of a person's secret sins. Indeed, there are times when prophecy *forth-tells,* declaring the general teachings of Scripture. And these anointed words so pierce a sinner's heart that he *thinks* the speaker knows the secrets of his life. Yet at other times, the gift of prophecy may be specific, as was the insight of Jesus to the woman at the well. Therefore, *"the secrets"* of a sinner's heart may be *"laid bare,"* through a word of prophecy that is either general or specific (1 Cor. 14:24-25).

Prophecy may be heart-telling. One of the authors relates his experience: I was attending a class, working on my doctoral studies. About 15 of us were studying together—all ordained ministers from several denominations. A pastor, whom I will refer to as Reuben, shared a problem he faced in his church. Four families in leadership were involved in sexual sins. Reuben feared that exposing the sinning members would divide the church and destroy its testimony in the community. The class wrestled with the problem until a professor announced that it was time to close the discussion. He said it would be best to let Reuben find the solution. Suddenly, my heart began to pound within me. Through a gift of prophecy, the Lord told me that the main reason why Pastor Reuben was not confronting the sexual problems in his church was his own sin—he was having a sexual affair with the choir director. I was shocked at this insight. At first I prayed silently, "Lord, you know that I am the only Assemblies of God minister here. If Reuben denies this sin, it will cast a shadow on me, the Assemblies of God, and even You." But a voice within me said, "If you do not want spiritual gifts, then stop asking Me for them." I responded in silent prayer, "All right, Lord. But please help me talk to the class about this." Then I raised my hand and asked for permission to speak. A professor stared at me and nodded his head. I imagined that his eyes were saying, "I told you it was time to close the discussion. But if you want to make a fool of yourself, go ahead!"

Quietly I said, "We are all here to learn. And if this class rebukes me for what I say, I will accept it as a lesson to humble me. But I have two questions I would like to ask Pastor Reuben." My first question to Pastor Reuben was, "Could you tell us more about the choir director?" With much emotion, Reuben began to talk about the choir director. He praised her with one compliment after another, and he commented that her husband was a jerk. After several minutes, he stopped abruptly when he said, "I wish I had met this choir director before I married my wife!" Reuben looked shocked, as if he could not believe what he had just said. And all of us were shocked. Meanwhile, I was feeling more confident! I broke the silence, saying, "My second question is difficult for me to ask. And the class may rebuke me for it. If so, I will accept the discipline." My second question was, "Is one of the reasons why you do not confront your church members with their sin that you are having a sexual problem with the choir director?" Again, there was silence for a minute or two. All of us were afraid to speak or move. Finally, Reuben said, "Yes, I have been having a sexual affair with her for 2 years." One of the professors suggested that Reuben get some counseling, and Reuben agreed. As for me, I was weak with grief and relief. And I had learned that spiritual gifts may test your courage and break your heart.[17]

A woman was known for praying several hours a day. At home, she asked her husband a question. "Do you hear that sound of crackling—like a fire that is burning?" "No," replied her husband, "I do not hear it." "It is coming from the closet," she said. When she opened the closet door, she said, "It is coming from a pocket in your shirt." She reached into the pocket and pulled out a large roll of money. "Oh," said the wife, "It is not fire burning; it is the sound of new money shuffling in a person's hands. Why do you have such a large amount of money in your pocket?" Amazed, the husband confessed, "I was stealing this money from the place where I work. But I will return it tomorrow."[18] Whether we call this a prophetic insight or a word of knowledge, it revealed the secret of a sinful heart. And it encouraged a man to turn in the right direction. Husbands and wives, fathers and mothers, sons and daughters—all of us may prophesy as we seek God and walk in the Spirit.

Q 29 ↖ How are some today like Gehazi?

D. The gift of prophecy **is not** given to help us make money (as a business).

Throughout the history of mankind, people have used spiritual power—and fake spiritual power—to gain money. Sad examples include palm reading, fortune-telling, reading tea leaves, reading animal intestines, gazing at crystal balls, sorcery, witchcraft, and horoscopes. Simon the Sorcerer used demonic power to tell people the future. He used this spiritual power from Satan to gain influence, popularity, and money (Acts 8:9-24). Likewise, in Philippi, some men owned a slave girl who was demon-possessed. They used her satanic powers to make money (Acts 16:16-18). Paul warned Titus about false teachers who ruin *"whole households"* for dishonest gain (Tit. 1:11). And Peter warned about false teachers who *"in their greed they will exploit you with false words"* (2 Pet. 2:3). Such stories often include false accounts of spiritual gifts and false prophecies. In contrast, it is not God's will for us to use any spiritual gifts to gain wealth.

The gift of prophecy is a service or free ministry by believers. As we prophesy, let us keep the focus on Jesus, not self. And let us remember the words of Christ: *"Freely you received, freely give"* (Matt. 10:8). May none of us ever make the mistake of Gehazi who tried to use spiritual gifts as a handle to grab money (2 Kings 5:20-27). For because of his greed, the inheritance he passed on to his children was the legacy of leprosy.[19]

Principles for Using Spiritual Gifts in Ministry (1 Cor. 14:1-26)
Goal: *Explain 4 principles for tongues, interpretation, and prophecy in a service.*

Paul's big theme in 1 Corinthians 12–14 is edification in the Church. Alone, like Paul, we should pray in tongues often to build ourselves up (1 Cor. 14:18). But when we come together, we should seek to edify one another. Just as Paul emphasizes this principle of edification, we will study four principles on tongues and prophecy.

A. The direction and content of tongues may vary.

Q 30 ↗ According to 1 Corinthians 14:16, tongues may be from _____ to _____.

1. Tongues may be prayer and praise from man to God. At Pentecost, believers spoke in languages they never learned, *"speaking of the mighty deeds of God"* (Acts 2:11). And Paul writes, *"If you are praising God with your spirit"* (that is, praying in tongues—1 Cor. 14:16), *"you may be giving thanks well enough"* when speaking in tongues (1 Cor. 14:17). But note the caution and uncertainty in Paul's words: *"may be giving thanks."* For when no person understands the unknown tongue, no one can say what the content is. Thus Paul says, *"No one understands him; he speaks mysteries with his spirit"* (1 Cor. 14:2).

Q 31 ↗ According to 1 Corinthians 14:21, tongues may be from _____ to _____.

2. Tongues may be a message from God to man. Some say that the content of tongues is always prayer and praise. These people claim that the direction of tongues is always from man to God. But in this very chapter of 1 Corinthians 14, Paul uses the example of the Assyrians speaking to unbelieving Israel in a tongue that Israel did not

Christian Edification and Spiritual Gifts

understand (1 Cor. 14:21). *"Through men of strange tongues and through the lips of foreigners I will speak to this people."* Through the Assyrians, God spoke to His people through a language they did not understand. It is true that this was a learned language, but that did not prevent Paul from using it as an example of God speaking to man in unknown tongues.

Another example of God speaking to man through an unknown tongue is the handwriting on the wall that Daniel explained through the gift of interpretation (Dan. 5:25-28). Tongues and interpretation may be a message from God to man.

Q 32 *In Daniel 5:25-28, the unknown tongue was a message from _____ to _____.*

Dr. Anthony Palma, former Dean of the Assemblies of God Theological Seminary, notes that tongues and interpretation are equally valid for edifying believers. And Palma refers to Carson, saying it appears that tongues with an interpreter can have the same function as prophecy.[20]

Dr. Palma notes that interpreted tongues and prophecy are of equal value in edifying the church.[21] Likewise, Dr. Stanley Horton and Don Stamps concur that tongues with interpretation may be from God to man—it "may contain a revelation, knowledge, prophecy, or teaching for the assembly (see 1 Cor. 14:6)."[22]

We have cited several scholars and two examples to emphasize that tongues may be a message from God to man and may function as prophecy. But the greatest example of God speaking to man through tongues is on the Day of Pentecost. The crowd thought those speaking in tongues were drunk. But Peter said: [16] *"But, this is what was spoken of through the prophet Joel:* [17] *'AND IT SHALL BE IN THE LAST DAYS,' God says, 'THAT I WILL POUR FORTH OF MY SPIRIT ON ALL MANKIND; AND YOUR SONS AND YOUR DAUGHTERS SHALL PROPHESY...'"* (Acts 2:16-17). Dr. Horton explains: "Evidently, Peter, through the Spirit, saw that tongues, when understood, are the equivalent of prophecy."[23] On the Day of Pentecost, it is easy for us to see that believers were praising God in tongues (Acts 2:11). But let us not lose sight of the big picture. For as the believers spoke in tongues, God was speaking through them to the unbelievers! While speaking in tongues, the believers were also prophesying, as Joel had foretold. For prophecy occurs when a person supernaturally speaks for God (Exod. 4:15-16; 7:1). As the prophets spoke for God, believers spoke for God through the power of Pentecost. Likewise, as Acts 2:4 predicts, Spirit-filled believers are God's witnesses—prophesying, speaking God's message through supernatural power all over the earth. As Roger Stronstad emphasizes, the pouring out of the gift of the Spirit is the Spirit of prophecy and is for the community of God's people.[24] The Day of Pentecost makes it clear that through the gift of tongues, God can speak to man.

Q 33 *Did God use the gift of tongues to speak to man at Pentecost? Explain.*

Q 34 *What error does Charles Russell guide us to avoid?*

We do not understand any tongue or language we have not studied or learned. A Baptist pastor, J. J. Ross, wrote a tract accusing Charles Taze Russell, founder of the Jehovah's Witnesses. Ross claimed that Russell made statements he was not qualified to make. Ross wrote that Russell was "totally ignorant" of languages such as Greek and Hebrew. Russell sued Ross for libel (untrue, damaging statements in print). Ross wrote the tract because Russell gave explanations about the Greek language, yet Russell was not fluent in Greek. And in court, Russell admitted that he was not familiar with Greek and might not even be able to identify letters of the Greek alphabet. So in court, Russell lost his case against Ross.[27] Our day in a bema court is coming when we will give account for every word we have spoken. So let us be humble and careful in our explanations about the content or direction of tongues. For we are *totally ignorant* of such languages.

Figure 8.5 Charles Russell, in a court of law, admitted that he was not familiar with Greek.[25] **This was after Russell had given explanations about the Greek language.**[26] **Those who do not know a tongue or language should not try to explain the language.**

Q 35 ⬉ *As we pray in tongues, why is it important to listen?*

3. Praying in tongues should include talking and listening. All agree that tongues can be a form of *prayer,* for Paul says, *"If I pray in a tongue, my spirit prays"* (1 Cor. 14:14). But let us remember that prayer is talking *with* God, not just talking *to* God. Prayer is conversing with God—which should include talking *and* listening. Pastor Bill Hybels says it is ironic that, when we think of prayer, we often think of talking to God and forget that prayer includes listening to what God says to us.[28] Likewise, others refer to *listening prayer.*[29] So let us realize that prayer in tongues may be us speaking to God or God speaking to us—as we listen and seek the interpretation.

"So what shall I do? I will pray with my spirit, but I will also pray with my mind; I will sing with my spirit, but I will also sing with my mind" (1 Cor. 14:15). This verse encourages us to pray in tongues, and then listen—in church and in private. Then, we may receive the interpretation—either of what we are saying to God or what He is saying to us.

In passing, let us note the joy in Paul's words—*"I will sing with my Spirit; but I will also sing with my mind"* (1 Cor. 14:15). Such singing, as a form of prayerful worship, may include songs of praise we know, new songs the Spirit gives us, and songs in an unknown tongue. And if we listen, we may even discover that God is singing over us, as Zephaniah prophesied that God would sing over Israel (Zeph. 3:17). *"See how great is the love the Father has bestowed on us, that we would be called children of God"* (1 John 3:1). Let us take time now, and every day, to rejoice in tongues and sing in the Spirit. For in Christ, *"...the love of God has been poured out within our hearts through the Holy Spirit who was given to us"* (Rom. 5:5).

Q 36 ⬉ *Give some examples of people to whom God spoke as they practiced "listening prayer."*

Peter prayed at lunchtime, and his prayer included listening. God sent him to the home of Cornelius (Acts 10:9-19). Paul prayed for God to deliver him from a thorn in the flesh. And Paul's prayer included listening. God assured Paul that His grace is sufficient and that His strength is made perfect in weakness (2 Cor. 12:9). While believers in Antioch, Syria worshiped (prayed) and fasted, they listened. God spoke and told them to separate Barnabas and Paul to be missionaries (Acts 13:1-2).

When we realize that prayer includes listening, it is easier for us to *"pray without ceasing"* (1 Thess. 5:17 KJV). Prayer is not a monologue or a one-way street. Indeed, multitudes of believers can testify that in private prayer God has often spoken to them through tongues and interpretation. Praying in tongues includes us talking to God AND God talking to us if we listen.

> PRAYER INCLUDES LISTENING.

Many dreams are not from God. Yet especially under the old covenant, there were times when God spoke to people through dreams or visions. These communications from God were often like languages they did not understand. However, as people prayed and looked to God, He gave them the interpretations of the dreams and visions (Gen. 40–41). Likewise, Joel prophesied that God would continue to speak to us through dreams and visions when He poured out His Spirit on all flesh. From the apostles to the present, God continues to speak to us through dreams and visions (Acts 10, 16; Rev. 1–22). Yet we need supernatural help from God to interpret the mysterious language of dreams and visions when God speaks to us. For dreams are like a message in tongues—we need supernatural help to interpret them.

B. Praying in tongues in church must be interpreted so that all are edified (1 Cor. 14:7-17, 26).

Q 37 ⬉ *Does God want believers to pray aloud in tongues in church **without** an interpretation? Explain.*

Paul encourages praying in tongues in private to build up a believer. He thanked God that he prayed in tongues more than all of those in Corinth. But in church, Paul insists that tongues must be interpreted so that others are edified.

Christian Edification and Spiritual Gifts

Paul gives three illustrations (1 Cor. 14:7-11) to show that tongues without interpretation cannot be understood—so they are unprofitable to others present.

> ⁶*Now, brothers, if I come to you and speak in tongues, what good will I be to you, unless I bring you some revelation or knowledge or prophecy or word of instruction?*
> - ⁷*"Even in the case of lifeless things that make sounds, such as the **flute or harp**, how will anyone know what tune is being played unless there is a distinction in the notes?"*
> - ⁸*"Again, if the **trumpet** does not sound a clear call, who will get ready for battle? ⁹So it is with you. Unless you speak intelligible words with your tongue, how will anyone know what you are saying? You will just be speaking into the air."*
> - ¹⁰*"Undoubtedly there are all sorts of languages in the world, yet none of them is without meaning. ¹¹If then I do not grasp the meaning of what someone is saying, I am a **foreigner** to the speaker, and he is a foreigner to me. ¹²So it is with you."*
>
> *Since you are eager to have spiritual gifts, try to excel in gifts that build up the church* (1 Cor. 14:7-12).

Q 38 Which 3 illustrations does Paul give of things not profitable because they are not understood?

C. Anyone who speaks in a tongue should pray that he may interpret what he says (1 Cor. 14:13).

> ¹³*For this reason anyone who speaks in a tongue should pray that he may interpret what he says. ¹⁴For if I pray in a tongue, my spirit prays, but my mind is unfruitful. ¹⁵So what shall I do? I will pray with my spirit, but I will also pray with my mind; I will sing with my spirit, but I will also sing with my mind. ¹⁶If you are praising God with your spirit, how can one who finds himself among those who do not understand say "Amen" to your thanksgiving, since he does not know what you are saying? ¹⁷You may be giving thanks well enough, but the other man is not edified* (1 Cor. 14:13-17).

Note that 1 Corinthians 14:13 begins with *"For this reason..."* The reason is the topic of 1 Corinthians 14:6-12. Throughout 1 Corinthians 12–14, Paul emphasizes one purpose of church meetings. It will surprise some today that the main purpose Paul emphasizes is **not** worship. Rather, the big theme of 1 Corinthians 12–14 is building up one another when we come together. This theme is like a nail that Paul hammers ten times in these chapters. *"Excel in gifts that build up the church"* (1 Cor. 14:12). Paul just gave three illustrations to show that, in church, speaking in tongues without interpreting does not edify others. Can you name these three illustrations of 1 Corinthians 14:6-11? *"For this reason"* (since tongues without interpretation do not edify others), he who speaks in a tongue should pray to interpret.

Q 39 To which reason does 1 Corinthians 14:13 refer?

Q 40 What is the main purpose of church services?

Paul puts the most responsibility for interpretation on the person who speaks in tongues:

- *"He who prophesies is greater than one who speaks in tongues, unless he interprets, so that the church may be edified"* (1 Cor. 14:5).
- *"Since you are eager to have spiritual gifts, [you] try to excel in gifts that build up the church"* (1 Cor. 14:12).
- *"...anyone who speaks in a tongue should pray that he may interpret what he says"* (1 Cor. 14:13).
- ²⁷*"If anyone speaks in a tongue, two—or at the most three—should speak, one at a time, and someone must interpret. ²⁸If there is no interpreter, the speaker should keep quiet in the church and speak to himself and God"* (1 Cor. 14:27-28).

Q 41 When there is a message in tongues, who has the greatest responsibility to interpret?

Q 42 What are some ways in which a speaker may know if someone will interpret the tongues?

The question arises, How will the speaker know whether he or someone else will interpret the message in tongues? Believers should be patient and tolerant in the area of spiritual gifts. We should be more concerned about the pattern than about each case. There are three things that may encourage a believer to speak in tongues in a group:

- *First,* does a believer often pray in tongues at home, and then interpret? If the answer is yes, then this believer may expect to interpret tongues in a group setting. For if in private he prays with his spirit and then his mind, he may expect this same pattern in a group setting (1 Cor. 14:15).
- *Second,* are there one or more believers in the local church to whom God often gives the gift of interpretation? If the answer is yes, then this may encourage a believer to speak out in tongues.
- *Third,* is a person experiencing a great urging of the Holy Spirit to speak out in tongues? Is his or her heart pounding loudly? Does the believer feel, like Jeremiah, compelled to speak?

"But if I say, 'I will not remember Him or speak anymore in His name,' then in my heart it becomes like a burning fire shut up in my bones; and I am weary of holding it in, and I cannot endure it" (Jer. 20:9). If a believer feels a strong urge to speak, then let him step forward in child-like faith, at the right time. For our first and foremost obligation is to seek to obey God. And even if we fail while trying to please Him, He will not condemn us. In the manifestation of every spiritual gift, there is a point when a believer must choose to step forward by faith. So let us spend much time with God, praying in tongues privately, building ourselves up in our most holy faith, praying in the Holy Spirit (Jude 20). Then we can be bold in public. Otherwise, we may quench the Spirit (1 Thess. 5:19) and forfeit the ministry of spiritual gifts God intends to give the church through us. Which is worse, to be humbled in public, or to fail because of pride and fear? Yet those known for spiritual gifts can testify that time after time, day after day, and year after year, faith is the hand that reaches out and receives the gifts our heavenly Father graciously offers us.

If none of the three cases above applies, then a believer should probably pray silently in tongues, speaking to himself and to God (1 Cor. 14:28).

Q 43 *What does the illustration about Amit emphasize?*

Amit sat in a church service at the close of the message. His heart was pounding. He had been praying for spiritual gifts. He felt the Spirit guiding him to give a message in tongues, but he had never done this before. Would someone interpret? He did not know! Wanting to please God and strengthen the church, he stood and spoke the message. There was a brief silence, and God gave Him the interpretation, so he also spoke it. The church was blessed. Later, Amit explained to the pastor that he almost remained silent. The pastor assured him that even if there were no interpretation, the church would be understanding and patient. They wanted spiritual gifts in their midst and wanted to encourage believers to respond to the Spirit.

Figure 8.6 Pastors should encourage believers in the use of spiritual gifts.

Q 44 *What are 2 extreme errors about sharing a message in tongues?*

There are times when a believer should pray quietly in tongues to God. Many do not understand the cooperation between a believer and the Holy Spirit. Some err by thinking it is the Holy Spirit, not the believer, who speaks. These never speak in tongues because they are still waiting for the Spirit to begin speaking through them. Others err in the opposite direction, thinking that when they feel the Spirit's presence, they must begin speaking loudly in tongues. The truth is in between these two extreme errors. It is the Holy Spirit who enables us to speak in tongues, but we control the speaking—whether

Christian Edification and Spiritual Gifts

to be silent, whisper, speak with a normal voice, or speak with a loud voice (See 1 Cor. 14:30-33). The Spirit gives the gifts to believers. But believers control the expression of the spiritual gifts they receive. A parent may give his son a trumpet, but the son decides when, where, and how loudly to blow the trumpet.

D. Tongues and prophecy serve as signs (1 Cor. 14:20-25).

[20]Brothers, stop thinking like children. In regard to evil be infants, but in your thinking be adults. [21]In the Law it is written: "Through men of strange tongues and through the lips of foreigners I will speak to this people, but even then they will not listen to me, says the Lord. [22]Tongues, then, are a sign, not for believers but for unbelievers; prophecy, however, is for believers, not for unbelievers (1 Cor. 14:20-22; Isa. 28:11-12).

As we interpret 1 Corinthians 14:20-22, it is important to review the context. In these verses, Paul is emphasizing his big theme: Do all to edify others when the church meets. Let us look at four examples on signs: two examples on tongues as a sign and two examples on prophecy as a sign (Figure 8.6).

> TONGUES AND PROPHECY SERVE AS SIGNS.

1. Tongues are a sign to unbelievers. The apostle contrasts tongues and prophecy in a church service. When believers meet together, tongues (without interpretation) do not edify. So in this context, tongues are not a sign or a blessing to believers. To illustrate this point, Paul refers to Isaiah 28:11-12. Those verses are about a time when Israel was rebelling. The Israelites would not obey God or believe His prophets. Near 800 B.C., Isaiah prophesied that Assyria would conquer Israel (Isa. 28:11-12). Through the actions and words of the Assyrians, God would be speaking to Israel. That is, God would be saying, "Israel, you need to repent, turn from sin, and return to Me." But even when Assyria conquered Israel in 722 B.C., Israel did not believe God. Thus Paul gives an illustration that a foreign tongue was a sign to unbelievers. Paul's point is that since tongues were a sign for unbelievers, do not use tongues (without interpretation) as a sign or blessing for believers.

In a church service, many believers began to pray in tongues at the same time. Like the Corinthians, they sensed the Spirit's presence, and they enjoyed praying in tongues. However, there was great confusion, and no one interpreted the tongues. Believers thought that the tongues would be a sign to the unbelievers. The church members thought tongues would cause the sinners to recognize that God was present. Tongues were indeed a sign to the unbelievers. But the sign did not say what the church members expected. Rather, to the unbelieving sinners, the sign of tongues said, "Exit now! You do not belong here. These people are insane" (1 Cor. 14:23). So the sinners left and never returned to the church. And their testimony discouraged many others from attending that Pentecostal church.

 Q 45 *What kind of sign are tongues to unbelievers?*

2. Tongues are a sign to believers. In another biblical context, Luke reveals that tongues can be a sign to believers. Peter and his Jewish friends heard the household of Cornelius speak in tongues. This was a sign to Peter and other Jews that the Gentiles had been filled with the Spirit (Acts 10:44-46). And today, when we hear believers speaking in tongues, this is an outward sign that they are filled with the Spirit.

Q 46 *In what way are tongues a sign to believers?*

Likewise, in a church service, tongues and interpretation are a sign to believers. For all spiritual gifts in a service are a sign that God is present. Spiritual gifts are a sign that believers are allowing the Holy Spirit to manifest Himself. Tongues and interpretation are a sign that the ministry of the Holy Spirit through believers is welcome and active. In contrast, the absence of spiritual gifts is a sign that a church is living below its privileges, below God's will and plan (1 Cor. 1:7).

		A Sign for Unbelievers	A Sign for Believers	
Tongues	Isa. 28:11-12	Israel did not believe God when the Assyrians spoke to them in 722 B.C. Exit now!	Tongues and interpretation edify believers. Peter and others believed the Gentiles had received the Spirit when they heard them speak in tongues.	1 Cor. 12:7,10; 14:5 Acts 10:44-46; 11:15-17
	1 Cor. 14:23			
Prophecy	1 Cor. 14:24-25	The secrets of their hearts are laid bare.	Strengthens, encourages, comforts, and instructs	1 Cor. 14:3, 21

Figure 8.7 Tongues and prophecy may be a sign for unbelievers or believers, depending on the context.

Q 47 *How is prophecy a sign to believers?*

3. **Prophecy is a sign to believers.** When a believer prophesies in church, this edifies other believers. They are encouraged, comforted, strengthened, and instructed by the Spirit. So the gift of prophecy in church is a sign to believers—a sign that God is present and cares for them. Paul emphasizes this in 1 Corinthians 14:3 and 21.

Q 48 *How is prophecy a sign to unbelievers?*

4. **Prophecy is a sign to unbelievers.** Paul also teaches us that the gift of prophecy is a sign to unbelievers. For if several prophesy, Paul assumes that these messages will reveal the secrets of a sinner's heart. Thus these prophecies will be a sign to the unbeliever that God is present, and it is time to repent.

Conclusion

The gift of tongues, by itself, is not understood. In private, praying in tongues edifies a believer. But in church, if a believer speaks out loud in tongues without an interpretation, confusion reigns. This will cause unbelievers to criticize and stumble (1 Cor. 14:23). So in a group meeting, there should be an interpretation of any message in tongues.

Prophecy is spoken in the language of the people, so all understand it. Through prophecy, God can speak to all—believers and unbelievers. God can use prophecy to encourage believers or convict unbelievers. So prophecy is a powerful tool of the Holy Spirit.

Lesson 26: Guidelines for Order With Spiritual Gifts (1 Cor. 14:26-40)

Goal: *Explain 6 guidelines for maintaining order as believers manifest spiritual gifts in a service.*

In this lesson, we will examine several guidelines (A–F) for maintaining order when believers minister spiritual gifts.

A. Paul writes three guidelines for tongues in a service (1 Cor. 14:26-28).

[26] What then shall we say, brothers? When you come together, everyone has a hymn, or a word of instruction, a revelation, a tongue or an interpretation. All of these must be done for the strengthening of the church. [27] If anyone speaks in a tongue, two—or at the most three—should speak, one at a time, and someone must interpret. [28] If there is no interpreter, the speaker should keep quiet in the church and speak to himself and God (1 Cor. 14:26-28).

Note that 1 Corinthians 14:26-28 lists several types of gifts. It is God's plan for there to be a variety of spiritual gifts when believers meet. The Corinthian church emphasized speaking in tongues—but without interpretation. To correct this, Paul gave three guidelines:

Q 49 *What are 3 guidelines for tongues in a service?*

- At the most, there should be three messages in tongues in a service (1 Cor. 14:27). Limiting the number of messages in tongues encourages the manifestation of other spiritual gifts.[30]
- Messages in tongues must be one at a time. It is confusing in church when two people speak at once.
- There must be an interpretation. Paul taught this truth earlier (1 Cor. 14:5, 6-13, and 14-19), but he emphasizes it again here because it was a problem in Corinth.

Christian Edification and Spiritual Gifts

B. Believers must examine and judge tongues and interpretation or prophecy (1 Cor. 14:29-31).

²⁹Two or three prophets should speak, and the others should weigh carefully what is said. ³⁰And if a revelation comes to someone who is sitting down, the first speaker should stop. ³¹For you can all prophesy in turn so that everyone may be instructed and encouraged (1 Cor. 14:29-31).

Paul did not limit the number of believers who can prophesy in a service, as he did with the gift of tongues. Thus he wrote than an unbeliever may come in when *"everybody is prophesying"* (1 Cor. 14:24). Again he wrote, *"you can all prophesy in turn"* (1 Cor. 14:31).³¹

Picture the scene in the Corinthian church. Two or three believers stand up to prophesy—one at a time. In between these prophecies, believers take time to examine what is said. Meanwhile, someone sitting down receives a revelation from God (1 Cor. 14:30). Since love is patient, the one speaking pauses and gives someone else the opportunity to minister. Taking turns prevents one believer from doing all the talking.

It is important to examine messages in tongues or prophecy. Earlier, under the gift of discernment, we noted three sources of speech: the Holy Spirit, evil spirits, and human spirits. Like Peter, sincere believers may be inspired by God (Matt. 16:16), guided by Satan (Matt. 16:22), or led by the flesh (Matt. 17:4). Furthermore, a prophecy may be a *mixture* of divine truth and human interpretation. For example, believers in Tyre *"through the Spirit"* urged Paul not to go to Jerusalem (Acts 21:4). And when Agabus prophesied that Jerusalem Jews would bind Paul, believers again urged him not to go (Acts 21:11-12). Yet Paul knew it was God's will for him to go to Jerusalem. Dr. Stanley Horton explains that these believers were mixing their own feelings and interpretations with what the Spirit was saying.³² The Spirit was predicting that Paul would suffer, so believers jumped to the conclusion that he should not go. We understand their conclusion, but their thoughts were being led by their feelings and not by the Spirit. So today, when we examine a prophecy, we must be careful to separate the Spirit's message from human emotions and interpretations.

Q 50 *What are 4 questions for examining a prophecy? Explain each.*

Here are four questions for examining a prophecy or message in tongues.

- ***First:* Is the message right—is it biblical?** God does not contradict Himself. No message in tongues or prophecy is from God if it contradicts Scripture. The Bible is our basis for judging all doctrine. We are never told to examine Scripture to see whether it is true. For the Bible is fully *inspired (God-breathed), *inerrant (without error), and *infallible (incapable of error). In contrast, we must examine prophecies that believers give today to be sure they contain no mixture of truth and error. So we measure all prophecies with the ruler of Scripture, God's standard for truth.

    In Thessalonica, someone prophesied that the Lord had already returned to earth. Thus Paul wrote,

    ¹Now we request you, brethren, with regard to the coming of our Lord Jesus Christ and our gathering together to Him, ²that you not be quickly shaken from your composure or be disturbed either by a spirit or a message or a letter as if from us, to the effect that the day of the Lord has come (2 Thess. 2:1-2).

    Paul contrasts the false prophecy at Thessalonica with his true apostolic teaching: *"So then, brothers, stand firm and hold to the traditions which you were taught, whether by word of mouth or by letter from us"* (2 Thess. 2:15). Let us reject any teachings that contradict Scripture.

- ***Second*: Is the messenger right—with God and man?** If the tree is bad, we should not expect good fruit from it. Do men gather grapes from thorns or figs from thistles (Matt. 7:15-20)? Only those who live godly lives may minister to the church.

Q 51 *If Diotrephes had prophesied, should believers have paid attention to him (3 John)? Explain.*

Q 52 *What are 2 reasons why believers listened when Agabus prophesied?*

Q 53 *To what problem does 1 Corinthians 14:34-35 refer?*

Q 54 *What disturbing position does Fee take on 1 Corinthians 14:33-35?*

In the church of Thyatira, the pastor and deacons tolerated a woman named Jezebel. She called herself a prophetess, but she led many into false teachings. Her purpose and her life were corrupt. Jesus warned that He would discipline the church with severe suffering if they did not repent (Rev. 2:20-23). It is the pastor's responsibility to examine all teachings and to guide the church away from error. Church leaders must fear God more than man, or the King of kings will judge them and His Church.

- **Third: Is the motive right?** Is the message to edify—strengthen, encourage, comfort, or instruct? The wisdom from heaven is *"pure... unwavering, without hypocrisy"* (James 3:17). Paul teaches that all spiritual gifts must be used in *love*—not in anger, revenge, or other selfish concerns.

A believer we will call "Queen Bee" often tried to control others. One evening, the church met to vote about building a new room for children's ministry. Queen stood and with a loud voice (that sounded like a prophecy) declared that the Lord did not want people to vote for the new building. But the people did not pay attention to her. For they knew she was just seeking to get her own way.

- **Fourth: Is the timing right?** Is the message orderly, or does it interrupt? The wisdom from above is peace-loving, considerate, and submissive. Love is patient and waits its turn to speak (1 Cor. 13:4). We will study more about the relationship between order and spiritual gifts in the next lesson.

While the pastor was preaching, a believer stood up and began speaking in tongues. The pastor said, "My brother, please do not interrupt. This is not yet the time for your message in tongues. The Holy Spirit is speaking through God's Word. This is what we need to hear right now. I know you want to help, but please wait until the pastor finishes the sermon."[33] The believer agreed and sat down. Later in the service, he stood and gave the tongues and interpretation.

C. Believers must submit to spiritual authority in the church (1 Cor. 14:34-38).

[33]...As in all the congregations of the saints, [34]women should remain silent in the churches. They are not allowed to speak, but must be in submission, as the Law says. [35]If they want to inquire about something, they should ask their own husbands at home; for it is disgraceful for a woman to speak in the church (1 Cor. 14:34-35).

First Corinthians 14:34-35 refers to a problem in Corinth. The men probably sat on one side of the church, and the women on the other.[34] This is still the case in some churches today. It appears that there was a problem with women calling out across the room to ask their husbands a question. This caused confusion, so Paul guided women to ask their husbands questions at home. But Paul was not forbidding women to prophesy in church. He had already written in favor of women who prophesy in a proper relation to their husbands (1 Cor. 11:3-5).

		May Speak in Church	May Not Speak in Church	
Women	1 Cor. 11:5	To pray and prophesy, while honoring their husbands	To yell across the aisle and ask their husbands questions	1 Cor. 14:33-35

Figure 8.8   Paul encouraged women to minister in church, but he emphasized order.

It saddens and shocks us that our brother, Dr. Gordon Fee, does not think 1 Corinthians 14:33-35 belongs in our Bibles.[35] Although Fee speaks in tongues, he is not always in harmony with Pentecostals. Fee believes that believers are baptized in the Holy Spirit at conversion. Thus Dr. Roger Stronstad wrote, "Fee writes as an iconoclast [a person who attacks cherished beliefs], tearing down the hermeneutical pillars upon which the structure of Pentecostal doctrine is built. He objects to the Spirit baptism being distinct from conversion."[36] Likewise, Fee's rejection of 1 Corinthians 14:33-35 from the Bible alarms many of us Pentecostals. Our view of inspiration does not permit us to remove this text from our Bibles when the best Greek manuscripts affirm it, and every Bible translation we know of includes it.

So let us approach texts like 1 Corinthians 14:33-35 with humility and faith. We can understand and accept these verses in the context of order and edification. For it is not only women whom Paul restricts in speaking. When the church meets, Paul does not want women to speak across the aisle, he does not want any two people to speak at the same time, and he does not want anyone to speak aloud in tongues if there is no interpretation. As believers, we must submit to the authority of God's Word and to spiritual authority in the Church.

Q 55 *Is it only women whom Paul restricts in speaking in the church? Explain.*

At times, Debbie spoke messages of prophecy. The church appreciated and affirmed most of what she said. But one Sunday morning, at the end of the sermon, she stood and spoke in an angry tone. Her words were harsh, mean, and hurtful. Pastor Warren did not say anything at the time. Debbie's unsaved husband was sitting beside her, and the pastor felt it best to talk with Debbie in private. Later, the pastor and his wife met with Debbie. Pastor Warren suggested that her message the previous Sunday expressed her frustration over her lost husband. He said that the message did not seem to be a mixture of truth and love that the Spirit inspires. Debbie became angry and said, "How dare you question what God has given me!" She did not respect the pastor's authority or submit to it. Rather, she left the church. This saddened the pastor, who had been building a relationship with Debbie's husband and felt that he was close to accepting Christ. Still, the pastor knew he had done the right thing in talking to Debbie. Although some may have an unteachable spirit, it is the pastor's duty to confront in love those who go astray with spiritual gifts.[37] And it is the responsibility of believers to submit to spiritual leaders of the church.

D. A pastor needs to encourage spiritual gifts in the church.

- A pastor needs to sense the moving of the Spirit and invite people to respond.
- A pastor needs be an example. Believers need a mentor and example to follow. So a pastor needs to pray for the gifts of the Spirit and manifest them before the people.
- A pastor needs to teach the value and purpose of tongues and interpretation.
- A pastor needs to teach how to cooperate with the Spirit. The keys to these *speaking gifts* include faith, desire for the gifts, and private praying in tongues. Little steps come before big steps. So pastors should encourage believers to take the small steps of praying often in tongues in private. Then, we can expect some of them to speak a message of tongues in the church.

Q 56 *What are some ways in which the pastor can encourage spiritual gifts?*

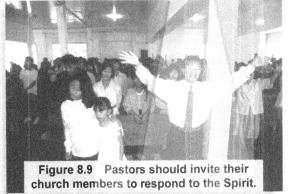

Figure 8.9 Pastors should invite their church members to respond to the Spirit.

Also, the pastor should teach that the Spirit does not usually give the speaker the complete message all at once. The believer who sees a mental image or feels the leading of the Spirit to speak (such as the strong pounding of the heart) must learn to step out in faith—trusting the Spirit to complete the message that is building up inside. A believer must learn to begin with only a word or a phrase.[38]

E. A pastor should explain spiritual gifts when visitors or new converts are present.

For example, explain that an interpretation is not necessarily a translation. Rather, an interpretation gives the essence and meaning of the message in tongues. So the length of the message in tongues may not be the same as that of the interpretation.

After tongues and interpretation, a pastor may explain like this:

Q 57 *As a pastor, what would you say to visitors just after tongues and interpretation?*

"Some of our guests may not be familiar with what just happened. The Bible refers to the spiritual gifts of speaking in tongues and interpretation. You may read more about these gifts in 1 Corinthians 12–14. Through the Holy Spirit, Jesus gave these gifts to the early church. And Jesus Christ is the same yesterday, today, and forever. We believe that God still wants to communicate directly with us through these gifts today. This morning, the message of these gifts is: (the pastor should summarize what the message in tongues said)."[39]

F. A pastor should lead the church in responding to tongues and prophecy. He should affirm or correct.

Q 58 *How should a pastor lead the church to respond to tongues or prophecy? Give examples.*

Believers may err as they speak in tongues or prophecy. As we said earlier, they may mix their own thoughts with what God is saying. Still, misuse should not lead to disuse.[40] Rather, let the pastor affirm the good, correct the error in love, and encourage more spiritual gifts. For as Paul said, [19]*"Do not quench the Spirit;* [20]*do not despise prophetic utterances"* (1 Thess. 5:19-20). Rather, *"Follow the way of love and eagerly desire spiritual gifts, especially the gift of prophecy"* (1 Cor. 14:1).

A retired minister we will call Leonard began attending Pastor Warren's church. At times, Leonard stood and gave a message in tongues and then interpreted it at once. At first, these messages seemed helpful. But believers began to notice that the messages were almost the same, time after time. So they became dull, and church members stopped listening to them. Pastor Warren knew he must do something. Since Leonard was an elder, Pastor Warren did not want to rebuke or correct him in public (1 Tim. 5:1). So in private, he said gently to Leonard, "I have some questions about your message in tongues last Sunday. It seemed more like something for your private prayer time." Leonard humbly agreed. And for several weeks he did not give a message in tongues. Then, one Sunday after an early morning time of prayer, Leonard stood and gave his usual message and interpretation. So Pastor Warren needed to stand and say something like: "Sometimes, God enables us to pray in tongues as we worship Him. Often, we do not interpret these tongues as our spirits worship God. But at other times, we speak in tongues in church, and these need to be interpreted so others will benefit. Sometimes, we may not be sure whether God intends us to worship in tongues quietly or speak aloud for the whole church. I believe that this morning, this speaking in tongues overflowed into our public service, but God intended it to be used in private. So let us continue to learn and grow in this area."[41]

If there is a message in tongues, but after waiting there is no interpretation, a pastor should explain. He may say something like: "We believe in the gifts of the Spirit, such as the gift of speaking in tongues. First Corinthians 12–14 teaches us about this gift. But it says that whenever someone speaks in tongues in church, there needs to be an interpretation. The purpose of spiritual gifts is to strengthen and build us up. Yet this cannot happen if we hear an unknown tongue without an interpretation. So 1 Corinthians 14 says that whoever speaks in an unknown tongue should pray to interpret it. The lack of an interpretation does not mean that the message in tongues was not from God. Perhaps God gave someone the interpretation, but he or she lacked the courage to share it. Or perhaps this message in tongues was a praise that should have been prayed quietly to God. Today, we did not benefit from this message in tongues, because we could not understand it. However, let us remember that although our use of spiritual gifts is not perfect, we should continue to seek and encourage their use. Let us continue to grow in our understanding and use of these gifts. For spiritual gifts are from God, and He delights to give them to us today."[42]

Test Yourself: Circle the letter by the *best* completion to each question or statement.

1. A message in tongues is
a) understood only by the listeners.
b) in a language unlearned by the speaker.
c) understood in heaven, but not on earth.
d) for the purpose of evangelism.

2. We know the tongues-speaker is in control
a) because the speaker may remain silent.
b) because experience proves this is the case.
c) because all believers testify that this is true.
d) because the interpretation soon follows.

3. The gift of prophecy is
a) the same as the office of a prophet.
b) the same as anointed preaching.
c) the result of meditating on Scripture.
d) a flash of insight from the Spirit.

4. The gift of prophecy is
a) 0% rooted in human reasoning.
b) 10% human and 90% divine.
c) a message to make believers stronger.
d) mostly about the future.

5. Which is NOT a function of prophecy?
a) Telling the message of the gospel
b) Telling the steps of personal guidance
c) Telling the events of the future
d) Telling the secrets of the heart

6. Which of these statements is FALSE?
a) Tongues may be a praise from man to God.
b) Tongues may be a message from God to man.
c) Tongues should include talking and listening.
d) Tongues may be a message, but not a song.

7. The most responsibility to interpret tongues
a) is on the one who speaks in tongues.
b) is on the pastor of the local church.
c) is on the one known to have this gift.
d) is on the most mature believers.

8. Paul emphasizes that prophecy is a sign to
a) unbelievers.
b) believers.
c) believers and unbelievers.
d) those with eyes to see.

9. Which is TRUE?
a) There is no limit on tongues in a service.
b) There is no limit on prophecy in a service.
c) Prophecy has the same authority as Scripture.
d) Prophecy may supersede Scripture.

10. Which church had an unbiblical prophecy?
a) Corinth
b) Philippi
c) Thessalonica
d) Galatia

 Essay Test Topics: Write 50-100 words on each of these goals that you studied in this chapter.

The Gifts of Tongues and Interpretation (1 Cor. 14:1-25)

Goal: *Explain what speaking in tongues is not and is.*

The Gift of Prophecy (1 Cor. 14:1-32)

Goal: *Explain what the spiritual gift of prophecy is not and is.*

Principles for Using Spiritual Gifts in Ministry (1 Cor. 14:1-26)

Goal: *Explain 4 principles for tongues, interpretation, and prophecy in a service.*

Guidelines for Order With Spiritual Gifts (1 Cor. 14:26-40)

Goal: *Explain 6 guidelines for maintaining order as believers manifest spiritual gifts in a service.*

Chapter 9:
Doctrine and Worship
(1 Corinthians 15–16)

Introduction

In a small village in Switzerland, there are a series of three chapels on a mountain (Figure 9.1). These chapels are along a trail that leads up the mountain. In each chapel there is a picture of some scene in the last hours of Christ. For example, as a person enters the first chapel, he sees a painting of Jesus before Pilate or Herod. As the person continues to climb the mountain, he comes to the second chapel, with a picture of Jesus on the cross. At the top of the mountain is the final chapel, with a painting of the Resurrection.

A visitor climbed the mountain. He noticed that many people had walked before him. The path past the first chapel and up to the cross was wide, because many people had walked on the trail to Calvary. However, the path that led beyond the chapel of the cross was hard to see. Most of the climbers had stopped at the chapel of the cross. Few had gone beyond Calvary. The visitor kept climbing on the faint path up the mountain. Soon he came to the chapel of the Resurrection. Those who had built the three chapels did not leave out this part of the gospel. But most of the people had not traveled beyond Calvary.

Figure 9.1 Many people visited the first chapel, and most went on to the chapel of the cross. But few continued to the chapel of the Resurrection.

The cross is the center of the gospel. Christians have been correct to discern this. The problem is not that the path to the cross is worn. We are thankful that believers follow the steps of Jesus to Calvary. But the problem is that few people travel the path to the empty tomb! Paul gloried in the cross. But he preached the cross in the light of the Resurrection! Alone, the cross is not good news. By itself, the cross is defeat, not victory. Only after the Resurrection did the disciples see the meaning of the cross. The empty tomb revealed that the cross was the Lord's victory over sin, death, and the grave. For as Paul wrote to the Corinthians, without Christ's resurrection, our gospel is a false witness, our lives are useless, and our hope is fruitless.[1]

Lessons:

The Resurrection of Believers—Part 1 (1 Cor. 15:1-19, 29-32)
Goal A: *Explain why we must believe in the resurrection of Christ.*
Goal B: *Analyze why the gospel is bad news if Christ was not raised from the dead.*

The Resurrection of Believers—Part 2 (1 Cor. 15:20-58)
Goal A: *Relate the resurrection of Christ to the firstfruits and the first Adam.*
Goal B: *Explain how the doctrine of the Resurrection affects the daily living of believers.*
Goal C: *Summarize 5 truths about the resurrection body.*

The Stewardship of Money, Opportunity, and God's Family (1 Cor. 16:1-24)
Goal A: *Summarize 6 ways in which we should be stewards of the wealth God entrusts to us.*
Goal B: *Explain 2 ways in which we should be stewards of the opportunities God gives us.*
Goal C: *Analyze the importance of being stewards of relationships in the church.*
Goal D: *Define "anathema" and "maranatha" in your own words.*

Lesson 27: The Resurrection of Believers—Part 1 (1 Cor. 15:1-19, 29-32)

Goal A: *Explain why we must believe in the resurrection of Christ.*
Goal B: *Analyze why the gospel is bad news if Christ was not raised from the dead.*

Setting

As we have studied 1 Corinthians 1–14, we have seen that the church in Corinth had many problems.

- They were divided over leaders (1 Cor. 1–4).
- They did not discipline the member who committed sexual sins with his father's wife (1 Cor. 5).
- Believers were cheating each other and fighting in court (1 Cor. 6).
- Some were attending pagan feasts and committing sexual sins with pagans (1 Cor. 6–10).
- Some women were not showing respect to their husbands (1 Cor. 11).
- Some were abusing the Lord's Supper (1 Cor. 11).
- There was confusion in the worship services, as many spoke in tongues at the same time and no one interpreted (1 Cor. 12–14).
- And as we will see in this lesson, some had stopped believing in the Resurrection (1 Cor. 15).

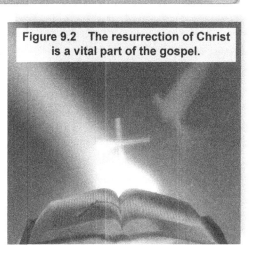

Figure 9.2 The resurrection of Christ is a vital part of the gospel.

Wow, what a mess of problems, and all in one church! Yet God did not give up on the believers in Corinth. Instead, He guided the apostle Paul to write and help them grow through their problems. All of us believers have problems. But God delights to love us, teach us, forgive us, and enable us to grow and triumph. And in the end, as we continue to be good stewards of the grace He gives us, He will save us completely and perfect us to be like Jesus.

Perhaps some in Corinth thought that those who are spiritual do not need resurrection bodies. The Greeks made a similar error. Greeks thought the body was only for our years on earth. But Christianity teaches that the resurrection of the body is important. We know that some in the Corinthian church said there was no Resurrection (1 Cor. 15:12). So Paul takes some time to correct this false teaching. He explains several truths about the resurrection of believers.

A. The Resurrection is a vital part of the gospel (1 Cor. 15:1-11).

1. The gospel is fixed, permanent, unchangeable truth that we must accept or reject.

Q 1 *What is the gospel? Does it change with generations and locations? Explain.*

*Now, brothers, I want to remind you of **the gospel** I preached to you, which you received and on which you have taken your stand* (1 Cor. 15:1).

There is only one gospel, and we cannot change it. When people tried to change the gospel, it caused Paul to get red in the face, angry, and loud! When some in Galatia tried to change the gospel, Paul called down an eternal curse from heaven on them.

⁶I am amazed that you are so quickly deserting Him who called you by the grace of Christ, for a different gospel; ⁷which is really not another; only there are some who are disturbing you and want to distort the gospel of Christ. ⁸But even if we, or an angel from heaven, should preach to you a gospel contrary to what we have preached to you, he is to be accursed! (Gal. 1:6-8).

No one made Paul angrier than people who tried to change the gospel. For changing the gospel is like destroying the foundation of the house while people are living in it. Those who change the gospel destroy their only chance of salvation.

Q 2 *To what can you liken or compare the gospel?*

2. The gospel is the sure foundation on which we stand.

*Now, brothers, I want to remind you of the gospel I preached to you, which you received and **on which you have taken your stand*** (1 Cor. 15:1).

There are a lot of slippery places in these times. We live in a dangerous world. In some places, the finances of nations are failing. Believers may lose their jobs and even their possessions due to wars, rebellions, financial crises, earthquakes, famines, floods, and other hard times. In many nations, believers suffer from poverty, sickness, and persecution. Many believers are in prison. This year, perhaps as many as 160,000 Christians will be killed because they believe in Jesus.[2] Yet in all of these trials, the gospel gives us a firm place to stand. For we know that we have peace with God through our Lord Jesus Christ. And even after death kills this earthly body, the gospel declares that there is a resurrection day coming. So in all times, we stand firm on the gospel of Christ. "On Christ the solid Rock I stand; all other ground is sinking sand."[3]

¹God is our refuge and strength, A very present help in trouble. ²Therefore we will not fear, though the earth should change And though the mountains slip into the heart of the sea; ³Though its waters roar and foam, Though the mountains quake at its swelling pride. Selah (Ps. 46:1-3).

And a modern song says, "Find rest my soul in Christ alone. Know His power in quietness and trust. When the oceans rise and thunders roar, I will soar with You above the storm. Father, You are King over the flood. I will be still and know You are God."[4]

3. Those who stop believing in the resurrection of Christ lose their salvation.

By this gospel you are saved, if you hold firmly to the word I preached to you. Otherwise, you have believed in vain (1 Cor. 15:2).

Q 3 *What are the promise, condition, and warning in 1 Corinthians 15:2?*

Salvation has a beginning, a middle, and a completion. It has a past, present, and future. As John Wesley said, "I was saved, I am being saved, and I will be saved." Salvation begins when people are born again. It continues as we obey Christ and follow His teachings. And salvation will be complete when we receive our new bodies and enter into eternity with Christ.

To be saved, a person must have a spiritual beginning—a time of being born again. But the Scriptures teach that it is not enough to begin well. We must continue in the process of salvation. As we saw in 1 Corinthians 10, many began well on the journey to Canaan, but they died in the desert, short of the Promised Land.

²⁷I beat my body and make it my slave so that after I have preached to others, I myself will not be disqualified for the prize. ¹For I do not want you to be ignorant of the fact, brothers, that our forefathers were all under the cloud and that they all passed through the sea. ²They were all baptized into Moses in the cloud and in the sea. ³They all ate the same spiritual food ⁴and drank the same spiritual drink; for they drank from the spiritual rock that accompanied them, and that rock was Christ. ⁵Nevertheless, God was not pleased with most of them; their bodies were scattered over the desert (1 Cor. 9:27–10:5).

4. The gospel that the apostles preached emphasized the resurrection of Christ.

*¹Now, brothers, I want to remind you of **the gospel I preached to you**, which you received and on which you have taken your stand. ²By this gospel you are saved, if you hold firmly to **the word I preached to you**. Otherwise, you have believed in vain. ³For **what I received I passed on to you** as of first importance: that Christ died for our sins according to the Scriptures, ⁴that he was buried, that he was raised on the third day according to the Scriptures, ⁵and that he appeared to Peter, and then to the Twelve. ⁶After that, he appeared to more than five hundred of the brothers at the same time, most of whom are still living, though some have* *fallen asleep. ⁷Then he appeared to James, then to all the apostles, ⁸and last of all he appeared to me also, as to one abnormally born. ⁹For I am the least of the apostles and do not even deserve to be called an apostle, because I persecuted the church of God. ¹⁰But by the grace of God I am what I am, and his grace to me was not without effect. No, I worked harder than all of them—yet not I, but the grace of God that was with me. ¹¹Whether, then, it was I or they, **this is what we preach**, and this is what you believed* (1 Cor. 15:1-11).

Look closely at the four parts in the gospel of the apostles. We could call these four basic truths the A, B, C, and D of the gospel.

Q 4 *What are the A, B, C, and D of the gospel?*

- **Christ died for our sins (according to the Scriptures).** He was our sacrifice. He was the Lamb of God who died to take away the sins of the world (John 1:29). He was our Passover Lamb, sacrificed for our sins (1 Cor. 5:7). Through the death of Christ on the cross, God was reconciling the world to Himself, not counting men's sins against them (2 Cor. 5:18).

   ⁵But He was pierced through for our transgressions, He was crushed for our iniquities; the chastening for our well-being fell upon Him and by His scourging we are healed. ⁶All of us like sheep have gone astray, each of us has turned to his own way; but the LORD has caused the iniquity of us all to fall on Him (Isa. 53:5-6; see 1 Pet. 2:24-25).

- **He was buried.** Muslims say that the Son of God did not die upon the cross. They claim that He departed, and only the man, Jesus, died. But the gospel says that Jesus Christ, the Son of God, died for our sins and was buried.

- **He was raised on the third day (according to the Scriptures).** The same Jesus Christ who lived, died on the cross for our sins, and was buried—this same Jesus rose from the dead. And notice that the gospel does not say, "He arose with our sins!" No! He died with our sins on His shoulders. But He arose from the dead without them. Hallelujah!

   The Resurrection is proof that God accepted the sacrifice of Christ for our sins, and they are gone! Stand up and shout about this good news for awhile! Our sins are gone! Jesus left them in the grave! In government offices, they place a seal or stamp on a document to show that it is approved and official. The resurrection of Jesus is the seal or stamp of approval that the Judge of Heaven placed on the death of Jesus Christ. The Resurrection validates our faith. Because the tomb is empty, our faith is full!

- **He appeared to hundreds of witnesses.** The resurrection of Jesus Christ is a historical fact. Both the Old and New Testaments emphasize that we establish truth by two or three witnesses. Complete Figure 9.3 to discover the great emphasis the Bible places on two or three witnesses of truth.

Q 5 *Complete Figure 9.3 on the relationship between truth and 2 or 3 witnesses.*

Scripture	Summary of Scripture
Num. 35:30	
Deut. 17:6	
Deut. 19:15	
Matt. 18:16	
John 8:13-18; 10:25	
2 Cor. 13:1	
1 Tim. 5:19	
Heb. 10:28	

Continued on next page

Continued from previous page

| Rev. 11:3 | |

Figure 9.3 Biblical verses emphasizing that truth and certainty are based on two or more witnesses

Q 6 *Mention 5 different times the risen Lord appeared to believers (1 Cor. 15:5-8).*

Q 7 *Why did Jesus appear to so many witnesses?*

Q 8 *Are Bible teachers who do not believe in the resurrection of Christ saved? Explain.*

The Old Testament, the New Testament, and courts of law today base truth on the testimony of two or three witnesses. But to emphasize the truth of the resurrection of Jesus Christ, our Lord appeared to *hundreds* of witnesses! Mormonism is based on the testimony of one man, Joseph Smith, who claimed to read secret documents with special eyeglasses that no witness ever saw.[5] Likewise, Islam is based on the testimony of one man, Muhammad, who could not read, but told people what he alone claimed to have seen and heard.[6] But Christianity is based on the resurrection of Jesus Christ. And He appeared to so many witnesses that it is impossible to deny His resurrection (1 Cor. 15:5-8).[7]

Q 9 *Explain 2 truths about the parable of the bus.*

The parable of the bus. Three men from the country walked to a town nearby. They wanted to ride a bus to the capital city. The first man asked some people which bus to get on. They decided to play a cruel trick on this man, who could not read. So they told him to get on a certain bus, although they knew it would take him in the wrong direction. He thanked them, bought his ticket, and believed he was on the right bus. Hours later, when the bus arrived in a strange town, he was shocked! The other two men from the country also wanted to go to the capital city. Unlike the first man, they got on the correct bus. But after a time, one of the men changed his mind. No one on the bus was sure why he got off the bus early. Perhaps he doubted that it was the right bus. Or maybe it was the feast he saw beside the road that drew him off the bus. In the end, only one of the three men reached the capital city, though all had desired to go there.

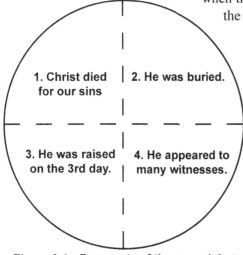

Figure 9.4 Four parts of the gospel that we believe in order to be saved (1 Cor. 15:1-2)

B. If Christ has not been raised from the dead, the good news is bad news (1 Cor. 15:12-19; 29-32).

Some in Corinth did not believe in the resurrection of the body. *"But if it is preached that Christ has been raised from the dead, how can some of you say that there is no resurrection of the dead?"* (1 Cor. 15:12). Paul guides believers to consider the results of this error. *"If there is no resurrection of the dead, then not even Christ has been raised ... your faith is futile; you are still in your sins"* (1 Cor. 15:13, 17). Complete Figure 9.5 to discover some results if Christ has not been raised from the dead.

Q 10 *Complete Figure 9.5 on the results if there is no resurrection (1 Cor. 15:14-32).*

1 Cor.	If (Condition)	Then (Result)
15:13	If there is no resurrection of the dead	
15:14	If Christ has not been raised	
15:15	If Christ has not been raised	
15:16	If the dead are not raised	
15:17	If Christ has not been raised	
15:18	If Christ has not been raised	
15:19	If only in this life we have hope in Christ	
15:29		What will those do who are baptized for (in reference to) *the dead* (Jesus)?
15:30-32a	If there is no resurrection	
15:32b	If the dead are not raised	

Figure 9.5 If/then statements about the Resurrection (1 Cor. 15:14-32)

A Christian song that was once popular said that even if there were no resurrection and no heaven, it has been good to know the Lord in this life. But this was a silly song. For if there is no resurrection, then we have been deceived in this life. Christianity stands on the truth of the Resurrection. If there is no resurrection, then Christianity is a false religion.

History is full of stories about those who followed wrong leaders, like Theudas, Judas, and others.

36 "For some time ago Theudas rose up, claiming to be somebody, and a group of about four hundred men joined up with him. But he was killed, and all who followed him were dispersed and came to nothing 37After this man, Judas of Galilee rose up in the days of the census and drew away some people after him; he too perished, and all those who followed him were scattered" (Acts 5:36-37).

And if Christ is not risen from the dead, we are wasting our lives and following the wrong leader!

> IF CHRIST IS NOT RISEN FROM THE DEAD, WE ARE WASTING OUR LIVES AND FOLLOWING THE WRONG LEADER!

First Corinthians 15:29 has been interpreted up to 40 different ways.[8] *"Now if there is no resurrection, what will those do who are baptized for the dead? If the dead are not raised at all, why are people baptized for them?"* (1 Cor. 15:29). Some have wondered if the Corinthians thought a believer could be baptized to help someone who had died. But as Dr. Palma notes, this belief is not good theology, and Church history "does not record such a practice in the first century."[9] The Mormons have an unbiblical doctrine about being baptized for the dead. They do a lot of work on family genealogies and teach that a Mormon may be baptized for (on behalf of) a dead family member who was not a member of the Mormon Church. In contrast, the Bible teaches that our only chance for salvation is in this life. The Scriptures never offer anyone a second chance for salvation *after* death. Rather, they teach: *"And as it is appointed unto man once to die, but after this the judgment"* (Heb. 9:27 KJV). Being baptized to help someone who has died is unbiblical, and probably un-Corinthian.

So what does 1 Corinthians 15:29 mean? The easiest way to understand this verse is in the context Paul has already given us. In 1 Corinthians 15, Paul refers to *the dead* as a group at least 15 times. We find many phrases like *if the dead are not raised*, or *if Christ has not been raised* (1 Cor. 15:12-32). Paul emphasizes that if the dead are not raised, Jesus is among the dead. So if Jesus is dead, then all believers who are baptized in the name of Jesus are being baptized for (with reference to) one among the dead. This interpretation makes sense in the context and also in the Greek. For the Greek word translated *for* is *huper*—which can mean "with reference to."[10] So the plainest, easiest way to understand this verse is that if the dead are not raised, we believers are wasting our time being baptized *in reference to* Jesus, who is just another man among the dead. This interpretation obeys the rule of hermeneutics: When the plain sense makes sense, seek no other sense (or meaning).

Q 11 *If Jesus is still dead, are believers today baptized for or on behalf of the dead? Explain.*

Also, this is the favored view of Richard C. H. Lenski and the *Beacon Bible Commentary.* These scholars believe that 1 Corinthians 15:29 refers to the baptism of all believers. They emphasize that our water baptism connects us to the death and resurrection of Christ (Rom. 6:3-5). So if Christ is dead, we are being baptized for the dead, or one among the dead.[11] Paul is using a literary device called metonomy, in which the whole may represent one.[12] In this case, the group of the dead represents or includes Christ, for whom we were baptized. As the Beacon commentators note, this interpretation is in harmony with Paul's theology of redemption *and* the practices of the early church.

> ## Lesson 28: The Resurrection of Believers—Part 2 (1 Cor. 15:20-58)
> **Goal A:** Relate the resurrection of Christ to the firstfruits and the first Adam.
> **Goal B:** Explain how the doctrine of the resurrection affects the daily living of believers.
> **Goal C:** Summarize 5 truths about the resurrection body.

A. Because Christ has been raised, the gospel affects all for good or bad (1 Cor. 15:20-34).

The resurrection of Christ affects everyone.

1. The resurrection of Christ means defeat for His enemies. Because Christ has been raised from the dead, His enemies will be under His feet (1 Cor. 15:25). The resurrection of Christ makes us certain that He will conquer every enemy—Satan, demons, humans who reject Him, and even death.

Q 12 *Why does the Bible refer to death as our enemy?*

The Bible refers to death as an enemy. On the one hand, death is the boundary or door between us and God. For as Paul said, to be absent from the body is to be present with the Lord.

> *⁶Therefore we are always confident and know that as long as we are at home in the body we are away from the Lord. ⁷We live by faith, not by sight. ⁸We are confident, I say, and would prefer to be away from the body and at home with the Lord* (2 Cor. 5:6-8).

> GOD WILL PUT ALL ENEMIES UNDER THE FEET OF CHRIST.

So if death is the last barrier between us and Christ, why does Scripture call death an enemy? Death is our enemy because it represents the opposite of all God is and desires. Death is surrounded by such friends as darkness, sickness, suffering, and crying. In contrast to death and its friends, God is light and life. And He desires for us to have health and happiness. So the Bible sees death as it is—the final enemy that our Lord will conquer. Jesus is reigning now, but God will put all enemies under the feet of Christ. And the last enemy that Christ will destroy is death (1 Cor. 15:25-26).

The apostle John saw a vision of Christ's final judgment over death. For *after* the Second Coming, *after* the Millennium, and *after* the final rebellion of Satan, John saw that *"death and Hades were thrown into the lake of fire"* (Rev. 20:14).

Q 13 *How is Christ's resurrection related to the Feast of the Firstfruits?*

2. The resurrection of Christ means resurrection and reward for His followers. Because Christ has been raised from the dead, His followers will be raised from the dead when He comes. Paul clarifies this truth with two powerful illustrations—the firstfruits and the Adams. Let us look at these two examples.

First, Paul assures us of our resurrection by using the example of the firstfruits.

> *But Christ has indeed been raised from the dead, the firstfruits of those who have fallen asleep* (1 Cor. 15:20).

The Feast of Firstfruits took place when Israel celebrated the barley harvest in the spring. They planted the barley seeds in the fall, and this crop of grain was ready to harvest in the spring. The Jews used wheat and barley to make bread, so these were the most important crops.[13] But before Jews could enjoy the barley crop, God required them to bring him the firstfruits—a ripe sheaf of the grain—as an offering (Lev. 23:10-14). So when the barley crop was ripe, the people brought a ripe sheaf of grain to the temple on the first Sunday after the Passover. The High Priest then waved this sheaf of grain to God. Afterward, because of this firstfruits, the rest of the harvest was acceptable and certain. Through the New Testament, we understand that offering the firstfruits was a prophecy about Jesus. For Jesus died on Thursday, the day Jews killed the Passover lamb (Figure 9.6). And 3 days later, on Sunday morning as the high priest of Jerusalem waved the firstfruits of barley to God, Jesus arose from the tomb, becoming the firstfruits of those who are resurrected from the dead (1 Cor. 15:20). Take time to worship as you meditate on this amazing truth. About 1500 years before the Son of God in heaven became the Son of Man on earth, God told Moses the exact days to celebrate the Feasts of the Passover and the Firstfruits. These feasts pointed to Jesus, who died on the Day of the Passover and arose from the dead on the Day of the Firstfruits! And since He is the firstfruits, His resurrection is the guarantee that all who follow Him as Savior and Lord will one day rise from death as the complete harvest God has planned.[14]

```
           Unleavened Bread
Passover      Firstfruits                              Pentecost
—— + ———————— + ——————————————————————— + ——
Thursday      Sunday                                   Sunday
```

Figure 9.6 Jesus died on the Day of Passover, and arose on the Day of Firstfruits.

Q 14 ↖ *What is the prophetic fulfillment of the Feast of Unleavened Bread?*

Spring Feast	Old Testament Explanation	New Testament Prophetic Fulfillment
1. Passover	Jews killed a lamb on the 14th day of the first month of the Jewish calendar (March/April). Passover celebrated their deliverance from the bondage of Egypt, when the death angel passed over them as he saw the blood of the lamb on their door posts (Exod. 12).	Jesus was crucified on the exact day of the Passover. He was our Passover Lamb (1 Cor. 5:7), sacrificed to free us from the bondage of sin.
2. Unleavened Bread	Jews killed the Passover lamb on the 14th. Then at sunset, which began the new Jewish day (the 15th), they ate the Passover meal. This day also began the 7-day Feast of Unleavened Bread, which celebrated their deliverance from Egypt (Matt. 26:17).[15] Recall that at the first Passover in Egypt, they ate unleavened bread—flat bread without yeast—because they left Egypt in a hurry, and the bread did not have time to rise (Exod. 12:8-20).	Paul teaches that leaven represents sin (1 Cor. 5:8). He exhorts us to celebrate and fulfill this feast as we allow Jesus to remove sin from our daily lives.
3. Firstfruits	This feast was on Sunday, the day after the Sabbath that followed Passover (Lev. 23:11). It celebrated the barley harvest. Jews planted the barley seeds in the fall, and the seeds sprouted and matured in the spring. But before the full harvest, the Jews took a sheaf of barley grain to the priest. He waved it to the Lord as the "firstfruits." Then, the full harvest was acceptable to God and certain to man.	Jesus rose from the dead on Sunday, the exact day of the Feast of Firstfruits.[16] Thus Paul refers to Him as *"the firstfruits of those who have fallen asleep"* (1 Cor. 15:20) and the reason we *"all will be made alive"* or resurrected (1 Cor. 15:22).
4. Pentecost	*Pentecost* means "fiftieth," and this feast was on the 50th day after the Sabbath of Passover week (Lev. 23:15-16; 1 Cor. 16:8). It celebrated the wheat harvest. Pentecost is also called the Feast of Weeks (7 weeks after Passover, Deut. 16:10) and the Feast of Harvest (Exod. 23:16).[17]	At Pentecost, God filled believers with the Holy Spirit, giving them power to witness for Christ, and thus reap the worldwide harvest of people into God's kingdom (Acts 1:8; 2:1-4).

Figure 9.7 The New Testament explains the prophetic fulfillment of four spring feasts of the Old Testament.

Second, Paul assures us of our resurrection by using the illustration of the two Adams.

[21]For since death came through a man, the resurrection of the dead comes also through a man. [22]For as in Adam all die, so in Christ all will be made alive. [23]But each in his own turn: Christ, the firstfruits; then, when he comes, those who belong to him (1 Cor. 15:21-23).

So it is written: "The first man Adam became a living being," the last Adam, a life-giving spirit (1 Cor. 15:45).

First, the bad news. God put Adam in the garden of Eden. He told him he could eat of every tree in the garden, except one—the tree of the knowledge of good and evil. But Adam disobeyed God. And this one act of disobedience opened the door for sin to enter the world. So through Adam, we all face death. This is the bad news.

Q 15 *Contrast the results of the first Adam and the last Adam.*

But the good news is that Jesus died for our sins and arose from the dead. Now, all who trust and obey Him are forgiven, receive new life, and will conquer death and live forever. For death entered the world through the first Adam, but through the last Adam—Jesus Christ—resurrection and life come to *"those who belong to him"* (1 Cor. 15:23). All of the paths of life lead *to* the grave. Only the path through Jesus Christ leads *from* the grave to glory.

Q 16 *What great promise does Romans 8:11 contain?*

3. The gospel of the resurrection of Christ requires His followers to stop sinning (1 Cor. 15:32-34). There is a sugar-coated gospel today that says followers of Jesus are still slaves of sin. This false gospel says that God does not see it when believers sin, because they are covered with the blood of Jesus. In contrast, Paul taught that those who have evil friends and live in sin have lost their senses (1 Cor. 15:34). And earlier in this letter, Paul wrote that some of the Corinthians had died, and others were sick, because they were living in sin (1 Cor. 11:30). And Paul wrote that if we would judge ourselves and turn from sin, God would not judge us (1 Cor. 11:31). Throughout the New Testament, the Scriptures warn that God sees us when we sin and that we must confess our sins and turn away from them.

Q 17 *If we are following Jesus, can we have evil friends and live in sin (1 Cor. 15:34)? Explain.*

³³Do not be misled: "Bad company corrupts good character." ³⁴Come back to your senses as you ought, and stop sinning; for there are some who are ignorant of God—I say this to your shame (1 Cor. 15:33-34).

Q 18 *Does anyone who abides in Christ continue to be a slave of sin? Explain.*

²Beloved, now we are children of God, and it has not appeared as yet what we will be. We know that when He appears, we will be like Him, because we will see Him just as He is. ³And everyone who has this hope fixed on Him purifies himself, just as He is pure. ⁴Everyone who practices sin also practices lawlessness; and sin is lawlessness. ⁵You know that He appeared in order to take away sins; and in Him there is no sin. ⁶No one who abides in Him sins; no one who sins has seen Him or knows Him (1 John 3:2-6).

Q 19 *What must all followers of Jesus do (2 Tim. 2:20-21)? Explain.*

¹⁸Men who have gone astray from the truth saying that the resurrection has already taken place, and they upset the faith of some ¹⁹Nevertheless, the firm foundation of God stands, having this seal, "The Lord knows those who are His," and, "Everyone who names the name of the Lord is to abstain from wickedness (2 Tim. 2:18-19).

Q 20 *Why should a believer refuse to date or be close friends with a sinner?*

We must avoid being close friends with evil people who corrupt good character. A rotten potato will soon ruin the potato next to it. And a sinful person will corrupt his friends. This truth related to the Corinthians who were eating at the wild pagan feasts. There, they ate meat offered to idols and committed sexual sins (1 Cor. 6–10). Paul warned them and us to avoid friendships that corrupt character and cause sinning. Why? Because those who practice sin are not followers of Jesus. We should greet sinners and try to lead them to Christ. But our close friends must be followers of Jesus.

A young woman graduated from a university and was engaged to be married. In this period of time she found Christ as her Savior, and He transformed her life. She had long talks with her fiancé about her new-found joy. He told her he still loved her and still wanted to marry her, but she must understand that he would not change his way of life.

The girl dreamed of winning him to Christ someday. She felt that this young man did not have any other contact with the gospel but through her. None of his friends or family members were Christians. Her new friends at church began to warn her that it would be very difficult to walk in the Christian way and still share life with him. But she was sure that she could win him.

She spoke with a pastor who told her that the Bible warns believers not to enter into a relationship with non-believers. "But, pastor," she protested with tears. "I am responsible for his salvation…he has no one else to help him."

The pastor gently warned her with 1 Corinthians 15:33-34. He said, "This sinful young man may wear you down day by day until you lose fellowship with the Lord. Instead of risking your own soul, it would be wise to realize that God is responsible for his salvation, not you. God can use another means to bring him to the light."

Easter is an important part of our message to everyone. Yet some churches emphasize only half the gospel—the cross. Many people know that Jesus died on the cross. They see Him hanging from the cross on every crucifix of a necklace. People see Jesus on the cross as they enter houses. They see a dead Jesus hanging from mirrors in cars and buses. And they see a dead Jesus nailed to a cross at the front of every Catholic Church in every nation. The death of Jesus is not news to many.

> EASTER IS AN IMPORTANT PART OF OUR MESSAGE TO EVERYONE.

We rejoice in the message of forgiveness through the death of Jesus. We give thanks that God pardons our guilt because of the cross. But so many have only this first half of the gospel. And the second half is Easter. The first half of the gospel says "I am *saved from sin* by Christ's death." The second half says "I am *saved from sinning* by His life." The first half of the gospel declares freedom from the *penalty of sin*. The second half proclaims freedom from the *power of sin*.

There is pardon through the cross. Yet many feel condemned to repeat the cycle of sin, confession, and forgiveness. Dear friends, there is good news—Jesus lives! And because He lives, we can have new life—through the power of the Spirit that overcomes our sinful desires! There is pardon, but there is also power. There is forgiveness, but there is also freedom.

When the Catholic Church preaches only the first half of the gospel, the result in society is a tragedy—for men. Why? Because the gospel we preach defines the roles of men and women. If we emphasize a dead Jesus on the cross, then this becomes the model for men. Men see a weak Jesus, who lacks power. So the Jesus men imitate is weak. Men see Him hanging helpless on the cross. Or they think of Him dead, lying with His head in the lap of His mother. And if a man's model is weak and helpless, so is the man. A man is not above his model.

In contrast to the weak and helpless Jesus, the model for a Catholic woman is Mary, mother of Jesus. She is strong, faithful, true, loving, and caring. She is the one who gives help. Thus the female in Catholic society becomes the strong and faithful one—while the male is weak and pitiful!

Then one day a new message is heard in the land of the *conquistador (Spanish conqueror). Jesus is Risen! Christ is no longer the weak and dying one. He is the Conqueror of death, the Risen One. Now the male has a new model—one who is strong. This new powerful Jesus is not helpless. This new Jesus is not like a slave who hangs his head or shuffles as helpless as a beggar. No! This new Jesus is the One who overcomes the grave. He is the Mighty One who triumphs over every foe of hell. And those who follow this Jesus act like Him. Because Jesus lives, we live also!

So we see the *new man*, filled with resurrection life. He takes his place in the home and in society. He is strong, and filled with the Spirit. He overcomes because Christ lives in his heart by faith!

> WE HAVE A *POWERFUL* MESSAGE. IT CHANGES LIVES; IT CHANGES SOCIETY.

We have a *powerful* message. It changes lives; it changes society. Easter gives hope to all. So let us proclaim both halves of the gospel. Jesus died, and then He arose from the grave. Jesus Christ is alive. He is Risen![18]

B. Paul teaches several truths about the resurrection body (1 Cor. 15:35-58).

Many today, like the Sadducees of yesterday, do not believe in the Resurrection. And others do not think that the resurrection body is important. But our salvation is not complete until God gives us new bodies. And these bodies we receive at the Resurrection are the ones we will live in forever. Our earthly bodies get weaker as we grow older.

1. What is sown differs from what is grown (1 Cor. 15:35-44).[19] Burying a body is like planting a seed. Remember the first time you planted a seed? Perhaps you planted a vegetable, fruit, or flower. As a child, you were amazed at the beautiful plant that grew from the plain seed. As years pass, we may lose the awe and wonder of nature. But Paul reminds us that death is like planting a seed. What is sown differs from what is grown. Figure 9.8 contrasts the *earthly body* one plants at death with the *heavenly body* one reaps at the Resurrection.

Q 21 *Which 2 types of bodies does Paul contrast in 1 Corinthians 15:35-44?*

Q 22 *Complete Figure 9.8 on contrasts of how the resurrection body is sown and raised (1 Cor. 15:42-44).*

1 Cor.	The body is sown	The body is raised
15:42	As perishable	
15:43		
15:43		
15:44		

Figure 9.8   Contrasts on how the resurrection body is sown and how it is raised (1 Cor. 15:42-44)

A plant is more glorious than the seed it grows from. Likewise, our heavenly bodies will be more glorious than the earthly bodies we plant in the grave.

2. As we are like the first Adam, we will be like the Last Adam (1 Cor. 15:45-49). Our salvation is not complete until our bodies are transformed. Jesus died to redeem our bodies as well as our souls (1 Thess. 5:23). On earth, we are like and linked to the first Adam. But at the Resurrection, we will be like and forever with the Last Adam, Jesus Christ.

Q 23 *Complete Figure 9.9 on contrasts of the first and Last Adam (1 Cor. 15:21-22; 45-49).*

1 Cor.	The First Adam	The Last Adam (Christ)
15:21	Brought death to men.	
15:22	All die in him.	
15:45	Became a	
15:46		
15:47		
15:48-49	Is the pattern for those on earth.	

Figure 9.9   Contrasts of the first Adam and the Last Adam (1 Cor. 15:21-49)
[Related Scriptures: Matt. 17:22; Phil. 3:21; 1 John 3:2]

Q 24 *Why do we need new bodies for heaven?*

3. We need new bodies to inherit a new kingdom (1 Cor. 15:50).

I declare to you, brothers, that flesh and blood cannot inherit the kingdom of God, nor does the perishable inherit the imperishable (1 Cor. 15:50).

Imagine trying to live forever in the bodies we have now! As the years go by, our wrinkles increase and our stiffness increases, but our energy, memory, and health decrease. So living forever in the bodies we have now would not be heaven! But God has planned new bodies for us, to match the holiness, happiness, and eternity of heaven. Then, we will never grow old, and we will never be tired! We will live in *spiritual bodies* forever.

4. We will receive new bodies in the twinkling of an eye, at the last trumpet (1 Cor. 15:51-52).

⁵¹*Listen, I tell you a mystery: We will not all sleep, but we will all be changed—* ⁵²*in a flash, in the twinkling of an eye, at the last trumpet. For the trumpet will sound, the dead will be raised imperishable, and we will be changed* (1 Cor. 15:51-52).

Q 25 ↖ *Why do you think God chose a trumpet to announce the return of Christ and our resurrection?*

The twinkling of an eye is a fraction of a second. Note that the trumpet signals a great victory and triumph.[20] At the Rapture, when Jesus returns, believers receive their new bodies and enter into the joys of heaven. Note the words *last trumpet*. These words do not mean that we will never hear another trumpet in heaven. But the trumpet at the Rapture is the last trumpet we will hear on earth *before* Jesus returns.

¹³*But we do not want you to be uninformed, brethren, about those who are asleep, so that you will not grieve as do the rest who have no hope.* ¹⁴*For if we believe that Jesus died and rose again, even so God will bring with Him those who have fallen asleep in Jesus.* ¹⁵*For this we say to you by the word of the Lord, that we who are alive and remain until the coming of the Lord, will not precede those who have fallen asleep.* ¹⁶*For the Lord Himself will descend from heaven with a shout, with the voice of the archangel and with the trumpet of God, and the dead in Christ will rise first.* ¹⁷*Then we who are alive and remain will be caught up together with them in the clouds to meet the Lord in the air, and so we shall always be with the Lord.* ¹⁸*Therefore comfort one another with these words* (1 Thess. 4:13-18).

Q 26 ↖ *Which verse in 1 Thessalonians 4:13-18 bases the resurrection of believers on the resurrection of Jesus?*

Q 27 ↖ *What sounds does 1 Thessalonians 4:16 mention that are not in 1 Corinthians 15:52?*

It is important to live ready to meet Jesus at any moment. For when Christ returns, there will be no time to prepare. The Rapture and the Resurrection will happen in less than a second! Live ready!

5. The resurrection of believers completes Christ's victory over death (1 Cor. 15:53-56).

Paul refers to verses in the Old Testament (Isa. 25:8; Hos. 13:14). The sting of death is sin. And the Law makes sin powerful because it lists the many types of sin. But since Jesus has saved us from our sins, death has lost its sting for us. So in some ways, death is like a bee with no stinger. And at the Resurrection, death will lose its hold on us. *"But thanks be to God! He gives us the victory* [over sin and death of the body] *through our Lord Jesus Christ"* (1 Cor. 15:57).

Q 28 ↖ *How does following Jesus take the sting out of death?*

Figure 9.10 All hell sang and danced at the crucifixion, but LOOK WHAT JESUS DID TO DEATH at the Resurrection!

Christ's victory over death began when He arose from the grave. And His victory over death will be complete when He resurrects every one of His followers. Then our salvation will be complete. Afterward, God will throw death and *Hades* into the lake of fire (Rev. 20:14).

Conclusion

Paul closes this chapter with words of encouragement and exhortation. *"Therefore, my dear brothers, stand firm. Let nothing move you. Always give yourselves fully to the work of the Lord, because you know that your labor in the Lord is not in vain"* (1 Cor. 15:58).

The word *therefore* is very important in Scripture. Paul has spent an entire chapter teaching about the Resurrection. Finally, he comes to the *therefore* (1 Cor. 15:58). This is the apostle's way of saying, "So what?" The word *therefore* is like a bridge that connects 1 Corinthians 15:1-57 to the practical application of 1 Corinthians 15:58. The Resurrection is certain and glorious. Now what?

Q 29 ↖ *What is the significance of "therefore" and the words that follow it (1 Cor. 15:58)?*

The Resurrection inspires and motivates us to action. It gives us assurance to stand firm and keep serving Christ. The resurrection of Christ reminds us that what we do now matters. For the path to glory passes through the grave.²¹ So in spite of the graves and tombstones around us, we live now as people who belong to the future. Our resurrection day is coming. So let us stand firm in the truth and do our part in the work of the Church. Let us live so that we will not regret working too little for Christ. God will reward us for every cup of cold water we give (Matt. 10:38)—every good deed we do in the name of Jesus.

The enemies of Jesus nailed Him to a cross on a hill outside of Jerusalem. And all hell sang and danced as the disciples wrapped the dead body of Jesus in a cloth and sealed it in a tomb. But within 3 days, the people in Jerusalem were not crying, "Look what death did to Jesus." Rather, they were exclaiming, "Look what Jesus did to death!"²² And because He arose, we will arise also. But today, let us be busy for Him.

The Stewardship of Money, Opportunity, and God's Family (1 Cor. 16:1-24)

Lesson 29

Goal A: Summarize 6 ways in which we should be stewards of the wealth God entrusts to us.
Goal B: Explain 2 ways in which we should be stewards of the opportunities God gives us.
Goal C: Analyze the importance of being stewards over relationships in the church.
Goal D: Define "anathema" and "maranatha" in your own words.

Setting

Our theme for this Unit has been worship. In chapters 11–14, Paul dealt with matters of worship in a church service. Chapter 15 reminds us that worship is useless without right doctrine. As Paul said, believers are saved if they hold on to the teaching of the gospel, which includes the Resurrection. So we must relate worship to doctrine. Jesus said that worship is useless unless it is based on the Word of God (Matt. 15:1-9).

Likewise, it is important to remember that worship relates not only to church services, but also to our time outside the church. Worship should be the theme of our entire lives. As Paul said, *"Therefore, I urge you, brethren, by the mercies of God, to present your bodies a living and holy sacrifice, acceptable to God, which is your spiritual service of worship"* (Rom. 12:1).

> WORSHIP IS A *WAY* OF LIFE, NOT JUST AN *INTERSECTION* WITH GOD IN A CHURCH SERVICE.

So we see that worship is a *way* of life, not just an *intersection* with God in a church service. In this final lesson of 1 Corinthians, we relate worship to stewardship in three areas of life: money, opportunity, and the family of God.²³

A. Be a faithful steward of the money God gives you (1 Cor. 16:1-4).

Geographical setting

On his third missionary trip, Paul collected an offering for the poor believers in Jerusalem, in the province of Judea (1 Cor. 16:3). Paul gathered money, mostly from Gentile churches, in three provinces:
- Galatia—cities such as Lystra, Iconium, Derbe, and Pisidian Antioch (1 Cor. 16:1);
- Macedonia—cities such as Philippi, Thessalonica, and Berea (2 Cor. 9:1-4);
- The Achaian church of Corinth (1 Cor. 16:1-4; 2 Cor. 8–9).

Q 30 *How many events and people do these provinces remind you of: Galatia? Asia? Macedonia? Achaia?*

Paul wrote 1 Corinthians while he was at Ephesus, in the province of Asia. Review the map of Figure 9.11. Remind yourself of events and teachings connected to each place. Reviewing biblical places makes learning easier and more fun.

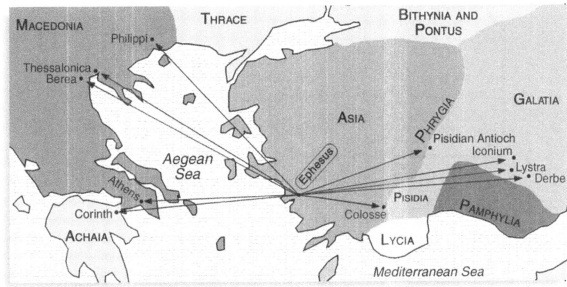

Figure 9.11 Ephesus was a strategic center for missions.

This missionary offering for Jerusalem was for a special purpose. Still, in 1 Corinthians 16 (and later in 2 Corinthians 8–9), we find principles about giving. Needs vary, but principles remain the same. Let us examine six principles on giving.

1. We should give to show compassion (1 Cor. 16:1, 3). Perhaps believers in Jerusalem needed help because of the famine (Acts 11:27-30). Or maybe their poverty was a result of the persecution that began at Stephen's death (Acts 8:1). At that time, believers were scattered. As they slowly returned, no doubt much of their property had been stolen (Compare Heb. 10:34). So Paul collected an offering to help these poor, Jewish believers. The Scriptures teach us that if we have love in our hearts, we must show it by giving to believers in need (Matt. 25:34-46; Gal. 6:10; James 2:14-17; 1 John 3:17-18).

Q 31 What does James 2:14-17 teach about showing compassion?

Q 32 Why do you think the Bible emphasizes this order in sharing: 1) family, 2) believers, 3) unbelievers (1 Tim. 5:8; 1 John 3:17-18; Gal. 6:10)?

Imagine that you lived in Corinth 20 centuries ago. Paul asked you to give in the offering for Jerusalem. At first, you might have refused for four reasons:
- The believers in Jerusalem were total strangers and far away. They were at least a month's journey from Corinth. Why give to people you would never see?
- Most believers in Corinth were Gentiles. But Jerusalem was the center for Jews. And besides, the Jews were slow to welcome Gentiles into the Church. Jesus told Jewish believers to go into all the world and share the gospel. But they did not leave Jerusalem until persecution, at Stephen's death, forced them to leave. And the Council of Acts 15 revealed that some Jews thought Gentiles should live like Jews. Why give to help people of a prejudiced ethnic group?
- There were people in need in Corinth. Why help with needs far from home?
- God knows the needs of everyone. Why should you help when God has power to help all?

Your flesh might have raised all these objections about giving. But as you listened to Paul and the Spirit, in the end, you would have given to help the poor believers in Jerusalem. And the first reason you would have given is for compassion. For as we listen to the Spirit of God within us, He opens our hearts to have mercy on those in need. In 1 Corinthians 16, the first principle on giving is that we should give to show compassion (1 Cor. 16:1, 3).

2. We should give as an act of worship (1 Cor. 16:2).

On the first day of every week, each one of you should set aside a sum of money in keeping with his income, saving it up, so that when I come no collections will have to be made (1 Cor. 16:2).

Q 33 What are the first 2 principles on giving in 1 Corinthians 16?

> THE EARLY CHURCH MET ON SUNDAY TO CELEBRATE THE RESURRECTION OF CHRIST AND THE OUTPOURING OF THE HOLY SPIRIT.

The early church met on Sunday, the first day of the week. The Jewish Sabbath or holy day was Saturday, the last day of the week. But Jesus rose from the dead on the first day of the week (Mark 16:2), and God poured out the Holy Spirit at Pentecost on the first day of the week (Acts 2:1-4; Lev. 23:15-16). So the early church met on Sunday to celebrate the resurrection of Christ and the outpouring of the Holy Spirit.

Paul told the Corinthians to bring an offering each Sunday when they met. Worship and giving must be wed together. For words of worship, without generous giving, are like clouds without water and trees without fruit.

Q 34 *How are those who worship with words only like a person with a sandal on one foot and a boot on the other?*

Worship includes words and wealth. Those who worship with words, but not money, are like the man who wore a sandal on one foot and a boot on the other, or the man who played his guitar in one key, but sung in another key. The great commandment teaches us to worship God with all of our heart (Matt. 22:37-38). Jesus said that treasure and heart are linked together (Matt. 6:21). So worship from the heart must include giving generous offerings.

Figure 9.12 Those who worship with words only are inconsistent and contradict themselves—like a person with a sandal on one foot and a boot on the other. What they claim with their words, they deny with their actions.

The magi worshiping Jesus knew little about God. Because they did not know the Scriptures, they had to ask others where the Messiah would be born (Matt. 2:1-6). Yet even with *little* knowledge, these Wise Men knew to give their best gifts as they worshiped (Matt. 2:11). What we express with our tongues, we should express with our treasure. The hands we raise up in praise must be the same hands that reach down into our pockets to give an offering. A closed hand reveals a closed heart, but an open hand giving a generous offering reveals an open heart!

Q 35 *How does God weigh our offerings? Explain.*

3. We should give in proportion to how God blesses us (1 Cor. 16:2). *"Each one of you should set aside a sum of money in keeping with his income"* (1 Cor. 16:2). The Scriptures do not teach equal giving. Some should give more, others should give less. God measures the size of our offerings not by the amount we give, but by the amount we keep! Jesus said that the poor widow who put in only two copper coins gave more than the rich man who gave gold (Luke 21:1-4). It does not matter how much wealth we have, so long as we give a generous part of it to God. In 1 Corinthians 16, the third principle on giving is that we give in proportion. The more God gives us, the more we share with others.

Q 36 *Where you live, what are some financial commitments people make each month?*

4. We should give in a regular way—such as on the first day of every week (1 Cor. 16:2).

On the first day of every week, each one of you should set aside a sum of money in keeping with his income, saving it up, so that when I come no collections will have to be made (1 Cor. 16:2).

The Bible does not teach us to give *only when we feel like it*. Rather, it teaches us to plan and give in a way that is regular, systematic, and organized. Paul guided believers to give on Sunday, on the first day of every week.

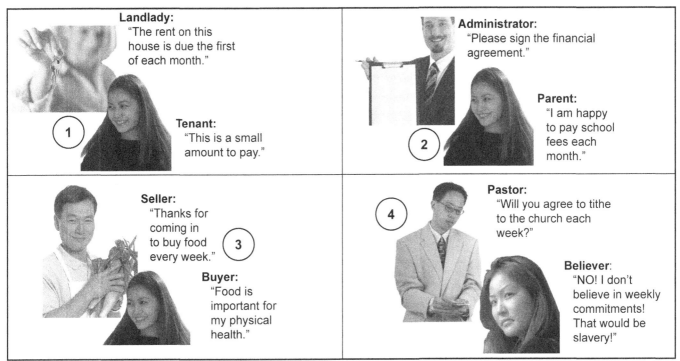

Figure 9.13 Shall we make regular payments for earthly things, but not spiritual things?

5. We should give to build relationships (1 Cor. 16:3). Note that the offering was for Jews, but the people who gave were mostly Gentiles. Paul used this offering to strengthen the relationship between Jews and Gentiles. Earlier, about A.D. 50, the Jewish church in Jerusalem had a big discussion about the relationship between Jews and Gentiles (Acts 15). At that meeting, the Jerusalem church asked Paul to teach Gentiles to remember the poor (Gal. 2:10). Paul agreed. This offering fulfilled Paul's promise. The Gentiles had been blessed spiritually by Jewish believers, such as Paul (Rom. 15:25-27). Now they were saying "Thank you" and "We love you" by giving an offering to Jewish believers in need. This offering wove a cord of love between Jews and Gentiles.

Q 37 *How did the offering from Corinth help build relationships? Explain.*

Pastor Phillip heard that a man died near his church. This man had never attended, so the pastor did not know him well. But the pastor collected a food offering to share with the family. He knew that many relatives and neighbors would come for the funeral, and the family would appreciate the help. When he delivered the food, he expressed his sorrow. Pastor Phillip said, "We did not know this man well, for he never attended our church. Now, all we can do is put him in the hands of our loving heavenly Father. Our church wanted you to know that we care when people hurt. So we brought this offering of food to show our love. Also, it is too late to pray for our brother who has died. But I would like to pray for God to comfort and guide those of you who remain." The family welcomed his prayer of concern. The next Sunday, six new families visited his church. Within a few weeks, he baptized many of them, and they became members of his church![24] Giving is a great way to build relationships with other believers *and* unbelievers.

Q 38 *What are some ways in which you can use money to build relationships, as Pastor Phillip did?*

6. We should give only to ministries that handle money in an open, accountable way (1 Cor. 16:3-4).

When I arrive, I will give letters of introduction to the men you approve and send them with your gift to Jerusalem (1 Cor. 16:3).

Some believers give offerings to ministers or ministries that do not give an account for the money they receive. This is like throwing an offering out the window of a car or bus and hoping it will be used well. In contrast, every minister has a responsibility to show people how funds are spent.

Q 39 *Whom does God hold responsible: those who give money, those who receive it, or both? Explain.*

God expects believers to be wise stewards. Paul did not ask the Corinthians to put their money in his pocket or the pocket of a stranger. Rather, the apostle guided the Corinthians to choose men (two or more) whom they approved. These men would carry the offering to the people who needed it. That is accountability. Paul handled money in a way that gave the givers confidence. He was honest and open in the eyes of all men (2 Cor. 8:21). Givers felt guaranteed then that their money went for the purpose they gave it. When Paul collected offerings, there were no secrets about how the offerings were used.

Q 40 *Do you know people who give to ministries that do not account for funds? Explain.*

Application. Many ministries today collect money but do not tell people how they spend it. In other words, these ministries are not accountable for the funds they receive. Sometimes, the government audits these ministries and puts the leading bandits in prison. But at other times, the leaders and family members of these ministries continue to build bigger houses with the money believers give. Using ministry as a business to get money is not new. Some Bibles record that Jesus rebuked the Pharisees for devouring the houses of widows (Matt. 23:13). Unfortunately, some believers are gullible—easy to deceive—because they have love and zeal without knowledge. So wolves in sheep's clothing steal the wool of God's sheep. Like Eli's sons, Hophni and Phinehas, they keep the offerings for themselves (1 Sam. 2:12-25). God will hold everyone accountable for the offerings they collect in His name. However, he will also judge all believers as stewards. If we want God to say "Well done" for how we handled His money, we must give to ministers who, like Paul, account well for funds they receive. (For more on this topic, see chapter 12 in this book, Lesson 40B.)

B. Be a faithful steward of the opportunities God gives you (1 Cor. 16:5-9).

Q 41 *Why do you think God may choose to guide us one step at a time?*

1. We should walk softly as faith guides us to make plans for ministry (1 Cor. 16:5-7). Notice that the great apostle's plans included the words *perhaps* and *if the Lord permits*. Sometimes we only discover the Lord's will one step at a time. (For more about how Paul changed his plans to minister in Corinth, see the *Faith & Action Series* course *Survey of the New Testament,* chapter 6, Lesson 18, point A. Also, we will discuss Paul's travels to Corinth when we come to 2 Corinthians 1:12-23.)

Figure 9.14 Jonathan went forward with a *perhaps* to see if the Lord would help Him.

When Jonathan attacked the Philistines, he went forward on a *perhaps* (1 Sam. 14:6). He had not heard a clear word that the Lord would help him. However, he had a great desire to do all he could. So with a strong faith in God, he felt an urge to take a bold step. God honored the desire of his heart and enabled him to win a battle. Likewise, as we desire to please God, depend on Him, and dare to take steps of faith, He will help us.

2. We should be faithful with great opportunities in spite of great opposition (1 Cor. 16:8-9).

⁸But I will stay on at Ephesus until Pentecost, ⁹because a great door for effective work has opened to me, and there are many who oppose me (1 Cor. 16:8-9).

Q 42 *Should believers expect open doors without enemies to conquer? Explain.*

Some see open doors, but expect no enemies. Others see enemies, and then fear to walk through open doors nearby. But the wise recognize that open doors come with open opposition.

Once, Paul had wanted to go to Ephesus in the province then called Asia. But the door was closed. For at that time, the Spirit forbade them to go to Asia (Acts 16:6). Later, when the timing was right, God led Paul to Ephesus, the queen city of Asia. The door to Ephesus opened for Paul to preach the gospel. But inside the door, Paul met

Doctrine and Worship 191

many enemies, like demons, paganism, the occult, and Demetrius and those who sold silver idols. Yet these challenges did not discourage Paul, for the Holy Spirit had told him that in every city he would face prison and difficulties (Acts 20:23). He knew that with open doors, there were mountains to climb, rivers to cross, robbers to survive, beatings to endure, tents to sew, and many sleepless nights. Paul understood the words "No pain, no gain."

A harvest of wheat does not come easily. Before the harvest, someone must clear the field of trees, stumps, bushes, thorns, weeds, and stones. Then someone must plow and plant the field. Finally, even reaping the crop requires a lot of sweat. Likewise, a spiritual harvest does not come easily. Success always comes at a high price. But God gives us the grace to face and overcome the problems that come with open doors.

God gave Nehemiah an open door to rebuild the walls of Jerusalem. He had the favor of God and the favor of King Artaxerxes. Still, he faced many foes. The journey from Persia (Iran) to Israel was long and dangerous. And God did not carry the people. They either had to walk or ride animals for 4 months—a distance of more than 1400 kilometers (900 miles). And when they arrived, many enemies were waiting inside the open door. There were social enemies—those who abused the poor. There were economic challenges—most of the Jews were poor. There were political enemies like Sanballat and Tobiah. So Nehemiah and *"each wore his sword girded at his side as he built"* (Neh. 4:18). But they completed the wall (Neh. 6:15)! Open doors come with open resistance. But God gives the grace for success.

Q 43 *What forms of opposition do pastors and other believers face today where you live?*

C. Be a faithful steward of the friends and family members God gives you (1 Cor. 16:10-20).

In this lesson, we have studied about being faithful stewards of money and opportunities. But these are useless without friends. The most important thing in life is relationships with people. As faith is the substance of the things we hope for, relationships are the building blocks of the things we dream of.

Q 44 *What are some keys to making and keeping friends?*

The apostle Paul not only won souls, he made friends! Friends in the family of God are our greatest wealth. As the proverb says, ***Make new friends, and keep the old; one is silver, and the other is gold.*** Figure 9.15 lists the friends Paul mentions in 1 Corinthians 16. Look over the list of these people and Paul's kind words about them.

Q 45 *How many friends does Paul mention in Romans 16?*

People	Kind words from Paul about them	1 Cor. 16
1. Brother Timothy	¹⁰*...See to it that he has nothing to fear while he is with you, for he is carrying on the work of the Lord, just as I am.* ¹¹*No one, then, should refuse to accept him. Send him on his way in peace so that he may return to me.*	16:10-11
2. Brother Apollos	*I strongly urged him to go to you with the brothers. He was quite unwilling to go now, but he will go when he has the opportunity.* (Recall that some preferred Paul and others Apollos, 1 Corinthians 1:12. Paul wanted them to know that he encouraged Apollos to visit them.)	16:12
3. Brothers and sisters at Corinth	¹³*Be on your guard; stand firm in the faith; be men of courage; be strong.* ¹⁴*Do everything in love.* (Note that men must use their strength with love, so that as leaders, they are not like dictators! With spiritual gifts, and with others, love is always the path.)	16:13-14
4. The household of Stephanas	[They] *were the first converts in Achaia, and they have devoted themselves to the service of the saints. I urge you, brothers, to submit to such as these.*	16:15-16
5. Brothers: Stephanas, Fortunatas, and Achaicus	¹⁷*I was glad when* [they] *arrived, because they have supplied what was lacking from you.* ¹⁸*For they refreshed my spirit and yours also.*	16:17-18
6. Brothers and sisters in the churches of Asia	[They] *send you greetings.*	16:19

Continued on next page

7. Aquila and Priscilla, and the church that meets in their house	[They] *greet you warmly.* (This was a great husband and wife team. Priscilla is often mentioned first, and seems to be the stronger leader of the two. They moved from Corinth to Ephesus to Rome, always helping in the ministry. There is a great need in the church for husbands and wives who serve together like this team!)	16:19
8. All the brothers here (in Ephesus)	[They] *send you greetings.*	16:20

Figure 9.15 Brothers and sisters Paul mentions in the family of God (1 Cor. 16)

D. Conclusion (1 Cor. 16:21-24)

²¹I, Paul, write this greeting in my own hand. ²²If anyone does not love the Lord—a curse be on him [anathema]. *Come, O Lord!* [maranatha] *²³The grace of the Lord Jesus be with you. ²⁴My love to all of you in Christ Jesus. Amen* (1 Cor. 16:21-24).

Three words stand out in these verses. (The NIV omits *Anathema* and *Maranatha*, because it translates them.)

- ***Anathema*** is a Greek word that means "cursed." Paul used this word earlier, saying that no one, by the Spirit, can say that Jesus is cursed (1 Cor. 12:3). Paul is not putting a curse on a personal enemy. Elsewhere Paul wrote, *"Bless those who persecute you; bless and do not curse"* (Rom. 12:14). Rather, he is saying, "May the curse or wrath of God be on anyone who does not love the Lord" (Compare John 3:18; Rom. 1:18; Eph. 2:1-3; 5:3-7).

- ***Maranatha*** is an Aramaic word that means "Come, our Lord." This was a common prayer of the early church for the Second Coming of Christ. It reminds us of the prayer that closes Revelation, *"Come, Lord Jesus"* (Rev. 22:20). Every believer should live ready to meet Jesus, abounding in the work of the Lord, and praying, Maranatha—"Come, our Lord."

- **Love.** Paul has been stern with the Corinthians in this letter. Review the outline of this book to recall the hard problems and questions about which he wrote. But he reminds all of the believers of his love for them in Jesus Christ (1 Cor. 16:24).

Q 46 Did Paul put a curse on unbelievers? Explain.

Q 47 What prayer does *maranatha* summarize?

Q 48 Does it seem unusual to you that Paul unites rebuke, strong teaching, and love? Explain and apply.

Doctrine and Worship

 Test Yourself: Circle the letter by the *best* completion to each question or statement.

1. Why must we believe in the Resurrection?
a) The Resurrection encourages us to persevere.
b) The Church has always taught the Resurrection.
c) Only weak believers doubt the Resurrection.
d) To reject the Resurrection is to reject salvation.

2. What assures us of the resurrection of Christ?
a) Jonah was in the whale 3 days and nights.
b) The Pharisees paid the soldiers to lie.
c) Many witnesses saw the risen Christ.
d) Many Old Testament saints arose with Christ.

3. If there is no resurrection from the dead, then
a) being a Christian is still the best path to walk.
b) we are baptized in the name of a dead man.
c) we can still look forward to heaven.
d) one religion is as good as another.

4. Which Old Testament feast pointed to the Resurrection?
a) Passover
b) Unleavened Bread
c) Firstfruits
d) Pentecost

5. In 1 Corinthians 15, faith in the Resurrection
a) requires us to stop sinning.
b) unites us to those before and after us.
c) inspires us to give generously.
d) prevents us from turning back.

6. What completes Christ's victory over death?
a) Christ's resurrection from the grave
b) Christ's death, resurrection, and ascension
c) The resurrection of believers
d) The final judgment of Satan

7. What does 1 Corinthians 16 teach about giving?
a) Equal giving, equal sacrifice
b) What you sow is what you grow.
c) Give as a seed you sow, not a debt you owe.
d) Give in proportion to your income.

8. A balanced view about opportunities is:
a) Open doors come with many enemies.
b) When God opens doors, enemies scatter.
c) Open doors depend on open minds.
d) The doors God opens stay open forever.

9. "One is silver and the other gold" refers to
a) minerals of earth.
b) spiritual parables.
c) friends that endure.
d) wealth that vanishes.

10. What thought does *maranatha* express?
a) A curse on the Lord's enemies
b) A prayer for the Lord's return
c) A declaration of the Lord's faithfulness
d) A question about the Lord's justice

Essay Test Topics: Write 50–100 words on each of these goals that you studied in this chapter.

The Resurrection of Believers—Part 1 (1 Cor. 15:1-19, 29-32)

Goal: *Explain why we must believe in the resurrection of Christ.*

Goal: *Analyze why the gospel is bad news if Christ was not raised from the dead.*

The Resurrection of Believers—Part 2 (1 Cor. 15:20-58)

Goal: *Relate the resurrection of Christ to the firstfruits and the first Adam.*

Goal: *Explain how the doctrine of the Resurrection affects the daily living of believers.*

Goal: *Summarize 5 truths about the resurrection body.*

The Stewardship of Money, Opportunity, and God's Family (1 Cor. 16:1-24)

Goal: *Summarize 6 ways in which we should be stewards of the wealth God entrusts to us.*

Goal: *Explain 2 ways in which we should be stewards of the opportunities God gives us.*

Goal: *Analyze the importance of being stewards over relationships in the church.*

Goal: *Define "anathema" and "maranatha" in your own words.*

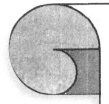

Unit 3: Paul's Apostolic Ministry (2 Cor. 1–13)

In a recent meeting, a leader asked a group of believers this question: "Do apostles walk at the front of the line, or the back? With one voice the group replied, "The front!" This confused thinking explains why the number of false apostles is growing today. Many want to be apostles because they think this means more money, more privileges, and more respect. But those who study 2 Corinthians discover that being an apostle, which is by God's choice, not man's, means less money, fewer privileges, less respect—and more beatings, more enemies, and more sacrifice. In most of 2 Corinthians, the apostle Paul is defending himself against the crowd of critics who attacked his character and ministry.

In Chapter 10 Paul reviews his recent past (2 Cor. 1:1–2:13). You will learn to:
- *Analyze the background, setting, and three-point outline of 2 Corinthians.*
- *Analyze the problem of tight places and identify six sources of comfort in difficult times.*
- *Explain how Paul's visit to Corinth differed from his earlier plans (2 Cor. 1:15-16).*
- *Identify six principles on relationships, in the context of Paul's change of plans.*

In Chapter 11 Paul defends his apostolic ministry (2 Cor. 2:12–7:16). In this chapter we will guide you to:
- *Explain and illustrate a principle for each of these: the open door, the victory march, and the open letter.*
- *Summarize a principle for each of these: a pointing finger, a helping hand, a veil, and the moon.*
- *From 2 Corinthians 4, explain and illustrate five reasons why we do not lose heart.*
- *Analyze and apply seven truths that prepare us for death (2 Cor. 5:1-10).*
- *State and apply five test questions of a faithful ministry.*
- *Analyze the foundation stones, pressures, powers, and paradoxes of ministry (2 Cor. 6:1-13).*
- *Analyze the commands, contrasts, promises, and invitation to holiness (2 Cor. 6:14–7:1).*
- *Explain and illustrate five principles for helping others repent (2 Cor. 7:2-7).*
- *Explain and illustrate four principles for helping self and others repent (2 Cor. 7:8-16).*

In Chapter 12 Paul teaches principles of giving (2 Cor. 8–9). You will learn to:
- *State a principle on giving for each of these: gold medal, faith, queen bee, grace, love, widow's mite.*
- *Explain and Ilustrate each of the six principles you stated in the previous goal.*
- *State a principle on giving related to each of these: equality, accountability, enthusiasm, harvest, and praise.*
- *Explain and illustrate each of the five principles you stated in the previous goal.*

In Chapter 13 Paul confronts his critics (2 Cor. 10:1–13:14). As you complete this final chapter, you will be able to:
- *Summarize and illustrate three reasons why bad thoughts are worse than most people think.*
- *State and illustrate five principles for overcoming evil thoughts.*
- *Contrast the two roads and destinies before each person in regard to his thoughts.*
- *Explain four characteristics of humility in the context of Paul and his critics.*
- *Contrast the characteristics of bad and good jealousy (2 Cor. 11:1-2).*
- *Contrast the tactics of Satan as a lion and as a serpent (2 Cor. 11:3-6, 13-15).*
- *Contrast Paul and false apostles on the topic of money (2 Cor. 11:7-12).*
- *Explain and apply five principles about spiritual experiences (2 Cor. 11:16–12:10).*
- *State and illustrate six concerns of a leader for spiritual children.*

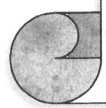

Chapter 10:
Paul Reviews His Recent Past
2 Corinthians 1:1–2:11

Introduction

A man in the Navy wanted to be the commander of a big ship. Finally, he succeeded and became the Captain of the newest, biggest, most powerful ship. One night in a storm, he was guiding the ship forward at a fast speed. In the darkness, he saw a strange light. As the light became closer, the Captain thought it was another ship about to smash into him. At sea, people use lights to send messages. So the captain sent a message: "Change the direction you are traveling by steering to the south. At once, a message came back, "No, you change your direction by steering to the north." The proud Captain did not want to submit to anyone. At once he answered, " Steer to the south. I am the Captain!" The response was, "Steer to the north. I am the man who works here at night." Full of anger, the Captain replied, "Steer to the south. I am on a big ship!" The reply was, "Steer to the north. I am a lighthouse—a building on the land!"

All of us must be flexible with our plans—we must allow the Holy Spirit to guide us. This principle is why Paul changed his plans about visiting Corinth (See Lesson 31). Likewise, in our relationships, we must practice being sensitive to God's Spirit.

Figure 10.1 The captain of a ship at sea learned the value of being flexible, and he changed his plans.

Lessons:

Comfort in Tight Places (2 Cor. 1:1-11)
Goal A: *Analyze the background, setting, and three-point outline of 2 Corinthians.*
Goal B: *Analyze the problem of tight places and identify 6 sources of comfort in difficult times.*

Guidelines for Relationships (2 Cor. 1:12–2:11)
Goal A: *Explain how Paul's visit to Corinth differed from his earlier plans (2 Cor. 1:15-16).*
Goal B: *Identify 6 principles on relationships, in the context of Paul's change of plans.*

Lesson 30 Comfort in Tight Places (2 Cor. 1:1-11)

Goal A: Analyze the background, setting, and three-point outline of 2 Corinthians.
Goal B: Analyze the problem of tight places and identify 6 sources of comfort in difficult times.

Background: First and Second Corinthians (Note: For a full review of Second Corinthians and explanations on the outline, see the *Faith & Action* course *Survey of the New Testament,* chapter 6.)

Paul traveled to Corinth at least three times and wrote several letters to the church in Corinth.[1] And we know that the Corinthians wrote at least one letter to Paul (1 Cor. 7:1).

Q 1 Where was Paul when he wrote 2 Corinthians?

Date (A.D.)	Background and Settings of First and Second Corinthians	Scriptures
52	**Beginning.** Paul was the spiritual father of the Corinthians. He planted the church there on his second missionary trip. Paul ministered in Corinth for 18 months with Priscilla and Aquila. They had fled from Rome when the emperor Claudius persecuted Jews. In Corinth, some Jews accused Paul, but Gallio threw his case out of the Roman court.	1 Cor. 4:15 Acts 18:1-17
Spring 55-56	**1 Corinthians.** Paul traveled from Antioch, Syria, to Ephesus on his third missionary trip. He ministered in Ephesus for 3 years. During this time, he wrote 1 Corinthians. Timothy carried the letter to the church.[2]	Acts 18:23– 21:26; 1 Cor. 16:5-8
Fall 55-56	**2 Corinthians.** Paul traveled from Ephesus up to Troas after the Feast of Pentecost. Titus had agreed to meet him there, but was late with the report on Corinth.[3] So Paul continued from Troas to Macedonia on his third missionary trip. There he met Titus, then wrote 2 Corinthians. Afterward, Paul went to see the Corinthians for the third time.	2 Cor. 2:13; 7:5-7; 12:14; 13:1

Figure 10.2   Dates and events related to 1 and 2 Corinthians

Paul ministered for 3 years in Ephesus on his third missionary trip. From there, he sent the letter we call 1 Corinthians (Figure 10.2). This was not the first letter he ever sent the Corinthians.[4] First Corinthians 5:9 refers to an earlier letter. Paul may have sent many letters that we do not have.[5] Our Bibles contain two letters to the Corinthians. We call them First and Second Corinthians based on the order in which they appear in the Bible. Our concern is for the letters God has given us, and not for letters we do not have. Our responsibility is always for what we have been given.

Outline

Q 2 What are the 3 main parts of the outline of 2 Corinthians?

Q 3 About how far is it from Ephesus to Philippi in Macedonia?

Theme	2 Corinthians
A. Ephesus to Macedonia: Paul Defends His Apostolic Ministry	**1–7**
Greeting	1:1-2
Thanks for God's comfort	1:3-11
The reason Paul changed his travel plans	1:12–2:4
Forgive the disciplined believer.	2:5-11
Ministers of the new covenant	2:12–3:6
The glory of the new covenant	3:7-18
Treasures in clay jars	4
Our heavenly dwelling	5:1-10
The ministry of reconciling the lost	5:11–6:10
A spiritual father's appeal to his children	6:11–7:4
The meeting with Titus	7:5-16

Continued on next page

Theme	2 Corinthians
B. Macedonia's Example: The Collection for Poor Believers in Jerusalem	8–9
Paul encourages being generous.	8:1-15
Titus and others will care for the offering.	8:16–9:5
The results of sowing generously	9:6-15
C. Macedonia to Corinth: Paul Contrasts Himself With False Apostles	10–13:10
Paul defends his authority and mission.	10
Paul is forced into foolish boasting to defend his apostleship.	11–12
Final warnings	13:1-10
Conclusion	13:11-14

Continued from previous page

Figure 10.3   Outline of 2 Corinthians

A. The Problem: All of God's children must endure *tight places* in this life.

A key Greek word in this lesson is *thlipsis* (pronounced thlip´sis), which means "troubles, distress, or pressures." Look at the four times a form of *thlipsis* occurs in 2 Corinthians 1:3-11:

- (2 Cor. 1:4) *"who comforts us in all our **troubles**,..."*
- (2 Cor. 1:4) *"...so that we can comfort those in any **trouble**..."*
- (2 Cor. 1:6) *"If we are **distressed**, it is for your comfort..."*
- (2 Cor. 1:8) *"We were under great **pressure**,..."*

The Greek verb *thlibo* and the noun *thlipsis* always describe pressure on a person. As the crowds *pressed* against Jesus (Mark 3:9), troubles often *press* against us. Paul wrote about *tight places* where trouble *pressed* him *"on every side"* (2 Cor. 4:8; 7:5). The *thlipsis* (pressures) of life, cause some young believers to fall away from Christ (Matt. 13:21). As people press against others on a crowded bus, the trials and troubles of life often press against us.

> THERE IS A FALSE TEACHING TODAY THAT SAYS CHRISTIANS SHOULD NOT HAVE TROUBLES.

There is a false teaching today that says Christians should not have troubles. This false doctrine boldly declares that those with faith are free from trials. Others, like the confused friends of Job, think that trouble only visits those who live in sin. We all wish these false teaching were true! But sin is not the cause of every problem (John 9:1-3). And faith does not exempt or deliver us from rust, dust, flies, or taller troubles. Jesus warned His followers, *"In the world you have tribulation"* (John 16:33). Victory in Jesus is sure, but trouble is also certain.

> ³*Praise be to the God and Father of our Lord Jesus Christ, the Father of compassion and the God of all comfort,* ⁴*who comforts us in all our troubles, so that we can comfort those in any trouble with the comfort we ourselves have received from God.* ⁵*For just as the sufferings of Christ flow over into our lives, so also through Christ our comfort overflows.* ⁶*If we are distressed, it is for your comfort and salvation; if we are comforted, it is for your comfort, which produces in you patient endurance of the same sufferings we suffer.* ⁷*And our hope for you is firm, because we know that just as you share in our sufferings, so also you share in our comfort.*

Q 4 What is the title of the lesson on 1 Corinthians 1:1-11?

Q 5 What are some meanings of the Greek word "thlipsis"? Give examples.

Q 6 Do troubles, trials, and pressures come only to the unspiritual? Explain.

Q 7 In 2 Corinthians 1:3-11, underline the 13 words or phrases that refer to trouble or suffering.

⁸*We do not want you to be uninformed, brothers, about the hardships we suffered in the province of Asia. We were under great pressure, far beyond our ability to endure, so that we despaired even of life. ⁹Indeed, in our hearts we felt the sentence of death. But this happened that we might not rely on ourselves but on God, who raises the dead. ¹⁰He has delivered us from such a deadly peril, and he will deliver us. On him we have set our hope that he will continue to deliver us, ¹¹as you help us by your prayers. Then many will give thanks on our behalf for the gracious favor granted us in answer to the prayers of many* (2 Cor. 1:3-11).

It would take too much time to give all the biblical examples of God's people who faced trouble. But for a quick review, read Hebrews 11. It lists many who were pressed by trials and overcame by faith. Likewise books like James and 1 and 2 Peter were written to believers who were squeezed, pushed, and pressed by trials. Many of these believers lost their homes and possessions. And the book of Revelation reveals a multitude that lost their lives in great *thlipsis* (Rev. 1:9; 2:9-10, 22; 7:14).

There are two forms of *thlipsis*: outer and inner. Paul had both kinds of troubles. *Inner* trouble came to him through the Corinthians themselves. They were proud and fleshly—resisting Paul's spiritual authority. Paul made a painful visit to them (2 Cor. 2:1; 12:14; 13:2). Later, he wrote a severe letter to the Corinthian church (2 Cor. 2:3, 4, 9; 7:8, 12). The visit and the letter brought inner pain and pressure to both Paul and the Corinthians. Often, people we love the most cause us the most heartache. Those Jesus loved caused Him so much inner pressure that His soul was overwhelmed with sorrow to the point of death, and His sweat became like drops of blood (Matt. 26:38; Luke 22:44).

Outer and *inner* trouble came to Paul in Asia. God's apostle does not tell us the specific kind of trouble he had or the specific place. Earlier, Paul told the Corinthians that he fought with wild beasts in Ephesus (1 Cor. 15:32). Since this was in Asia, Paul may be referring to that. Whether these beasts were animals or humans, we know that Paul's enemies were as fierce as wild beasts.⁶ Read 2 Corinthians 1:8 again, then answer Questions 9 and 10.

B. The Solution: 2 Corinthians 1:1-11 reveals six sources of comfort in our tight places.

Comfort #1: For tight places, God gives us Scripture through the apostles (2 Cor. 1:1-2).

¹*Paul, an apostle of Christ Jesus by the will of God, and Timothy our brother, To the church of God in Corinth, together with all the saints throughout Achaia: ²Grace and peace to you from God our Father and the Lord Jesus Christ* (2 Cor. 1:1-2).

Paul was an apostle, chosen and sent by Jesus Christ. It was God's will for Paul to be an apostle to bless all believers, in all places, at all times. The Holy Spirit guided Paul to write God's thoughts to help us.

The name *Paul* (*Paulos*) means "little one" in Greek. Tradition of the second century describes Paul as a small man, bald, with eyebrows that met, a hooked nose, and bandy legs (with knees that could not touch)—but full of grace.⁷ One ancient writer called Paul *a three-cubit man.* Like John Wesley and Napoleon, he was probably short—perhaps 5 feet tall or less.⁸ Paul himself was small and weak. In contrast, the words he wrote in our Bibles are powerful, because they are words from God Almighty. As humans, we have no insight or help for ourselves or others without the revelation and authority of God. So God has given us the Scriptures, a light in our darkness. In this world, we all face troubles—trials, pressures, and tight places. But in *every* situation, we have the Word of

Q 8 *In 2 Corinthians 1:3-11, what are 2 types of thlipsis?*

Q 9 *The pressure on Paul was so heavy that he thought he would _____.*

Q 10 *In your troubles, have you ever felt near death's door? Explain.*

Q 11 *Is Achaia a city or a province? Find it on the map.*

Q 12 *Contrast Paul and the Scriptures he wrote.*

Q 13 *What are some of your favorite Scriptures for comfort?*

God to comfort, encourage, and guide us. Figure 10.4 matches some Scriptures with the *tight places* we all face.[9]

Tight Place	Read
In sorrow or sadness	Psalm 34; John 14
Men fail you	Psalm 27; 2 Tim. 4:16-17
You have sinned	Psalm 51; 1 John 1:5-10
You worry	Matthew 6:19-34
You are in danger	Psalm 91
God seems far away	Psalm 139; Job 19:25-27 (For a DVD on Job, go to http://www.youtube.com/watch?v=ATBLXyJxyTI)
You are discouraged	Isaiah 40
You are lonely or fearful	Psalm 23; Matt. 28: 20; Hebrews 13:5
You feel down and out	Romans 8:39
You want courage for your task	Joshua 1
The world seems bigger than God	Psalm 90
You want rest and peace	Matthew 11:25-30
You leave home for labor or travel	Psalm 121; 107:23-31
You become bitter or critical	1 Corinthians 13

Figure 10.4 The Scriptures are a major source of comfort for believers in tight places.

In our tight places, the Word of God is a major source of comfort. Read the Scriptures, meditate on them, pray them, sing them, and worship as others sing them. The Word of God will inspire your faith to victory in Jesus Christ—in any situation.

Comfort #2: In tight places, God delights to encourage us (2 Cor. 1:3-11).

³*Praise be to the God and Father of our Lord Jesus Christ, the Father of compassion and the God of all comfort,* ⁴*who comforts in all our troubles...* (2 Cor 1:3-4a).

Q 14 *What are some sources of our trials?*

Hard times can twist and warp our attitudes about God. Trials pressed Job on every side, threatening to crush him. At first, Job kept a good attitude. But as the weight of the trials continued to press down on Job's shoulders, he became angry with God. A problem with Job's theology was that there was no devil in it. So Job blamed God, rather than Satan, for every trouble. Likewise, many believers today blame God instead of Satan, demons, evil people, their own mistakes, and the results of sin in our world.

Paul and other biblical writers remind us that Satan is totally evil, but God is completely good. Like a thief, the devil comes *"only to steal and kill and destroy"* (John 10:10). In contrast,

Every good thing given and every perfect gift is from above, coming down from the Father of lights, with whom there is no variation or shifting shadow (James 1:17).

Q 15 *What are 3 reasons why we should always praise God?*

From the beginning, the devil has exalted himself, and defamed God—attacking His reputation. But as one preacher said, God is a good God, and the devil is a bad devil! With Paul, let us always <u>praise</u> God for at least three reasons:

- **He is the Father of our Lord Jesus Christ (2 Cor. 1:4).** The proverb "like father, like son" emphasizes that a father and son are often alike. This is true of the Father and Son in heaven. When trouble comes, let us praise our heavenly Father! He is the Father of our Lord and Savior, Jesus Christ. Every good thing we can say about Jesus we can say about His Father! They are one—completely alike in their attitudes, values, and natures. As Jesus said: *"Anyone who has seen me has seen the Father"* (John 14:9).

- **He is the Father of compassion (2 Cor. 1:4).** ¹³*"Just as a father has compassion on his children, So the LORD has compassion on those who fear Him.* ¹⁴*For He Himself knows our frame; He is mindful that we are but dust"* (Ps. 103:13-14).
- **He is the God of all comfort (2 Cor. 1:4).** As *all* evil is linked to the devil, our heavenly Father is the God of *all* comfort. Earlier, you underlined the 13 words and phrases that refer to trouble in 2 Corinthians 1:3-11. In contrast, a form of the word *comfort* appears *10 times* in 2 Corinthians 1:3-7 (in many Bibles).

Q 16 Circle each form of the word "comfort" in 2 Corinthians 1:3-7.

God comforts us in many ways. We have already noted that He comforts us through the Scriptures—like the letters the apostle Paul wrote. And God may comfort us through family members, friends, the prayers of other believers, or even the ministry of angels (Acts 27:23-24). But since *all* comfort is from God, and God works on earth through His Spirit, we should recognize that *any comfort* is through the ministry of the Holy Spirit, the Comforter.

The Greek noun for comfort is *paraklesis,* and the Greek verb is *parakaleo. Para* means "beside," and *kaleo* means "to call." In John 14:16, Jesus promised to send the Comforter (*Paraklete*), the One called to be beside us and in us (John 14:17). Here are some examples of how God comforts and encourages us through the Holy Spirit:

Q 17 What are some ways in which God comforts us by the Spirit?

- He gives us **grace** to endure trials that are beyond our human strength and ability (2 Cor. 1:8; 11:16–12:10).
- He provides **spiritual gifts** such as prophecy that encourages (1 Cor. 14:3); healings, miracles, and other acts of deliverance; and insights and words of knowledge or wisdom that encourage us.
- He **reminds** us of Scriptures, causing us to remember the promises of God (John 14:26).
- He gives us **songs** to sing in the night, even when we are beaten and bleeding (Acts 16:22-25).
- He gives **inner assurance** that we are God's children (Rom. 8:17), inner confidence, and peace that passes all understanding (Phil. 4:7).
- He blesses us with **prayer** through other believers (2 Cor. 1:11) and through the Spirit Himself (Rom. 8:26-27).
- He gives **prayer in tongues** so that we often, like Paul, build ourselves up in our most holy faith (1 Cor. 14:4, 18; Jude 20).
- We experience **God's presence.** Jesus did not come to explain suffering. Nor did He come to deliver us from suffering in this world. But He has promised that He will always be with us in our suffering (Matt. 28:20; 2 Tim. 4:17; Heb. 13:5; Ps. 23). The greatest sorrow for humans is to be separated from God's presence (Gen. 4:14-16; 2 Thess. 1:9). The worst thing about hell is not being in the fire or near the devil, but being away from God forever. In contrast, the most valuable, encouraging, comforting experience is being close to God. In God's presence is fullness of joy (Ps. 16:11; 1 Thess. 3:9). So we daily pray with Moses, *"If your Presence does not go with us, do not send us up from here"* (Exod. 33:15). As the song says, " In the presence of Jehovah, God Almighty, Prince of Peace; Troubles vanish, hearts are mended, in the presence of the King." Being in the presence of God is our greatest need and our greatest privilege.

In many ways, through the Holy Spirit's ministry to us and in us, God comforts, encourages, and strengthens us in our inner being (Eph. 3:16). The suffering of Christ overflows in our lives, but so does His comfort (2 Cor. 1:5).

Comfort #3: In tight places, God equips us to comfort others (2 Cor. 1:4).

³*Praise be to the God and Father of our Lord Jesus Christ, the Father of compassion and the God of all comfort,* ⁴*who comforts us in all our troubles,*

so that we can comfort those in any trouble with the comfort we ourselves have received from God (2 Cor. 1:3-4).

Q 18 *How does 2 Corinthians 1:4 comfort us?*

Our ministry is born in our tight places. We can only give what we receive. We can only pass on the insight and comfort God passes to us. David wrote many of the Psalms based on his own experiences in tight places. But Solomon wrote no psalms of comfort, because he spent his life living in a palace! *"Blessed are those who mourn, for they will be comforted"* (Matt. 5:4). And blessed are those who mourn, for the comfort they receive enables them to comfort others.

What comfort has God given you in hard times? Did He forgive you when you cried out in repentance? Did He lift your eyes at the grave of a loved one? Did He sustain you in a time of low finances? Did He cheer your heart in a time of sickness? Did He send a friend in a time of loneliness? Was His presence precious in the lowest valley? What comfort have you received from God? This is the comfort you can pass on to others.

Comfort #4: In tight places, God's comfort is in direct proportion to our suffering (2 Cor. 1:5).

Q 19 *What principle does Figure 10.5 illustrate? Give an example.*

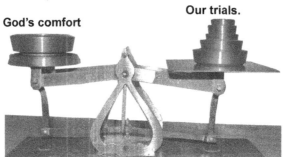

For just as the sufferings of Christ flow over into our lives, so also through Christ our comfort overflows (2 Cor. 1:5).

Figure 10.5   God's comfort is in direct proportion to our trials.

This verse reveals *a blessed proportion.*[10] God has a pair of scales. On one side He puts our trials, and on the other side, our comfort. When the side of the scales with trials is almost empty, the side with comfort is nearly empty. But when the side with trials is almost full, the side with comfort is just as heavy. When the black clouds gather the most, the light of His presence is the brightest. When the storm is the greatest, His presence is the closest.

> TROUBLES MAKE ROOM FOR GOD.

Troubles make room for God. The shovel of trouble digs the hole for God to fill with comfort. When the barn is very full, we feel less need for God. When our strength is the greatest, His strength in us is the least. For His *"power is made perfect in weakness"* (2 Cor. 12:9). When the wallet is full, we tend to depend on ourselves. But when we are the lowest, we call to God the loudest. When we are at the bottom of the sea, like Jonah, we cry out to God with all of our hearts. *"I cried for help from the depth of Sheol; You heard my voice"* (Jonah 2:2). When we are in a horrible pit, like David, we reach up a hand to God for help (Ps. 40:2). When we are on the ground, under the horns of the wild ox, we pray with emotion (Ps. 22:21)! The comfort of God comes to us in direct relation to the amount of trouble we face.

Comfort #5: In tight places, God produces endurance in us (2 Cor. 1:6).

Q 20 *Give an example of the comfort of 2 Corinthians 1:6.*

If we are distressed, it is for your comfort and salvation; if we are comforted, it is for your comfort, which produces in you patient endurance of the same sufferings we suffer (2 Cor. 1:6).

It is a comfort to know that trials have a purpose. God uses trials to produce endurance in us. James reminds us:

Paul Reviews His Recent Past

²Consider it all joy, my brethren, when you encounter various trials, ³knowing that the testing of your faith produces endurance. ⁴And let endurance have its perfect result, so that you may be perfect and complete, lacking in nothing (James 1:2-4).

Comfort #6: In tight places, we learn to rely on God, not ourselves (2 Cor. 1:8-9).

⁸We do not want you to be uninformed, brothers, about the hardships we suffered in the province of Asia. We were under great pressure, far beyond our ability to endure, so that we despaired even of life. ⁹Indeed, in our hearts we felt the sentence of death. But this happened that we might not rely on ourselves but on God, who raises the dead (2 Cor. 1:8-9).

> GOD USES TRIALS TO HUMBLE PEOPLE AND TEACH THEM TO TRUST IN GOD.

God uses trials to humble people and teach them to trust in God. Trials taught kings like Nebuchadnezzar (Dan. 4) and Belshazzar (Dan. 5) to trust in God, not self. Likewise, tight places taught apostles like Peter (Matt. 26:33-35) and Paul to rely on God rather than self (2 Cor. 1:8-9; 11:16–12:10).

"I have often been driven to my knees in prayer, because I had no where else to go."¹¹ In hard times, turn toward God, not away from Him.

Q 21 *Give some biblical examples of people who trusted in themselves.*

Q 22 *In your hard times, are you learning to depend on God? Explain.*

Conclusion

Trials in life are as certain as rain. In our tight places, we want to get in bed and pull the covers over us.

But 2 Corinthians 1:1-11 offers us six sources of comfort when pressure comes:

- **Comfort #1:** For tight places, God gives us Scripture through the apostles (2 Cor. 1:1-2).
- **Comfort #2:** In tight places, God delights to encourage us (2 Cor. 1:3-11).
- **Comfort #3:** In tight places, God equips us to comfort others (2 Cor. 1:4).
- **Comfort #4:** In tight places, God's comfort is in direct proportion to our sufferings (2 Cor. 1:5).
- **Comfort #5:** In tight places, God produces endurance in us (2 Cor. 1:6).
- **Comfort #6:** In tight places, we learn to rely on God, not ourselves (2 Cor. 1:8-9).

Lesson 31: Guidelines for Relationships (2 Cor. 1:12–2:11)

Goal A: *Explain how Paul's visit to Corinth differed from his earlier plans (2 Cor. 1:15-16).*
Goal B: *Identify 6 principles on relationships, in the context of Paul's change of plans.*

Setting

Paul's main purpose in 2 Corinthians was to defend his ministry. Rebels in the Corinthian church caused problems and attacked Paul's ministry. They criticized his character and questioned his authority. These false teachers said Paul was not a true apostle. Why did they accuse Paul? Because they wanted his title and power for themselves (2 Cor. 11:11-12)!

False teachers criticized Paul for changing his plans to visit Corinth. *First,* he had planned to sail from Ephesus to Corinth (2 Cor. 1:15-16). *Later,* he decided to travel by land up to Macedonia, and then down to Corinth. The false teachers used Paul's change of plans to accuse him. They said believers could not trust his word—for he might change his mind. Also, they accused Paul of planning to steal the offering for the poor saints in Jerusalem. In response to these attacks, Paul wrote 2 Corinthians.

Q 23 *What was the main reason why Paul wrote 2 Corinthians? Explain.*

Q 24 *How did false apostles use Paul's change of plans to criticize him?*

Q 25 *Use the map to explain Plan A—Paul's first plan to re-visit Corinth.*

He exposed the false apostles for their greed. In contrast, Paul asked the Corinthians to remember his unselfish life among them. He urged them to stand firm on the truth of his gospel.

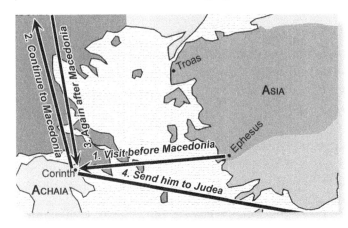

Figure 10.6 (Plan A) There were two routes for Paul from Ephesus to Corinth: by sea, (Plan A) and by land (Plan B). Paul first planned to visit Corinth twice, sailing from Ephesus to Corinth for a visit and then traveling up to Macedonia, and later back to Corinth for another visit.

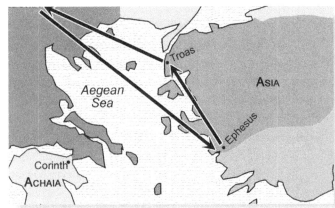

Figure 10.7 (Plan B) Because of sexual sin at Corinth, Paul decided it was better to write the Corinthians than to visit them. This gave them time to discipline the sinner in the church and avoid embarrassment in his presence. So he went by land from Ephesus to Macedonia, and then visited Corinth on his third missionary journey.

Q 26 *Use the map to explain Plan B—Paul's second plan to re-visit Corinth.*

Q 27 *Why did Paul change from Plan A to Plan B?*

Paul's critics in Corinth looked for reasons to accuse him. Among Paul's critics were the man living with his father's wife (1 Cor. 5:1-8), false teachers and false apostles (2 Cor. 11–12), and carnal Christians (1 Cor. 3:1). As Paul said, they were *"looking only on the surface of things"* (2 Cor. 10:7). Paul's critics lacked spiritual maturity and discernment. His critics were like some believers today who criticize church leaders.

In contrast to the critics in Corinth, Paul was a mature believer. This great apostle was concerned about his relationship with believers at Corinth. In this lesson we will study six principles on relationships, in the context of Paul's change of plans.

Q 28 *Which of the 6 principles do you think you will like best?*

A. Relationship Principle #1: Live with a clear conscience—be holy and sincere (2 Cor. 1:12).

Now this is our boast: Our conscience testifies that we have conducted ourselves in the world, and especially in our relations with you, in the holiness and sincerity that are from God (2 Cor. 1:12).

Some at Corinth criticized Paul because he changed his plans about visiting Corinth. Look at Figures 10.6 and 10.7 and answer questions 25 and 26.

Q 29 *What did Paul's conscience testify about his relationship with the Corinthians?*

God gives each person a conscience—an inner judge of thoughts, speech, and actions. (For a thorough study on the conscience, see the *Faith & Action Series* book *Acts of the Holy Spirit,* chapter 13, Lesson 38, Point A: "God Uses the Conscience to Help Guide People," Acts 24:15-16.)

Living with a clear conscience means living a life of integrity, holiness, and sincerity. For believers, living with a clear conscience includes:
- Being honest, telling the truth, never deceiving people;
- Paying our bills, being good stewards, and keeping our promises;
- Being faithful to our families with our thoughts, time, emotions, finances, and actions; and
- Being faithful to God in prayer, Bible study, church attendance, witnessing, and holy living.

Paul's conscience was his friend and witness. Paul had an inner witness that he had lived with integrity in relation to the Corinthians. Living with a clear conscience is a key in relating well to others. What is behind us, before us, and around us is small compared to what is within us. Live with a clear conscience, and you may live well with others. It takes integrity to make a friend and keep one. People admire the brilliant, envy the wealthy, fear the powerful, and clap for the talented, but they trust only the honest.

B. Relationship Principle #2: Be sensitive to the Spirit—be flexible (2 Cor. 1:15-17 and 1:23–2:3).

Paul was confident that the Corinthians would understand him and trust him more and more (2 Cor. 1:14). Because of this confidence, Paul planned to visit the Corinthians twice (Figure 10.6, Plan A).

> ...I hope that, ¹⁴as you have understood us in part, you will come to understand fully that you can boast of us just as we will boast of you in the day of the Lord Jesus. ¹⁵Because I was confident of this, I planned to visit you first so that you might benefit twice. ¹⁶I planned to visit you on my way to Macedonia and to come back to you from Macedonia, and then to have you send me on my way to Judea. ¹⁷When I planned this, did I do it lightly? Or do I make my plans in a worldly manner so that in the same breath I say, "Yes, yes" and "No, no?" (2 Cor. 1:13b-17).

Q 30 *To what does "this" refer, near the beginning of 2 Corinthians 1:15?*

Instead of visiting the Corinthians twice, Paul wrote to them, and later visited them once.

Q 31 *Why did Paul change his plans about visiting the Corinthians twice?*

> ²³I call God as my witness that it was in order to spare you that I did not return to Corinth. ²⁴Not that we lord it over your faith, but we work with you for your joy, because it is by faith you stand firm. 1 So I made up my mind that I would not make another painful visit to you. ²For if I grieve you, who is left to make me glad but you whom I have grieved? ³I wrote as I did so that when I came I should not be distressed by those who ought to make me rejoice. I had confidence in all of you, that you would all share my joy. (2 Cor. 1:23–2:3).

Paul changed his plans because circumstances changed. The sexual sin in Corinth was an awkward situation. Paul decided it was better to write the Corinthians first and visit them later. This gave them time to discipline the sinner in the church and avoid embarrassment in his presence. So, he went by land from Ephesus to Macedonia and visited Corinth afterward, on his third missionary journey. Paul believed that people's feelings were important. As he prayed, courtesy, love, and wisdom counseled him to change his plans. Being sensitive to the Holy Spirit and to others is an important principle of relationships.

How about you? Do you move ahead like a horse charging into battle or a tank into war? Are you like Balaam, moving ahead with less sense than a donkey? Or are you like Ahab, who walked on tiptoes after Elijah rebuked him?

Q 32 *When you talk to people, how do their actions, feelings, and responses affect what you say?*

> It came about when Ahab heard these words, that he tore his clothes and put on sackcloth and fasted, and he lay in sackcloth and went about despondently (1 Kings 21:27).

Are you like Diotrephes, *"who loves to be first,"* trampling on the rights of others (3 John 9)? Do you act like a big boss and lord it over those around you (2 Cor. 1:23; Matt. 20:25; 1 Pet. 5:1-3)? Are you sensitive to the rights of your children, spouse, friends, and coworkers?

When something surprises you, are you like the workers in the vineyard who became angry (Matt. 20:9-15)? Or do you pray each step of the day? As we listen to the Holy Spirit, He teaches us to be sensitive to the feelings of others. This is a key to healthy relationships.

C. Relationship Principle #3: Emphasize the positive (2 Cor. 1:18-22).

18But as surely as God is faithful, our message to you is not "Yes" and "No." 19For the Son of God, Jesus Christ, who was preached among you by me and Silas and Timothy, was not "Yes" and "No," but in him it has always been "Yes." 20For no matter how many promises God has made, they are "Yes" in Christ. And so through him the "Amen" is spoken by us to the glory of God. 21Now it is God who makes both us and you stand firm in Christ. He anointed us, 22set his seal of ownership on us, and put his Spirit in our hearts as a deposit, guaranteeing what is to come (2 Cor. 1:18-22).

Q 33 *What are 4 blessings or positive things in 2 Corinthians 2:18-22?*

Q 34 *Does 2 Corinthians 1:20 mean we can claim Deuteronomy 28:7?*

Bad interpretation. Some have tried to be too positive, and have therefore abused this verse. Does 2 Corinthians 1:20 mean we can claim all the promises made to the nation of Israel under the old covenant? Paul wrote 2 Corinthians 1:20, but he did not claim that his enemies would flee seven different directions (Deut. 28:7). Paul's enemies did not flee from him—they followed him. Jesus did not promise that enemies would flee from apostles. Rather, he told apostles to flee from their enemies (Matt. 10:23). It is good to emphasize the positive, when it is the truth!

Good interpretation. So what does 2 Corinthians 1:20 mean? Let us review the context. Some of Paul's enemies were accusing him, saying he was not trustworthy. He had told the Corinthians that he would return soon. Then, he heard about the sexual sin of incest among them. So Paul delayed his visit to spare them pain and shame (2 Cor. 1:23). He sent a letter telling them to deal with the sin in the church. Paul gave them a chance to avoid the shame they would feel if he came and found sin among them (1 Cor. 5:1-13). When Paul changed the timing of his visit, his enemies said that people could not believe Paul's word or his gospel. Paul responded by saying that both his word and his gospel were reliable.

Q 35 *What does 2 Corinthians 1:20 mean?*

Notice that in 2 Corinthians 1:20, Paul places the emphasis on Christ—through whom God fulfills all of His promises to us.
- Through Jesus, God fulfills the promises the prophets made about the Messiah (Luke 1:69; 24:44).
- The promises God made to Abraham come to us through Jesus Christ (Gal. 3:16).
- In Him all the fullness of God dwells (Col. 1:19).
- In Jesus Christ alone we have wisdom, righteousness, holiness, and redemption (1 Cor. 1:30).
- He is the Cornerstone of the Church, God's holy temple (Eph. 2:20-21).
- He is the First and Last, the Beginning and the End (Rev. 22:13).
- Through Christ, we receive all that God has promised and planned for us (2 Cor. 1:20).[12] Amen!

Q 36 *How does being negative or positive affect relationships? Explain.*

Good application. There is a time to be negative—to talk about problems, like those in Corinth. And there is a time to talk about the trials we have suffered (2 Cor. 11:16–12:10). But being positive is an important part of relationships. Some whine their way to alienation, isolation, and loneliness. People do not enjoy being close to those who complain, criticize, and emphasize the negative. All of us tend to move away from those who are always frowning and move toward those who smile. Paul liked to emphasize all of the blessings we have in God. He said that our sufferings are small compared to our blessings (2 Cor. 4:17). And so, dear friends, as we seek to relate well to others, let us emphasize the positive.

Our day goes the way the corners of our mouth turn—up or down.[13] Like Paul and Silas, let us practice singing, even in hard times (Acts 16:25). Just as a magnet pulls metal and honey draws bees, a positive attitude attracts friends.

D. Relationship Principle #4: Have balanced love that is tough and tender (2 Cor. 2:4).

⁴For I wrote you out of great distress and anguish of heart and with many tears, not to grieve you but to let you know the depth of my love for you (2 Cor. 2:4).

At times, love must be tough. Biblical love confronts the faults of those near and dear.

- *"If your brother sins, go and show him his fault in private; if he listens to you, you have won your brother"* (Matt. 18:15).
- *"FOR THOSE WHOM THE LORD LOVES HE DISCIPLINES"* (Heb. 12:6).
- *"He who withholds his rod hates his son, but he who loves him disciplines him diligently"* (Prov. 13:24).
- *"Faithful are the wounds of a friend, but deceitful are the kisses of an enemy"* (Prov. 27:6).

Q 37 *Give some examples to show that biblical love must be tough.*

Love must be tough—tough enough to talk truth face to face. But love must also be tender. When Paul talked about tough topics, there were tears on his face, not just in his voice. When he wrote to the Corinthians about sexual sin, he was crying. *"I wrote you out of great distress and anguish of heart and with many tears, not to grieve you but to let you know the depth of my love for you"* (2 Cor. 2:3-4). Paul's love was tough and tender. Even when he talked about false teachers, it brought tears to his eyes:

Q 38 *Give examples emphasizing that biblical love must be tender.*

"For many walk, of whom I often told you, and now tell you even weeping, that they are enemies of the cross of Christ" (Phil. 3:18). Biblical love is tough, but also tender.

When I was a boy, there were times when my mother had to discipline me. Sometimes she used a belt on my behind, after I bent over the bed. When she hit me, it did not hurt much physically. But it always hurt me on the inside—because she was always crying when she spanked me. Her love was tough enough to correct me, but tender enough to cry for me.¹⁴

E. Relationship Principle #5: When discipline is needed, use it to restore, not to hurt (2 Cor. 2:6-9).

⁶The punishment inflicted on him by the majority is sufficient for him. ⁷Now instead, you ought to forgive and comfort him, so that he will not be overwhelmed by excessive sorrow. ⁸I urge you, therefore, to reaffirm your love for him (2 Cor. 2:6-9).

Discipline hurts and causes sorrow, but this is not its purpose. The purpose of discipline is to correct, train, and restore. The discipline should always match the sin. Paul warns against harsh discipline that *overwhelms*—like the waters of the Red Sea overwhelmed the Egyptians (Heb. 11:29). Also, he teaches fathers to be fair and gentle—never harsh with wives or children (Eph. 5:25-33; 6:4; Col. 3:19, 21). Because a believer in Corinth was sinning sexually with his father's wife, Paul told the church to discipline him (1 Cor. 5:1-13). A church must discipline members who sin. Paul gives three reasons why church discipline is necessary: to prevent sin from spreading through the entire church (1 Cor. 5:6), to correct and restore the sinner (2 Cor. 2:5-9), and to protect the reputation of the Church (2 Cor. 6:3-4).

Q 39 *How can we avoid using discipline that is too harsh—that "overwhelms" with sorrow (2 Cor. 2:7)?*

In 2 Corinthians 2:6, the Greek word for discipline is *epitimia,* which appears only once in the New Testament. It can mean "discipline, reprimand, rebuke, penalty, or punishment."†

---

† In the New Testament, the word *punishment* often refers to eternal judgment (Matt. 25:46; 1 Pet. 2:14; Heb. 10:29). So in 2 Corinthians 2:6, we prefer to translate *epitimia* as "rebuke, penalty, or discipline" to avoid confusion. The purpose of discipline is always to restore, but punishment may be only for justice, such as capital punishment or the eternal punishment of hell.

In Corinth, the church disciplined the sinning believer. Discipline causes the sinner to suffer the results of his sin so that he will repent and be restored to fellowship. In the Bible, the purposes of discipline are always redemptive: to correct, restore, and train a person to be righteous.

Q 40 *What happens if parents are too weak to discipline their children? Give examples.*

Cowards cannot confront, for biblical love belongs only to the brave.

> COWARDS CANNOT CONFRONT, FOR BIBLICAL LOVE BELONGS ONLY TO THE BRAVE.

⁷It is for discipline that you endure; God deals with you as with sons; for what son is there whom his father does not discipline? ⁸But if you are without discipline, of which all have become partakers, then you are illegitimate children and not sons. ⁹Furthermore, we had earthly fathers to discipline us, and we respected them; shall we not much rather be subject to the Father of spirits, and live? ¹⁰For they disciplined us for a short time as seemed best to them, but He disciplines us for our good, so that we may share His holiness. ¹¹All discipline for the moment seems not to be joyful, but sorrowful; yet to those who have been trained by it, afterwards it yields the peaceful fruit of righteousness (Heb. 12:7-11).

Q 41 *Explain: Discipline reveals love, and the lack of discipline reveals a lack of love.*

Q 42 *According to Hebrews 12:7-11, does the blessing of discipline come before, during, or after it? Explain.*

F. Relationship Principle #6: Be quick to forgive (2 Cor. 1:24; 2:10-11).

⁵If anyone has caused grief, he has not so much grieved me as he has grieved all of you, to some extent—not to put it too severely. ⁶The punishment inflicted on him by the majority is sufficient for him. ⁷Now instead, you ought to forgive and comfort him, so that he will not be overwhelmed by excessive sorrow. ⁸I urge you, therefore, to reaffirm your love for him. ⁹The reason I wrote you was to see if you would stand the test and be obedient in everything. ¹⁰If you forgive anyone, I also forgive him. And what I have forgiven—if there was anything to forgive—I have forgiven in the sight of Christ for your sake, ¹¹in order that Satan might not outwit us. For we are not unaware of his schemes (2 Cor. 2:5-11).

Q 43 *Explain: "Too much sorrow causes people to drown."*

Some are quick to discipline, but slow to forgive; ever ready to throw the first stone, but never ready to help someone up after a fall. Second Corinthians 2 gives us at least three reasons why we should forgive.

First, we should forgive for the sake of the one who has done the wrong. Paul says, *"so that he will not be overwhelmed by excessive sorrow."* The Greek word for *overwhelmed* occurs several times in the New Testament:
- First Peter 5:8 refers to a lion that *overwhelms* or devours his prey.
- Hebrews 11:29 says the Egyptians were *overwhelmed* or drowned in the sea.
- First Corinthians 15:54 declares that the resurrection of Jesus swallows or *overwhelms* death.

At Corinth, Paul does not want loneliness and sorrow to *overwhelm* the believer who has repented. Paul says that if the Corinthians do not forgive him, they will cause this person to drown in his sorrow. They must forgive and comfort. The word *forgive* means "to give grace and to encourage."

When people do wrong and then repent, we must forgive for their sake. We do not want people to suffer more sorrow than God desires. Too much sorrow discourages people too much—it drowns them with sorrow upon sorrow (Phil. 2:27).

The *second* reason why we should forgive is to pass the test of obedience to Jesus. Paul wrote, *"The reason I wrote you is to see if you would stand the test and be obedient in everything"* (2 Cor. 2:9). Paul tested the obedience of the Corinthians. They were obedient to discipline the sinner. Then, he asked them to obey by forgiving and restoring. Likewise, Jesus commands us, *"Be on your guard! If your brother sins, rebuke him; and if he repents, forgive him"* (Luke 17:3). Love must be tough and tender—tough enough to rebuke when one sins, but tender enough to forgive when one repents.

Third, we forgive so that Satan will not get an advantage over us. Paul wrote, *"...in order that Satan might not outwit us. For we are not unaware of his schemes"* (2 Cor. 2:11). The Greek word for schemes is *nous,* which means "mind or pattern of thinking." We are not unaware of how Satan thinks. Satan influences people and churches to be unforgiving. Why is this Satan's scheme? Because people who refuse to forgive are harsh and judgmental. And nothing will kill the work of God more quickly than people, like the Pharisees, who are harsh, critical, and judgmental. So if Satan can guide people to hold grudges and be harsh, cold, and mean, he gets the advantage over the work of God.

Q 44 *How does Satan use unforgiveness to defeat some?*

Paul says that we are not unaware of what Satan is trying to do. It was time for the Corinthians to forgive. And it is time for us to forgive those who repent.

In wars, many people are wounded. Some are hurt worse than others. In some places, if medical help is scarce, doctors practice *triage. They use colored tags to divide the wounded into three groups. For example, a red tag on a soldier means that it is hopeless—death is sure; a yellow tag means a soldier will probably die, even after medicine; but a green tag predicts hope if a doctor helps the wounded.

On one battlefield, a man named Lew was wounded and bleeding. The doctor decided Lew was a hopeless case and would not recover, even with medical help. So on his arm the doctor put a red tag, which meant "leave him alone." But a nurse noticed that Lew was conscious and began to talk to him. While talking, they discovered that they came from the same part of the country. The nurse felt compassion and hope for Lew. She was not willing to let him die, so she changed the color of his tag from red to green. Soon, workers carried Lew to a truck that took him to the hospital. After months in the hospital and the amputation of one leg, Lew recovered! And while in the hospital, he met a girl who later became his wife. He went on to live a full, happy life with only one leg—all because a nurse changed his tag.

Q 45 *What lesson does Lew illustrate?*

It is the church's task to change the tags on sinners. That is what Paul was doing in Corinth. There was a man who had been disciplined and "tagged as hopeless," so the church excluded him. But Paul said it was time to change the color of his tag. With forgiveness and love, this wounded believer would recover.[15]

Test Yourself: Circle the letter by the *best* completion to each question or statement.

1. Paul may have written 2 Corinthians from
   a) Ephesus.
   b) Philippi.
   c) Jerusalem.
   d) Syria.

2. Corinth was in the province of
   a) Galatia.
   b) Asia.
   c) Macedonia.
   d) Achaia.

3. The main purpose of 2 Corinthians was
   a) to prepare believers for an offering.
   b) to repair divisions in the church.
   c) to teach about spiritual gifts.
   d) to defend Paul's ministry.

4. The Greek word *thlipsis* means
   a) "joy, encouragement, hope."
   b) "pressure, trouble, distress."
   c) "attitude, value, view."
   d) "thistles, thorns, briars."

5. God gives comfort in direct proportion to our
   a) faith.
   b) prayers.
   c) trials.
   d) friends.

6. In Plan A, Paul wanted to go to Corinth
   a) from Ephesus.
   b) from Macedonia.
   c) from Troas.
   d) from Galatia.

7. Why did Paul change to Plan B?
   a) He was delayed by a storm at sea.
   b) Satan hindered him.
   c) There was much sin at Corinth.
   d) There was an open door in Troas.

8. What does 2 Corinthians 1:20 mean?
   a) Our enemies must flee seven directions.
   b) We should be known for yes, not no.
   c) God fulfills all His promises through Christ.
   d) Eye has not seen what God has prepared.

9. What is the purpose of discipline?
   a) To train, correct, and restore
   b) To punish people who do wrong
   c) To warn of future judgment
   d) To teach that God is holy

10. Biblical love is known for being
    a) tender, but not tough.
    b) tough, but not tender.
    c) neither tough nor tender.
    d) both tough and tender.

Essay Test Topics: Write 50-100 words on each of these goals that you studied in this chapter.

Comfort in Tight Places (2 Cor. 1:1-11)

Goal: *Analyze the background, setting, and three-point outline of 2 Corinthians.*

Goal: *Analyze the problem of tight places and identify 6 sources of comfort in difficult times.*

Guidelines for Relationships (2 Cor. 1:12–2:11)

Goal: *Explain how Paul's visit to Corinth differed from his earlier plans (2 Cor. 1:15-16).*

Goal: *Identify 6 principles on relationships, in the context of Paul's change of plans.*

Chapter 11:
Paul Defends His Apostolic Ministry
(2 Corinthians 2:12–7:16)

Introduction

The triumphal procession was a major event for the Roman Empire. It was a part of Roman culture. The celebration lasted a day or more, but the highlight was the victory parade. The general was the hero who rode in a chariot pulled by white horses. In front of the general were the prisoners, his soldiers, and the spoils of war. For a general, this parade of victory was the highest honor. It celebrated his great success. At the end of the parade were those captives condemned to die in the arena (1 Cor. 4:9).[1] (See also the arches in Figures 11.2 and 11.3.)

The apostle Paul knew about the triumphal procession. So he used this event to describe how Jesus conquers all evil and leads us in eternal victory. The victory march is one of three pictures we will study in Lesson 32 of this chapter.

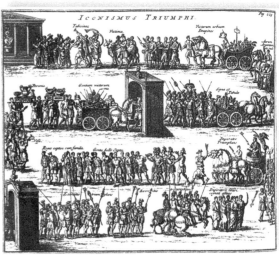

Figure 11.1 The victory parade (triumphal procession) was a great event in Roman history. This drawing from the late 1600's shows the main parts of a march of triumph.[2]

Lessons:

 Pictures and Principles for Ministers of the New Covenant (2 Cor. 2:12–3:3)
  Goal: *Explain and illustrate a principle for each of these: the open door, the victory march, and the open letter.*

 Contrasts Between the Ministries of the Old and New Covenants (2 Cor. 3:4–4:6)
  Goal: *Summarize a principle for each of these: a pointing finger, a helping hand, a veil, and the moon.*

 Keys to Staying Encouraged (2 Cor. 4:7-18)
  Goal: *From 2 Corinthians 4, explain and illustrate 5 reasons why we do not lose heart.*

 Facts for Facing Death (2 Cor. 5:1-10)
  Goal: *Analyze and apply 7 truths that prepare us for death (2 Cor. 5:1-10).*

 Test Questions for a Fruitful Ministry (2 Cor. 5:11-21)
  Goal: *State and apply 5 test questions of a fruitful ministry.*

 Pressures, Powers, and Paradoxes of Ministry (2 Cor. 6:1-13)
  Goal: *With an open Bible, analyze the foundation stones, pressures, powers, and paradoxes of ministry (2 Cor. 6:1-13).*

 Reasons for Holiness (2 Cor. 6:14–7:1)
  Goal: *Analyze the commands about, contrasts and promises of, and invitation to holiness (2 Cor. 6:14–7:1).*

 Insights on Repentance (2 Cor. 7:2-16)
  Goal A: *Explain and illustrate 5 principles for helping others repent (2 Cor. 7:2-7).*
  Goal B: *Explain and illustrate 4 principles for helping self and others repent (2 Cor. 7:8-16).*

Lesson 32
Pictures and Principles for Ministers of the New Covenant (2 Cor. 2:12–3:3)

Goal: *Explain and illustrate a principle for each of these: the open door, the victory march, and the open letter.*

Setting

Second Corinthians is a precious book, because Paul shares some of his inner, personal life with us. There are times in life when we must live by inner insights, or what we see on the outside will overcome us. As we have pictures and paintings in our homes, we need pictures within to strengthen and encourage us. For we live and overcome based on inner truth that we think about.

This lesson give us three mental pictures:
- The picture of an open door that Paul could not walk through;
- The picture of the march of victory that Jesus leads us in;
- The picture of believers as open letters to those we meet.

As you study these three pictures, allow the Holy Spirit to paint them on the inner walls of your mind and heart. Each of these pictures is linked to a principle for believers, God's ministers of the new covenant.

Q 1 *What are the 3 pictures we will study in this lesson?*

A. Principle of the open door: It is better to finish one work for God than to start two and finish neither (2 Cor. 2:12-13).

¹²Now when I went to Troas to preach the gospel of Christ and found that the Lord had opened a door for me, ¹³I still had no peace of mind, because I did not find my brother Titus there. So I said good-by to them and went on to Macedonia (2 Cor. 2:12-13).

Paul had planted a church in Corinth. The church grew and was several years old. But in time, a sexual sin in the church became a big problem. The sinner was a man who was living with his father's wife. Paul wrote that this type of sin was not even found among pagans (1 Cor. 5:1)! It appears that this sinful man had influence and power. Still, Paul sent a letter insisting that the Corinthians discipline this man and put him out of the church (1 Cor. 5:1-5). Meanwhile, instead of visiting Corinth as he had planned, Paul sent Titus to visit the Corinthians. Paul and Titus agreed to meet later on a certain day in the city of Troas.

Q 2 *Whom did Paul plan to meet at Troas? Why?*

Paul chose Troas as a meeting place because he wanted to preach the gospel there and plant a new church. When Paul arrived in Troas, he found that the Lord had opened a door to the gospel. An open door is what every missionary prays for. The New Testament emphasizes that good results come when God opens doors. Paul depended on God to open doors of ministry, and he wrote often about these open doors:

- *"When they had arrived and gathered the church together, they began to report all things that God had done with them and how He had **opened a door** of faith to the Gentiles"* (Acts 14:27).
- In Corinth, God had assured Paul that he was **opening the door** for ministry (Acts 18:9-10).
- *"Praying at the same time for us as well, that God will open up to us a door for the word, so that we may speak forth the mystery of Christ, for which I have also been imprisoned"* (Col. 4:3).

Paul had prayed for an open door in Troas. When he arrived there, the door was open. Did he walk through that door? Read again the shocking words the Bible records:

¹²Now when I went to Troas to preach the gospel of Christ and found that the Lord had opened a door for me, ¹³I still had no peace of mind, because I did not

Q 3 Why did Paul walk away from the open door at Troas?

find my brother Titus there. So I said goodbye to them and went on to Macedonia (2 Cor. 2:12-13).

Paul did not walk through the door in front of him—the door that God had opened! Why? Titus had not yet come back with a good report about Corinth. Paul said that his anxiety was so great—that he had no rest, no ease in his spirit—that he went to Macedonia (2 Cor. 2:13). He said goodbye to the open door and went to Macedonia—toward Corinth.

God's apostle walked away from an open door. How hard that must have been for Paul. Yet it contains a great lesson for us. Paul had to finish what needed to be done at the open door in Corinth before he walked through another open door. It is one thing to begin a building, but it is another thing to complete it.

Q 4 Give an example of something that was easier for you to start than to finish.

Finish what you start! Do not start things left and right without completing what God has given you to do. Like Paul, there are times when we must leave the open door. And we should not feel guilty about leaving some doors open. There will always be more open doors than we should walk through in life. There will always be opportunities that we lack the time, energy, and money to accept. So we must have priorities in life and finish what we start. As a proverb says, "The man who is always available is not worth much when he is available."

Success is measured not by what we start, but by what we finish. Have you begun a program of education? Continue until graduation! Have you married and vowed to be faithful? Finish the race you have started. Have you become a parent of children? Fulfill your responsibilities to your children. Have you agreed to support the church with your time, talents, and finances? Fulfill your commitments. Eat the food that is on your plate before you look for more. Fulfill the responsibilities of the door you have walked through before you seek another open door.

B. Principle of the victory parade: Believers are in a march of triumph led by Jesus, the Conqueror of death and evil (2 Cor. 2:14-16).

After a victory parade, the city often built a stone arch as a memorial. For example, the Arch of Titus was built in A.D. 81. The stone arch honored General Titus and his victory over Judea in A.D. 70—when he conquered Jerusalem and destroyed the temple. One carving on the arch shows the triumphal procession of Titus. Another carving shows his soldiers carrying off sacred items from the temple.

Figure 11.2
A stone arch built in A.D. 81 celebrated the victory of General Titus over Jerusalem. Scenes in the arch include the march of triumph and soldiers carrying treasures from the temple.

The second picture in this lesson was one of Paul's favorite—the march of triumph!

¹⁴But thanks be to God, who always leads us in triumphal procession in Christ and through us spreads everywhere the fragrance of the knowledge of him. ¹⁵For we are to God the aroma of Christ among those who are being saved and those who are perishing. ¹⁶To the one we are the smell of death; to the other, the fragrance of life (2 Cor. 2:14-16).

Paul reminds his readers of a famous scene, the Roman march of triumph—the victory parade. This event celebrated a great victory by a Roman general. (Review Figure 11.1 and the comments under it.)

Q 5 What are some of the qualifications for a general in a victory parade?

Here is one version of the qualifications and order of the march of triumph or victory parade.[3]

Qualifications of the General. There were certain qualifications that a leader needed in order to be honored in a march of triumph.

- The general had to be the top commander of an army that was in a war.
- The war had to be finished and peace be ruling in the region.
- The soldiers had to be home.
- Five thousand of the enemy must have died in one battle.
- Rome must have expanded its territory and boundaries in the war.
- There had to be a victory over a foreign foe.

If a general and his army met these six qualifications, the government spent months to prepare the march of triumph. At the event, thousands of citizens gathered to celebrate.

Order or plan of the march. There was an order or plan for the march—from outside the city of Rome through the streets to the capital.

Q 6 *What did the parade look like? Describe the order and those in it.*

- The parade began with state officials, the senate, and other honored nobles.
- Those blowing the trumpets followed them.
- Next came pictures and models of defeated people, cities, or ships. These huge models told the story of what had happened in the war.
- Following the models was the white bull to be sacrificed.
- After the bull came the captives, walking in chains. Many of them were on their way to death that same day. They were walking to their own execution.
- Next in the parade were the guards bearing rods.
- Following them were musicians.
- Behind the musicians were the priests, swinging censors of incense that had a sweet smell. To the captives, this was the smell of death (2 Cor. 2:16), but to the Romans, the incense was the smell of victory.
- After the priests was the general of the army. He rode in a chariot led by four white horses. The general wore his purple tunic or robe.
- Following the general was his family.
- At the end of the parade was the army he commanded and captives condemned to die in the arena.[4]

Paul compares the Roman victory march to our journey as Christians. Jesus is like the general. He has conquered death and defeated Satan.

Figure 11.3 The Arch of Constantine next to the Roman Colosseum is a triumphal arch, erected about 315 A.D. to commemorate the triumph of Constantine I after his victory over Maxentius in the battle at the Milvian Bridge in 312 A.D. The arch is located in the valley of the Colosseum, between the Palatine Hill and the Colosseum, along the road taken by the triumphal processions.

¹³When you were dead in your transgressions and the uncircumcision of your flesh, He made you alive together with Him, having forgiven us all our transgressions, ¹⁴having canceled out the certificate of debt consisting of decrees against us, which was hostile to us; and He has taken it out of the way, having nailed it to the cross. ¹⁵When He had disarmed the rulers and authorities, He made a public display of them, having triumphed over them through Him (Col. 2:13-15).

At Calvary, Jesus defeated Satan and more than 5,000 demons in one battle. He expanded the boundaries of God's kingdom to include millions of believers all over the earth! In time, General Jesus will conquer and judge all evil.

The good news of the gospel is like the sweet incense in the march of triumph. Just as the priests carried the incense, believers carry and spread the good news. The gospel always has a sweet smell, but people respond to it in two ways. To those who receive it, the gospel is the fragrance of life. But to those who reject it, the gospel is the smell of judgment and death. Though the gospel has a sweet smell, it is a matter of life or death.

Q 7 *Complete Figure 11.4 about the march of triumph (2 Cor. 2:14-16).*

Topic in the march of triumph	Comparison
Roman general who conquered	Jesus, who has conquered death and Satan
Incense with sweet smell	
Priests who carry the incense	
Those who smell death	
Those who smell life	

Figure 11.4   Paul compared the Roman march of triumph to our journey as Christians.

In this second letter to the Corinthians, Paul has already talked about tight places that bring hard times. His trials in Asia were too tough for a human to survive in his own strength. Later, at Troas, he had no peace. And before the end of this letter, Paul will tell more of his sufferings —beatings with rods, stripes from whips, time in prison, shipwrecks, robberies, lack of sleep, no food, not enough clothes to stay warm, and a constant thorn in his flesh (2 Cor. 11:16–12:10). And yet, whatever the circumstances, Paul meditated on a picture in his mind. He chose to remember that we are in a march of victory. Our General, Jesus Christ, is the Conqueror of death, Satan, demons, and evil people. Likewise, whatever trials we have on earth, we can remember this picture— hanging on an inner wall of our minds. We are members of a victory parade from earth to the capital city of the New Jerusalem. In good times and in bad, we can encourage ourselves, because we are marching with a Great General.

C. Principle of the open letter: Believers are open, living letters from Christ to those we meet (2 Cor. 2:16b–3:3).

¹⁶...And who is equal to such a task? ¹⁷Unlike so many, we do not peddle the word of God for profit. On the contrary, in Christ we speak before God with sincerity, like men sent from God (2 Cor. 2:16-17).

¹Are we beginning to commend ourselves again? Or do we need, like some people, letters of recommendation to you or from you? ²You yourselves are our letter, written on our hearts, known and read by everybody. ³You show that you are a letter from Christ, the result of our ministry, written not with ink but with the Spirit of the living God, not on tablets of stone but on tablets of human hearts (2 Cor. 3:1-3).

Q 8 *What kind of letters do false apostles, like those in Corinth, have?*

As Paul reflects on the picture of the victory march, he asks: "*...And who is equal to such a task?*" (2 Cor. 2:16b). He refers to the task of carrying the incense—spreading the sweet smell of the gospel. Paul felt our huge responsibility to share the good news. Many misuse or abuse this opportunity. Some *"peddle the Word of God for profit"*— using religion as a profitable business (2 Cor. 2:17). Hypocrites like these need false letters to commend them, false stories, fake degrees, and lofty titles to make them seem honorable. Paul was not against letters of recommendation. Such letters were common in the early church, as with Silas and Judas (Acts 15:22-29), Apollos (Acts 18:27), and Phoebe (Rom. 16:1). But the false apostles were carrying their own letters and asking, "Where are Paul's letters?"

Q 9 *What kind of letters did Paul have to recommend him?*

Read Paul's response again (2 Cor. 3:1-3). He says:
- *"You are our letter."*
- You are *"a letter from Christ."*
- You are *"a letter written with the Spirit."*

Q 10 *In what sense is each believer an open letter?*

And as the Corinthians were a letter from Christ, all of us believers today are letters. This truth can make us feel guilty. All of us may feel that we fall short. But with all their failures, Paul still praises and compliments the Corinthians. When we first learned to write, our teachers kept working with us to shape our letters. With practice, we wrote

Paul Defends His Apostolic Ministry

the letter "a" until it conformed to the letter on the board at the front of the classroom. Likewise, God keeps working with us today until our lives conform to what Jesus wants to say to those around us.

Every letter has a sender. Each believer is *"a letter from Christ"* (2 Cor. 3:3).

Every letter has an address. To whom are you sent? You are sent to those around you.

Every letter has a message. When people *read* your life—hear your words and watch your examples—what message do they receive? What message do you give about Jesus and your church? Are there things in your letter that need to be marked out? Jesus will help you with these as you seek Him, submit to Him, and allow Him to write the message of your life.

Conclusion. The pictures inside of us are more important than the pictures around us. In this lesson, we have studied three pictures that should be on the inner walls of our hearts and minds. Think of these three pictures often and the principle that each picture teaches:

- **The principle of the open door:** It is better to finish one work for God than to start two and finish neither (2 Cor. 2:12-13).
- **The principle of the victory march:** Believers are in a march of triumph led by Jesus, the Conqueror of death and evil (2 Cor. 2:14-16).
- **The principle of the open letter:** Believers are open, living letters from Christ to those we meet (2 Cor. 2:16b–3:3).

Lesson 33 Contrasts Between the Ministries of the Old and New Covenants (2 Cor. 3:4–4:6)

Goal: *Summarize a principle for each of these: a pointing finger, a helping hand, a veil, and the moon.*

Setting

When there is something valuable, a counterfeit is not far away. Money is valuable, so some make counterfeit money. Fake money looks real, but it is worthless. Likewise, there are fake copies and imitations of such things as valuable paintings, jewelry, watches, and clothes. There is a Christ, but there is a fake imitation or substitute called the Antichrist. There are true healings, miracles, and gifts of the Spirit. But Satan also produces counterfeits to deceive people and lead them astray (2 Thess. 2:9-10).

In Paul's day, one of the big problems was counterfeit religion. The true gospel teaches that we are saved by faith in Jesus. But false teachers, called Judaizers, emphasized salvation through Judaism—based on the Law of Moses. These taught that we are saved by following Jesus *and* Moses. In parts of 2 Corinthians, Paul writes to correct the teachings of these Judaizers and other false teachers.[5]

Figure 11.5 shows seven contrasts between the ministries of the old and new covenants.

The ministry of the old covenant (Law)	The ministry of the new covenant (by the Spirit)	2 Cor.
1. Was written on tablets of stone	Is written on tablets of the human heart	3:3, 7
2. Kills through the letter	Gives life through the Spirit	3:6-8, 17-18
3. Condemns	Brings righteousness	3:9
4. Was temporary (fading glory)	Is permanent (eternal glory)	3:11
5. Brought bondage (legalism)	Brings freedom	3:17
6. Concealed God's presence, like a veil	Reflects the Lord, like a mirror	3:18
7. Centered on the face of Moses	Centers on the face of Christ	4:6

Figure 11.5 Seven contrasts between the ministries of the old and new covenants[6]

In this lesson, we will contrast the ministries of the old covenant (Law) and the new covenant (by the Spirit). The key verse in this lesson is 2 Corinthians 3:6.

⁴Such confidence as this is ours through Christ before God. ⁵Not that we are competent in ourselves to claim anything for ourselves, but our competence comes from God. ⁶He has made us competent as ministers of a new covenant—not of the letter but of the Spirit; for the letter kills, but the Spirit gives life (2 Cor. 3:4-6).

Unlike the Judaizers, Paul did not call attention to himself. He did not need letters of recommendation as the Judaizers needed, for the Corinthians themselves proved that Paul was a minister from God. And Paul's confidence was not in himself, but in God and the power of the Holy Spirit.

In the previous lesson, we noted one contrast between the ministries of the Law and the Spirit. The Law was written on tablets of stone. In contrast, under the new covenant, God writes His truth, not on stone, but on human hearts with the Spirit of the living God (2 Cor. 3:3). Believers are open, personal letters from Christ to those we meet.

In this lesson, we continue to study contrasts between the ministries of Law and the Holy Spirit.[7] We will study 4 truths that are illustrated by a pointing finger, a helping hand, a veil, and the moon.

A. A pointing finger: The ministry of the Law was negative—it killed and condemned (2 Cor. 3:6-9, 17).

Q 11 Circle the 3 negative words about the Law in 2 Corinthians 2:6-9.

⁶He has made us competent as ministers of a new covenant—not of the letter but of the Spirit; for the letter kills, but the Spirit gives life. ⁷Now if the ministry that brought death, which was engraved in letters on stone, came with glory, so that the Israelites could not look steadily at the face of Moses because of its glory, fading though it was, ⁸will not the ministry of the Spirit be even more glorious? ⁹If the ministry that condemns men is glorious, how much more glorious is the ministry that brings righteousness! (2 Cor. 3:6-9).

Q 12 How was the Law like a pointing finger, a policeman, and a stern teacher?

The Law was right, but it was negative.
- The Law was like a pointing finger that accused and condemned.
- The Law was like a mirror that showed dirt on a person's face, but gave no water for washing. And it is impossible to wash your face with only a mirror!
- The Law was like a policeman: it cited violations, but gave no money to help pay the tickets!
- The Law was like an official at a sports match: it blew the whistle for a foul, but did not give power to play better.
- The Law was like a stern teacher: it said we failed the test, but did not help us do better.
- The Law was like a judge: it accused us and sentenced us to prison and death.

Paul is not saying that the Law of the Old Testament was a mistake or a failure. The Law fulfilled its purpose. The Law showed us that we need grace. It taught us that we were guilty sinners. The Law was like John the Baptist: it preached a strong message of repentance. This prepared people to receive the grace that Jesus offers us. But although the Law could point the way to life, it could not take anyone there. Like a flashlight, the Law of the old covenant revealed the problem—it shone a light on our sins. But there has never been a law that can change a person's life![8] Rather, without Christ, law is like a pointing finger that accuses and condemns.

B. A helping hand: The ministry of the New Testament is positive—it brings spiritual life and righteousness (2 Cor. 3:6, 9).

For the letter kills, but the Spirit gives life (2 Cor. 3:6).

If the ministry that condemns men is glorious, how much more glorious is the ministry that brings righteousness! (2 Cor. 3:9).

> THE LAW WAS A POINTING FINGER THAT ACCUSED, BUT THE SPIRIT REACHES OUT A HAND TO HELP US.

The Law was a pointing finger that accused, but the Spirit reaches out a hand to help us (2 Cor. 3:6). Under the old covenant, people were always guilty. Their relationship to God was like criminals before a judge. But the new covenant offers us a relationship of love. The new covenant began when *"God so loved the world that he gave his one and only Son"* (John 3:16). The old and the new covenants both contain laws and commands. But under the new covenant, the Spirit gives us the power to obey the laws by giving us a new heart. The book of Hebrews quotes a prophecy in Jeremiah about the new covenant:

Q 13 Which covenants does 2 Corinthians 3:6 contrast?

Q 14 Under the New Testament, are we responsible to obey God's laws? Explain.

⁷For if that first covenant had been faultless, there would have been no occasion sought for a second. ⁸For finding fault with them, He says, "BEHOLD, DAYS ARE COMING, SAYS THE LORD, WHEN I WILL EFFECT A NEW COVENANT WITH THE HOUSE OF ISRAEL AND WITH THE HOUSE OF JUDAH; ⁹NOT LIKE THE COVENANT WHICH I MADE WITH THEIR FATHERS ON THE DAY WHEN I TOOK THEM BY THE HAND TO LEAD THEM OUT OF THE LAND OF EGYPT; FOR THEY DID NOT CONTINUE IN MY COVENANT, AND I DID NOT CARE FOR THEM, SAYS THE LORD. ¹⁰FOR THIS IS THE COVENANT THAT I WILL MAKE WITH THE HOUSE OF ISRAEL AFTER THOSE DAYS, SAYS THE LORD: I WILL PUT MY LAWS INTO THEIR MINDS, AND I WILL WRITE THEM ON THEIR HEARTS. AND I WILL BE THEIR GOD, AND THEY SHALL BE MY PEOPLE" (Heb. 8:7-10).

What the old covenant told us to do, the new covenant enables us to do. The old covenant told us to be righteous—to be in a right relationship with God. But the new covenant gives us righteousness through faith in Jesus Christ. As we repent, God forgives our sins. He accepts Jesus as our substitute who died on the cross for our sins. God puts His Spirit within us, and we are born again. God gives us spiritual life (Rom. 6:23; John 20:31). He adopts us into His family as His children (John 1:12). And He gives us the power to live a holy life (2 Cor. 7:1) as we are filled with and led by the Spirit and resist sinful desires of the flesh (Gal. 5:16).

Q 15 How is the ministry of the Spirit like a helping hand?

The ministry of the old covenant was negative. It brought guilt, condemnation, and death. But the ministry of the new covenant is positive. Through the Holy Spirit, God gives us forgiveness, new life, righteousness in Christ, and righteous deeds to do (Eph. 2:10). The ministry of the Spirit is like a helping hand that lifts us up.

C. A veil is a symbol of the Old Testament because it hid the glory of God (2 Cor. 3:7-16; 4:3-4).

A veil hides and covers. It prevents seeing clearly.

The background of 2 Corinthians 3:7–4:6 is Exodus 34:29-35.

Q 16 What effect did the veil on Moses have?

²⁹It came about when Moses was coming down from Mount Sinai (and the two tablets of the testimony were in Moses' hand as he was coming down from the mountain), that Moses did not know that the skin of his face shone because of his speaking with Him. ³⁰So when Aaron and all the sons of Israel saw Moses, behold, the skin of his face shone, and they were afraid to come near him. ³¹Then Moses called to them, and Aaron and all the rulers in the congregation returned to him; and Moses spoke to them. ³²Afterward all the sons of Israel came near, and he commanded them to do everything that the LORD had spoken to him on Mount Sinai. ³³When Moses had finished speaking with them, he put a veil over

Figure 11.6
A veil hides and covers

his face. ³⁴*But whenever Moses went in before the LORD to speak with Him, he would take off the veil until he came out; and whenever he came out and spoke to the sons of Israel what he had been commanded,* ³⁵*the sons of Israel would see the face of Moses, that the skin of Moses' face shone. So Moses would replace the veil over his face until he went in to speak with Him* (Exod. 34:29-35).

The glory of the Lord caused the face of Moses to shine. This caused the Israelites to be afraid of him (Exod. 34:30; 2 Cor. 3:7). One of the reasons why Moses put a veil over his face was to calm the fears of the people.⁹ Another reason for the veil was *"to keep the Israelites from gazing at it* [his face] *while the radiance was fading away"* (2 Cor. 3:13). For whatever reasons, the veil hindered the vision of the people—it prevented them from clearly seeing the fading glory on the face of Moses.

Q 17 How many times do "veil" or "veiled" appear in 2 Corinthians 3:7–4:6? Circle them beside this question.

⁷*Now if the ministry that brought death, which was engraved in letters on stone, came with glory, so that the Israelites could not look steadily at the face of Moses because of its glory, fading though it was,* ⁸*will not the ministry of the Spirit be even more glorious?* ⁹*If the ministry that condemns men is glorious, how much more glorious is the ministry that brings righteousness!* ¹⁰*For what was glorious has no glory now in comparison with the surpassing glory.* ¹¹*And if what was fading away came with glory, how much greater is the glory of that which lasts!* ¹²*Therefore, since we have such a hope, we are very bold.* ¹³*We are not like Moses, who would put a veil over his face to keep the Israelites from gazing at it while the radiance was fading away.* ¹⁴*But their minds were made dull, for to this day the same veil remains when the old covenant is read. It has not been removed, because only in Christ is it taken away.* ¹⁵*Even to this day when Moses is read, a veil covers their hearts.* ¹⁶*But whenever anyone turns to the Lord, the veil is taken away* (2 Cor. 3:7-16).

Paul mentions at least four things related to the veil.

Q 18 Which of the 4 truths about the veil means the most to you? Explain.

- *First,* as the glory under the veil of Moses was fading (Exod. 34:29-35), the Old Testament was fading and temporary. In contrast, the glory of the New Testament is increasing and permanent. In Moses' fading glory, the Holy Spirit showed Paul a deeper spiritual meaning.
- *Second,* it was necessary for Moses to wear a veil to hide the glory of God. In contrast, *"we are very bold. We are not like Moses, who would put a veil over his face to keep the Israelites from gazing at it while the radiance was fading away"* (2 Cor. 3:12b-13).
- *Third,* there is a veil over the hearts of Jewish unbelievers today that prevents them from seeing the truth about Jesus (2 Cor. 3:15-16).
- *Fourth,* there is a veil over the hearts and eyes of all unbelievers. Some put blinders over the eyes of a horse in the city so that it cannot see the cars. Likewise, Satan veils and blinds the minds of unbelievers.

³*...And even if our gospel is veiled, it is veiled to those who are perishing.* ⁴*The god of this age has blinded the minds of unbelievers, so that they cannot see the light of the gospel of the glory of Christ, who is the image of God* (2 Cor. 4:3b-4).

Q 19 How was the Old Testament like a veil?

The Old Testament veiled the truth. The truth shone dimly through the veil of rituals, types, and symbols. The high priest represented Jesus. The animal sacrifices were types of Jesus, the Lamb of God who takes away the sin of the world (John 1:29). But the Israelites could not see these truths clearly. And in the temple, a veil kept people at a distance. This veil separated God from everyone except the high priest. The veil over the face of Moses hid the glory of God. Likewise, the Old Testament was like a veil—it prevented people from seeing the truth clearly.

D. The moon illustrates our relationship to the new covenant. As the moon reflects the glory of the sun, the Spirit enables us to reflect God's glory (2 Cor. 3:16–4:6).

Figure 11.7
The moon reflects the glory of the sun.

¹⁶But whenever anyone turns to the Lord, the veil is taken away. ¹⁷Now the Lord is the Spirit, and where the Spirit of the Lord is, there is freedom. ¹⁸And we, who with unveiled faces all reflect the Lord's glory, are being transformed into his likeness with ever-increasing glory, which comes from the Lord, who is the Spirit.

¹Therefore, since through God's mercy we have this ministry, we do not lose heart. ²Rather, we have renounced secret and shameful ways; we do not use deception, nor do we distort the word of God. On the contrary, by setting forth the truth plainly we commend ourselves to every man's conscience in the sight of God. ³And even if our gospel is veiled, it is veiled to those who are perishing. ⁴The god of this age has blinded the minds of unbelievers, so that they cannot see the light of the gospel of the glory of Christ, who is the image of God. ⁵For we do not preach ourselves, but Jesus Christ as Lord, and ourselves as your servants for Jesus' sake. ⁶For God, who said, "Let light shine out of darkness," made his light shine in our hearts to give us the light of the knowledge of the glory of God in the face of Christ (2 Cor. 3:16–4:6).

In this lesson, we are studying some contrasts between the ministries of the Old and New Testaments. Some say that the contrast between the Old Testament and the New Testament is Law and grace.¹⁰ For sure, the Law was the core of the old covenant. Likewise, Paul in his letters to the Corinthians emphasizes grace, love, and faith in Christ. Grace, love, and faith are always present in our relationship with God. But for Paul, the power of ministry in the New Testament is the Holy Spirit. So in Corinthians, when we contrast the ministries of the Old and New Testaments, we

Q 20 ⤴ *In Corinthians, is the main contrast between Law and grace? Explain.*

Figure 11.8a   The Law was the core of the old covenant.

Figure 11.8b   The power of ministry in the New Testament is the Holy Spirit.

prefer to contrast the Law and the Spirit. Grace is a thing, not a person. Grace cannot hear us when we talk about it. In contrast, the Holy Spirit is a person who is always present and deserves all the credit, honor, and respect we can give Him. Sometimes, believers emphasize grace but say little about the Holy Spirit. To the authors of this course, it seems good to keep the emphasis on the Spirit, whom God gives us by grace.

Names and titles of the Holy Spirit.   The New Testament refers to the Holy Spirit, in relation to the Trinity, in several ways.

Q 21 ⤴ *What are some names and titles of the Spirit?*

- In Romans 8:9, the Holy Spirit is referred to as *the Spirit, the Spirit of God,* and *the Spirit of Christ.*
- In Acts 16:6-7, the Holy Spirit is also called *the Spirit of Jesus.* The Spirit comes from the Father and the Son (John 14:16-18), and the Father and Son do their work on earth through the Holy Spirit.
- In 2 Corinthians 3:17, *the Spirit of the Lord* seems to refer to the Holy Spirit.

There is unity in the Trinity. The Father, Son, and Spirit are three persons with the same character, essence, and purpose. Jesus is the exact representation of the Father (Heb. 1:3). Jesus is the image of God (2 Cor. 4:4). So Jesus said, *"Anyone who has seen me has seen the Father"* (John 14:9). Likewise, the Spirit exactly represents Jesus.

When Jesus said, *"I will not leave you as orphans; I will come to you"* (John 14:18), He meant that the Holy Spirit would come. The unity in the Trinity helps us understand what Paul means by *"the Lord is the Spirit"* (2 Cor. 3:17). The Lord Jesus and the Spirit are one in nature, essence, and purpose.

Ministry of the Spirit. In First Corinthians, Paul wrote about the ministry and gifts of the Spirit. And in Second Corinthians, Paul mentions several things about the Spirit's ministry.

Q 22 *In your own words, complete the chart on the Spirit's ministry (Figure 11.9).*

2 Cor.	Summary of the Spirit's ministry
3:3	
3:6	
3:17	
3:18	

Figure 11.9 Summary of the Spirit's ministry

- **The Spirit gives us new life and birth.** *"You show that you are a letter from Christ, the result of our ministry, written not with ink but with the Spirit of the living God, not on tablets of stone but on tablets of human hearts"* (2 Cor. 3:3).
- **The Spirit equips us to minister.** *"He has made us competent as ministers of a new covenant—not of the letter but of the Spirit; for the letter kills, but the Spirit gives life"* (2 Cor. 3:6).
- **The Spirit gives us freedom—from the Law, the world, and the flesh.** *"Now the Lord is the Spirit, and where the Spirit of the Lord is, there is freedom"* (2 Cor. 3:17; see Gal. 5:16).
- **The Spirit transforms us, day by day, to be like Jesus and reflect Him.** *"And we, who with unveiled faces all reflect the Lord's glory, are being transformed into his likeness with ever-increasing glory, which comes from the Lord, who is the Spirit"* (2 Cor. 3:18).

The moon illustrates the final truth of this lesson. At night, the moon graces the heavens with its beautiful light. But scientists have learned that the moon has no light of its own—it only reflects the light of the sun. Likewise, Paul says that we reflect the Lord's glory. The moon reflects the glory of the sun, but the moon is not being changed to look like the sun. In contrast, we reflect the Lord's glory, and we are being transformed (Greek: *metamorphosis*) to be like Jesus.

There are *three faces* in this lesson (2 Cor. 3:4–4:6).
- The face of Moses shone. It reflected the glory of God after being in His presence (2 Cor. 3:7). Moses wore a veil to hide the glory from the Israelites.
- The face of Jesus shines with the glory of God. The apostle Paul first met Jesus at noon on the road to Damascus. Jesus shone down on Saul as a light brighter than the sun (Acts 26:19). Likewise, when John saw the risen Christ in a vision, *"His face was like the sun; shining in its strength"* (Rev. 1:16).
- Our faces reflect and radiate the glory of Jesus. Read 2 Corinthians 3:18 again. *"And we, who with unveiled faces all reflect the Lord's glory, are being transformed into his likeness with ever-increasing glory, which comes from the Lord, who is the Spirit."*

Q 23 *Read 2 Corinthians 4:2. As the Spirit transforms us, how are we different from sinners?*

Q 24 *Read 2 Corinthians 4:5. As the Spirit transforms us, we preach and testify about _____.*

> **WE ARE BEING TRANSFORMED TO BE LIKE JESUS—*SANCTIFIED*.**

We are being transformed to be like Jesus. Another word for this process is *sanctification*. From the time we are born again, God's plan is for us to grow in grace and become more like Christ. Little by little, one step at a time, as we cooperate

Paul Defends His Apostolic Ministry

with the Spirit, study the word, and pray, God is transforming us. Christianity is not only about what Jesus did *for* us on the cross, but also what He does *in* us by the power of His Spirit, through *"the face of Christ"* (2 Cor. 4:6).

Q 25 *Review: Write 2 sentences about each of these: a pointing finger, a helping hand, a veil, and the moon.*

Lesson 34 — Keys to Staying Encouraged (2 Cor. 4:7-18)

Goal: *From 2 Corinthians 4, explain and illustrate 5 reasons why we do not lose heart.*

Setting

2 Cor.	A	B
3:4–4:6	Ministry of the Law	Ministry of the Spirit
4:7	The treasure of God's Spirit	
4:8-9, 16	Outwardly	
4:17	Light affliction now	
4:17-18		
4:18		
5:1-10	Earthly body	

Figure 11.10 Some contrasts in 2 Corinthians 3–5

Q 26 *Complete Figure 11.10 on some contrasts in 2 Corinthians.*

Second Corinthians 4 begins and ends with the words *"We do not lose heart"* (2 Cor. 4:1, 16). These words are like two brackets that set off or enclose the chapter. *We do not lose heart* is a sign over the front door and the back door of 2 Corinthians 4. Paul gives us five reasons why we do not lose heart—why we have courage for the conflict.[11]

Q 27 *With which words does 2 Corinthians 4 begin and end?*

A. Reason 1: We focus on the treasure, not the clay jar it is in (2 Cor. 4:7, 10-11).

But we have this treasure in jars of clay to show that this all-surpassing power is from God and not from us (2 Cor. 4:7).

The *first* reason why we do not lose heart is that we remember the source of our power. All of God's famous servants have been *weak* believers who did great things for God <u>because</u> they depended on Him.[12] Paul reminded the Corinthians of this in his first letter to them (1 Cor. 1:26-31).

Q 28 *Name 5 types of people God uses so that He will receive the glory (1 Cor. 1:26-31).*

> [26]*Brothers, think of what you were when you were called. Not many of you were wise by human standards; not many were influential; not many were of noble birth.* [27]*But God chose the foolish things of the world to shame the wise; God chose the weak things of the world to shame the strong.* [28]*He chose the lowly things of this world and the despised things—and the things that are not—to nullify the things that are,* [29]*so that no one may boast before him.* [30]*It is because of him that you are in Christ Jesus, who has become for us wisdom from God—that is, our righteousness, holiness and redemption.* [31]*Therefore, as it is written: "Let him who boasts boast in the Lord* (1 Cor. 1:26-31).

There is something wrong when the container robs the treasure of its glory. It is sad when the casket attracts more attention than the person in it. It is wrong when the picture takes second place to the frame. It is a shame when the dish distracts people from the food in it. It is a deadly sin when the power is from us and not from God.[13]

Q 29 *Give examples of the treasure taking second place to the container.*

Read 2 Corinthians 4:7 again. God delights to put the treasure of His Spirit in clay jars. He loves to put His fullness in common people. How often He shows His power through those who are last on the list! Samuel chose Eliab, the most handsome and the best looking. But God chose David, the youngest and the least.

Q 30 *What is "this treasure" (2 Cor. 4:7)?*

Q 31 *Why does God put the treasure in clay jars?*

What mighty power God pours through plain people with simple speech! He ignores long, loud prayers on the street corners that call attention to those who are praying (Matt. 6:5). Yet He answers the humble prayers of those like Hannah who pray in only a whisper (1 Sam. 1:12-13). An empty cart rattles the loudest.

Those who trust in man will lose heart. People and organizations will disappoint us. Let us not be like the disciples, who called attention to big religious *buildings* (Matt. 24:1). Or like those who admired Saul because he was taller than the others. Let us remind ourselves that the battle is not to the strong or to the swift, but to the Lord. Let us beware of human jars that absorb the glory which belongs to God alone. *"God is opposed to the proud, but gives grace to the humble"* (James 4:6).

God places no value on laziness, ignorance, or disorder. We must make every effort to offer God our best as we pray, study, and walk in the Spirit. But let us avoid all that calls attention to ourselves. We must present to the Lord a pure vessel—a clay jar that is pure, clean, and holy. And remember that our great treasure and power is the Holy Spirit within us.

²⁰Now to him who is able to do far more abundantly beyond all that we ask or think, according to the power that works within us, ²¹to Him be the glory in the church and in Christ Jesus to all generations, forever and ever! Amen (Eph. 3:20-21).

We have this treasure in jars of clay to show that this all-surpassing power is from God and not from us (2 Cor. 4:7).

Q 32 *How does Isaiah 40:28-31 relate to 2 Corinthians 4:7?*

B. Reason 2: We are wasting away outwardly, but inwardly we are renewed day by day (2 Cor. 4:8-12, 16).

The second reason why we do not lose heart is that God renews us within.

⁸We are hard pressed on every side, but not crushed; perplexed, but not in despair; ⁹persecuted, but not abandoned; struck down, but not destroyed. ...¹⁶Therefore we do not lose heart. Though outwardly we are wasting away, yet inwardly we are being renewed day by day (2 Cor. 4:8-9, 16).

Q 33 *How are believers wasting away outwardly?*

The problem. To survive, Paul needed a lot of help from the Holy Spirit. In 2 Corinthians 1:8, Paul mentioned suffering that was beyond human ability to endure. Later in this letter, he lists more of his sufferings, such as prison, floggings, 39 lashes, beatings, stoning, shipwreck, and robbers. He was often without food, clothing, sleep, and friends. And Paul lived with a thorn in the flesh that tormented him. Insult, hardship, pain, persecution, difficulty, and weakness walked with him wherever he went (2 Cor. 11:16–12:10).

In lesser ways we all have our struggles. Sickness beats us. Business robs us. Friends desert us. Strength fails. Loved ones disappoint us. Satan mocks us.

Q 34 *What are some ways in which we enable the Spirit to renew us within?*

The solution. *"Though outwardly we are wasting away, yet inwardly we are being renewed day by day"* (2 Cor. 4:16). In the hot, dry desert, Paul had plenty of cool water. He drank often from the spring of water welling up to eternal life (John 4:13-14). He prayed in tongues to build himself up more than all the Corinthians prayed (1 Cor. 14:18). He meditated on the promises of God. He enjoyed the presence of Christ at all times. Thus he could say, *¹⁶"At my first defense no one supported me, but all deserted me; may it not be counted against them. ¹⁷But the Lord stood with me and strengthened me"* (2 Tim. 4:16-17).

A great Scottish preacher wrote, "There are times when things look very dark to me—so dark that I have to wait, even for hope. Yet I have learned to wait for hope. When I see no light, I refuse to despair. When I have nothing but dark night around me, still I keep the curtains open in case a star may appear. Although I have an empty place in my heart, I refuse to allow defeat to fill that space. Waiting for hope is the greatest patience in the universe! When we wait for hope, and trust in God, we are like Job in the storm, like Abraham on the road to Moriah, like Moses in the desert of Midian, and like Jesus in Gethsemane."[14]

Why are you in despair, O my soul? And why have you become disturbed within me? Hope in God, for I shall yet praise Him, the help of my countenance and my God (Ps. 42:11).

When the mountains are on both sides of us, Pharaoh's army is behind us, and the Red Sea is before us, the Holy Spirit is *a sea of peace* within us.[15]

As a young woman, Annie Johnson Flint suffered from rheumatoid arthritis. It left her crippled and unable to rise from bed. To avoid some pain, she rested and slept on soft pillows. Her body developed bed sores, and cancer finally conquered her. All her years she struggled as a captive of disease and pain. Still, her heart was filled with faith. She daily trusted God to give her the grace and strength she needed. Her fingers were bent, stiff, sore, and swollen from arthritis. Yet these very fingers wrote comfort for herself, her friends, and the world. One of her poems that later became a famous hymn, was "He Giveth More Grace":[16]

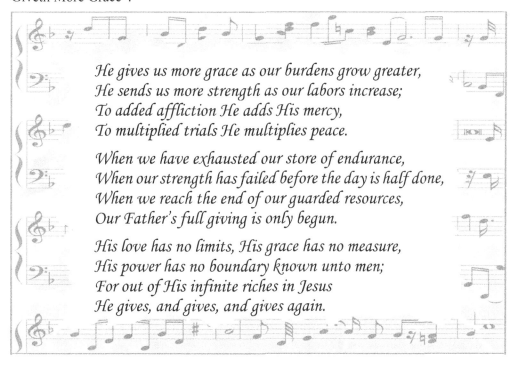

He gives us more grace as our burdens grow greater,
He sends us more strength as our labors increase;
To added affliction He adds His mercy,
To multiplied trials He multiplies peace.

When we have exhausted our store of endurance,
When our strength has failed before the day is half done,
When we reach the end of our guarded resources,
Our Father's full giving is only begun.

His love has no limits, His grace has no measure,
His power has no boundary known unto men;
For out of His infinite riches in Jesus
He gives, and gives, and gives again.

So Paul could say, *"In all our troubles my joy knows no bounds"* (2 Cor. 7:4).

Therefore we do not lose heart. Though outwardly we are wasting away, yet inwardly we are being renewed day by day (2 Cor. 4:16).

C. Reason 3: We encourage ourselves and others by what we speak (2 Cor. 4:13-14).

[13]*It is written: "I believed; therefore I have spoken." With that same spirit of faith we also believe and therefore speak,* [14]*because we know that the one who raised the Lord Jesus from the dead will also raise us with Jesus and present us with you in his presence* (2 Cor. 4:13-14).

Faith talks. In 2 Corinthians 4:13, Paul quotes Psalm 116:10: *"I believed; therefore I have spoken."* Like the writer of Psalm 116, Paul believed—he had *"that same spirit of faith"* (2 Cor. 4:13). What did Paul believe? He believed the gospel, including the resurrection (2 Cor. 4:14). Paul was trained as a Pharisee, and unlike the Sadducees, he

Q 35 *How does faith reveal itself in our speech?*

believed in the resurrection of the dead (2 Cor. 5:1; Matt. 22:22-34; Acts 23:6). He was sure that when his body, like a tent, was worn-out, torn down, and destroyed, God would provide a new one. Paul's belief caused him to speak—to testify and preach the good news.

Belief causes us to speak. As Jesus said, *"the mouth speaks out of that which fills the heart"* (Matt. 12:34). A heart full of faith causes the mouth to speak words of faith. Light shines, fire produces heat, and faith speaks.

Faith talks—it quotes the promises of God. This helps others hear the gospel. And "faith talk" also helps the person who is talking. Faith comes from hearing the Word of God (Rom. 10:17). We strengthen our faith and the faith of others as we declare the Scripture.

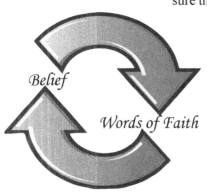

Figure 11.11 Belief speaks words of faith, and words of faith strengthen belief.

Watch what you say. Both faith and doubt are contagious—they spread like yeast. Your words can either encourage or discourage. Words have power to shape our attitudes, emotions, and actions. When the ten spies spoke words of doubt and discouragement, they infected an entire nation with unbelief. In contrast, in the midst of his sufferings, Job believed and spoke words of faith. In his darkest hour he affirmed, [25]*"As for me, I know that my Redeemer lives, and at the last He will take His stand on the earth.* [26]*Even after my skin is destroyed, Yet from my flesh I shall see God;* [27]*Whom I myself shall behold, And whom my eyes will see and not another. My heart faints within me"* (Job 19:25-27). When no one else encouraged Job, he encouraged himself with the truth that he knew. Train yourself to speak words of faith and encouragement.

Q 36 What does Ephesians 4:29 say about our speech?

Q 37 Is there a time for negative words? Explain.

For everything there is a time (Eccl. 3:1, 7). There is a time to mourn (Eccl. 3:4). There is a time to admit that we are sick and ask for prayer. There is a time to tell God and others about our troubles, as Jesus did in Gethsemane and Paul did in 2 Corinthians. There is a time to confess our sins, our faults, and our needs (James 5:13-16). The authors of this course do NOT agree with those who say that there is never a time for negative words. The Scriptures give many examples of godly people talking about their feelings, needs, and problems. There is a time for this. However, the Bible also teaches us, *"Let the word of Christ richly dwell within you, with all wisdom teaching and admonishing one another with psalms and hymns and spiritual songs, singing with thankfulness in your hearts to God"* (Col. 3:16).

Feed your faith and starve your doubts. Speak the words of God to yourself and others. Practice self talk (what you tell yourself) that is guided by the Word and the Spirit. *"We do not lose heart"* (2 Cor. 4:1, 16).

D. Reason 4: We weigh our present troubles against the weight of our future glory (2 Cor. 4:17).

For our light and momentary troubles are achieving for us an eternal glory that far outweighs them all (2 Cor. 4:17).

This is a verse of great contrasts. Paul sets things present and things to come side by side.

Q 38 Complete Figure 11.12 on the contrasts in 2 Corinthians 4:17.

Present Troubles	Future Glory
Light as a feather	
Short as a moment	

Figure 11.12 Second Corinthians 4:17 contrasts present troubles with future glory.

Read 2 Corinthians 4:17 again. Paul is not teaching that by suffering we earn future glory. Rather, he is contrasting our light, short sufferings with the eternal glory God will give us by His grace. Our sufferings for Jesus do not earn future glory, but they are part of the process. For as we suffer outwardly, we experience fellowship with God inwardly (2 Cor. 4:8-12, 16).

Paul's troubles were severe, year after year—beyond his human ability to endure (2 Cor. 1:8; 11:16–12:10). Yet he calls these sufferings *light* and *short* (2 Cor. 4:17). The Holy Spirit shows Paul the great contrast between our time on earth and eternity in heaven. Present sufferings are lighter than a feather. Future glory is heavier than a boulder. Present sufferings are as short as a moment—measured by a second on a watch. But a millennium is too short of a stick to measure the glory of eternity. Heaven is a bargain no matter how much it costs you.[17]

Q 39 *What contrast is in Romans 8:18?*

E. Reason 5: We focus on the unseen, not the seen (2 Cor. 4:18).

So we fix our eyes not on what is seen, but on what is unseen. For what is seen is temporary, but what is unseen is eternal (2 Cor. 4:18).

Second Corinthians 4:18 mentions two types of vision: the first is sight, and the second is insight. The first method of seeing is natural, but the second is spiritual. The mind of the flesh can see the visible. But only the spirit can see the invisible. Eyes of the flesh see only outward circumstances. But spiritual eyes discover secrets of the kingdom of God.

Q 40 *What are some examples of fixing our eyes on the unseen?*

The Bible often contrasts fleshly sight and spiritual insight. For example, an army of enemies surrounded Elisha (2 Kings 6:1-15). Elisha's servant was surprised to see an army with horses and chariots in the morning. His fleshly eyes saw that they were shut in by *"the things which are seen."* Who has not shared an experience like his? Sometimes circumstances, such as financial problems, sickness, conflict, and confusion, press on us from every side. Like Elisha's servant, we may be tempted to think that *"the things that are seen"* are the only things. But the prophet had eyes of faith. His spiritual eyes saw the hills full of horses and chariots of fire (2 Kings 6:8-22). The servant had fleshly sight, but the prophet had spiritual insight. One had reason; the other had faith.[18]

Like Paul, let us *"live by faith, not by sight"* (2 Cor. 5:7).

[42]*A poor widow came and put in two small copper coins, which amount to a cent.* [43]*Calling His disciples to Him, He said to them, "Truly I say to you, this poor widow put in more than all the contributors to the treasury;* [44]*for they all put in out of their surplus, but she, out of her poverty, put in all she owned, all she had to live on"* (Mark 12:42-44).

Those with only eyes of flesh saw little in the widow's offering. Perhaps some laughed when she gave only *"two very small copper coins."* This was not much to support such a big temple! But Jesus was watching with spiritual eyes. And He saw the unseen—her invisible spirit of worship. The treasurer saw two copper coins, but Jesus saw an offering that heaven would remember forever.

In this lesson, we have looked at five principles of encouragement—five reasons why we do not lose heart.

- We focus on the treasure, not the clay jar it is in (2 Cor. 4:7, 10-11).
- We are wasting away outwardly, but inwardly we are renewed day by day (2 Cor. 4:8-12, 16).
- We encourage ourselves and others by what we speak (2 Cor. 4:13-14).
- We weigh our present troubles against the weight of our future glory (2 Cor. 4:17).
- We focus on the unseen, not the seen (2 Cor. 4:18).

Lesson 35: Facts for Facing Death (2 Cor. 5:1-10)

Goal: *Analyze and apply 7 truths that prepare us for death (2 Cor. 5:1-10).*

A believer named Marcos went to visit Julio, a neighbor. Julio's father had just died, and soon the family would gather for the funeral. Marcos sensed that this could be the opportunity for which he had prayed. Marcos expressed sorrow and sympathy for the father's death. He mentioned the death of his grandfather, who had prepared well for death. Then came a great surprise. Julio said, "I am very afraid of death." So Marcos shared some things the Bible teaches us about death.

Death is a visitor that comes to every home. Are we prepared to face death? In this lesson we will study seven biblical truths about death.[19] Use these truths to prepare yourself and to help others be ready.

A. Our earthly body is like a tent—it is temporary (2 Cor. 5:1, 4).

At the end of 2 Corinthians 4, Paul contrasted the seen and the unseen. He continues this by contrasting the body we see now and the future body we will receive at the resurrection (read 2 Corinthians 5:1-10, especially 5:7).

Figure 11.13 Like Abraham, some people today live in tents. They move the tent from place to place so their sheep and goats have grass and water.

¹Now we know that if the earthly tent we live in is destroyed, we have a building from God, an eternal house in heaven, not built by human hands. ²Meanwhile we groan, longing to be clothed with our heavenly dwelling, ³because when we are clothed, we will not be found naked. ⁴For while we are in this tent, we groan and are burdened (2 Cor. 5:1-4).

Paul sewed tents to support his ministry (Acts 18:3). So it does not surprise us that he used a tent to illustrate truth. Paul says that living in our earthly body is like living in a tent. Tents are modest and temporary. Unlike the best houses, tents have no foundation. They are made of cloth, fabric, or animal skins. Strong winds may cause the wall of a tent to move or even fall. People drive pegs in the ground and tie ropes to the tent walls to help hold the walls up. Those who live in tents do not stay long in one place. They are visitors and pilgrims—just passing through.

Q 41 *What are some ways in which a tent differs from a home?*

The book of Hebrews contrasts living in a tent on earth with living in permanent buildings in heaven.

⁹By faith he lived as an alien in the land of promise, as in a foreign land, dwelling in tents with Isaac and Jacob, fellow heirs of the same promise; ¹⁰for he was looking for the city which has foundations, whose architect and builder is God (Heb. 11:9-10).

Paul compares a tent and a permanent building to our present and future bodies.[20] Our earthly body is temporary, like a tent.

B. The earthly tent we live in may be destroyed (2 Cor. 5:1).

*Now we know that **if the earthly tent we live in is destroyed**, we have a building from God, an eternal house in heaven, not built by human hands* (2 Cor. 5:1).

Q 42 *Is it spiritual for believers to prepare for death? Explain.*

Note the word *if* in 2 Corinthians 5:1. Earlier, in a letter to the Thessalonians, Paul explained that some will not die.

¹⁵For this we say to you by the word of the Lord, that we who are alive and remain until the coming of the Lord, will not precede those who have fallen asleep. ¹⁶For the Lord Himself will descend from heaven with a shout, with the voice of the archangel and with the trumpet of God, and the dead in Christ will rise first. ¹⁷Then we who are alive and remain will be caught up together with them in the clouds to meet the Lord in the air, and so we shall always be with the Lord. ¹⁸Therefore comfort one another with these words (1 Thess. 4:15-18).

All of us should live so that we are ready to meet the Lord at any moment. Still, we should also prepare for death.

Paul Defends His Apostolic Ministry

Death is a subject that many avoid. But most believers must face death. Paul hoped that he would not die. He did not want his earthly tent or body to be destroyed. He groaned at the thought of dying, because he did not want his soul to be unclothed. *"For while we are in this tent, we groan and are burdened, because we do not wish to be unclothed"* (2 Cor. 5:4). In Jewish and Christian thought, the body, soul, and spirit are united. Paul sees the soul as naked when death separates the soul from the body. Even though our earthly body is weak and tends to lust, we do not want to exist only as a *naked* soul and spirit. God has created the human soul and spirit with a desire to be *clothed* with a body. Likewise, even demons desire to live in a body (Matt. 12:43-45). As our bodies get older and weaker, they are not all we would like them to be. Still, we appreciate having a body to live in!

We groan at the thought of dying. And we groan while waiting for our new bodies.

²²For we know that the whole creation groans and suffers the pains of childbirth together until now. ²³And not only this, but also we ourselves, having the first fruits of the Spirit, even we ourselves groan within ourselves, waiting eagerly for our adoption as sons, the redemption of our body (Rom. 8:22-23).

Solomon described old age in Ecclesiastes 12:1-7. Take time to read these verses.

Q 43 *In Ecclesiastes 12:1-7, how does Solomon represent few teeth, dim vision, poor hearing, white hair, and weakness?*

Most of the people who live on earth must die. But the return of Christ is *"the blessed hope"* for all of us (Tit. 2:11-14). We would love to hear the final trumpet today. Then, we would escape death, and we would replace this old tent with something better.

Even if death separates the believer's soul from the body, God will give us a beautiful white robe to wear until the Resurrection (Rev. 6:10-11). And perhaps while we wait for a new body, God may glorify us as He did Moses and Elijah (Matt. 17:3).

Q 44 *What are some reasons why we call the return of Christ the "Blessed Hope" (Tit. 2:11-14)?*

C. Our future body is like a heavenly building—it is eternal (2 Cor. 5:1-4).

Our earthly body is like a tent—temporary. But our heavenly body is like a building in heaven—eternal. The body we receive at the Resurrection will provide a *permanent* covering for the naked soul.²¹ Recall that Paul wrote about our new bodies in 1 Corinthians. Our heavenly bodies are eternal; they cannot die, perish, or grow old!

Q 45 *What are some characteristics of the spiritual body God will give us at the Resurrection (1 Cor. 15)?*

Paul built tents with his own hands. Likewise, all that we build on earth requires the work of our hands. In contrast, God, who spoke the worlds into existence, will create our new bodies without any help from us!

D. God has given us the Holy Spirit as a deposit to guarantee our future beyond death (2 Cor. 5:4-5).

⁴For while we are in this tent, we groan and are burdened, because we do not wish to be unclothed but to be clothed with our heavenly dwelling, so that what is mortal may be swallowed up by life. ⁵Now it is God who has made us for this very purpose and has given us the Spirit as a deposit, guaranteeing what is to come (2 Cor. 5:4-5).

What happens after death? People have different opinions.

- Some say that after death, nothing happens. These atheists think that humans are an accident—a collection of atoms.
- Others, like Hindus and New Age followers, say that death is a door to the next life. These think that after death, we may be a tree, a cow, a snake, or a god. Followers of Jesus believe that these teachings on reincarnation are either myths or *"doctrines of demons"* (1 Tim. 4:1).

Q 46 *What do non-Christians think happens at death?*

What happens after death? Our answer is, "We are with Jesus!" This answer is not just a guess or an "I think so." We KNOW! Paul begins 2 Corinthians 5:1 with the words: *"Now we know."* We know whom we have believed.

Q 47 *How is the Spirit like a deposit that God has given us?*

- *⁸"Therefore do not be ashamed of the testimony of our Lord or of me His prisoner, but join with me in suffering for the gospel according to the power of God, ⁹who has saved us and called us with a holy calling, not according to our works, but according to His own purpose and grace which was granted us in Christ Jesus from all eternity, ¹⁰but now has been revealed by the appearing of our Savior Christ Jesus, who abolished death and brought life and immortality to light through the gospel, ¹¹for which I was appointed a preacher and an apostle and a teacher. ¹²For this reason I also suffer these things, but I am not ashamed; for **I know whom I have believed** and I am convinced that He is able to guard what I have entrusted to Him until that day"* (2 Tim. 1:8-12).

- *²"Beloved, now we are children of God, and it has not appeared as yet what we will be. We know that **when He appears, we will be like Him,** because we will see Him just as He is. ³And everyone who has this hope fixed on Him purifies himself, just as He is pure"* (1 John 3:2-3).

We know because God's Spirit gives us an inner witness and assurance.

- *¹⁶"The Spirit Himself testifies with our spirit that we are children of God, ¹⁷and if children, heirs also, heirs of God and fellow heirs with Christ, if indeed we suffer with Him so that we may also be glorified with Him"* (Rom. 8:16-17).

When a person wants to buy a house, he must give a deposit—a large amount of money that assures the seller. Likewise, God gives us the great deposit of His Spirit to guarantee that the gospel is true. Those without God fear death. But we do not fear to cross death's river, for we are sure that our Father, our Savior, and many beloved others are there. The Spirit inspires us to sing the old song, "Blessed assurance, Jesus is mine, O what a foretaste of glory divine!"²²

E. To be absent from the body is to be present with the Lord (2 Cor. 5:6-8).

⁶Therefore we are always confident and know that as long as we are at home in the body we are away from the Lord. ⁷We live by faith, not by sight. ⁸We are confident, I say, and would prefer to be away from the body and at home with the Lord (2 Cor. 5:6-8).

Q 48 *Did Paul believe in purgatory or soul sleep? Explain.*

When Paul considers death, he is not thinking about purgatory—a doctrine that is nowhere in the Bible. Nor does Paul believe in soul sleep—the false teaching that when believers die, they take a long nap. Paul says that at death, we are at once in the presence of the Lord. Death may separate our bodies from our spirits, but *nothing can separate us from the love of God in Christ Jesus.*

³⁵Who will separate us from the love of Christ? Will tribulation, or distress, or persecution, or famine, or nakedness, or peril, or sword? ³⁶Just as it is written, "FOR YOUR SAKE WE ARE BEING PUT TO DEATH ALL DAY LONG; WE WERE CONSIDERED AS SHEEP TO BE SLAUGHTERED." ³⁷But in all these things we overwhelmingly conquer through Him who loved us. ³⁸For I am convinced that neither death, nor life, nor angels, nor principalities, nor things present, nor things to come, nor powers, ³⁹nor height, nor depth, nor any other created thing, will be able to separate us from the love of God, which is in Christ Jesus our Lord (Rom. 8:35-39).

To be absent from the body is to be present with the Lord.

F. It is better and preferred to be with the Lord in heaven (2 Cor. 5:8).

Q 49 *Which 2 options did Paul face?*

*We are confident, I say, and would **prefer** to be away from the body and at home with the Lord* (2 Cor. 5:8).

Paul saw life through spiritual eyes. He knew that living in heaven was far better than living on earth.

Paul Defends His Apostolic Ministry

²¹For to me, to live is Christ and to die is gain. ²²But if I am to live on in the flesh, this will mean fruitful labor for me; and I do not know which to choose. ²³But I am hard-pressed from both directions, having the desire to depart and be with Christ, for that is very much better (Phil. 1:21-23).

Sometimes Christians fear and fight death too much. A country preacher was preaching on heaven. He asked: "How many of you want to go to heaven?" Except for one boy, everyone raised his hand. The preacher asked, "Son, don't you want to go to heaven?" "Sure, I want to go to heaven," said the boy. "But I thought you were getting a group ready to go tonight!"

A preacher told the story of a family he knew.²³ There was a little boy who was ill with a disease that no doctor could cure. Month by month the mother cared for him. In time, as the boy watched other boys playing outside his window, the truth came to him. He realized that he was dying. One day he asked the question that was heavy on his childish heart. "Mama, what is it like to die? Does it hurt?"

Quick tears filled her eyes, and she fled to the kitchen to hide her sorrow. Alone, she prayed that the Lord would give her an answer that would bring peace to her little boy. The Lord gave her that answer. She came back and said to him, "Do you remember when you played hard all day? At the end of the day you came in and lay down on mama's bed with all of your clothes on and fell asleep. When you woke up in the morning, you found yourself with your pajamas on and in your own bed. What happened during the night was that your daddy came in. With his strong arms he lifted you from mommy's bed to your own bed. He carried you. And death is like that. We wake up one morning in another room—the room where we belong. It will be a room that the Lord gives us because He loves us and died for us and rose again." With a smile on his face, the little boy told his mother that he understood. His father's big strong arms would carry him to his own room.

Q 50 *What is death like for a believer?*

Death is not a dungeon. It is a door to heaven and to our eternal reward.

Q 51 *What was the bema in Corinth?*

G. After death, we must all stand before Christ to be judged (2 Cor. 5:9-10).

⁹So we make it our goal to please him, whether we are at home in the body or away from it. ¹⁰For we must all appear before the judgment seat of Christ, that each one may receive what is due him for the things done while in the body, whether good or bad (2 Cor. 5:9-10).

The Greek word for *judgment seat* is *bema*. The Corinthians were familiar with the *bema*. The Romans punished crime in public. So the judge sat in the open, at the top of the stairs to a government building.²⁴ There, the public watched and listened. Some citizens served as a jury, as the judge heard cases.²⁵ Some Jews accused Paul in Corinth and brought him to the bema court to be judged (See Figure 11.14). When Gallio refused to judge Paul's case, the Jews beat Sosthenes, the synagogue ruler, in front of the bema (Acts 18:12-17).

Figure 11.14 Remains of the judgment seat (*"bema"*) in Corinth, where Jews accused Paul before Gallio (Acts 18:12-17). In the background is the high hill called the Acrocorinth. (Internet users, search for "Bema Acts 18:12-17")

The Bible teaches that believers will one day give an account at the bema—the judgment seat of Christ. (In the *Full Life Study Bible,* or *Life in the Spirit Study Bible,* see the article "The Judgment of Believers" in 2 Corinthians 5:10.) Truth about the bema judgment is very important. In a church, it would be good to preach an entire sermon on this great event. Let us study four facts about the bema judgment of believers.

Q 52 *According to 2 Corinthians 5:10, who must stand before the judgment seat of Christ?*

1. All believers must stand before the judgment seat of Christ. There will be no exceptions.²⁶ *"We must all appear before the judgment seat of Christ"* (2 Cor. 5:10). At the bema, judgment is not as a group, but is one by one—*"that **each one** may receive what is due him"* (2 Cor. 5:10).

The judge is Christ. Other verses, such as Romans 14:10, refer to God as Judge.

¹⁰But you, why do you judge your brother? Or you again, why do you regard your brother with contempt? For we will all stand before the judgment seat of God. ¹¹For it is written, "AS I LIVE, SAYS THE LORD, EVERY KNEE SHALL BOW TO ME, AND EVERY TONGUE SHALL GIVE PRAISE TO GOD." ¹²So then each one of us will give an account of himself to God (Rom. 14:10-12).

God judges, but as John clarifies, the Father judges through the Son, who is Himself God (John 5:22-23).

The bema judgment seems to be for believers only. Yet the parallel passage in Romans 14:10-12 states that *"EVERY KNEE SHALL BOW TO ME, AND EVERY TONGUE SHALL GIVE PRAISE TO GOD."* Does this mean that the bema judgment is also for sinners?

Some passages, like Daniel 12:2 and John 5:28-29, mention the judgment of the righteous and the wicked together, emphasizing the event of judgment. In contrast, other verses, like Revelation 20:4-5, explain that there is a gap of 1000 years between the judgment of saints and the judgment of sinners. All people must stand before the judgment seat of Christ. But it seems that we believers stand at the bema a thousand years before Christ judges sinners from His great white throne (Rev. 20:11-15).

Q 53 *Does justification by faith take away our responsibility to obey? Explain.*

2. The doctrines of justification and *retribution balance each other.²⁷

Eternal life is a free gift that comes to us by God's grace (Eph. 2:8-9). We are justified—counted righteous—on the basis of Christ's death on the cross (Rom. 5:1). This is the doctrine of *justification*. Still, Christ will judge each believer. This is the doctrine of *retribution*. Each Christian will *"receive what is due him for the things done while in the body, whether good or bad"* (2 Cor. 5:9-10). God's free gift of salvation does not free us from obedience. On the Day of Judgment, all Christians must give an account of how they lived in the body.²⁸ Justification is not a substitute for obedience. And justification does not negate obedience; rather, justification makes obedience possible and necessary. Earlier, Paul warned that it is possible for him and others to be lost on the basis of his actions (1 Cor. 9–10). We must renew our decision to follow and obey Christ day by day.²⁹ At the end of our days, God will judge each of us (Eccl. 12:14; Rom. 14:10-12; 2 Cor. 5:10).

Figure 11.15
The doctrines of justification and retribution balance each other. Either doctrine without the other is extreme and unbalanced.

Q 54 *What is the purpose of the bema judgment?*

3. The bema judgment is not for salvation, but for eternal rewards (2 Cor. 5:10).

In Paul's day, cities and towns used the bema to judge crime, give speeches, and give awards. The bema was the place to give awards each year for the annual Olympic contests.

In 1 Corinthians, Paul wrote about the bema judgment for rewards.

¹²If any man builds on this foundation using gold, silver, costly stones, wood, hay or straw, ¹³his work will be shown for what it is, because the Day will bring it to light. It will be revealed with fire, and the fire will test the quality of each man's work. ¹⁴If what he has built survives, he will receive his reward. ¹⁵If it is burned up, he will suffer loss; he himself will be saved, but only as one escaping through the flames (1 Cor. 3:12-15).

Worthless building is destroyed by fire, but the builder is not destroyed with it.³⁰ What a person does may be worthless, and yet this does not exclude him from the kingdom of God.³¹

Picture each person walking into the fire, holding his works in his arms. Those who have lived wisely on earth will carry many works into and out of the fire. Others may carry many works into the fire, but have part or all of them destroyed. This will be because they lived fleshly lives, selfish lives, and did good deeds for the wrong reasons. And there will be some who do not carry any works into or out of the fire. This group may contain many *baby believers who did not mature.* At the bema, Christ does not whip anyone, but He rewards the faithful.

John Wesley lived on 30 British *pounds a year and gave more than 1000 pounds to spread the gospel. He prayed 2 hours a day and led 250,000 people to Christ. Imagine how many works he will carry through the fire! Likewise, there are many believers today who are not famous but live godly lives. At the bema judgment, these will receive great rewards (Rev. 22:12).

Sometimes schools and colleges give awards and rewards on graduation day. At the end of several years of studies, schools honor students who have worked hard and learned well. Likewise, after the contests in the Olympics, some receive honor for their success. But these types of rewards are very different from the rewards of the bema judgment. At a school or at the Olympics, only those who have done well are called to the front. Others clap after a person receives a reward. But at the bema judgment, each person will have a time to come to the front. And all will see whether the person lived wisely or foolishly. Some will have great joy, but others great sorrow (1 John 2:28; 2 John 8).

People soon forget who received the rewards at graduation or at the Olympics. But the rewards at the bema judgment will last for all eternity. What kind of rewards will God give to those who are faithful? Perhaps He will give them crowns with many jewels in them. Or perhaps He will give them positions of high responsibility and honor, over those who were less faithful on earth (Matt. 25:21, 23; Luke 19:16-19). In heaven, some who were poor and lowly on earth will be honored above those who were once wealthy and famous. Some of the first will be last, and some of the last will be first. Use well what God has given to you, and He will add to it in eternity. But neglect will cause God to subtract. God adds to the diligent and subtracts from the negligent. There is a direct relationship between how we live on earth and the level of honor we will enjoy for eternity.[32]

4. The bema judgment should cause us to judge ourselves now (2 Cor. 5:10). As Paul wrote to the Corinthians, *"If we judged ourselves, we would not come under judgment"* (1 Cor. 11:31). Here are some questions for each person to ask himself in preparation for the bema judgment:

Q 55 *What questions should we ask ourselves now to prepare for judgment day?*

- Am I a good son or daughter, bringing honor to my father and mother?
- Am I a good and faithful father or mother?
- Am I a good citizen, obeying the laws and doing my part to make the world a better place?
- Am I a good neighbor, treating others as I want to be treated?
- Am I a good church member, faithful in tithing, attending, and participating in church ministries?
- Am I a good Christian, pleasing the Lord, being holy, reading the Bible, praying, and walking in the Spirit?
- Am I a good witness, daily seeking to lead others closer to Christ by my actions and words?
- Am I a good mentor, discipling and training others to follow me, as I follow Christ?
- Am I a good steward of my body, mind, eyes, money, time, and abilities—things that God has entrusted to me to serve Him?
- Am I a cheerful giver—reaching out a full hand to give, as often as I reach out an empty hand to take?

- Am I hiding sin in a closet? Is my conscience clear? Is there anything of which I need to repent and ask God to help me change now—to prevent shame and loss in the future?

Select a song or hymn, such as "Take My Life And Let It Be." Sing it often as a prayer of commitment to God.

Q 56 *Complete Figure. 11.16 by summarizing what each passage teaches about the judgment of believers.*

Conclusion: As a review, complete Figure 11.16. Let the truth of God's Word sink deep into your heart as you read and summarize these Scriptures related to the bema judgment and our eternal rewards.

Verses	Summary of teaching about the judgment of believers
Eccl. 12:14	
Rom. 14:10-12	
1 Cor. 3:12-15	
2 Cor. 5:9-10	
Gal. 6:7-10	
Matt. 10:40-42	
Matt. 12:36-37	
Matt. 19:29	
Matt. 25:21, 23	
Luke 19:13-24	
Eph. 6:8	
Heb. 6:10-12	
1 John 2:28	
2 John 8	
Rev. 2:4-5	
Rev. 22:12	

Figure 11.16 Practice chart on verses related to the bema judgment

Lesson 36: Test Questions for a Fruitful Ministry (2 Cor. 5:11-21)

Goal: *State and apply 5 test questions of a fruitful ministry.*

Setting

Throughout 2 Corinthians, Paul speaks of his ministry and our ministry. All of us have a ministry. Some believers may think that the only ministers stand behind pulpits and preach, while all other believers just watch. But as we mature and grow in understanding, we discern that all of God's people are God's servants or ministers. All who serve God and serve others for God are His ministers.

Second Corinthians gives us helpful insights about our ministry as Christians. This passage shows us principles that made Paul a fruitful servant or minister of Jesus Christ. All of us want to be faithful and fruitful for the Lord. Let us study five principles, in the form of questions, which will guide us to be fruitful ministers for Jesus.

Take a few minutes to read 2 Corinthians 5:11-21.

The first question that each of us should ask ourselves is:

A. Does the fear of the Lord affect what I say to others?

Since, then, we know what it is to fear the Lord, we try to persuade men (2 Cor. 5:11).

There are two types of fear of God—the fear of sinners and the fear of believers. Sinners have a fear that is a dread and terror. They are afraid to stand before God on judgment day. This is the kind of fear in Revelation 6:12-15, as sinners see Jesus returning to judge them. Take a moment to read these verses.

Like all sinners, the sinners of Revelation 6:15 would rather die than meet God face to face. So when the Lord returns, those who are unprepared will cry out in fear. They will pray to die rather than face God Almighty.

In contrast to sinners, believers are free from this type of fear. We are God's children. He has forgiven our sins and adopted us into His family. His Spirit lives within us and guides us. With great joy, we look forward to Christ's return. We are delivered from the type of fear that Revelation 6:12-15 describes. God is our Father, and Jesus is our Savior and Lord. We have peace with God. Unlike sinners, we do not fear to stand before our Father.

Q 57 How do sinners fear God?

The fear that Paul writes about in 2 Corinthians 5:11 is reverence for the Lord. This fear is an attitude of respect and awe. The bema judgment is the background for this fear (2 Cor. 5:10). Paul knows that at the end of our days, we must stand before the judgment seat of Christ. So we walk *"in the fear of the Lord"* (Acts 9:31). Judgment day causes us to fear God. This fear affects what we say to others to persuade them to honor and obey Him.

Q 58 In what sense do we saints fear God?

> WHAT WE SAY TO OTHERS IS EVIDENCE OF WHAT IS IN OUR HEARTS.

What we say to others is evidence of what is in our hearts. If the fear of God is in us, this causes us to talk to others about Him. If we saw a fire burning a building, we would fear the harm that the fire could do. Knowing the fear of the fire, we would warn people in or near the building. Likewise, since we know that God will judge the world, we seek to persuade others to get ready.

Q 59 How does our fear of God affect our witness?

The first question that guides me to fruitful ministry is: **Does the fear of the Lord affect what I say to others?** Those who do not witness do not believe that a fiery day of judgment is coming. These are not fruitful in their service and ministry. These sleeping saints feel no need to warn others or *"blow a trumpet in Zion"* (Joel 2:1, 15). They seem to think that tomorrow will be okay for everybody. But the prophet warned those at ease in Zion (Amos 6:1). And the Spirit says to us, "Use your influence to prepare people for the judgment day." Paul said, *"Since, then, we know what it is to fear the Lord, we try to persuade men"* (2 Cor. 5:11). May the fear of the Lord affect what I say to others!

John Wesley often asked those he met: "Do I meet you praying?" The fear of the Lord guided him to talk to others about their walk with God.

Now let us look at the second question that guides us to a fruitful ministry.

B. Is my conscience clean?

¹¹What we are is plain to God, and I hope it is also plain to your conscience. ¹²We are not trying to commend ourselves to you again, but are giving you an opportunity to take pride in us, so that you can answer those who take pride in what is seen rather than in what is in the heart. ¹³If we are out of our mind, it is for the sake of God; if we are in our right mind, it is for you (2 Cor. 5:11-13).

Paul writes, *"What we are is plain to God, and I hope that it is also plain to your conscience"* (2 Cor. 5:11b). In Corinth, critics slandered Paul to destroy his integrity. These false teachers wanted to gain wealth and attention by leading the church away from God's apostle. Paul defended himself in order to protect the integrity of the church. Likewise, there are times when we must defend ourselves, not for our own ego, but for the sake of others. Because enemies attacked Paul's character, he told the Corinthians that his character was plain to God and should be plain to them also.

The false apostles in Corinth misjudged Paul. At the bema, there would be a true judgment. But in Corinth, false apostles judged by human standards alone, and not by the heart (2 Cor. 5:12). In contrast, Paul emphasized that God looks on the inside and speaks through our consciences.

Throughout his ministry, Paul testified often of a clean conscience.

- To the Corinthians Paul wrote, *"Our conscience testifies that we have conducted ourselves in the world, and especially in our relations with you, in the holiness and sincerity that are from God. We have done so not according to worldly wisdom but according to God's grace"* (2 Cor. 1:12).
- *"We commend ourselves to every man's conscience in the sight of God"* (2 Cor. 4:2).
- To Felix, Paul said, *"I also do my best to maintain always a blameless conscience both before God and before men"* (Acts 24:16).
- Near Paul's death, he wrote, *"I thank God, whom I serve with a clear conscience the way my forefathers did, as I constantly remember you in my prayers night and day"* (2 Tim. 1:3).

Q 60 *What enables a conscience to be clear and clean?*

> OUR CONSCIENCE FEELS GUILTY WHEN WE TREAT SOMEONE IN A WAY WE BELIEVE IS WRONG.

Conscience means "with knowledge" or "co-knowledge." It refers to knowledge of self in relation to what we believe is right and wrong. Our conscience is not clear when we profess what we do not possess. Our conscience feels guilty when we treat someone in a way we believe is wrong. Our conscience accuses us if we disobeyed God in areas of money or morals.

A child named George, only 10 years old, bought a piece of candy at a store. When the clerk gave change, he erred by giving the child one coin too many. Then the small boy erred by keeping it. Even then, his conscience told him to be honest and return the money. When George was a young man of 16, the Holy Spirit convicted him. He repented and cleared his conscience by not keeping the small coin. Likewise, we must practice keeping the conscience clean in small things. For as Jesus said, it is through being faithful in small things that we climb the steps to be faithful with greater things:

> *"He who is faithful in a very little thing is faithful also in much; and he who is unrighteous in a very little thing is unrighteous also in much"* (Luke 16:10).

One preacher wrote, "I stole a test in college and did well on it. But for a whole year, my relationship with the Lord suffered, until I made things right and cleansed my conscience. I could not pray when my conscience was stained. I could not witness when my conscience was stained. I did not even enjoy reading God's Word when my conscience was stained. Paul knows that fruitful ministry depends on a clean conscience. To relate well to God and others, we must keep our consciences clear. When we do something wrong—offend God or another, what will we do? Will we repent and see our conscience cleansed, or rebel and live with a guilty conscience? When our conscience is clean, we can worship God and minister to others."[33]

Jesus was so busy with ministry that He missed a meal. His family members said, *"He is out of his mind"* (Mark 3:21). Likewise, Paul's critics said he was *out of his mind*. Perhaps they thought he worked too much, witnessed too much, gave too much, or prayed in tongues too much (1 Cor. 14:18, 23). When we walk in the Spirit, people may say that we are fanatics or are out of our minds in ministry. We cannot control what people say. But we can please God in all our thoughts, attitudes, and actions. When we live with a clean conscience, we can say with Paul, *"If we are out of our mind, it is for the sake of God; if we are in our right mind, it is for you"* (2 Cor. 5:13).

Paul Defends His Apostolic Ministry

We come now to the third question to guide us in a fruitful ministry.

C. Does the love of Christ compel me?

¹⁴For Christ's love compels us, because we are convinced that one died for all, and therefore all died. ¹⁵And he died for all, that those who live should no longer live for themselves but for him who died for them and was raised again (2 Cor. 5:14-15).

Earlier, we saw that *"the fear of the Lord"* guided Paul to persuade people to make peace with God (2 Cor. 5:11). Likewise, *"the love of the Lord"* compelled him to lead people to Jesus (2 Cor. 5:14).

Gasoline powers a car to go forward. Batteries energize a flash light. Wood enables a fire to burn and produce heat. Food provides energy to work. The love of Christ inspires us to minister to others.

Love of money drives many forward in business. Love of pleasure leads multitudes astray. Love of praise motivated Pharisees (Matt. 6). Love of self guides us to serve ourselves. Love of power and position pushes some to cheat, steal, and even murder. But the love of Christ—that love He showed on Calvary—compels us to share the gospel.

The love of Christ is a force—a power that compels. The love of Christ made it impossible for Him to remain in heaven. It led Him down millions of stairs—from a throne in heaven to a manger in Bethlehem and to a cross on Calvary. When we have the love of Christ in us, it compels us to witness to others about Jesus.

Q 61 *What are some examples of those compelled by the love of Christ?*

The love of Christ is a love for the lost.
- *When the love of Christ fills us,* we love a beggar, like Jesus loved Bartimaeus (Mark. 10:46-52).
- *When the love of Christ fills us,* we love those led astray by sexual sins, like Jesus loved the woman caught in adultery (John 8), the woman at the well (John 4), and the sinful woman who washed his feet (Luke 7:36-38).
- *When the love of Christ fills us,* we love thieves, like Jesus loved the thief on the cross (Luke 23:38-43).
- *When the love of Christ fills us,* we love lost rich people like Jesus loved the rich young ruler (Mark 10:17-21).
- *When the love of Christ fills us,* we love the poor, like Jesus loved them when the Spirit anointed Him to preach the gospel to them (Luke 4:18).
- *When the love of Christ fills us,* we love the sick, like Jesus loved the multitude at Peter's house (Matt. 8:14-17).
- *When the love of Christ fills us,* we love those of other tribes and nations, like Jesus loved the Samaritans (John 4), and the Canaanite woman (Matt. 15:22-28).
- *When the love of Christ fills us,* we love national traitors, like Jesus loved Matthew, who betrayed his fellow Jews to collect taxes for the Romans.
- *When the love of Christ fills us,* we love children, as Jesus loved them when His disciples wanted to send them away (Matt. 19:13-15).
- *When the love of Christ fills us,* we love the multitudes of lost people, whom Jesus loved and compared to sheep without a shepherd (Matt. 9:35-36).
- *When the love of Christ fills us,* we love the one lost sheep, like the good shepherd who left the 99 to find the lost sheep and bring it home (Luke 15:3-7).

When we lack love, we are content to sit and count God's blessings, and ask for more. But when the love of Christ fills us, we must be up and about the Master's business. Those who are low on love live to grab all they can. But those who are filled with the love of Christ *"no longer live for themselves but for him who died for them"* (2 Cor. 5:15).

Q 62 *What are the characteristics of believers who lack love?*

Does the love of Christ compel us? Too often it does not. What can we do to solve this problem? When we find that our love is low, here are some steps to increase our love for the lost:
- Repent and turn from anything that causes a guilty conscience.
- Forgive everyone who has sinned against you.
- Limit the time you spend to please yourself. Invest some time in others.
- Take time for devotions—to read the Bible, pray, and worship each day.
- Keep the Sabbath. Take time off from work to rest, relax, and worship.
- Sow a good deed of love, and reap a harvest of love. Feelings often follow actions.

Review the first three questions that guide us to a fruitful ministry. Then move on to question four.

D. Do I look at others through spiritual eyes?

[16]So from now on we regard no one from a worldly point of view. Though we once regarded Christ in this way, we do so no longer. [17]Therefore, if anyone is in Christ, he is a new creation; the old has gone, the new has come! (2 Cor. 5:16-17).

"We no longer look at anybody from a human or a worldly point of view," Paul says. "I once did this to Jesus. I saw Him as just a man, a human being." It may be that before he was converted, Paul heard Jesus in Jerusalem. No doubt Paul heard others talk about Christ. Back then, Paul thought of Jesus as a false teacher. Before conversion, Paul hated and opposed Jesus and all who followed Him. He persecuted them, tried to force them to blaspheme, put both men and women in prison, and rejoiced when the Sanhedrin stoned believers (Acts 26:9-11).

But everything changed when Paul met Jesus as Savior and Lord. As a believer, Paul wrote, *"So from now on we regard no one from a worldly point of view"* (2 Cor. 5:16). Paul discovered that Jesus was not only a man of the earth, but He was the Son of God, the One from heaven. Paul's view changed after He met Jesus on the road to Damascus. And because of that, his view of others changed.

When we are born again, Jesus changes us. Each of us becomes a new creation. Only the power that created the world can create a Christian—*"a new creation."*[34] And when He gives us this new life, *"the old has gone"*—as one season fades away—and behold, *"the new has come!"* (2 Cor. 5:17). At the new birth, God gives us new life, new desires, new appetites, new friends, new ideas, new behavior, and a new purpose. Redeemed by the blood of the Lamb, all of life looks new to us—as if we were living in a new world. As believers, we relate to God, others, and the world in a whole new way.

It is important to relate these verses to the context of 2 Corinthians 5. Paul is defending his ministry as an apostle. His enemies *"take pride in what is seen rather than what is in the heart"* (2 Cor. 5:12). This is the worldly point of view Paul had before he met Jesus. But as a new creation in Christ, he no longer sees anyone from a worldly point of view. As a new creation, Paul sees people as God sees them.[35] He knows that Jesus is Savior, Lord, and Judge. He knows that Jesus died for all and that all must stand before Him. So as a new creation in Christ, Paul sees all people as in need of a Savior. The rich and the poor need a Savior, so he will witness to both of them. All people are lost without Christ, including Jews, Gentiles, free men and slaves, educated and ignorant. So as a new creation in Christ, Paul testifies to Agrippa—a king, a jailer in Philippi—a Roman, Lydia—a businesswoman, Sosthenes—a synagogue leader, Onesimus–a slave, Philemon—his master, and many other types of people. As a new creation in Christ, Paul's old way of looking at life is gone. He no longer cares more about the rich and famous than the poor and unknown. In Christ, he has become a debtor to all men—the wise and the foolish—so he is eager to preach to everyone (Rom. 1:14-15). As a new creation in Christ, the Spirit guides Paul to witness to all, regardless of the color of their skin, their gender, their age, their tribe or nation, or their sins.[36] The fear of the Lord *and* the love of the Lord compel him to witness about Jesus. And as we will see in Point E, the Great Commission also guides him to witness.

Application: What about you and me? As new creations in Christ, do we see others with spiritual eyes? Do we recognize that everyone we meet needs Jesus? Do we criticize some, exclude some because of prejudice, and seek only those like us? Or do we look for every opportunity to minister to others? Do we forgive those who offend us and continue to reach out to them in love? Or do we still relate to others like sinners relate to them? Do we look at people for what they can give us or for what we can give them? Has the old gone and the new come?

Q 63 *How does a believer with spiritual eyes see people? Explain.*

Jesus changes how we see others. As a new creation in Christ, Paul did not look at people like the world and the flesh looked. He did not ask, "What can I get from you?" Rather, as a new creation in Christ, he learned to ask, "How can I bless you?" As he said goodbye to believers in Ephesus, Paul was able to testify:

> [33]*"I have coveted no one's silver or gold or clothes.* [34]*You yourselves know that these hands ministered to my own needs and to the men who were with me.* [35]*In everything I showed you that by working hard in this manner you must help the weak and remember the words of the Lord Jesus, that He Himself said, 'It is more blessed to give than to receive'"* (Acts 20:33-35).

Now let us look at the final question that guides us to fruitful ministry.

E. Am I Christ's ambassador of reconciliation?

> [18]*All this is from God, who reconciled us to himself through Christ and gave us the ministry of reconciliation:* [19]*that God was reconciling the world to himself in Christ, not counting men's sins against them. And he has committed to us the message of reconciliation.* [20]*We are therefore Christ's ambassadors, as though God were making his appeal through us. We implore you on Christ's behalf: Be reconciled to God.* [21]*God made him who had no sin to be sin for us, so that in him we might become the righteousness of God* (2 Cor. 5:18-21).

We have seen that the fear of the Lord and the love of the Lord motivated, compelled, and guided Paul. In 2 Corinthians 5:18-21, we see that the commission of the Lord also guided him.[37] Jesus gave Paul, the apostles, and all believers a Great Commission. He commanded us to share the good news with everyone and teach them to obey Him (Matt. 28:19-20).

Second Corinthians 5:18-21 contains four key words:

- **Reconciliation.** *To reconcile* means "to bring to fellowship those separated by hostility." Philemon and Onesimus were separated and hostile to each other—they had bad feelings between them. Onesimus was a slave whom Philemon owned. Slavery was common in Rome. Some estimate that there were 60,000,000 slaves in the Roman Empire.[38] Sixty million! Paul reconciled one slave, Onesimus, to his master. He brought them back together. Paul said that he would pay any debt Onesimus owed. And Paul told Philemon to treat the slave as a brother, not just a worker. Why? Because Paul had also reconciled Onesimus to God!

Q 64 *What is reconciliation? Give an example.*

Likewise, we were separated from God—far away from Him. God was angry with us because of our sins. But Jesus Christ reconciled us to God. Through His death on the cross, Jesus became our substitute. He bore our sins in His own body on the cross (1 Pet. 2:23). *"God made him who had no sin to be sin for us"* (2 Cor. 5:21). Jesus paid our debt. He died so that we might live in relation to God. He reconciled us to God!

Q 65 ↗ *What is God's "special offer" related to sins?*

- **Not counting.** *"God was reconciling the world to himself in Christ, **not counting** men's sins against them"* (2 Cor. 5:19). Look at this amazing verse. We were guilty before God because of our rebellion and disobedience. We were like the servant who owed his master millions of dollars (Matt. 18:24). But God, the Judge of all the earth, made a special offer. He is willing **not to count** our sins if we surrender our lives to Jesus and obey Him as Savior and Lord! God knows everything. He counts the stars and knows them all by name. But He promises that He will **not count** our sins if we receive Jesus! Wow! What an amazing invitation the Judge offers to the criminals! The only thing more amazing than this offer is that most people refuse it and choose to pay for their sins in hell for eternity.

Q 66 ↗ *In which 2 ways do we become the righteousness of God?*

- **Righteousness.** God does not leave us as criminals, with bad character and hearts of rebellion. The Judge not only refuses to count our sins, He transforms us from criminals into good citizens. *"God made him who had no sin to be sin for us, so that in him we might become the **righteousness** of God"* (2 Cor. 5:21). What an exchange! Jesus took our sins and gave us His righteousness. *First,* He justifies us and calls us righteous. *Then,* little by little, He transforms us to be righteous like Jesus (2 Cor. 3:18). As we submit to the Spirit, we grow in grace. And when God is through changing us from criminals to saints, we will be completely righteous. Praise God for what Jesus did for us (justification) and what He does in us (sanctification, which begins at regeneration). In Christ, we become the righteousness of God.

Q 67 ↘ *How much authority does an ambassador have? Explain.*

- **Ambassadors.** An ambassador is a diplomat—a person who speaks for and in place of the king or president he represents. When Paul lived, Rome ruled the world. A Roman ambassador spoke terms and conditions of war or peace to nations. On a higher level, Paul ministered as an ambassador from God to humanity. When Paul preached the gospel, his voice was equal to the voice of God. The king of heaven had entrusted Paul with the news that humans needed to hear. Paul, as an ambassador, saw men as God saw them—lost. Feel the emotion in Paul's words as he brings news from God Almighty:

> ALL BELIEVERS ARE CHRIST'S AMBASSADORS.

We are therefore Christ's ambassadors, as though God were making his appeal through us. We implore you on Christ's behalf: Be reconciled to God (2 Cor. 5:20).

All believers are Christ's ambassadors. We represent the King of kings. God has given us the good news to reconcile people to Him. Today, God waits for people to accept His offer of peace. But a day is coming when God will declare war on earth. Then, Jesus will return to judge all of God's enemies—all who refuse to submit to Jesus Christ as Lord and Savior (2 Thess. 1:3-10; Rev. 19:11-21).

We are all ministers, servants of God. In this lesson, we studied five questions that guide us to a fruitful ministry:

A. Does the fear of the Lord affect what I say to others?
B. Is my conscience clean?
C. Does the love of Christ compel me?
D. Do I look at others through spiritual eyes?
E. Am I Christ's ambassador of reconciliation?

Figure 11.17
Then Jesus will return to judge all of God's enemies—all who refuse to submit to Jesus Christ as Lord and Savior.

Pressures, Powers, and Paradoxes of Ministry (2 Cor. 6:1-13)

Lesson 37

Goal: With an open Bible, analyze the foundation stones, pressures, powers, and paradoxes of ministry (2 Cor. 6:1-13).

Setting

Paul lived with one desire—to be a faithful and fruitful minister of Jesus Christ. Why? In 2 Corinthians 5, we saw that Paul knew the fear of the Lord, the love of the Lord, and the commission of the Lord. He also knew that the reputation of the gospel depends on those who claim to believe it. Paul summarizes his strategy for living: ³*"We put no stumbling block in anyone's path, so that our ministry will not be discredited. ⁴Rather, as servants of God we commend ourselves in every way: in great endurance"* (2 Cor. 6:3-4a).

Q 68 *What were 3 reasons why Paul lived to be a faithful minister?*

In Corinth, enemies criticized Paul. These false apostles turned many away from God's true apostle. It is hard to imagine, but some believers in Corinth did not love and appreciate Paul. He wrote, *"We are not withholding our affection from you, but you are withholding yours from us"* (2 Cor. 6:12). Throughout 2 Corinthians, Paul defends his ministry. The false apostles in Corinth claimed to be apostles, but they did not have the signs of an apostle, the power of an apostle, the character of an apostle, or the scars of an apostle who fought spiritual warfare.

In 2 Corinthians 6:1-13, Paul looks back over the years of his ministry. *First*, he explains three foundation stones of his ministry. *Then* he describes the pressures, the power, and the paradoxes of ministry (Figure 11.19). We might call this passage "The Song of God's Ambassador." Let us begin with the foundation for any ministry.

A. Three foundation stones of Paul's ministry were grace, integrity, and endurance (2 Cor. 6:1-4a).

1. Grace. Followers of John Calvin misinterpret 1 Corinthians 6:1-2 at their own peril. These believe that once you are saved, you are always saved. Read these two verses, and then we will analyze their form and meaning:

Q 69 *In 2 Corinthians 6:1-2, what does "grace" mean?*

¹*As God's fellow workers we urge you not to receive God's <u>grace</u> in vain.*
²*For he says, "In the time of my <u>favor</u> I heard you, and*
    in the day of <u>salvation</u> I helped you."
I tell you, now is the time of God's <u>favor</u>,
    now is the day of <u>salvation</u> (2 Cor. 6:1-2).

The big topic of 2 Corinthians 6:1-2 is grace. Paul urges the Corinthians not to receive God's grace in vain. It is possible to receive God's grace, accept His salvation, and then *"let it go for nothing"* (2 Cor. 6:1, NEB).³⁹ As Dr. James Hernando rightly explains, Paul fears that some of the Corinthians may receive God's grace for no lasting purpose. God's Ambassador is afraid that some Corinthians may depart from the faith, follow false apostles, reject God's *favor*, and lose their *salvation*.⁴⁰

Q 70 *What was Paul's great concern about the Corinthians?*

But what does Paul mean by grace? Paul answers this question in 2 Corinthians 6:2, where he uses synonyms for *grace*.⁴¹ In 2 Corinthians 6:1-2, the words *grace, God's favor,* and *salvation* refer to the same thing.

In 2 Corinthians 6:2, lines 1 and 2 are parallel, like the tracks of a train. Lines 1 and 2 of 2 Corinthians 6:2 are synonymous with each other—they mean the same thing. When two parallel lines of poetry are synonymous, the second line echoes or repeats the thoughts of the first line. So we can use the two lines to interpret each other—each clarifies the other. Study the parallel lines of 2 Corinthians 6:2. Then we will use them to interpret each other.

²*For he* [God, through Isaiah] *says,*
Line 1:   *"In the time of my favor I heard you, and*
Line 2:   *in the day of salvation I helped you."*

I [Paul, God's Ambassador) *tell you,*
Line 1:   *now is the time of God's favor,*
Line 2:   *now is the day of salvation* (2 Cor. 6:1-2).

Q 71 *Read 2 Corinthians 6:2 and fill in the empty boxes in Figure 11.18.*

Parallel Lines:	Synonyms	Synonyms
Line 1:	Time	Favor
Line 2:		

Figure 11.18
Second Corinthians 6:2 has parallel lines that are synonymous. Line 2 echoes Line 1.

Q 72 *Did Paul believe that it is possible to receive grace and then lose it? Give examples.*

> GRACE WAS ONE OF PAUL'S FAVORITE WORDS.

Grace was one of Paul's favorite words. He knew that his life and ministry depended on grace—God's favor, help, and salvation. Paul wrote:

But by the grace of God I am what I am, and his grace to me was not without effect. No, I worked harder than all of them—yet not I, but the grace of God that was with me (1 Cor. 15:10).

Paul was thankful for grace. And he realized that grace is a precious gift to use wisely. Paul believed that it is possible to receive God's grace, be born again, and then throw grace away and return to sin.

- Paul told believers in Antioch to *"continue in the grace of God"* (Acts 13:43).
- He told believers in Galatia, *"you have fallen from grace"* (Gal. 5:4).
- He told the Corinthians *"we urge you not to receive God's grace in vain"* (2 Cor. 6:1).

Paul was concerned about the Corinthians. They had begun the race well. But some Corinthian believers were attending pagan feasts, having sex with prostitutes, and participating in fellowship meals with demons (1 Cor. 6–10). Some had received the truth but later denied the Resurrection and thus turned away from the only gospel that offers salvation (1 Cor. 15:1-2, 12). Many believers in Corinth were rejecting Paul, God's chosen representative, and the gospel God gave him to preach (2 Cor. 5:11-21). Many had turned their hearts away from him (2 Cor. 6:13). So Paul's heart is troubled for these Corinthians. He urges them not to waste the grace they have received. Paul does not want them to forfeit the grace, favor, and salvation God gave them. As Paul closes this letter, he will warn all of them to examine themselves to see whether they are in the faith and Christ is still in them (2 Cor. 13:5). For he fears that some have received the grace of God—but *in vain.*

God once delivered the Israelites from bondage. With miracles, He led them from the slavery of Egypt through the Red Sea, toward Canaan. They started the journey well. But many began to neglect God's grace and favor. Soon, they forsook Moses, God's ambassador, and followed new leaders on the path of doubt. As a result, an entire generation of more than a million people died in the wilderness and never inherited the Promised Land. Earlier, Paul reminded the Corinthians of this example (1 Cor. 10:1-13; see also Heb. 3–4). As the Israelites turned away from Moses, the Corinthians were turning away from Paul, God's true ambassador. So in 2 Corinthians 6:1, Paul again urges believers in Corinth not to receive God's grace in vain. Grace is a major stone in the foundation of our lives. Without foundation stones, a house falls to destruction. The time to guard grace is always now (2 Cor. 6:3). The day to be sure of salvation is always today (Heb. 3:7, 15; 4:7).

Q 73 *Do you know someone who received the grace of God in vain? What happened?*

Paul Defends His Apostolic Ministry

2. **Integrity was another stone in the foundation of Paul's life and ministry.**

Q 74 *What is integrity?*

³*We put no stumbling block in anyone's path, so that our ministry will not be discredited.* ⁴*Rather, as servants of God we commend ourselves in every way* (2 Cor. 6:3-4).

Integrity means "honesty and truthfulness." People with integrity are in private what they claim to be in public. The opposite of integrity is hypocrisy. If believers are hypocrites—people who lack integrity—sinners stumble over their examples. So our deeds must match our words.

King David is an example of someone who was once a hypocrite—a man without integrity. He wrote many psalms and led people in worship. But in private, he committed adultery and murdered Uriah. This life of hypocrisy led his sons, like Absalom, to follow his steps, deceive people, and live void of integrity. Hypocrites cause many to stumble and blame God. David repented. But because he lacked integrity, many watching his life continued to stumble toward hell. The prophet Nathan told David, *"The Lord also has taken away your sin; you shall not die. However, because by this deed you have given occasion to the enemies of the Lord to blaspheme..."* (2 Sam. 12:13-14).

We are people of integrity as we:

Q 75 *How can you recognize those with integrity?*

- Pay our financial debts and our social debts to government leaders (Rom. 13:1).
- Keep our word so that our *yes* means yes and *no* means no (2 Cor. 1:17; Matt. 5:37) and tell the truth and never lie (Col. 3:9).
- Work hard instead of begging or borrowing from those who work (2 Thess. 3:10-12).
- Do what is honest and right in the sight of everyone (Rom. 12:17).
- Avoid sexual sins (Col. 3:5) and present our bodies as living sacrifices (Rom. 12:1).
- Live with a clear conscience (2 Cor. 1:12).
- Resist evil desires of the flesh and walk in the Spirit (Gal. 5:16; Rom. 8:1-17).

The reputation of the gospel and the integrity of God's name depend on how we live (Ps. 23:3). As Paul wrote earlier, we are open letters from God to society. Let us live as people of integrity, avoiding whatever causes others to stumble and leaving footprints that all can follow to heaven.

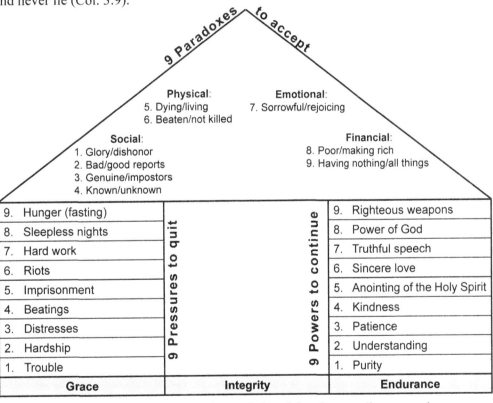

Figure 11.19 Grace, integrity, and cheerful endurance (*hupomone*) were foundation stones of Paul's ministry (2 Cor. 6:1-10).

3. **Endurance** in 2 Corinthians 6:4 is the translation of the Greek word *hupomone* (pronounced hoo-pa-mo-NAY'). *Hupomone* is "endurance, patience, steadfastness, and perseverance."⁴² It is the spiritual power to cheerfully endure, stand firm, continue, and not give up. A person with *hupomone* (cheerful endurance) remains constant, faithful

Q 76 *What is endurance?*

to a purpose, and loyal to the end. As we will see, endurance is a quality or virtue that helped Paul through all of the 27 problems, challenges, and solution he describes in 2 Corinthians 6:4-10 (Figure 11.19). So we will emphasize and illustrate this quality of endurance often throughout the lesson.

B. Nine pressures that tempt us to quit (2 Cor. 6:4b-5). (See the left pillar of Figure 11.19)

We will divide these nine pressures into three groups: inner conflicts, outer conflicts, and daily efforts. Note that there are three topics in each group.

Inner conflicts press upon all who minister (2 Cor. 6:1-4a). Grace, integrity, and endurance enabled Paul to stand firm under the pressure of inner conflicts. He gives three examples. (Many of the topics in this lesson overlap, but we have grouped them to assist memory and study.)

1. Trouble. The word *trouble* translates the Greek word *thlipsis*. Recall that we studied *thlipsis* in 2 Corinthians 1:3-11. Trouble or *thlipsis* describes the squeeze (vice) of circumstances, the pressures of life—things that weigh upon us. For Paul, these inner pressures included dangers, concern for the churches (2 Cor. 11:28), and spiritual warfare with God's enemies. Take a moment to review the various kinds of *thlipsis* we studied earlier.

2. Hardship. This word describes the things in life from which we cannot escape; the steep hills we cannot change on the road of life. For Paul, hardships included his thorn in the flesh (2 Cor. 12:7) and the hills to climb in every city where he preached! *"The Holy Spirit solemnly testifies to me in every city, saying that bonds and afflictions await me"* (Acts 20:23). Paul's life was harder than the lives of most. The road he walked on was paved with hardship.

Some people in life face more hardships than others. Yet all may overcome hardship by grace, integrity, and endurance—walking in the Spirit. Fanny Crosby was born blind. Still, she refused to complain, quit, or pity herself. Instead, she let Jesus take her by the hand and lead her to write over 8,000 songs and hymns! She died at the age of 95 and is known as one of the most famous women in the history of the church.

Life contains many stories of people who climbed the hill of hardship. There are people with no hands who have painted famous pictures, holding the paint brush with their teeth. There are cripples who have become presidents and great leaders. There are millions who have overcome prejudice, unfairness, abuse, and other hardships; by the grace of God, they live a life of integrity and use the endurance that the Spirit gives them. We can do all things through Christ who strengthens us (Phil. 4:13).

3. The word distresses means "narrow places." It describes an army, caught in a narrow pass between two rock walls on a mountain road —unable to escape to the left or the right. We could say that Israel was in a distress, with the Red Sea before them and Pharaoh's army behind them. As one proverb says, they were "between a rock and a hard place."

In times of distress, we must learn to stand firm and not fret because we cannot go forward or backward, left or right. There are times when moving in any direction is wrong. Sometimes we must endure distress by standing firm, waiting for God to help us.

Outer conflicts come to many who minister (2 Cor. 6:4). Paul was not a stranger to physical problems. He mentioned three types of this physical persecution that he endured.

4. Beatings. Paul was often beaten. He tells us that five times he received from the Jews forty lashes minus one (2 Cor. 11:24). In Philippi, Paul and Silas preached the good news. God enabled them to deliver a slave girl from a demon. As a result, the town leaders beat Paul and Silas. They flogged them severely (Acts 16:22-23). With cheerful

---

Q 77 *Is it possible to avoid the troubles and hardships of life? Explain.*

Figure 11.20 Although Fanny Crosby was blind, she depended on God to overcome hardship.

Q 78 *What hardship did Fanny Crosby overcome? What resulted?*

Q 79 *What were some outer conflicts that Paul endured?*

Paul Defends His Apostolic Ministry

endurance, Paul and Silas sang praises to God at midnight. After an earthquake and a brief witness for Jesus, the jailer and his family were saved! Often, our greatest ministry comes as we endure conflicts!

5. Prison. Paul testified that he was in prison *"more frequently"* than the other apostles (2 Cor. 11:23). For an active person like Paul, being in prison must have been tough. Prisons are not nice today, but they were worse in the first century. Clement of Rome, a church leader in the first century, wrote that Paul was in prison seven times. Likewise, many believers today suffer this outer, external conflict of prison. Do we visit believers in prison (Matt. 25:39)? Do we *"sympathize with those in prison"* (Heb. 10:34)? Will we endure if we must go to prison for following Jesus?

6. Riots erupt like a volcano, just as a group of people goes wild with violence. Paul knew what it was like to be caught in a riot as he preached Jesus Christ to the lost.

⁹*And there occurred a great uproar; and some of the scribes of the Pharisaic party stood up and began to argue heatedly, saying, "We find nothing wrong with this man; suppose a spirit or an angel has spoken to him?"* ¹⁰*And as a great dissension was developing, the commander was afraid Paul would be torn to pieces by them and ordered the troops to go down and take him away from them by force, and bring him into the barracks* (Acts 23:9-10).

Likewise, recall the riot at Derbe when the angry crowd stoned Paul and dragged him out of the city, thinking he was dead (Acts 14:19-20).

John Wesley wrote about an experience he had in England: a mob "came pouring down like a flood. To attempt speaking was in vain, because the noise on every side was like the roaring of the sea. So they dragged me along until we came to the town. Seeing the door of a large house open, I attempted to go in. But a man caught me by the hair, and pulled me back into the middle of the crowd. They made no more stops until they had carried me to the main street— from one end of town to the other."⁴³

Outer conflicts like beatings, prison, and riots are not locked within the pages of the Bible—they continue today. It will surprise some to learn that this year there will be at least 160,000 martyrs. These believers will be killed for only one reason—they love Jesus Christ.⁴⁴ As in Bible times, some believers must endure outer conflicts, even as you read this sentence.

Daily efforts require us to depend on the Holy Spirit at all times (2 Cor. 6:5).

7. Hard work is a part of the Christian life. Paul gave the Thessalonians this rule: *"If a man will not work, he shall not eat"* (2 Thess. 3:10). To support his ministry of preaching and teaching, Paul had a second job of making tents. We cannot reach our goals by dreaming, but many dreams come true through hard work. God gives us the grain for our daily bread, but he expects us to bake it.⁴⁵

Q 80 *What are some daily efforts that tempt some to quit?*

8. Sleepless nights. Paul taught all night, though Eutychus fell asleep (Acts 20:7-12). Once, he spent a night and a day in the sea (2 Cor. 11:25). And like Jesus, he may have prayed all night from time to time. Likewise, there are times when we must endure with cheer a night without sleep.

9. Hunger (fasting). To the Corinthians, Paul wrote:

¹¹*To this very hour we go hungry and thirsty, we are in rags, we are brutally treated, we are homeless.* ¹²*We work hard with our own hands* (1 Cor. 4:11-12).

I have labored and toiled and have often gone without sleep; I have known hunger and thirst and have often gone without food; I have been cold and naked (2 Cor. 11:27).

We have looked at nine pressures that tempt us to quit serving Jesus. Now, let us look at nine powers that enable us to be faithful and fruitful.

C. Nine powers that enable us to continue to be faithful and fruitful (2 Cor. 6:6-7). (See the right pillar of Figure 11.19.)

Q 81 *What are some examples of "purity power"?*

1. *Purity* means "cleanness of heart, soul, motives, and mind." Pure water is clean, free from dirt and disease.

A pure person is:
- Clean in the conscience—living a life that pleases God in all areas.
- Clean in the mind—free from the bondage of evil thoughts of bitterness, unforgiveness, impure motives, lust, and false teachings (2 Cor. 10:5-6). Evil thoughts may knock at the door, but a pure person sends Jesus to answer.
- Clean in the heart and soul—free from anger and evil desires.
- Clean in the spirit—washed by the blood of Jesus, filled with the Spirit, walking in the light.

Purity gives us power to know God and enter into His presence. As Jesus said, *"Blessed are the pure in heart, for they shall see God"* (Matt. 5:8).

Q 82 *Explain: "Understanding brings power."*

2. Understanding (knowledge) in the mind is like money in the bank—it gives power. But people without knowledge perish in many ways. Those who lack medical knowledge may drink impure water, which leads to sickness and death. Those lacking medical knowledge may not know that God has given us vaccinations. These people in darkness do not discern that diseases, not demons, kill their children. Likewise, a third of the world is illiterate. These people lack the knowledge to read the Bible and lesser books that bring God's blessings to us. Those without knowledge are poor, sick, and lost. They need to know Jesus, *"in whom are hidden all the treasures of wisdom and knowledge"* (Col. 2:3).

There are many things we do not know. But we know the most important things in life. We know that Jesus died to redeem us and the Holy Spirit fills us to be victorious. We know that God is for us and Jesus is preparing a place for us. And it is God's will that we continue to grow in knowledge and understanding. You are on the right track, because you are studying God's Word!

⁹And this I pray, that your love may abound still more and more in real knowledge and all discernment, ¹⁰so that you may approve the things that are excellent, in order to be sincere and blameless until the day of Christ (Phil. 1:9-10).

Q 83 *Who is the most patient person you have known?*

3. Patience gives power to stand, to succeed, and to overcome. We inherit the kingdom of God through patient endurance (Rev. 1:9). You have heard of the patience of Job and seen what the Lord did for him (James 5:11).
- *"He who is slow to anger has great understanding, but he who is quick-tempered exalts folly"* (Prov. 14:29).
- *"A hot-tempered man stirs up strife, but the slow to anger calms a dispute"* (Prov. 15:18).
- *"He who is slow to anger is better than the mighty, and he who rules his spirit, than he who captures a city"* (Prov. 16:32).

4. Kindness. Being kind is the opposite of being mean, harsh, uncaring, or severe. Kindness expresses itself with love, gentleness, compassion, and thoughtfulness. Love is patient and kind (1 Cor. 13:4).

Kindness enables and empowers us to build strong relationships and influence others for good. Just as the sun melts ice, kindness melts misunderstanding, mistrust, and hostility. Kindness has converted more sinners than zeal or eloquence have won. Through kindness, Abigail won David's favor and saved many lives (1 Sam. 25).

Q 84 *How does kindness help us be fruitful?*

- A kind, soft answer turns away wrath (Prov. 15:1).
- A kind man benefits himself, but a cruel man brings trouble on himself (Prov. 11:17; Gal. 6:7).

- Some people are right in what they say, but wrong in how they say it—lacking kindness.
- One way to please our Father in heaven is to be kind to His children on earth.
- Kind actions begin with kind thoughts.[46]

Kindness is a fruit that the Holy Spirit enables us to bear (Gal. 5:22). When we are kind, we reflect God.

5. Holy Spirit (Anointing). The presence of the Holy Spirit in our lives is the source of all our spiritual power. He enables us to edify ourselves by praying in tongues, so we can serve others (1 Cor. 14:4; Jude 20).

- The Holy Spirit gives us power to be the right kind of people—He preaches through our lives and helps us. Power to become more and more like Jesus (2 Cor. 3:18). For [22]*"...the fruit of the Spirit is love, joy, peace, patience, kindness, goodness, faithfulness,* [23]*gentleness, self-control"* (Gal. 5:22-23).
- The Holy Spirit gives us power to witness with words (Acts 1:8) and with powerful deeds (1 Cor. 12).
- He gives us the power to pray in tongues to build ourselves up in our most holy faith.

The Holy Spirit appears 53 times in the book of Acts. He is the One who enabled the first believers to overcome their problems and challenges. And He is the One Jesus sent to help us every step of our journey.

6. Sincere love is not fake or false. It is *agape* love—the kind of love God showed by giving His Son to die on the cross for us. Paul tells us that love is greater than even faith or hope (review the characteristics of love in 1 Corinthians 13). The command, *"LOVE YOUR NEIGHBOR AS YOURSELF"* sums up all of God's commands about relating to others (Rom. 13:9).

Love is like age—we cannot hide it. Love is the prettiest flower that blooms in God's garden. Works, more than words, are the proof of love.[47]

Paul was able to resist the pressures to quit because the Spirit empowered him with six qualities of mind and heart (1–6 above). Also, God gave Paul tools for the work of spreading the gospel. Let us examine three tools of the ministry.

7. Truthful speech may refer to two things. *First,* truthful speech could be translated *message of truth* (Greek: *logoi aletheias*). Sometimes this refers to the gospel message that Paul preached.[48] In Ephesians 1:13, Paul refers to the gospel as the *"message of truth."*

Second, truthful speech may refer to the words that Paul spoke to people. Truthful speech helps us overcome the pressures of life, because truth puts us on God's side. *"God is light; in Him there is no darkness at all"* (1 John 1:5). Speaking the truth enables us to walk close to God and receive His blessings. When Satan lies, *"he speaks from his own nature, for he is a liar and the father of lies"* (John 8:44). Likewise, children of darkness speak lies, and God must judge them (Rev. 21:8). In contrast, God's children walk in the light and speak the truth in love (Eph. 4:15).

8. The power of God. Earlier in Corinthians, Paul emphasized speaking the truth in the power of God.

> [3]*I came to you in weakness and fear, and with much trembling.* [4]*My message and my preaching were not with wise and persuasive words, but with a demonstration of the Spirit's power,* [5]*so that your faith might not rest on men's wisdom, but on God's power* (1 Cor. 2:3-5).

Those of the world depend on human gifts and abilities. But members of the Church depend on the power of God to do God's work.

Q 85 *What are some righteous weapons that we need?*

9. Righteous weapons. Roman soldiers carried a sword or spear in one hand and a shield in the other. Likewise, Paul held righteous weapons in both hands. Our righteous, spiritual weapons include:

- the Bible, which is God's truth, the sword of the Spirit (Eph. 6:10),
- prayer and the power of God to pull down spiritual strongholds (2 Cor. 10:3-5; Eph. 6:18),
- likewise, all of the eight things Paul lists in 2 Corinthians 6:6-7—purity, understanding, patience, and kindness; in the Holy Spirit and in sincere love; in truthful speech and in the power of God. (See Ephesians 6:10-18.) For example, with purity, we *conquer* immorality, wrong motives, and lust. With truth, we *defeat* false teachings. In the power of the Holy Spirit, we *overcome* Satan, demons, the world, and the flesh. With love we *triumph over* hate.

We have studied three foundation stones for ministry, nine pressures to make us quit, and nine powers to help us continue. To complete this lesson, we come to the roof of Figure 11.19.

D. Nine paradoxes or contrasts we must accept (2 Cor. 6:8-10).

A *paradox* is a statement or situation that contrasts opposites. A paradox is like a coin, it has two sides that face opposite directions, but are stuck together—like sunshine and rain, or midnight and noon.[49] Here are some examples of paradoxes:

- Water can be a liquid or a solid (ice).
- Though it should not, the tongue praises God and curses men (James 3:9-11).

Paul lists nine paradoxes (contradictions or opposites). We will divide these nine contrasts into four groups: social, physical, emotional, and financial.

Q 86 *Explain: Do not take too seriously the best or the worst things that people say about you.*

1. The social paradox: The judgments of the world are fickle. Like the wind, they blow one direction and then another. As we witness for Christ, we will have friends and foes, honors and insults. Paul gives four examples of social contrasts or paradoxes in the ministry. ⁸*"Through glory and dishonor, ...bad report and good report; ...genuine, yet regarded as impostors; ...⁹known, yet regarded as unknown"* (2 Cor. 6:8-9).

Sometimes, people are fickle. At Lystra, people called Paul a god when he healed a cripple (Acts 14:11). A few minutes later, they thought he was a criminal and stoned him (Acts 14:19). At Malta, the people first thought that Paul was a murderer because a snake bit him (Acts 28:4). But when he did not die from the bite, they said he was a god (Acts 28:6)! Likewise, many said that Jesus was the Messiah and Son of God, while others said that He had a demon and was insane (John 10:20). So as God's ministers, we can expect the world, and even those in the church, to say both good and bad things about us. A servant in not above his master (John 15:18).

Principle: Do not take *too* seriously the best or the worst things that people say about you. The truth is probably somewhere in between them. Some may think you are a genius, while others call you an idiot. Or the same person may say to your face that you are a blessing, but behind your back call you a plague!

If people speak well of us, we should not become proud. Rather, we should consider ourselves as unworthy servants (Luke 17:10). And if others insult or criticize us, we should see whether there is any truth in the accusations. Sometimes, even words that wound contain truth. In every case, let us cast all our care on the Lord (1 Pet. 5:7). There is a comfort and peace in living to please God. Let us say with Paul, *"We make it our goal to please him"* (2 Cor. 5:9).

Q 87 *What are some physical paradoxes?*

2. The physical paradox. *"Dying, and yet we live on; beaten, and yet not killed"* (2 Cor. 6:9). Life is full of physical paradoxes. Paul healed many, yet remained with a thorn in his flesh. And many were healed from Paul's handkerchief, but he left Trophimus at Miletum sick. And Paul told Timothy to take wine for his stomach trouble. Healing Evangelist Smith Wigglesworth suffered greatly from kidney stones. Raymond T. Richie was so weak at times that people had to carry him to the place where he preached. Still, many were healed when he prayed for the sick! God often heals, and sometimes He delivers us from persecutions. But in this body, the fiery trial of our faith should not be strange to us. Healing and suffering, living and dying are paradoxes to walk through by faith.

3. The emotional paradox. *"Sorrowful, yet always rejoicing"* (2 Cor. 6:10). There were times when Paul cried, as at Ephesus (Acts 20:19). And he often knew the sorrow of persecution and prison (2 Cor. 11:23; Phil. 2:27). Yet he chose to practice thinking on things that are true, right, pure, and lovely (Phil. 4:8). Even in jail in Philippi, beaten and bleeding, locked in stocks, unable to sleep at midnight, he allowed the Holy Spirit to give him a song (Acts 16:25).

Q 88 How is it possible to be sad, but always rejoicing?

Principle: No night is too dark for us to sing, if we choose to look up.

4. The financial paradox. *"Poor, yet making many rich; having nothing, and yet possessing everything"* (2 Cor. 6:10).

Q 89 Does faith bring wealth in this life? Explain.

Some today teach that those with faith must be wealthy. In contrast, God meets our needs, but not our "greeds." Wealthy apostles were as rare as fast chameleons. Jesus was born in a barn and buried in a borrowed tomb. Paul rebukes those who teach that godliness is a path to money (1 Tim. 6:5). The most spiritual of God's ministers may, like Paul, be poor. Believers at Smyrna were poor, yet spiritually rich (Rev. 2:9). Believers at Laodicea were rich, but poor spiritually (Rev. 3:17). Neither riches nor poverty reveals the level of faith in a person's heart. True riches are those that last forever (Luke 16:11; Matt. 6:19-20). Those who follow Jesus will inherit the riches of heaven.

Q 90 Complete the practice house in Figure 11.21.

Conclusion. We have studied nine pressures that rage like the waves of a sea in a storm. But all the water in an ocean cannot sink a ship as long as the water is outside the ship. Within us, God gives us nine powers that enable us to continue. As the left pillar matches the right pillar (Figure 11.19), God gives us grace to match every trial that we face. And by faith we learn to accept the paradoxes of life. As we mature in Christ, we learn to say with Paul:

> ¹²I know how to get along with humble means, and I also know how to live in prosperity; in any and every circumstance I have learned the secret of being filled and going hungry, both of having abundance and suffering need. ¹³I can do all things through Him who strengthens me (Phil. 4:12-13).

Paul opened his heart wide to the Corinthians. But their hearts were cold and closed (2 Cor. 6:11-13).

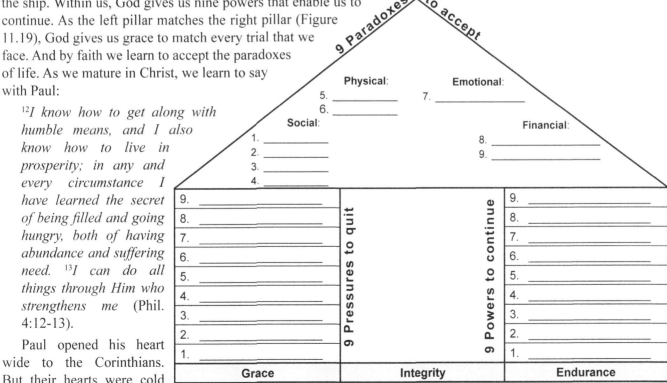

Figure 11.21 Practice house to complete on 2 Corinthians 6:1-10

Lesson 38: Reasons for Holiness (2 Cor. 6:14–7:1)

Goal: Analyze the commands about, contrasts and promises of, and invitation to holiness (2 Cor. 6:14–7:1).

Perhaps this second letter to them unlocked their hearts. Likewise, God has opened His heart and kingdom to us. Are our hearts open to Him today? This is a fair exchange (2 Cor. 6:13).

Setting

Holy is a word that some people have used in a wrong way. Ask a person, "What do you think of when you hear the word *holy*?" You might hear words like *weird, odd,* or *self-righteous.* To some, holiness is a list of rules about things we cannot do. To others, "holy" only describes special believers, or "saints" like Paul and Peter.

People have many ideas about holiness. But the Bible explains that a holy person is someone who is separated, or set apart, *from* evil and *to* God.

It is good to separate some things. For example, my toothbrush is separated for me to use. I set it aside for myself. I do not want anyone else to use it. So in a sense, my toothbrush is holy—separated for me to brush my teeth with it. I do not use it to put polish on my shoes. It is separated for one purpose—brushing my teeth. Likewise, a holy person is someone separated *from* evil and *to* God—for Him to love and use as He desires.

Like a triangle, **holiness** has three sides or aspects.
- **Holiness includes our *position*.** We are justified—called holy and righteous—because of our faith in Christ and His sacrifice on the cross.
- **Holiness includes our *orientation*.** We turn away from sin and toward God. The Scriptures teach us that in addition to facing God, we are to act like Him—to be holy, like He is, in all we *do* (1 Pet. 1:15).
- **Holiness includes our *condition*—what we *are*.** This inner holiness of character begins at the new birth. At regeneration, we partake of God's nature and become His children. Little by little, we grow in grace and perfect (increase) holiness as we submit to the Holy Spirit (2 Cor. 3:18; 7:1). This process reaches a new level at glorification (Figure 3.6). Throughout the history of the Church, theologians have debated the question: "Do we grow in holiness, or is our holiness complete at the moment when we are born again?" But the Scriptures teach that holiness, also called sanctification, is a process.

Paul gives three reasons (A–C) for all believers to live a separated, holy life (2 Cor. 6:14-18).

A. The Commands: God commands us to separate ourselves from sin and sinners (2 Cor. 6:14, 17).

The *first* command is: *"Do not be yoked together with unbelievers"* (2 Cor. 6:14). In Bible times, and in some places today, people plow with a yoke. The yoke is a wooden frame that fits across the necks of two animals, joining them together to plow. Peter said that the Law was like a yoke on the neck with which no one could plow—it was too heavy (Acts 15:10). In contrast, Jesus said that the yoke He gives us is light and easy on us. A good yoke does not cause sores on an animals neck. Likewise, Christ's commandments are not heavy or harmful (Matt. 11:29-30).

Animals in a yoke should match each other in size and strength. Otherwise, the yoke will hurt the necks of both animals. Deuteronomy 22:10 forbade yoking together the ox and the donkey to plow. Those two animals do not match. An ox is stronger and bigger than a donkey. Yoking them together would be cruel.

Figure 11.22
Deuteronomy 22:10 forbade yoking together an ox and a donkey.

Q 91 *How would both animals suffer if an ox and a donkey were yoked together to plow?*

In the Middle East, one man saw a camel and a donkey yoked together to plow. The camel walked with long steps, but the donkey ran to keep up. And since the camel was taller, the yoke pulled up on the donkey's throat and down on the camel's neck. It was both unwise and unkind to yoke together these two animals.

Likewise, the Bible commands: *"Do not be yoked together with unbelievers"* (2 Cor. 6:14). A yoke binds two together. A yoke does not allow one person to act alone or independent of another. Two people may be yoked together in such things as marriage, business, or friendship. Scripture forbids the sin of the unequal yoke.

Q 92 What are 3 examples of unequal yokes?

The *second* command restates the first in a positive way. *"Therefore come out from them and be separate, says the Lord. Touch no unclean thing, and I will receive you"* (2 Cor. 6:17). The first command emphasizes *do not,* while the second emphasizes *do.* Like a toothbrush is separated for a specific purpose, we are separated from sin to God for His purposes.

Application. As a Christian single person prepares for marriage, it is very important to be separate from sin and to avoid being unequally yoked with an unbeliever. To follow Jesus as Lord, we must obey Him. This means that a believer must marry another believer. Why? If a believer marries an unbeliever, this is an act of rebellion and disobedience against Christ. If married, a believer and an unbeliever will seldom pray together, read the Bible together, or go to church together. They will have different friends. There will be conflicts about raising their children. There will be a constant pull toward the world and away from serving the Lord.

Q 93 What conflicts arise if a believer marries an unbeliever?

Sometimes a young Christian will want to marry a non-Christian, hoping to lead this person to Christ. The young believer may say, "If I marry him, he will get saved." This seldom works. People change more before the wedding than after it. Also, we should beware of standards or conversions that are required for dating or marriage. Often, an unbeliever may make a shallow change that does not last, and it brings a harvest of grief down the road. So in choosing a mate, each believer should seek to be yoked together with someone who is already a mature believer. Love for a mate should always be second, behind our first love for the Lord.

Misinterpretations. The first reason to be holy—to be separated from sinners—is that God commands it. However, some have misunderstood this command. Before leaving this first reason to be holy, let us consider four truths that clarify separation.

1. Although we are not yoked with sinners, we still have some communication with them. Jesus taught us to greet everyone, not just our friends (Matt. 5:47-48). So we believers should be friendly to sinners whom we meet. Recall what Paul wrote the Corinthians about associations with sinners.

> *⁹I have written you in my letter not to associate with sexually immoral people—¹⁰not at all meaning the people of this world who are immoral, or the greedy and swindlers, or idolaters. In that case you would have to leave this world. ¹¹But now I am writing you that you must not associate with anyone who calls himself a brother but is sexually immoral or greedy, an idolater or a slanderer, a drunkard or a swindler. With such a man do not even eat. ¹²What business is it of mine to judge those outside the church? Are you not to judge those inside? ¹³God will judge those outside* (1 Cor. 5:9-13).

Q 94 Is it possible to live on earth and not associate with sinners? Explain.

2. Believers should attend some social events with unbelievers.

> *²⁷If some unbeliever invites you to a meal and you want to go, eat whatever is put before you without raising questions of conscience. ²⁸But if anyone says to you, "This has been offered in sacrifice," then do not eat it, both for the sake of the man who told you and for conscience' sake* (1 Cor. 10:27-28).

Q 95 What is an example of a social event that Jesus attended?

Q 96 What are some examples of social events that believers and sinners attend?

Many social events, such as weddings, funerals, and public meetings, are good. Often, believers meet new people at social events and discover opportunities to witness. Still, at all social events, we must show integrity, avoid the appearance of all evil, and remain separate from sin. There are some places where believers must not go, or they will hurt their reputation and lose their holy testimony.

Q 97 *What does 1 Corinthians 7:12-13 teach?*

3. In a marriage, a believer should not leave an unbeliever, except for biblical reasons. The commandment that forbids the unequal yoke does not mean to break apart a marriage. For example, if two sinners marry, and one becomes a believer, the Bible says that they should not separate, but remain together.

> *¹²If any brother has a wife who is not a believer and she is willing to live with him, he must not divorce her. ¹³And if a woman has a husband who is not a believer and he is willing to live with her, she must not divorce him* (1 Cor. 7:12-13).

The Bible gives only two reasons for which a believer may divorce an unbeliever. *One* is if the unbeliever is sexually unfaithful. The *other* reason is if the unbeliever refuses to live with the believer. Paul says that if the unbeliever leaves the marriage, the believer is no longer bound (1 Cor. 7:15). In such a case, the believer is free to marry another believer (1 Cor. 7:39).

Q 98 *What things today do some call unholy, but others call acceptable?*

4. The command, *"Touch no unclean thing"* **is not a banner for the church to wave over everything new.** Looking back in Church history, we see that believers have made many mistakes in this area. Some pastors have used the word *unclean* to refer to such things as deodorant, toothpaste, perfume, radio, television, colored shirts or ties, cosmetics for women, and electric guitars. In fact, there are a few pastors today who preach that cars, buses, trains, airplanes, and all machines are *unclean,* including the printing press that prints the Bible! This is not preaching the Bible—it is not *preaching* at all!

It is good to separate ourselves from evil. But we must discern between evil and personal preference (favorites). For example, an older believer may not enjoy the Christian music that a younger believer likes. But if the young person's music has a good message, the older believer should not discourage the younger by calling the music *unholy* or *unclean.* In personal matters (such as music, hairstyles, clothing, athletic games, and other entertainment), we must be modest and biblical, but never legalistic or outdated.

Q 99 *Which pastor was wiser, Anthony or Jeff? Explain.*

Many years ago, when television was first invented, the leaders of some churches said that watching it was a sin. Pastor Anthony agreed and forbade his children to watch television. As these children matured, they left the church. Another pastor, Jeff, took a different path. Pastor Jeff heard that his son went to a bar to watch television. Learning of this, the pastor decided to buy a television for his home and watch it with his son. They avoided evil television programs, but enjoyed some TV programs that were good. Which pastor was wiser, Anthony or Jeff?

B. The Contrasts: Believers have nothing in common with unbelievers (2 Cor. 6:14-16a).

God divides all of humanity into two groups: the holy (those in Christ, separated from sin to God) and the unholy (those of the world). Figure 11.23 gives some characteristics of each group.

Q 100 *Which words answer Paul's 5 questions (2 Cor. 6:14-16)?*

The *second* reason to be holy is based on contrast. In spiritual matters, believers have nothing in common with unbelievers. Paul writes: *"Do not be yoked together with unbelievers"* (2 Cor. 6:14). Then he uses five questions that contrast the two groups—the holy and the unholy (2 Cor. 6:14-16):

- *"For what do righteousness and wickedness have in common?"* The righteous and the wicked have different tastes and appetites. The righteous eat at the table with Christ, but the wicked choose from the menus of the flesh, the world, and the devil.
- *"Or what fellowship can light have with darkness?"* Believers and unbelievers are as different as night and day. Unbelievers lie, cheat, steal, slander, lust, hate, fight, use dirty language, serve themselves, and disobey God. Unbelievers are sinners and have no inheritance in the kingdom of God (Eph. 5:5; 1 Cor. 6:9-11). In contrast, Paul says that we believers must put away all these sins—like a person takes off dirty clothes (Eph. 5:25-30). And we must put on the new clothes of righteousness, forgiveness, compassion, kindness, gentleness, patience, love, and holiness (Eph. 5:8; Col. 3:12-14).

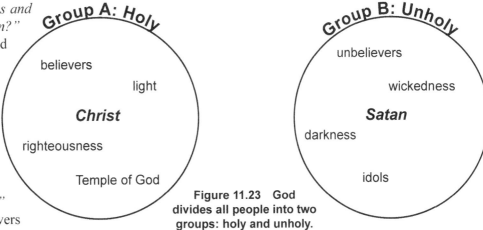

Figure 11.23 God divides all people into two groups: holy and unholy.

- *"What harmony is there between Christ and Belial?"* Can you imagine an angel marrying a demon? Can the most honest policeman be in business with the worst criminal? Can a sheep eat side by side with a wolf? Believers and unbelievers are on different sides, with different values and goals.
- Christ is different from Belial (a name for Satan or the Antichrist).[50] Likewise we are different from sinners.
- *"What does a believer have in common with an unbeliever?"* Believers share life with Jesus. We love what He loves and hate what He hates. But sinners love what Satan loves. Sinners do not want to pray with us, worship with us, or sing with us. The contrast between believers and sinners is like the contrast between sheep and wolves (Matt. 10:16). Therefore, we must live separated from sinners and not be yoked together with them in marriage, business, or social events.
- *"What agreement is there between the temple of God and idols?"* We are God's temple. He lives in us (1 Cor. 6:19), and we live in Him. In contrast, idols belong in pagan temples. God's temple and idols are in different places. What do they have in common?

Paul has used five questions to contrast believers and unbelievers. What does north have in common with south, up with down, or forward with backward? Putting opposites together makes an unequal yoke. Therefore, God calls us to be holy—separated *from* sin and *to* Him.

We have considered two reasons to be holy: the commands and the contrasts. This brings us to the third reason why we desire to be holy.

C. The Promises: God promises to receive the holy as sons and daughters (2 Cor. 6:16-18).

16For we are the temple of the living God. As God has said: "I will live with them and walk among them, and I will be their God, and they will be my people." 17"Therefore come out from them and be separate, says the Lord. Touch no unclean thing, and I will receive you." 18"I will be a Father to you, and you will be my sons and daughters, says the Lord Almighty" (2 Cor. 6:16-18).

Q 101 *In 2 Corinthians 6:16b-18, underline the possessive pronouns.*

The promises. Most languages have *possessive pronouns—words like *my*, *your*, and *their*. These words show ownership, relationship, and fellowship. God, the Lord

Q 102 *What promises does God give to the holy?*

Almighty, is the Creator of everything. But to the holy, He gives special promises: *"I will be their God, and they will be my people. I will be a Father to you, and you will be my sons and daughters, says the Lord Almighty"* (2 Cor. 6:16, 18).

Consider the worth and dignity of our place in God's family.⁵¹ You can say: "He is *my* Father, and I am *His* child." God is my Father, who has pledged to protect me and provide all my needs. This is the true claim of all who live a holy life. As one song says: *Now I belong to Jesus; Jesus belongs to me.*

Q 103 *In 2 Corinthians 6:16-18, what conditions must we fulfill to receive the promises?*

The conditions. There is a false theology that says all people are God's children. It is true that we are all God's creation. But it is not true that we are all His children. Jesus once told a religious group of people, *"You are of your father the devil, and you want to do the desires of your father"* (John 8:48). Sin separates us from God, as it separated Adam and Eve from God in Eden.

We become the children of God when we submit our lives to Jesus as Savior and Lord (John 1:12). The moment we receive Jesus into our lives by faith, we are born again and become children of God. And we remain children of God, and grow in grace, as we walk in the Spirit and live holy lives. *"For all who are being led by the Spirit of God, these are sons of God"* (Rom. 8:14).

Are you holy? Do you separate yourself from the sin and stains of the world? Do you present yourself to God for Him to love and use for His own personal pleasures and purposes? If you practice fulfilling these responsibilities and conditions, you belong to God.

The choice. Every promise in the Bible is based on a condition. The promise that God will be our Father is based on the condition that we live holy lives, allowing the Spirit to lead us from sin to God's will. The *third* reason we want to be holy is to receive the promise that He is *our* God, and we are *His* people. There are two groups of people. The unholy belong to the devil and the world. Only the holy belong to God.

D. The Invitation: Let us grow in holiness (2 Cor. 7:1).

Since we have these promises, dear friends, let us purify ourselves from everything that contaminates body and spirit, perfecting holiness out of reverence for God (2 Cor. 7:1).

Q 104 *Which aspect of our holiness is already perfect?*

This verse contains one of the most encouraging invitations in the Bible. It assures us that God accepts us as we are when we repent of our sins and receive Jesus to sit on the throne of our hearts. What a wonderful assurance. As His children, God does not expect us to grow to maturity in a day. Rather, He invites us to *perfect* holiness, that is, to grow in grace and holiness, as we submit to the Spirit, day by day.

There are three sides to our holiness. *First,* we are holy in our position because of what Jesus did *for* us on the cross. What Jesus did *for* us on the cross is already perfect, finished, and complete. We can never add to or increase this aspect of our holiness. We refer to this side of holiness with terms like justification. Through the blood of Jesus, all of our past sins are forgiven. By faith in Jesus we are justified—counted holy and righteous in God's sight.

Q 105 *What does it mean to "perfect holiness?" Identify 3 phases.*

In contrast, the holiness that Jesus develops in us is progressive. It has a beginning, a middle, and an end.

- The beginning of holiness in us starts at *regeneration*. At the moment of the new birth, a change occurs in us. We receive new life from God. As Paul wrote, *"all things become new"* (2 Cor. 5:17). *Justification* is a legal term that describes our relationship to God, the Judge of all. At justification—positional holiness—God *counts* us holy. But in *sanctification*—inner holiness—God *makes* us holy. As Peter writes, we experience God, receiving and partaking of the divine nature (2 Pet. 1:4).

- The middle part of holiness describes the process of growing in grace (2 Pet. 3:18). The new birth occurs suddenly, at once, in a moment. But God is not through with us at regeneration. The new birth is only the beginning of spiritual life. As a baby grows into a mature adult, a new Christian will grow into the full likeness of Christ. As Paul said, *"we are being transformed into his likeness with ever increasing glory"* (2 Cor. 3:18). As we submit to the Bible, submit to the Holy Spirit, and submit to mature leaders in the church, God transforms us little by little to be more and more holy like Christ (2 Cor. 3:18). This process of holiness centers in our attitudes. As we have the attitude to separate *from* sin and *to* God, we become more holy. Right attitudes lead to right choices, right actions, and right character. Like a person walking up a ramp, we perfect holiness, from one level of maturity to the next (2 Cor. 7:1). Review Figure 3.6.
- The goal of our holiness is *glorification*. This will happen when Jesus returns (1 Cor. 15). He will transform our lowly bodies to heavenly bodies, with completely holy, heavenly desires. Then, we will reach the goal of perfect holiness in our condition.

Q 106 *What are some keys to perfecting holiness?*

Holiness is both instantaneous and progressive. (To study more on holiness, see the article "Sanctification [1 Pet. 1:2]" in the *Full Life Study Bible* or *Life in the Spirit Study Bible*.)

Praise God for the exciting adventure of holiness. Even now, we are accepted in Jesus, the beloved (Eph. 1:6). And day by day, we are perfecting holiness in body (avoiding outer sins) and in spirit (overcoming inner sins).[52]

We have looked at three reasons to be holy, and an invitation to grow in holiness. As we walk in the light of these truths, let us always remember that the key to holiness is submitting to the Holy Spirit. For as we allow the Spirit to guide us, we grow in holiness as easily as a sailboat glides across the water, blown by the wind.

Lesson 39: Insights on Repentance (2 Cor. 7:2-16)
Goal A: Explain and illustrate 5 principles to help others repent (2 Cor. 7:2-7).
Goal B: Explain and illustrate 4 principles to help self and others repent (2 Cor. 7:8-16).

Dr. J. Edwin Orr once preached a sermon called: "The First Word of the Gospel." If you ask a person, "What's the first letter of the alphabet?", all who read can answer this question. But what is the first word of the gospel? Is it believe, or confess, or behave? If we look in the Scriptures, we find that the first word of the gospel is *repent*.

Q 107 *What is the first word of the gospel?*

- John the Baptist came preaching, *"Repent, for the kingdom of heaven is at hand"* (Matt. 3:2).
- Jesus came preaching, *"Repent, for the kingdom of heaven is at hand"* (Matt. 4:17).
- Jesus sent the twelve on their first mission. *"They went out and preached that men should repent"* (Mark 6:12).
- Peter spoke to the crowd on the Day of Pentecost. He explained that Jesus had ascended, and God was pouring out the Spirit. When people wanted to know what they should do, Peter replied: *"Repent..."* (Acts 2:38).
- Paul spoke to King Agrippa. This great apostle summed up all that he had preached to both Jews and Gentiles. *"I preach that they should repent and turn to God"* (Acts 26:20).

Repentance is the first word of the gospel, and the first step into the Christian life.

Background. We must all repent as a step toward the new birth. But we also need to repent, from time to time, throughout our life on earth. All believers need to repent for things that do not please God and are not good for us.

Repentance was needed at Corinth when Paul wrote 2 Corinthians. Take a minute to review the chart in Figure 10.2. Paul evangelized Corinth on his second missionary trip.

Q 108 *What problems did Paul write about in 1 Corinthians?*

On his third missionary trip, he ministered in Ephesus for 3 years. During that time, Paul wrote 1 Corinthians, discussing several problems at Corinth. Problems at Corinth included divisions (1 Cor. 1–4), incest (1 Cor. 5), lawsuits among believers (1 Cor. 6:1-11), and sexual sins (1 Cor. 6:12-20). Also, there were questions about marriage, conscience, head coverings, communion, spiritual gifts, and the Resurrection (1 Cor. 7–15).

Q 109 *On which topics did Paul answer questions in 1 Corinthians?*

Q 110 *What event prepared Paul to write 2 Corinthians?*

The first letter to the Corinthians did not solve all the problems. So Paul sent Titus, his co-worker, to minister to the Corinthians and bring back a report of their progress. Paul agreed to meet Titus at Troas, after the Feast of Pentecost. When Titus did not arrive at Troas, Paul was concerned about him, and traveled across the Aegean Sea into Macedonia north of Corinth. There, he rejoiced when Titus finally came with the good news. Titus reported that the Corinthians had repented in some areas, and were accepting some of Paul's words of correction and guidance. With this knowledge, Paul wrote 2 Corinthians.

We have reviewed the background. Now we are ready for our lesson: Insights on Repentance. We divide this lesson into two parts: principles to help others repent (2 Cor. 7:2-7) and principles to help others and ourselves repent (2 Cor. 7:8-16).

Part 1: Principles to help others repent (2 Cor. 7:2-7)

Each person is responsible for being in a right relationship with God. All must repent for themselves. But our attitudes can be a bridge or a stumbling block between God and others. We can make it easier or harder for a person to repent. Paul gives us five principles to help us bring others to repentance or change.

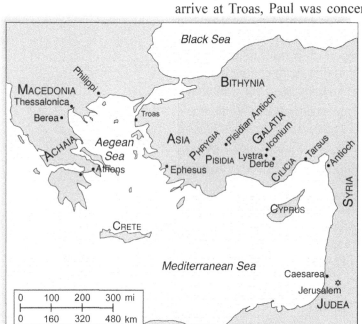

Figure 11.24
Some places related to First and Second Corinthians

A. Before you try to lead someone else to repent, look inside yourself (2 Cor. 7:2).

Q 111 *What did Paul do before he talked about the faults of others?*

There were people at Corinth who said that Paul needed to repent. Some said he was not trustworthy, because he changed his travel plans to Corinth (2 Cor. 1:12–2:4). Others said he corrupted people with his doctrine of grace. These accused him of teaching too much grace, and too little Law. Paul replied to these accusations in 2 Corinthians 3:6. And critics always accused preachers of financial scandals—exploiting people, eating the sheep instead of feeding them. Paul was collecting an offering for the poor saints in Jerusalem (1 Cor. 16; 2 Cor. 8–9). Paul's enemies said he was using those funds for himself.

Before Paul asked others to repent, he searched himself. There was no truth in the accusations his critics brought against him. Paul's heart and conscience assured him that his relationship with the Corinthians was pure and righteous. So he affirmed his integrity to believers at Corinth.

Make room for us in your hearts. We have wronged no one, we have corrupted no one, we have exploited no one (2 Cor. 7:2).

Q 112 *Where is the first place to look for faults?*

Sad to say, there are believers in the body of Christ who are guilty of sins. Some have taught false doctrines. Others have committed sexual sins. A few have stolen money, time, or honor that belongs only to God. There will always be sin around us. But Paul knew that if we are going to bring change, our own hearts must be clean before God.

Jesus said to take the log out of our own eye, and then we can see clearly to remove the speck from someone else's (Matt. 7:5). We should wash the dirt off our own face, before we tell a friend his face is dirty. We should hoe our own garden, before we point at weeds across the fence. Before you rebuke another, look closely at your sister's brother. The first place to look for faults is in a mirror.

B. Never criticize or condemn a person you want to help repent.

I do not say this to condemn you (2 Cor. 7:3a).

There is a big difference between correcting and condemning. Condemning puts a person down. In contrast, correcting is to lift a person up. If we want to help people, we cannot succeed with an attitude of condemnation. The voice and the face are either *signs* of love, or condemnation. When we ask someone to change, what is our tone of voice? Listening to adults talk to kids, it is sometimes amazing to hear tones of voice that suggest condemnation. Some say to a child: "You're in my way." Or "I don't like the way you look." And some rebuke with a face that looks mean enough to frighten a bad dog. If the voice or the face of the speaker shows condemnation, this causes the listener to close up, turn away, and resist. Do we pray for the person we are trying to correct? If we are praying, this will help the tone of our voice, and the look on our face.

Q 113 *What are 3 signs of criticizing?*

Another *sign* of condemnation is self-pity in the speaker. Someone may complain: "I'd be a lot further down the road if it were not for you!" When we blame someone for our situation, a person feels condemned. If we live with self-pity, then we seek to blame someone for our problems. This prevents others from changing or repenting, because people who feel condemned do not feel like changing. They feel resentment, rebellion, anger, and hurt. If you want to gather honey, don't kick the bee hive.

Most people would rather be ruined by praise, than saved by criticism. People respond to criticism the same way they respond to being kicked. They kick back! So if you want to criticize a mule, stand in front of it! Criticism is like a big, bitter pill—it is easy to give, but hard to swallow. Running a person down is the quickest way to running him off. A wise person never criticizes those he hopes to change. It is better to offer a helping hand than to point a criticizing finger.

Q 114 *How do people respond to criticism?*

C. Affirm your commitment to the person you want to help repent (2 Cor. 7:3b).

We need to affirm our commitment to people we hope will change. Paul wrote: *"I have said before that you have such a place in our hearts that we would live or die with you"* (2 Cor. 7:3b). There were some unpleasant things about the Corinthians. But Paul said, I love you so much that no matter what—warts and wrinkles—I would live with you and I would die with you. I'm committed to you.

Q 115 *What is the purpose of affirmation before confrontation?*

Some of the Corinthians rejected and criticized Paul. But he did not return insult for insult. Paul was proactive, not reactive. He practice the rule: *"Do not be overcome by evil, but overcome evil with good"* (Rom. 12:21).

"They drew a circle that shut me out—called me a rebel and a person to doubt.
But love and I had the wit to win—we drew a circle that took them in."

Love has many languages, such as words, actions, time, money, or touch. Words of praise, gratitude, and encouragement affirm people. Actions may speak louder than words. An action such as a kind deed says, "I love you. You are worth my efforts." Likewise, spending time with people is a way of affirming them. It makes them feel valuable. We also affirm people when we spend our money on them. Buying lunch for someone or giving a person a small gift is affirming. And touch may also affirm, with a hug, a hand on the shoulder, or holding hands to pray. People reject those who reject them. But they often respond to those who love them.

Q 116 *How can we affirm a person with the 5 languages of love?*

Q 117 *Interpret the story of the wind and sun.*

Q 118 *How do some pastors and parents discourage people?*

Q 119 *Has anyone brought out the best in you by believing in you? Explain.*

The wind and the sun had a contest to see who could cause a person to take off his coat. The wind blew and blew, but this only made the man hold his coat closer to him. Yet as the sun shone warmly on the man, he unbuttoned his coat and took it off.

D. To help a person repent, believe that the person can and will change.

I have great confidence in you; I take great pride in you (2 Cor. 7:4a).

What a great statement: "I have confidence in you; I am proud of you." Paul could have said negative things about the Corinthian church. He could have said "What a difficult church you are. You're not like the Ephesian church, filled with love. You are not like the Philippian church—so generous. You are a church that is a pain and a problem!" Some pastors in the ministry talk that way. They say "My church is difficult. It has so many problems. It is like a field that has been burned." But the burning is often in our own mind. And the way we describe a person often shapes our relationship to that person. Paul *believed in* the Corinthians—in spite of all their problems. He believed that the power of Jesus Christ in their lives was strong enough to change them and bring them to maturity.

Some people think that believing in others is childish. They frown and say, "This person will never change! It's too late." For sure, only God knows who will change. But our attitude toward those we hope will change is important. Faith is not blind, but neither is it cold. True faith has its roots in love. And faith rooted in love is patient, as it hopes for change.

PAUL TELLS US THAT LOVE NEVER FAILS.

Paul tells us that love never fails. It keeps on believing that all things are possible with God. If we love people, we can continue believing, praying, and hoping the best for them. We can focus on the smallest spark of good in them, and fan that spark into a fire of goodness. Love practices hoping and believing that good things can happen. Love keeps reaching out to people—hoping and believing the best for them.

Evangelist Dwight Moody began his ministry with a Sunday school that several thousand kids attended. On a cold January day, a little boy came in shaking and shivering. He wore thin, ragged pants and a torn coat. His small cap did not protect his ears from the winter wind, so his ears were red from the cold. The greeter asked, "Where have you come from to attend Sunday school today?" The boy described the poor area of town where he lived. He had walked 2 miles through that icy wind to reach Moody's Sunday school class. The greeter said, "There are a lot of churches on the way. Why did you come all the way here?" His response was, "Because they know how to love a boy here."

A cynic is a person who claims to know everything, but believes nothing.[53] He looks both ways before crossing a one-way street. He smells manure at the root of every flower. And an onion is the only thing that brings tears to his eyes. But those who have faith and love believe that a national traitor like Matthew can become an apostle, and a blasphemer like Saul can become the apostle Paul. To the person with faith in God, all things are possible (Mark 11:22).

E. To help a person repent, share your feelings and emotions (2 Cor. 7:4b-7)

⁴...I am greatly encouraged; in all our troubles my joy knows no bounds. ⁵For when we came into Macedonia, this body of ours had no rest, but we were harassed at every turn—conflicts on the outside, fears within. ⁶But God, who comforts the downcast, comforted us by the coming of Titus, ⁷and not only by his coming but also by the comfort you had given him. He told us about your longing for me, your deep sorrow, your ardent concern for me, so that my joy was greater than ever (2 Cor. 7:4b-7).

Notice the flow of emotions in these verses. Paul does not hide his feelings. He tells the Corinthians when he was down and restless about them. And he lets them know that he rejoiced when Titus brought good news about them.

These verses about joy stand out like light shining through a dark cloud, because Paul mentions the tough times in the background. Paul said, *"we were harassed at every turn"* (2 Cor. 7:5). Why is it that trouble seems to run in a pack, like dogs? It would be easier to manage our problems if they came one at a time. But often, they arrive in a group. Paul opened his heart to those he wanted to change. He talked about what it felt like to lack rest, battle conflicts, and be surrounded by fears. Then, he said, "I'm so glad for the comfort you've given me now."

Paul opens his heart. As he shares his feelings, this creates warmth. Likewise, our emotions communicate warmth and draw people to us and to God. If we do not reach out with our emotions to embrace people, then we cannot complete *the circle of repentance*. For example, recall the cold way David treated Absalom—how David broke the circle of repentance. Absalom had sinned. He killed Amnon, his half-brother, because Amnon had raped Tamar, the sister of Absalom. After the murder, Absalom fled and stayed away for 3 years. In time, David longed to go to Absalom (2 Sam. 13:39). Joab, David's general, brought Absalom back to Jerusalem, where King David reigned. Still, David let him sit in his household for 2 years without ever going to see him. When the prodigal son came back to Father God, the first thing the Father did was put his arms around him. The father wept and gave him the best clothes. The Father communicated emotions. This led to a healing of the relationship. In contrast, David's relationship with his son, Absalom, remained shattered. The king did not help Absalom complete the circle of repentance. David kept his arms at his sides, when he should have had them around the son whom he loved.

Q 120 What did Paul say to share his feelings about the Corinthians?

Q 121 Why does sharing emotions help bring change?

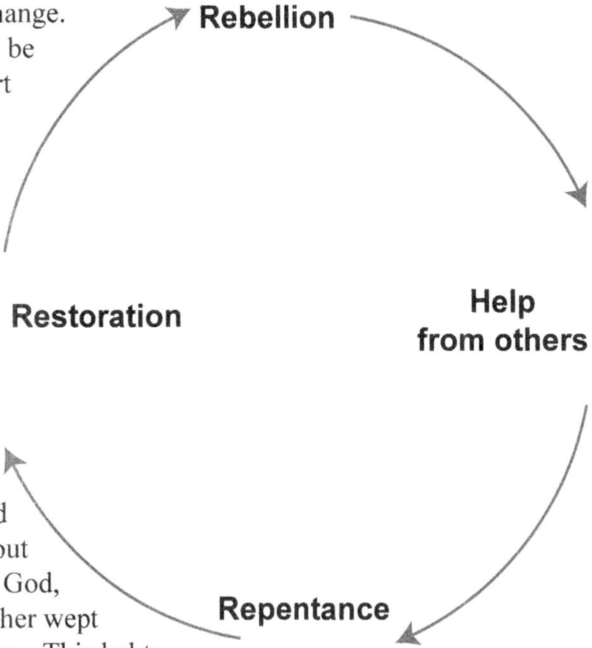

Figure 11.25
The circle of repentance

Part 2: Principles to help others and ourselves repent (2 Cor. 7:8-16)

A. Remember that repentance cannot begin until someone loves enough to confront (2 Cor. 7:8-9).

⁸Even if I caused you sorrow by my letter, I do not regret it. Though I did regret it—I see that my letter hurt you, but only for a little while— ⁹yet now I am happy, not because you were made sorry, but because your sorrow led you to repentance. For you became sorrowful as God intended and so were not harmed in any way by us (2 Cor. 7:8-9).

Have you ever sent a letter, and later wished you could take it back? Often, if a letter is to correct someone, it is wise to write it, wait a day or two, and then make a few changes before you send it. Paul, led by the Spirit, wrote his first letter to the Corinthians. He realized the letter was going to hurt. It caused him sorrow and regret to send the letter. But he knew that the result would be good *after* the Corinthians repented.

To bring repentance, God must confront us with truth. He may use the Bible, our conscience, a whisper of the Holy Spirit, or the voice of a preacher or friend. So do not shoot the messenger! *"Faithful are the wounds of a friend, but deceitful are the kisses of an enemy"* (Prov. 27:6). Beware of those who always praise you. Only those who love you enough will confront you with the truth.

One question divides the sheep from the goats: "How do I respond when God calls me to repent and change?" The Holy Spirit asks, "What are you going to do about this

Q 122 What does this mean: "Don't shoot the messenger"?

Q 123 Which question divides the sheep from the goats?

sin or weakness in your life?" I may respond in several ways. I might say, "I'm not ready to do anything about it yet." Or, "I tried to do something about it before, but had no success." Or, "It's not my fault. Let the other person change." Or "I don't feel like doing anything." Or I might have attitude of the Corinthians, "Lord, I repent."

Someone has said that sin is like a cancer. In its early stages it is easy to cure, yet hard to detect. But in its later stages it is easy to detect, yet hard to cure. Since this is true, God repeats the same truth three times:

Q 124 *Why does God repeat "Today" 3 times?*

- *"Today, if you hear his voice, do not harden your hearts, as you did in the rebellion"* (Heb. 3:7-8).
- *"TODAY IF YOU HEAR HIS VOICE, ⁸DO NOT HARDEN YOUR HEARTS AS WHEN THEY PROVOKED ME, AS IN THE DAY OF TRIAL IN THE WILDERNESS"* (Heb. 3:15).
- *"TODAY, IF YOU HEAR HIS VOICE, DO NOT HARDEN YOUR HEARTS"* (Heb. 4:7).

Repentance in the believer's life should be an ongoing process, so we correct little faults before they become deadly. John says to Christians, *"If we confess our sins, He is faithful and righteous to forgive us our sins and to cleanse us from all unrighteousness"* (1 John 1:9). It is much easier to be cleansed each day than to wait until the end of the year. That is why the Spirit says, *"Today. Today. Today."*

Q 125 *What made David better than Saul?*

King Saul and King David both had their faults. But one thing led them to opposite destinies. When God confronted Saul for his faults, Saul always defended himself. When Saul did wrong, he claimed that he had done right (1 Sam. 15:20). And when a prophet confronted him for his sin, He blamed others, saying, "The people made me do it" (1 Sam. 15:15). David's sins were as bad or worse than Saul's sins. But when God confronted David, his response was " I have sinned" (2 Sam. 12:13). All of us have sinned, and we may make more mistakes or poor judgments in the future. But when God confronts us, our destinies will depend on whether we are like Saul or David.

B. Repentance is a step beyond godly sorrow (2 Cor. 7:10-11).

¹⁰Godly sorrow brings repentance that leads to salvation and leaves no regret, but worldly sorrow brings death. ¹¹See what this godly sorrow has produced in you: what earnestness, what eagerness to clear yourselves, what indignation, what alarm, what longing, what concern, what readiness to see justice done. At every point you have proved yourselves to be innocent in this matter (2 Cor. 7:10-11).

Q 126 *What is the difference between worldly and godly sorrow?*

Paul makes two contrasts. *First,* he contrasts the *reasons* for worldly sorrow and godly sorrow. The sorrow of this world is because of self pity. Worldly sorrow says, "I am sorry that I got caught! I'm sorry for the embarrassment, shame, loss, and punishment that I must bear." But godly sorrow is for falling short of righteousness. Godly sorrow says, "I am sorry that I did wrong. I am sorry that I hurt someone."

Second, Paul contrasts the *results* of worldly sorrow and godly sorrow. Worldly sorrow is just penance. It produces tears, but not change. Those with worldly sorrow may confess their sins and faults—week after week. They may say, "I'm sorry. I repent. Please forgive me." Then, they do the same sins again, and again, and again. Several times along the way, they may say, "I'm sorry. I repent. Please forgive me." This is worldly sorrow, and the result is spiritual death— separation from God (2 Cor. 7:10).

While editing this paragraph, I received both glad and sad news. The glad news was that an Assemblies of God (AG) believer accepted a position in the government. The sad news was that this angered the Muslims, so they murdered the General Superintendent of the AG in that nation. The martyrs remind us that we are in a spiritual battle that is real. It is good for us to recognize the seriousness of repentance. Sooner or later, in one way or another, the first death will come to most all of us on earth. But those who refuse to repent will face the second death—separation from God in the lake of fire forever (Rev. 20:11-15).

In contrast to worldly sorrow, godly sorrow leads to repentance. Notice that godly sorrow is different from repentance. Godly sorrow is a feeling, but repentance is a decision, a change in direction. In the New Testament, the word *repentance* comes from the Greek word *metanoia*—which means "a change (*meta*) of mind." To *repent* means "to change your mind and your direction." We recognize godly sorrow, because it always leads to repentance—a change in the way we think and act. *Repentance* is the first word of the gospel. Those who repent *turn away* from sin. Repentance makes footprints on the path of righteousness. And righteousness is the path *"that leads to salvation and leaves no regret"* (2 Cor. 7:10).

Q 127 *How does godly sorrow differ from repentance? Give an example.*

Zacchaeus is an example of a person who felt godly sorrow, repented, and received salvation. Since Jesus came to seek and help sinners, he went to the home of Zacchaeus—a Jewish traitor that collected taxes for the Romans. Jesus loved Zacchaeus and ate a meal with him. As they talked, Zacchaeus felt godly sorrow. In his heart and conscience, he felt guilty—convicted of his sins.

> ⁸*Zaccheus stopped and said to the Lord, "Behold, Lord, half of my possessions I will give to the poor, and if I have defrauded anyone of anything, I will give back four times as much."* ⁹*And Jesus said to him, "Today salvation has come to this house, because he, too, is a son of Abraham"* (Luke 19:8-9).

In 2 Corinthians 7:10, Paul mentions three characteristics of godly sorrow; unlike worldly sorrow, it brings repentance, leads to salvation, and leaves no regrets. Then, in 2 Corinthians 7:11, Paul lists eight more characteristics, qualities, or fruits of godly sorrow (See Figure 11.26).

Q 128 *What are 8 things that come with repentance (2 Cor. 7:11)?*

2 Cor.	Key words	Principles related to godly sorrow that brings repentance
7:8-9	Confrontation	Repentance cannot come until confrontation comes.
7:10	Godly sorrow	Repentance is the result and proof of godly sorrow.
7:10	Salvation	Repentance leads to salvation.
7:11	No regret	Repentance leaves no regrets.
7:11	Earnestness	Repentance is sincere. It does not deny or hide sin, but confesses sin, as David admitted his sin to Nathan.
7:11	Eagerness	Repentance reveals a desire to make things right. It does not excuse sin, but corrects wrongs, as Zacchaeus did. It is eager to restore its testimony and reputation.
7:11	Indignation	Repentance is angry about sin. It hates what is wrong, as Jesus hated thievery in the temple. The Corinthians were upset with sin among them and with themselves for tolerating it.
7:11	Alarm	Repentance feels the danger of sin. It hears the sound of the trumpet that announces a deadly enemy.
7:11	Longing (Affection)	Repentance brings the desire for restored relationships. The Corinthians longed to have the right relationship with God, and with Paul, God's ambassador. How wonderful it is to repent and experience cleansing and righteous emotions.
7:11	Concern (Zeal)	Repentance has energy and enthusiasm for what is right. The Corinthians were not apathetic or uncaring. Rather, they had a passion to honor God and Paul.
7:11	Justice	Repentance is always ready to bring justice. The Corinthians were ready to discipline sinners among them and put their house in order.⁵⁴
7:12-13a	Perspective	Repentance renews our perspective of who we are. After repentance, the Corinthians saw themselves as God's sheep, who loved God's apostle.
7:13-16	Fellowship	Repentance is a step toward restoring fellowship. When the Corinthians repented, their relationship with God, Paul, and Titus returned to health.

Figure 11.26 Characteristics of repentance, based on 2 Corinthians 7:8-11

So we see that repentance is a step beyond godly sorrow. And repentance does not live alone. It is surrounded by a host of fruits and friends—godly qualities and characteristics.

C. Repentance renews our perspective of who we are (2 Cor. 7:12-13a).

¹²So even though I wrote to you, it was not [only] on account of the one who did the wrong or of the injured party, but rather that before God you could see for yourselves how devoted to us you are. ¹³By all this we are encouraged (2 Cor. 7:12-13a).

Paul wrote to correct the wrongs at Corinth—like the man living in incest. But this man's sin was not the only reason for Paul's letter. For as long as the Corinthians allowed the sin, the whole church was not in a right relationship with God. They were falling short of what God had called them to be—the light of the world. God is never pleased with us if we tolerate sin. He rebuked the church at Thyatira because they permitted sin among them. He said if they did not repent, He would strike them down with sickness and death (Rev. 2:20-23).

When we have the wrong attitude toward sin, we forgot who we were. Psalm 73 says it well: ²¹*"When my heart was embittered and I was pierced within,* ²²*then I was senseless and ignorant; I was like a beast before You"* (Ps. 73:21-22).

Q 129 *How did repentance affect the attitude of the Corinthians toward themselves and Paul (2 Cor. 7:12)?*

When the Corinthians repented, the fog lifted, and their view of themselves changed. Once again, they realized they were the people of a holy God. And when their lives were right, they could see that they loved Paul. Sin clouds our view of who we are. But when we are in a right relationship with God, we see ourselves as His children, under the guidance of godly leaders.

Q 130 *Are some believers mad at the preacher, because their attitude toward sin is wrong? Explain.*

D. Repentance restores fellowship with God and others (2 Cor. 7:13b-16).

¹³...In addition to our own encouragement, we were especially delighted to see how happy Titus was, because his spirit has been refreshed by all of you. ¹⁴I had boasted to him about you, and you have not embarrassed me. But just as everything we said to you was true, so our boasting about you to Titus has proved to be true as well. ¹⁵And his affection for you is all the greater when he remembers that you were all obedient, receiving him with fear and trembling. ¹⁶I am glad I can have complete confidence in you (2 Cor. 7:13b-16).

Q 131 *Give an example of a relationship that was healed through repentance.*

When the Corinthians repented, God restored their fellowship with Paul and with Titus.

Where do we need to restore fellowship in our lives? Is it between us and the Lord? Is it in the church? Is it among friends? Is it at work? Is it in the home? True repentance is a step toward restoring fellowship.

There are so many stories of broken relationships between husbands and wives, family members, and friends. In most of these cases, the relationship could be healed if one or more people humbled themselves, repented, and reached out in love.

Q 132 *Is there a broken relationship you can heal by repenting of a bad attitude?*

Test Yourself: Circle the letter by the ***best*** completion to each question or statement.

1. In the victory march, what is like the gospel?
   a) The chariot of the General
   b) The cheering of the crowd
   c) The sword of the soldier
   d) The incense of the priest

2. The Law was like
   a) a clinched fist.
   b) a pointing finger.
   c) a helping hand.
   d) a withered hand.

3. In 2 Corinthians 4, a reason why we do not lose heart is that
   a) we know godly sorrow leads to repentance.
   b) we are renewed outwardly day by day.
   c) we focus on the treasure, not the container.
   d) we depend on others for encouragement.

4. What is the purpose of the bema judgment?
   a) Salvation
   b) Rewards
   c) Punishment
   d) Justification

5. What helps guide us to a fruitful ministry?
   a) The fear of rejection
   b) The fear of failure
   c) The fear of death
   d) The fear of the Lord

6. In 2 Corinthians 6:1-2, a synonym of *grace* is
   a) salvation.
   b) loveliness.
   c) graciousness.
   d) pleasure.

7. A paradox of Paul's ministry was that
   a) he was educated, but humble.
   b) he was poor, but made many rich.
   c) he was happy, but made many sad.
   d) he was successful, but unknown.

8. God will be our Father if we
   a) are born again but are slaves of sin.
   b) pray, read the Bible, and worship.
   c) practice the Golden Rule.
   d) separate ourselves from sin.

9. To help lead others to repentance,
   a) we should share our feelings with them.
   b) we should frown on their behavior.
   c) we should compare them with the righteous.
   d) we should remind them of their past.

10. Which of these is repentance?
    a) Confessing our sins
    b) Being sorry for our sins
    c) Turning away from sins
    d) Paying for our sins

Essay Test Topics: Write 50-100 words on each of these goals that you studied in this chapter.

Pictures and Principles for Ministers of the New Covenant (2 Cor. 2:12–3:3)

Goal: *Explain and illustrate a principle for each of these: the open door, the victory march, and the open letter.*

Contrasts Between the Ministries of the Old and New Covenants (2 Cor. 3:4–4:6)

Goal: *Summarize a principle for each of these: a pointing finger, a helping hand, a veil, and the moon.*

Keys to Staying Encouraged (2 Cor. 4:7-18)

Goal: *From 2 Corinthians 4, explain and illustrate 5 reasons why we do not lose heart.*

Facts for Facing Death (2 Cor. 5:1-10)

Goal: *Analyze and apply 7 truths that prepare us for death (2 Cor. 5:1-10).*

Test Questions for a Fruitful Ministry (2 Cor. 5:11-21)

Goal: *State and apply 5 test questions for a faithful ministry.*

Pressures, Powers, and Paradoxes of Ministry (2 Cor. 6:1-13)

Goal: *With an open Bible, analyze the foundation stones, pressures, powers, and paradoxes of ministry (2 Cor. 6:1-13).*

Reasons for Holiness (2 Cor. 6:14–7:1)

Goal: *Analyze the commands, contrasts, promises, and invitation to holiness (2 Cor. 6:14–7:1).*

Insights on Repentance (2 Cor. 7:2-16)

Goal: *Explain and illustrate 5 principles to help others repent (2 Cor. 7:2-7).*

Goal: *Explain and illustrate 4 principles to help self and others repent (2 Cor. 7:8-16).*

Figure 11.27 Ruins of Doric columns in Corinth

Chapter 12:
Paul Teaches Principles of Giving
(2 Corinthians 8–9)

Introduction

Figure 12.1 A woman who gave a wooden bowl and two chopsticks inspired people to give more than a million dollars.

  A widow in Korea was old and poor. She had little to offer. Her greatest possessions were the chopsticks and the bowl she ate rice from each day. The church she attended wanted to build a large new building. The amount of money they needed was more than a million dollars. It did not appear that the people would be able to give enough. Then one day this widow stepped forward. The offering she gave was the chopsticks and the only bowl she had for her rice. It was not worth much money, but this offering inspired the people. They all began to give generously. It took the elders a long time to count the money in the offering. They found that it was more than enough to meet the need. Today, that church has grown to more than 800,000 members! God does miracles as we give what we have to Jesus.[1]

Likewise, the Macedonians were the poorest of the poor. But God opened their hearts, and they gave all they could. And God used them to inspire others, like the Corinthians and us, to give generously.

Lessons:

Principles on the Grace of Giving—Part 1 (2 Cor. 8)

Goal A: *State a principle on giving for each of these: gold medal, faith, queen bee, grace, love, widow's mite.*

Goal B: *Explain and illustrate each of the 6 principles you stated in Goal A.*

Principles on the Grace of Giving—Part 2 (2 Cor. 8–9)

Goal A: *State a principle on giving related to each of these: equality, accountability, enthusiasm, harvest, and praise.*

Goal B: *Explain and illustrate each of the 5 principles you stated in Goal A.*

266

Lesson 40: Principles on the Grace of Giving—Part 1 (2 Cor. 8)

Goal A: State a principle on giving for each of these: gold medal, faith, queen bee, grace, love, widow's mite.

Goal B: Explain and illustrate each of the 6 principles you stated in Goal A.

Setting: Why was Paul collecting an offering?

Four of Paul's letters help us understand the setting before and after the offering Paul collected:

- When Paul wrote Galatians (A.D. 49), he was concerned about the poor (Gal. 2:9-10).
- When Paul wrote 1 Corinthians (A.D. 55), the churches of Galatia had given an offering for poor Jewish saints in Jerusalem, the capital of Judea (1 Cor. 16:1-2).
- When Paul wrote 2 Corinthians (A.D. 56), the churches of Macedonia had already given an offering (2 Cor. 8:1-7).
- And when Paul wrote Romans (A.D. 57), the Corinthian church of Achaia had also given (Rom. 15:26).

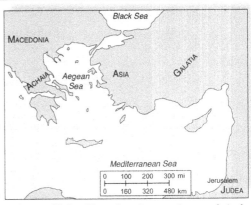

Figure 12.2 Map showing regions related to the Corinthian letters

Believers in Jerusalem suffered financially for at least three reasons.

First, when Stephen was stoned, persecution forced Jewish believers to flee from Jerusalem throughout Judea and Samaria (Acts 8:1-2). These believers lost most or all of their possessions. Even those who returned later suffered great loss.

Second, following Christ closed many doors of business, prosperity, and justice to believers (James 5:1-7). Unbelieving Jews continued to persecute Jews who believed (Heb. 10:32-34). Local cults rejected those who followed Jesus. And the Roman government did not protect those who would not bow to Caesar.

Third, a famine in Judea hurt many believers (Acts 11:28-29).

The Corinthians had begun collecting the offering a year earlier (2 Cor. 8:6; see also 1 Cor. 16:1-4). Then, conflicts at the church in Corinth delayed its completion. After Paul wrote to the Corinthians, Titus brought good news to Paul. They had repented and were making progress. So Paul felt confident to urge them to complete their offering.

As we study 2 Corinthians 8–9, we must recall that Paul is not teaching about tithing or about meeting needs in a local church. The offering of 2 Corinthians 8–9 was for poor saints in another place. So that offering was much like a missions offering today. Still, these chapters contain biblical principles that apply to all types of giving. In this lesson and the next, we will study a total of eleven principles about giving.

Q 1 For whom was Paul collecting an offering?

Q 2 Why were saints in Jerusalem poor?

A. The Gold Medal Principle: The outstanding generosity of others inspires us to give (2 Cor. 8:1-2).

¹*And now, brothers, we want you to know about the grace that God has given the Macedonian churches.* ²*Out of the most severe trial, their overflowing joy and their extreme poverty welled up in rich generosity* (2 Cor. 8:1-2).

Throughout history, society has honored its heroes. Caleb gave his daughter as a prize to the man who conquered the city of Kiriath Sepher (Judges 1:12). King Saul offered great honor and wealth to the man who killed Goliath (1 Sam. 17:25). In most wars, those who are the bravest receive medals of honor. In the early Greek Olympic games, the fastest runners received public honor and rewards. These days, the world gives gold medals to those who are the best in the Olympic contests. And in every nation, we give medals and awards, prizes and rewards, ribbons, trophies, and plaques to honor those who are good examples.

Figure 12.3 Examples of some god medals that society gives to heroes

Q 3 How does society honor heroes in your culture? Give examples.

Those who receive medals serve as an inspiration to others. Boys and girls want to run as fast as their favorite Olympic runner. Soldiers want to be as brave as those who have won medals. Christians seek to serve God, like the heroes of Hebrews 11. Heroes inspire all of us to be and to do our best.

To inspire believers in Corinth, Paul pins a gold medal on the Macedonians. That is, he gives them special recognition. And they deserved it!

Q 4 *Should the rich be the only ones who give? Explain.*

Some teach the poor that they cannot give. But this is not true. The principles of giving work for everyone, in every nation, and in every generation. God delights to use the foolish, the weak, the lowly, and the despised to build His kingdom (1 Cor. 1:26-31). As a result, we realize that success is by grace, and God gets the credit.

Look at the grace God gave the Macedonian Christians. They were suffering from a severe trial. And they were the poorest of the poor. But by the grace of God, they overflowed with joy and generosity! Hallelujah! This inspired the Corinthians, who were wealthy and prosperous, to be generous. If the Macedonians could give, then everyone can give—all of us can be generous!

Q 5 *How do generous givers inspire others? Give an example.*

Mary, the sister of Lazarus, poured her perfume on the feet of Jesus. This perfume was the treasure of a lifetime—worth a year's wages! To honor her, and to inspire others, Jesus said this story would be told wherever the gospel is preached (Matt. 26:6-13).

Application. Some today say, "Let's stop giving to others and just take care of our own needs." But to be good stewards and to obey the Great Commission, we must give to missions. We must follow the example of the Macedonians. They were poor and could have used the little money they had on themselves. But even in their poverty and affliction, they found the joy of giving to others. Giving blesses two people—the one who receives and the one who gives.

B. The Faith Principle: When we depend on God, we can give beyond our human ability (2 Cor. 8:3-4).

³For I testify that they gave as much as they were able, and even beyond their ability. Entirely on their own, ⁴they urgently pleaded with us for the privilege of sharing in this service to the saints (2 Cor. 8:3-4).

Q 6 *How is it possible to give beyond your ability? Give an example.*

This verse sounds like a riddle: *"They gave as much as they were able, and even beyond their ability."* How can we give more than we are able? Only with supernatural help. This explains why the word *grace* appears six times in 2 Corinthians 8–9. Look at how grace opened the hearts of the Macedonians. No one pushed or pulled them to give—no one except the Holy Spirit. But as faith and love filled their hearts, they begged for the opportunity to share the little that they had. True faith enables believers to heal the sick, cast out demons, speak in tongues, prophesy, and give in supernatural ways—beyond human ability (1 Cor. 12:4-12).

Q 7 *How do we know how much to give?*

There must be a balance in giving. And we must be led by the Spirit. Some people are foolish and give too much to others, neglecting the needs in their own families. But the Bible does not call the unwise *heroes*—it calls them traitors! Scripture says that those who do not provide for their own families have denied the faith (1 Tim. 5:8).

Millions of believers can testify about the results of a *faith* promise. These believers have learned to listen to the voice of the Holy Spirit and obey when He speaks. Often, they give more than what seems possible.

A widow lacked money and food during a famine. But when a man of God visited her, she felt led to give him the last little bit of flour and oil that she had. She only had enough to feed the prophet one time. However, as a result of her faith and obedience, she fed the prophet for more than 3 years and had plenty left over for herself and her son (1 Kings 17:7-16).

C. The Queen Bee Principle: Where the queen bee flies, the entire swarm follows (2 Cor. 8:5).

And they did not do as we expected, but they gave themselves first to the Lord and then to us in keeping with God's will (2 Cor. 8:5).

In every hive of honey bees, there is one queen bee, larger than the rest. She lays thousands of eggs that develop into bees. When the time is right, she lays some special eggs—one of which will become the new queen. But before the new queen hatches, the old queen bee will leave the hive, and thousands of bees will follow her to begin a new hive. Often the bees will swarm around the old queen and all join together in a group (Figure 12.4).

Just as the smaller bees follow the queen, our smaller desires follow the gift of *self* to Christ. The Macedonian Christians *"gave themselves first to the Lord,"* and then they gave their money. The one followed the other. If the gift of self to Christ is complete, the giving of money is certain. But if the gift of self is partial, then we will feel reluctant, hesitant, and unsure about giving our money to Him.

When we have yielded all of self—the whole heart—to the Lord, then every part of our lives will bear the mark of Christ. For the healthy Christian life is not a series of small surrenders, but a lifetime of total surrender.

In a war, after a battle, people found a soldier dead on the battlefield. A letter in his pocket contained words to his parents. "You know that I made the sacrifice of my life before I left for the war. That was the total surrender that included everything that might follow. I prayed, 'Dear God, I give you my life. All that I have now belongs to you, no matter what happens.'" This was the attitude of the Macedonians. They gave themselves completely to the Lord. This is the secret of the Christian life—to give ourselves wholly to God. In contrast, the Christian life lacks joy and depth if a person offers God a part of the heart but holds back the central throne. It is one thing to surrender a few dollars to the Lord, but it is a different thing to give Him all of our wealth. It is one thing to pray from time to time along the road, but it is another thing to commit the whole journey to Him. If a person withholds himself and his heart from the Lord, this person will often be annoyed and irritated with the demands of following Christ. Every day will bring the question, "How much of my life shall I give Christ today?" And this is the trouble that so many people face. They try to follow Christ by making small surrenders, but the great surrender of self has never been made. But when we, like the Macedonians, give ourselves first to the Lord, then all the lesser offerings follow without a struggle—as the bees follow their queen. And as God's children, His will becomes our song.²

D. The Grace Principle: God expects us to excel in giving as much as we excel in other gifts of grace (2 Cor. 8:6-7).

⁶So we urged Titus, since he had earlier made a beginning, to bring also to completion this act of grace on your part. ⁷But just as you excel in everything—in faith, in speech, in knowledge, in complete earnestness and in your love for us—see that you also excel in this grace of giving (2 Cor. 8:6-7).

As we study this fourth principle about giving, notice the words *"this act of grace"* (2 Cor. 8:6). Giving is a spiritual deed—one of many gifts the Holy Spirit makes possible. Therefore, giving depends as much on grace as any other manifestation of the Spirit does. Do you believe this? Do you believe that healing the sick and giving both depend on grace that the Spirit brings?

The Greek text of the New Testament makes it clear that grace is the root of all spiritual gifts. In Greek, the word for grace is *charis,* and the word for spiritual gifts is *charismata.* Charismatics are those who emphasize spiritual gifts, *charismata.* As *charis* (grace) is the root of *charismata,* grace is the root of all spiritual gifts. Paul lists nine

 Q 8 What does the queen bee represent?

Figure 12.4
A swarm of bees following a queen to a new place

 Q 9 What enabled the Macedonians to be so generous with their money?

Q 10 Circle the 6 times "grace" appears in 2 Corinthians 8–9. Read each verse that contains "grace."

Q 11 Does giving depend as much on grace as healing the sick does? Explain.

Q 12 Where did the term "Charismatics" come from?

charismata (spiritual gifts of grace) in 1 Corinthians 12:4-11. And in Romans 12:3-8, he lists seven more *charismata*—and one of these is the gift of giving (by grace).[3]

Q 13 *Why must giving always be on the list of spiritual gifts?*

The Corinthians are famous as a church that had spiritual gifts. All of these gifts were evidence of the grace God gave them by the Holy Spirit. Paul mentions gifts in the groups of *faith, speech, and knowledge* (2 Cor. 8:7). With the gift of *faith,* they could *"remove mountains"* (1 Cor. 13:2). Gifts of *speech* included the supernatural gifts of speaking in tongues, interpretation, and prophecy (1 Cor. 12:10). And grace gifts related to *knowledge* probably included the spiritual gifts of knowledge and wisdom (1 Cor. 12:8). Paul praised the Corinthians for these gifts and encouraged them to seek for the best spiritual gifts (1 Cor. 12:31). Early in his first letter to the Corinthians, Paul praised them because they did not lack any of the spiritual gifts as they waited for the Lord to return to earth (1 Cor. 1:7). And Paul adds that the Corinthians should excel in the graces of sincerity and love (2 Cor. 8:7). It is God's will *today* that we excel and overflow with spiritual gifts—gifts of grace that the Spirit works through common believers.

Paul emphasized that we need all the spiritual gifts of faith, speech, knowledge, sincerity, and love. And then he added, *"See that you also excel in this grace of giving"* (2 Cor. 8:6-7). *Giving* must always be on the list of spiritual gifts we value the most today. For life is out of balance if we emphasize gifts of faith, speech, and knowledge, but neglect giving. And giving is an *act of grace* God desires for every believer. About giving, Paul wrote: *"On the first day of every week, each one of you should set aside a sum of money in keeping with his income"* (1 Cor. 16:2).

So remember these two truths about giving. *First,* each believer should practice the spiritual gift of giving. *Second,* to please God in our giving, we must depend on the Spirit to give us *grace* and make us *gracious.*

As we seek to excel in spiritual matters, let us be known for excelling in the grace of giving. We can give without loving, but we cannot love without giving.

E. The Love Principle: We should give in love, following the example of Jesus (2 Cor. 8:8-9).

⁸*I am not commanding you, but I want to test the sincerity of your* **love** *by comparing it with the earnestness of others.* ⁹*For you know* **the grace of our Lord Jesus Christ**, *that though he was rich, yet for your sakes he became poor, so that you through his poverty might become rich* (2 Cor. 8:8-9).

There are at least four reasons why people give offerings:[4]
- **Duty.** Some people give because they feel it is their responsibility. This is a good reason to give.
- **Self-satisfaction.** Some give because it keeps them from feeling guilty and makes them feel good about themselves. They see a need, and they respond. Then they think, "I am a good person." Giving to keep a clear conscience and giving to feel good about one's self are not bad reasons to give.
- **Prestige.** Some give so that others will clap. Jesus said that this is a bad reason to give (Matt. 6:1-4).
- **Love.** There are many good reasons to give, but the best reason is love. So Paul wrote, *"I want to test the sincerity of your love"* (2 Cor. 8:8). Jesus is the greatest example of giving because of love. And here is that word *grace* again: *"For you know the grace of our Lord Jesus Christ, that though he was rich, yet for your sakes he became poor"* (2 Cor. 8:9). Jesus was *"full of grace"* (John 1:14). And grace enabled Him to love us so much that He became poor so that He could save us.

To see how poor Jesus was financially, we must look at the number of times He borrowed things. At His birth, He did not have a crib, so Joseph and Mary borrowed a manger. Throughout His ministry, unlike even the foxes and birds, He did not have His own home or bed. So He borrowed a place to sleep—on a boat, on the ground, or in the home of a friend under a tree (Matt. 8:20; Mark 1:30-35). He once borrowed food to feed the multitude. Another time He borrowed a coin to give an illustration (Matt. 22:19). When He needed an animal to ride into Jerusalem, He borrowed a donkey. When He needed a place to be buried, He borrowed a tomb. Such love! Imagine the riches, wealth, and honor Jesus had in heaven. If there were a stairway from His throne to the manger, imagine how many stairs someone would need in order to come down to where we live! It is a long way from the riches of heaven to the poverty of earth. But He loved us so much that He gave up everything He had. And He became poor financially so that we can become rich spiritually and enjoy the riches of heaven forever. When we think of the love Jesus showed us, can we be less than generous? Can we open both of our hands to receive all that Jesus gives us but refuse to reach out one hand to pass on that love to others?

Sabio says that the reason why there are so many small coins and small bills in the offering is that there are none smaller to give. Giving is the *thermometer of our love.⁵ Those who love little give little, and those who love much give much—in proportion to what they have.

Q 14 *What does James 2:15-16 teach about the grace of giving?*

Q 15 *What does 1 John 3:17-18 teach about the grace of giving?*

Q 16 *Riddle: Why are there so many small coins and bills in the offering?*

F. The Widow's Mite Principle: We should give what we can, even if it is less than we desire to give (2 Cor. 8:10-12).

¹⁰*And here is my advice about what is best for you in this matter: Last year you were the first not only to give but also to have the desire to do so.* ¹¹*Now finish the work, so that your eager willingness to do it may be matched by your completion of it, according to your means.* ¹²*For if the willingness is there, the gift is acceptable according to what one has, not according to what he does not have* (2 Cor. 8:10-12).

Q 17 *Should we teach children to give (John 6:1-13)?*

God looks at what we have, not what we lack. He does not ask all of us to give the same amount. Some eat steak every day, while others eat rice and beans. So the Bible says to give *"according to your means"* (2 Cor. 8:11). It does not matter how good our best is so long as we offer our best to God. Some can give gold, incense, and myrrh (Matt. 2:11), while others can only give copper (Mark 12:42-43). One can wash His feet with expensive perfume (John 12), while another can only give her tears to wash His feet (Luke 7:38). God is pleased with both if they both offer their best. From the early days of giving, God allowed the poor to give less than the rich. The Lord was pleased when Joseph and Mary sacrificed two pigeons because they could not afford to sacrifice a lamb (Lev. 12:8; Luke 2:24). God looks at the heart. If a person is willing and offers the best he has, God is pleased.

Q 18 *Why did God accept pigeons from some, but require a bull from others?*

God does not measure our offerings by what we put in, but by what we have left. Read the story of the widow in Mark 12:41-44. *"Many rich people were putting in large sums"* (Mark 12:41). The poor widow gave only two copper coins—they were worth less than a penny. Yet Jesus said she *"put in more than all of them"* (Luke 21:3). Therefore, we should give what we can, even if it is not as much as we would like to give.

Why did Paul write these verses to the Corinthians? Perhaps, when he first told them about the offering, they promised to give a lot of money. Maybe they pledged more than they were able to give or trusted God to provide. Or maybe their financial situation changed after they pledged. Some may have been embarrassed that they could not give more. But Paul says, "That is okay. Give what you have, and that will please God." So Paul releases the Corinthians from feeling guilty or carrying a heavy load on their backs. Some may have been saying, "I don't have much to give, so I won't give anything." But Paul says, "Give what you have. That is all God ever asks of any of us." So when you make a faith promise to give to a missionary or to help build a church, use your faith *and* your wisdom. If God gives you the faith to pledge more than you would be able to give on your own, trust Him to provide the resources for you. In the end, give what you can, even if it is less than you hoped to give.

God gives some the grace to give more than others. The Lord blessed R. G. LeTourneau with great grace. As his business grew and made millions of dollars, he gave 90 percent to God's work and lived well on the other 10 percent.[6] These days, God has enabled some Christian businessmen to give more than $1 million per month to the work of the Lord!

Q 19 *What did the poor widow in Korea give?*

Read the first illustration at the beginning of this chapter again. A poor widow in Korea gave what she could.

Lesson 41: Principles on the Grace of Giving—Part 2 (2 Cor. 8–9)

Goal A: State a principle on giving related to each of these: equality, accountability, enthusiasm, harvest, and praise.

Goal B: Explain and illustrate each of the 5 principles you stated in Goal A.

A. The Equality Principle: We should love others as we love ourselves, sharing with those in need (2 Cor. 8:13-15).

¹³Our desire is not that others might be relieved while you are hard pressed, but that there might be equality. ¹⁴At the present time your plenty will supply what they need, so that in turn their plenty will supply what you need. Then there will be equality, ¹⁵ as it is written: "He who gathered much did not have too much, and he who gathered little did not have too little" (2 Cor. 8:13-15).

Q 20 *Does the equality principle teach equal giving? Explain.*

A key word in these verses is *equality* or sufficiency—having enough for everyone. Paul refers to the 40 years when the children of Israel gathered manna in the wilderness (Exod. 16:18). When they gathered the manna, some gathered more than others. The young and strong gathered more than the old and weak. Then, they divided the manna. For each person in the tent, God said to take an *omer* (about two liters or two quarts). This was so that each person could have daily bread. No doubt the largest adults ate more than the smallest children. But the omer gave an average measure that would provide for each family.

Paul applies this illustration to the situations in Jerusalem and Corinth. When Paul wrote, those in Jerusalem did not have enough to eat, while believers in Corinth had more than they needed. God's will is that everyone has enough food, clothing, and shelter for his daily needs. This does not mean that those who work should feed the lazy. For Paul also wrote this rule: *"if anyone is not willing to work, then he is not to eat, either"* (2 Thess. 3:10). The point is that in the body of Christ, we are all one family. Like the Israelites, we are all passing through the wilderness of earth. And we have a responsibility to share with our brothers and sisters in need. We are to care equally about ourselves and others—loving our neighbors as ourselves (Matt. 22:39). And Paul explains that we should especially do good deeds to neighbors of the household of faith (Gal. 6:10).

Figure 12.5 Israelites picking up manna in the wilderness

Q 21 *Is it God's will for believers to have equal wealth and talents on earth? Explain.*

Equality, in the New Testament, does not mean uniformity. Equality does not mean that all believers live at the same social or financial level. Under the new covenant, God has not given us an *omer* or any other standard for how much we eat. The Scriptures recognize that some believers are richer than others. Some have more talents than others. There are masters and servants, parents and children. There are the greatest of the brothers and the least. Paul was not a social revolutionary. He did not tell Philemon to release Onesimus, but rather to receive him and treat him as a Christian brother.

Likewise, he told all masters to be kind and fair to their servants (Col. 4:1). Spiritually, we are all equal—joint heirs in the eternal kingdom with Christ. But on earth, there are great differences in the social and economic conditions of believers.[7]

Equality, in the New Testament, means that we treat one another with mutual love and respect. In our times of prosperity, we share with those in need. In our times of adversity, others will help supply our needs. This equal sharing of love and concern is God's plan and will for all in the body of Christ (2 Cor. 8:13). As Paul writes elsewhere, *"From whom* [Christ] *the whole body, being fitted and held together by what every joint supplies, according to the proper working of each individual part, causes the growth of the body for the building up of itself in love"* (Eph. 4:16).

Q 22 *What type of equality does Paul want (2 Cor. 8:13)?*

B. The Accountability Principle: We should give only to ministries that are accountable (2 Cor. 8:16-24).

Take a moment to read this long passage. All of these verses are for one reason—accountability. Paul uses more than 200 words to ensure the givers that their money will go to help poor believers in Jerusalem. As Paul said, *"We want to avoid any criticism of the way we administer this liberal gift"* (2 Cor. 8:20).

Q 23 *Why did Paul have several people handle the offering?*

To inspire people to give, Paul was accountable with the funds. If only one person collects the offering and is responsible for it, this causes many doubts, questions, and criticism. Note that there are *four* trusted people to collect, handle, and distribute the offering for Jerusalem:

- *First,* Titus was collecting the offering at Corinth. The Corinthians knew Titus well and trusted him.
- *Second,* there was a brother [18]*"...praised by all the churches for his service to the gospel.* [19]*What is more, he was chosen by the churches to accompany us as we carry the offering"* (2 Cor. 8:18-19). If Paul had chosen this man, the assurance would have been less. But since those who were giving chose a representative to go with the offering, the accountability was high.
- *Third,* there was a fellow minister of Paul. *"In addition, we are sending with them our brother who has often proved to us in many ways that he is zealous, and now even more so because of his great confidence in you"* (2 Cor. 8:22). This unnamed brother was also a representative of the churches (2 Cor. 8:23).
- *Fourth,* the apostle Paul was helping with the offering. He did not collect it, but he was helping carry and distribute the money to the poor.

Accountability is good for all of us. It is wise to have several people collect, count, and administer church funds. These team members should not all be from the same family! And the pastor or leader should not be the one who chooses these team members. The givers should choose some of them. Those who give offerings and those who collect offerings should insist on proper guidelines for accountability. This ensures five things: that the church has a good name, that givers are not cheated, that people are not tempted to steal funds, that those in need receive help, and that God is glorified.

Q 24 *Which 5 things does accountability ensure?*

The principle of accountability is vital in stewardship. As one man said that the way the church handles funds should be cleaner than a bride's wedding dress! There must not be any hidden funds. There must not be anything about money *in the closet.* Everything should be in the open and accounted for. All offerings must be counted with more than one person present. Every check a church writes must have two signatures on it. This is a guarantee and safeguard to protect givers, spenders, and receivers. Sometimes it is not convenient in a church to find the second person whom the church has chosen to sign checks. But the second signature is necessary. Church finances must be open for examination.

Q 25 *What are some keys to financial accountability of church funds?*

Today, some are unwise and unbiblical in how they give offerings. They hear a preacher on the radio or television and send an offering. But there is no accountability!

Q 26 *Why is it wise to give through a local church?*

Those who give do not know how their money is used. This is why it is wise to give through the local church. The church chooses representatives to help count money. Each year, deacons examine the financial books. This is accountability. The Bible requires it.

Figure 12.6 Even a dumb sheep knows better than to trust a wolf to guard the lambs.

As we give to ministries that are accountable, we are good stewards and are sowing to reap a harvest. But those who give their money without requiring accountability are not being good stewards. They are wasting God's money. Do these unwise stewards think that God will praise and bless them? They are like the sheep that trusted a wolf to guard the lambs. Not all who carry Bibles are honest. And even good men fall without accountability. Those who give have a right and a responsibility to ask wise questions about the use of their offerings.[8]

A believer heard a preacher on the radio tell about children who needed food. With love and compassion, the listener sent an offering to the preacher. Will any or all of this money help hungry children? Does the believer have any way of checking to find out how the funds are used? Will God bless the person who gave the offering, no matter what the preacher does with the money? Let us add that it is okay to give to reputable ministries if radio or TV preachers are raising money for them and you can give it directly to the organization.

C. The Enthusiasm Principle: Enthusiasm is *contagious—it spreads from one to another (2 Cor. 9:1-2).

¹There is no need for me to write to you about this service to the saints. ²For I know your eagerness to help, and I have been boasting about it to the Macedonians, telling them that since last year you in Achaia were ready to give; and your enthusiasm has stirred most of them to action (2 Cor. 9:1-2).

Q 27 *What are some examples of the enthusiasm principle?*

Both bad and good things are contagious. We may catch the flu or measles by being close to a sick person. Likewise, when people give with enthusiasm, this is contagious. It affects others to open their hearts and give. Paul told the Corinthians *"your enthusiasm has stirred most of them* [the Macedonians] *to action"* (2 Cor. 9:2).

A cold church is like cold butter—it does not spread well.[9] In contrast, the Corinthians were a hot church, aflame with enthusiasm. Their zeal influenced others to give. *"See how great a forest is set aflame by such a small fire!"* (James 3:5). In the same way, the enthusiasm of one person can ignite an entire church to be generous. But only those with fires in themselves can kindle fires in others.

Enthusiasm is contagious. Children catch it from their parents. Students catch it from their teachers. New church members catch it from the elders.

Enthusiasm is contagious, but so is the lack of it. When ten spies were negative, an entire nation caught their pessimism and missed the Promised Land (Num. 14). What do people catch from you?

Years wrinkle the skin, but a lack of enthusiasm wrinkles the soul.[10]

D. The Harvest Principle: We reap in proportion to what we sow (2 Cor. 9:6-11).

⁶Remember this: Whoever sows sparingly will also reap sparingly, and whoever sows generously will also reap generously. ⁷Each man should give what he has decided in his heart to give, not reluctantly or under compulsion, for God loves a cheerful giver (2 Cor. 9:6-7).

Q 28 *To what does Paul compare giving? Explain.*

Sometimes, when it is time to give, the voice of doubt whispers to us, "Giving is losing." Or as the deacons pass the offering plate, the flesh may say, "The more you give, the less you have." At such times, we should respond, "But God has said that giving is sowing."[11]

Neither the devil nor the flesh prevents people from planting seeds in their gardens and fields. For we know the truth about sowing and reaping. The law of the harvest states that generous sowing is the key to generous reaping. Likewise, we know that God's Word is true, and it likens giving to sowing.

Some have abused this principle of the harvest. They have tried to manipulate people to give to a certain ministry. These false teachers promise that if people send them an offering, God will multiply it back 100 times to the givers. As proof, they quote Matthew 19:29. But if we read Matthew 19:29, we soon discover that it is not about sending offerings to a preacher. Rather, it was a promise Jesus gave to those who left their homes and families to serve Him. And we note that there were no wealthy apostles, although they left everything for Christ. This leads us to understand that Matthew 19:29 does not focus on earthly possessions, but rather on provisions. For example, Peter did not own 100 new homes because he left one home behind. But the doors of 100 homes opened to him as he traveled from place to place to preach the gospel. When we give to help believers or to help people become believers, God keeps records. The blessings He gives back to us are not only money; they include money and *all* else we need. When Paul wrote about God's blessings, he used the word *all* four times in one verse! *"And God is able to make **all** grace abound to you, so that in **all** things at **all** times, having **all** that you need, you will abound in every good work"* (2 Cor. 9:8).

Q 29 What is the condition of Matthew 19:29?

Q 30 In what sense did the apostles receive 100 times what they gave?

It is true that some have twisted and misused verses like Matthew 19:29 and 2 Corinthians 9:6-7. So we want to reject and turn away from false and selfish interpretations of verses on giving. Still, we must continue to emphasize the truth of God's Word. The Bible teaches the law of the harvest. *"Remember this: Whoever sows sparingly will also reap sparingly, and whoever sows generously will also reap generously"* (2 Cor. 9:6). This is the Word of God Almighty to us, and many other verses in the Bible declare it.

Q 31 What is the law of the harvest?

The plain truth is this: No one ever loses by obeying what the Spirit says to give. Giving is like sowing seed.

It would be fleshly to give for the sole purpose of reaping a harvest. But the New Testament is not ashamed or afraid of mentioning the blessings that come to us as we serve God. We do not give just so that we will receive. However, we give with the assurance that God blesses those who share wealth with others. Here are some verses that encourage us to sow generously:

Q 32 What are some of your favorite verses on giving?

- *"He has scattered abroad his gifts to the poor; his righteousness endures forever"* (2 Cor. 9:9; Ps. 112:9).
- *⁷"If there is a poor man with you, one of your brothers, in any of your towns in your land which the LORD your God is giving you, you shall not harden your heart, nor close your hand from your poor brother; ⁸but you shall freely open your hand to him, and shall generously lend him sufficient for his need in whatever he lacks. ⁹Beware that there is no base thought in your heart, saying, 'The seventh year, the year of remission, is near,' and your eye is hostile toward your poor brother, and you give him nothing; then he may cry to the LORD against you, and it will be a sin in you. ¹⁰You shall generously give to him, and your heart shall not be grieved when you give to him, because for this thing the LORD your God will bless you in all your work and in all your undertakings. ¹¹For the poor will never cease to be in the land; therefore I command you, saying, 'You shall freely open your hand to your brother, to your needy and poor in your land'"* (Deut. 15:7-11; 2 Cor. 9:7).
- *"God loves a cheerful giver"* (2 Cor. 9:7). This verse is not in the Hebrew version of Scripture, but the Spirit leads Paul to refer to Proverbs 22:9 in the Septuagint (Greek version of the Old Testament). Also, Paul substitutes the word *loves* for *blesses*.[12] So

the meaning of the verses is that God blesses a cheerful giver—one who is happy to share with those in need.

- *24"There is one who scatters, and yet increases all the more, and there is one who withholds what is justly due, and yet it results only in want. 25The generous man will be prosperous, and he who waters will himself be watered"* (Prov. 11:24-25).
- *"Give, and it will be given to you. They will pour into your lap a good measure—pressed down, shaken together, and running over. For by your standard of measure it will be measured to you in return"* (Luke 6:38). The context of this verse is about judging and forgiving. So the primary meaning is moral. Still, scholars agree that it contains a principle that applies to many areas of life, like giving.
- *10"Now he who supplies seed to the sower and bread for food will also supply and increase your store of seed and will enlarge the harvest of your righteousness. 11You will be made rich in every way so that you can be generous on every occasion"* (2 Cor. 9:10-11).

Does God love cheerful givers more than He loves those who are stingy? Does God seek cheerful givers and set them aside to bless in a special way? Sometimes. It is God's will to bless everyone. But those who give cheerfully cooperate with God's plan—which enables God to bless them. The sunshine always warms those who stand in it more than it warms those in the shade. It is God's will to bless all people. But each one of us decides whether we will allow Him to bless us.

Someone asked Aunt Denny, "Why do you love and bless that child more than other children?" She replied, "I am not partial to that child; he is partial to me! He comes and sits on my lap. He smiles at me and sings to me. He reaches out his hands and asks me to pick him up. He brings me little pictures and flowers he has picked. He always gets the closest to me. He allows me to love him more than I can love other children."[13]

Q 33 *What does the story about Aunt Denny teach?*

E. The Praise Principle: Generous giving causes people to thank God (2 Cor. 9:12-15).

12This service that you perform is not only supplying the needs of God's people but is also overflowing in many expressions of thanks to God. 13Because of the service by which you have proved yourselves, men will praise God for the obedience that accompanies your confession of the gospel of Christ, and for your generosity in sharing with them and with everyone else. 14And in their prayers for you their hearts will go out to you, because of the surpassing grace God has given you. 15Thanks be to God for his indescribable gift! (2 Cor. 9:12-15).

Q 34 *What does the praise principle teach?*

People's attitude toward God in heaven depends on His children on earth. When Christians are selfish and stingy, fewer people praise God. In fact, some people curse God because of the way His children behave on earth. But when God's children love, share, and give, many people look up and worship. They say, "These people are so much like their Father in heaven." So Jesus said, *"Let your light shine before men in such a way that they may see your good works, and glorify your Father who is in heaven"* (Matt. 5:16).

When Christians are stingy, everyone loses. But when we are generous givers, everyone wins. Those in need receive help. Those who give reap a harvest. And most of all, God receives glory, praise, and thanksgiving. Yet let us always remember this: Nothing we give compares with the gift that God has given us. *"Thanks be to God for his indescribable gift!"* (2 Cor. 9:15).

Test Yourself: Circle the letter by the *best* completion to each question or statement.

1. Who won Paul's Gold Medal award?
   a) The Syrians
   b) The Achaians
   c) The Judeans
   d) The Macedonians

2. *"They gave themselves first to the Lord"*
   a) is the basis of the Gold Medal Principle.
   b) is the basis of the Faith Principle.
   c) is the basis of the Queen Bee Principle.
   d) is the basis of the Love Principle.

3. The Faith Principle teaches that we can
   a) give beyond our human ability.
   b) expect to receive 100 times what we give.
   c) believe God to multiply our offerings.
   d) trust those who are accountable.

4. What is the highest and best motive for giving?
   a) Rewards
   b) Faith
   c) Love
   d) Inspiration

5. Which is based on the Greek word for *grace*?
   a) Pentecostals
   b) Charismatics
   c) Evangelicals
   d) Gracinomials

6. Who illustrates the Widow's Mite Principle?
   a) A poor woman in Korea
   b) A sinful woman in Judea
   c) A famous widow in Asia
   d) An unknown woman in Moab

7. Which emphasizes "love others as self"?
   a) The Queen Bee Principle
   b) The Equality Principle
   c) The Praise Principle
   d) The Sharing Principle

8. Paul compared giving to
   a) building.
   b) fasting.
   c) prophesying.
   d) sowing.

9. The Enthusiasm Principle is related to
   a) a fire.
   b) an earthquake.
   c) a famine.
   d) a harvest.

10. The Praise Principle teaches that
    a) we should worship as we give.
    b) everything with breath should give.
    c) peoples' attitude toward God depends on us.
    d) we should give so God will commend us.

 Essay Test Topics: Write 50-100 words on each of these goals that you studied in this chapter.

Principles on the Grace of Giving—Part 1 (2 Cor. 8)

Goal: *State a principle on giving for each of these: gold medal, faith, queen bee, grace, love, widow's mite.*

Goal: *Explain and illustrate each of the 6 principles you stated in the above goal.*

Principles on the Grace of Giving—Part 2 (2 Cor. 8–9)

Goal: *State a principle on giving related to each of these: equality, accountability, enthusiasm, harvest, and praise.*

Goal: *Explain and illustrate each of the 5 principles you stated in the above goal.*

Chapter 13:
Paul Confronts His Critics
2 Corinthians 10–13

Introduction

Today, there are cults outside the Church—cults like Jehovah's Witnesses, Mormons, and the New Age movement. And there are many false teachings inside the Church. It was similar in Paul's day. False teachers in the Church opposed the teachings of Jesus and the apostles. These false teachers attacked apostles like Paul and claimed to be the true leaders. So it was necessary for the apostles to defend themselves and defend the truth that Jesus entrusted to them.

Figure 13.1 Church tradition says the apostle Paul was a small man who did not look like a powerful preacher.

Some were attacking Paul because he did not look and sound like a powerful man of God (2 Cor. 10:1-6). He was *timid face to face* (2 Cor. 10:1). Earlier, we noted that Paul did not look like a powerful apostle. The name Paul (*Paulos*) means "little one" in Greek. Second-century tradition describes Paul as a small man, bald, with eyebrows that met, a hooked nose, and bandy legs (with knees that could not touch)—but full of grace.[1] One ancient writer called Paul *a three-cubit man*. Like John Wesley and Napoleon, he was probably short—perhaps 5 feet tall or less.[2] Physically, Paul was small and weak. And his voice, manner, and speaking were not very powerful—*unimpressive* (2 Cor. 10:1, 10). In short, Paul did not look like an apostle or sound like an apostle. But as we emphasize in this chapter, the world measures apostles with a different ruler than God uses. Many whom the world says are the tallest are the shortest in God's eyes. And those whom God declares the greatest, society calls the least.

Lessons:
Spiritual Thinking (2 Cor. 10:1-6)

Goal A: *Summarize and illustrate 3 reasons why bad thoughts are worse than most people think.*
Goal B: *State and illustrate 5 principles for overcoming evil thoughts.*
Goal C: *Contrast the 2 roads and destinies before each person in regard to his thoughts.*

Spiritual Humility (2 Cor. 10:7-18)

Goal: *Explain 4 characteristics of humility in the context of Paul and his critics.*

Spiritual Insights (2 Cor. 11:1-15)

Goal A: *Contrast the characteristics of bad and good jealousy (2 Cor. 11:1-2).*
Goal B: *Contrast the tactics of Satan as a lion and as a serpent (2 Cor. 11:3-6, 13-15).*
Goal C: *Contrast Paul and false apostles on the topic of money (2 Cor. 11:7-12).*

Spiritual Highs and Lows (2 Cor. 11:16–12:10)

Goal: *Explain and apply 5 principles about spiritual experiences (2 Cor. 11:16–12:10).*

Spiritual Concerns (2 Cor. 12:11–13:14)

Goal: *State and illustrate 6 concerns of a leader for spiritual children.*

Spiritual Thinking (2 Cor. 10:1-6)

Goal A: *Summarize and illustrate 3 reasons why bad thoughts are worse than most people think.*
Goal B: *State and illustrate 5 principles for overcoming evil thoughts.*
Goal C: *Contrast the 2 roads and destinies before each person in regard to his thoughts.*

Setting

Someone outlined 2 Corinthians with three themes:
- Living (2 Cor. 1–7),
- Giving (2 Cor. 8–9), and
- Guarding (2 Cor. 10–13).

Chapter 10 begins the third part of Second Corinthians. Chapters 10–13 are different in tone from the earlier parts of this letter. They are more severe as Paul defends his apostleship. Many believers in Corinth accepted Paul's authority. Yet false teachers led a group that opposed Paul.

At times, even spiritual people can err by *"looking only on the surface"* (2 Cor. 10:7). Like Samuel the great prophet, we can look at a tall, strong, eloquent man like Eliab and think that God's anointing is upon him.

> *⁶When they entered, he looked at Eliab and thought, "Surely the LORD'S anointed is before Him." ⁷But the LORD said to Samuel, "Do not look at his appearance or at the height of his stature, because I have rejected him; for God sees not as man sees, for man looks at the outward appearance, but the LORD looks at the heart"* (1 Sam. 16:6-7).

Looking only on the surface was a major fault of the Corinthians. In Paul's first letter to them, Paul wrote about the problem of divisions. Some followed Peter, some Paul, some Apollos, and some Christ. Why? Because these young, immature believers were *looking only on the surface.* They admired things like appearance, style, tone of voice, and eloquence. Paul reminded them that these are worldly standards, but not godly standards (2 Cor. 10:3-4). Paul's message in Corinth was in weakness, fear, and much trembling. He did not use big, wise, persuasive words. Rather, he ministered in the Spirit's power. Why? So that their faith would be based on God, not on human wisdom, talent, or personality. And in his second letter to the Corinthians, Paul continues to deal with this same problem—*looking only on the surface.* Some of the Corinthians were masters at taking *"pride in what is seen rather than in what is in the heart"* (2 Cor. 5:12).

Application. This type of *worldly thinking* was a big problem in Corinth. And it is a big problem today. Immature believers want a pastor as tall as King Saul (1 Sam. 9:2), as handsome and diplomatic as Absalom (2 Sam. 14:25; 15:1-6), as eloquent as Apollos (Acts 18:24-28), and with a voice *"like the sound of many waters"* (Rev. 1:15). Immature and fleshly believers do not recognize many anointed leaders, but they follow those whom God rejects. These shallow disciples think that meekness is weakness, self confidence is anointing, loud volume is power, and prosperity is spiritual blessing. In 2 Corinthians 10–13, we will study much about how a true apostle looks. And we will examine the characteristics of false apostles and teachers.

In this lesson, we will contrast worldly thinking and spiritual thinking. One of the biggest problems in the Church today is the lack of spiritual thinking. Many of God's people have been led astray. They are losing, or have already lost, fellowship with God because they do not honor God with their thoughts. For many, this lesson will be *the most helpful lesson you will ever study in your lifetime.* For as we learn to take our thoughts captive and practice thinking spiritual thoughts that please the Lord, we enter the dimension of constant communion with God. A title for this lesson could have been:

Q 1 *What is Paul guarding in 2 Corinthians 10–13?*

Q 2 *What things did the Corinthians admire, looking only on the surface?*

Q 3 *What do those who are immature look for in a pastor?*

"Thoughts About Thought."

Biblical text:

*¹By the meekness and gentleness of Christ, I appeal to you – I, Paul, who am "timid" when face to face with you, but "bold" when away! ²I beg you that when I come I may not have to be as bold as I expect to be toward some people who think that we live by the standards of this world. ³For though we live in the world, we do not wage war as the world does. ⁴The weapons we fight with are not the weapons of the world. On the contrary, they have divine power to demolish strongholds. ⁵We demolish arguments and every pretension that sets itself up against the knowledge of God, and **we take captive every thought to make it obedient to Christ**. ⁶And we will be ready to punish every act of disobedience, once your obedience is complete (2 Cor. 10:1-6).*

Introduction: How many different thoughts are possible in only one minute? 20? 30? How many thoughts can you think in an hour? 100? 1,000? How many thoughts are possible in a day? A week? A month? A year? Thoughts can be so many! They swarm like bees. They fly in flocks like birds. They are like links of a chain—one leads to another. Thoughts are like grains of sand. A single grain does not matter, but a ton of sand is made up of single grains!³

Thesis or theme of this lesson: Because our thoughts are many, we must make them our friends. Then they will escort us into God's presence and up to heaven. But if our thoughts are our enemies, they will become a mighty army that will drag us down to hell.

I. The Problem: Bad thoughts are worse than some people realize.

A. God knows when we welcome evil thoughts.

A policeman cannot fine you or put you in jail because of your thoughts. A parent or teacher cannot discipline a child because of bad thoughts. A judge cannot take you to court for bad thoughts. Why? Because no one can see inside another person's mind. Our thoughts are invisible and unknown to other humans.

In contrast, God sees our thoughts within us. *"The LORD knows the thoughts of man"* (Ps. 94:11). Dirty thoughts are as repulsive and offensive to the Holy Spirit as dirty sheets are to a king.⁴

A man once saw a glass beehive. You could see all the bees inside it. Likewise, God sees our thoughts inside our minds.

B. God says that meditating on evil thoughts is sinful.

Jesus said that befriending thoughts of lust is adultery (Matt. 5:27-28). Keeping thoughts of hate is murder (1 John 3:15). Continued thoughts of bitterness become a root that defiles many (Heb. 12:15). Thoughts of unforgiveness can cause us to lose the pardon that God gives us (Matt. 18:21-35). Thoughts of greed are the same as idolatry (Col. 3:5). Thoughts of fear or worry dishonor God.

C. Welcoming evil thoughts leads to the bondage of sin.

- A match will not light dry charcoal. But soak charcoal in kerosene, and a match will light it. Likewise, sin will one day burst into flame in a person who soaks his mind with evil thoughts.
- Evil thoughts are the nest in which the eggs of sin hatch.
- An arrow leaves no trail as it flies through the air. In contrast, dwelling on evil thoughts leaves a slimy trail like a snail leaves.

Q 4 Why is it important to make our thoughts our friends?

Q 5 What are 3 reasons why bad thoughts are worse than some realize?

Q 6 When do evil thoughts become sin?

Q 7 How do evil thoughts prepare the way for sin? Explain.

- Nurse evil thoughts and they will grow into a giant who will conquer you.
- It was not a demon that led King David to commit adultery with Bathsheba. It was his own thoughts that he refused to rule.
- Pornography, sinful books and magazines, and worldly movies or videos lower our resistance to temptation. They move us step by step to sin.
- As surely as John the Baptist prepared the way for Jesus, welcoming evil thoughts prepares the way for sin.

II. The Solution: We can live a life of freedom and victory in our thoughts.

Many have believed the devil's lie that we cannot control our thoughts. But the truth is that we can live a life of mental freedom and victory. Here are five keys to *"take captive every thought to make it obedient to Christ"* (2 Cor. 10:5).

A. Depend on God to help you.

All of us need a Savior to save us from our sins (Matt. 1:21; Rom. 3:23; 6:23). *Jesus* is the Greek form of *Joshua*, which means "the LORD saves." The angel told Joseph, *"You shall call His name Jesus, for He will save His people from their sins"* (Matt. 1:21). It is the delight and mission of Jesus to save us from sin through the ministry of the Holy Spirit.

Invite the Spirit to control you moment by moment. Submit your mind and will to Him (Rom. 8:9-14). Walk in the Spirit, and He will lead you to think good thoughts (Gal. 5:16-26).

Q 8 Can we free ourselves from the bondage of evil thoughts? Explain.

B. Be aware of your thoughts.

You can know what is in your pocket by emptying its contents on the table in front of you. Likewise, you can keep your thoughts out in front of you. Be aware of what you are thinking. Be alert and watchful. A person who owns a store keeps an inventory — a list of what is in his store. Likewise, we must keep a constant inventory of what we allow to stay in our heart and mind.

When we eat, we pay attention to the food, for our physical health depends on what we eat. Likewise, our spiritual health depends on the thoughts we think. Therefore, we must pay attention to what we are thinking. The devil and the world constantly seduce people to sin. Those who are not alert are led into sin before they know it. One sinful thought leads to another, like links of a chain. And soon, those who do not pay attention are enslaved by sin. For if we eat from the devil's menu, we will become his slaves. So we must be alert and pay attention to our thoughts.

Being watchful and aware of our thoughts is a key to being free. Watchfulness is the price of mental freedom. Guide your thoughts as a rider steers a bicycle. Do not allow your thoughts to float along in life, like sticks in a river. Be aware of what you are thinking. Censor your thoughts. Approve or disapprove each thought that comes to you.

Q 9 Why is it vital to be aware of our thoughts?

C. Let the Spirit train you to hate what God hates.

Hate sinful thoughts because they are an enemy that wants to destroy you. Sinful thoughts led to the fall of Adam and Eve. Sinful thoughts led Samson into defeat. Sinful thoughts stole Reuben's birthright. Sinful thoughts seduced David into the shadows of shame. Sinful thoughts cost Ananias and Sapphira their lives. Sinful thoughts cost Judas his soul.

Q 10 What are some reasons why we should hate evil thoughts?

Learn to hate sinful thoughts, because they are a deadly enemy that wants to destroy your reputation, steal your wealth, separate you from God, and condemn you to hell.

Christian was climbing a mountain when he saw a poisonous snake. He picked up a rock to kill the viper. But as the man delayed, the snake began to talk. "Please do not kill me," pleaded the serpent. "I promise not to hurt you. Have mercy on me. I am so cold. Please pick me up and carry me under your coat to where the sun is shining at the top of the mountain." After much discussion, and with many words, the snake convinced Christian to carry him. All went well until Christian was near the top of the mountain. But when he unbuttoned his coat and set the snake down, it bit him. Christian cried out in shock and in pain. "Why did you bite me? You promised not to hurt me, but now I will die." The snake laughed and said, "You fool. You knew I was your enemy when you took the time to talk with me and picked me up!"

I was talking with a man once when a pretty woman walked by. His eyes followed every step she took. He seemed hypnotized by her body and movements. Finally, he returned from his mental safari. I said to him, "It looks like you have a problem with your thoughts." He answered, "Oh, I cannot help that. Besides, it was just a thought!"

We cannot keep from being tempted. Even Jesus was tempted by evil thoughts. Thoughts fly to us as swiftly as birds. You cannot keep a bird from flying over your head. But you can prevent it from building a nest in your hair! You cannot prevent a thief from coming to your door, but you do not have to invite him in!

A person turns a piece of candy over in his mouth because he likes it. Likewise, a person turns an evil thought over in his mind because it is sweet to the flesh. In contrast, we spit out what we do not like. We reject food that we hate, and we reject thoughts that we hate. As we learn to hate evil thoughts, we will reject them as quickly as Jesus rejected Satan's temptations to sin.

Q 11 *What are some verses that teach us to hate evil?*

Many verses in the Bible teach us to hate what is wrong.

- *"Hate evil, you who love the LORD, who preserves the souls of His godly ones; He delivers them from the hand of the wicked"* (Ps. 97:10).
- *"The fear of the LORD is to hate evil; pride and arrogance and the evil way and the perverted mouth, I hate"* (Prov. 8:13).
- *15"Do not love the world nor the things in the world. If anyone loves the world, the love of the Father is not in him. 16For all that is in the world, the lust of the flesh and the lust of the eyes and the boastful pride of life, is not from the Father, but is from the world"* (1 John 2:15-16).
- *"Yet this you do have, that you hate the deeds of the Nicolaitans, which I also hate"* (Rev. 2:6).

Be like Joseph—flee from sinful thoughts as you would flee from a poisonous snake (Gen. 39:10-12). Turn away from signs, scenes, pleasures, and pictures that God's enemies promote.

D. Let the Spirit lead you to love what God loves.

Q 12 *Upon which 2 things does our fellowship with God depend?*

Hating evil is half of our fellowship with God. The other half is loving what is good.

- *"You have loved righteousness and hated lawlessness; therefore God, your God, has anointed you with the oil of gladness above your companions"* (Heb. 1:9).
- *"Hate evil; love good"* (Amos 5:15).
- *"Abhor what is evil; cling to what is good"* (Rom. 12:9).

Q 13 *Why did God exalt Jesus (Heb. 1:9)? Apply this principle.*

Hating evil and loving good belong together, like two sides of a coin.

Hate the evil thoughts of darkness, because Satan slithers in the darkness. But love the pure thoughts of light, because God lives there.

> *⁵This is the message we have heard from Him and announce to you, that God is Light, and in Him there is no darkness at all. ⁶If we say that we have fellowship with Him and yet walk in the darkness, we lie and do not practice the truth* (1 John 1:5-6).

To fellowship with God, we must walk with Him in the light. We must learn to hate what God hates and love what God loves.

Philippians 4:8-9 tells us to think about things that are true, noble, right, pure, lovely, admirable, excellent, and worthy of praise. As you love good thoughts, your will stands like a guard at the door of your mind (Phil. 4:8). When a temptation comes to your mind the first time, it must knock at the door of your mind. If you choose to welcome the evil thought, it will not knock the next time. Instead, it will boldly rush into your mind, because your will is not guarding the door. In contrast, as you practice loving good thoughts, *"the God of peace will be with you"* (Phil. 4:9). And your will, like an armed guard, protects the door of your mind.

Q 14 *What does Philippians 4:8-9 command about thinking?*

When a mother decides to wean a nursing child, a battle takes place. The child has become used to the warm milk and the pleasant feelings of resting on its mother's breast. But after only a few days of protesting, the child will learn to be content with other food. Likewise, if you have developed the habit of savoring sinful thoughts, your fleshly nature will cry like a baby when you try to wean it. But as you stand firm in Christ and decide to hate what He hates and love what He loves, the voice of the flesh will become quieter and quieter. As you daily choose to hate evil thoughts, they will pass by you like birds. You will not give an evil thought a second thought! Temptations to a pure mind are like matches thrown into a barrel of water.

Q 15 *What happens when we cooperate with the Spirit to break the habit of evil thoughts? Explain the process.*

E. Use the weapons God has given us for spiritual warfare (2 Cor. 10:4).

> *³For though we live in the world, we do not wage war as the world does. ⁴The weapons we fight with are not the weapons of the world. On the contrary, they have divine power to demolish strongholds. ⁵We demolish arguments and every pretension that sets itself up against the knowledge of God, and **we take captive every thought to make it obedient to Christ*** (2 Cor. 10:3-5).

To win a spiritual battle, we must use spiritual weapons. Some of our spiritual weapons are the power of the Holy Spirit, the Scriptures, prayers, faith, righteousness, truth, honesty, and thinking good thoughts (2 Cor. 6:6-7; 10:4-5).

Q 16 *What are some spiritual weapons God gives us to conquer evil thoughts?*

Rizpah became tired trying to keep the birds away from her dead sons (2 Sam. 21:10). All day long she chased the vultures away. No doubt this wore her out. Likewise, a person could become weary trying to chase away every evil thought. The easy way to keep dirty things out of a bucket is to fill it with good things. So once the Savior has cleansed your mind, do your part to think good thoughts. It is impossible to think a bad thought and a good thought at the same time!

Fill your mind with good thoughts. How? Read and meditate on the Bible. Pray and sing. Listen to worship music or preaching at church or on a radio, a television, the internet, a cassette, a CD, or an MP3 player. Fellowship with other godly people and talk about godly things. When you seek entertainment, such as books, music, movies or television programs, it is important that you reject evil things and approve only what is good. You will defeat yourself if you have devotions in the mornings and then watch bad movies in the evenings! Refuse to watch any movies that use the Lord's name in vain or show nudity. Fill your heart, mind, and soul with good thoughts. Hate what God hates, and love what God loves. Good thoughts are a spiritual weapon to defeat bad thoughts.

III. The Choice: Two roads are before us today. Each person must decide which road to travel.

Q 17 How does our destiny depend on our thoughts? Explain the 2 roads.

  A. ***Future good result:*** If you choose the road of good thoughts, you choose to walk with God. A year from now, you will be so different. You will be experiencing peace instead of guilt. You will have freedom instead of bondage. You will be walking away from shame and toward honor. Others will rise up and bless you because you honor God in your private thoughts. Your good example will influence your family and many others.

  B. ***Future bad result:*** If you decide to welcome and indulge sinful thoughts, you will become a slave to your thoughts—a prisoner of your own imagination. Little by little, you will slide further into the pit of sin. Thoughts that once embarrassed you will no longer alarm you. Your appetite for spiritual things will lessen. Your hunger for filth will increase. You will make the decision to welcome evil thoughts in private. But the day will come when everyone will know the road you chose to travel. If you travel the road to destruction, one day you will arrive at that destination. Your name could easily be added to the long list of those whose names and reputations have been shamed—names like Achan, Samson, Ananias and Sapphira, and Judas.

Q 18 Do you need Jesus to deliver you from evil thoughts? Explain.

Invitation. If you are on the wrong road, you can find the right one today. Perhaps your thoughts are out of control. You are in bondage, and at times the thoughts that come to you cause you agony and torment. There is another road for you to walk. Regardless of the lies the devil has told you, he cannot keep you as a prisoner against your will. Jesus forgives, cleanses, and empowers those who repent and ask Him for help. The Savior's work is to set the captive free, whether the bondage is great or small. Call on His name and He will save and deliver you. If the Son sets you free, you will be free indeed (John 8:36).

Paul Confronts His Critics

Lesson 43: Spiritual Humility (2 Cor. 10:7-18)

Goal: *Explain 4 characteristics of humility in the context of Paul and his critics.*

Setting

As we begin this lesson, recall that in 2 Corinthians 10–13, Paul is defending his ministry. This was necessary because critics and false teachers were attacking him. We know that some of Paul's critics were Judaizers. From the beginning of the church in Corinth, some Jews persecuted those who turned to Jesus. Acts 18 records the earliest days of the church in Corinth. As Paul preached in the synagogue, Jews opposed Paul and became abusive (Acts 18:6). So he left the synagogue and went next door to preach. Crispus, the ruler of the synagogue, and his household believed in the Lord. Paul baptized Crispus, who became a part of the new community of believers (1 Cor. 1:14). Also, many others believed and were baptized (Acts 18:8). Gallio, a government leader (proconsul), refused to listen when local Jews accused Paul. Jewish leaders became desperate to stop the revival in Corinth. To frighten other Jews from following Jesus, they beat Sosthenes, the new ruler of the synagogue. So we know that in Corinth, unbelieving Jews—those with no faith in Jesus—opposed Paul.

Yet other Jews, with *some* faith in Jesus, also opposed Paul. These were the Judaizers. They believed that salvation came through following Moses and Jesus. So they insisted that all believers must obey the Law of Moses *and* follow Jesus. But the gospel does NOT recognize two saviors—Moses and Jesus. We are saved by faith in Jesus Christ alone. And the council in Jerusalem affirmed this truth for Jews and Gentiles (Acts 15).

Paul, in response to the Judaizers, defended his ministry by emphasizing his Jewish roots (2 Cor. 11:22). Paul was the first pastor of the Corinthian church. And the salvation of his converts depended on his gospel and reputation. So as we study 2 Corinthians 10–13, remember that Paul was not talking about himself for personal reasons. He was not patting himself on the back so he would feel better. Rather, the salvation of believers in Corinth depended on them recognizing that he was God's apostle.

Paul was not proud or self-centered. He was humble and Christ-centered. In this lesson we will examine four characteristics or principles about humility. These four principles become clear as we contrast Paul and his critics.

A. A humble person has an accurate measure of himself (2 Cor. 10:7).

Consider two errors that a humble person avoids as he measures himself.

1. A humble person does not think he is taller than he is. He is not proud—like the tom cat who looked at himself in the mirror and thought he saw a lion. Paul emphasized this truth when he wrote:

> *For through the grace given to me I say to everyone among you not to think more highly of himself than he ought to think; but to think so as to have sound judgment, as God has allotted to each a measure of faith* (Rom. 12:3).

Q 19 *How many times does a form of the word "boast" appear in 2 Corinthians 10:7-18? Circle them.*

Q 20 *Why did Paul explain his Jewish background and Jewish roots (2 Cor. 11:22)?*

Q 21 *What are the 2 errors in Figure 13.2*

Figure 13.2 A humble person has an accurate measure of self.

A story about a rooster illustrates the problem of *too-tall-thinking*. In the beginning, a rooster on the farm saw himself clearly. He knew it was his duty to announce the sunrise to the farmer and his wife. So as the sun rose, the rooster crowed. But as time went by, the rooster became confused. He began to think that he was more important than he

Q 22 *What error did the rooster make?*

Q 23 *What error did the donkey make?*

really was. He began to think of himself too highly. He became so tall in his own eyes that he thought that his crowing *caused* the sunrise! As pride filled his life, he began to crow earlier and earlier, even in the middle of the night, to cause the sunrise. In the end, he was unable to sleep. So the farmer and his wife ate the rooster for supper. Even chickens suffer when they think of themselves too highly!

The story of a little donkey also reminds us not to take ourselves too seriously. At then end of a certain day in Jerusalem, a little donkey was singing. At home, it told an older donkey about the events of the day. "I am famous," said the young donkey. "People spread their garments in front of me on the road. They cut palm branches and laid them before me. The children were all singing about me." The older donkey laughed and said, "Stop braying. The praises were not for you, but for the Messiah you were carrying."

Saul was once small in his own eyes, but he became proud (1 Sam. 15:17-23). Saul, Satan, and many others can testify that *"Pride goes before destruction, and a haughty spirit before stumbling"* (Prov. 16:18). *"Do not be wise in your own eyes"* (Prov. 3:7). Do not think of yourself as taller than you are.

2. A humble person does not think he is shorter than he is. He does not have *false humility*—like the lion who looked at himself in the mirror and thought he saw a cat.

Paul's critics were void of humility. They wanted to drag him down to the ground and stand on him so they would look taller.

"You are looking only on the surface of things. If anyone is confident that he belongs to Christ, he should consider again that we belong to Christ just as much as he" (2 Cor. 10:7). Look behind these words and between the lines. Paul's critics were saying, "Paul may be a Christian, but he is not as good of a Christian as we are. So Paul must respond, must say, *"we belong to Christ just as much as he."* A humble person stands up for who and what he is. If a person has two talents, it is not humble to deny these talents. Rather, the person who has two talents should be thankful for these, declare that talents come through the grace of God, and humbly use them for God. Some believers say that they have no talents for God. This is not humility; it is false humility. God has created every person with at least one talent. It was not humility that caused the servant with one talent to bury it (Matt. 25:18). He hid the talent because he was lazy and rebellious. Many believers who do little or nothing for God have *just as much* talent as some who are fruitful. So let us remember that a humble person does not claim to be shorter than he is. Paul was humble, but he testified about how God's grace worked through him (2 Cor. 10:7; 11:1–12:21).

Q 24 *Why did the servant with one talent bury it?*

Q 25 *Contrast the wrong and right attitudes toward receiving correction.*

B. A humble person has a correct attitude toward correction (2 Cor. 10:8-11).

The core of the problem at Corinth was that Paul's critics were not open to correction.

⁸For even if I boast somewhat freely about the authority the Lord gave us for building you up rather than pulling you down, I will not be ashamed of it. ⁹I do not want to seem to be trying to frighten you with my letters. ¹⁰For some say, "His letters are weighty and forceful, but in person he is unimpressive and his speaking amounts to nothing." ¹¹Such people should realize that what we are in our letters when we are absent, we will be in our actions when we are present (2 Cor. 10:8-11).

A humble person has a correct attitude toward correction in two ways.

1. A humble person receives correction well. When people are proud and think they are taller than they are, they may feel *super-spiritual.* Like Paul's critics in Corinth, they reject God's messengers. These proud rebels are like the sinful Israelite who said to Moses, *"Who made you a prince or a judge over us?"* (Exod. 2:14). They are like Aaron

Paul Confronts His Critics

and Miriam, when they said, *"Has the LORD indeed spoken only through Moses? Has He not spoken through us as well?"* (Num. 12:2). They are like Korah, who rebuked Moses and Aaron saying, *"You have gone far enough, for all the congregation are holy, every one of them, and the LORD is in their midst; so why do you exalt yourselves above the assembly of the LORD?"* (Num. 16:3).

Proud people are like Paul's critics in Corinth—they have a bad attitude toward correction. But God resists the proud and gives grace to the humble. And we all need discipline and correction from time to time. So may God help us to take the least important seats at the feast and not exalt ourselves (Luke 14:7-11). *"For those whom the Lord loves he disciplines, and he scourges every son whom he receives"* (Heb. 12:6; see also Rev. 3:19). Those who are humble are open to correction—even if it comes from a person at the bottom of the ladder. If the Pharisees had been humble, they would have repented when the man who had been blind testified. He said, ³²*"'Since the beginning of time it has never been heard that anyone opened the eyes of a person born blind. ³³If this man were not from God, He could do nothing.'* ³⁴*They answered him, 'You were born entirely in sins, and are you teaching us?' So they put him out"* (John 9:32-34).

Likewise, the critics in Corinth rejected Paul. And proud, smug people reject words of correction that the Spirit gives. But the humble welcome God's correction as God's love. And a mature person in Christ can receive a word of correction directly from the Spirit, a pastor, a parent, a friend, or even a child (Matt. 11:25-26).

2. A humble person has the right attitude toward giving correction. Like Paul, a humble person realizes that authority and correction are *"for building you up rather than pulling you down"* (2 Cor. 10:8). Humble parents do not scold their children often, or use correction like a club. Rather, they are gentle, mixing correction with love, patience, praise, and wisdom. Read what Jesus said to the five churches He corrected (Rev. 2–3). Notice that when possible, He spoke praise and encouragement *before* and *after* words of correction. Children respond better when parents mix words of praise with words of correction. A sandwich is easy to eat because the meat is surrounded by bread. Likewise, correction is easier to swallow if it is surrounded by praise. Sabio says, "A spoonful of sugar helps the medicine go down."

Q 26 *What is wise to give with correction?*

Also, let us remember that humble people do not try to do the work of the Spirit. For everything there is a time. And often, only the Holy Spirit can open a person's heart, from the inside out. Only God can open a flower and cause it to bloom. And if we try to force a flower open, we will ruin God's plan and cause its petals to fall to the ground. A wise and humble person discerns that the Holy Spirit has many ways of correcting the faults and weaknesses in God's people. Seeing a fault does not mean that we should say anything about it. Sometimes, the best things we can do to help others are to love them, encourage them, be a good friend and example to them, and pray for them.

C. A humble person has a proper focus on ministry (2 Cor. 10:12–16).

¹²*We do not dare to classify or compare ourselves with some who commend themselves. When they measure themselves by themselves and compare themselves with themselves, they are not wise.* ¹³*We, however, will not boast beyond proper limits, but will confine our boasting to the field God has assigned to us, a field that reaches even to you.* ¹⁴*We are not going too far in our boasting, as would be the case if we had not come to you, for we did get as far as you with the gospel of Christ.* ¹⁵*Neither do we go beyond our limits by boasting of work done by others. Our hope is that, as your faith continues to grow, our area of activity among you will greatly expand,* ¹⁶*so that we can preach the gospel in the regions beyond you. For we do not want to boast about work already done in another man's territory* (2 Cor. 10:12-16).

Notice three things in these verses about the focus of a humble person toward ministry.

Q 27 *What advice does Proverbs 27:2 give us?*

1. A humble person does *not* compare himself with others in ministry (2 Cor. 10:12). Those who compare themselves to others will commit one of three errors—they will fall into one of three pits. *First,* some say, "I am better than others" and fall into the pit of pride. *Second,* some say, "I am as good as others" and relax in the pit of laziness. *Third,* some say, "I am less than others" and fall into the pit of discouragement. In contrast, a person who is humble does not compare himself with others. If he is a singer, he does not say, "I can sing better than someone else." If she is the hand, she does not say, "I am less important than the eye."

The person who compares himself with others cannot enjoy the success of others. Instead, this person who is always comparing feels bad, focusing on self. We are saying that the person who compares himself with others is proud. Think about it. One form of pride is to always be thinking about self. In Luke 15, the son who remained at home was proud. He was more concerned about himself than about his sinful brother who had come home. Read this parable again. Notice that the older brother, like the Pharisees, was always looking in the mirror. He compared himself with others (Luke 15:25-30; 18:9-14).

A father attended a church to hear his son speak. The son was a missionary. As the missionary told about all God had done, the people rejoiced. They had prayed for the missionary and had given offerings to help make his ministry possible. So they all celebrated together. Everyone was smiling except the missionary's father. He was thinking, "No one has ever rejoiced over what I have done."

Q 28 *Was the missionary's father a humble person? Explain.*

Q 29 *In what ways should we share our successes with others?*

2. A humble person does *not* take credit for what others have done for God (2 Cor. 10:13-15a). Paul wrote, *"Neither do we go beyond our limits by boasting of work done by others"* (2 Cor. 10:15a). History has many examples of those who have stolen the credit that others deserved. Dishonest people have received awards, recognition, and money for the writings, paintings, songs, inventions, sermons, or discoveries of others. This is not humble, but it is unethical.

There is another form of stealing credit that is much more common. This occurs when one person takes the credit for what a group of people have done. One athlete enjoys all the applause, although it was his team that made his success possible. One singer smiles on the stage, although others wrote the song, played the song, and taught her to sing. An author takes the credit for a book, although his parents, pastors, teachers, and friends deserve much of the credit. In contrast, humble people realize that the eye is nothing without the rest of the body.

> WE HUMANS HAVE A BASIC NEED TO BE APPRECIATED.

We humans have a basic need to be appreciated. We feel good when we do something right or helpful. God has created all of us with the need to feel loved, respected, and appreciated. Still, as Paul said, there are limits that we should respect. But let us always share honor with others who have helped and not steal their credit. And let us always reflect praise upward to God. His grace enables our success. His Spirit causes us to be fruitful. It is God who created us and not we ourselves. All praise be to God, who always leads us in a victory march in Christ (2 Cor. 2:14).

3. A humble person focuses on what God has called him to do (2 Cor. 10:15b). The call of God led Paul to *"preach the gospel in the regions beyond"* (2 Cor. 10:16). His concern was for fulfilling his own calling and responsibilities. A humble person does not waste time either criticizing or glorifying others. Rather, he keeps his mind on his own ministry. For he knows that the bema judgment is ahead for each one of us.

Paul Confronts His Critics

God must remind even apostles that each person needs to focus on his own ministry, not the ministry of another. This was one of the last things on earth that Jesus taught Peter.

20Peter, turning around, saw the disciple whom Jesus loved following them; the one who also had leaned back on His bosom at the supper and said, "Lord, who is the one who betrays You?" 21So Peter seeing him said to Jesus, "Lord, and what about this man?" 22Jesus said to him, "If I want him to remain until I come, what is that to you? You follow Me" (John 21:20-22).

Q 30 — *What was the lesson of John 21:20-22?*

A humble believer does not criticize the pastor's sermon or complain about the music or waste time gossiping about others. Humble people discipline themselves to fulfill their own callings, ministries, and areas of service.

D. A humble person leaves it to the Lord to commend (2 Cor. 10:17–18).

17But, "Let him who boasts boast in the Lord." 18For it is not the one who commends himself who is approved, but the one whom the Lord commends (2 Cor. 10:17-18).

A wise man said, "Success corrupts, and absolute success corrupts absolutely." Some with titles, degrees, trophies, and awards are as puffed up and inflated as a tire. Some with wealth strut like a rooster, a turkey gobbler, or a peacock.

A coach told his players, "If you succeed and make a goal, act like you have done it before. Do not call attention to yourself, like it is your first goal, or act like you are the greatest athlete who ever lived." An empty cart rattles the loudest.

Jesus taught His disciples that we can succeed with faith as small as a mustard seed. Then He told them not to be proud when they succeeded in ministry.

7"Which of you, having a slave plowing or tending sheep, will say to him when he has come in from the field, 'Come immediately and sit down to eat'? 8But will he not say to him, 'Prepare something for me to eat, and properly clothe yourself and serve me while I eat and drink; and afterward you may eat and drink'? 9He does not thank the slave because he did the things which were commanded, does he? 10So you too, when you do all the things which are commanded you, say, 'We are unworthy slaves; we have done only that which we ought to have done'" (Luke 17:7-10).

Q 31 — *What advice does Luke 17:10 give us?*

A wise woman once said that at the judgment, success means faithfulness. In God's eyes, those who succeed are those who are faithful. So let each of us, like Paul, live to please the Lord (1 Cor. 4:3-5). Let us live our lives in such a way that God will say to us, "Well done, good and faithful servant." For in the end, the only thing that matters is whether the Lord commends or condemns.

 Lesson 44

Spiritual Insights (2 Cor. 11:1-15)
Goal A: *Contrast the characteristics of bad and good jealousy (1 Cor. 11:1-2).*
Goal B: *Contrast the tactics of Satan as a lion and as a serpent (1 Cor. 11:3-6, 13-15).*
Goal C: *Contrast Paul and false apostles on the topic of money (1 Cor. 11:7-12).*

In this lesson we will study three principles, in the context of Paul and the false apostles.

A. Godly jealousy loves enough to confront (2 Cor. 11:1-2).

1I hope you will put up with a little of my foolishness; but you are already doing that. 2I am jealous for you with a godly jealousy. I promised you to one husband, to Christ, so that I might present you as a pure virgin to him (2 Cor. 11:1-2).

The word *jealous* is related to the Greek verb *zeloo* and means "to have zeal, strong desire, or envy." Jealousy is a strong emotion that causes a person to act for or against a person, group, or idea.[5]

Jealousy can be bad or good—evil or godly.

Q 32 *What are some examples of ungodly jealousy?*

The Bible gives many examples of sinful jealousy. Cain killed Abel because of jealousy and anger (1 John 3:12).[6] Rachel was jealous of Leah because God gave Leah children but left Rachel barren (Gen. 30:1). Joseph's brothers were jealous of the favor his father showed him (Gen. 37:11). Some husbands are jealous (suspicious) of their wives in a way that is fleshly and shows a lack of trust (Num. 5:14). King Saul was jealous of David's success and popularity (1 Sam. 18:9). David was jealous of another man's wife, which led to adultery and murder (2 Sam. 11:1-27). The Pharisees were jealous (envious) of the people's love for Jesus (Matt. 27:18). There was strife and jealousy among the Corinthian believers (1 Cor. 3:3). Sinful jealousy is a problem that can lead to criticism, complaining, division, anger, hatred, and even murder.

Evil jealousy wants for self what God or people have given to others. We can be tempted to be jealous over the looks, success, friends, wealth, popularity, or talents that others have. But God commands us not to covet—not to be jealous.

Q 33 *What does this mean: "Godly jealous loves enough to confront"? Give examples.*

In contrast, 2 Corinthians 11:2 speaks of a jealousy that is godly. Godly jealousy is a strong emotion that stands up for what is right. God is jealous for our affections, worship, and obedience (Deut. 32:16, 21; Zech. 8:2). He is our Creator, and it is righteous for Him to desire our love. Likewise, a husband should feel a righteous jealousy to protect the health and reputation of his wife and family.

Paul felt a zeal and jealousy for believers in Corinth. When he preached to them, they accepted the message and were born again. Then he watched them grow spiritually. A father watches his daughter grow and desires for her to have a godly marriage. Likewise, Paul desired to present the Corinthian church *"as a pure virgin to him"* [Christ] (2 Cor. 11:1-2). Some of the Corinthians were once sexually immoral, idolaters, adulterers, prostitutes, homosexuals, thieves, drunks, slanderers, and swindlers. But they became a *virgin* bride, washed, made holy, and justified by the Spirit in the name of the Lord Jesus (1 Cor. 6:9-11). Hallelujah for the grace of God that transforms sinners into saints—that changes the sexually impure into spiritual virgins! But false teachers were leading the virgin bride away from Christ. This made it necessary for Paul to confront the false teachers and the Corinthians, who were going astray. A lesser, weaker love would have remained silent. But godly jealousy loves enough to confront.

In the book *Caring Enough to Confront,* the author explains *five* responses to conflict:

- **Repay.** We may say, "I'll get him back—I'll get revenge. I'll hurt this person like he hurt me." This is one unbiblical response.

Q 34 *What happened to Eli's sons and to Israel because Eli lacked godly jealousy that confronts (1 Sam. 2:12-36)?*

- **Retreat.** We may say, "I'll get out. Solving this problem is not worth the pain. I'm checking out of this relationship."
- **Concede.** We may say, "I surrender. I give in. I will be a doormat and let them do what they want."
- **Compromise.** We may say, "I'll meet you half way. I will agree to a mixture of good and evil."

Q 35 *In which of the 5 ways do you respond to conflict? Explain and grow.*

- **Confront.** This was Paul's response. He said, "I love you enough to tell you the truth."[7]

B. False teachers may be charming speakers (2 Cor. 11:3-6, 13-15).

³But I am afraid that just as Eve was deceived by the serpent's cunning, your minds may somehow be led astray from your sincere and pure devotion to Christ. ⁴For if someone comes to you and preaches a Jesus other than the Jesus we preached, or if you receive a different spirit from the one you received, or a different gospel from the one you accepted, you put up with it easily enough. ⁵But I do not think I am in the least inferior to those "super-apostles." ⁶I may not be a trained speaker, but I do have knowledge. We have made this perfectly clear to you in every way (2 Cor. 11:3-6).

In this passage on deception, Paul refers to the devil as a cunning serpent that deceived Eve in the Garden of Eden. Elsewhere, Peter compares the devil to a lion. *"Be of sober spirit, be on the alert. Your adversary, the devil, prowls around like a roaring lion, seeking someone to devour"* (1 Pet. 5:8). This raises the question, *Is the devil like a snake or a lion?* The answer is *both*.

In times of outward persecution, Satan comes as a lion. He roars, threatens, and devours. As a lion, Satan drags Christians to the Colosseum, to jail, to be whipped, and to be robbed of their property or even their lives. But to Christians living in prosperity and freedom, Satan comes as a serpent—deceiving, as an angel of light. The devil may be as scary as a lion or as attractive as the serpent in Eden.

We resist Satan best when he comes as a lion, because we see his evil nature. But he may appeal to us when he comes disguised as a serpent, an angel of light, a false teacher, or a tempter. He seeks to trick us as he tricked Eve. When he came as a serpent, he did not say to Eve, "I am the devil. I have come to ruin your life. If you listen to me, you will forfeit paradise and inherit the curse of death. I want to destroy your walk with God. I want to guide one of your sons to kill the other. Then I'm going to curse the whole human race through you." If Satan had talked like this, Eve would have screamed and run the other way. When Satan comes as a lion, he frightens us closer to God. But when he comes as a serpent, he lures us away from God.

Consider the deceit Satan uses when he comes as a serpent. He says, "I'm your friend. I'm here to help you. I want you to have fun. You are missing so much excitement and fulfillment." Satan sells his products like companies sell beer and cigarettes. Beer advertisements never show a drunk driver beside a child lying dead in the road. And cigarette companies never show those dying from lung cancer—those who lack the breath to warn you about smoking. Telling the truth about alcohol and cigarettes would kill sales, just as their products kill people. Satan is the father of lies and deceit. And he is the partner and master planner behind all who seek to ruin us.

When the devil comes to you with the temptation of fornication, he does not show a picture of how he will twist your sexuality, confuse your values, and turn you against God. Nor does he show any pictures of babies to abort, hate, shame, or abandon. When he tempts you with adultery, he does not show your children crying, your family shamed, and your name in the mud. It is the same way when a false teaching comes. Satan does not show you the danger of the false teaching. It looks good and attractive. False teachings often come through those who speak with great confidence. *"In their greed these teachers will exploit you with stories they have made up"* (2 Pet. 2:3 NIV).

False teachers were leading believers astray at Corinth, and they are leading people astray today. They spoke well. But they did not speak the truth. They twisted Bible verses to deceive people. So Paul emphasizes that the message is more important than the messenger.

The power is in the seed, not the sower. We have this treasure of the gospel and the Spirit in clay jars (2 Cor. 4:7). Paul says, *"I may not be a trained speaker, but I do have knowledge"* [from God] (2 Cor. 11:6). Twice, Paul told the Corinthians, *"You are looking only on the surface of things"* (2 Cor. 5:12; 10:7). Today, believers must beware. We must look deep into the Bible rather than *"on the surface of things."* Many have skill with the microphone. But we must ask questions like these:

- Does this speaker preach the whole Bible? Or does he just emphasize verses that make me feel good? Is the message he preaches true in every country of the world?

Q 36 What is our response when Satan comes as a lion?

Q 37 What are some examples of Satan coming as a serpent?

Q 38 What are some questions that help us discern false teachers?

- Are the stories the speaker tells true, or are they just *made up* to exploit and deceive people?
- Does this speaker live what he preaches? Does he have a good reputation and character? Who are some ministers with good reputations that speak well of this speaker?
- To whom is this speaker accountable? Which organization gives him a license to preach and makes sure he lives by godly standards?
- Does this speaker hide behind the cross and lift up Jesus Christ? Or does he call attention to himself?

A man trained in drama and speaking stood to recite Psalm 23. He was a handsome man—tall and confident. His motions were smooth and skillful. His voice was professional as he whispered or spoke powerfully in a loud voice. When he finished, the crowd clapped with a loud applause. It was a masterpiece of oration. Then, from the audience came a simple, humble man. He stood before the people and began to quote the same psalm. At the beginning, his words stumbled a little, because he was not used to speaking in front of so many people. Some smiled a little, and others laughed, because he was so common. But as he continued through the psalm, the group became silent as the man of God quoted the 23rd Psalm. When he finished, no one clapped. The people were thinking about the Shepherd in the Psalm, not the man who quoted it. The orator who had spoken first went over to the godly man and said, "Sir, I know the psalm, but you know the Shepherd."[8] Likewise today, there are many charming speakers with great ability, but they do not know Jesus. And one day He will say to them, *"I never knew you. Away from me, you evildoers"* (Matt. 7:23). Beware lest one of these powerful talkers lead you away from Jesus of Nazareth.

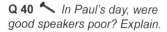

Q 39 What does the word "masquerade" mean (2 Cor. 11:13)? Give an example.

13For such men are false apostles, deceitful workmen, masquerading as apostles of Christ. 14And no wonder, for Satan himself masquerades as an angel of light. 15It is not surprising, then, if his servants masquerade as servants of righteousness. Their end will be what their actions deserve (2 Cor. 11:13-15).

Some of the best speakers are Satan's best servants.

C. We cannot measure people's ministry by the amount of money they receive (2 Cor. 11:7-12).

Q 40 In Paul's day, were good speakers poor? Explain.

7Was it a sin for me to lower myself in order to elevate you by preaching the gospel of God to you free of charge? 8I robbed other churches by receiving support from them so as to serve you. 9And when I was with you and needed something, I was not a burden to anyone, for the brothers who came from Macedonia supplied what I needed. I have kept myself from being a burden to you in any way, and will continue to do so. 10As surely as the truth of Christ is in me, nobody in the regions of Achaia will stop this boasting of mine. 11Why? Because I do not love you? God knows I do! 12And I will keep on doing what I am doing in order to cut the ground from under those who want an opportunity to be considered equal with us in the things they boast about (2 Cor. 11:7-12).

Long before Paul lived, those who spoke well became rich and famous. Demosthenes was well known for making political speeches (about 350 B.C.). As a child, he stuttered and did not speak clearly. He learned to pronounce words better by practicing speeches with small stones in his mouth. He strengthened his voice by reciting sentences while running and also by speaking beside the sea, more loudly than the roar of the waves.[9] Demosthenes became wealthy and powerful.[10]

Figure 13.3 Demosthenes gave powerful political speeches in Athens about 350 B.C.

In Paul's day, people looked down on poor speakers and up to good speakers. Those who spoke well earned a lot of money. The Roman Emperors Augustus and Tiberius paid Verrius Flaccus a huge salary each year (the equivalent of $300,000 US) because he spoke and taught well.¹¹ The Corinthians believed that those who spoke well should be paid well.

In contrast, it appears that Paul lived by a financial principle: He received no offerings from those where he was planting a new church. A church could support him only *after* he had left. Why? This enabled him to say, "I am leading you to the Lord—not for your money, but because I love you. Others are helping support my ministry to you." Corinth was in the province of Achaia. When Paul preached in Corinth, believers in the province of Macedonia (especially the Philippians) sent him gifts (Acts 18:5; Phil. 4:15). Thus he preached the gospel *"free of charge"* (2 Cor. 11:7).

Q 41 *Who paid Paul when he planted the church in Corinth? Explain.*

Meanwhile, the false *super apostles* at Corinth got large offerings from the believers in Corinth. They were like parasites—like amoebas, leeches, and mosquitoes that suck the life out of something and give it nothing but disease. These false teachers lived by the worldly standard of the day—that everyone who spoke well got big offerings. They used this fleshly standard to justify the offerings they demanded and to criticize Paul. They said that the reason why Paul did not receive offerings at Corinth was because he was a poor speaker. They said, "Paul does not take any money because he is embarrassed by his lack of ability. He is worth what you paid him—nothing!"

Q 42 *Why did some Corinthians like the false apostles?*

The world measures people by the amount of money they receive. Paul does teach that those who preach the gospel should live by the gospel (1 Cor. 9:14). But we cannot measure ministry by money. Some of the wealthiest preachers end up in scandals and prison for being dishonest. And some who receive the least are of great value in God's eyes. As Paul said, the apostles were often the poorest and walked at the end of the parade (1 Cor. 4:9).

Lesson 45: Spiritual Highs and Lows (2 Cor. 11:16–12:10)
Goal: *Explain and apply 5 principles about spiritual experiences (1 Cor. 11:16–12:10).*

Setting

The verses in this lesson are part of a larger section, 2 Corinthians 10–13. In these final chapters, Paul defends his ministry as God's apostle. The false apostles at Corinth were attacking Paul's ministry and character. They criticized him so that the Corinthians would turn away from Paul and follow them. These "super-apostles" were parasites and con men. Their goal was to get money, attention, and power.

These circumstances forced Paul to defend and promote himself. He was God's ambassador—the true apostle whom God sent to Corinth. He spoke truth, inspired by God Almighty. Turning away from Paul meant turning away from God. Although Paul did not like to talk about himself, it became necessary so that the Corinthians would follow him, not the false apostles. In 2 Corinthians 11:16–12:10, Paul talks about the valleys and mountains of his spiritual experiences. These verses contain at least five principles on spiritual experiences.

A. Spiritual thirst leads some astray (2 Cor. 11:16-21).

The Bible teaches us to have an interest in spiritual matters. Consider these verses that encourage spiritual hunger and thirst:

Q 43 *Does the Bible encourage spiritual experiences? Explain.*

- *"For I will pour out water on the thirsty land and streams on the dry ground; I will pour out My Spirit on your offspring and My blessing on your descendants"* (Isa. 44:3).
- *"Blessed are those who hunger and thirst for righteousness, for they shall be satisfied"* (Matt. 5:6).
- *"If anyone is thirsty, let him come to Me and drink"* (John 7:37).
- *"Follow the way of love and eagerly desire spiritual gifts"* (1 Cor. 14:1).

- *"Be filled with the Spirit"* (Eph. 5:18).
- *"And let the one who is thirsty come; let the one who wishes take the water of life without cost"* (Rev. 22:17).

These are only a few of the biblical verses that guide us to have spiritual thirst.

Q 44 *How does spiritual thirst lead some astray today? Give examples.*

However, spiritual thirst leads many astray. King Saul's thirst for spiritual insight led him to consult with a witch (1 Sam. 28). Many today seek to satisfy their spiritual thirst through horoscopes, palm readers, witches, cults, and false religions. In Corinth, some believers had a thirst for spiritual things, but they were following false teachers.

Q 45 *How do false teachers enslave and exploit people today? Give examples.*

Paul was forced to confront his critics and talk about his own ministry. Up to this point in 2 Corinthians, Paul had been rather mild. But note his boldness, irony, and satire in these verses:

> ¹⁹*You gladly put up with fools since you are so wise!* ²⁰*In fact, you even put up with anyone who enslaves you or exploits you or takes advantage of you or pushes himself forward or slaps you in the face.* ²¹*To my shame I admit that we were too weak for that!* (2 Cor. 11:19-21).

The Corinthians were claiming to be wise, but they showed immaturity and a lack of spiritual insight—the opposite of the apostle Paul. False teachers were taking advantage of them. Paul mentions several characteristics of the false teachers who were leading believers astray:

- **False teachers** *enslave.* In Corinth, the false teachers enslaved believers to Judaism. They guided them away from salvation by grace and insisted that they obey Jewish laws. Other false teachers today enslave their followers with guilt. They make them feel guilty if they do not give enough, clap enough, and bow down enough. These proud leaders act with great authority and treat their followers like slaves. Such leaders act like dictators, not servants. They demand obedience without questions or accountability.

- **False teachers** *exploit* and *take advantage* of others. Leaders like this in Corinth served their own bellies (Rom. 16:18). They lived on a high financial level, paid for by their followers. Like the Pharisees, they robbed widows. Like many TV preachers today, they built mansions with the offerings of the poor. The Corinthians were proud that these leaders had a high lifestyle. They looked up to them. But the Corinthians and all of us are God's stewards. We will give an account to God for how we use His money. There are great needs in the world, and we should refuse to pay the expenses of leaders who want to live like kings. Did Jesus or the apostles live like kings? We should not let leaders exploit us, for we are God's stewards.

Q 46 *Whose authority do false teachers recognize?*

- **False teachers** *push themselves forward.* These are like many independent ministries today that do not cooperate and coordinate with local denominations and churches. In contrast to these is the Billy Graham Evangelistic Association. When its leaders come into a city, they meet with local leaders and work closely with them. But false teachers do not recognize any authority except their own.

Q 47 *Why do you think some believers follow rude, unkind leaders?*

- **False teachers** *abuse* others—they *slap* them *in the face.* These words may refer to physical, emotional, or spiritual abuse. Some leaders physically slap people in the face, as Ananias struck Paul (Acts 23:2-3). Such leaders rule through terror and force. Why do some believers follow rude, unkind leaders like this? Why do some women marry rude, abusive husbands? The answer may be that their fathers were abusive, and their mothers chose them. In contrast, Paul says that no church leaders should be strikers (1 Tim. 3:3). God approves leaders who are gentle—even to those who oppose them (2 Tim. 2:25).

Q 48 *How are false teachers like clouds, actors, and wolves?*

Jude called false teachers *"clouds without water"* (Jude 12). They make great boasts, but are unable to satisfy spiritual thirst. False teachers wear masks—they disguise themselves as God's servants (2 Cor. 11:13-15). They are wolves in sheep's clothes (Matt. 7:15). They are hypocrites—skilled actors in a theater. So as we follow after God, let us beware of false teachers. There are many spiritual roads in life, but God's blessings are on the path of biblical truth.

B. True apostles share the lows of Christ's sufferings (2 Cor. 11:22-33).[12]

Some in Corinth claimed to be apostles. To them, being an apostle meant having the top title, walking at the front of the parade, strutting on the stage, showing off as speakers, ruling with authority, pushing people around, gloating over the respect others gave them, collecting big offerings, and living like kings. These liars were not apostles. And they did not have an idea or a clue about what it meant to be an apostle. Paul had already written that being an apostle means being last:

⁹For it seems to me that God has put us apostles on display at the end of the procession, like men condemned to die in the arena... ¹¹To this very hour we go hungry and thirsty, we are in rags, we are brutally treated, we are homeless. ¹²We work hard with our own hands. When we are cursed, we bless; when we are persecuted, we endure it; ¹³when we are slandered, we answer kindly. Up to this moment we have become the scum of the earth, the refuse of the world (1 Cor. 4:9, 11-13).

Q 49 *Did being an apostle have a lot of earthly benefits? Explain.*

In 2 Corinthians 11:22-33, Paul continues to explain what it means to be an apostle. Against his will, these false apostles have forced him to defend his apostleship. So he describes the road that apostles walk on. It is a road of intense pain and great suffering. And it cannot be otherwise. For apostles live in the middle of the battle—at the center of spiritual warfare. And as warfare increases, suffering increases.

Q 50 *On what kind of road do apostles walk?*

²⁴Five times I received from the Jews the forty lashes minus one. ²⁵Three times I was beaten with rods, once I was stoned, three times I was shipwrecked, I spent a night and a day in the open sea, ²⁶I have been constantly on the move. I have been in danger from rivers, in danger from bandits, in danger from my own countrymen, in danger from Gentiles; in danger in the city, in danger in the country, in danger at sea; and in danger from false brothers. ²⁷I have labored and toiled and have often gone without sleep; I have known hunger and thirst and have often gone without food; I have been cold and naked. ²⁸Besides everything else, I face daily the pressure of my concern for all the churches (2 Cor. 11:24-28).

³⁰If I must boast, I will boast of the things that show my weakness. ³¹The God and Father of the Lord Jesus, who is to be praised forever, knows that I am not lying. ³²In Damascus the governor under King Aretas had the city of the Damascenes guarded in order to arrest me. ³³But I was lowered in a basket from a window in the wall and slipped through his hands (2 Cor. 11:30-33).

We may divide Paul's hardships and sufferings as an apostle into five groups.

1. Suffering throughout his ministry as an apostle.
"I have worked much harder, been in prison more frequently, been flogged more severely, and been exposed to death again and again" (2 Cor. 11:23b).

Q 51 *What were some characteristics of Paul's life as an apostle?*

Paul's life as an apostle was rugged and painful. Those who fight wars do not sit in the shade and drink pink lemonade. And those God calls to be apostles do not wear fine linen in a palace (Matt. 11:8).

> PAUL'S LIFE AS AN APOSTLE WAS RUGGED AND PAINFUL.

It is interesting to compare the list of Paul's sufferings in 2 Corinthians 11:23-29 with the trials Luke mentions in the book of Acts. As one writer notes, Acts does not tell us about even ¼ of Paul's sufferings.[13] Acts only records a small amount of what happened to Paul. So Paul opens a window of his soul and reveals that, in general, his ministry as an apostle has included hard work, great pain, rejection, harsh treatment, and self-denial. If this makes you want to sign up to be an apostle, keep reading!

Q 52 *Of the times when Paul faced death, which would you have hated most?*

2. **Suffering the times he faced death as an apostle.** False apostles want to be paid at any cost, but true apostles pay a great price to serve the Church.

- *"Five times I received from the Jews the forty lashes minus one"* (2 Cor. 11:24). Deuteronomy 25:1-3 ordered 40 lashes for certain sins. The person who used the leather whip was responsible for counting. It became a Jewish practice to stop at 39. Then if the person who was whipped died, the one who did the whipping was not guilty. But if he miscounted and lashed 41, he could be whipped himself.[14] Can you imagine being in a synagogue and having your hands tied to two posts—one on each side—and then being whipped until you were too weak to stand, as you hung by your hands at death's door? Paul endured this five times in Jewish synagogues! Acts does not mention any of these five beatings.
- *"Three times I was beaten with rods"* (2 Cor. 11:25). The Jews used leather whips, but the Gentiles used rods or canes.
- *"Once I was stoned"* (2 Cor. 11:25). Unlike Stephen, Paul was pelted with rocks until he was unconscious, but still alive. This happened at Lystra, the hometown of Timothy. ¹⁹*"But Jews came from Antioch and Iconium, and having won over the crowds, they stoned Paul and dragged him out of the city, supposing him to be dead. ²⁰But while the disciples stood around him, he got up and entered the city The next day he went away with Barnabas to Derbe"* (Acts 14:19-20).
- *"Three times I was shipwrecked"* (2 Cor. 11:25). These occurred before the shipwreck described in Acts 27, since Paul wrote Corinthians 5 years before Luke wrote Acts in A.D. 61-62. And Paul writes, *"I spent a night and a day in the open sea."* This probably means that after a shipwreck, he clung to a piece of wood, as wave after wave beat upon him—a night and a day in the deep water. Any volunteers to be an apostle?

Altogether, these accounts show us eleven times when Paul was at death's door for the sake of the gospel.

3. **Suffering in his journeys as an apostle.** God's apostle to the Gentiles lists eight dangers he faced as a traveling preacher. *"I have been constantly on the move. I have been in danger from rivers, in danger from bandits, in danger from my own countrymen, in danger from Gentiles; in danger in the city* [like Damascus, 2 Cor. 11:32-33]*, in danger in the country, in danger at sea; and in danger from false brothers"* (2 Cor. 11:26).

Q 53 *Does it surprise you that God lets apostles face danger and lack food and clothes? Explain.*

4. **Suffering in times of great need as an apostle.** *"I have labored and toiled and have often gone without sleep; I have known hunger and thirst and have often gone without food; I have been cold and naked"* (2 Cor. 11:27). Paul worked long hours and endured sleepless nights. Often he was cold and naked in prison. This was the situation later when he wrote the second letter to Timothy. He asked Timothy to bring him a coat before winter. Paul knew what it was like to be freezing and have his teeth chattering. As an apostle, he suffered for the gospel.

5. **Suffering from the daily pressures of the concerns of an apostle.** ²⁸*"Besides everything else, I face daily the pressure of my concern for all the churches. ²⁹Who is weak, and I do not feel weak? Who is led into sin, and I do not inwardly burn?"* (2 Cor. 11:28-29). Apostles carry the weight of the churches on their shoulders. They live with emotional, mental, and spiritual stress. They are troubled when believers follow false doctrines. They cry when people fall into sin. They are shepherds who sacrifice their lives for the sheep. Note the contrast between Paul and the false apostles at Corinth, who wanted to sacrifice the sheep for their own egos and lusts.

When we read the list of Paul's sufferings, most of us feel small standing in his shadow. But Paul does not give this list to make us feel guilty. These sufferings show us the true standards and measure of an apostle. Most of the people who call themselves apostles today are not like Paul; rather, they are like the false apostles at Corinth.

Applications. The word *apostle* means "one sent." Apostles do not live in castles or sit in comfortable chairs. If you find an apostle today, he will not be in front of a TV camera. He will be on the move, in the battle or in prison, and covered with scars from spiritual warfare. Like Paul, a true apostle does not announce a list of his converts, church plants, or miracles. He boasts only in his weakness and in his sufferings.

God does not call most of us to be apostles—missionaries who climb mountains and cross rivers to sow the seed of the gospel in hard places. However, the Church would be stronger if we were willing to suffer even a little. Today, believers walk away from each other, turn away from responsibility, and even leave the church—not because they were whipped, beaten, or stoned, but because their feelings were scratched. Paul might have said after his first whipping, "One whipping is enough for me. If this is the kind of thanks I get for serving Christ, forget it!" Always in the body of Christ, we face the fact that people may not appreciate what we do. They may say careless things to us or others. These words can sting a little like a whip or a lash can sting. But we need to remember that we are in a spiritual battle. And the Church needs some examples of people who will act a little like apostles and *refuse* to quit when there are small hills to climb.

> Q 54 ↖ *Do you know anyone who claims to be an apostle? If so, is this person like Paul or like the false apostles in Corinth? Explain.*
>
> Q 55 ↖ *Where might you find an apostle today?*
>
> Q 56 ↖ *What would make the Church better today?*

C. Some spiritual experiences should be kept private (2 Cor. 12:1-6).

> Q 57 ↖ *When should we talk about a spiritual experience?*

As we study this principle, keep in mind that we are talking about *spiritual experiences* and not other experiences, such as common dreams that are not spiritual. How do we know whether to share a spiritual experience or remain silent about it? Here are four guidelines.

1. We should keep spiritual experiences to ourselves if our motives are impure. Some like to talk about spiritual gifts and spiritual experiences to make themselves look taller. Why did the false apostles in Corinth claim that they had dreams and visions? So that others would look up to them. We must guard against the temptation to share spiritual experiences that exalt us.

Paul tells about a spiritual experience of the third heaven. (The *first heaven* is the atmosphere and clouds around earth. The *second heaven* contains the stars and planets. The *third heaven* is the place where God dwells. Most modern scholars[15] think that Paul refers to *paradise* as the *"third heaven."*)[16] As Paul describes this experience, he says that it happened *"fourteen years ago."* This may have been when he was in Damascus or perhaps Antioch, Syria. It appears that Paul had not told the Corinthians about this spiritual experience. He had been silent about it for 14 years. But because the false apostles were bragging about visions, dreams, and revelations, the Spirit guided Paul to share this experience. Many Bible teachers think that Paul was the man caught up to paradise, but in humility he says, *"I know a man in Christ...who was caught up to the third heaven"* (2 Cor. 12:2). Paul shared very little about this spiritual experience. The only reason why he shared the experience was to silence the false apostles and encourage the Corinthians to accept him as God's apostle.

2. We should keep spiritual experiences private if God gave them to encourage us, but not others. At the birth of Christ, the shepherds had a spiritual experience. An angel told them the good news about Jesus, and many other angels joined in to praise God (Luke 2:8-15). The shepherds *"made known the statement"* that they heard from the angels. But notice that Mary did not talk much about this *spiritual experience.* Rather, she *"treasured all these things, pondering them in her heart"* (Luke 2:19). Perhaps if she had talked more, her words might have helped Herod, or other enemies, who wanted to kill the young king (Matt. 2). For everything there is a time… *"a time to be silent and a time to speak"* (Eccl. 3:7).

3. We should not share most of our spiritual experiences with unbelievers. For example, Joseph shared his dreams with his brothers. They already hated him. When he shared his dreams, they hated him even more (Gen. 37:5). Do not share your spiritual experiences with those who will mock you. The Bible warns us not to cast our pearls before pigs (Matt. 7:6).

4. We should share our spiritual experiences to edify others, as the Holy Spirit leads us. Paul often shared the spiritual experience he had at conversion (Acts 9:1-19; 23:3-16; 26:9-18). The Holy Spirit guides us believers to share our personal testimonies about being born again, healed, and filled with the Spirit. These spiritual experiences may lead many closer to God.

Paul's first letter to the Corinthians teaches us to share spiritual experiences and spiritual matters with other believers. We may share *"a hymn, or a word of instruction, a revelation, a tongue, or an interpretation"* (1 Cor. 14:26). We may give a prophecy. There is a great need in the body of Christ for believers to edify others when we gather together. However, many spiritual experiences are meant just to encourage us, and we should cherish these in private, between ourselves and God. May the Holy Spirit guide us into many spiritual experiences and give us the wisdom to know when to keep them private and when to share them.

Q 58 *Have you had a spiritual experience that encouraged you? Explain.*

D. Spiritual experiences are not the basis for doctrine, but they may give personal help (2 Cor. 12:1-6).

Bible doctrines are teachings like our 16 fundamental truths. These include topics like the inspiration of Scripture, the One True God, the deity of Christ, salvation, water baptism, and the Second Coming of Christ. We base all Bible doctrines on Scripture, *not* on spiritual experiences. Sometimes, spiritual experiences confirm and illustrate biblical doctrines. At other times, the experiences of life puzzle and confuse us. But at all times, our faith rests upon God's Word and not on our feelings or our spiritual experiences.

Figure 13.4 The Spirit may build us up through our personal spiritual experiences.

Although spiritual experiences are not the foundation of doctrine, the Spirit often uses these to encourage, strengthen, or guide us. The Spirit may speak to us, as we pray in tongues or prophesy, to build us up. God may assure or reassure us through spiritual gifts, visions, or dreams. Through spiritual experiences, the Spirit guided Philip to the Ethiopian, Ananias to Saul, Peter to Cornelius, and Paul to Macedonia. And many can testify that God has spoken to them as a pastor preached in a local church. These spiritual experiences are of great value and help us in various ways.

Last month, I was with a young man named Ben, who had suffered a great tragedy. He and his wife are strong believers and wonderful examples in the church. But when the time came for their first child to be born, it had already died. After many people prayed, the life of the child did not return, so they had a small funeral. Seeking to encourage this young man, I took him to a public event. We walked around, ate together, and looked at some exhibits about hunting. As we were talking, I felt impressed to give him a gift of $100. So I told him the amount and promised to give him the money. At that moment, in a crowded room, with hundreds of people walking around, the Lord guided my attention to a small piece of paper on the floor. Several people stepped on it as I went to pick it up. When I unfolded it, Ben and I were amazed to discover that it was $100! This encouraged Ben that even in our sorrows, God is with us.

E. In spiritual lows, when God does not remove a thorn, He will give us grace to live with it (2 Cor. 12:7-10).

The Problem: Paul's thorn reminds us that life contains some pain that *we* cannot remove and pain that *God* will not remove.

> *⁷To keep me from becoming conceited because of these surpassingly great revelations, there was given me a thorn in my flesh, a messenger of Satan, to torment me. ⁸Three times I pleaded with the Lord to take it away from me* (2 Cor. 12:7-8).

Paul's thorn (Greek *skolops*) may have been small or large, physical, mental, or spiritual.[17] It seems to have been a constant or recurring source of great pain and weakness. Over the centuries, Bible teachers have tried to guess what Paul's thorn was.
- Tertullian thought Paul's thorn was an earache.
- Chrysostom thought it was a headache, perhaps caused by the fever of malaria.
- Lietzmann thought that Paul's eyes ached (Gal. 4:13-15; 6:11).[18]
- Augustine and Luther thought it was all the aches Paul suffered from persecution.

The authors of this course lean toward this last interpretation. In Paul's ministry, it seems that a messenger of Satan went everywhere Paul went and stirred up enemies against him. There is a summary of these afflictions (2 Cor. 11:23-27) just before the mention of Paul's thorn. Still, we are not sure what Paul's thorn was. Perhaps God did not describe the thorn so that all believers with the "thorn" of trials could relate to this famous passage.

Paul prayed three times for God to remove the thorn. Likewise, Jesus prayed three times in Gethsemane for the Father to remove the cup from Him.[19] But the Father did not remove the cup from Jesus or the thorn from Paul. God receives all of our petitions with compassion. But like Paul, we must all learn the lesson that God may answer "No," but reassure us with His grace and presence. In the life of every believer, there are sufferings in the will of God (Phil. 1:29; 2 Tim. 3:12; 1 Pet. 1:21; 4:1, 12-19; Rev. 2:8-11).

The Promise: God will perfect His power in believers who seek His strength (2 Cor. 12:9-10).

God saw a better solution than removing Paul's thorn. Our Lord does not explain our trials, nor promise deliverance in this life. But He does promise to be with us and give us the grace we need in our sufferings. God's promise to us is *"My grace is sufficient for you, for my power is made perfect in weakness"* (2 Cor. 12:8). Or, as the New English Bible says, *"My grace is all you need."* Some call this verse "the summit of the Epistle"—the highest peak from which we can view all of Paul's ministry as an apostle.[20] From this mountaintop of grace, we understand Paul's calling, conversion, empowerment, weakness, trials, labors, and victories—all by grace!

God's grace enables us to walk with joy on the path He chooses. John Wesley preached 42,000 sermons. He traveled 4,500 miles a year by riding a horse 60 to 70 miles a day! On an average day, he preached three times. At the age of 83, he wrote in his diary, " I am a wonder to myself. I am never tired, either with preaching, writing, or traveling."[21] God's grace was like energy in his body.

The Response: Our response to a thorn may either deform or transform us.

> *⁹...Therefore I will boast all the more gladly about my weaknesses, so that Christ's power may rest on me. ¹⁰That is why, for Christ's sake, I delight in weaknesses, in insults, in hardships, in persecutions, in difficulties. For when I am weak, then I am strong* (2 Cor. 12:9b-10).

Q 59 — *What do you think Paul's thorn was? Explain.*

Q 60 — *Why does God allow all believers to have "thorns"?*

Paul prayed about his thorn until he had a definite answer from God. Many times, believers may accept sickness, financial problems, and various trials. Throughout the Bible, we find that often God's answer was "Yes" to those who came to Him for help. So let us be sure that we do not scratch like chickens when God has created us to soar like eagles. Who among us has been so exalted by heavenly revelations that he needs a thorn to keep him humble? Let us keep praying, like the widow who went to the unjust judge (Luke 18). This was Paul's method of prayer, and it should be ours. For most often, God's answer to us will be yes, rather than no.

Q 61 *Explain: Our response to a thorn may either deform us or transform us.*

Our attitude in accepting God's will is vital. As we pray, if God assures us that a *thorn* is His will for us, let us accept our trials with faith, hope, and confidence in God's grace. Some accept the will of God with their shoulders drooped, their heads hanging low, and a frown on their faces. Others accept God's will with a song and a smile. God's grace (His presence and help) was sufficient for Paul to endure weariness, pain, opposition, and slander. By God's grace, this apostle endured all without bitterness, and he sang with cheerfulness.

Q 62 *What is the lesson from Archelaus?*

Once a man threw a bucket of water on Archelaus of Macedonia. Although soaking wet, Archelaus said nothing at all. A friend asked how Archelaus endured this harsh treatment, yet kept such peace. Archelaus replied, "He threw the water on the man he thought I was, not on the man I really am." Likewise, Paul, by the grace of God, focused on what God knew about him, not what mistaken men said about him.

In the painful times of our lives, as we open our hearts to the Word and to prayer, the Lord speaks to us. Often it is from Scripture that God gives us strength to carry us through difficult moments. Paul had his word from the Lord—*"My grace is all you need."*

A Sunday school teacher was asked by a child, "Why did Jesus come to his disciples and tell them *'Watch and pray'* the first two times but *'Sleep on and take your rest'* (KJV) the third time? Why didn't He say the same thing all three times?" The teacher found it difficult to answer the child's question. Suddenly, the small child said, "I think I know! It was because Jesus had seen the face of His Father and He didn't need their help any more."

A missionary faced persecution and trials in many forms. In response to these problems, he wrote (like Paul), "It is great to be in the middle of the fight—to receive the devil's strongest attacks! It is wonderful to have Satan hit you with discouragement, slander, and disease! He does not waste time on a lukewarm believer. But he hits hard when a person is hitting him. You can always measure your own success in ministry, by the opposition that comes back to you!"[22]

Lesson 46: Spiritual Concerns (2 Cor. 12:11–13:14)

Goal: *State and illustrate 6 concerns of a leader for spiritual children.*

Setting

Q 63 *Which problems at Corinth do you think were the hardest for Paul?*

We have come to the final lesson on Paul's letters to the Corinthians. Do you wish you had been the pastor in Corinth? Recall the problems and questions there:

- The problem of divisions (1 Cor. 1:10–4:21)
- The problem of the immoral brother (1 Cor. 5:1-13)
- The problem of lawsuits (1 Cor. 6:1-11)
- The problem of sexual immorality (1 Cor. 6:12-20)
- Questions about marriage (1 Cor. 7:1-40)
- Questions about conscience (1 Cor. 8:1–10:33)

- Questions about head coverings (1 Cor. 11:1-16)
- Questions about communion (1 Cor. 11:17-34)
- Questions about spiritual gifts (1 Cor. 12:1–14:40)
- Questions about the resurrection of the dead (1 Cor. 15:1-58)
- Questions about giving (1 Cor. 16:1-4)
- The problem of following false apostles and accusing Paul (2 Cor. 1–7)
- The problem of not completing the offering they promised (2 Cor. 8–9)
- The problem of rebelling against Paul and accepting false apostles (2 Cor. 10–13)

In spite of all the problems and questions in Corinth, Paul loved believers there. In this final lesson, we will study six spiritual concerns of an apostle or leader for spiritual children.

A. Leaders grieve when unspiritual children follow the wrong messengers (2 Cor. 12:11-13).

¹¹I have made a fool of myself, but you drove me to it. I ought to have been commended by you, for I am not in the least inferior to the "super-apostles," even though I am nothing. ¹²The things that mark an apostle—signs, wonders and miracles—were done among you with great perseverance. ¹³How were you inferior to the other churches, except that I was never a burden to you? Forgive me this wrong! (2 Cor. 12:11-13).

One of the ways in which we can recognize an apostle is *"signs, wonders and miracles"* (2 Cor. 12:12). It appears that the false or "super-apostles" lacked these signs. Likewise, most of the leaders who claim to be apostles today lack the signs and wonders of an apostle. In some ways, people have not changed much. Many still like big titles that they do not deserve. And unspiritual people still follow these smooth talkers.

In contrast, Paul was a true apostle, with signs and wonders that confirmed the pure gospel he preached. Believers at Corinth should have commended Paul. Instead, many rejected him and followed false shepherds.

Throughout the history of the world, people have rejected God's messengers and followed the ministers of Satan. Consider a few examples:

- **Moses.** *"This Moses whom they disowned, saying, 'WHO MADE YOU A RULER AND A JUDGE?' is the one whom God sent to be both a ruler and a deliverer with the help of the angel who appeared to him in the thorn bush"* (Acts 7:35).
- **Jesus and the Prophets.** ³⁷*"Jerusalem, Jerusalem, who kills the prophets and stones those who are sent to her! How often I wanted to gather your children together, the way a hen gathers her chicks under her wings, and you were unwilling. ³⁸Behold, your house is being left to you desolate! ³⁹For I say to you, from now on you will not see Me until you say, 'BLESSED IS HE WHO COMES IN THE NAME OF THE LORD!'"* (Matt. 23:37-39).
- **Paul.** *"I have made a fool of myself, but you drove me to it. I ought to have been commended by you"* (2 Cor. 12:11).

Some of the Corinthians had closed their hearts to Paul—withholding their love from him (2 Cor. 6:12). Instead, they were accepting, loving, and submitting to false apostles (2 Cor. 11:19).

Paul had a great concern for the young believers at Corinth. He was their spiritual father. They were born again when he preached the gospel to them. Many of them had been filled with the Spirit and received spiritual gifts. But false teachers were leading some astray. This departure from the truth deeply disturbed God's apostle. So he prayed for them, and he confronted them with the truth.

Application. Wherever there are true believes, false shepherds will come. Jesus said they are like wolves in sheep's clothing (Matt. 7). Paul also compared the false teachers

Q 64 *Is it common for people to reject God's leaders? Give examples.*

Q 65 *What are some false teachings today that lead people astray? Why?*

to *"savage wolves"* who *"will not spare the flock"* (Acts 20:29). So let us seek to protect ourselves and our spiritual children. For the rewards of heaven are not for those who begin the journey, but for those who finish it.

B. Leaders delight in spending themselves for their spiritual children (2 Cor. 12:14-18).

Q 66 *How do true and false apostles differ on giving?*

One of the ways in which we can recognize true leaders today is that they would rather give than receive. The false apostles at Corinth were exploiting the bride and *fleecing the sheep. In contrast, Paul did not seek the wealth of the Corinthian believers. Rather, he said,

> ¹⁴*...What I want is not your possessions but you. After all, children should not have to save up for their parents, but parents for their children.* ¹⁵*So I will very gladly spend for you everything I have and expend myself as well. If I love you more, will you love me less?* (2 Cor. 12:14-15).

Examine the ministers you respect and support in the church. Ask some questions about them. The truth can bear examination. Is their purpose to get what you have or to share what they have with you? One of the ways in which we can discern false teachers is that they focus on what they can get rather than what they can give.

Examine yourself. What are your attitudes about giving? Do you delight in helping others? Do you look for opportunities to give your money, time, and talents to help believers in the church? If you want to become more spiritual, take small steps to bless others. Little by little, you will enjoy giving more than taking. For as we give our time and treasure, our hearts follows (Matt. 6:21). Those who are spiritually healthy and mature practice giving—edifying and encouraging others in small and big ways. When you reach out your hand, is it empty or full?

C. Leaders mourn when they must discipline their spiritual children (2 Cor. 12:19–13:4).

Q 67 *What were 9 sins that Paul feared he would find in the Corinthian church?*

Take time to read 2 Corinthians 12:19–13:4. Then answer questions 67 and 68.

Parents rejoice in their children. Likewise, Paul felt great joy, pride, and delight in his spiritual children at Corinth. But if he went to Corinth and found his children sinning, it would break his heart, humble him, make him ashamed, and grieve him. His spiritual authority was to build people up, and it grieved him to use his authority for discipline (2 Cor. 13:10).

Q 68 *Was Paul afraid he would find one case of sexual sin, or many? Explain.*

Application. Paul had a great concern for sin in the lives of believers. He could not ignore sin, for like cancer, it kills. As Jesus said, we must deal severely with sin. Whatever the cost, it is better to get rid of sin than to allow it to drag people into eternal hell.

> PAUL HAD A GREAT CONCERN FOR SIN IN THE LIVES OF BELIEVERS.

> ²⁹*If your right eye makes you stumble, tear it out and throw it from you; for it is better for you to lose one of the parts of your body, than for your whole body to be thrown into hell.* ³⁰ *If your right hand makes you stumble, cut it off and throw it from you; for it is better for you to lose one of the parts of your body, than for your whole body to go into hell* (Matt. 5:29-30).

Q 69 *In what way did Paul fear he would be humbled on his third visit to Corinth (2 Cor. 12:21)?*

In one way, sin is like cancer. If a person ignores it in himself, it will kill him. But in another way, sin is worse than cancer. For unlike cancer, sin spreads from one person to another. So wherever Paul found sin in a believer, it was necessary for him to eliminate it—through teaching, discipline, and even *excommunication.

However, note Paul's attitude toward sin in believers. He was not cold and harsh. Sin in believers made Paul cry. He could not ignore it. But it broke his heart to discipline those who sinned.

When a boy disobeyed, his father had to discipline him. The dad and his son went into a private room together. As they talked, the father wept. He told his son, "The Bible teaches me that I must discipline you when you disobey me. You will feel the pain when I whip you with this belt. But someday you will understand that whipping you hurts me more than it hurts you." Paul felt like this father felt. Likewise, all spiritual parents grieve over sin in their children. They grieve because sin is evil, offends God, and brings a harvest of sorrow. And they grieve because they must discipline sin in their children.

Q 70 *Did your parents cry when they disciplined you?*

Some today ignore sin in the lives of believers. Others falsely teach that all believers sin day by day. But the Bible teaches us that we cannot spare discipline whenever sin appears. Although it grieves us, we must be severe with sin or it will be severe with us. It is better to cry a little now than a lot later.

Q 71 *Should pastors and parents cry when they must discipline? Explain.*

D. Leaders want their spiritual children to pass the frequent test of truth (2 Cor. 13:5-8).

Examine yourselves to see whether you are in the faith; test yourselves. Do you not realize that Christ Jesus is in you—unless, of course, you fail the test? (2 Cor. 13:5).

The Corinthians had been examining Paul. Now, he turns the table on them. It is themselves, not him, they must examine. Like the Galatians, the Corinthians began the race well (Gal. 5:7). But were they still in the faith?

Q 72 *How were the Corinthians like the Galatians?*

Paul was not among those who believed "once in grace, always in grace." He believed it was possible to *fall from grace* and be lost forever. He taught that wise believers do not base their future on past experiences. Wise believers do not say, "I was born again 10 years ago, so I must be on the right road today." No! The wise examine themselves from time to time.

Q 73 *What are some ways in which believers should examine themselves spiritually?*

People examine metals like gold and silver to see whether they are pure. We examine money, bills, and coins to see whether they are counterfeit. We examine food to see whether it is good to eat or has spoiled. We examine clothes before we buy them. We examine ourselves to see whether we are healthy. How much more should we examine ourselves to see if our lives are based on the truth.[23]

Paul says that *truth* is the standard we use to examine ourselves. As an apostle, Paul was committed to the truth. Truth was his message, his standard, his judge. All of Paul's ministry was based on and united with the truth. As he said, *"we cannot do anything against the truth, but only for the truth"* (2 Cor. 13:8).

Like fire, truth is an impartial judge. It is a standard that tests and measures our beliefs, motives, and actions.

The meter is an official standard for measuring—it is used all over the world. At first, scientists defined the meter as $\frac{1}{10{,}000{,}000}$ of the distance from the equator to the North Pole, through Paris. They created a platinum metal bar to represent this exact length and called it a meter (Greek *metron*, which means "a unit of length"). Later, in 1983, the length of a meter remained the same, but scientists redefined it as the distance light travels in space in $\frac{1}{299{,}792{,}458}$ of a second.[24] People may have various opinions and claims about their height. But if they want to know the truth, they can measure themselves with a meter stick—a true standard. Likewise, the Bible is God's standard of truth to measure our lives. Regardless of what we claim about ourselves, God will test and measure us by His Word.

Riddle: How many legs does a donkey have if you count the tail as one leg? Sabio says, "Four. The tail is not a leg, whether you count it as one or not."

Q 74 *How many legs does a cow have if you count the tail as a leg?*

Paul feared that many of the Corinthians would fail the test when he examined them by the standard of the gospel. He wrote to them, *"As God's fellow workers, we urge you not to receive God's grace in vain"* (2 Cor. 6:1). Some of the Corinthians were rejecting Paul and following false teachers. On his third visit to them, he feared that he would find *"quarreling, jealousy, outbursts of anger, factions, slander, gossip, arrogance and disorder…*and *many who* had *not repented of impurity* and *sexual sin"* (2 Cor. 12:20-21). Some claimed to follow Jesus but practiced these sins. Paul is warning them that those who practice sin fail the test of biblical truth.

Q 75 *Why should each person take the truth test?*

Today, some who are slaves of sin claim to be saved. But we might ask them, "Saved from what?" If we save a man from the fire, is he still burning? If we save a man from drowning, is he still under water? If we save a man from prison, is he still locked up? If Jesus saves a person from sin, that person is washed, cleansed, set free, and delivered from sin. Recall what Paul wrote earlier:

> ⁹*Do you not know that the wicked will not inherit the kingdom of God? Do not be deceived: Neither the sexually immoral nor idolaters nor adulterers nor male prostitutes nor homosexual offenders* ¹⁰ *nor thieves nor the greedy nor drunkards nor slanderers nor swindlers will inherit the kingdom of God.* ¹¹*And that is what some of you were. But you were washed, you were sanctified, you were justified in the name of the Lord Jesus Christ and by the Spirit of our God* (1 Cor. 6:9-11).

If anyone is in Christ, he is a new creation; the old has gone, the new has come (2 Cor. 5:17).

Not all who talk about heaven are going there (Matt. 7:21). To inherit the Kingdom, we must pass the test of truth—we must live by God's standards.

Q 76 *According to 2 Thessalonians 2:10, why will some perish?*

As believers, we need to recognize that the truth is one our greatest friends. We should never fight with the truth, but be its ally. Let us embrace the truth as we embrace those we love the most. We need to bring our beliefs to the Bible—God's written book of truth. We must allow the Bible to examine our doctrines. We must be careful not to twist the Bible, using an occasional verse out of context to approve our false beliefs. As Benjamin Franklin said, "A lie stands on one leg, but truth on two." And the easiest person to deceive is yourself.²⁵ So let us allow the Bible and the Spirit of truth (Acts 5) to examine our lives. With David, wise believers pray:

> ²³*Search me, O God, and know my heart; try me and know my anxious thoughts;* ²⁴ *And see if there be any hurtful way in me, and lead me in the everlasting way* (Ps. 139:23-24).

SEARCH ME, O GOD, AND KNOW MY HEART.

As we daily submit our lives to God's Word and His Spirit, we pass the test of truth. Thus we abide in Christ, have spiritual life, and fellowship with God. Those who love the truth are safe in Christ. But those who refuse to love the truth will perish. They will be led astray by Satan and the world (2 Thess. 2:10).

Q 77 *Is truth a friend or an enemy?*

Q 78 *What price is truth worth?*

Truth divides all people into two groups: those who love it and those who do not. Those who love the truth are the children of God and are part of the family of Jesus, who is the Truth (John 14:6). Those who reject the truth are children of the devil, the father of lies (John 8:44). Those who love the truth are members of the bride of Christ, but those who reject truth may become members of the harlot of the Antichrist (Rev. 17:18). So let us humbly welcome every test of truth. "The truth will make you free, but first it will make you miserable." ²⁶ Still we must embrace truth. Let us affirm with Martin Luther: "Peace if possible, but truth at any price. For truth, though crushed to the earth, will rise again."²⁷

E. Leaders pray for their spiritual children to grow to perfection—which is maturity (2 Cor. 13:9-11).

Q 79 *What does it mean to "Aim for perfection"?*

⁹*…Our prayer is for your perfection. …* ¹¹*…Aim for perfection* (2 Cor. 13:9, 11).

We will only mention this principle on perfection, since we have already covered it. To be perfect means to be complete and mature in Christ. Earlier, Paul encouraged believers to be *"perfecting holiness in the fear of the Lord"* (2 Cor. 7:1). Paul was like the writer of the Hebrews, who wrote, *"Therefore leaving the elementary teaching about the Christ, let us press on to maturity"* (Heb. 6:1).

No believer stands still for long. We either go forward or slowly slip backward. Healthy spiritual children grow in grace, whereas children who do not grow are in danger of dying. So may our motto be, "forward ever, backward never."

Let us aim for perfection, although we will never be perfect in this life. Consider these proverbs:
- It is better to aim at a good thing and miss it than to aim at a bad thing and hit it.
- Following the path of least resistance makes men and rivers crooked.
- Better to aim at the moon and hit the light post than to aim at the dirt and hit it.
- Failure is not missing the target, but aiming too low.
- The lazy person aims at nothing and hits it.
- Progress depends little on speed, but much on direction.
- Perfection is impossible by the meter, but possible by the centimeter.[28]

Aim for perfection, and depend on the Holy Spirit and God's grace to make progress.

F. Leaders want their spiritual children to believe *and* experience the Trinity (2 Cor. 12:19-21).

May the grace of the Lord Jesus Christ, and the love of God, and the fellowship of the Holy Spirit be with you all (2 Cor. 13:14).

We have come to the final verse in our study of 1 and 2 Corinthians. Paul closes with a benediction—a final prayer for believers. This beautiful prayer is Trinitarian in form, that is, it refers to the three members of the Trinity.

In the New Testament, the doctrine of the Trinity is not just for the head. Rather, biblical teachings about the Trinity are practical. We experience the Trinity in our salvation and daily living. Paul reminds us of how the Trinity (Father, Son, and Holy Spirit) is involved in our salvation.

Q 80 *Explain: The Trinity is for the head, heart, hands, and feet.*

- *"The grace of the Lord Jesus Christ"* (2 Cor. 13:14) reminds us of His birth in Bethlehem and His death on Calvary. As Paul wrote earlier, *"For you know the grace of our Lord Jesus Christ, that though he was rich, yet for your sakes he became poor, so that you through his poverty might become rich"* (2 Cor. 8:9). It was the grace of Christ that led Him to the cross to die for us.

Q 81 *Memorize 2 Corinthians 13:14 and quote it to a friend.*

- *"The love of God"* [the Father] (2 Cor. 13:14) reminds us of John 3:16. God loved us so much that He gave His One and Only Son to redeem us. We know and have experienced this love.
- *"The fellowship of the Holy Spirit"* (2 Cor. 13:14) reminds us that the Spirit entered us at the new birth and later filled us when we were baptized in the Spirit and first spoke in tongues.

God is too big, and our minds are too small to understand Him fully. Trying to put the full knowledge of the Trinity in a human mind is like trying to put the ocean in a teacup. Still, although the full knowledge of God is beyond us, we understand the Trinity in part because we have experienced the Father, Son, and Holy Spirit in our saving relationship with God. We have experienced the grace of the Lord Jesus Christ, the love of God the Father, and the fellowship of the Holy Spirit.

Paul prays that all believers may continue to experience the Trinity. For if our experience with God is "not an abiding reality, it is not a saving reality."[29] So Paul prays that we may continue to know and experience the grace, love, and fellowship of the Son, Father, and Holy Spirit. Amen!

Test Yourself: Circle the letter by the *best* completion to each question or statement.

1. Why are evil thoughts dangerous?
a) Most evil thoughts are sin.
b) Evil thoughts prepare the way for sin.
c) The source of all evil thoughts is Satan.
d) Evil thoughts are evil deeds.

2. A key to overcoming evil thoughts is to
a) keep your thoughts in front of you.
b) keep the devil behind you.
c) keep a friend beside you.
d) keep your courage within you.

3. The right attitude toward wrong is:
a) resent it.
b) examine it.
c) tolerate it.
d) hate it.

4. In our lesson on thoughts, we contrasted
a) two valleys.
b) three attitudes.
c) two roads.
d) three perspectives.

5. False apostles in Corinth were like
a) a cat that looked in a mirror.
b) a lion that looked in a mirror.
c) a dog that sat under a table.
d) a wolf killed by a shepherd.

6. Which is TRUE about jealousy?
a) It is good most of the time.
b) It is good in the context of marriage.
c) It was a bad habit of the Corinthians.
d) It may be either good or bad.

7. We resist Satan best when he comes as
a) a serpent.
b) a lion.
c) a wolf.
d) a dragon.

8. Who paid Paul when he was in Corinth?
a) Believers in Corinth
b) The Council in Jerusalem
c) Those who bought his tents
d) Believers in other cities

9. Who is a good example for most on sharing spiritual experiences?
a) Joseph
b) Mary
c) Aquila
d) Timothy

10. A key test in 2 Corinthians 13 is
a) the bema test.
b) the persecution test.
c) the truth test.
d) the post test.

Essay Test Topics: Write 50-100 words on each of these goals that you studied in this chapter.

Spiritual Thinking (2 Cor. 10:1-6)

Goal: *Summarize and illustrate 3 reasons why bad thoughts are worse than most people think.*

Goal: *State and illustrate 5 principles for overcoming evil thoughts.*

Goal: *Contrast the 2 roads and destinies before each person in regard to his thoughts.*

Spiritual Humility (2 Cor. 10:7-18)

Goal: *Explain 4 characteristics of humility in the context of Paul and his critics.*

Spiritual Insights (2 Cor. 11:1-15)

Goal: *Contrast the characteristics of bad and good jealousy (2 Cor. 11:1-2).*

Goal: *Contrast the tactics of Satan as a lion and a serpent (2 Cor. 11:3-6, 13-15).*

Goal: *Contrast Paul and false apostles on the topic of money (2 Cor. 11:7-12).*

Spiritual Highs and Lows (2 Cor. 11:16–12:10)

Goal: *Explain and apply 5 principles about spiritual experiences (2 Cor. 11:16–12:10).*

Spiritual Concerns (2 Cor. 12:11–13:14)

Goal: *State and illustrate 6 concerns of a leader for spiritual children.*

Definitions

The right-hand column lists the chapter in the textbook in which the word is used.

	Chapter
antithesis—opposite; hate is the antithesis of love; good is the antithesis of evil.	3
asceticism—denying the desires of the body for religious reasons	3
celibacy—a state of being unmarried, or abstaining from sexual intercourse, or vowing not to marry	3
charismania—emphasizing spiritual gifts too much	6
charisphobia—fear of spiritual gifts	6
chiasm—a literary device named for the Greek letter "X" (chi, pronounced kee). There are four parts of a basic chiasm: A, B, and B1, A1 (Figure 7.2).	7
communion/Lord's Supper—in the early church, a meal that celebrated the death of Christ for us; today, partaking of tokens of bread and juice to celebrate the death of Christ	5
conquistador—a Spanish conqueror; famous warriors from Spain who conquered various parts of the world	9
conscience—an inner voice from God that either approves or condemns our actions	4
contagious—known for spreading from one to another	12
Corinth—a key city in Achaia, a few miles southeast of Athens	1
discipline—training or corrective action by God to redeem, restore, or refine	3
diversity—variation, differences	7
eschatological—end times; the Great Tribulation is an eschatological period.	4
excommunicating—putting a sinning believer out of the church for a time, for the purpose of correcting a sin and restoring him or her to fellowship	3
excommunication—separation from fellowship for the purpose of correcting a fault	13
fleecing—taking the wool off of sheep; often refers to stripping a person of money or valuables by cheating, overcharging, or robbing	13
Ghandi—a famous leader of India; he led them to political freedom, and died in 1948.	Unit 1
gibberish—syllables without meaning that a person makes up	8
head covering—a veil that covered only the hair; or that covered the face and shoulders	5
head—an authority over another	5
holy—sanctified; sacred; uncommon; set apart for a godly purpose	1
illumination—revelation from the Holy Spirit that enables a person to understand, grasp, know, and experience spiritual truth that is beyond mere human knowledge	2
imparted—given or bestowed; Isaac imparted his blessing to Jacob; Jesus imparted the Holy Spirit to believers at Pentecost; teachers impart knowledge to students.	1, 3

imputed—credited, attributed, reckoned to, accounted to; the righteousness of Christ is imputed or credited to believers, apart from any works of their own. — 1, 3

inerrant—without error — 8

infallible—incapable of containing error — 8

inspired—God-breathed; all Scripture came about this way. — 8

interpretation—an explanation that gives the essence and meaning of the message of a statement — 8

isthmus—a short neck of land between two seas or bodies of water — 1

koinonia—[Greek] fellowship or sharing with someone — 4

libertinism—liberty, or total freedom, to satisfy appetites of the body — 3

love feast—in the early church, a meal that celebrated the death of Christ for redemption — 5

manifestation—a revelation, appearance, or happening — 6

metonomy—derived from the Latin, and means "change of name"; a figure of speech in which one word represents another — 4

possessive pronouns—words, like *my, your,* and *their* that substitute for proper nouns and show ownership or relationship — 11

pound—the unit of currency used in Great Britain, as dollars are used in the US — 11

prophecy—a sudden, supernatural message from God through a believer by the Holy Spirit — 8

retribution—judgment or punishment given as repayment for what someone deserves — 11

rights—privileges that may result from position, works, or grace — 4

sacraments—the sacred events of water baptism and communion — 4

signal lights—colored lights that guide drivers at intersections so they will know when it is safe to go forward — 4

spiritual gifts—expressions of grace that God gives through believers to confirm the gospel, assist in the ministry, and build up the body of Christ — 1, 6

steroids—drugs that enhance physical strength — 4

thermometer—an instrument that measures heat — 12

tongues—a spiritual gift that enables a believer to speak a language he or she has not learned and does not understand — 8

triage—the use of colored tags to divide the wounded into three groups to determine degrees of urgency to treat the wounds — 10

woodpecker—any of a group of birds with long, pointed beaks, and known for pecking the trunks of trees in search of insects for food — 4

Scripture List

Genesis
2:18 65
25:28 28

Exodus
2:14 286
4:15-16 163
7:1 163
14:13 87
16:14-16 84
32:4-6 83
32:19 83
33:15 201
34:29–35 219

Leviticus
23:10-14 180

Numbers
12:2 287
14:22-24 84
14:28-35 84
16:3 287
16:41 83
16:49 83
17:5 83
17:10 83
25:1-9 83

Deuteronomy
21:23 29

Judges
7 30

1 Samuel
16:4-13 30
16:6-7 279
16:7 30
17:28 144
19:23-24 155

2 Samuel
14:20 160

1 Kings
21:27 205

2 Kings
6:12 160

1 Chronicles
21:1 126

Nehemiah
9:17-18 144

Job
19:25-27 226
38:11 86

Psalms
19:14 82
24:1 89
42:11 225
46:1-3 176
90:12 38
94:11 280
97:10 282
103:12 145
103:13-14 201
103:14 86
139:23-24 304

Proverbs
3:7 286
4:18-19 33
8:13 282
11:17 246
11:24-25 276
13:24 . . . . 47, 207
14:29 246
15:1 246
15:18 246
16:18 286
16:32 246
27:2 143
27:4 142
27:6 . . . . 207, 259

Ecclesiastes
3:1 67
3:7 298
4:12 63

Isaiah
1:2-9 124
53:5-6 177

Jeremiah
9:1 137
20:9 166

Amos
5:15 283

Matthew
1:21 . . . . 23, 281
3:2 255
4:1 126
4:17 255
5:4 202
5:8 58
5:16 276
5:29-30 302
5:43-46 130
10:8 78
10:38 185
12:25 27
13:13 32
13:19 32
16:23 126
18:15 207
18:15-18 51
18:29-30 140
19:10-12 65
19:22 32
22:36-40 130
23:37-39 . . . . 124, 301

Mark
5:19 66
12:41-44 271
12:42-44 227

Luke
2:19 297
4:18-19 156
5:8 106
6:38 276
9:54-56 128
11:14-15 124
13:11-16 125
14:7-14 157
16:10 236
17:3 209
17:7-10 289
19:8-9 261
19:41-44 124
23:34 141

John
1:12-13 33
1:14 270
1:29 104
3:27 142
5:22-23 232
7:37-39 117
8:36 284
8:44 . . . . 32, 247
8:48 254
9:32-34 287
10:10 200
13:2 126
14:9 221
14:18 222
17:4-5 101
17:17 146
17:22-23 101
18:6 155
19:11 60
21:7 124
21:20-22 289

Acts
1:4-5 109
2:6 153
2:16-17 163
2:17-18 158
5:3 126
5:15 27
5:36-37 179
6 28
7:35 301
8:23 161
9:4 155
9:15-16 159
9:32-35 134
9:35 . . . . 112, 122
9:36 142
9:39 142
10:9-13 155
13:6-12 43
14:19-20 296
14:27 213
15:29 72
16:16 77
16:16-18 124
18:1-17 20
18:4 20
18:5 20
18:6 20
18:9-10 20
18:24-26 27
19:1-41 18
20:31 18
20:33-35 239
23:1 41
24:16 236
24:25 32
26:18 32
26:20 255

Romans
1:7 22
5:5 164
6 23
6:23 109
8:8-9 128
8:9 . . . . 33, 34
8:14 254
8:16-17 230
8:22-23 229
8:29 . . . . 22, 55
8:35-39 230
12:1 . . . . 186, 58, 56
12:1-2 22
12:3 285
12:3-8 109
12:9 283
12:21 63
13:3-4 50
13:10 130
14:10-12 232
14:20 74
14:22-23 73

1 Corinthians
1–4 . . . . 19, 31
1–6 18
1–14 175
1:1 21
1:1-2 18
1:1-9 27
1:2 . . . . 21, 22, 58
1:4 27
1:4-7 23
1:7 . . . . 19, 23, 110
1:8-9 24
1:11 . . . . 18, 27
1:12 27
1:13 27
1:14-16 27
1:17-18 29
1:18-25 28
1:20 29
1:21 29
1:22 29
1:24 29
1:26-31 . . . . 223, 29
1:30 . . . . 29, 58
1:31 143
2:1-5 30
2:3-5 247
2:6–3:4 31
2:6 33
2:9-10 32
2:14 . . . . 31, 32
2:15-16 35
3:1 33
3:1-3 . . . . 33, 34, 35
3:3 128
3:5 37
3:7 37

3:11 38
3:12. 38
3:12-15 232
3:16-17 39
3:21-23 39
4:1-2 40
4:6. 42
4:8-13 43
4:9. 295
4:11-13 295
4:14. 51
4:18-19 34
5 19
5:1-2 47
5:1-13 34
5:2. 47
5:3-5 47
5:6-8 49
5:7. 104
5:9-13 . . . . 49, 251
6:1. 50
6:1-2 241
6:1-11 19
6:2-3 50
6:5. 51
6:7. 52
6:7-8 51
6:8. 34
6:9. 57
6:9-10 53
6:9-11 . . . . 20, 22, 23, 32, 304
6:11 55
6:12. 59
6:12-14 59
6:12-20 19
6:13-20 34
6:15-18 60
6:18. 62
6:19-20 . . . . 21, 62
7–15 19
7:5. 126
7:7-9 64
7:12. 98
7:12-13 252
7:12-16 66
7:17-20 66
7:21-27 66
7:26. 67
7:29-31 67
8:1. . . . . 73, 143
8:4-8 72
8:9. 74
8:9-13 74
9:15-18 77
9:19-23 79
9:24. 82
9:24-27 80
9:27–10:5 176
9:27. . . . . 80, 81
10:1-5 83
10:3-4 84
10:5. 84
10:6. . . . . 84, 85
10:7. 83
10:8. 83
10:9. 83
10:10. 83
10:11 . . . . 84, 85
10:12. 85
10:13. 86
10:16. 87
10:19-20 88
10:21. 34
10:21-22 83
10:26. 89
10:27-28 251
11–14 19
11:3. . . . . 96, 97, 99
11:4-6 99
11:17. 102
11:23-26 103
11:26. 104
11:26-32 105
11:30. 182
11:31. 233
11:33-34 102
12–14 23
12:1. 113
12:1-3 114
12:4-13 23
12:8. 115
12:8-10 23
12:12-13 131
12:15-26 133
12:27-29 157
12:27-30 134
13:1-3 137
13:4. . . . . 143, 246
13:4-7 139
13:5. . . . . 143, 144, 145
13:6. 145
13:7. 146
13:8-12 110
13:8-13 147
14:1. . . . . 110, 153, 172
14:2. . . . . 153, 154
14:4. 109
14:5. 165
14:7-12 165
14:12. 165
14:13. 165
14:13-17 165
14:14. . . . . 154, 164
14:15. 164
14:18. 155
14:20. . . . . 144, 156
14:20-22 167
14:21. 163
14:26. 298
14:26-28 168
14:27-28 165
14:28. 109
14:29-31 169
14:33. 152
14:34-35 170
15:1. . . . . 175, 176
15:1-11 177
15:2. 176
15:5-8 178
15:10. 242
15:12. . . . . 175, 178
15:12-32 179
15:13. 178
15:17. 178
15:20. . . . . 180, 181
15:20-23 181
15:22. 181
15:24-28 99
15:25. 179
15:25-26 180
15:29. 179
15:33-34 182
15:35-44 183
15:35-58 183
15:45. 181
15:45-49 184
15:50. 184
15:51-52 184
15:53-56 185
15:57. 185
15:58. 185
16:2. . . . . 187, 188
16:3. 189
16:8-9 190
16:21. 18
16:21-24 192

2 Corinthians

1:1-2 199
1:3-4 . . . . 200, 202
1:3-11 199
1:4. 1984,
1:5. 202
1:6. . . . . 198, 202
1:8. 198
1:8-9 203
1:12. 236
1:13-17 205
1:18-22 206
1:23–2:3 205
2:1-3 216
2:3-4 207
2:5-11 208
2:6-9 207
2:9. 208
2:11. 209
2:12-13 . . . . 213, 214
2:13. 214
2:14-16 214
2:16-17 216
2:17. 216
3:3. 222
3:4–4:6 222
3:4-6 218
3:6. . . . . 218, 222
3:6-9 218
3:7-16 220
3:9. 219
3:12-13 220
3:13. 220
3:16–4:6 221
3:17. 222
3:18. . . . . . 22, 23, 55, 58, 222
4:1. . . . . 223, 226
4:2. 236
4:3-4 220
4:7. . . . . 30, 223
4:8-9 224
4:13-14 225
4:16. . . . . . 223, 224, 225, 226
4:17. 226
4:18. . . . . 222, 227
5:1. 228
5:1-4 228
5:4-5 229
5:6-8 . . . . 180, 230
5:7. 227
5:8. 230
5:9. 248
5:9-10 231
5:10. 38
5:11 . . . . 234, 235
5:11-13 235
5:12. 279
5:14-15 237
5:16. 238
5:16-17 238
5:17. 238
5:18-21 239
5:21. . . . . 104, 239
6:1. 304
6:3-4 241
6:9. 248
6:10. 249
6:14. 250
6:14-18 34
6:16-18 253
6:16, 18. 254
6:17–7:1 23
6:17. 251
7:1. . . . . 56, 58, 89, 254
7:3. 257
7:4. 258
7:4-7 258
7:8-9 259
7:10-11 260
7:12-13 262
7:13-16 262
8:1-2 267
8:3-4 268
8:6-7 . . . . 269, 270
8:8-9 270
8:9. 305
8:10-12 271
8:11. 271
8:13-15 272
8:18-19 273
8:20. 273
8:22. 273
9:1-2 274
9:6. 275
9:6-7 274
9:7. . . . . 78, 275
9:9. 275
9:10-11 276
9:12-15 276
10:1-6 280
10:4. 283
10:5. 281
10:8. 287
10:8-11 286
10:12. . . . . 28, 287
10:15. 288
10:17-18 289
11:1-2 289
11:3. 34
11:3-6 291
11:6. 291
11:7-12 292
11:13-15 292
11:19-21 294
11:22-33 295
11:23-27 299
11:26. 296
11:27. . . . . 245, 296
11:29-30 296
11:32-33 296
12:1-10 299
12:7-10 . . . . 125, 299
12:8. 299

2 Corinthians (cont.)
- 12:9-10 299
- 12:11 301
- 12:11-13 301
- 12:14 79
- 12:14-18 302
- 12:20-21 304
- 13:5 . . . . 34, 303
- 13:8 303
- 13:9, 11 304
- 13:14 305

Galatians
- 1:6-8 175
- 1:6-9 42
- 3:13 29
- 3:28 96
- 5:16 . . . . 128, 127, 35
- 5:16-21 34
- 5:16-26 23
- 5:21 34
- 5:22-23 34
- 6:1 35
- 6:7 246

Ephesians
- 1:1 22
- 1:4 58
- 1:7 21
- 2:1-3 32
- 2:20 21
- 3:6 40
- 3:17-19 32
- 3:20-21 224
- 4:11 109
- 4:11-12 157
- 4:12 273
- 4:15 . . . . 73, 146
- 4:29 159
- 5:5 34
- 5:25-33 97
- 6:10-12 126
- 6:18 155

Philippians
- 1:1 22
- 1:9-10 246
- 1:21-23 231
- 3:9-10 21
- 3:18-19 207
- 4:6-7 32

Colossians
- 2:2-3 115
- 2:13-15 215
- 3:14 130
- 3:16 226
- 4:3 213
- 4:6 158

1 Thessalonians
- 2:18 126
- 4:3-4 58
- 4:13-18 185
- 4:15-18 228
- 5:19-20 172
- 5:23 . . . . 58, 184

2 Thessalonians
- 2:1-2 169
- 2:1-4 125
- 2:9-10 146
- 2:15 169
- 3:10 272

1 Timothy
- 4:1 229
- 4:1-2 125
- 4:3-4 145
- 4:3-5 72

2 Timothy
- 1:6 118
- 1:8-12 230
- 2:18-19 182
- 2:21 . . . . 22, 56
- 3:1-2 62
- 3:1-4 145
- 3:4-5 62
- 3:7 32
- 4:16-17 224

Titus
- 1:16 56
- 2:11-12 59

Philemon
- 16 66

Hebrews
- 1:9 283
- 3:7-8 260
- 3:12-13 61
- 3:15 260
- 3:17 84
- 4:7 260
- 5:11-14 33
- 8:7-10 219
- 8:10-13 158
- 9:27 179
- 10:10 . . . . 55, 58
- 10:17 145
- 10:32-34 67
- 10:37 67
- 11:9-10 228
- 12:6 207
- 12:7-11 208
- 12:10 58
- 12:11 48
- 12:14 . . . . 56, 57

James
- 1:2-4 203
- 1:5 109
- 1:14 127
- 1:17 109
- 1:27 73
- 3:5 274
- 3:17 170
- 5:11 246

1 Peter
- 1:15-16 . . . . 56, 58
- 2:2 33
- 2:23 239
- 4:8 130
- 5:8 . . . . 28, 291
- 5:8-9 86

2 Peter
- 1:3-11 37
- 1:4 . . . . 22, 33, 55
- 1:21 158
- 2:1-3 127
- 2:2 291
- 2:3 162
- 2:12 32
- 3:17-18 34

1 John
- 1:5 247
- 1:5-6 283
- 1:9 260
- 2:15-16 . . . . 32, 282
- 3:1 164
- 3:2-3 230
- 3:2-6 182
- 3:27 136
- 4:1 125
- 4:16 130

2 John
- 1-3 146
- 6 146

Jude
- 12 294
- 20 155

Revelation
- 1:16 222
- 1:17 155
- 2:20-23 170
- 3:15-17 112
- 12:9-11 126
- 20:11-15 232
- 20:14 180
- 21:5 148
- 21:27 58
- 22:11 58
- 22:20 . . . . 105, 192

Bibliography

Augsburger, David W. *Caring Enough to Confront,* 3rd ed. Ventura, California: Regal Books, 2009.

Barker, Kenneth, gen. ed. *The NIV Study Bible*. Grand Rapids, Michigan: Zondervan Publishing House, 1985.

Barclay, William. *The Daily Study Bible Series: The Gospel of Matthew.* Rev. ed. Vol. 1, Philadelphia, Pennsylvania Westminster Press, 1975.

Barclay, William. *The Daily Bible Study Series: The Letters to the Corinthians.* Rev. ed. Philadelphia, Pennsylvania Westminster Press, 1975.

Barrett, C. K. *The First Epistle to the Corinthians.* London, England: Adam & Charles Black, 1968.

Barrett, C. K. *The Second Epistle to the Corinthians.* Great Britain: University Printing House, Cambridge, 1973.

Barrett, C. K. *The Second Epistle to the Corinthians, Black's New Testament Commentaries.* London: Adam and Charles Black, 1976.

Barrett, C. K. *The Second Epistle to the Corinthians.* London, England: Adam and Charles Black, 1976.

Barrett, David. *International Bulletin of Missionary Research,* Fall 2000, p. 25.

Baxter, J. Sidlow. *Baxter's Explore the Book.* Grand Rapids, Michigan: Zondervan Publishing House, 1966.

Beasley-Murray, G. R. *Christ is Alive.* Cambridge, England, United Kingdom: Lutterworth Press, 1947.

Beers, Ronald A., ed. *Life Application Study Bible.* Carol Stream, Illinois: Tyndale House Publishers, 1997.

Bradford, James. Sermon on 1 Corinthians 15, December, 2009.

Brayer, Menachem M. *The Jewish Woman in Rabbinic Literature: A Psychosocial Perspective.* Hoboken, N.J: Ktav Publishing House, 1986.

Bromiley, Geoffrey W. *The International Standard Bible Encyclopedia,* Vols. III-V. Grand Rapids, Michigan: Wm. B. Eerdmans Publishing Co., 1979.

Bruce, F. F. *New Testament History.* New York: Doubleday, 1971.

Brueggemann. Dale A. *The Gifts of the Spirit.* www.Lulu.com, 2009.

Bullock, Warren. *When the Spirit Speaks.* Springfield, Missouri: Gospel Publishing House, 2009.

Carter, Tom. *Spurgeon at His Best.* Grand Rapids, Michigan: Baker Book House, 1988.

Carver, Frank G. *Beacon Bible Commentary, Romans, 1&2 Corinthians.* Kansas City, Missouri: Beacon Hill Press, 1968.

Cho, Paul Yonggi. *The Fourth Dimension.* Plainfield, New Jersey: Logos International, 1979.

Cowman, Mrs. Charles E. *Springs in the Desert Sampler.* Grand Rapids, Michigan: Zondervan Publishing House, 1983.

Drummond, Henry. *The Greatest Thing in the World,* http://silkworth.net/henry_drummond/hd_tablecontents.htm

Elliot, Jim. http://www.brainyquote.com/quotes/quotes/j/jimelliot189244.html

Fee, Gordon D. *Corinthians, New International Commentary on the New Testament.* Grand Rapids, Michigan: Wm. B. Eerdmans Publishing Co., 1987.

Fee, Gordon D. *The First Epistle to the Corinthians, New International Commentary on the New Testament.* Grand Rapid, Michigan: Wm. B. Eerdmans Publishing Co., 1991.

Garfield, James A. http://www.quotegarden.com/truth.html

Gee, Donald. *Concerning Spiritual Gifts.* Springfield, Missouri: Gospel Publishing House, 1972.

Gilbrandt, Thoralf. *Complete Biblical Library, The New Testament Greek-English Dictionary, Alpha-Gamma.* Springfield, Missouri: World Library Press, Inc., 1990.

Gilbrandt, Thoralf. *Complete Biblical Library, The New Testament Greek-English Dictionary, Pi-Rho*. Springfield, Missouri: World Library Press, Inc., 1991.

Gilbrandt, Thoralf. *Complete Biblical Library, The New Testament Greek-English Dictionary, Sigma-Omega*. Springfield, Missouri: World Library Press, Inc., 1991.

Gilbrandt, Thoralf. *Complete Biblical Library, Greek English Dictionary, Zeta-Kappa*. Springfield, Missouri: World Library Press, Inc., 1991.

Gingrich, F. Wilbur. *Shorter Lexicon of the Greek New Testament*. Chicago, Illinois: The University of Chicago. Press, 1975.

Godet. Frederic L. *Commentary on First Corinthians*. Grand Rapids: Kregel Publications, 1977 repr. ed.

Grams, Rocky. *In Awe In Argentina*. Lake Mary, Florida: Creation House, 2006.

Grosheide, F. W. *Commentary on the First Epistle to the Corinthians, .New International Biblical Commentary on the New Testament*. Grand Rapids, Michigan: Wm. B. Eerdmans Publishing Co., 1963.

Grossman, Cathy Lynn. "Survey of Clergy Abuses Suggests Previous Estimates Were Low," *USA Today,* February, 2004.

Grudem, Wayne "The Meaning of *Kephale*. "head": An Evaluation of New Evidence, Real and Alleged," *Journal of the Evangelical Theological Society* 44/1. March 2001: 25-65.

Gundry, Robert H. *A Survey of the New Testament*. Grand Rapids, Michigan: Zondervan Publishing House, 1994.

Gundry, Stanley N., Series Editor. *Counterpoints: Five Views on Sanctification*. Grand Rapids, Michigan: Zondervan, 1987. [Stanley M. Horton, Pentecostal View; J. Robertson McQuilken, Keswick View]

Harris, Ralph W., ed. *The Complete Biblical Library, The New Testament Study Bible, Romans–Corinthians,* Vol. 7. Springfield, Missouri: World Library Press, Inc., 1989.

Hayes, Doremus Almy. *Paul and His Epistles,* Published by Methodist Book Concern, 1915. http://books.google.com/books?id=FO02AAAAMAAJ&pg=PA35&lpg=PA35&dq=Apostle+paul+bandy-legged&source=web&ots=Igwf Fj5zVd&sig=QjHTKOhUUi1-8okkOOOA_fPqzxY&hl=en&sa=X&oi=book_result&resnum=4&ct=result

Horton, Stanley M. *Acts, A Logion Press Commentary*. Springfield, Missouri: Gospel Publishing House, 1981.

Horton, Stanley M. *1 & 2 Corinthians, A Logion Press Commentary. Springfield, Missouri:* Gospel Publishing House, 1999.

Horton, Stanley M. *What the Bible Says About the Holy Spirit*. Springfield, Missouri: Gospel Publishing House, 1976.

Hughes, Philip E. *The Second Epistle to the Corinthians, New International Commentary on the New Testament*. Grand Rapids, Michigan: Wm. B. Eerdmans Publishing Co., 1977.

Hybels, Bill. *Too Busy Not To Pray*. Downers Grove, Illinois: InterVarsity Press, 1988.

Jowett, J. H. *Life in the Heights, Studies in the Epistles*. New York: The Christian Herald, 1925.

Keener, Craig S. *The IVP Bible Background Commentary: New Testament*. Downer's Grove, Illinois: InterVarsity Press, 1993.

MacArthur, John. Sermon on 1 Corinthians 13:1-3. http://www.gty.org/Resources/Sermons/1863_The-Prominence-of-Love

Martin, Walter. *Kingdom of the Cults*. Minneapolis, Minnesota: Bethany House Publishers, 1992.

McGhee, Quentin and Carl Gibbs. *General Principles for Interpreting Scripture.* Springfield, Missouri: Faith & Action, 2006.

McKenzie, E. C. *Mac's Giant Book of Quips and Quotes*. Grand Rapids, Michigan: Baker Book House, 1980.

Menzies, William W. and Stanley M. Horton. *Bible Doctrines*. Springfield, Missouri: Gospel Publishing House, 1993.

Metz, Donald S. *First Corinthians, Beacon Bible Commentary.* Kansas City, Missouri: Beacon Hill Press, 1968.

Mote, Edward. [Hymn] "The Solid Rock," 1834, http://library.timelesstruths.org/music/The_Solid_Rock/

Mounce, Robert H. *The Book of Revelation, New International Commentary on the New Testament*. Grand Rapids, Michigan: Wm. B. Eerdmans Publishing Co., 1998.

Nelson, P. C. *Bible Doctrines,* Rev. ed. Springfield, Missouri: Gospel Publishing House. 1971.

Nicholson, Dick. "Communique," April, 2007.

Palma, Anthony. "First Corinthians" in *Life in the Spirit New Testament Commentary*. Grand Rapids, Michigan: Zondervan Publishing House, 1999.

Palmer, John. Sermon series on 1 Corinthians, preached at First Assembly of God, Des Moines, Iowa.

Pfeiffer, Charles, Howard Vos, and John Rea. *Wycliffe Bible Encyclopedia,* Vol. 1. Chicago, Illinois: Moody Press, 1975.

Plummer, Alfred. *International Critical Commentary, Second Epistle of St. Paul to the Corinthians*. Edinburgh: T&T Clark, 1975.

Robertson, Archibald and Alfred Plummer. *The International Critical Commentary, First Corinthians.* Edinburgh: T&T Clark, 1978.

Rockhill, David. *Parables,* January, 1984, Rockport, Indiana.

Spurgeon, C. H. *John Ploughman's Talks*. Ann Arbor, Michigan: Baker Book House, 1976.

Spurgeon, Charles Haddon. *Morning and Evening*. McClean, Virginia: Macdonald Publishing Co., n.d.

Stamps, Donald C., gen. ed. *The Full Life Study Bi*ble. Grand Rapids, Michigan: Zondervan Publishing House, 1992.

Stamps, Donald C., gen. ed. *Life in the Spirit Study Bible*. Grand Rapids, Michigan: Zondervan Publishing House, 2003.

Stott, John R. W. *The Message of Acts: The Spirit, the Church and the World*. Downers Grove, Illinois: InterVarsity Press, 1994.

Stronstad, Roger. *Prophethood of All Believers—A Study in Luke's Charismatic Theology*. London: Sheffield Academic Press, 1999.

Stronstad, Roger. *Spirit, Scripture & Theology—A Pentecostal Perspective*. Bagio City, Philippines: Asia Pacific Seminary Press, 1995.

Tan, Paul Lee. *Encyclopedia of 7700 Illustrations: Signs of the Times*. Rockville, Maryland: Assurance Publishers, 1984.

Tasker, R. V. G. *Tyndale New Testament Commentaries: The Second Epistle of Paul to the Corinthians*. Grand Rapids, Michigan: Wm. B. Eerdmans Publishing Co., 1977.

Tozier, A. W. *A Treasury of A. W. Tozier.* Harrisburg, Pennsylvania: Christian Publications Inc., 1980.

Tuttle, Robert G. Jr. "John Wesley and the Gifts of the Holy Spirit," http://ucmpage.org/articles/rtuttle1.html

Wesley, John. *Wesley's Notes on the New Testament,* Vol. 2 (Grand Rapids, Michigan: Baker Book House, 1983.

Wiersbe, Warren W. *Be Wise 1 Corinthians*. Colorado Springs, Colorado: Chariot Victor Publishings, A Division of Cook Communications, 1983.

Wiersbe, Warren W. *The Bible Exposition Commentary, Matthew to Galatians,* Vol. 1. Wheaton, Illinois: Victor Books, 1994.

Wiersbe, Warren W. *The Bible Exposition Commentary, Ephesians to Revelation,* Vol. 2. Wheaton, Illinois: Victor Books, 1994.

Wood, George O. *Acts–A Study Guide*. Irving, Texas: ICI University Press, 1996.

Wood, George O. *Study in Acts,* Acts 18, cassette tape. Costa Mesa, California: Newport-Mesa Christian Center, 1988.

ALL George O. Wood sermons can be found on the website http://georgeowood.com. Then look under Expositional Sermons, New Testament, and choose 1st Corinthians or 2nd Corinthians.

Wood, George O. Sermon on 1 Corinthians 3:5-23, "God's Possessions."

Wood, George O. Sermon on 1 Corinthians 4, "How Christians Should Regard Pastors and Themselves."

Wood, George O. Sermon on 1 Corinthians 6:1-11, "The Wrong Way to Right Wrongs."

Wood, George O. Sermon on 1 Corinthians 7:1-9, "Sexual Freedom God's Way."

Wood, George O. Sermon on 1 Corinthians 8, "Social Drinking, Dancing, Movies, and Other Sins."

Wood, George O. Sermon on 1 Corinthians 9, "What About My Rights?"

Wood, George O. Sermon on 1 Corinthians 11:2-16, "The Veiled Woman."

Wood, George O. Sermon on 1 Corinthians 11:17-34,. "The Lord's Supper."

Wood, George O. Sermon on 1 Corinthians 12:1, "Spiritual Gifts—Unopened and Misused."

Wood, George O. Sermon on 1 Corinthians 12:10, "The Gift of Prophecy."

Wood, George O. Sermon on 1 Corinthians 13:1-3, "What's Important to You?"

Wood, George O. Sermon on 1 Corinthians 13:4-7, "How to Be More Loving."

Wood, George O. Sermon on 1 Corinthians 15:1-19, "He Is Alive!"

Wood, George O. Sermon on 1 Corinthians 15:20-34, "What Christ's Resurrection Means."

Wood, George O. Sermon on 1 Corinthians 15:35-58, "The Glorious Destiny of Our Bodies."

Wood, George O. Sermon on 2 Corinthians 5:1-10, "Confronting Death."

Wood, George O. Sermon on 2 Corinthians 5:11-21, "The Test of a Fruitful Minister."

Wood, George O. Sermon on 2 Corinthians 12:1-10, "Spiritual Ecstasy and Agony."

http://ag.org/top/Beliefs/sptlissues_prophets_prophecies.cfm

http://en.wikipedia.org/wiki/Agabus

http://en.wikipedia.org/wiki/Demosthenes

http://en.wikipedia.org/wiki/Edwin_M._Stanton

http://en.wikipedia.org/wiki/Isthmus_of_Corinth

http://en.wikipedia.org/wiki/Metre

http://en.wikipedia.org/wiki/Plutarch

http://en.wikipedia.org/wiki/Truth

http://en.wikipedia.org/wiki/William_J._Seymour

http://gracethrufaith.com/selah/holidays-and-holy-days/the-feast-of-first-fruits/

http://ntreadthrough.blogspot.com/2007/08/triumphal-procession-2-corinthians-2.html

http://thinkexist.com/quotes/with/keyword/holiness/

http://www.americanbible.org/brcpages/MadeaLiving

http://www.ascendingleaders.org/synapse/homepage/view.cfm?Edit_id=242&website=ascendingleaders.org

http://www.bible-history.com/court-of-women/jewish_encyclopedia.html

http://www.biblebb.com/files/MAC/sg1863.htm

http://www.biblebb.com/files/spurgeon/2603.htm

http://www.BibleGateway.com

http://www.corsinet.com/braincandy/qtruth.html

http://www.cyberhymnal.org/htm/r/i/riseupom.htm

http://www.google.com/imgres?imgurl=http://www.andreaharner.com/BabyPufferFish.jpg&imgrefurl

http://www.growingchristians.org/dfgc/legacy.htm

http://www.logos.com/product/1500/mormonism-changes-contradictions-and-errors
http://www.preceptaustin.org/holiness_quotes.htm
http://www.squidoo.com/bible_farming
http://www.tgm.org/hayfordOnTongues.html
http://www.thebody.com/content/prev/art2301.html
http://www.themillionaireblog.com/gods-shovel-is-bigger-than-mine/
http://www.watchman.org/jw/jwcourt.htm
http://www.youtube.com/watch?v=JJZqxuKShDc

Endnotes

Chapter 1

[1] Robert H. Gundry, *A Survey of the New Testament* (Grand Rapids, Michigan: Zondervan Publishing House, 1994), p. 285.

[2] Philip E. Hughes, *The Second Epistle to the Corinthians, New International Commentary on the New Testament* (Grand Rapids, Michigan: Wm. B. Eerdmans Publishing Co., 1977), p. xvii.

[3] John R. W. Stott, *The Message of Acts: The Spirit, the Church and the World* (Downers Grove, Illinois: InterVarsity Press, 1994), p. 293.

[4] Charles Pfeiffer, Howard Vos, and John Rea, *Wycliffe Bible Encyclopedia,* vol. 1 (Chicago, Illinois: Moody Press, 1975), p. 380.

[5] Kenneth Barker, gen. ed., *The NIV Study Bible* (Grand Rapids, Michigan: Zondervan Publishing House, 1985), p. 1732.

[6] David Barrett, *International Bulletin of Missionary Research,* Fall 2000, p. 25.

[7] Stott, p. 292.

[8] George O. Wood, *Acts–A Study Guide* (Irving, Texas: ICI University Press, 1996), p. 289.

[9] George O. Wood, *Study in Acts,* Acts 18, cassette tape (Costa Mesa, California: Newport-Mesa Christian Center, 1988).

[10] F. F. Bruce, *New Testament History* (New York: Doubleday, 1971), p. 367.

[11] Stott, p. 296.

[12] Wood, *Acts* (ICI), p. 289.

[13] Stott, pp. 295-296.

[14] Donald C. Stamps, gen. ed., *The Full Life Study Bible* (Grand Rapids, Michigan: Zondervan Publishing House, 1992), Acts 28:30 comment, p. 1704.

[15] Stanley N. Gundry, series editor, *Counterpoints: Five Views on Sanctification* (Grand Rapids, Michigan: Zondervan, 1987), Stanley M. Horton [Pentecostal View], p. 115.

[16] Stanley N. Gundry, *Counterpoints* [Horton referring to Myer Pearlman], p. 114.

[17] See Gordon D. Fee, *The First Epistle to the Corinthians, New International Commentary on the New Testament* (Grand Rapids, Michigan: Wm. B. Eerdmans Publishing Co., 1991), pp. 39-40.

[18] The term *charisma* appears only 17 times in the New Testament, and except for 1 Peter 4:10, all occurrences are in Paul's letters. See Siegfried S. Schatzmann, *A Pauline Theology of Charismata* (Peabody, Massachusetts: Hendrickson Publishers, 1987), pp. 1-11.

[19] Rocky Grams, *In Awe In Argentina* (Lake Mary, Florida: Creation House, 2006), p. 169.

[20] Grams, p. 170.

Chapter 2

[1] R. H. Jowett, *Life in the Heights, Studies in the Epistles* (New York: The Christian Herald, 1925), p. 72.

[2] http://en.wikipedia.org/wiki/William_J._Seymour

[3] Donald C. Stamps, gen. ed., *Life in the Spirit Study Bible* (Grand Rapids, Michigan: Zondervan Publishing House, 2003), "Three Kinds of People" (1 Cor. 2:14-15).

[4] Adapted from a sermon by Dr. George O. Wood, "God's Possessions," 1 Corinthians 3:5-23. http:"georgeowood.com.

[5] Fee, *The First Epistle to the Corinthians, NICNT,* pp. 5-6, 8.

[6] George O. Wood, "How Christians Should Regard Pastors and Themselves," sermon on 1 Corinthians 4. http://georgeowood.com

[7] The movie *Ben Hur* shows rowers under a captain.

Chapter 3

[1] This story was told by Edgar Muñoz, Argentina.

[2] We assume from the way Paul describes it that this is not his mother, but stepmother. Still, incest was forbidden by Jewish law (Lev. 18:8; Deut. 22:22).

[3] Incest between parent and child was one sexual sin that was universally condemned in the Greco-Roman world. See Craig S. Keener, *The IVP Bible Background Commentary: New Testament* (Downer's Grove, Illinois: InterVarsity Press, 1993), p. 462.

[4] Fee, *The First Epistle to the Corinthians, NICNT,* p. 2.

[5] Fee, *The First Epistle to the Corinthians, NICNT,* p. 3.

[6] William Barclay, *The Daily Bible Study Series: The Letters to the Corinthians,* rev. ed. (Philadelphia, Pennsylvania: Westminster Press, 1975), p. 45.

[7] Barclay, *The Letters to the Corinthians,* pp. 49-50.

[8] Barclay, *The Letters to the Corinthians,* p. 49.

[9] George O. Wood, "The Wrong Way to Right Wrongs," sermon on 1 Corinthians 6:1-11. http://georgeowood.com

[10] Fee, *The First Epistle to the Corinthians, NICNT,* p. 240.

[11] Fee, *The First Epistle to the Corinthians, NICNT,* pp. 239-242.

[12] Geoffrey W. Bromiley, *The International Standard Bible Encyclopedia,* vol. IV (Grand Rapids, Michigan: Wm. B. Eerdmans Publishing Co., 1979), p. 2682.

[13] Geoffrey W. Bromiley, *The International Standard Bible Encyclopedia,* vol. III (Grand Rapids, Michigan: Wm. B. Eerdmans Publishing Co., 1979), p. 1403.

[14] Stanley N. Gundry, *Counterpoints* [Horton], p. 116.

[15] Stanley N. Gundry, *Counterpoints* [J. Robertson McQuilken, Keswick View], p. 54.

[16] Stanley N. Gundry, *Counterpoints* [Horton], p. 116.

[17] Stanley N. Gundry, *Counterpoints* [Horton referring to Myer Pearlman], p. 114.

18 Bromiley, vol. IV, p. 2685.

19 Tom Carter, *Spurgeon at His Best* (Grand Rapids, Michigan: Baker Book House, 1988), p. 354.

20 http://www.preceptaustin.org/holiness_quotes.htm

21 William W. Menzies and Stanley M. Horton, *Bible Doctrines* (Springfield, Missouri: Gospel Publishing House, 1993), p. 149.

22 Stanley N. Gundry, *Counterpoints* [Horton], p. 116.

23 Alfred Plummer, *International Critical Commentary, Second Epistle of St. Paul to the Corinthians* (Edinburgh: T&T Clark, 1975), p. 212.

24 P. C. Nelson, *Bible Doctrines,* rev. ed. (Springfield, Missouri: Gospel Publishing House. 1971), p. 103.

25 Stanley M. Horton, *What the Bible Says About the Holy Spirit* (Springfield, Missouri: Gospel Publishing House, 1976), p. 258.

26 Carter, p. 101.

27 Carter, p. 100.

28 http://thinkexist.com/quotes/with/keyword/holiness/

29 Carter, p. 354.

30 http://www.preceptaustin.org/holiness_quotes.htm

31 http://www.preceptaustin.org/holiness_quotes.htm

32 Bromiley, vol. IV, p. 2685.

33 *Full Life Study Bible,* John 19:11 comment, p. 1623; See also *NIV Study Bible,* John 19:11 comment, p. 1630.

34 http://www.thebody.com/content/prev/art2301.html

35 See Fee, *The First Epistle to the Corinthians, NICNT,* p. 275.

36 Stanley M. Horton, *1 & 2 Corinthians, A Logion Press Commentary* (Springfield, Missouri: Gospel Publishing House, 1999), p. 68.

37 George O. Wood, "Sexual Freedom God's Way," sermon on 1 Corinthians 7:1-9. http://georgeowood.com

38 Cathy Lynn Grossman, "Survey of Clergy Abuses Suggests Previous Estimates Were Low," *USA Today,* February, 2004, p. 2A.

39 Barclay, *The Letters to the Corinthians,* p. 64.

40 Archibald Robertson and Alfred Plummer, *The International Critical Commentary, First Corinthians* (Edinburgh: T&T Clark, 1978), p. 144.

41 Ralph W. Harris, ed., *The Complete Biblical Library, The New Testament Study Bible, Romans–Corinthians,* vol. 7 (Springfield, Missouri: World Library Press, Inc., 1989), p. 335.

Chapter 4

1 Barclay, *The Letters to the Corinthians,* p. 72.

2 Dr. George O. Wood related this story that was told by Dr. H. A. Ironside. "Social Drinking, Dancing, Movies, and Other Sins," sermon on 1 Corinthians 8. http://georgeowood.com

3 George O. Wood, "Social Drinking, Dancing, Movies, and Other Sins," sermon on 1 Corinthians 8. http://georgeowood.com

4 George O. Wood, "What About My Rights?" sermon on 1 Corinthians 9. http://georgeowood.com

5 http://www.squidoo.com/bible_farming

6 http://en.wikipedia.org/wiki/Isthmus_of_Corinth

7 Gordon D. Fee, *Corinthians, New International Commentary on the New Testament* (Grand Rapids, Michigan: Wm. B. Eerdmans Publishing Co., 1987), p. 437.

8 Harris, *CBL,* vol. 7, p. 375.

9 Warren W. Wiersbe, *The Bible Exposition Commentary,* vol 2, (Colorado Springs, Colorado: Victor [an imprint of Cook Communications Ministries], 1992), pp. 594-602.

10 Jim Elliot, quoted in the book *Through Gates of Splendor.* http://www.brainyquote.com/quotes/quotes/j/jimelliot189244.html

11 Fee, *Corinthians, NICNT,* p. 441.

12 Fee, *Corinthians, NICNT,* p. 450.

13 http://www.biblebb.com/files/spurgeon/2603.htm

14 Fee, *Corinthians, NICNT,* p. 460.

15 C. K. Barrett, *The First Epistle to the Corinthians* (London, England: Adam & Charles Black, 1968), p. 229.

16 Paul Lee Tan, *Encyclopedia of 7700 Illustrations: Signs of the Times* (Rockville, Maryland: Assurance Publishers, 1984), pp. 1445-1447.

17 C. K. Barrett, *The First Epistle to the Corinthians,* p. 234.

18 *Full Life Study Bible,* 1 Corinthians 10:21 comment, p. 1765.

19 Barclay, *The Letters to the Corinthians,* p. 92.

20 Fee, *Corinthians, NICNT,* p. 481.

21 John Palmer, sermon on 1 Corinthians 10:14–11:1, preached at First Assembly of God, Des Moines, Iowa, 2004.

Chapter 5

1 This story is related by missionary Mary Beggs.

2 Menachem M. Brayer, *The Jewish Woman in Rabbinic Literature: A Psychosocial Perspective* (Hoboken, N.J: Ktav Publishing House, 1986), p. 239.

3 Geoffrey W. Bromiley, *The International Standard Bible Encyclopedia,* vol. V (Grand Rapids, Michigan: Wm. B. Eerdmans Publishing Co., 1979), p. 3047.

4 George O. Wood, "The Veiled Woman," sermon on 1 Corinthians 11:2-16. http://georgeowood.com

5 http://www.bible-history.com/court-of-women/jewish_encyclopedia.html

6 William Barclay, *The Daily Study Bible Series: The Gospel of Matthew,* rev. ed. vol. 1 (Philadelphia, Pennsylvania: Westminster Press, 1975), p. 17.

7. See Dr. George O. Wood, sermon on 1 Corinthians 11:2-16, "The Veiled Woman"; *Full Life Study Bible*, 1 Corinthians 11:3 comment, p. 1766; Grosheide, *Corinthians*, NICNT [see below], pp. 249-250; *Complete Biblical Library*, vol. 7, p. 395; Wayne Grudem, "The Meaning of *Kephale* ("head"): An Evaluation of New Evidence, Real and Alleged," *Journal of the Evangelical Theological Society* 44/1 (March 2001): 25-65.
8. See Horton, *1 and 2 Corinthians*, p. 99. Note also that in *"subjecting themselves"* they are to ask *"their own husbands"* (1 Cor. 14:34).
9. Barclay, *The Letters to the Corinthians*, pp. 97-98.
10. *NIV Study Bible*, 1 Corinthians 11:5-6 comment, p. 1750.
11. F. W. Grosheide, *Commentary on the First Epistle to the Corinthians, New International Biblical Commentary on the New Testament* (Grand Rapids, Michigan: Wm. B. Eerdmans Publishing Co., 1963), p. 258.
12. George O. Wood, "The Lord's Supper," sermon on 1 Corinthians 11:17-34. http://georgeowood.com
13. George O. Wood, "The Lord's Supper," sermon on 1 Corinthians 11:17-34. http://georgeowood.com
14. George O. Wood, "The Lord's Supper," sermon on 1 Corinthians 11:17-34. http://georgeowood.com
15. Warren W. Wiersbe, *Be Wise 1 Corinthians* (Colorado Springs, Colorado: Chariot Victor Publishings, A Division of Cook Communications, 1983), p. 117.
16. John Palmer, sermon on 1 Corinthians 11:17-34, 2004.
17. Words and music by Ronald Michael Payne and Ronnie Hinson.
18. Grosheide, p. 275.
19. George O. Wood, "The Lord's Supper," sermon on 1 Corinthians 11:17-34. http://georgeowood.com

Chapter 6

1. George O. Wood, referring to a story by Dr. Norman McClean, "Spiritual Gifts—Unopened and Misused," sermon on 1 Corinthians 12:1. http://georgeowood.com
2. Robert G. Tuttle, Jr., "John Wesley and the Gifts of the Holy Spirit," http://ucmpage.org/articles/rtuttle1.html
3. http://www.cyberhymnal.org/htm/r/i/riseupom.htm
4. Harris, *CBL*, vol. 7, 1 Corinthians, p. 415.
5. Jimmy Beggs, interview, January 18, 2006.
6. Donald Gee, *Concerning Spiritual Gifts* (Springfield, Missouri: Gospel Publishing House, 1972), p. 15.
7. Gee, p. 34.
8. Gee, p. 30.
9. Gee, p. 31.
10. Gee, pp. 37-38.
11. Gee, pp. 38-39, 111-119.
12. The young pastor was Quentin McGhee.
13. Horton, *1 & 2 Corinthians*, p. 115.
14. *NIV Study Bible*, 1 Corinthians 12:10 comment, p. 1752.
15. Gee, p. 46.
16. This miracle occurred at an Assemblies of God revival in Mombasa, Kenya.
17. Harris, *CBL*, vol. 7, p. 417.
18. http://www.logos.com/product/1500/mormonism-changes-contradictions-and-errors

Chapter 7

1. Henry Drummond, *The Greatest Thing in the World*, http://silkworth.net/henry_drummond/hd_tablecontents.htm
2. This list is adapted from Phoenix First Assembly of God, which has over 200 ministries by church members.
3. Adapted from a poem written by Rafael Pombo, Colombian poet (1833-1912).
4. Frederic L. Godet. *Commentary on First Corinthians* (Grand Rapids: Kregel Publications, 1977 repr. ed.), pp. 657-58. See also Fee, *Corinthians, NICNT*, pp. 623-625 for a full discussion of the various interpretations.
5. Koran 55:56-58.
6. Drummond.
7. John MacArthur, sermon on 1 Corinthians 13:1-3, http://www.gty.org/Resources/Sermons/1863_The-Prominence-of-Love
8. George O. Wood, "What's Important to You?" sermon on 1 Corinthians 13:1-3. http://georgeowood.com
9. John MacArthur, sermon on 1 Corinthians 13:1-3, http://www.gty.org/Resources/Sermons/1863_The-Prominence-of-Love
10. Dale A. Brueggemann, *The Gifts of the Spirit*, www.Lulu.com, 2009, p. 41.
11. John MacArthur, sermon on 1 Corinthians 13:1-3, http://www.gty.org/Resources/Sermons/1863_The-Prominence-of-Love
12. http://en.wikipedia.org/wiki/Edwin_M._Stanton
13. Thoralf Gilbrandt, *Complete Biblical Library, The New Testament Greek-English Dictionary, Sigma-Omega* (Springfield, Missouri: World Library Press, Inc., 1991), p. 516.
14. http://www.google.com/imgres?imgurl=http://www.andreaharner.com/BabyPufferFish.jpg&imgrefurl
15. George O. Wood, "How to Be More Loving," sermon on 1 Corinthians 13:4-7. http://georgeowood.com
16. This story told by Mike McClaflin.
17. http://en.wikipedia.org/wiki/Truth
18. Fee, *Corinthians, NICNT*, p. 639.

Chapter 8

1. *Full Life Study Bible*, 1 Corinthians 14:2 comment, pp. 1773-1774.
2. Drummond, *The Greatest Thing in the World*, http://silkworth.net/henry_drummond/hd_contrast.html
3. John MacArthur, sermon on 1 Corinthians 13:1-3, http://www.gty.org/Resources/Sermons/1863_The-Prominence-of-Love

4. Thoralf Gilbrandt, *Complete Biblical Library, The New Testament Greek-English Dictionary, Alpha-Gamma* (Springfield, Missouri: World Library Press, Inc., 1990), p. 628.
5. http://www.tgm.org/hayfordOnTongues.html
6. Harris, *CBL*, vol. 7, p. 435.
7. *Full Life Study Bible,* "Spiritual Gifts for Believers," 8b, p. 1799.
8. Wilbur F. Gingrich, *Shorter Lexicon of the Greek New Testament* (Chicago, Illinois: The University of Chicago Press, 1975), p. 42.
9. http://ag.org/top/Beliefs/sptlissues_prophets_prophecies.cfm
10. Harris, *CBL,* vol. 7, p. 505.
11. http://ag.org/top/Beliefs/sptlissues_prophets_prophecies.cfm
12. Thoralf Gilbrandt, *Complete Biblical Library, The New Testament Greek-English Dictionary, Pi-Rho* (Springfield, Missouri: World Library Press, Inc., 1991), pp. 62-63.
13. Robertson and Plummer, p. 306.
14. http://en.wikipedia.org/wiki/Agabus
15. Fee, *Corinthians, NICNT,* pp. 632-633.
16. Gilbrandt, *CBL, The New Testament Greek-English Dictionary, Pi-Rho,* p. 429.
17. This spiritual gift came to Quentin McGhee in some of his studies.
18. This illustration shared by Quentin McGhee.
19. http://www.growingchristians.org/dfgc/legacy.htm
20. Anthony Palma, "First Corinthians" in *Life in the Spirit New Testament Commentary* (Grand Rapids, Michigan: Zondervan Publishing House, 1999), pp. 881-882.
21. Palma, p. 881.
22. *Full Life Study Bible,* "Spiritual Gifts for Believers," 8c, p. 1799.
23. Stanley M. Horton, *Acts, A Logion Press Commentary* (Springfield, Missouri: Gospel Publishing House, 1981), pp. 67-68.
24. Roger Stronstad, *Prophethood of All Believers—A Study in Luke's Charismatic Theology* (London: Sheffield Academic Press, 1999), pp. 68-70.
25. Walter Martin, *Kingdom of the Cults* (Minneapolis, Minnesota: Bethany House Publishers, 1991), p. 44.
26. http://www.watchman.org/jw/jwcourt.htm
27. http://www.watchman.org/jw/jwcourt.htm
28. Bill Hybels, *Too Busy Not To Pray* (Downers Grove, Illinois: Intervarsity Press, 1988), p. 132.
29. http://www.ascendingleaders.org/synapse/homepage/view.cfm?Edit_id=242&website=ascendingleaders.org
30. Horton, *1 and 2 Corinthians,* p. 141.
31. Fee, *Corinthians, NICNT,* p. 693.
32. Horton, *1 and 2 Corinthians,* p. 142.
33. Warren Bullock, *When the Spirit Speaks* (Springfield, Missouri: Gospel Publishing House, 2009), p. 86.
34. Harris, *CBL,* vol. 7, pp. 452-453.
35. Fee, *Corinthians, NICNT,* pp. 699-705.
36. Roger Stronstad, *Spirit, Scripture & Theology—A Pentecostal Perspective* (Bagio City, Philippines: Asia Pacific Seminary Press, 1995), p. 23.
37. Bullock, p. 86.
38. George O. Wood, "The Gift of Prophecy," sermon on 1 Corinthians 12:10. http://georgeowood.com
39. Bullock, p. 83.
40. Bullock, p. 26.
41. Bullock, pp. 85-86.
42. Bullock, pp. 84-85.

Chapter 9

1. George O. Wood, referring to story in the book *Christ is Alive* [Cambridge, England, United Kingdom, Lutterworth Press] by G. R. Beasley-Murray, sermon on 1 Corinthians 15:20-34 "What Christ's Resurrection Means," personal notes.
2. David Barrett, *International Bulletin of Missionary Research,* p. 25.
3. Edward Mote, [Hymn] "The Solid Rock," 1834, http://library.timelesstruths.org/music/The_Solid_Rock/
4. http://www.youtube.com/watch?v=JJZqxuKShDc
5. http://www.crookedlakereview.com/books/saints_sinners/martin9.html Also see: http://www.northforest.org/Religions/worldreligions.html#mormonism
6. http://hermetic.com/sabazius/mohammed.htm
7. Dr. Stanley Horton, January, 2006, principles on 1 and 2 Corinthians.
8. Palma, p. 905.
9. Palma, p. 905.
10. Gilbrandt, *CBL, The New Testament Greek-English Dictionary, Sigma-Omega,* p. 356.
11. Donald S. Metz, *First Corinthians, Beacon Bible Commentary* (Kansas City, Missouri: Beacon Hill Press, 1968), p. 465.
12. Quentin McGhee and Carl Gibbs, *General Principles for Interpreting Scripture* (Springfield, Missouri: Faith & Action, 2006), pp. 130-131.
13. http://www.americanbible.org/brcpages/MadeaLiving
14. George O. Wood, "What Christ's Resurrection Means," sermon on 1 Corinthians 15:20-34. http://georgeowood.com
15. *NIV Study Bible,* Matthew 26:17 comment, p. 1481.
16. http://gracethrufaith.com/selah/holidays-and-holy-days/the-feast-of-first-fruits/
17. *NIV Study Bible,* Acts 2:1 comment, p. 1648.
18. Illustration by Dick Nicholson, Assemblies of God Regional Director for Latin America and the Caribbean, "Communique," April, 2007.

[19] George O. Wood, "The Glorious Destiny of Our Bodies," sermon on 1 Corinthians 15:35-58. http://georgeowood.com

[20] Jim Hernando, unpublished *Faith & Action Series* comments on 1 Corinthians.

[21] George O. Wood, "He Is Alive!" sermon on 1 Corinthians 15:1-19. http://georgeowood.com

[22] James Bradford, sermon on 1 Corinthians 15, December, 2009.

[23] Warren W. Wiersbe, *The Bible Exposition Commentary*, vol. 1, (Colorado Springs, Colorado: Victor [an imprint of Cook Communicatons Ministries], 1994), p. 621.

[24] Testimony of Pastor Phillip Sindani, Kenya.

Chapter 10

[1] Harris, *CBL*, vol. 7, p. 313.

[2] Robert H. Gundry, p. 285.

[3] Hughes, p. xvii.

[4] C. K. Barrett, *The Second Epistle to the Corinthians* (London, England: Adam and Charles Black, 1976), pp. 17-19.

[5] Hughes, p. xvi.

[6] *NIV Study Bible*, 1 Corinthians 15:32 comment, p. 1759.

[7] Doremus Almy Hayes, *Paul and His Epistles*, Published by Methodist Book Concern, 1915, p. 35. (http://books.google.com/books?id=FO02AAAAMAAJ&pg=PA35&lpg=PA35&dq=Apostle+paul+bandy-legged&source=web&ots=IgwfFj5zVd&sig=QjHTKOhUUi1-8okkOOOA_fPqzxY&hl=en&sa=X&oi=book_result&resnum=4&ct=result) footnote 23, Ante-Nicean Fathers, vol. viii, p. 487.

[8] Hayes, p. 35 (see reference 7 above).

[9] Based on information from http://www.BibleGateway.com

[10] Charles Haddon Spurgeon, *Morning and Evening* (McClean, Virginia: Macdonald Publishing Co., n.d.), p. 86.

[11] Barclay, *The Letters to the Corinthians*, p. 173.

[12] Hughes, pp. 31-38.

[13] E. C. McKenzie, *Mac's Giant Book of Quips and Quotes*. (Grand Rapids, Michigan: Baker Book House, 1980), p. 68.

[14] This illustration shared by Quentin McGhee.

[15] David Rockhill, *Parables*, January, 1984, Rockport, Indiana.

Chapter 11

[1] Fee, *Corinthians, NICNT*, p. 174.

[2] http://ntreadthrough.blogspot.com/2007/08/triumphal-procession-2-corinthians-2.html

[3] William Barclay, *The Letters to the Corinthians*, pp. 182-185.

[4] Fee, *Corinthians, NICNT*, p. 174.

[5] Wiersbe, vol. 1, p. 637.

[6] J. Sidlow Baxter, *Baxter's Explore the Bible* (Grand Rapids, Michigan: Zondervan Publishing House, 1966), p. 128.

[7] James Hernando, *Life in the Spirit Study Bible*, 2 Corinthians, p. 934.

[8] Wiersbe, vol. 1, p. 638.

[9] C. K. Barrett, *The Second Epistle to the Corinthians* (Great Britain: University Printing House, Cambridge, 1973), p. 119.

[10] Wiersbe, vol. 1, p. 637.

[11] Wiersbe, vol. 1, p. 641.

[12] Paraphrase of Hudson Taylor, referred to by Warren Wiersbe, vol. 1, p. 642.

[13] Jowett, p. 72.

[14] Mrs. Charles E. Cowman, *Springs in the Desert Sampler* (Grand Rapids, Michigan: Zondervan Publishing House, 1983), p. 84.

[15] A. W. Tozier, *A Treasury of A. W. Tozier* (Harrisburg, Pennslyvania: Christian Publications Inc., 1980), p. 80.

[16] http://www.jlfoundation.net/songs-in-the-night.html

[17] McKenzie, p. 234.

[18] Jowett, pp. 75-79.

[19] George O. Wood, this lesson is adapted from the message "Confronting Death," 2 Corinthians 5:1-10, http://georgeowood.com

[20] Hughes, p. 164.

[21] Harris, *CBL*, vol. 7, p. 547.

[22] "Blessed Assurance" was written by Fanny J. Crosby in 1873.

[23] George O. Wood, "Confronting Death," sermon on 2 Corinthians 5:1-10, refers to this illustraton by Peter Marshall. http://georgeowood.com

[24] Harris, *CBL*, vol. 7, p. 549.

[25] Barclay, *The Letters to the Corinthians*, p. 206.

[26] Plummer, *ICC, Second Corinthians*, p. 155.

[27] R. V. G. Tasker, *Tyndale New Testament Commentaries: The Second Epistle of Paul to the Corinthians* (Grand Rapids, Michigan: Wm. B. Eerdmans Publishing Co., 1977), p. 83.

[28] Ronald A. Beers, ed., *Life Application Study Bible* (Carol Stream, Illinois: Tyndale House Publishers, 1997), 2 Corinthians 5:10 comment.

[29] C. K. Barrett, *The Second Epistle to the Corinthians* (London, England: Adam & Charles Black, 1976), p. 161.

[30] C. K. Barrett, *The Second Epistle to the Corinthians* (London, England: Adam & Charles Black, 1976), p. 161.

[31] Plummer, *ICC, Second Corinthians*, p. 160.

[32] Frank G. Carver, *Beacon Bible Commentary, Romans, 1&2 Corinthians* (Kansas City, Missouri: Beacon Hill Press, 1968), p. 546.

[33] George O. Wood, "The Test of a Fruitful Minister," sermon on 2 Corinthians 5:11-21. http://georgeowood.com

[34] John Wesley, *Wesley's Notes on the New Testament*, vol. 2 (Grand Rapids, Michigan: Baker Book House, 1983), commentary on 2 Corinthians 5:17.

[35] Hughes, p. 210.

[36] Harris, *CBL*, vol. 7, p. 553.

[37] Wiersbe, vol. 1, p. 649.

[38] Robert H. Mounce, *The Book of Revelation, New International Commentary on the New Testament* (Grand Rapids, Michigan: Wm. B. Eerdmans Publishing Co., 1998), p. 334.

39 Horton, *1 & 2 Corinthians,* p. 211.
40 Harris, *CBL,* vol. 7, p. 557.
41 Plummer, *ICC, Second Corinthians,* p. 190.
42 Gingrich, p. 226.
43 Barclay, *The Letters to the Corinthians,* p. 214.
44 David Barrett, *International Bulletin of Missionary Statistics,* p. 25.
45 McKenzie, p. 563.
46 McKenzie, p. 283.
47 McKenzie, pp. 312-314.
48 Hughes, p. 229.
49 Jowett, p. 97.
50 Gingrich, p. 37.
51 Wesley, commentary on 2 Corinthians 6:18.
52 Wesley, commentary on 2 Corinthians 7:1.
53 McKenzie, p. 119.
54 Hughes, p. 274.

Chapter 12

1 Paul Yonggi Cho, *The Fourth Dimension* (Plainfield, New Jersey: Logos International, 1979), p. 139.
2 Jowett, pp. 80-82.
3 Gilbrandt, *CBL, The New Testament Greek-English Dictionary, Sigma-Omega,* pp. 491-493.
4 Barclay, *The Letters to the Corinthians,* pp. 232-233.
5 McKenzie, pp. 205-206.
6 http://www.themillionaireblog.com/gods-shovel-is-bigger-than-mine/
7 Hughes, pp. 305-310.
8 Some organizations, such as Evangelical Council for Financial Accountability (ECFA), give information on ministries that choose to be members.
9 McKenzie, p. 157.
10 McKenzie, p. 157.
11 Hughes, p. 329.
12 Alfred Plummer, *ICC, Second Corinthians,* p. 259.
13 Jimmy Beggs, interview, December, 2007.

Chapter 13

1 Hayes, (See chapter 10, reference 7).
2 Hayes, (See chapter 10, reference 7).
3 Many of the thoughts in this sermon are adopted from a sermon "Thoughts about Thought" by C. H. Spurgeon, in the book *John Ploughman's Talks* (Ann Arbor, Michigan: Baker Book House, 1976), pp. 50-53.
4 Tozier, p. 80.
5 Thoralf Gilbrandt, *Complete Biblical Library, Greek English Dictionary, Zeta-Kappa* (Springfield, Missouri: World Library Press, Inc., 1991), p. 24.
6 *Life Application Study Bible,* 1 John 3:12-13 comment.

7 David W. Augsburger, *Caring Enough to Confront* 3rd ed. (Ventura, California: Regal Books, 2009), mentioned in George Wood's sermon on 1 Corinthians 4:14–5:5 "Caring Enough to Confront." http://georgeowood.com
8 Barclay, *The Letters to the Corinthians,* p. 247.
9 http://en.wikipedia.org/wiki/Plutarch — http://en.wikipedia.org/wiki/Demosthenes
10 http://en.wikipedia.org/wiki/Demosthenes
11 Barclay, *The Letters to the Corinthians,* p. 249.
12 Hughes, p. 405.
13 Barclay, *The Letters to the Corinthians,* p. 253.
14 Plummer, *ICC, Second Corinthians*, p. 324.
15 Hughes, p. 435.
16 *NIV Study Bible,* 2 Corinthians 12:2-4 comment, p. 1777.
17 Gilbrandt, *CBL, The New Testament Greek-English Dictionary, Sigma-Omega,* p. 71.
18 C. K. Barrett, *The Second Epistle to the Corinthians, Black's New Testament Commentaries* (London: Adam and Charles Black, 1976), p. 315.
19 George O. Wood, "Spiritual Ecstasy and Agony," sermon on 2 Corinthians 12:1-10. http://georgeowood.com
20 Hughes, p. 451.
21 Barclay, *The Letters to the Corinthians,* p. 259.
22 George O. Wood sermon on 2 Corinthians 12:1-10, "Spiritual Ecstasy and Agony," referring to Ray Steadman quoting a missionary.
23 Harris, *CBL,* vol. 7, p. 645.
24 http://en.wikipedia.org/wiki/Metre
25 http://www.corsinet.com/braincandy/qtruth.html
26 Quote attributed to James A. Garfield, President of the United States (1881), http://www.quotegarden.com/truth.html
27 http://www.corsinet.com/braincandy/qtruth.html
28 McKenzie, pp. 206-207.
29 Hughes, p. 490.

The Plan of Salvation

1. Introduction: God is holy, good, and pure—completely righteous. *"God is light; in him there is no darkness at all"* (1 John 1:5).

2. The Problem: Our sins have separated us from God. Because we have sinned—done things that we know are wrong—we cannot fellowship with God. Our sins make us too dirty to come into God's holy presence. As we cannot enter a clean room with muddy shoes, we cannot come into God's presence with our sins. *"All have sinned"* (Rom. 3:23). The wages for our sin is death—spiritual death—which is eternal separation from God. Those who reject Jesus will die in their sins. They will spend eternity tormented in the flames of hell, away from the presence of God.

3. The Solution: God loves us so much that he sent Jesus to rescue us. His name is *Jesus*, which means "Savior," because He will save us from our sins (Matt. 1:21). Jesus, the Son of God, became a man and lived a perfect, sinless life. He died on the cross as our substitute—He took the penalty for our sins. Whoever believes in Jesus—submits his or her life to Him—God declares to be forgiven, clean, and righteous. Jesus said, *"I am the way and the truth and the life. No one comes to the Father except through me"* (John 14:6).

4. Invitation: Repent of your sins; that is, turn away from what you know is wrong. Put your trust in Jesus Christ, the Son of God. Believe that He died to save you from your sins. Ask Him to forgive you and free you from being a slave to sin. *"If we confess our sins, he is faithful and just and will forgive us our sins and purify us from all unrighteousness"* (1 John 1:9).

Welcome Jesus into your life. Promise to seek to obey His teachings in the Bible. To all who receive Him, He gives the right to become God's children (John 1:12). Jesus says, *"Here I am! I stand at the door* [of your heart] *and knock. If anyone hears my voice and opens the door, I will come in"* (Rev. 3:20). Invite Jesus into your life, and He will enter. He will lead you into fellowship with God. Be baptized in water, and become part of a local church that preaches and teaches the Bible.